List of figures and tables

The 'last appeared' and the 'previous number' columns refer to the Social Trends (ST) edition and location in which the same or similar chart or table last appeared. The 'type' column provides information on the status of the statistics included in this edition; National Statistics (NS) or Non-National Statistics (Non-NS). Page number refers to the page on which the table or chart can be found in Social Trends 40.

DATA

Hover and click over tables and graphs on the online pdf of Social Trends and you can download them in Microsoft Excel. It's as simple as that.

www.statistics.gov.uk/socialtrends

3: Education and training

13: Lifestyles and social participation

Contributors and acknowledgements

The Editor would like to thank colleagues in contributing Departments and other organisations for their generous support and helpful comments, without which this edition of *Social Trends* would not have been possible.

Authors:	Grace Anyaegbu
	Sonia Carrera
	Tania Corbin
	Julie Crowley
	Anna Donabie
	Joanne Evans
	Steve Howell
	Ian Macrory
	Rittah Njeru
	Chris Randall
	David Sweet
Production managers:	Ann Corp
	Steve Howell
Production team:	Andrew Barnard
	Angela Collin
	Marc Evans
	Rebecca Holley
	Tony James
	Andrew White
Lead reviewers:	Paul Allin
	Stephen Hicks
Design:	ONS Design
Typesetting:	Academic + Technical
Publishing management:	Alison Sarioglu
Index:	ONS Library and Information
Maps:	Jeremy Brocklehurst

Introduction

Croeso (welcome) to the 40th edition of *Social Trends*, one of the flagship publications from the Office for National Statistics (ONS). *Social Trends* provides an up to date and comprehensive description of society, drawing on statistics from a wide range of government departments and other organisations to show how society is changing, as well as some of the factors which may be driving these trends.

Social Trends is aimed at a wide audience: policy makers in the public and private sectors, service providers, people in local government, journalists and other commentators, academics and students, schools, and the general public.

Social Trends – Present – Future

In response to user feedback, this edition of *Social Trends* has undergone several changes. The overview page has again been used, to highlight at a glance some of the key and emerging trends in today's society. This year's theme, 'forty years of *Social Trends* in the UK' has been supported by an article drawing on past editions, and a time line, to show some of the ways in which the UK and the world are very different places now, compared with 40 years ago. Both can be found as part of the summary pages.

Social Trends is itself evolving and this will be the last edition in book form. From now on, *Social Trends* will be disseminated wholly as web publication, with material being published throughout the year. This will provide more timely releases of statistics and commentary on changes in UK society. ONS is also planning to publish regular statistical reports highlighting particular areas of interest.

New material, definitions and terms

Each year, to preserve topicality around one-third of data used in *Social Trends* is new. The remainder, where possible have been carried forward from previous editions and updated.

Due to variations in coverage and definitions, some care may be needed when comparing data from more than one source. Anyone seeking to understand the figures and tables in detail will find it helpful to read the Appendix and Symbols and conventions pages towards the end of the book. A list of further reading and websites is also provided.

Availability on electronic media

Social Trends 40 is available electronically on the National Statistics website, www. statistics.gov.uk/socialtrends. The full report is available as an interactive PDF file where excel spreadsheets containing the data used in the publication can be accessed and downloaded by clicking on the relevant chart or table.

Contact

Matthew Hughes

Editor: Social Trends
Office for National Statistics
Room: 1.059
Government Buildings
Cardiff Road
Newport
Gwent
NP10 8XG

Email: social.trends@ons.gov.uk

In this year's edition...

- **Rise in proportion of UK population aged 85 and over**
  The number of people aged 85 and over in the UK reached 1.3 million in mid-2008 and accounted for 2 per cent of the population compared with 1 per cent in 1971.

- **Trend towards smaller household sizes continues**
  The average household size in Great Britain in Q2 2009 was 2.4 people per household compared with 2.9 people per household in 1971.

- **More than three-fifths of three and four-year-olds in early years education**
  In 2008/09, the proportion of three and four-year-olds enrolled in all schools in the UK was 63 per cent, triple the rate in 1970/71 but slightly down from a peak of 65 per cent in 2003/04.

- **Fall in employment rates for men and women**
  Between Q2 2008 and Q2 2009, UK employment rates for men fell from 79 per cent to 76 per cent, while for women the rate fell from 70 per cent to 69 per cent.

- **Households continue to spend more on services than goods**
  In 2008, the proportion of UK household spending on services was just over half (52 per cent) of total domestic household expenditure, an increase from around a third (35 per cent) in 1970.

- **Just under a quarter of adults are obese**

  In England in 2008, 24.5 per cent of adults aged 16 and over had a body mass index (BMI) classed as obese, compared with 15.7 per cent in 1994.

- **Plastic card fraud at record high**

  In 2008, the value of transactions resulting from fraudulent use of UK credit and debit cards totalled £609.9 million, an increase of 14 per cent on the previous year and over 350 per cent since 1998.

- **Increase in electricity generated from renewable sources**

  UK electricity generated from renewable sources amounted to 4.3 million tonnes of oil equivalent in 2008, an increase of around 5 per cent since 2007 and 564 per cent since 1991.

- **Fewer than half of primary school children walk to school**

  The proportion of children aged 5 to 10 walking to school in Great Britain fell from 62 per cent in 1989–91 to 48 per cent in 2008.

- **UK adults most likely in EU to buy online**

  In 2009, a higher percentage of UK adults bought or ordered goods and services over the Internet for private use in the previous 12 months than in any other EU country.

Overview

Social Trends provides a unique overview of the state of the nation. In this year's edition, there are updated statistics on population changes, labour market participation, key health indicators, travel patterns and environmental behaviour. In addition to these staple items, this edition also highlights some of the major social changes over the 40 years since *Social Trends* was first published.

Chapter 1: Population shows that demographic patterns in the UK continue to change. In 2008, there were 61.4 million people resident in the UK, an increase of 5.5 million since 1971. In addition to births and deaths, changes in the population in the UK have been caused by international migration and by people moving around within the UK. In 2008, England experienced a net loss to other countries in the UK of around 7,800 people. Scotland, Wales and Northern Ireland all experienced small net gains.

As the UK population continues to grow there are notable changes in family and household types. Chapter 2: Households and families highlights the growing trend towards smaller household sizes. Between 1961 and quarter 2 (Q2) 2009, the average household size in Great Britain fell from 3.1 people per household to 2.4 people. In Q2 2009, more than 8 million children lived with married parents, equivalent to just under two-thirds (63 per cent) of all dependent children. A number of demographic trends have influenced families and households in recent times. The statistics reveal a change in attitudes to both marriage and motherhood. For women born in England and Wales in 1981, 16 per cent had married by the time they were 25, compared with 71 per cent of women born in 1956. Similarly, there has been a fall in the proportion of younger mothers in England and Wales. In 2008, 25 per cent of babies were born to women aged under 25, compared with 47 per cent in 1971.

Chapter 3: Education and training reflects on the major expansion in early years education and highlights the growth in number of early years places available to three and four-year-olds in schools in the UK, from 723 state nursery schools in 1970/71 to 3,209 in 2008/09. For an increasing number of people, their experience of formal education is no longer confined to their years in school. There has been an expansion in further education since the 1970s as more students in the UK continue in full-time education beyond school-leaving age. Figures show that there were almost 2.5 million students in higher education in 2007/08, nearly four times the total of 621,000 in 1970/71. In addition to following these traditional education routes, there has been an increase in job-related training and in the award of vocational qualifications.

Despite evidence of young people remaining in education for longer, the increasing population has contributed to growth in the UK labour market, although its composition has been changing. In Chapter 4: Labour market we examine the decline in the proportion of employee jobs in the manufacturing sector over the last 30 years, from 28.5 per cent in 1978 to 10.0 per cent in 2009. This chapter also highlights the impact of the recession which began in 2008; the working-age employment rate fell to 72.7 per cent in Q2 2009 and the unemployment rate for people aged 16 and over rose to 7.8 per cent. Reflecting this upturn in unemployment, the proportion of households which were workless increased to 16.9 per cent in Q2 2009 and the overall redundancy rate rose to 11.0 per 1,000 employees aged 16 and over during the same period.

The downturn in the economy and the contraction in the labour market have impacted on the level of economic activity in the UK. In Chapter 5: Income and wealth we highlight a 0.4 percentage point decrease in gross domestic product per head between 2007 and 2008. Over the same period, the UK National Accounts measure of household wealth reports a 15 per cent fall in real terms in household net wealth per head, the first annual fall since 2001. Perceptions of the current economic situation vary by age; 62 per cent of people aged 16 to 21 judged the economic situation in the UK as 'bad' or 'very bad' compared with 84 per cent of people aged 60 and over. We also find that the ability of households to save is affected by contractions in the economy. The household saving ratio in the UK in 2008 was 1.7 per cent of total resources, the lowest recorded since 1970.

The impact of the economic recession is also reflected in Chapter 6: Expenditure where the total number of insolvencies in England and Wales reached 134,142 in 2009. The amount of lending in the UK secured on dwellings fell from a peak of £33.3 billion in the last quarter of 2003 to £1.9 billion by the third quarter (Q3) of 2009. The level of consumer credit lending has also been falling and in Q3 2009 it reached -£1.0 billion. The chapter also examines changes over the last 40 years in the way in which households in the UK allocate expenditure between different goods and services. Between 1970 and 2008 the proportion of total household expenditure spent on services increased from 35 per cent to 52 per cent. The expenditure patterns of children in the UK are also reported in this chapter. In 2007/08, the average household expenditure by children aged 7 to 15 was £12.50, and the largest category of children's expenditure was recreation and culture, accounting for 36 per cent of their average weekly spend.

There is further focus on children statistics in Chapter 7: Health which reports a record low in infant and neonatal mortality rates in the UK in 2008, falling by around 90 per cent since records began in 1930. Improvements in nutrition and the advancement of medical science and technology means we are living longer, though individual behaviours such as diet, drinking and smoking can impact on morbidity and mortality. The proportion of adults in England classified as obese has increased by 9 percentage points between 1994 and 2008 to reach 25 per cent. Figures indicate that over the last decade the proportion of adult regular smokers in Great Britain has fallen to 22 per cent for men and 21 per cent for women.

Chapter 8: Social protection highlights a 122 per cent increase in social security expenditure in the UK over the last 30 years, to reach £152 billion in 2008/09. In the same year, there were just under 2.7 million working age recipients of incapacity benefit and other benefits in the UK, 18,000 less than 2007/08, continuing the downward trend since 2005/06. In addition to this financial support, sick and disabled people are entitled to assistance through the provision of services. In this edition, we examine the role of home care services in helping to allow those with disabilities, dementia and mental health problems to encourage and maintain their independence and live in their own homes. In 2008, an average of 35 hours per week of home care was provided by councils in England to households in receipt of care. The main support given to sick and disabled people in care is provided through the National Health Service. Between 1991/92 and 2007/08, the average length of stay in hospital in the UK decreased from 6.0 days to 3.9 days.

In Chapter 9: Crime and justice, we learn that 10.7 million crimes were reported to the British Crime Survey in England and Wales in 2008/09, almost half the level of the peak in 1995. Household crime accounted for almost two-thirds of crimes reported in 2008/09, of which vandalism was the most common household crime experienced. Credit card fraud has become more apparent over the last 10 years. In 2008, the value of transactions resulting from fraudulent use of UK credit and debit cards totalled £609.9 million, a 350 per cent increase since 1998. In 2008, immediate custody was the most common type of sentence given to offenders for fraud and forgery in England and Wales, with 30 per cent of offenders receiving this sentence.

Changes in family and household structure combined with recent economic pressures have impacted on housebuilding and the housing market. In Chapter 10: Housing, we examine a 20 per cent decrease in the number of housebuilding completions in England between 2007/08 and 2008/09, the lowest number recorded since 2001/02. The economic recession which began in 2008 has made it more difficult for people to arrange finance to purchase a home, or move. In this chapter we highlight a fall in the proportion of young homeowners and the increasing difficulty in the UK for young people to become homeowners. Between Q2 1997 and Q2 2009 the proportion of households aged under 30 buying their homes with a mortgage decreased from 43 per cent to 29 per cent.

In Chapter 11: Environment, climate change is still a key environmental concern and in June 2009 the UK signed up to the European Union (EU) Renewable Energy Directive. In 2008, biofuels accounted for the largest proportion of electricity generated from renewable sources (3.2 million tonnes of oil equivalent) in the UK followed by wind power and hydroelectricity (0.6 million and 0.4 million tonnes of oil equivalent respectively). However, conventional fuel methods continue to be the main generators of electricity, with natural gas taking over from coal in 2008 as the most commonly used fuel for electricity generation in the UK. We also learn in this chapter that 78 per cent of people aged 15 and over in the EU felt recycling was the most common action they had undertaken in 2009 to help fight climate change.

In Chapter 12: Transport, we examine the continuation of long-term trends in many areas of transport and travel. In 2008, a total of 28.4 million cars were licensed in Great Britain, of which 4.0 million cars had an engine capacity of 2,001 cubic centimetres or over, almost double the number recorded a decade earlier. We also learn that over the last two decades children in Great Britain have become more reliant on cars as a mode of transport to and from school. In 1989–91, the proportion of children aged 5 to 10 walking to school was 62 per cent, but by 2008 this had dropped to only 48 per cent. Over the same period, the proportion of children travelling to school by car increased from 27 to 43 per cent.

Finally, Chapter 13: Lifestyles and social participation highlights the growing popularity of Internet usage. In 2009, a higher percentage of UK adults (66 per cent) bought or ordered goods and services over the Internet in the previous 12 months than in any other EU country. This chapter also shows the rise in popularity of Internet-based reading material for children. In England in 2007, websites were the second most popular source of reading material outside school for boys aged 9 to 14, at 58 per cent. For girls in the same age group, emails were the second most common type of reading material, at 59 per cent. Despite these advancements in technology traditional leisure activities also remain popular: watching TV remained the most common activity undertaken in free time by men and women in England in 2007/08. Going on holiday still remains a popular activity and in 2008 UK residents made a record 45.5 million holiday trips.

Social Trends – past, present, future

I am delighted to introduce this edition of *Social Trends*, the latest statistical picture of life in the UK compiled by the Office for National Statistics and colleagues across the Government Statistical Service. There have been marked social changes over the last 40 years, since *Social Trends* was first published in 1970. Changes in the pattern of our working lives – who is employed, where and how – have accompanied changes in household and family structure. There is greater material wealth, although there are still large variations in income and wealth, as well as in health and educational attainment.

To mark the 40th anniversary, this edition includes some description of long term trends in every chapter. The *Social Trends* team has also prepared an article drawing on past editions, and a time line, to show some of the ways in which the UK and the world are very different places now, compared with 40 years ago.

The statistical landscape was changed by the arrival of *Social Trends*. Historically it had been economic, production and labour market statistics that were predominantly used in political and public discussion and debate, with social statistics tending to be limited to tracking the size of the population. *Social Trends* was created in response to the growing need for economic progress to be measured, at least in part, in terms of social benefits. This need remains, as exemplified by the publication in 2009 of the Stiglitz-Sen-Fitoussi report recommending ways of measuring economic performance and social progress.

In an article in the first edition of *Social Trends*, Professor Claus Moser, then the director of the Central Statistical Office, suggested that *Social Trends* would be a success if it helped public understanding and discussion of social policy. The publication was indeed a success – it has attracted enormous publicity and featured on lists of Christmas reading recommended by a number of national papers. *Social Trends* has remained a flagship publication from the ONS for the whole of the Government Statistical Service. It is regularly welcomed as a 'must-read for anyone working in advertising, marketing or social policy' (*The China Post*) and even 'a sort of up-market Guinness Book of Records, recording the way we live now' (*The Guardian*).

While the mission of *Social Trends* is unchanged, the content has developed. New data have become available and areas of interest change. For example, chapters on the environment and on transport have been introduced. The lifestyles and social participation chapter has grown. A chapter specifically on our 'e-society' is being prepared for future editions.

Social Trends is itself evolving and this will be the last edition in book form. *Social Trends* and supporting data tables have been available from the ONS website for 10 years. From now on, *Social Trends* will be disseminated wholly as a web publication, with material being published throughout the year. This will provide more timely releases of statistics and commentary on changes in UK society.

I regularly refer to *Social Trends*, and with not a little pride as the editor for four editions that spanned the turn of the millennium. Looking back through the cuttings, I was amused to see one from that time headlined 'Women swap sewing needles for DIY'. Long may *Social Trends* continue to capture and present social trends of all kinds. Statistics matter. *Social Trends* helps deliver my vision: statistics, analysis and advice used in debate and decision-making.

Thank you to everyone involved in compiling *Social Trends*.

Jil Matheson

Jil Matheson
National Statistician
June 2010

Social Trends through the decades

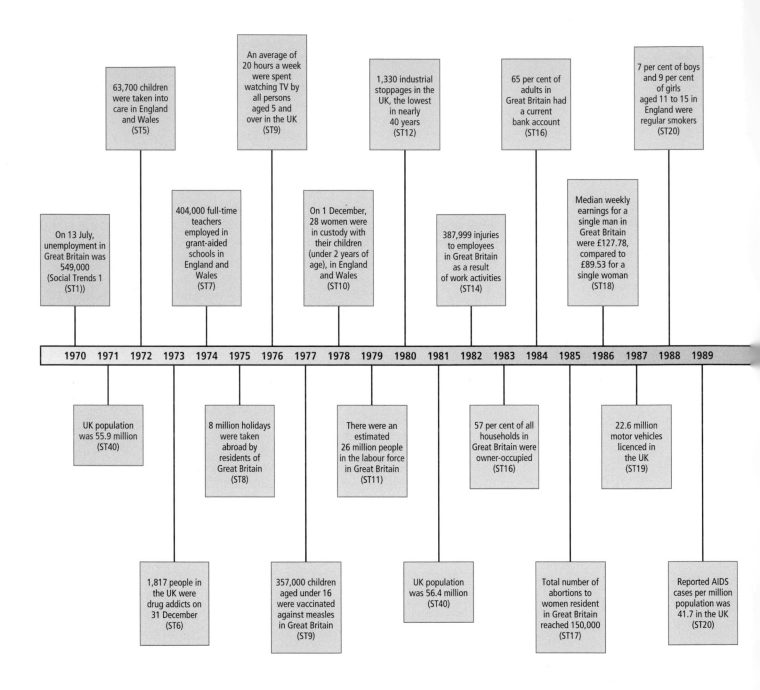

63,700 children were taken into care in England and Wales (ST5)

An average of 20 hours a week were spent watching TV by all persons aged 5 and over in the UK (ST9)

1,330 industrial stoppages in the UK, the lowest in nearly 40 years (ST12)

65 per cent of adults in Great Britain had a current bank account (ST16)

7 per cent of boys and 9 per cent of girls aged 11 to 15 in England were regular smokers (ST20)

404,000 full-time teachers employed in grant-aided schools in England and Wales (ST7)

On 1 December, 28 women were in custody with their children (under 2 years of age), in England and Wales (ST10)

387,999 injuries to employees in Great Britain as a result of work activities (ST14)

Median weekly earnings for a single man in Great Britain were £127.78, compared to £89.53 for a single woman (ST18)

On 13 July, unemployment in Great Britain was 549,000 (Social Trends 1 (ST1))

1970 1971 1972 1973 1974 1975 1976 1977 1978 1979 1980 1981 1982 1983 1984 1985 1986 1987 1988 1989

UK population was 55.9 million (ST40)

8 million holidays were taken abroad by residents of Great Britain (ST8)

There were an estimated 26 million people in the labour force in Great Britain (ST11)

57 per cent of all households in Great Britain were owner-occupied (ST16)

22.6 million motor vehicles licenced in the UK (ST19)

1,817 people in the UK were drug addicts on 31 December (ST6)

357,000 children aged under 16 were vaccinated against measles in Great Britain (ST9)

UK population was 56.4 million (ST40)

Total number of abortions to women resident in Great Britain reached 150,000 (ST17)

Reported AIDS cases per million population was 41.7 in the UK (ST20)

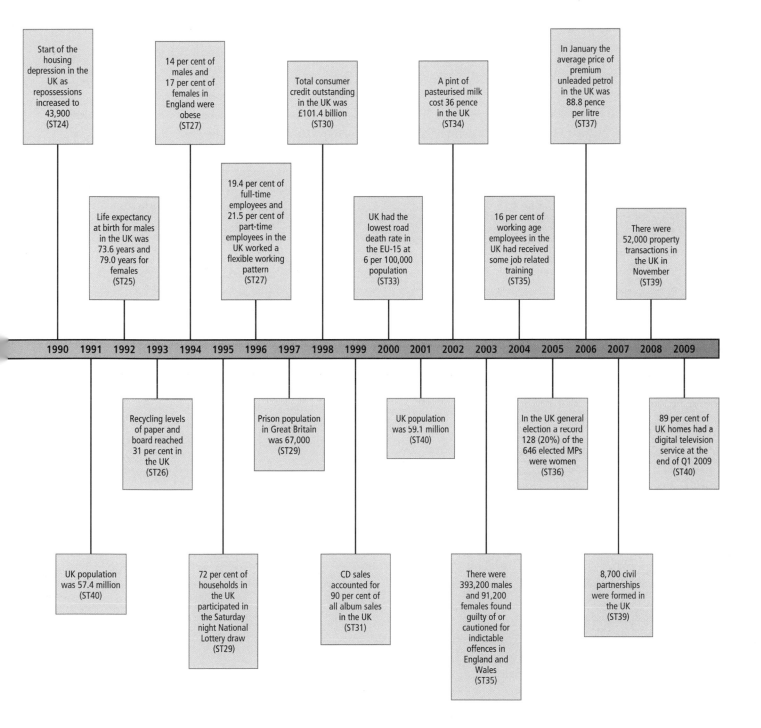

Start of the housing depression in the UK as repossessions increased to 43,900 (ST24)

14 per cent of males and 17 per cent of females in England were obese (ST27)

Total consumer credit outstanding in the UK was £101.4 billion (ST30)

A pint of pasteurised milk cost 36 pence in the UK (ST34)

In January the average price of premium unleaded petrol in the UK was 88.8 pence per litre (ST37)

Life expectancy at birth for males in the UK was 73.6 years and 79.0 years for females (ST25)

19.4 per cent of full-time employees and 21.5 per cent of part-time employees in the UK worked a flexible working pattern (ST27)

UK had the lowest road death rate in the EU-15 at 6 per 100,000 population (ST33)

16 per cent of working age employees in the UK had received some job related training (ST35)

There were 52,000 property transactions in the UK in November (ST39)

1990 1991 1992 1993 1994 1995 1996 1997 1998 1999 2000 2001 2002 2003 2004 2005 2006 2007 2008 2009

Recycling levels of paper and board reached 31 per cent in the UK (ST26)

Prison population in Great Britain was 67,000 (ST29)

UK population was 59.1 million (ST40)

In the UK general election a record 128 (20%) of the 646 elected MPs were women (ST36)

89 per cent of UK homes had a digital television service at the end of Q1 2009 (ST40)

UK population was 57.4 million (ST40)

72 per cent of households in the UK participated in the Saturday night National Lottery draw (ST29)

CD sales accounted for 90 per cent of all album sales in the UK (ST31)

There were 393,200 males and 91,200 females found guilty of or cautioned for indictable offences in England and Wales (ST35)

8,700 civil partnerships were formed in the UK (ST39)

Social Trends through the decades

Anna Donabie, Matthew Hughes and Chris Randall

Social Trends 40 marks 40 years of social reporting in the UK. This publication has been one of the flagships of the Government Statistical Service since it was first published in 1970. In the first edition, Professor Claus Moser, the then Director of the Central Statistical Office, said in his article on developments in social statistics:

'Our aim is to bring together, initially once a year, a number of significant statistical series relating to social policies and conditions ... but even so the combination and confrontation of tables bearing on different aspects of social life may produce a more rounded picture of the social scene than now exists. If it is a success, *Social Trends* will help public understanding and discussion of social policy'.

This publication has indeed been a success and the Office for National Statistics are proud to publish *Social Trends*, and to continuously develop it. In this article we highlight some of the main changes over the past four decades since *Social Trends* began. Through each decade we will reflect on the statistics and commentary we reported on in these editions[1].

The 1970s

The 1970s was a decade in which a wave of strikes paralysed the country, and the three day working week and winter of discontent became potent symbols.

The mid-1970s saw levels of unemployment not known in the UK since World War Two. In *Social Trends 9, Table 5.12* highlighted the unemployment levels and rates over the decade. Unemployment rates in the UK increased from 3.5 per cent in 1971 to 5.7 per cent in 1976, before further rises to 6.0 per cent by quarter 2 (Q2) 1978. Working days lost in industrial disputes were also particularly high during this decade. The 1972 miners' strike was the first strike of British

miners since 1926, and on 9 January all British miners came out on strike. In *Social Trends 8, Table 5.23* (Table 1970.1) reported a total of 23.9 million days lost in the UK associated with labour disputes in 1972.

The majority (91 per cent) of these working days lost were a result of pay claims and disputes. The number of industrial disputes fell in 1973 before rising sharply in 1974 to 14.8 million. Again, this coincides with a decision by British miners to take industrial action. Their 1974 dispute lasted for 16 weeks.

The pattern of fuel used for energy generation changed during the period covering the miners' strike. In *Social Trends 40, Figure 11.1* examines the trends in fuel used for electricity generation over the last 40 years. In 1970, coal was the most commonly used fuel for electricity generation in the UK, providing over 67 per cent of the fuel input. However, the provision of coal declined during the British mining strike periods and in 1972 and 1974 coal use accounted for 56 per cent of fuel input.

Measuring education participation and attainment has been a key feature of *Social Trends* since the first edition. In *Social Trends 1* the tables and commentary provided trends in 'stock' or the total number of pupils in primary and secondary schools since the 1960s. Although attendance at school has not been compulsory until a child is five, throughout the decades *Social Trends* have highlighted the expansion of early years education in the UK. In *Social Trends 40, Figure 3.1* examines the proportion of three and four-year-olds enrolled in all schools in the UK between 1970/71 and 2008/09. Since records began in the early 1970s this proportion has increased from 21 per cent to 63 per cent. The number of early years places has also increased over the same period, from 723 state nursery schools in the UK in 1970/71 to 3,209 in 2008/09.

The 1970s was a period of expansion for the education system in the UK, a major event reported in *Social Trends 7* was the raising of the school leaving age from 15 to 16 in 1972/73. *Table 3.5* in *Social Trends 7* examined the number of children at school by age of child. In 1971, prior to the raising of the

Table 1970.1

Industrial disputes

United Kingdom   Millions

	1966	1970	1971	1972	1973	1974	1975	1976
Working days lost:								
Pay claims and disputes	1.6	9.2	12.3	21.7	5.1	13.1	4.4	1.8
All other causes	0.8	1.7	1.3	2.3	2.0	1.7	1.5	1.7
Total days lost	2.4	10.9	13.6	23.9	7.1	14.8	5.9	3.5

Source: Department for Employment

Table 1970.2

Secondary education

England & Wales   Percentages

	1970	1971	1972	1973	1974	1975
Public sector secondary schools						
Middle deemed secondary	1.2	1.8	2.3	3.7	4.6	5.4
Modern	40.3	37.0	33.4	28.7	23.0	18.2
Grammar	19.9	18.2	16.6	14.8	11.0	9.0
Technical	1.4	1.2	1.0	0.8	0.6	0.5
Comprehensive	30.8	35.9	41.1	47.0	57.4	64.3
Others	6.5	5.9	5.5	5.1	3.3	2.6
All pupils (=100%) (thousands)	3,046.0	3,143.9	3,251.4	3,362.6	3,723.7	3,826.6
Average number of pupils per qualified teacher[1]	17.8	17.9	17.6	17.1	17.5	17.2

1 Including full-time equivalent of part-time and visiting teachers.

Source: Statistics of Education, Volume I, Schools, Department of Education and Science

statutory minimum school-leaving age to 16, there were 272,000 pupils aged 16 in schools in the UK, accounting for 3 per cent of the school pupil population. By 1974, the number of pupils aged 16 at school rose to 400,000, accounting for 4 per cent of the pupil population.

Between 1965 and 1975 many secondary modern schools and grammar schools were amalgamated to form large neighbourhood comprehensives. By the mid-1970s, *Social Trends* reported on the closure of many grammar and modern schools and the amalgamation of the remainder into comprehensives. In *Social Trends 7, Table 3.6* (Table 1970.2) reported a total of just over 3.0 million pupils in public sector secondary schools in England and Wales in 1970. Of these, the largest proportion (40.3 per cent) attended modern schools, while 30.8 per cent attended comprehensives and 19.9 per cent attended grammar schools. By 1975, the proportion of pupils attending comprehensive schools had reached 64.3 per cent, while there had been rapid declines in the proportions attending modern and grammar schools (18.2 per cent and 9.0 per cent respectively).

The introduction of the General Household Survey (GHS, now the General Lifestyle Survey) in 1970 provided regular data on the social conditions in Great Britain. Since the first edition the GHS has been an important source of information for *Social Trends*. Along with changes in the labour market and the education system, *Social Trends* in the 1970s highlighted a significant increase in the ownership of many consumer durables and household amenities. One change reported was the proportion of households owning a telephone, which increased from 35 per cent in 1970 to 52 per cent by 1975.

Technological change in the 1970s was beginning to transform lives and was laying the foundations for the explosion of global communications in future decades. The 1970s marked a period of rapid developments in the telecommunications sector, many new services, such as international dialling were added. To support this expansion Post Office Telecommunications was set up as a separate department of the UK Post Office.

In *Social Trends 10, Table 10.18* (Table 1970.3) examined the calls to information services reported by the Post Office. In 1970–71, a total of 366 million information service calls were made in the UK. Of these, 297.3 million calls were made to the speaking clock and 45.5 million calls to Dial-a-Disc, which enabled callers to listen to a song down a telephone line.

Table 1970.3

Calls to information services

United Kingdom   Millions

	1970–71	1978–79
Speaking clock	297.3	431.2
Dial-a-Disc	45.5	110.3
Weather	11.6	29.0
Cricket	5.0	18.0
Financial Times index	1.4	4.0
Motoring	1.0	2.7
Recipe	2.7	2.3
Teletourist	1.1	0.6

Source: Telecommunication Statistics, Post Office

By 1978–79 these figures had increased to 431.2 million and 110.3 million respectively, possibly reflecting the larger number of households with a telephone.

Lifestyle choices in the UK were high on the household agenda during the 1970s. One way of illustrating changes in lifestyles is to look at how spending patterns changed during this decade. In *Social Trends 9*, *Table 7.6* was able to examine patterns of change in consumer spending in the UK throughout the decade. Overall, consumers' expenditure fell in real terms between 1973 and 1977. Spending on items such as food, housing, water and fuel remained fairly stable throughout the 1970s. However, expenditure on less essential items – including communication, spending abroad, and recreation and culture – rose sharply. The largest category of expenditure in 1977 was food (£12.1 million), accounting for 19.5 per cent of total consumers' expenditure during that year. However, between 1970 and 1977, the largest proportional growth in consumer spending was on housing, which increased 2.6 percentage points to account for 15.4 per cent of consumer spending in 1977. Spending on transport and vehicles was the second largest increase (0.8 percentage points) over this period, and accounted for 12.5 per cent of consumer spending in 1977,

followed by spending on alcohol which increased by 0.5 percentage points and accounted for 7.8 per cent of consumer spending in 1977.

The 1980s

In 1979 unemployment stood at around 1.4 million, and the Conservative party swept to power on the message that 'Labour isn't working'. However, during the early 1980s, unemployment rose further still, topping 3.0 million in 1982. The two main factors behind the rise in the jobless total at the start of the 1980s were an economic recession with high inflation and industrial restructuring, which included closure of many factories in the UK's industrial heartlands.

As well as the high unemployment total, the duration of unemployment for many was also long. In *Social Trends 15*, *Table 4.20* (Table 1980.1) showed the duration of incomplete spells of unemployment for unemployed claimants in April 1984 in the UK that were reported at the time. A quarter (24.6 per cent) of unemployed males aged 16 and over had been unemployed for over two years, while a further 18.9 per cent were unemployed for between one and two years. The proportion

Table 1980.1

Unemployed claimants: by sex, age and duration, April 1984

United Kingdom | | | | | | Percentages

	Duration of unemployment (weeks)					
	Up to 2	Over 2, up to 8	Over 8, up to 26	Over 26, up to 52	Over 52, up to 104	Over 104
Males aged:						
16–19	5.8	12.8	28.0	29.4	18.8	5.1
20–24	5.2	10.9	23.9	20.5	18.6	20.9
25–34	4.6	9.8	21.6	17.8	19.2	27.0
35–49	4.3	8.8	19.6	16.4	19.1	31.8
50–59	3.6	6.5	16.9	17.3	20.5	35.3
60 and over	6.6	9.9	28.0	32.6	11.4	11.4
All males aged 16 and over	4.7	9.7	22.0	20.1	18.9	24.6
Females aged:						
16–19	5.9	12.8	29.8	30.4	17.1	4.1
20–24	6.2	12.8	29.0	24.7	14.2	13.0
25–34	6.5	13.7	30.9	27.4	12.9	8.6
35–49	6.2	12.3	25.4	22.5	17.9	15.7
50 and over	3.3	6.5	16.3	18.4	22.0	33.5
All females aged 16 and over	5.8	12.1	27.5	25.5	16.2	12.9

Source: Claimant Count, Department of Employment

of men who were long-term unemployed in April 1984 increased with age, 55.8 per cent of unemployed men aged 50 to 59 were unemployed for more than a year, compared with just under a quarter (23.9 per cent) of those aged 16 to 19. However, those aged 16 to 19 were helped by special training and employment measures that were around at the time.

The data for women was affected by women's entitlement to unemployment benefit at the time. But the table still shows that a higher proportion of older women were long-term unemployed with 55.5 per cent of unemployed women aged 50 and over unemployed for over a year. Overall, just under three in ten (29.1 per cent) unemployed women aged 16 and over were unemployed for over a year.

Social Trends 15 also included a table (Table A.2) from the 1983 British Social Attitude Series that showed the expectations of employees and unemployed people in Great Britain as to the estimated time to find an acceptable job. Just over a third (34 per cent) of employees thought that the estimated time taken to find an acceptable job from the time they became unemployed would be two months or less with a further 26 per cent estimating three to six months. While just under a fifth (19 per cent) of those unemployed thought that the estimated time taken to find an acceptable job from the time of their interview would be two months or less with a further 21 per cent estimating three to six months.

The 1980s will also be remembered for a new disease to come to the forefront of the medical world – Acquired Immune Deficiency Syndrome or AIDS, a disease of the human immune system caused by the Human Immunodeficiency Virus (HIV). The disease was first reported in the medical world in 1981. By 1982, there had been just seven reported cases of AIDS in the UK, compared to over 1,000 in the United States. It wasn't until 1987 that the first item about AIDS appeared in Social Trends 17 (Figure 7.5). The item showed that around 400 cases had been reported by 1986 in the UK and of those cases around 200 people had died. In 1990, Social Trends 20, Table 7.9 contained more in-depth coverage in a table showing the number of HIV antibody positive reports, of which there were 10,794 to the end of June 1989, with 2,372 AIDS cases and 1,272 deaths. The chart also contained the exposure category which showed that the vast majority of HIV and AIDS cases were to homosexual and bisexual males.

A table in the article of Social Trends 19 (Table A.6) reported on attitudes to discrimination against AIDS sufferers from the 1987 British Social Attitude Series. It showed that nearly four in ten (38 per cent) adults aged 18 and over in Great Britain felt that there should be definitely or probably a legal right for employers to dismiss employees with AIDS. Just under a third

(31 per cent) felt that there should be definitely or probably a legal right for doctors and nurses to refuse treatment to AIDS sufferers and just under a quarter (24 per cent) felt that there should be definitely or probably a legal right for schools to expel children with AIDS.

Two government policies were popular with the general public in the 1980s. They were the privatisation of various nationalised industries and the associated shares bought by the public and the right to buy council homes. According to Social Trends 19, 8 per cent of the adult population owned shares only in privatised companies in 1988, including the Trustees Saving Bank Group (TSB). The substantial growth in share ownership began with the British Telecom privatisation in 1984 in which 2 million people bought shares. The TSB and British Gas flotation, in September and November 1986 attracted 3 million and 4.5 million shareholders respectively.

The legislation to implement the right to buy was passed in the Housing Act 1980. The sale price of a council house was based on its market valuation but also included a discount to reflect the rents paid by tenants and also to encourage take-up. The legislation gave council tenants the right to buy their council house at a discounted value, depending on how long they had been living in the house, with the proviso that if they sold their house before a minimum period had expired they would have to pay back a proportion of the discount. The sales were an attractive deal for many tenants and hundreds of thousands of homes were sold. According to Social Trends 19, sales of local authority and new town dwellings in the UK increased from about 93,000 in 1980 to over 228,000 in 1982 before falling back to 109,000 in 1986. Total sales reached 142,000 in 1987 and between 1980 and 1987 reached over one million.

A reflection of the times can be observed by looking at the durable goods that were owned in households. Table 1980.2 overleaf draws on two tables that appeared in Social Trends 13 (Table 6.12) and Social Trends 22 (Table 6.4) showing durable goods owned in 1981 and 1989–90 in Great Britain. In 1981, just under three-quarters (74 per cent) of households owned a colour television and under a quarter (23 per cent) owned a black and white television only. By the end of the decade the proportion of households owning a colour television had increased to 93 per cent and just 5 per cent owned only a black and white television. Ownership of a deep-freezer showed the largest percentage increase between the two dates (31 percentage points), from just under half (49 per cent) of households in 1981 to four-fifths (80 per cent) in 1989–90. Ownership of a home computer was also reported for the first time in Social Trends with just under one in five (19 per cent) households owning one in 1989–90.

Table 1980.2

Household ownership of selected durable goods[1]

Great Britain		Percentages
	1981	1989–90
Colour television	74	93
Telephone	75	87
Washing machine	78	86
Deep-freezer[2]	49	80
Video	..	60
Microwave oven	..	47
Tumble drier	23	45
Home computer	..	19
CD player	..	16
Dishwasher	4	12
Black and white television only	23	5
Vacuum cleaner	94	..
Refrigerator[2]	93	..
Central heating	59	..

1 Data is as reported in Social Trends 13 for 1981 and Social Trends 22 for 1989–90.
2 Includes fridge-freezers.

Source: General Household Survey, Office for National Statistics

Recently, the Treasury Committee launched an enquiry into the abolition of the cheque, which is scheduled for 31 October 2018. However, *Social Trends 16* reported methods of payments for purchase of goods and services in 1984 in

Table 1980.3

Household division of labour, 1987[1]

Great Britain			Percentages
	Mainly men	Mainly women	Shared equally
Washing and ironing	2	88	9
Looking after sick children[2]	2	67	30
Household cleaning	4	72	23
Preparing evening meal	6	77	17
Household shopping	7	50	43
Teaching children discipline[2]	13	19	67
Doing evening dishes	22	39	36
Organising household bills	32	38	30
Repairing household equipment	82	6	8

1 Asked of respondents who were married or living as married.
2 Asked of respondents who were married or living as married and with children aged under 16 living in household.

Source: British Social Attitude Series, Social and Community Planning Research

Great Britain when using cheques was the main non-cash method of payment. There were 1,180 million cheque transactions compared with 610 million standing orders/direct debits and 280 million credit card transactions, while the debit card was yet to be introduced.

And finally in this decade, the age old question as to who does what in the home? According to *Table A.9* in *Social Trends 19*, it was still overwhelmingly the case that the woman was responsible for looking after the house in Great Britain in 1987. Table 1980.3 shows that it was mainly the woman that performed household tasks like washing and ironing, looking after sick children or household cleaning. Only in repairing household equipment, organising bills and doing the evening dishes did men play a significant role.

The 1990s

The 1990s began with the continuation of the late 1980s economic downturn in which the UK saw interest rates rise. This in turn caused mortgage rates to rise from 9.8 per cent in the second quarter (Q2) of 1988 to 13.4 per cent a year later. The result of increased payments led to a rise in financial difficulties, arrears and repossessions in the late 1980s with the number of mortgages in arrears reaching a peak in 1992.

In *Social Trends 29*, *Table 10.27* (Table 1990.1) reported a total of 76,000 properties repossessed in the UK in 1991 and a further 69,000 in 1992. The total number of mortgages in arrears in 1992 was 352,000, the highest number recorded to date.

The growth in technology in the 1990s showed an increase in the use of computers at work, at home and at school which began in the 1980s and continued throughout the 1990s, with the introduction of the World Wide Web which led to the dot-com boom in the mid to late 1990s.

Social Trends 27 reported the importance of computer use in schools showing that in secondary schools, word processing was the most common form of use in England in 1994, with 39 per cent of pupils' time using computers being spent for this purpose in Year 11.

Social Trends 29 reported the ratio of pupils to computers had fallen in England. In primary schools in 1993/94 there were 18 pupils per computer compared with 107 in 1984/85. Secondary schools had an even lower ratio with 10 pupils per computer in 1993/94 compared with 60 in 1984/85.

In *Social Trends 29*, *Table 13.6* reported the increase in ownership of home computers, showing that the proportion of households in the UK with a home computer increased from 16 per cent in 1986 to 26 per cent in 1996–97. Households

Table 1990.1

Mortgages, arrears and repossessions[1]

United Kingdom   Thousands

| | | Loans in arrears at end-period | | |
	Mortgages	By 6–12 months	By over 12 months	Properties repossessed in period
1981	6,336	22	..	5
1982	6,518	27	6	7
1983	6,846	29	8	8
1984	7,313	48	10	12
1985	7,717	57	13	19
1986	8,138	52	13	24
1987	8,283	56	15	26
1988	8,564	43	10	19
1989	9,125	67	14	16
1990	9,415	123	36	44
1991	9,815	184	92	76
1992	9,922	205	147	69
1993	10,137	165	152	59
1994	10,410	134	117	49
1995	10,521	127	85	49
1996	10,637	101	67	43
1997	10,738	74	45	33

1 Estimates cover only members of the Council of Mortgage Lenders; these account for 98 per cent of all mortgages outstanding.

Source: Council of Mortgage Lenders

Figure 1990.2

Households with a mobile phone: by age of head of household, 1997–98

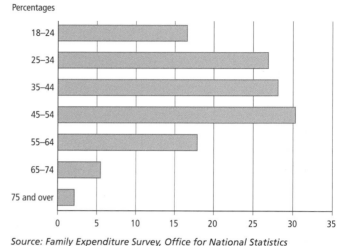

United Kingdom
Percentages

Source: Family Expenditure Survey, Office for National Statistics

a mobile phone in 1997–98. In comparison, this edition of *Social Trends* reports that 79 per cent of households in the UK own a mobile phone (Chapter 6: Expenditure, Figure 6.9).

Throughout the decades *Social Trends* has reported on various aspects of transport and travel throughout Britain, reporting on the rise in car ownership and the decline in the use of public transport, together with increasing costs of motoring.

October 1994 saw a new alternative to air and sea travel when a limited car carrying service was introduced through the Channel Tunnel. In *Social Trends 27, Table 12.18* data was first reported on traffic travelling through the Tunnel. In 1995, 1.8 million visits to the UK were through the Channel Tunnel together with 1.9 million visits abroad.

The 1990s was the decade that saw the increase in the number of 'road-rage' incidence amongst car drivers, and this was reported on in *Social Trends 28. Table 12.11* stated that in Great Britain women were almost as likely as men to say they had felt like swearing or gesturing but men were much more likely to have felt like committing the more dangerous forms of 'road-rage'. Not surprisingly people under the age of 35 were three times as likely as people aged 65 or over to have actually sworn or gestured at another driver, however, these younger drivers were only twice as likely as the older drivers to have felt like swearing or gesturing.

Social Trends 26 reported on what activities people carried out during a typical week. *Table 13.2* (Table 1990.3 overleaf) showed that in 1995 men working full time spent 53 hours a week in Great Britain on either work, travel or study which was five hours more than women in full time work. However, these

comprising families with children were more likely than one person households to own a computer, and in 1996–97 around two-fifths of households with children in the UK owned a computer compared with around a fifth of one person households aged 16 to 59, and only 2 per cent of those aged 60 and over.

The 1990s also saw the growth in the ownership and use of mobile phones. Although the first British mobile phone call was made on 1 January 1985, *Social Trends* did not report on the number of households with a mobile phone until towards the end of the 1990s, in *Social Trends 29, Figure 13.7* (Figure 1990.2). In 1997–98, a fifth of households in the UK owned at least one mobile phone with ownership being most common among households headed by 45 to 54-year-olds. *Social Trends* also reported that two-fifths of households headed by a professional owned a mobile phone compared with around 6 per cent of those headed by someone who was retired or unoccupied. The South East region had the greatest proportion of mobile phone owners where three in ten households owned

Table 1990.3

Time use: by employment status and gender, May 1995

Great Britain   Hours

	In full-time employment		In part-time employment		Retired		All adults
	Males	Females	Males	Females	Males	Females	
Weekly hours spent on							
Sleep	57	58	62	60	67	66	61
Free time	34	31	48	32	59	52	40
Work, study and travel	53	48	28	26	3	4	32
Housework, cooking and shopping	7	15	12	26	15	26	16
Eating, personal hygiene and caring	13	13	13	21	15	17	15
Household maintenance and pet care	4	2	6	3	9	3	4
Free time per weekday	4	4	6	4	8	7	5
Free time per weekend day	8	6	8	6	10	8	8

Source: Economic and Social Research Council Research Centre on Micro-social Change, from Omnibus Survey

women spent eight hours more than their male counterparts on housework, cooking or shopping each week. As a result of these differences, at weekends men in full-time employment had around two more hours a day of free time than women who worked full time, although on weekdays they have the same amount at nearly four hours of free time each day.

The 2000s

The year 2001 marked the end of the 20th century and the 30th birthday for *Social Trends*. The previous three decades had already shown the rate at which UK society was changing, and the impact that economic cycles, government policies and evolving technology had on people's lives.

The start of the 21st century coincided with an upturn in the UK economy. Gross domestic product (GDP), the UK National Accounts measure of overall level of activity in the economy, showed strong growth, and *Social Trends* began to highlight the early signs of a housing boom in the UK market. Past editions of *Social Trends* have demonstrated the mirroring of economic cycles and the housing market in the UK, with booms and slumps in one also occurring in the other.

The post-war housebuilding boom led to a shift in tenure patterns in the UK. We have already examined the right to buy legislation launched in the 1980s which proved extremely popular, and contributed to the substantial growth in the number of owner-occupied homes since the 1980s. In *Social Trends 40, Figure 10.4* examines the rise in the owner-occupation in the UK. In quarter 2 (Q2) 2000, there were

17.0 million owner-occupied households in the UK, by Q2 2005 this figure had reached 17.7 million. Despite falling to 17.5 million in Q2 2009, owner-occupation still remained the dominant feature of UK tenure, accounting for 68 per cent of household tenure in this period.

In *Social Trends 36, Figure 10.22* (Figure 2000.1) examined the average dwelling prices in the UK. There have been steep increases in house prices since the series began in 1980. In more recent years, in 2004 the average price paid by first-time

Figure 2000.1

Average dwelling prices:[1] by type of buyer

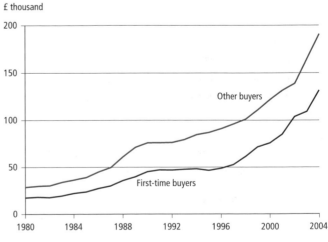

United Kingdom

£ thousand

1 Uses simple average prices.

Source: Office of the Deputy Prime Minister

buyers reached £131,700, 74 per cent higher than in 2000. For former owner-occupiers, the average price paid reached £191,000 in 2004, 56 per cent higher than in 2000.

Directly linked to the average dwelling price are changes in the number of property transactions. The methodology used to calculate residential property transactions was changed in 2008, as a result the system only enables a consistent time series to be backdated to April 2005. Even over this limited period, *Figure 10.17* in *Social Trends 40* highlights the large increases in residential property transactions in the UK. There were 105,000 property transactions in May 2005. Transactions then increased sharply to a peak of 153,000 in December 2006. Housing market conditions changed substantially at the start of 2007, there were decreases in the number of property transactions almost every month throughout that year, the largest monthly decrease was between November 2007 and December 2007, with a 21 per cent fall in transactions from 131,000 to 104,000. Similarly, *Figure 6.10* in *Social Trends 40* measures the amount of lending to individuals in the UK secured on dwellings. Mirroring the property boom, lending increased sharply from 2000 to a peak of £33.3 billion in the last quarter of 2003. Lending fell in 2004 but started to increase again in 2005, to reach £32.4 billion in the last quarter of 2006. The amount of secured lending then decreased sharply from the last quarter of 2007 and following the announcement that the UK was officially in recession in January 2009 lending figures fell further and were £1.9 billion by the third quarter of 2009.

People in the UK now travel more and further than 40 years ago. This is one aspect of what is known as our 'carbon footprint'. In order to moderate and reduce the negative impact that human activity has upon the environment, governments both at the UK and global level have developed environment-related policies. In *Social Trends 38*, *Figure 11.15* (Figure 2000.2) examined the disposal of domestic and commercial waste in England. At the end of the 20th century, 84 per cent of the 24.6 million tonnes of municipal waste was disposed to landfill, while recycling accounted for 7 per cent of this total. During the 2000s, households have taken more accountability of environmental issues and by 2006/07, municipal waste disposed to landfill had fallen to 16.9 million tonnes, 58 per cent of the total amount of waste produced, while recycling had increased to 8.9 million tonnes, accounting for 31 per cent of total municipal waste.

In addition to improvements in recycling rates, renewable energy developments have been at the forefront of environmentally friendly campaigning. In *Social Trends 40*, *Table 11.2* examines electricity generation by renewable

Figure 2000.2

Management of municipal waste: by method

England
Million tonnes

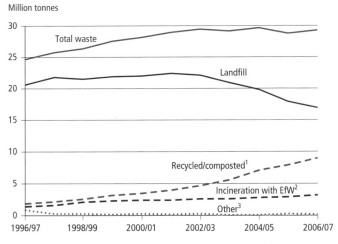

1 Includes household and non-household sources collected for recycling or for centralised composting; home composting estimates are not included in this total.
2 Energy from waste. Includes refuse derived fuel.
3 Includes incineration without energy from waste and other disposal that excludes any processing before waste is sent to landfill or materials reclamation.

Source: Department for Environment, Food and Rural Affairs

sources in the UK. In 2008, renewable energy accounted for 5.5 per cent of all electricity generated in the UK, the equivalent of 4.3 million tonnes of oil equivalent. This represented an increase of around 110 per cent since 2001. In both periods, biofuels accounted for the largest proportion of electricity generated from renewable sources.

We have already seen in the previous decades that rapid advances in technology have affected many aspects of people's lives. Undoubtedly, people today are more technologically minded than ever before, laptops, mobile phones and social networking sites appear to be a primary tool for arranging social activities. However, traditional activities such as watching television, reading and spending time with family and friends have not been completely abandoned in favour of new technology.

A particular focus of *Social Trends 33* was to examine the concept of social capital and its impact upon society. One measure of social capital in this edition was data on 'neighbourliness' and the strength of community spirit. *Table 13.5* (Table 2000.3 overleaf) examined the number of times people speak to their neighbours and the number of people they know within their area.

The proportion of people who say they know many people in their neighbourhood increases with age. In Great Britain in 2000/01, 35 per cent of people aged between 16 and 29 said

Table 2000.3

Indicators of neighbourliness: by age, 2000/01

Great Britain   Percentages

	16–29	30–39	40–49	50–59	60–69	70 and over
Frequency of speaking to neighbours						
Daily	17	25	21	28	39	43
3–6 days per week	20	23	25	24	23	22
1–2 days per week	32	31	37	32	27	23
Less than once per week	30	21	17	16	11	12
Number of people known in the neighbourhood						
Most/many	35	39	48	50	54	57
A few	51	54	48	47	44	41
None	14	8	4	3	2	3

Source: General Household Survey, Office for National Statistics

that they knew most or many people in their neighbourhood, compared with at least half of people aged 50 and over. Younger people were also the least likely of all age groups to speak to their neighbours on a daily basis. Almost a fifth (17 per cent) of people aged 16 to 29 reported doing this compared with more than two-fifths (43 per cent) of people aged 70 and over.

Individuals are also able to contribute to their community through volunteering. Table 13.16 in Social Trends 39 reported on the selected benefits from formal volunteering by age in England. Young people aged 16 to 34 were most likely of all age groups to feel that volunteering gave them a chance to gain new skills, enhance their employment prospect, gain a position in the community and get a recognised qualification. Older people aged 65 and over were most likely of all age groups to see volunteering as something that gave them the chance to meet people and make friends.

Social Trends – Life begins at 40

Throughout the decades Social Trends has remained a co-operative effort by the whole Government Statistical Service. ONS are proud to publish Social Trends, and to continuously develop it. Thanks goes to all, both past and present, who contributed, developed and quality assured the content of Social Trends, allowing each edition to provide accessible statistics about UK society.

Following publication of Social Trends 40, ONS intends to develop and launch web only editions of Social Trends in the future, with material being published throughout the year. This will provide more timely releases of statistics and commentary on changes in UK society. ONS is also planning to publish regular statistical reports highlighting particular areas of interest.

Notes

1   All statistics and sources presented in this article are as reported in the Social Trends edition quoted, and were correct at the time of publication. Methodological changes, revisions and survey design may have resulted in revised figures being published in more recent editions.

Contact

social.trends@ons.gov.uk

01633 455931

Chapter 1

Population

- In 2008, there were 61.4 million people resident in the UK, an increase of 400,000 on 2007, and an increase of 23.2 million since the start of the 20th century. (Table 1.1)

- The number of people aged 85 and over in the UK reached 1.3 million in mid-2008, 422,000 men and 914,000 women, and accounted for 2 per cent of the population. (Figure 1.3)

- During 2008, England experienced a net loss to other countries in the UK of around 7,800 people, with an outflow of 100,600 people and an inflow of 92,800 people, whereas Scotland, Wales and Northern Ireland all experienced net gains. (Table 1.10)

- There were around 25,900 applications for asylum (excluding dependants) to the UK in 2008, an increase of 11 per cent on the previous year. This was the first annual increase in applications since 2002. (Figure 1.12)

- In 1975, the population of the UK accounted for 1.4 per cent of the world's population. By 2005, this proportion had fallen to 0.9 per cent. (Table 1.15)

- For the EU as a whole, fewer than 5 babies per 1,000 live births were expected to die in infancy (during their first year) over the period 2005 to 2010, compared with 11 in 1970. (Table 1.16)

DATA

Download data by clicking the online pdf

www.statistics.gov.uk/socialtrends

Information on the size and structure of the population is essential in understanding various aspects of society, such as labour market and household composition. Changes in demographic patterns not only affect social structures but also the demand for services, such as education, healthcare, housing and pensions.

Population profile

In 2008 there were 61.4 million people resident in the UK, an increase of 400,000 on 2007, and an increase of 23.2 million since the start of the 20th century (Table 1.1). England accounted for 84 per cent of the UK population in 2008, Scotland 8 per cent, Wales 5 per cent and Northern Ireland 3 per cent and despite differences in population growth rates across the UK, these proportions have varied little since the first edition of Social Trends was published, almost 40 years ago.

Over the longer term, England has seen the most significant change of all the constituent countries since 1901, with a population increase of 69 per cent (almost 21 million). The populations of Wales and Northern Ireland have both increased by 50 per cent (1 million and 600,000 respectively) whereas the population of Scotland has increased by 16 per cent (700,000 people). Since 2001, Northern Ireland has seen the biggest percentage increase in population, at around 6 per cent.

Projections suggest that the population of the UK may reach 70 million by 2029. Projected growth rates differ for the constituent countries. Between 2008 and 2031, the population in England is expected to increase by 17 per cent to 60.1 million people; in Wales, by 11 per cent to 3.3 million; in Northern Ireland, by 13 per cent to 2.0 million; and in Scotland by 7 per cent to 5.5 million.

The age structure of the population in any given year reflects past trends in births, deaths and migration. The number of people in each age group within the population depends on how many people are born in a particular period and how long they live as well as the numbers and ages of migrants moving to, and from, the country.

For every 100 girls that are born each year in the UK, there are 105 boys born. However there are more females than males in the overall UK population: 31.2 million females compared with 30.2 million males in 2008 (Table 1.2). In 2008, males outnumbered females up to age 32, while from age 34 onwards women outnumbered men. The gap between the sexes increases markedly from the late 50s onward and is most pronounced among those aged 75 and over. At younger ages, the increase in the proportion of females is largely determined by differences in levels of net migration and, at older ages, the longer life expectancy of women compared with men drives the sex ratio. However, male life expectancy is improving at a faster rate than female life expectancy and the number of men in these older age groups is expected to increase, helping to close this gap.

Historically, the ageing of the UK population was largely the result of the fall in birth rates that began towards the end of the 19th century. Early in the 20th century lower infant mortality helped to increase the number of people surviving into adulthood. Over the past four decades, lower fertility rates and decreases in mortality rates have resulted in the UK population being skewed towards the older age groups.

The proportion of the UK population aged under 16 in mid-2008 was 19 per cent (11.5 million children), having fallen from 25 per cent in 1971 (Figure 1.3 overleaf). Projections

Table 1.1

Population[1] of the United Kingdom

Millions

	1901	1971	1981	1991	2001	2008	2011	2021	2031
United Kingdom	38.2	55.9	56.4	57.4	59.1	61.4	62.6	67.0	70.9
England	30.5	46.4	46.8	47.9	49.5	51.4	52.6	56.4	60.1
Wales	2.0	2.7	2.8	2.9	2.9	3.0	3.0	3.2	3.3
Scotland	4.5	5.2	5.2	5.1	5.1	5.2	5.2	5.4	5.5
Northern Ireland	1.2	1.5	1.5	1.6	1.7	1.8	1.8	1.9	2.0

1 Data are census enumerated for 1901; mid-year estimates for 1971 to 2008; 2008-based projections for 2011 to 2031. See Appendix, Part 1: Population estimates and projections.

Source: Office for National Statistics; General Register Office for Scotland; Northern Ireland Statistics and Research Agency

Table 1.2

Population:[1] by sex and age

United Kingdom   Thousands

	Under 16	16–24	25–34	35–44	45–54	55–64	65–74	75 and over	All ages
Males									
1971	7,318	3,730	3,530	3,271	3,354	3,123	1,999	842	27,167
1981	6,439	4,114	4,035	3,409	3,121	2,967	2,264	1,063	27,412
1991	5,976	3,800	4,432	3,949	3,287	2,835	2,272	1,358	27,909
2001	6,077	3,284	4,215	4,382	3,856	3,090	2,308	1,621	28,832
2008	5,898	3,823	3,985	4,533	4,027	3,566	2,447	1,873	30,151
2011	5,949	3,821	4,257	4,303	4,285	3,587	2,623	2,017	30,842
2016	6,128	3,622	4,731	4,043	4,474	3,630	3,032	2,326	31,986
2021	6,411	3,459	4,800	4,334	4,199	4,037	3,127	2,766	33,134
2026	6,489	3,641	4,566	4,800	3,948	4,229	3,201	3,337	34,210
Females									
1971	6,938	3,626	3,441	3,241	3,482	3,465	2,765	1,802	28,761
1981	6,104	3,966	3,975	3,365	3,148	3,240	2,931	2,218	28,946
1991	5,709	3,691	4,466	3,968	3,296	2,971	2,795	2,634	29,530
2001	5,786	3,220	4,260	4,465	3,920	3,186	2,640	2,805	30,281
2008	5,620	3,629	3,916	4,619	4,133	3,706	2,708	2,902	31,232
2011	5,673	3,639	4,128	4,357	4,420	3,743	2,878	2,970	31,807
2016	5,846	3,462	4,526	4,039	4,620	3,798	3,312	3,185	32,787
2021	6,122	3,306	4,606	4,222	4,301	4,254	3,424	3,589	33,824
2026	6,197	3,480	4,395	4,615	3,991	4,455	3,503	4,206	34,841

1 Mid-year estimates for 1971 to 2008; 2008-based projections for 2011 to 2026. See Appendix, Part 1: Population estimates and projections.

Source: Office for National Statistics; General Register Office for Scotland; Northern Ireland Statistics and Research Agency

suggest that this proportion will continue to fall, but at a slower pace, to 18 per cent by 2031.

The proportion of people aged 16 to 64 has increased from 61 per cent in 1971 to 65 per cent in mid-2008. This rise is not expected to continue, and the proportion of people in this age group is projected to fall to 60 per cent by 2031.

The number of people aged 85 and over in the UK reached 1.3 million in mid-2008, accounting for 2 per cent of the population compared with 1 per cent in 1971. There were more than twice as many women aged 85 and over than men: 914,000 compared with 422,000. The proportion of people aged 85 and over is projected to increase further, to reach 4 per cent by 2031. In mid-2008 the proportion of the UK population over state pension age (65 for men and 60 for women) was 19 per cent (11.8 million people). The increase in the number of older people has policy implications, for example, placing greater demand on healthcare and social services, and on social security arrangements. The state

pension age (SPA) is changing for both men and women. Between 2010 and 2020 the SPA for women will gradually increase to 65, the same as for men, and between 2024 and 2046 it is planned that the SPA for both men and women will gradually increase to 68.

The population of Great Britain is made up predominantly of people from a White British ethnic background and, in 2008, around 83 per cent of the population belonged to this ethnic group. However, during the second half of the 20th century, the pattern of migration into Great Britain produced a number of distinct ethnic minority groups within the general population. In 2008, the second largest ethnic group was Other White (5 per cent), for example, those born overseas, followed by Indian (2 per cent) and Pakistani (also 2 per cent). The remaining ethnic minority groups accounted for around 8 per cent of the population.

The age structure of the population varies across the different ethnic groups (Table 1.4 overleaf). The Mixed ethnic group,

Figure 1.3

Population age structure[1]

United Kingdom
Percentages

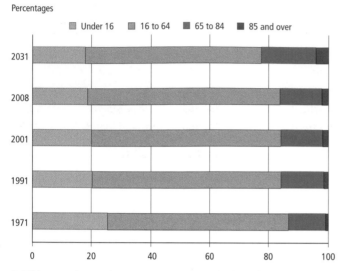

■ Under 16　■ 16 to 64　■ 65 to 84　■ 85 and over

1　Mid-year estimates for 1971 to 2008; 2008-based projections for 2031.
  See Appendix, Part 1: Population estimates and projections.

*Source: Office for National Statistics; General Register Office for Scotland;
Northern Ireland Statistics and Research Agency*

for example, people who identify with both of their parents'
differing ethnicities, had the youngest age profile in
Great Britain in 2008, with more than half (51 per cent) of
people in this group aged under 16. Only 2 per cent of people
in the Mixed ethnic group were aged 65 and over. The Other
Black group also had a young age profile, with 37 per cent of
people in this group being aged under 16. The majority of
people in the Chinese group in Great Britain in 2008 were
aged between 16 and 64 (83 per cent). Only 12 per cent of
people in the Chinese group were under 16 and 5 per cent
were aged 65 and over.

Within each age group, the White British group was the
largest at 91 per cent of those aged 65 and over, 82 per cent
of those aged 16 to 64 and 80 per cent of those aged under
16. The Mixed group made up less than half of 1 per cent of
those aged 65 and over and almost 1 per cent of those aged
16 to 64 compared with 3 per cent of those aged under 16.

The Labour Force Survey (LFS) (see Appendix, Part 4: Labour
Force Survey) provides information on socio-economic
classification based on occupation for those of working age
(men aged 16 to 64 and women aged 16 to 59). Students and
those whose occupation was not stated or who were not
classifiable for other reasons are excluded. The largest
population group in quarter 2 (Q2) 2009 was the lower
managerial and professional category at 22 per cent
(20 per cent of men and 24 per cent of women), followed by
the never worked and unemployed category at 19 per cent

Table 1.4

Population: by ethnic group[1] and age, 2008[2]

Great Britain　　　　　　　　　　　　　　　　　Percentages

	Under 16	16–64	65 and over	All people
White				
White British	18	65	17	100
White Irish	7	68	25	100
Other White	14	75	12	100
Mixed	51	47	2	100
Asian or Asian British				
Indian	20	72	8	100
Pakistani	34	62	4	100
Bangladeshi	36	61	4	100
Other Asian	23	73	5	100
Black or Black British				
Black Caribbean	20	66	13	100
Black African	33	64	2	100
Other Black	37	57	6	100
Chinese	12	83	5	100
Other ethnic group	20	75	4	100
All ethnic groups	19	65	16	100

1　See Appendix, Part 1: Classification of ethnic groups.
2　Data are at January to December. See Appendix, Part 4: Annual
  Population Survey.

Source: Annual Population Survey, Office for National Statistics

(17 per cent of men and 22 per cent of women) (Table 1.5).
Although the smallest category overall was the small employers
group, the smallest category for men was intermediate
occupations, which includes clerical workers and those working
in sales, at 5 per cent, compared with 14 per cent of women.
For women, the smallest category was small employers and
own account workers at 4 per cent compared with 11 per cent
of men.

The largest population differences between the sexes were in
the small employers and own account workers group. The
majority of workers in this category were men (74 per cent),
closely followed by the lower supervisory and technical group,
where 71 per cent of workers were men and 29 per cent were
women. Conversely, in the intermediate occupations,
71 per cent of workers were women and 29 per cent were
men.

By the mid-1800s, today's large cities were already established,
with London as the largest urban area in the UK. However,

Table 1.5

Working-age population: by sex and socio-economic classification,[1] 2009[2]

United Kingdom   Percentages

	Men	Women	All
Higher managerial and professional	16	7	12
Lower managerial and professional	20	24	22
Intermediate occupations	5	14	9
Small employers and own account workers	11	4	8
Lower supervisory and technical	11	5	8
Semi-routine occupations	9	16	12
Routine occupations	11	7	9
Never worked, unemployed and nec[3]	17	22	19

1 Population living in private households. Excludes those who did not state their current or last occupation, and those who had not worked in the last eight years. Men aged 16 to 64 and women aged 16 to 59. See Appendix, Part 1: National Statistics Socio-economic Classification (NS-SEC).
2 Data are at Q2 (April–June) and are not seasonally adjusted. See Appendix, Part 4: Labour Force Survey.
3 People unemployed for less than one year are classified according to their previous occupation. Includes those not elsewhere classified (nec).

Source: Labour Force Survey, Office for National Statistics

large scale movement into urban areas was not yet under way. This was in part because travel over large distances was still difficult and expensive, and industry providing employment was not yet centred on large towns but based around the existing rural craft centres. It was not until the last quarter of the 19th century that there was a large increase in urbanisation. Improvements in transport, better education, large scale industrialisation and agricultural depression were factors in this change.

The population of the UK was highly urbanised for much of the 20th century. The largest of these urban areas was Greater London which, with a resident population of 7.6 million in 2008, had more than the populations of the next three largest metropolitan counties combined (West Midlands, Greater Manchester and West Yorkshire).

In 2008, the largest local authority area in terms of population size was Birmingham, with a population of just over 1 million, followed by Leeds, with around 770,800 residents (Table 1.6). The Isles of Scilly and the City of London were the local authority areas with the smallest populations in the UK, with around 2,100 and 7,900 residents respectively.

The most densely populated local authority area within the UK in 2008 was the London borough of Kensington and Chelsea, with almost 14,900 people per square kilometre. The 10 most

Table 1.6

Ten most and least populated areas,[1] 2008

United Kingdom   Numbers

Most populated		Least populated	
Birmingham	1,016,840	Isles of Scilly	2,130
Leeds	770,830	City of London	7,940
Glasgow City	584,240	Moyle	16,880
Sheffield	534,460	Orkney Islands	19,890
Bradford	501,700	Shetland Islands	21,980
City of Edinburgh	471,650	Teesdale	24,800
Manchester	464,190	Berwick-upon-Tweed	25,920
Liverpool	434,860	Eilean Siar	26,200
City of Bristol	421,320	Ballymoney	30,110
Kirklees	403,940	Larne	31,290

1 Local or unitary authorities in England and Wales, council areas in Scotland and district council areas in Northern Ireland.

Source: Office for National Statistics

densely populated local authorities in the UK were all London boroughs.

Population change

Historically, net natural change – the difference between births and deaths – was the main driver behind population increase, accounting for 98 per cent of population growth in the UK between 1951 and 1961. Since 1971, the influence of net natural change has been much lower and net inflows of immigrants (people moving to the UK) have had a bigger impact on population growth, accounting for 62 per cent of growth between 2001 and 2008 (Table 1.7 overleaf). However, in the year to mid-2008, net immigration accounted for 46 per cent of population growth in the UK, compared with 52 per cent in the year to mid-2007 and 71 per cent in the year to mid-2002.

Over the period 2011–2021 natural change is expected to become more important in influencing population change, accounting for around 58 per cent of the increase in population. Just over two-fifths (42 per cent) of the projected increase in population over this period is expected to be directly attributable to the assumed level of net inward migration.

Since 2001, the UK population has increased by an average of 0.5 per cent per year although growth in the year to mid-2008 was slightly higher at 0.7 per cent. Population growth between mid-2007 and mid-2008 was highest in Northern Ireland, at 0.9 per cent. The population of England grew by 0.7 per cent

Table 1.7

Population change[1]

United Kingdom

Thousands

	Population at start of period	Annual averages				
		Live births	Deaths	Net natural change	Net migration and other[2]	Overall change
1951–1961	50,287	839	593	246	6	252
1961–1971	52,807	962	638	324	-12	312
1971–1981	55,928	736	666	69	-27	42
1981–1991	56,357	757	655	103	5	108
1991–2001	57,439	731	631	100	68	167
2001–2008	59,113	710	591	119	191	310
2008–2011	61,383	781	561	221	198	419
2011–2021	62,649	791	544	248	183	431

1 Mid-year estimates for 1951–1961 to 2001–2008; 2008-based projections for 2008–2011 and 2011–2021. The start population for 2008–2011 is the mid-year estimate for 2008. See Appendix, Part 1: Population estimates and projections.
2 The annual average for 'net migration and other' for 2008–2011 includes an adjustment to reconcile the transition from estimates to projected population data. See Appendix, Part 1: International migration estimates.

Source: Office for National Statistics; General Register Office for Scotland; Northern Ireland Statistics and Research Agency

over the same period and the populations of Scotland and Wales each grew by 0.5 per cent.

The two world wars had a major impact on births. There was a substantial fall in the number of births during the First World War, followed by a post-war 'baby boom' with the number of births reaching 1.1 million in 1920, the highest number of births in any single year during the 20th century (Figure 1.8). Births then decreased in number and remained low during the 1930s' depression and World War Two. A second 'baby boom' occurred after World War Two, followed by a further boom during the 1960s.

During the 1990s, the number of births fell gradually, to a low of 668,800 in 2002, but has since increased each year. There were 794,400 births in the UK in 2008, an increase of just under 3 per cent on 2007, and the sixth consecutive annual increase. Projections suggest that the number of births will decline over the next few years but then increase gradually to around 804,000 in 2041.

Despite considerable population growth since 1901, the annual number of deaths remained relatively constant during the 20th century. There were almost 580,000 deaths in the UK in 2008, compared with 632,000 in 1901. However, this masks large declines in mortality rates. In 2008, mortality rates in England and Wales were the lowest on record at 6,860 deaths per million population for males and 4,910 per million population for females.

In 2008, the total fertility rate (TFR – see text box) in the UK reached 1.96 children per woman, the highest level since 1973 when it was 2.05. This represents a rise from 1.90 in 2007 and is the seventh consecutive rise since a low of 1.63 in 2001.

Total fertility rate

The total fertility rate (TFR) is the average number of live children per woman that a group of women would have if they experienced the age specific fertility rates for a particular calendar year throughout their childbearing lifespan (generally considered to be from age 15 to 44). The number of births in the UK depends on both the fertility rates of women living in the UK and the size and age structure of the UK childbearing population. The TFR is commonly used to analyse fertility because it standardises for the changing age structure of the population and provides a snapshot of the current level of fertility.

Replacement level fertility

Replacement level fertility is the level of fertility needed for a population to replace itself in size in the long term, in the absence of migration. To replace themselves, women need to have, on average, one daughter who survives long enough to have a daughter herself. In developed countries replacement fertility is usually valued at 2.1 children per woman, slightly higher than two children per woman to take account female mortality and the fact that slightly more boys are born than girls.

Figure 1.8

Births[1] and deaths

United Kingdom

Millions

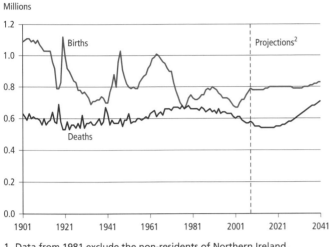

1 Data from 1981 exclude the non-residents of Northern Ireland.
2 2008-based projections for 2009 to 2041. See Appendix, Part 1:
   Population estimates and projections.

*Source: Office for National Statistics; General Register Office for Scotland;
Northern Ireland Statistics and Research Agency*

However, fertility rates remain much lower than the rates seen during the 1960s 'baby boom' when the TFR peaked at just under 3 children per woman. The TFR fell below the replacement level of 2.1 children per woman in 1973 and has remained below this level ever since.

Fertility fell below replacement level in both England and Wales in 1973 and in 1974 in Scotland (Figure 1.9). Over the last 35 years, fertility rates in the UK have been the highest in

Figure 1.9

Total fertility rate[1]

United Kingdom

Children per woman

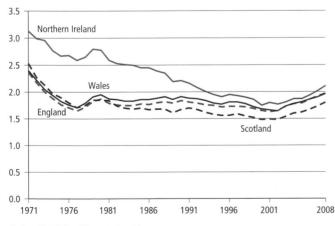

1 See Total fertility rate text box.

*Source: Office for National Statistics; General Register Office for Scotland;
Northern Ireland Statistics and Research Agency*

Northern Ireland. In 1974 the TFR was 2.77 in Northern Ireland compared with 1.97 in Scotland, 1.94 in Wales and 1.88 in England. Since the late 1980s, this difference has substantially reduced; Northern Ireland's TFR fell below replacement level in 1992 and by 2001 had fallen to 1.80, rising back to above replacement level in 2008, at 2.11 children per woman. TFRs in the remainder of the UK in 2008 remained below replacement level: 1.97 in England, 1.96 in Wales and 1.80 in Scotland.

In addition to births and deaths, changes in the population of the UK are caused by international migration and by people moving around within the UK. The extent of migration within the UK is estimated using information on re-registrations with NHS doctors (see Appendix, Part 1: Internal migration estimates). Population gains and losses due to internal migration have important implications for housing planning, as well as for the provision of welfare services.

During 2008, England experienced a relatively small net loss to other countries in the UK of around 7,800 people, with an outflow of 100,600 people and an inflow of 92,800 people (Table 1.10). Scotland, Wales and Northern Ireland experienced small net gains, of around 3,600 people, 2,500 people, and 1,600 people respectively.

At a regional level within England, Greater London experienced the most movement overall: around 209,700 people moved from the capital to other regions of the UK while 163,100 people moved into the area, resulting in a net loss of 46,600 people in 2008. The South West recorded the largest gain of 21,800 people with an outflow of 89,500 and an inflow of 111,300 people.

Table 1.10

Interregional movements within the UK,[1] 2008

Thousands

	Country of origin				
	United Kingdom	England	Wales	Scotland	Northern Ireland
Destination					
United Kingdom	.	100.6	48.4	42.1	9.8
England	92.8	.	46.3	38.3	8.3
Wales	50.9	49.0	.	1.5	0.4
Scotland	45.7	42.9	1.7	.	1.1
Northern Ireland	11.4	8.7	0.4	2.2	.

1 Based on patients re-registering with NHS doctors in other parts of the UK.

Source: National Health Service Central Register; General Register Office for Scotland; Northern Ireland Statistics and Research Agency

From the early 1970s onwards, more people have migrated from northern to southern areas of the UK than vice versa (see Appendix, Part 1: North–South divide), with a net gain to the south of 71,000 people in 1986. This net gain declined rapidly, eventually leading to a small net gain of around 1,000 people to the north in 1989 and again in 1991. During the 1990s the net flow was again towards the south but, between 2001 and 2007, the south recorded a net loss each year as more people moved to the north. In 2008, the north recorded a further net loss, of almost 14,000 people.

Since the beginning of the last century, the pattern of people entering and leaving the UK has varied. In the first 30 years of the 20th century there was a net loss of people each year. However, in the 1930s there was an overall net inflow of people, mainly refugees from other European countries. After a period of net outflow during the 1960s and 1970s, the direction of the trend reversed again and in most years since 1991–92 more people have entered the UK as migrants than left the UK (see Appendix, Part 1: International migration estimates).

In 2007–08, according to August 2009 figures, an estimated 554,000 people came to live in the UK for at least one year (Figure 1.11), equivalent to around 1,500 people per day. In total, this was a fall of around 41,000 people (around 7 per cent) compared with 2006–07. Around 371,000 people were estimated to have left the UK to live abroad for at least one year in 2007–08 meaning that the UK experienced a net gain of around 184,000 people.

An estimated 14 per cent of the long-term migrants into the UK in 2007–08 were British citizens, compared with 45 per cent of those moving abroad. Of those coming to live in the UK, 32 per cent were citizens of the European Union, 23 per cent were citizens of the New Commonwealth and around 8 per cent were citizens of the Old Commonwealth, which comprises Australia, Canada, New Zealand and South Africa.

Some people wish to move to the UK as refugees from the country in which they are living. Such people are able to apply for asylum (see Appendix, Part 1: Refugees). There were around 25,900 applications for asylum to the UK (excluding dependants) in 2008, an increase of 11 per cent on the previous year (Figure 1.12). This was the first time there had been an annual increase in applications since 2002, when applications peaked at 84,100. Including dependants, there were around 31,300 applications for asylum in 2008. Around 1 in 10 applications for asylum, excluding dependants, were made at the point of entry into the UK; the majority were made after the applicant had entered the country.

Around 40 per cent of asylum applications in 2008 were made by African nationals, 37 per cent were from nationals from Asia and Oceania, 19 per cent from Middle Eastern nationals, 3 per cent from European nationals and 2 per cent from nationals of the Americas.

A total of 19,400 initial decisions were made on asylum applications to the UK in 2008, excluding dependants. Just

Figure 1.11

Long-term international migration into and out of the UK[1,2]

Thousands

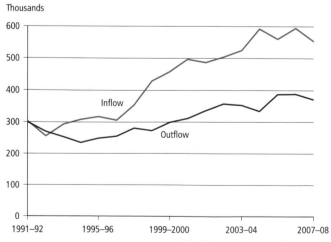

1 An international long-term migrant is defined as a person who moves to a country other than that of his or her usual residence for a period of at least 12 months.
2 Figures are derived from August 2009 estimates published before ONS revised figures in November 2009.

Source: Office for National Statistics

Figure 1.12

Asylum applications[1] excluding dependants

United Kingdom

Thousands[2]

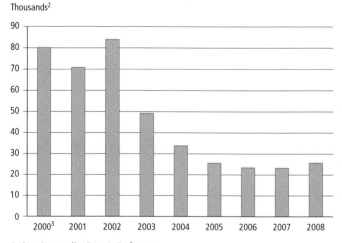

1 See Appendix, Part 1: Refugees.
2 Figures rounded to the nearest 100.
3 May exclude some cases lodged at local enforcement offices between January and March 2000.

Source: Home Office

Figure 1.13

Grants of British citizenship:[1] by basis of grant

United Kingdom

Thousands

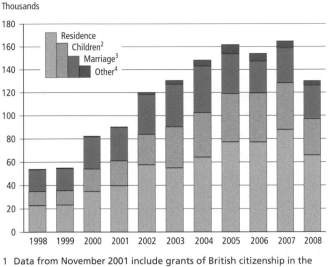

1   Data from November 2001 include grants of British citizenship in the
    Channel Islands and Isle of Man. See Appendix, Part 1: International
    migration estimates.
2   Children aged under 18.
3   Includes civil partnerships from 5 December 2005.
4   Includes British Overseas Territories citizens from Gibraltar registered as
    British citizens under section 5 of the *British Nationality Act 1981*.

Source: Home Office

over 13,500 of these decisions (70 per cent) were refusals. In 19 per cent of cases (3,700 applications) the applicant was granted asylum. The remaining initial decisions were either to grant discretionary leave to stay in the UK or, in less than 1 per cent of cases, to grant humanitarian protection. At the end of 2008, there were 10,600 cases awaiting an initial decision.

There were 241,300 applications for asylum, including dependants, received by member states of the EU-27 in 2008. France received the most applications (15 per cent) followed by the UK and Italy (13 per cent each). However, if population size is taken into consideration, the UK ranks 13th among the member states with 0.51 asylum seekers per 1,000 population. France had 0.57 applicants per 1,000 population and Italy had 0.52 applicants per 1,000 population. Malta had the highest number of asylum seekers, at 6.33 per 1,000 population, followed by Cyprus (3.7 asylum seekers). Estonia had the fewest, with 0.01 asylum seekers per 1,000 population.

In 2008, 156,000 applications were received for British citizenship, just over 1,000 fewer than in 2007. With the exception of a sharp rise in applications in 2005, (211,900 applications), just before requirements for applicants to demonstrate knowledge of life in the UK and English language ability came into force, the number of applications has remained fairly stable since 2003.

Around 129,400 people were granted British citizenship in 2008, 21 per cent fewer than in 2007 (Figure 1.13). Around 9,000 applications were refused, withdrawn or the applicant was found to be British already. The most common basis for granting British citizenship was residence of five or more years in the UK, accounting for slightly over half of all citizenships granted. The proportion of grants awarded to people married to British citizens was 22 per cent and 24 per cent of citizenships granted were to children (aged under 18).

The nationalities with the largest number of British citizenship grants awarded in 2008 were: Indian (11,825), Pakistani (9,440) and Iraqi (8,895). In total, 14,830 European nationals were granted British citizenship, around a quarter (27 per cent) of whom were nationals of the European Economic Area, which comprises all 27 EU member states plus Iceland, Liechtenstein and Norway.

Since 2004 it has been possible to attend a special ceremony to mark the granting of British citizenship, and in 2008 around 91,500 people did so. At local authority level, the highest proportions of ceremonies took place in Birmingham (4 per cent), Ealing (3 per cent), Brent (3 per cent) and Newham (3 per cent).

International perspectives

Population density varies considerably throughout the world, from 131 people per square kilometre (sq km) in Asia as a whole, to 4 people per sq km in Oceania (Table 1.14 overleaf). Comparing individual countries, the variation is far more pronounced: from less than 1 person per sq km in Greenland to more than 21,000 people per sq km in Monaco and in Macao. Countries with the highest population densities are not always those which have the largest populations. The population of China in 2005 was around 860 times that of Gambia but, as it is geographically around 850 times the size of Gambia, the densities of these countries were very similar – 137 and 135 people per sq km respectively. Population density data only give an indication of average land area per person – they do not take account of the dispersion or concentration of populations within countries nor the availability of habitable land.

Table 1.14 shows a selection of demographic indicators based on United Nations (UN) estimates and projections averaged over the period 2005 to 2010. The more developed regions of the world – Europe and North America – have total fertility rates below replacement level (see the Replacement level fertility text box) whereas the less developed regions have fertility rates above replacement level, for example 4.61 children per woman in Africa. These differences in fertility rates

Table 1.14

World demographic indicators, 2005–2010[1]

	Population (millions)[2]	Population density (sq km)[2]	Infant mortality rate[3]	Total fertility rate[4]	Life expectancy at birth (years)	
					Males	Females
Asia	4,167	131	41.5	2.35	67.1	70.8
Africa	1,033	34	82.6	4.61	52.9	55.3
Europe	732	32	7.2	1.50	71.1	79.1
Latin America and the Caribbean	587	29	21.8	2.26	70.2	76.7
North America	352	16	5.8	2.04	77.0	81.5
Oceania	36	4	22.8	2.44	74.1	78.9
World	6,909	51	47.3	2.56	65.4	69.8

1 Data are estimates and projections for the period 2005–2010, revised in 2008.
2 Data are projections for 2010.
3 Per 1,000 live births.
4 See Total fertility rate text box.

Source: United Nations

partly reflect infant mortality rates: on average across Europe and North America, fewer than 8 babies per 1,000 live births will die during their first year (estimates suggest 7.2 in Europe and 5.8 in North America) compared with 82.6 deaths per 1,000 live births in Africa. This is a considerable improvement from the period 1965 to 1970, when the infant mortality rate in Africa averaged 143.5 deaths per 1,000 live births. In Europe and North America, the infant mortality rate has fallen from around 29.8 and 22.2 infant deaths per 1,000 live births respectively since the period 1965 to 1970.

Estimates and projections show that average world-wide life expectancy at birth for males and females is less than 70 years (65.4 for males and 69.8 for females). For Africa, life expectancy is much lower: 52.9 for males and 55.3 for females.

In October 1999 the world's population exceeded 6 billion for the first time, and reached nearly 6.1 billion in 2000, which was more than three and a half times the size it had been 100 years earlier. The UN estimate the world population will be 6.9 billion people in 2010. China was the country with the largest population in 2005 with 1.31 billion people, representing 20 per cent of the world's population (Table 1.15), followed by India with 1.13 billion people (17 per cent). However, according to UN projections, India is expected to have overtaken China in population size by 2030. The country with the third largest population in the world in 2005 was the USA, with around 300 million people (almost 5 per cent of the world's population).

As home to the two countries with the largest populations in the world, Asia is by far the most populous continent, accounting for 60 per cent of the world's population in 2005, followed by Africa with 14 per cent and Europe with

Table 1.15

Selected regions' and countries' share of world population

Percentages

	1965	1975	1985	1995	2005
Asia	56.8	58.7	59.7	60.4	60.4
Africa	9.6	10.2	11.4	12.7	14.2
Europe[1]	19.0	16.6	14.6	12.7	11.2
Latin America and the Caribbean	7.6	8.0	8.3	8.5	8.6
North America	6.6	6.0	5.5	5.2	5.1
Oceania	0.5	0.5	0.5	0.5	0.5
China	21.8	22.8	22.0	21.2	20.2
India	14.8	15.1	15.9	16.7	17.4
EU-27[2]	12.6	11.0	9.5	8.3	7.5
USA	6.0	5.4	5.0	4.7	4.6
Russian Federation	3.8	3.3	3.0	2.6	2.2
Japan	3.0	2.7	2.5	2.2	2.0
United Kingdom	1.6	1.4	1.2	1.0	0.9

1 EU-27 and the Russian Federation, plus Albania, Andorra, Belarus, Bosnia and Herzogovina, Croatia, Faroe Islands, Iceland, Liechtenstein, the Former Yugoslav Republic of Macedonia, Republic of Moldova, Montenegro, Norway, Serbia, Switzerland and the Ukraine.
2 See Appendix, Part 4: Accession to the European Union (EU).

Source: Office for National Statistics; Eurostat; United Nations

Table 1.16

Demographic indicators: selected EU countries[1]

	1970						2005–2010[2]					
	Population (millions)	Population density (sq km)	Total fertility rate[3]	Infant mortality rate[4]	Life expectancy at birth (years)		Population (millions)[5]	Population density (sq km)[5]	Total fertility rate[3]	Infant mortality rate[4]	Life expectancy at birth (years)[2]	
					Males	Females					Males	Females
Germany	78.17	219	1.64	21.1	67.9	73.8	82.06	230	1.32	4.1	77.1	82.4
France	50.77	92	2.31	16.3	68.6	76.2	62.64	114	1.89	3.9	77.6	84.7
United Kingdom	55.66	229	2.44	17.4	69.0	75.2	61.89	253	1.94	4.7	77.2	81.6
Italy	53.36	177	2.35	26.7	69.1	75.1	60.10	199	1.38	3.9	78.1	84.1
Netherlands	13.04	314	2.06	11.7	71.1	77.0	16.65	401	1.74	4.5	77.8	82.0
Belgium	9.63	316	2.02	17.2	68.4	74.9	10.67	350	1.77	4.1	76.7	82.6
Denmark	4.93	114	1.97	12.0	70.9	76.4	5.48	127	1.84	4.4	76.0	80.6
Ireland	2.95	42	3.82	18.1	68.9	73.8	4.59	65	1.96	4.5	77.5	82.3
Luxembourg	0.34	131	1.72	17.1	67.2	74.1	0.49	190	1.66	4.2	76.7	82.1

1 The nine EU countries after the UK joined in 1973. See Appendix, Part 4: Accession to the European Union (EU).
2 Data are estimates and projections for the period 2005–2010, revised in 2008.
3 See Total fertility rate text box.
4 Per 1,000 live births.
5 Data are projections for 2010.

Source: Office for National Statistics; United Nations

11 per cent. Latin America and the Caribbean accounted for 9 per cent, North America 5 per cent and Oceania less than 1 per cent of the world's population.

Between 1965 and 2005, the EU-27 share of the world's population fell from 12.6 per cent to 7.5 per cent. Projections suggest that by 2050 this proportion will be just 5 per cent. The UK has accounted for around 1 per cent of the world's population since the mid-1970s.

Table 1.16 shows selected demographic indicators for the countries that were part of the EU when the UK joined in 1973. Over the last four decades, infant mortality rates have fallen dramatically. In 1970, at least 11 babies per 1,000 live births in each of the EU member states were expected to die in infancy (during their first year) compared with fewer than five in the period 2005 to 2010.

There have also been marked improvements in life expectancy in the years since the UK joined the EU. In 1970, Luxembourg had the lowest life expectancy at birth for males at 67.2 years

and Ireland and Germany had the lowest life expectancy for females at 73.8 years. Estimates and projections show that, in the period 2005 to 2010, life expectancy at birth for males in Luxembourg has risen to 76.7 years and life expectancy for females in Ireland and Germany has risen to 82.3 years and 82.4 years respectively.

Estimates averaged over the period 2005 to 2010 show that, of the EU-27 member states, Lithuania has the lowest life expectancy at birth for males, at 65.8 years. Romania has the lowest life expectancy for females at 76.2 years. Sweden and Italy have the highest life expectancies for males, at 78.7 years and 78.1 years respectively, and France has the highest for females at 84.7 years, closely followed by Italy and Spain at 84.1 years. The gap between life expectancy for males and females is greatest in Lithuania, where females are expected to live to 77.7 years which is 11.9 years longer than males. The gap is narrowest in Malta where females are expected to live 3.6 years longer than males, to 81.4 years.

Chapter 2

Households and families

- An increasing trend towards smaller household sizes has seen the average household size in Great Britain fall from 3.1 people per household in 1961 to 2.4 people in Q2 2009. (Table 2.1)

- The proportion of dependent children in the UK living with married parents fell from almost three-quarters (72 per cent) in Q2 1997 to less than two-thirds (63 per cent) in Q2 2009. (Table 2.5)

- The number of marriages in England and Wales fell for the third consecutive year in 2007, to around 231,500. (Figure 2.11)

- There were around 128,500 divorces in England and Wales in 2007, a fall of 3 per cent compared with 2006. This was the fourth fall in succession and is the lowest number of divorces in a single year since 1976. (Figure 2.15)

- Since the 1970s, there has been a fall in the proportion of babies born to women aged under 25 in England and Wales, from 47 per cent (369,600 live births) in 1971 to 25 per cent (180,700 live births) in 2008. (Figure 2.16)

- In 2007, the average age of women in England and Wales at their first childbirth (27.5 years) was below the average age at first marriage (29.8 years), as has been the case since 1992. (Figure 2.17)

DATA

Download data by clicking the online pdf

www.statistics.gov.uk/socialtrends

Home life, partnerships and other social relationships are important influences on personal development and well-being. Trends in household and family formation are of particular interest to policy makers, for example in determining educational or housing requirements. Traditionally most people in the UK have shared living arrangements for much of their life. However, over the past few decades, changes in social legislation, attitudes, and the age profile of the population have led to new structures and characteristics of households and families. More people spend time living on their own, whether before, after, or instead of marriage or cohabitation. This chapter looks at all of these changes and explores aspects of households and families in the UK.

Household composition

Households are defined, broadly, as people who live and eat together, or people who live alone. Families are defined by marriage, civil partnership or cohabitation and, where there are children in the household, child/parent relationships. Most households consist of a single family or someone living alone. The first section of this chapter looks at people living in private households, and so those living in institutions such as care homes, prisons, hospitals and other communal establishments are not included in the results.

There were 25.2 million households in Great Britain in Q2 (April to June) 2009, an increase of 8.9 million (55 per cent) since 1961 (Table 2.1). Although the population has increased considerably over this time (see Population chapter, Table 1.1),

Table 2.1

Households:[1] by size

Great Britain						Percentages
	1961	1971	1981	1991	2001[2]	2009[2]
One person	14	18	22	27	29	29
Two people	30	32	32	34	35	35
Three people	23	19	17	16	16	16
Four people	18	17	18	16	14	14
Five people	9	8	7	5	5	4
Six or more people	7	6	4	2	2	2
All households (=100%) (millions)	16.3	18.6	20.2	22.4	23.9	25.2
Average household size (number of people)	3.1	2.9	2.7	2.5	2.4	2.4

1 See Appendix, Part 2: Households, Families, and Multi-sourced tables.
2 Data are at Q2 (April–June) each year and are not seasonally adjusted. See Appendix, Part 4: Labour Force Survey.

Source: Census, Labour Force Survey, Office for National Statistics

the number of households has grown faster because of an increasing trend towards smaller household sizes. This is reflected in the fall in the average household size in Great Britain from 3.1 people per household in 1961 to 2.4 people per household in Q2 2009. Reasons for this increase in household numbers, and the fall in household size, include more lone parent families, smaller family sizes and, in particular, more one person households. However, the rise in one person households has levelled off in recent years. As a proportion of all households, one person households increased by 13 percentage points between 1961 and 1991, by a further 2 percentage points between 1991 and Q2 2001, and has since remained stable.

Over the same time period, there has been a marked fall in the proportion of households comprising six or more people. In 1961, 7 per cent of all households in Great Britain were home to at least six people. By 1991, this had fallen to 2 per cent, a proportion that has since remained stable.

In Northern Ireland there were estimated to be around 693,000 households in 2008–09 and the average household size was 2.5 people per household, compared with 2.7 people per household in 1998–99. More than a quarter (28 per cent) of households in Northern Ireland were home to just one person in 2008–09. Between 1998–99 and 2004–05 the proportion of large family households, comprising six or more people, fell from 5 per cent to 3 per cent, and has since remained stable.

In Q2 2009 the most common type of household in Great Britain was a couple family household, which accounted for more than half (56 per cent) of all households (Table 2.2). However, there has been a decline in the proportion of households containing a 'traditional' family unit – couple families with dependent children (children aged under 16 and those aged 16 to 18 who have never married and are in full-time education). In 1961, 38 per cent of households comprised couple families with dependent children but by Q2 2009 this had fallen to 21 per cent. Over the same period, the proportion of households comprising one person under state pension age (65 for men and 60 for women) increased more than threefold, from 4 per cent in 1961 to 14 per cent in Q2 2009. The proportion of households headed by one person over state pension age doubled between 1961 and 1981, and rose a further 2 percentage points between 1981 and 1991. By Q2 2009, the proportion of these older one person households had fallen back to 14 per cent.

Couple family households also accounted for 56 per cent of all households in Northern Ireland in 2008–09. Couple families with dependent children accounted for almost a quarter

Table 2.2

Households:[1] by type of household and family

Great Britain						Percentages
	1961	1971	1981	1991	2001[2]	2009[2]
One person households						
Under state pension age[3]	4	6	8	11	14	14
Over state pension age[3]	7	12	14	16	15	14
One family households						
Couple[4]						
No children	26	27	26	28	29	29
1–2 dependent children[5,6]	30	26	25	20	19	18
3 or more dependent children[5,6]	8	9	6	5	4	3
Non-dependent children only	10	8	8	8	6	6
Lone parent[4]						
Dependent children[5,6]	2	3	5	6	7	7
Non-dependent children only	4	4	4	4	3	3
Two or more unrelated adults	5	4	5	3	3	3
Multi-family households	3	1	1	1	1	1
All households						
(=100%) (millions)	16.3	18.6	20.2	22.4	23.9	25.2

1 See Appendix, Part 2: Households, Families, and Multi-sourced tables.
2 Data are at Q2 (April–June) each year and are not seasonally adjusted. See Appendix, Part 4: Labour Force Survey.
3 State pension age is currently 65 for men and 60 for women.
4 These households may contain individuals who are not family members. Couples data for 2009 include a small number of same-sex couples and civil partners.
5 Children aged under 16 and those aged 16 to 18 who have never married and are in full-time education.
6 These families may also contain non-dependent children.

Source: Census, Labour Force Survey, Office for National Statistics

(24 per cent) of all households, a fall of 4 percentage points since 1998–99. The proportion of one person households has remained broadly stable over the last 10 years, at around 27 per cent. In 2008–09, 14 per cent of these households comprised one adult over state pension age and 13 per cent comprised one adult below state pension age.

In Q2 2009, 59.2 million people lived in private households in Great Britain (Table 2.3 overleaf). The remainder of the population lived in one of a range of communal establishments, for example, prisons, hospitals and care homes, and hotels (live-in staff). For further information see Appendix, Part 4: Labour Force Survey.

The data in Table 2.2 showed that over half (56 per cent) of households were headed by a couple in Q2 2009, whereas Table 2.3 is based on people in households. It shows that over

Reference persons

Though the majority of households contain one family, some households contain multiple families, while others do not contain a family at all (for example, where the household consists of only one person or unrelated adults). This chapter mainly refers to data based on the household reference person although some data are based on the family reference person. The UK Census 2001 defined household reference person and family reference person as follows:

Household reference person (HRP)

A person living alone is the HRP. If the household contains one family, the HRP is the same as the family reference person (FRP, see below). If there is more than one family in the household, the HRP is chosen from the FRPs using the same criteria as for choosing the FRP. If there is no family, the HRP is chosen from the individuals living in the household using the same criteria.

Family reference person (FRP)

In a couple family the FRP is chosen from the two people in the couple on the basis of their economic activity in priority order of full-time job, part-time job, unemployed, retired, other. If both have the same economic activity, the FRP is defined as the elder of the two, or if they are the same age, the first member of the couple listed on the census form. In a lone parent family the FRP is the lone parent.

two-thirds (70 per cent) of people living in private households lived in couple family households in Q2 2009. However, between 1961 and Q2 2009 the proportion of people living in the 'traditional' family household of a couple with dependent children has fallen from just over half (52 per cent) to just over a third (36 per cent), while the proportion of people living in couple family households with no children increased from almost a fifth (18 per cent) in 1961 to a quarter (25 per cent) in Q2 2001, and has remained stable since.

The proportion of people living in lone parent households doubled between 1961 and 1981 (from 3 per cent to 6 per cent) and doubled again between 1981 and Q2 2009 (from 6 per cent to 12 per cent). Between 1961 and Q2 2009 the proportion of people living in other households, including multi-family households and households with unrelated adults only, halved from 12 per cent to 6 per cent.

Earlier in this section, the increase in the proportion of people living alone was highlighted as one of the most noticeable changes in household composition over the past few decades. The number of one person households increased from around 1.7 million in 1961 to more than 7 million in Q2 2009.

Table 2.3

People in households:[1] by type of household and family

Great Britain   Percentages

	1961	1971	1981	1991	2001[2]	2009[2]
One person households	4	6	8	11	12	12
One family households						
Couple						
No children	18	19	20	23	25	25
Dependent children[3]	52	52	47	41	38	36
Non-dependent children only	12	10	10	11	9	9
Lone parent[4]	3	4	6	10	11	12
Other households[5]	12	9	9	4	5	6
All people in private households						
(=100%) (millions)	49.5	53.4	53.9	54.1	56.7	59.2

1 See Appendix, Part 2: Households, Families, and Multi-sourced tables.
2 Data are at Q2 (April–June) each year and are not seasonally adjusted. See Appendix, Part 4: Labour Force Survey.
3 Children aged under 16 and those aged 16 to 18 who have never married and are in full-time education.
4 Includes those with dependent children only, non-dependent children only and those with both dependent and non-dependent children.
5 Includes same-sex couples and civil partners for 2009.

Source: Census, Labour Force Survey, Office for National Statistics

However, the percentage increase has not been uniform across all ages, or by sex. Data from the General Household Survey (see Appendix, Part 2: General Household Survey) show that older women were the most likely to be living alone in Great Britain in 2007, 61 per cent of women aged 75 and over,

compared with 34 per cent of men in the same age group (Figure 2.4). In recent years, the proportion of younger people living alone has halved, from 6 per cent of men and 4 per cent of women aged 16 to 24 in 2000, to 3 per cent and 2 per cent respectively in 2007.

The majority of dependent children in the UK live in families, of which there are three main types: a married couple, a cohabiting couple or a lone parent family. In Q2 2009 there were around 13 million dependent children living with at least one parent in the UK. More than three-quarters (76 per cent) of these children, equivalent to over 10 million children, lived with two parents (Table 2.5). The proportion of dependent children living with two parents fell during the 1970s, 1980s and 1990s: from 92 per cent in 1972, to 88 per cent in 1981 and to 83 per cent by 1992. In Q2 2001, 78 per cent of dependent children lived with two parents, a figure that has remained fairly stable since.

Almost 8.3 million dependent children (63 per cent) lived with married parents in the UK in Q2 2009 and around 1.7 million (13 per cent) lived with cohabiting parents. In comparison, 9.6 million children (72 per cent) lived with married parents in Q2 1997 and 1.0 million (8 per cent) lived with cohabiting parents.

The number of families with dependent children in the UK in Q2 2009 was around 7.6 million. Of these, 4.6 million (61 per cent) were married couple families. The second most common type was families headed by a lone mother (1.8 million), followed by cohabiting couple families (1.0 million) and lone father families (0.2 million).

Figure 2.4

People living alone: by sex and age

Great Britain

Percentages

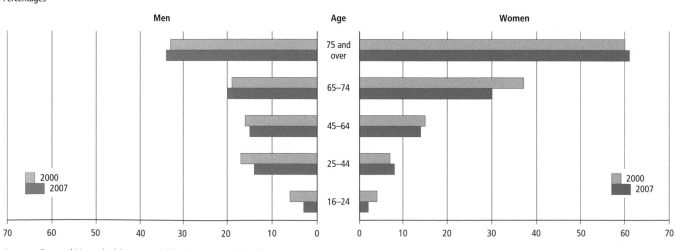

Source: General Household Survey, Office for National Statistics

Table 2.5

Dependent children[1] and their families[2]

United Kingdom   Millions

	1997	2001	2005	2008	2009
Number of dependent children: by family type					
Married couple[3]	9.6	9.0	8.6	8.3	8.3
Cohabiting couple[4]	1.0	1.3	1.5	1.7	1.7
Female lone parent	2.5	2.7	2.8	2.8	2.9
Male lone parent	0.2	0.2	0.3	0.2	0.3
Number of families with dependent children					
Married couple[3]	5.1	4.8	4.7	4.6	4.6
Cohabiting couple[4]	0.6	0.8	0.9	1.0	1.0
Female lone parent	1.5	1.6	1.7	1.7	1.8
Male lone parent	0.2	0.2	0.2	0.2	0.2

1 Children aged under 16 and those aged 16 to 18 who have never married and are in full-time education. See Appendix, Part 2: Families.
2 Data are at Q2 (April–June) each year and are not seasonally adjusted. See Appendix, Part 4: Labour Force Survey.
3 Data for 2008 onwards include civil partnerships.
4 Data for 2008 onwards include same-sex couples.

Source: Labour Force Survey, Office for National Statistics

In Q2 2009, married couple families with dependent children had an average of 1.8 dependent children living with them. Cohabiting couples with dependent children had an average of 1.7 dependent children. The figure for lone mothers was 1.6 dependent children whereas for lone fathers it was 1.4 dependent children.

Children live in an increasing variety of family structures during their lives. If their parents separate they will typically start to live in a lone parent family or a stepfamily. Stepfamilies are formed when an adult with a child (or children) lives in a partnership with someone who is not the parent of their child (or children). This can happen after the death of a spouse or partner but is more common after divorce or separation. In most cases, stepfamilies comprise a natural mother and a stepfather (86 per cent of stepfamilies in Great Britain in 2007) because it is usual for children to remain with the mother following a relationship breakdown (Table 2.6). In Great Britain in 2007, 10 per cent of stepfamilies comprised a natural father and a stepmother and around 4 per cent of stepfamilies were formed by two adults who both had one or more stepchildren in the household.

There has been a considerable increase in the proportion of families headed by a lone mother since 1971, when 7 per cent of families with dependent children in Great Britain were lone mother families, compared with 20 per cent in 2007. The marital status of these lone parents has changed markedly over

Table 2.6

Stepfamilies[1] with dependent children[2]

Great Britain   Percentages

	1991/92	1996/97	2000/01	2005[3]	2007
Child(ren) from the woman's previous marriage/cohabitation	86	84	88	86	86
Child(ren) from the man's previous marriage/ cohabitation	6	12	9	11	10
Child(ren) from both partners' previous marriage/cohabitation	6	4	3	3	4
Lone parent with child(ren) from a previous partner's marriage/cohabitation	1	-	-	-	-
All stepfamilies	100	100	100	100	100

1 Family reference person aged 16 to 59. See Appendix, Part 2: General Household Survey.
2 Children aged under 16, or aged 16 to 18 and in full-time education, in the family unit, and living in the household.
3 In 2005 General Household Survey data collection changed from financial to calendar year.

Source: General Household Survey, Office for National Statistics

this time. In 1971, only 1 per cent of families with dependent children were single (never-married) lone mothers, but by 2007 this proportion had risen to 10 per cent (Figure 2.7). These single lone parents may or may not have previously been in a

Figure 2.7

Lone mother families with dependent children:[1] by marital status

Great Britain

Percentages

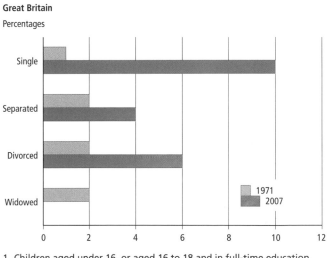

1 Children aged under 16, or aged 16 to 18 and in full-time education, in the family unit, and living in the household.

Source: General Household Survey, Office for National Statistics

cohabiting relationship with the father of their child (or children). In 1971, 2 per cent of families with dependent children were headed by widowed lone mothers but by 2007 this proportion fell to less than 0.5 per cent (rounded to zero). This trend probably shows a fall in lone mother families created by the death of a male partner (although the mother may have become a lone parent after becoming widowed). Between 1971 and 2007, there was a large increase in the proportion of families with dependent children that were separated or divorced lone mothers. The proportion that were separated lone mothers doubled (from 2 per cent to 4 per cent), and the proportion that were divorced lone mothers tripled (from 2 per cent to 6 per cent). Lone father families with dependent

children accounted for 3 per cent of all families with dependent children in 2007.

Household size and composition vary across ethnic groups. Demographic traditions and socio-economic characteristics of the ethnic groups in the UK underlie many of these differences. In Q2 2009, 86 per cent of dependent children from the Asian or Asian British ethnic group were living in married couple families (894,000 children). This compares with 62 per cent of dependent children from a White background (6.7 million children), 74 per cent of children from the Chinese group (25,000 children), and 78 per cent of children from the Other ethnic group (181,000 children) (Table 2.8). Fewer than half of

Table 2.8

Dependent children:[1] by family type and ethnic group[2,3]

United Kingdom

Thousands

	2001	2003	2005	2007	2009
Married couple[4]					
White	7,863	7,637	7,313	7,061	6,717
Mixed	125	126	151	167	188
Asian or Asian British	620	659	693	752	894
Black or Black British	131	148	152	215	196
Chinese	33	23	33	36	25
Other ethnic group	45	108	142	148	181
Total dependent children with married parents[5]	8,997	8,772	8,577	8,441	8,290
Cohabiting couple[6]					
White	1,256	1,300	1,383	1,492	1,567
Mixed	27	26	29	50	55
Asian or Asian British	3	7	2	5	7
Black or Black British	26	19	24	26	22
Chinese	2	*	*	2	3
Other ethnic group	*	4	5	7	12
Total dependent children with cohabiting parents[5]	1,339	1,366	1,455	1,597	1,682
Lone parent					
White	2,418	2,557	2,474	2,424	2,496
Mixed	127	128	133	134	150
Asian or Asian British	94	81	107	134	143
Black or Black British	198	206	206	240	279
Chinese	12	9	6	10	6
Other ethnic group	5	24	47	73	40
Total dependent children with lone parents[5]	2,900	3,020	2,995	3,028	3,146

1 Children aged under 16 and those aged 16 to 18 who have never married and are in full-time education.
2 See Appendix, Part 1: Classification of ethnic groups.
3 Data are at Q2 (April–June) each year and are not seasonally adjusted. See Appendix, Part 4: Labour Force Survey.
4 Data for 2007 onwards include civil partnerships.
5 Includes those who did not know or state their ethnicity.
6 Data for 2007 onwards include same-sex couples.

Source: Labour Force Survey, Office for National Statistics

all children in the Mixed (48 per cent) and Black or Black British (39 per cent) groups lived with married parents (188,000 children and 196,000 children respectively).

More than half of Black or Black British dependent children lived with a lone parent (56 per cent) in Q2 2009, a similar proportion as reported in 2001. Children from the Asian or Asian British group were least likely to live with a lone parent, at just 14 per cent of all dependent children in this group. The proportion of Asian or Asian British children living with lone parents was similar to 2001 (13 per cent) but the proportion of White children living with lone parents had risen since 2001, when it was 21 per cent of all children in this group, compared to 23 per cent in Q2 2009.

Partnerships

In 2007, the majority of the adult population in England and Wales were living as part of a couple, either cohabiting or married. Types of partnership vary according to age group, although by far the most common partnership type was marriage. More than half (55 per cent) of adults aged 30 and over were married in 2007. Adults aged 16 to 29 were the least likely age group to be living with a partner: 10 per cent were married and 16 per cent were cohabiting (Figure 2.9). In comparison, almost three-quarters (71 per cent) of adults aged 30 to 44 and just over three-quarters (76 per cent) of adults aged 45 to 64 were living with a partner, either as a married or cohabiting couple. In the older age group, people aged 65 and

Figure 2.9

Population: by partnership status and age

England & Wales

Percentages

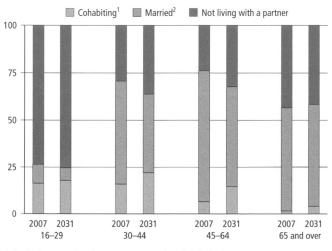

1 Includes people who are separated and cohabiting.
2 Includes people who are separated but not cohabiting; projections are not available for this group.

Source: Office for National Statistics

Table 2.10

Cohabiting population:[1] by marital status and sex, 2007[2]

England & Wales		Percentages
	Men	Women
Never married	72	74
Separated	3	2
Widowed	1	2
Divorced	24	21

1 Aged 16 and over.
2 2006-based estimates, incorporating estimates of the population cohabiting at mid-2007. See Appendix, Part 1: Population estimates and projections.

Source: Office for National Statistics

over, more than half (55 per cent) were married and less than 2 per cent were cohabiting.

The proportion of opposite-sex couples (either married or cohabiting) is projected to fall for most age groups over the next 25 years. However, expected improvements in life expectancy are projected to impact upon the proportion of adults who are currently living as part of a couple, leading to an increase in the proportion of married and cohabiting adults aged 65 and over in 2031. Overall, the number of cohabiting couples in England and Wales is projected to rise by almost two-thirds, from 2.25 million in 2007 to 3.70 million in 2031.

It is estimated that in 2007, around 10 per cent of the population aged 16 and over in England and Wales were cohabiting (4.5 million adults) and that the majority of cohabiting adults (72 per cent of men and 74 per cent of women) had never married (Table 2.10). Most of the remainder were divorced (24 per cent of cohabiting men and 21 per cent of cohabiting women).

Almost a fifth (19 per cent) of women aged between 16 and 30 were cohabiting compared with 14 per cent of men in the same age group in 2007. Of the men who were cohabiting, the largest proportion (42 per cent) were aged between 31 and 45, whereas female cohabitants tended to be younger: 45 per cent of women cohabiting in England and Wales in 2007 were aged between 16 and 30.

Tables 2.1, 2.2 and 2.3 showed estimates of households and families at a given point in time, but another consideration is the stability of household and family types over time. Changes in family type can occur because of partnership dissolution. A cohabitation separation causes a family change and marks the end of a cohabiting partnership. It only measures the flow of cohabiting couples who stop living together, and not when a cohabiting couple marry each other. In 2007, around 1 in 10 married (or civil partnered) adults aged between 16 and 59 had ever experienced a cohabitation separation (prior to their current partnership). In comparison, 1 in 5 cohabiting adults (of the same age) had experienced a cohabitation separation (not including their current cohabitation). In part this difference may be explained by the fact that younger people are both more likely to be currently cohabiting and to have experienced a cohabitation separation in the past. Divorced adults aged between 16 and 59 were also more likely than married adults to have experienced cohabitation separation at some point in their lives, while widowed adults were the least likely to have ever experienced cohabitation separation. Again, it is likely that age and generational differences explain some of this variation.

Marriage and divorce are two further types of family transition. The number of marriages in England and Wales fell for the third consecutive year in 2007, to 231,500 (Figure 2.11). With the exception of an increase between 2002 and 2004, there has been a steady decline since the early 1970s and this was the lowest number of marriages recorded in a single year in England and Wales since 1895 when there were just over 228,000 marriages.

The number of first marriages (first for both partners) in England and Wales has decreased substantially since the peak of 340,000 in 1970, equivalent to 82 per cent of all marriages registered that year. First marriages fell below three-quarters (73 per cent) of all marriages in 1972 and continued to decline, reaching a low of 58 per cent in 1996. However, in 2007 there

were around 143,000 first marriages, which accounted for almost two-thirds (62 per cent) of all marriages. The last time the proportion of marriages that were first marriages was this high was in 1992.

Almost 29,900 marriages were registered in Scotland in 2007. The highest number of marriages registered in Scotland in a single year was just over 53,500 in 1940. The lowest since records began was in 1858 when just under 19,700 marriages were registered.

In Northern Ireland there were 8,500 marriages registered in 2008, which was a decrease of around 2 per cent on the previous year. The highest number of marriages ever recorded in Northern Ireland was in 1970 (12,300 marriages). Since then, the number of marriages taking place in Northern Ireland has declined, and reached a low of 7,300 in 2001. In 2008, four-fifths (80 per cent) of marriages were first marriages for both partners and 7 per cent were remarriages for both partners.

Of the 231,500 marriages that were registered in England and Wales in 2007, a third (33 per cent) were religious marriages (Table 2.12). Of all religious ceremonies, 72 per cent were Church of England and Church in Wales, around 1 in 10 (11 per cent) were Roman Catholic, just under 1 in 10 (9 per cent) were nonconformist, and around 1 in 20 (4 per cent) were other types of Christian ceremony such as Presbyterian, Society of Friends (Quakers), Salvation Army,

Figure 2.11

Marriages: by previous marital status

England & Wales

Thousands

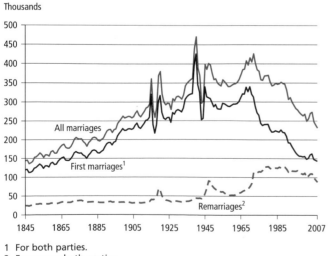

1 For both parties.
2 For one or both parties.

Source: Office for National Statistics

Table 2.12

Marriages: by type of ceremony

England & Wales
Thousands

	1981	1991	2001	2007
Civil ceremonies	172.5	151.3	160.2	154.0
in approved premises	.	.	50.1	99.8
Religious ceremonies	179.5	155.4	89.0	77.5
Church of England/Church in Wales	118.4	102.8	60.9	55.9
Roman Catholic	26.1	19.6	10.5	8.8
Nonconformist[1]	29.0	25.5	11.2	6.6
Other Christian bodies[2]	4.4	5.6	4.0	3.4
Other[3]	1.5	2.0	2.4	2.8
All ceremonies	352.0	306.8	249.2	231.5

1 Includes Methodist, Calvanistic Methodist, United Reformed Church, Congregationalist and Baptist.
2 Includes Presbyterian, Society of Friends (Quakers), Salvation Army, Brethren and Jehovah's Witnesses.
3 Includes Jewish, Muslim and Sikh.

Source: Office for National Statistics

Brethren and Jehovah's Witnesses. The remaining 4 per cent (2,800 ceremonies) were other religious ceremonies including Jewish, Muslim and Sikh marriages.

The proportion of religious marriages fell from just over half (51 per cent) of all marriages in 1981 to around a third (33 per cent) in 2007. During this period, the number of Church of England/Church in Wales marriages has more than halved, although they have increased from 66 per cent to 72 per cent of all religious marriages. Roman Catholic marriages, which accounted for 15 per cent of religious marriages in 1981, fell by around two-thirds and, in 2007, accounted for 11 per cent of religious marriages. The number of Other marriages, for example, Jewish, Muslim and Sikh marriages almost doubled, from 1,500 in 1981 to 2,800 in 2007.

Over four-fifths (81 per cent) of religious ceremonies in 2007 were first marriages for both partners compared with just over half (53 per cent) for civil ceremonies. Nearly a quarter (23 per cent) of civil marriages were remarriages for both partners, compared with 7 per cent of religious marriages.

In Scotland, just over half (52 per cent) of marriages were civil ceremonies in 2007. Just over a quarter (26 per cent) were Church of Scotland ceremonies and the remainder were other denominations. In Northern Ireland, 71 per cent of marriages in 2008 were religious marriages, a much higher proportion than in the rest of Great Britain. Although the number of civil marriages in Northern Ireland is low compared with England, Wales and Scotland, the popularity of the civil ceremony has

been increasing over the longer term. Civil marriages accounted for 7 per cent of all marriages in 1928 and 14 per cent in 1988.

According to the 2006 British Social Attitudes Survey, more than two-thirds of people believe that they did not need a partner to be happy and fulfilled in life. Falling marriage rates and an increasing number of cohabiting couples partly reflect differences between generations in addition to differences between age groups. For men born in 1956, the proportion who had ever married by age 25 was 50 per cent (503 men for every 1,000 born in 1956). Women in this generation were even more likely to have married by age 25: the equivalent proportion was 71 per cent (710 women for every 1,000 born in 1956) (Figure 2.13).

By comparison, younger generations are much less likely to have ever been married, particularly at younger ages. This reflects both a delay and a decline in marriage. For men born in 1981, 8 per cent had married by the time they were 25. For women the equivalent figure was 16 per cent.

It is difficult to compare different generations because a complete partnership history for each generation will only become available as the people in each generation come towards the end of their lives. Nevertheless, Figure 2.13 indicates that there has been a smaller proportion of ever married adults in each successive generation when comparing the proportion at every age. It remains to be seen whether younger generations will catch up with older generations in the proportion that have ever married by the end of their lives.

Figure 2.13

Proportion of adults[1] ever married: by age and year of birth[2]

England & Wales

Rates per 1,000 population

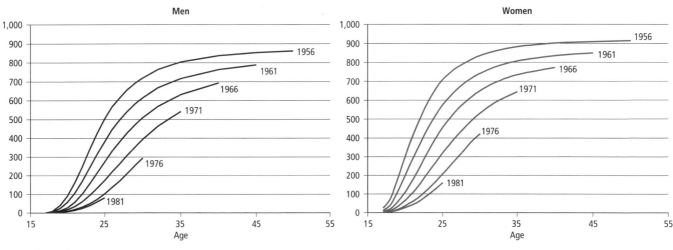

1 Aged 16 and over.
2 Each line is a birth cohort (year of birth).

Source: Office for National Statistics

Some catching up might be expected as the average age at marriage continues to rise.

The highest number of civil partnerships registered in the UK was in December 2005 (1,953), when the *Civil Partnership Act 2004* came into force (see Appendix, Part 2: Civil partnership) (Figure 2.14). The artificially high number of partnerships formed in this month, and throughout the following 12 months, reflected the number of same-sex couples in long-term relationships who took advantage of the opportunity to formalise their relationship as soon as possible after the legislation was implemented. There were a total of 7,169 civil partnerships registered in the UK in 2008, a fall of 18 per cent on the previous year.

A fall in the number of civil partnership registrations was recorded in all four countries of the UK. The largest annual fall was in Scotland (24 per cent) where 525 partnerships were registered in 2008 followed by Northern Ireland (23 per cent) where 86 partnerships were registered. England accounted for around 88 per cent (6,276) of all civil partnerships formed in the UK, a fall of 18 per cent in registrations compared with 2007. The smallest fall was recorded in Wales (4 per cent) where 282 partnerships were registered in 2008.

In order to obtain the dissolution of a civil partnership, a couple must have been in a registered partnership, or a recognised foreign relationship, for at least 12 months. In 2008 there were 180 civil partnership dissolutions granted in the UK. Of these, the majority took place in England, where there were

154 dissolutions. There were 14 dissolutions in Scotland, 12 in Wales and none in Northern Ireland.

The number of divorces that took place in England and Wales in the 1920s and the early 1930s averaged slightly more than 3,000 per year. Following an Act of Parliament in 1938 that extended the grounds on which divorce was allowed, numbers increased considerably throughout the 1940s, to a peak of around 60,300 in 1947 (Figure 2.15). Although the number of divorces then fell to a low of 22,700 in 1958, there was a further increase during the 1960s. The *Divorce Reform Act 1969*, which was subsequently consolidated into the *Matrimonial Causes Act 1973*, removed the concepts of a 'guilty party' and 'matrimonial offence' and introduced the idea of 'the irretrievable breakdown of marriage'. This had a considerable impact on divorce numbers in England and Wales, which exceeded the 100,000 mark in 1972 at 119,000, an increase of almost 60 per cent on the previous year.

From the 1970s onwards, England and Wales generally saw an upward trend in the number of divorces each year, reaching the highest recorded peak of 165,000 in 1993. There were around 128,500 divorces in England and Wales in 2007 (a rate of 11.9 divorcing people per 1,000 married population), a fall of 3 per cent compared with 2006 (12.2 divorcing people per 1,000 married population). This was the fourth successive annual fall and was the lowest number of divorces in a single year since 1976 when there were just under 126,700 divorces, 10.1 divorcing people per 1,000 population. In Scotland, there were around 11,500 divorces registered in 2008, a fall of 10 per cent on the previous year when 12,800 divorces were recorded. The number of divorces in Scotland peaked at just

Figure 2.14

Civil partnerships:[1] by sex, 2005 to 2008

United Kingdom

Number of partnerships

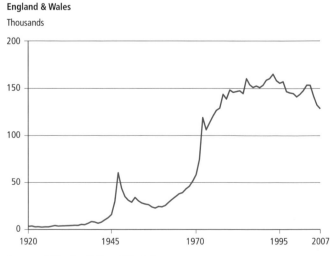

1 Data do not include civil partnerships of UK residents taking place abroad but will include non-UK residents who form a partnership in the UK. See Appendix, Part 2: Civil partnership.

Source: Office for National Statistics; General Register Office for Scotland; Northern Ireland Statistics and Research Agency

Figure 2.15

Divorces

England & Wales

Thousands

Source: Office for National Statistics

under 13,400 in 1985. In 2008, just under 2,800 divorces were recorded in Northern Ireland, around 100 fewer than in 2007. There were around 2,900 divorces in 2007, which was an increase of around 14 per cent on 2006 and the highest number of divorces recorded in Northern Ireland in a single year.

Family formation

A number of demographic trends have influenced families and households in recent times, most notably the decline and delay of marriage and childbearing. However, the number of births in England and Wales increased for the seventh successive year in 2008, rising from 690,000 in 2007 to 709,000 in 2008. The number of live births is now at its highest level since 1972, when there were 727,000 live births. During this period the average age for women giving birth for the first time has risen from 23.8 years to 27.5 years. Since the 1970s there has been a fall in the proportion of babies born to women aged under 25, from 47 per cent in 1971 (369,600 live births) to 25 per cent in 2008 (180,700 live births) (Figure 2.16).

Conversely, there has been an increase in the proportion of births to older women, with births to women aged 35 and over accounting for 20 per cent of all births each year for the past four years (142,600 live births in 2008). The last time the proportion of births to women in this age group was at this level was in 1945 (137,700 live births).

In Scotland, the number of births in 2008 among those aged 35 and over exceeded births to women aged 20 to 24. More than 60,000 births were registered in Scotland in 2008, which

was the sixth consecutive rise and the highest number recorded since 1995. There were 25,600 births registered in Northern Ireland in 2008, a rise of 5 per cent on the previous year and also the sixth successive annual rise in births.

Figure 2.17 compares the average age of women in England and Wales at their first marriage and the average age of mothers at their first childbirth. Overall, the average age of women at first marriage fell between the 1930s and 1960s, before beginning to rise, reaching 29.8 years in 2007. This partly reflects the choices many women make to live independently, to continue their education and to participate more fully in the labour market rather than follow the more 'traditional' route of early marriage. Along with changing attitudes to marriage have come changing attitudes to motherhood. Over the same period, the average age of first birth within marriage has followed a similar pattern. In 2007, it was 30.3 years: around six months more than the average age at first marriage.

The average age of all women at the birth of their first child, whether within marriage or not, also fell between the 1930s and 1960s but began to increase from the early 1970s, although at a much slower rate than the age at marriage and the age at first childbirth within marriage. In 1992, the average age for women at their first childbirth fell below the average age at marriage and in 2007 was 27.5 years (see Appendix, Part 2: Mean age).

Figure 2.16

Live births: by age of mother at birth of child

England & Wales
Thousands

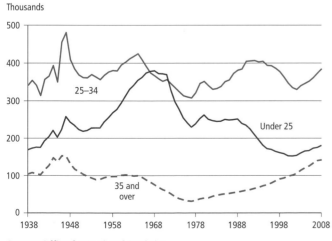

Source: Office for National Statistics

Figure 2.17

Average age of women at first marriage[1] and first live birth

England & Wales
Mean age (years)

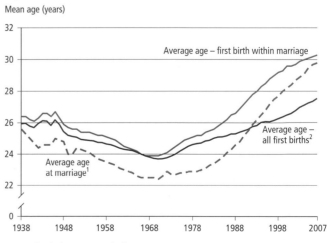

1 For single (never-married) women.
2 Standardised for the age-distribution of the population. This measure is more appropriate for use when analysing trends or making comparisons between different geographies.

Source: Office for National Statistics

Figure 2.18

Births outside marriage[1]

England & Wales
Percentages

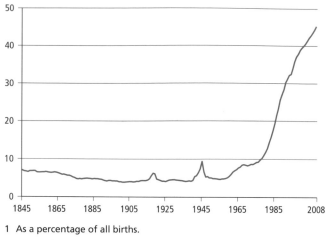

1 As a percentage of all births.

Source: Office for National Statistics

With the exception of the periods immediately following the two world wars, relatively few births occurred outside marriage during the first 60 years of the 20th century (Figure 2.18). Births outside marriage became more commonplace during the 1980s and 1990s, and by 2008 there were 320,800 live births outside marriage in England and Wales, accounting for 45 per cent of all live births that year. This was an increase of 1 percentage point on the previous year when there were 305,600 live births outside marriage. In 1971, less than 10 per cent of all live births in England and Wales were outside marriage (65,700 births). Of these, more than half (55 per cent) were solely registered. In 2008, 65 per cent of births were registered by parents living at the same address (most likely to be cohabiting parents), 21 per cent were registered by parents living at different addresses and 14 per cent were solely registered.

There were 42,000 births outside marriage to women aged under 20 in England and Wales in 2008, equivalent to 94 per cent of all births to women of that age. Almost three-quarters (72 per cent) of all live births to mothers aged 20 to 24 in 2008 were outside marriage. This compares with 43 per cent of live births to mothers aged 25 to 29 and 28 per cent to mothers aged 30 to 34. For older age groups the figures increase to 30 per cent for mothers aged 35 to 39, and 36 per cent for mothers aged 40 and over. In Scotland, the proportion of births outside marriage rose to 50 per cent for the first time in 2008. In Northern Ireland in 2008, there were almost 10,000 births outside marriage, around 39 per cent of all births.

Family patterns vary among the 27 European Union (EU-27) member states because of cultural differences, as well as variations in attitudes, values and behaviour. However the increase in the proportion of births taking place outside marriage seen in the UK is one factor common to almost the whole EU-27. In 2007, more than a third (35 per cent) of all births in the EU were outside marriage (Figure 2.19). Five countries in the EU-27 had a higher proportion of births outside marriage than within. Estonia had the highest proportion of live births outside marriage at 58 per cent, followed by Sweden at 55 per cent, France (52 per cent), Slovenia (51 per cent) and Bulgaria (just over 50 per cent). In Sweden, babies born to married parents have been in a minority for the last decade, with around 55 per cent of births occurring outside marriage since the mid-1990s. In Denmark, the proportion of births outside marriage has remained fairly stable over the past two decades, at between 45 and 47 per cent. Greece (6 per cent) and Cyprus (9 per cent) had the lowest proportions of births outside marriage in the EU-27, much lower than Poland, which was the third lowest (just under 20 per cent).

Figure 2.19

Births outside marriage: EU comparison, 2007

Percentages

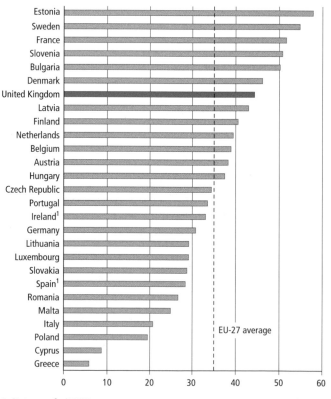

1 Data are for 2006.

Source: Office for National Statistics; Eurostat

Figure 2.20

Teenage conceptions: by outcome[1,2]

England & Wales
Thousands

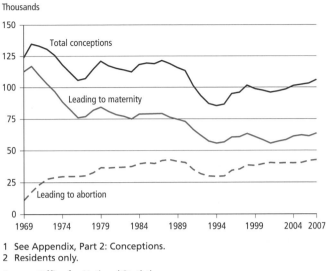

1 See Appendix, Part 2: Conceptions.
2 Residents only.

Source: Office for National Statistics

Figure 2.21

Legal abortions

England & Wales[1]
Thousands

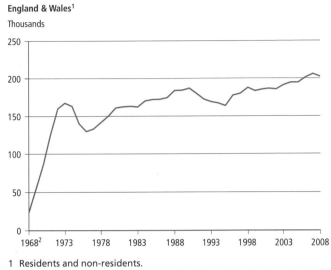

1 Residents and non-residents.
2 1968 figure contains only eight months data as the *Abortion Act 1967* came into effect on 27 April 1968.

Source: Department of Health

After the introduction of free contraception on the NHS in 1974, the rate of teenage conceptions to females aged 15 to 19 declined overall for around a decade but rose by 21 per cent between 1983 and 1990. The rates began to fall again in the early 1990s, increasing slightly between 1995 and 1998.

In England and Wales in 1969, the year after the *Abortion Act 1967* came into effect, there were around 124,000 conceptions to teenage females (a rate of 75.3 conceptions per 1,000 females aged 15 to 19) and around 9 per cent of these were terminated (Figure 2.20). In 2007, there were fewer teenage conceptions than in 1969, at around 106,000 and the rate was also lower at 61.7 conceptions per 1,000 females aged 15 to 19. However, a higher proportion (43 per cent) of these conceptions led to abortion.

In 1969, there were 6,600 conceptions to girls aged under 16 (6.9 conceptions per 1,000 girls aged 13 to 15), of which 25 per cent were terminated. The equivalent figures for 2007 were 8,200 conceptions (8.3 conceptions per 1,000 girls aged 13 to 15) and 62 per cent of these were terminated.

There were around 54,800 legal abortions in 1969, a rate of 5.2 abortions per 1,000 females aged 15 to 44. This figure more than doubled by 1971, when there were just under 126,800 legal abortions, a rate of 9.9 per 1,000 females in this age group (Figure 2.21).

During the early 1990s, the total number of abortions in England and Wales fell slightly, before rising again between 1995 and 1996. In 1995 the Committee on Safety of Medicines warned that several brands of the contraceptive pill

carried a relatively high risk of thrombosis. This warning is believed to have contributed to the increase in abortion rates in 1996, particularly among young women as they were more likely to have been using the pill. Since this pill scare, abortion rates have continued to rise for all age groups except those aged under 16, whose abortion rates have stayed broadly stable.

In 2008 there were 202,200 legal abortions, equivalent to 18.2 abortions per 1,000 females aged 15 to 44. This is a fall of around 2 per cent on the peak of 205,600 legal abortions in 2007. Almost 6,900 of the legal abortions in England and Wales in 2008 were to residents of other countries, mostly from Ireland (67 per cent) and Northern Ireland (17 per cent). The total number of legal abortions to non-residents in 2008 was the lowest number recorded since 1969.

Around 8 in 10 abortions (81 per cent) to England and Wales residents in 2008 were carried out for single women. Ethnicity was recorded in 94 per cent of cases: 76 per cent were reported as White, 10 per cent as Black or Black British and 8 per cent as Asian or Asian British.

There were 13,703 abortions in Scotland in 2007, a rate of 13.0 abortions per 1,000 females aged 15 to 44, compared with 3,566 in 1969, or 3.5 abortions per 1,000 females aged 15 to 44.

For some people, one way to have children is through adoption. Children can be adopted from birth up to and including 17 years of age. On 30 December 2005, the

2

Figure 2.22

Adoptions:[1] by whether child was born inside or outside marriage[2]

England & Wales

Thousands

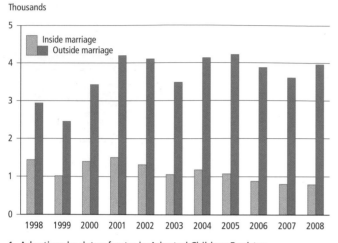

1 Adoptions by date of entry in Adopted Children Register.
2 Excludes cases where marital status was not stated. See Appendix, Part 2: Adoptions.

Source: Office for National Statistics

Adoption and Children Act 2002 was fully implemented. It replaced the *Adoption Act 1976* and modernised the legal framework for adoption in England and Wales. The Act provides for an adoption order to be made in favour of single people, married couples and, for the first time, civil partners, same-sex couples and unmarried couples. The Act also introduced Special Guardianship to provide permanence for children who cannot return to their birth families, but for whom adoption is not the most suitable option.

In 2008, the total population in England and Wales of under 18-years-old was 12.4 million. There were a total of 5,065 children entered onto the Adopted Children Register in 2008, of which, 3,960 children were born outside marriage, and 793 were born within marriage, the remainder (312 children) were recorded as marital status unknown. In comparison, 4,382 children were entered onto the Adopted Children Register in 1998, 2,941 children born outside marriage, and 1,441 children born within marriage (Figure 2.22).

Longer term trends show that in England and Wales there were 21,495 adoptions entered onto the Adopted Children Register in 1971. The number fell rapidly during the 1970s and continued to fall steadily over the 1980s and 1990s. There was an increase in adoptions at the start of this century and in the most recent period, between 2007 and 2008, there was a 9 per cent increase in the number of children entered onto the Adopted Children Register.

In Scotland, 441 children were adopted in 2007 compared with 470 children in 1997. Of those adopted in 2007, 30 per cent were adopted by a step parent and 66 per cent were adopted by someone unrelated to them. Figures for Northern Ireland show that 150 children were adopted in 1997, compared with 147 in 2007.

Chapter 3

Education and training

- In 2008, 38 per cent of respondents in Great Britain agreed that the main advantage of early years education to very young children was that it enabled them to interact and socialise with other children. (Table 3.2)

- In 2007/08, there were almost 2.5 million students in higher education in the UK, nearly four times as many as in 1970/71 (621,000). (Table 3.7)

- Of the 222,000 higher education students in the UK who left with a first degree in 2007/08, 60 per cent moved into UK employment within six months of graduation. (Table 3.9)

- In 2007/08, around 773,000 National Vocational Qualifications and Scottish Vocational Qualifications were awarded in the UK. The majority (64 per cent) of awards were at level 2, and awards at this level have increased more than fivefold since 1991/92. (Figure 3.18)

- Public expenditure on education in the UK as a proportion of gross domestic product (GDP) increased from 5.4 per cent in 2007/08 to 6.1 per cent in 2008/09. This was the highest proportion since records began in 1978/79 when it was 5.1 per cent. (Figure 3.20)

- In 2007/08, 42 per cent of full-time secondary school teachers in the UK were male, a 13 percentage point decrease since 1980/81 when the majority (55 per cent) of secondary school teachers were male. (Figure 3.21)

DATA

Download data by clicking the online pdf

www.statistics.gov.uk/socialtrends

For an increasing number of people, their experience of formal education is no longer confined to their years at school. Early years education has become more common since the 1970s and is seen as being vital in building important foundations for future learning in schools. There has also been an expansion in further and higher education since the 1970s as more people in the UK continue in full-time education beyond school-leaving age. Qualifications attained at school are increasingly supplemented by further education and training to equip people with the skills required by a modern labour market and to keep these skills current.

Early years education

Some form of free early years education aimed at developing young children's learning is available across all the countries of the UK, although it is delivered under different strategies (see Appendix, Part 3: Stages of education). For example the Early Years Foundation Stage (EYFS) in England aims to develop children in six broad areas: personal, social and emotional development; communication, language and literacy; problem solving, reasoning and numeracy; knowledge and understanding of the world; physical development; and creative development.

Since records began in the early 1970s, data for the UK show an expansion in early years education provided for young children in all settings. The proportion of three and four-year-olds enrolled in all schools in the UK rose from 21 per cent in

1970/71 to 63 per cent in 2008/09, although this is slightly down from a peak of 65 per cent in 2003/04 (Figure 3.1). This increase in participation partly reflects growth in the number of early years places available – in 1970/71 there were 723 state nursery schools in the UK compared with 3,209 in 2008/09.

In England the pattern of participation in early years education varies by region. In January 2009, the participation of children aged under five in maintained nursery and primary schools as a proportion of the population aged three and four was highest in the North East (80 per cent) compared with 42 per cent in both the South East and South West. However, a higher proportion of children aged three and four were enrolled with private and voluntary providers in the south of England than in other English regions (53 per cent in the South East and 58 per cent in the South West).

According to the Childcare and Early Years Providers Survey, there has been a steady increase in the number of providers offering full day child care in England to reach 13,800 in 2008, an increase of 77 per cent since 2001. This has been accompanied by a fall in the number of providers offering

Figure 3.1

Children under five[1] in schools

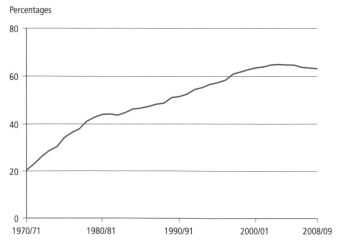

United Kingdom

Percentages

1970/71   1980/81   1990/91   2000/01   2008/09

1 Pupils aged three and four at 31 December each year as a proportion of all three and four-year-olds, with the exception of Scotland where census dates differ over the years. See Appendix, Part 3: Stages of education.

Source: Department for Children, Schools and Families; Welsh Assembly Government; Scottish Government; Northern Ireland Department of Education

Table 3.2

Perceptions of the main advantages of early years education:[1] by sex, 2008

Great Britain			Percentages
	Men	Women	All
Good for children to interact and socialise with other children	35	42	38
Helps children's educational development[2]	24	20	22
Enables parent to work	20	17	19
Prepares children for school	5	5	5
Enables parent to do other things[3]	5	4	5
Good for children's independence/ confidence	3	4	4
Good for children's behaviour	3	1	2
Good for children to interact and socialise with other adults	1	2	2
Children enjoy it	1	2	1
Other	-	-	-
No advantages	3	3	3

1 Respondents aged 18 and over were shown the above statements and asked 'What do you think is the main advantage, if any, when children under three years of age attend pre-school, nursery school or playgroups for about three mornings a week?' Excludes those who responded 'don't know' or did not answer.
2 Includes concentration, memory and language.
3 For example training, shopping or free time.

Source: British Social Attitudes Survey, National Centre for Social Research

sessional care (one session is care for up to 4 hours) to 8,500 in 2008, a fall of 39 per cent since 2001. This drop could be due to increasing parental demand for child care covering longer hours. In 2008, nearly one in five (18 per cent) full day care providers said they had changed from offering sessional care, and the majority of these (70 per cent) said they had done so because of parental demand for longer hours of care provision.

Research has been carried out to assess the value of early years education for very young children (under three years of age). One source of such research is the British Social Attitudes Survey, which in 2008 asked adults in Great Britain what advantage, if any, they thought attending an early years educational setting for about three sessions per week had for very young children. Although over a fifth of respondents (22 per cent) considered that a child's educational development was the main advantage of early years education, a higher proportion (38 per cent) agreed that the main advantage was that it enabled children to interact and socialise with other

children (Table 3.2). A higher proportion of women (42 per cent) than men (35 per cent) thought this to be the main advantage although it was the most common advantage suggested by both sexes. However, the other main perceived advantage, agreed by almost one in five (19 per cent) of respondents was that early years education for very young children allowed parents to work. This possibly reflects the other findings mentioned above regarding the demand by parents for longer hours of care.

Compulsory education

In 2008/09, there were 33,396 schools in the UK, a fall of 1,231 since 1990/91, attended by 9.7 million pupils (Table 3.3). Pupil numbers in the UK peaked in 1976/77 with 11.3 million pupils attending 38,500 schools, at a time when the children of women who were born in the baby boom after World War Two reached school age (See chapter 1: Population).

Table 3.3

School pupils:[1] by type of school[2]

United Kingdom   Thousands

	1970/71	1980/81	1990/91	2000/01	2008/09
Public sector schools[3]					
Nursery[4]	50	89	105	152	150
Primary	5,902	5,171	4,955	5,298	1,869
State-funded secondary[5]					
of which, admissions policy					
Comprehensive	1,313	3,730	2,925	3,340	3,243
Grammar	673	149	156	205	221
Modern	1,164	233	94	112	142
City technology colleges	.	.	8	17	3
Academies	.	.	.	.	122
Not applicable	403	434	298	260	197
All public sector schools	9,507	9,806	8,541	9,384	8,948
Non-maintained schools	621	619	606	609	621
All special schools	103	148	114	113	107
Pupil referral units	.	.	.	10	16
All schools	10,230	10,572	9,260	10,116	9,691

1 Headcounts.
2 See Appendix, Part 3: Stages of education, and Main categories of educational establishments.
3 Excludes maintained special schools and pupil referral units.
4 Figures for Scotland before 1998/99 only include data for local authority pre-schools, data thereafter include partnership pre-schools. From 2005/06, figures refer to centres providing pre-school education at a local authority centre, or in partnership with the local authority only. Children are counted once for each centre they are registered with.
5 Excludes sixth-form colleges from 1980/81 onwards.

Source: Department for Children, Schools and Families; Welsh Assembly Government; Scottish Government; Northern Ireland Department of Education

In 2008/09, 8.9 million pupils (92 per cent) attended public sector schools (not including special schools and pupil referral units (PRUs)), while over 0.6 million (6 per cent) attended one of the 2,547 non-maintained mainstream schools and a small proportion (1 per cent) attended one of the 1,378 special schools. These proportions have remained at similar levels since 1970/71 when records began. There were also around 511 PRUs attended by 16,000 pupils in the UK. PRUs provide suitable alternative education on a temporary basis for pupils who have been excluded from mainstream schools and children with medical problems. PRUs may also provide education for pregnant schoolgirls and school-aged mothers, school-phobics, and pupils awaiting placement in a maintained school.

Although they still form a small proportion of the total number of non-maintained schools in the UK, in England, academies are growing in number. The academies programme was introduced in 2000 to promote publicly funded independent schools managed by sponsors from a range of backgrounds including universities, businesses, faith communities and voluntary groups. They are aimed at pupils of all abilities, and all new academies are required to follow the National Curriculum programmes of study in English, mathematics, and information and communication technologies (ICT). All academies, like the large majority of secondary schools, have specialist school status, and have specialisms in one or more subjects. Most academies are located in areas of disadvantage and either replace existing schools or are established where there is a need for additional places. In 2008/09, there were 133 academies in England attended by 122,000 pupils and the Government is planning to open 400 academies in total.

One of the issues in education which has been debated over the years is class sizes in schools. Between 1978, when the series began, and 1984 class sizes in England fell to an average of 25.0 children per class for primary schools and 20.9 children for state-funded secondary schools (Figure 3.4). However, from the mid-1980s the average class size increased to a peak of 27.8 children in primary classes in 1998, and peaked at 22.2 in secondary schools in 2000. In the years that followed these peaks the average class size for both types of school fell, and in January 2009 the averages were 26.2 children per class and 20.6 children per class respectively. One of the contributory factors to the decline in average class size at primary level is the *School Standards and Framework Act 1998* whose aim was to reduce Key Stage 1 (pupils aged five to seven) class sizes in maintained schools in the UK to no more than 30 pupils by 2001/02. The average primary class size in Wales followed a similar pattern to England with a fall from 26.4 children per class in 1998 to 24.4 in 2002 and it has stayed at around this level since. The average number of children per class in

Figure 3.4

Average class sizes:[1] by type of school[2]

England
Number of pupils

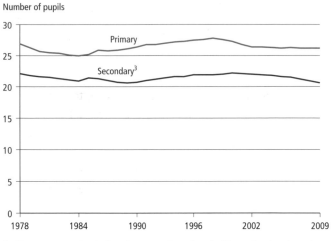

1 Classes as taught during the one selected period in each school on the day of the census in January. Figures relate to all classes, not just those taught by one teacher.
2 Includes middle schools as deemed.
3 Data are for state-funded only and include city technology colleges and academies. Excludes sixth-form colleges from 1980/81 onwards.

Source: Department for Children, Schools and Families

secondary schools in Wales fluctuated between 20 and 21 children throughout the period with a high of 21.3 in January 2001 and a low of 20.1 in January 2009. Primary level class sizes in Northern Ireland also followed a similar pattern to England and Wales, falling from an average of 25.8 in 1990/91 to 22.0 in 2008/09. In 2009, the average primary level class size in Scotland was 23.1 pupils, compared with 24.0 in 2002.

An alternative way to view class size is to measure the proportion of classes with 31 or more pupils. In January 2009, 9.9 per cent of classes in primary schools in England contained more than 30 pupils compared with 6.6 per cent of state-funded secondary schools.

Some pupils have special educational needs (SEN). That is, they have significantly greater difficulty in learning than other children of the same age, or have a disability that can make it difficult for them to use normal educational facilities. When a school identifies a child with SEN it has a duty to try to meet the child's needs in line with the provisions in the SEN Code of Practice. If their initial attempts do not meet the child's needs, an education authority or board may determine the education required for the child by drawing up a formal statement of their needs and the action it intends to take to meet them. In Scotland, local authorities' responsibilities towards children with additional support needs are set out in the *Additional Support for Learning Act 2004*, which also introduced a statutory document called a co-ordinated support plan (CSP).

These plans are aimed at pupils whose support needs are complex and require support from a range of sources.

In 2008/09, 258,200 pupils (2.7 per cent) in the UK had statements of SEN or CSPs. Of these, 221,700 were in England (equivalent to 2.7 per cent of its pupil population), 14,800 (3.0 per cent) in Wales, 8,800 (1.1 per cent) in Scotland and 13,300 (4.1 per cent) in Northern Ireland. Figure 3.5 shows the types of special educational needs among pupils with statements of SEN in England. In January 2009, the most common need of pupils in primary schools was extra help with speech, language and communication (24 per cent) followed by needs resulting from autistic spectrum disorder (20 per cent). The most common type of need among secondary school pupils was help with moderate learning difficulty (22 per cent).

The types of need in Wales were very similar to England, with the most common need at primary level in 2009 being for extra help with speech, language and communication (24 per cent) and, at secondary level, help with moderate

Figure 3.5

Pupils with statements of special educational needs (SEN):[1] by type of need, 2009[2]

England

Percentages

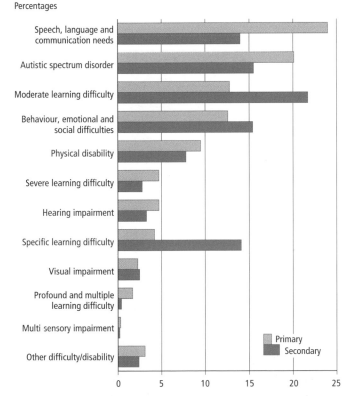

1 As a proportion of all children with statements of SEN in maintained primary and secondary schools, respectively. See Appendix, Part 3: Special educational needs (SEN) data.
2 Data are at January.

Source: Department for Children, Schools and Families

learning difficulty (25 per cent). In Scotland the most common additional support need in 2009 for primary level pupils was for social, emotional and behavioural difficulties (22 per cent).

In 2007/08, there were 8,130 permanent exclusions of pupils from primary, secondary and special schools in England (equivalent to 11 pupils per 10,000); that is, they were excluded from the school and their name removed from the school register. These pupils would then be educated at another school or through some other form of provision, for example PRUs (see above). This figure was the lowest total since 1996/97 when there were 12,668 permanent exclusions in England. Almost four in five (78 per cent) of permanent exclusions were for boys in 2007/08.

Table 3.6

Absence from school: by reason, 2008/09[1]

England   Percentages

	Primary[2]	Secondary[2,3]	Total[2,3]
Authorised absence			
Illness[4]	62.0	56.9	59.2
Agreed family holiday	11.2	4.6	7.7
Medical/dental appointments	4.8	5.9	5.4
Religious observance	2.6	1.4	1.9
Excluded, no alternative provision	0.3	2.4	1.4
Study leave	-	0.6	0.3
Traveller absence[5]	0.4	0.1	0.2
Agreed extended family holiday	0.4	0.1	0.2
Other authorised circumstances	6.4	7.8	7.2
Total authorised absence	88.1	79.8	83.6
Unauthorised absence			
Family holiday not agreed	2.0	1.7	1.8
Arrived late	1.1	1.1	1.1
Other reason	6.3	13.3	10.1
No reason yet	2.4	4.1	3.3
Total unauthorised absence	11.9	20.2	16.4

1 Data are absent sessions by reason as a proportion of all absent sessions during autumn term 2008 and spring term 2009.
2 Includes middle schools as deemed.
3 Includes maintained secondary schools, city technology colleges and academies.
4 Excludes medical and dental appointments.
5 Includes Roma, English and Welsh Gypsies, Irish and Scottish Travellers, Showmen (fairground people) and circus people, Bargees (occupational boat dwellers) and New Travellers.

Source: Department for Children, Schools and Families

In 2007/08, there were 241 permanent exclusions from schools in Wales, a fall of 17 per cent from 291 in the previous year. Boys accounted for the majority of exclusions, at 83 per cent. During 2007/08 there were 39,717 exclusions from local authority schools in Scotland, a fall of 11 per cent from 2006/07. The majority of these were temporary exclusions (39,553). There were also 25 permanent expulsions in Northern Ireland, and 5,205 fixed period suspensions of pupils.

Exclusion from school can be one of the reasons for a child being absent although only a small proportion of all absences are for this reason. There are a number of other reasons for a child's absence from school and these can be classified as either authorised or unauthorised. In 2008/09, the most common reason for absence from either the morning or afternoon school sessions in England was authorised absence because of illness (59 per cent of all school absent sessions) (Table 3.6). The next most common reason for a child's absence was also authorised, for an agreed family holiday (8 per cent), although a small proportion (2 per cent) of all absences were for family holidays which were not authorised by the school. Overall over four in five (84 per cent) absences from school were authorised, although unauthorised absence was more common in secondary schools (20 per cent) than in primary schools (12 per cent).

Post-compulsory education

There were around 3.5 million further education students in the UK in 2007/08, compared with 1.7 million in 1970/71 (Table 3.7), although it should be noted there have been changes to data coverage and methodology during this period (see Appendix, Part 3: Stages of education). In 2007/08, there were 2.0 million female further education students, nearly three times as many as in 1970/71, and 1.5 million male students, 49 per cent more than in 1970/71. Over the same period, the proportion of further education students who were female increased: in 1970/71, 42 per cent were female compared with 57 per cent in 2007/08 while the proportion who were male decreased from 58 per cent to 43 per cent. More women than men were taking part-time further education courses in 2007/08 compared with 1970/71: four in ten (41 per cent) of people taking part-time courses were female whereas in 2007/08, this had increased to 59 per cent.

There have also been substantial increases in the number of students in higher education in the UK, studying in both

Table 3.7

Students in further and higher education:[1] by type of course and sex

United Kingdom

Thousands

	Men				Women			
	1970/71	1980/81	1990/91	2007/08	1970/71	1980/81	1990/91	2007/08
Further education								
Full-time	116	154	219	520	95	196	261	534
Part-time	891	697	768	984	630	624	986	1,432
All further education	1,007	851	986	1,503	725	820	1,247	1,966
Higher education								
Undergraduate								
Full-time	241	277	345	574	173	196	319	717
Part-time	127	176	148	255	19	71	106	422
Postgraduate								
Full-time	33	41	50	124	10	21	34	125
Part-time	15	32	46	109	3	13	33	150
All higher education[2]	416	526	588	1,063	205	301	491	1,414

1 Home and overseas students attending further education or higher education institutions. See Appendix, Part 3: Stages of education.
2 Figures for 2007/08 include a small number of higher education students for whom details are not available by level.

Source: Department for Children, Schools and Families; Department for Business, Innovation and Skills; Welsh Assembly Government; Scottish. Government; Northern Ireland Department for Employment and Learning

further and higher education institutions (see Appendix, Part 3: Stages of education). In 2007/08, there were almost 2.5 million students in higher education, nearly four times the total of 621,000 in 1970/71. The proportion of higher education students who were female increased from 33 per cent to 57 per cent over the period, and there have been more female than male higher education students each year since 1995/96. There were almost seven times as many female higher education students in 2007/08 (1.4 million) than in 1970/71 (205,000) and more than two and a half times as many male students (1.1 million compared with 416,000).

Data from the Higher Education Statistics Agency show that there were 2.3 million students in higher education institutions in the UK (and therefore differs to the total in Table 3.7 which also includes those studying higher education courses in further education institutions). There are many subjects available for students studying in higher education institutions in the UK and these subjects can be classified into 19 headline areas. Analysis of these headline subject areas reveals that the most popular subject for men in 2007/08 was business and administrative studies, studied by 16.1 per cent of male higher education students (equivalent to 159,500 students), followed by engineering and technology studied by 11.8 per cent of male students (Table 3.8). For women in the same year, the largest proportion of higher education students (17.7 per cent) studied subjects allied to medicine (equivalent to 233,300 students) followed by education (11.7 per cent) and business and administrative studies (11.5 per cent). The least common subjects for both sexes were veterinary science, and agricultural and related subjects, which each accounted for less than 1 per cent of both male and female students.

Provision of education by UK institutions now extends outside the UK and data are available on the number of students studying entirely outside the UK for qualifications awarded by UK higher education institutions. The data shows that during 2007/08, 196,640 students were studying entirely overseas for qualifications at higher education level from 112 UK higher education institutions. Distance learning courses accounted for over half of this 'offshore provision' of UK higher education (equivalent to 100,360 students) while 7,090 students were studying at overseas campuses which were directly run by UK higher education institutions. The majority of the remaining 89,190 students were studying for awards offered by UK institutions in collaboration with overseas partners.

Students in four countries, Hong Kong, Singapore, Malaysia and China, accounted for 37 per cent of this 'offshore' UK

Table 3.8

Students in higher education:[1] by subject[2] and sex, 2007/08

United Kingdom   Percentages

	Men	Women	All
Business and administrative studies	16.1	11.5	13.5
Subjects allied to medicine	5.4	17.7	12.5
Education	4.9	11.7	8.8
Social studies	7.5	9.5	8.6
Biological sciences	5.9	7.8	7.0
Creative arts and design	6.3	7.3	6.9
Engineering and technology	11.8	1.7	6.0
Languages	4.5	6.9	5.9
Historical and philosophical studies	4.5	4.0	4.2
Computer science	7.8	1.4	4.1
Law	3.7	4.0	3.9
Physical sciences	4.9	2.6	3.6
Architecture, building and planning	4.4	1.5	2.7
Medicine and dentistry	2.6	2.7	2.7
Mass communications and documentation	2.1	2.1	2.1
Mathematical sciences	2.1	1.0	1.5
Agriculture and related subjects	0.7	0.8	0.8
Veterinary science	0.1	0.3	0.2
Combined[3]	4.6	5.5	5.1
All subject areas (=100%) (thousands)	988	1,318	2,306

1 Full-time and part-time, undergraduate and postgraduate, and home and overseas students in higher education institutions only. See Appendix, Part 3: Stages of education.
2 Subject data are classified using the Joint Academic Coding System. See Appendix, Part 3: Joint Academic Coding System.
3 Courses which are a mix of subject groups.

Source: Higher Education Statistics Agency

education provision and overall Asia accounted for 45 per cent. Almost a quarter (23 per cent) of offshore students were studying in other European Union countries.

Of those students studying at higher education institutions in the UK, their labour market status approximately six months after leaving their institution varied according to the level of qualification which they had obtained. For example, of the 222,000 students who left with a first degree in 2007/08, three-fifths (60 per cent) moved into UK employment while a small proportion (2 per cent) gained overseas employment (Table 3.9 overleaf). Around 1 in 12 (8 per cent) went on to combine employment with some form of studying, while 16 per cent continued with their studies only. Those who had gained undergraduate qualifications, other than a first degree,

Table 3.9

Destination of students leaving higher education:[1] by type of qualification, 2007/08

United Kingdom   Percentages

	First degree	Other undergraduate[2]	Postgraduate
UK employment only[3]	60	55	71
Overseas employment only[3]	2	1	7
Work and further study	8	18	9
Further study only	16	20	6
Assumed to be unemployed	8	4	4
Not available for employment	4	2	2
Other	1	1	1
All (=100%) (thousands)	222	44	79

1 Destination of UK and other European Union domiciled full-time and part-time students after leaving higher education institutions approximately six months after graduation. Excludes those where destination was not known.
2 Includes foundation degrees and all other higher education qualifications not included as first degree or postgraduate.
3 Includes self-employed and voluntary or unpaid work.

Source: Department for Children, Schools and Families; Higher Education Statistics Agency

were most likely to move into UK employment (55 per cent), continue studying (20 per cent) or combine study with employment (18 per cent). Those who left with postgraduate qualifications were most likely to move into employment either in the UK (71 per cent) or overseas (7 per cent).

Female first degree graduates were more likely than male graduates in 2007/08 to be in full or part-time employment, or combining employment with study six months after graduating (72.9 per cent of female first degree graduates compared with 67.9 per cent of male graduates). Similar proportions of male (16.2 per cent) and female (15.1 per cent) first degree graduates went on to further study only. Also, a higher proportion of male first degree graduates than females were assumed to be unemployed six months after graduation (10.3 per cent compared with 6.5 per cent) in 2007/08. The overall proportion of leavers with first degrees who were assumed to be unemployed rose to 8.1 per cent for 2007/08 graduates, up from 5.6 per cent for 2006/07 graduates.

Not everyone working towards a qualification beyond the age of 16 has worked their way continuously through the various levels of education. More than 2.9 million (44 per cent) people of working age (16 to 64 for men and 16 to 59 for women) studying towards a qualification in the UK in Q2 (April to June) 2009 were aged 25 and over, and around 1.2 million (18 per cent) were aged 40 and over. Adults aged 25 and over comprised 42 per cent of people of working age studying towards a degree or equivalent while those aged 40 and over comprised 14 per cent of those studying for this level of qualification.

Data from the Labour Force Survey also show the economic activity status of those who are studying for a qualification and show the proportions of people of working age who combine studying with work. For example, two-fifths (42 per cent) of

Table 3.10

People working towards a qualification:[1] by economic activity status, 2009[2]

United Kingdom   Percentages

	Degree or equivalent and higher	Higher education[3]	GCE A level or equivalent	GCSE or equivalent	Other qualifications	All qualifications
In employment						
Full-time	26	45	23	22	57	34
Part-time	24	23	30	20	17	23
All in employment	50	67	53	42	74	57
Unemployed	5	5	8	8	8	7
Inactive student	42	24	37	46	10	32
Other inactive	3	3	2	4	8	4
All people (=100%) (millions)	2.1	0.5	1.5	1.0	1.7	6.7

1 For those working towards more than one qualification, the highest is recorded. See Appendix, Part 3: Qualifications. Excludes those who did not answer and those who did not state the qualification they were working towards. Men aged 16 to 64 and women aged 16 to 59.
2 Data are at Q2 (April–June) and are not seasonally adjusted. See Appendix, Part 4: Labour Force Survey.
3 Below degree level but including National Vocational Qualification (NVQ) level 4.

Source: Labour Force Survey, Office for National Statistics

those people who were studying for a degree or equivalent and higher in Q2 2009 were economically inactive students, while half (50 per cent) were in employment, either full time or part time, and were therefore combining study with employment (Table 3.10). This pattern was more marked for those studying higher education qualifications (for example National Vocational Qualifications at level 4 or the equivalent) or GCE A level or equivalent. Overall, of the 6.7 million working-age people studying for a qualification, almost three-fifths (57 per cent) were in employment and almost a third (32 per cent) were economically inactive students. Of the remaining people studying, 7 per cent were unemployed and 4 per cent were economically inactive for some reason other than being a full-time student.

Adult training and learning

Work-based learning is often necessary in order that workers can keep their skills up-to-date and be able to satisfy the demands of the modern day labour market. In England, there are a number of initiatives which aim to increase the knowledge and skills base among the workforce. These include apprenticeships, which provide structured learning that combines work-based training with off-the-job learning. Apprenticeships offer training equivalent to National Vocational

Figure 3.11

Employees receiving job-related training: by sex and occupation, 2009[1]

United Kingdom
Percentages

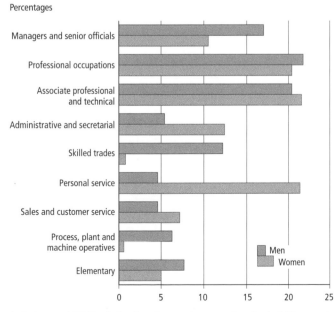

1 Data are at Q2 (April–June) and are not seasonally adjusted. Men aged 16 to 64 and women aged 16 to 59. See Appendix, Part 4: Labour Force Survey, and Standard Occupational Classification 2000 (SOC2000).

Source: Labour Force Survey, Office for National Statistics

Qualification (NVQ) level 2, and advanced apprenticeships offer training equivalent to NVQ level 3 (see Appendix, Part 3: Qualifications). Learning and Skills Council (LSC) data show that in 2008/09, 239,900 apprenticeship programmes were started, an increase of 7 per cent compared with 2007/08 when there were 224,800 apprenticeships started. Of those started in 2008/09, 158,500 were level 2 and 81,400 were advanced apprenticeships (level 3).

Young people are more likely than older workers to receive job-related training. The Labour Force Survey (LFS) includes questions about employment training, and in Q2 (April to June) 2009, 20 per cent of those aged between 16 and 24 had participated in job-related training in the four weeks prior to interview. This proportion fell to around 16 per cent of those aged 25 to 34 and fell further to 14 per cent of those aged 35 to 49. The proportions of men and women aged 16 to 24 in employment who received job-related training were the same, both 20 per cent. However, in the older age groups women were more likely than men to have received job-related training: 14 per cent of men and 18 per cent of women in the 25 to 34 age group, and 12 per cent of men and 16 per cent of women in the 35 to 49 age group.

The likelihood of receiving job-related training also varies by occupation. The LFS showed that in Q2 2009, among working-age employed men in the UK, those in professional occupations were most likely to receive job-related training whereas among working-age employed women, those in associate professional and technical occupations were most likely to receive job-related training, accounting for 21.8 per cent and 21.6 per cent respectively of employees (Figure 3.11). Those least likely to receive job-related training were men working in sales and customer service, and personal service (both 4.6 per cent) and women working as process, plant and machinery operatives (0.6 per cent). Overall, those people who worked in professional, and associate professional and technical occupations were most likely to receive job-related training (21.1 per cent) and those who were process, plant and machinery operatives were least likely (3.2 per cent).

Data from the Learning and Skills Council (LSC) shows that the number of adults in England participating in further education has fluctuated over recent years, with the number of learners dropping by nearly a fifth (19.5 per cent) between 2005/06 and 2006/07, but then rising again to reach 3.7 million in 2008/09, 7.2 per cent lower than in 2005/06 (Table 3.12 overleaf). One component of adult learning is Skills for Life which is an LSC-funded government strategy to improve the numeracy, literacy and language skills of adults by offering free

Table 3.12

Adult further education and skills participation: by level[1]

England   Thousands

	2005/06	2006/07	2007/08	2008/09[2]
Below level 2	1,032	590	533	427
Skills for Life	979	810	827	939
Full level 2	441	516	740	959
Full level 3	264	268	328	423
Level 2[3]	1,235	1,118	1,319	1,543
Level 3[3]	525	486	528	619
Level 4 and above	68	60	53	58
No level assigned	1,050	842	804	863
All learners	3,984	3,206	3,306	3,697

1 See Appendix, Part 3: Qualifications.
2 Data are not directly comparable with earlier years as the introduction of demand led funding changed how data were collected and how funded learners were defined.
3 Includes all those studying for a full level 2 or 3 and those studying for a part level 2 or 3.

Source: Learning and Skills Council

Figure 3.13

Distribution of skills gaps:[1] by occupation,[2] 2007

England
Percentages

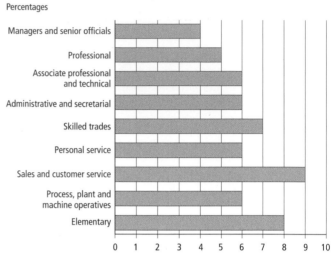

1 Skills gaps exist where employers consider that employees are not fully proficient in their job. Data show the proportion of employees considered to have skills gaps as a proportion of all employees in each occupation. See Appendix, Part 3: National Employers Skills Survey.
2 See Appendix, Part 4: Standard Occupational Classification 2000 (SOC2000).

Source: National Employers Skills Survey, Learning and Skills Council

tuition in these subject areas. Although participation in this type of learning fell between 2005/06 and 2006/07, it has since increased, and by 2008/09 939,000 adults in England were undertaking this training. Learners studying for a level 2 qualification (those studying for a full level 2 combined with those studying for a part level 2 qualification – see Appendix, Part 3: Qualifications) rose from 1.24 million in 2005/06 to 1.54 million in 2008/09, an increase of 25 per cent, whereas those studying for a full level 2 qualification more than doubled from 441,300 to 959,400 over the same period. For level 3 qualifications (equivalent to 2 GCE A levels), numbers increased by 18 per cent from 524,900 in 2005/06 to 619,300 in 2008/09. Those studying for a full level 3 rose by 60 per cent from 264,200 to 423,300 over the same period. It should be noted however, that comparisons over time are affected by changes in methodology (see Appendix, Part 3: Stages of education).

The National Employers Skills Survey in 2007 looked at the extent of skills deficiencies among employees in England, as reported by employers. They found that the occupation with employees most likely to have skills gaps was sales and customer service, where employers considered that 9 per cent of employees lacked at least some of the skills required to be fully proficient at their job (Figure 3.13). This group was closely followed by those in elementary occupations such as catering assistants, bar staff and shelf fillers, at 8 per cent. Managers

and senior officials were least likely to have skills gaps (4 per cent of employees). According to the Scottish Employers Skills Survey (see Appendix, Part 3: Scottish Employers Skills Survey), the pattern in Scotland was very similar. In 2008, those working in sales and customer service, and those in elementary occupations were most likely to have skills gaps (both 11 per cent), closely followed by those in personal service occupations (10 per cent). Those working in professional occupations were least likely to have skills gaps (5 per cent).

Employers in the North East were most likely to have reported skills gaps in 2007 (19 per cent of employers), followed by London (17 per cent) and the South West (16 per cent). All other English regions had reported levels of skills gaps at or below the average for all employers in England, which was 15 per cent.

Educational attainment

Assessment at Key Stages forms part of the National Curriculum in England (see Appendix, Part 3: The National Curriculum) and is carried out through a combination of teacher assessments and tests which measure pupils' attainment against the levels set by the National Curriculum. Wales, Scotland and Northern Ireland each have their own guidelines for assessing attainment against the curriculum.

Table 3.14 shows the differences in performance of boys and girls in England, as measured by teacher assessment, for Key

Table 3.14

Pupils reaching or exceeding expected standards:[1] by Key Stage and sex

England   Percentages

	1999		2009	
	Boys	Girls	Boys	Girls
Key Stage 1[2]				
English				
Reading	78	86	81	89
Writing	75	85	75	87
Mathematics	84	88	88	91
Science	85	88	87	91
Key Stage 2[3]				
English	62	74	75	84
Mathematics	69	70	80	80
Science	75	76	85	87
Key Stage 3[4]				
English	55	73	71	84
Mathematics	63	66	79	80
Science	59	62	76	79

1 By teacher assessment. See Appendix, Part 3: The National Curriculum.
2 Pupils achieving level 2 or above at Key Stage 1.
3 Pupils achieving level 4 or above at Key Stage 2.
4 Pupils achieving level 5 or above at Key Stage 3.

Source: Department for Children, Schools and Families

Stages 1 to 3. Between 1999 and 2009, although the proportion of girls reaching the required standard in Key Stage 1 was generally higher than that for boys, there were improvements in the performance of both sexes. At Key Stage 1, the proportion of boys who reached the required standard in reading by teacher assessment increased by 3 percentage points over the period to 81 per cent whereas for writing there was no change at 75 per cent. For girls, the proportions also increased between 1999 and 2009 by 3 percentage points for reading (to 89 per cent) and by 2 percentage points for writing (to 87 per cent).

Although the performance of both sexes improved between 1999 and 2009 at Key Stages 2 and 3, boys generally performed less well than girls by teacher assessment. However, at Key Stage 2 mathematics, boys performed as well as girls, with 80 per cent of both boys and girls reaching or exceeding the expected standard in 2009. In both 1999 and 2009 the performance of boys was close to that of girls for both mathematics and science, with the gap between the proportion of boys and girls reaching or exceeding the expected standard for each of these subjects being no more

than 3 percentage points in both years. However, the gap in performance for English was more marked with girls performing a lot better than boys. In 1999, the difference in the proportion of boys and girls reaching or exceeding the expected standard at Key Stage 2 was 12 percentage points and at Key Stage 3 it was 18 percentage points. By 2009, although the gaps had narrowed, there were still gaps of 9 percentage points at Key Stage 2 and 13 percentage points at Key Stage 3.

In Wales in 2009, 78 per cent of boys achieved the expected standard in Key Stage 1 English by teacher assessment, compared with 88 per cent of girls. At Key Stage 2 the percentage of boys gaining the expected standard was 76, compared with 87 per cent of girls. The marked difference between boys' and girls' level of attainment continued through to Key Stage 3, with 63 per cent of boys and 78 per cent of girls achieving at least level 5. For the Welsh language, which is used as a first language in some schools in Wales, at Key Stage 1, 87 per cent of boys achieved the expected level, whereas for girls it was 93 per cent. At Key Stage 2, these proportions dropped to 73 per cent of boys and 86 per cent of girls. The proportions of boys and girls achieving the expected levels dropped further at Key Stage 3, to 67 per cent and 83 per cent respectively.

There is also a difference in overall performance between boys and girls at GCSE level. In 2007/08, 69 per cent of girls in the UK in their last year of compulsory education achieved five or more GCSEs at grades A* to C or equivalent, compared with 60 per cent of boys (Figure 3.15 overleaf). This was an increase for both sexes of 19 percentage points since 1995/96. Overall, 64 per cent of pupils achieved five or more GCSEs at grades A* to C or equivalent in 2007/08 compared with 46 per cent in 1995/96.

A measure of pupils' academic performance which focuses more on core skills measures the proportion of pupils achieving at least five or more GCSEs at grades A* to C including English and mathematics. The proportion of pupils in the UK in their last year of compulsory education achieving this alternative measure in 2007/08 was 48 per cent of pupils, compared with 64 per cent for the rate based on five or more GCSEs at grades A* to C in any subject. A higher proportion of girls (52 per cent) than boys (44 per cent) achieved five or more GCSE grades A* to C including English and mathematics.

Five GCSEs at grades A* to C are the equivalent of a level 2 qualification in the UK (see Appendix, Part 3: Qualifications) which also include National Vocational Qualifications (NVQ) and Vocationally Related Qualifications (VRQ), both at level 2, General National Vocational Qualifications (GNVQ) and some

Figure 3.15

Pupils achieving five or more GCSE grades A* to C or equivalent:[1,2] by sex

United Kingdom
Percentages

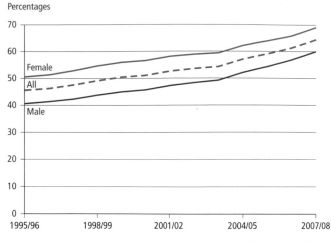

1 For pupils in their last year of compulsory education. Pupils aged 15 at the start of the academic year; pupils in year S4 in Scotland. From 2004/05, pupils at the end of Key Stage 4 in England.
2 From 1990/91, National Qualifications were introduced in Scotland but are not included until 2000/01. See Appendix, Part 3: Qualifications.

Source: Department for Children, Schools and Families; Welsh Assembly Government; Scottish Government; Northern Ireland Department of Education

Table 3.16

Attainment of level 2 qualifications[1] at age 16 and 17: by socio-economic classification of parent,[2] 2008

England
Percentages

	Age 16	Age 17	Proportion without Level 2 at 16 but gaining by 17	Proportion without Level 2 at 17
Higher professional	81	88	33	12
Lower professional	75	82	28	18
Intermediate	61	71	26	29
Lower supervisory	47	58	20	42
Routine	43	54	20	46
Other/not classified	37	49	19	51

1 Attainment of five or more GCSE grades A* to C, National Vocational Qualification level 2, Vocationally Related Qualification level 2, Intermediate General National Vocational Qualification. See Appendix, Part 3: Qualifications.
2 National Statistics Socio-economic Classification (NS-SEC) of parent. See Appendix, Part 1: National Statistics Socio-economic Classification (NS-SEC).

Source: Longitudinal Study of Young People in England, and Youth Cohort Study, from the Department for Children, Schools and Families

apprenticeships. Data from the Longitudinal Study of Young People in England show that at age 16, 61 per cent of those in the survey had attained level 2 qualifications in 2007, rising to 69 per cent by the age of 17. Therefore, just over one in five of the young people who had not achieved level 2 at 16 had gone on to do so by the age of 17.

The study also showed that those from lower socio-economic groups tended to have much lower levels of academic attainment at age 16 compared with the higher socio-economic groups. For example, 43 per cent of children whose parents were in the routine occupation group in England in 2008 had attained level 2, compared with 81 per cent of those in the higher professional group (Table 3.16). This gap continues to the age of 17 as those from the lower socio-economic groups who had not achieved level 2 at 16 were also less likely to have gone on to achieve it at 17 than young people from the professional socio-economic groups. In 2008, 46 per cent of those from the routine group were still without qualifications to this level at age 17 compared with 12 per cent of those from the higher professional occupation group.

GCE A level examinations are usually taken after two years post-GCSE study in a school sixth form, sixth-form college or further education college by those who stay in education full time beyond the age of 16. The performance gap between the

sexes seen at early stages of education can also be seen at this stage. In 2007/08, 41 per cent of young men aged 17 at the start of the academic year in the UK had gained two or more GCE A levels (or equivalent) by the end of the academic year compared with 52 per cent of young women.

Following further education many people continue to study towards higher education qualifications (see Table 3.9). In 2007/08 there were around 334,900 first degrees obtained by UK and overseas domiciled students at higher education institutions in the UK, including 308,600 classified degrees and 26,300 unclassified degrees (certain qualifications obtained at first degree level are not subject to classification, for example medical degrees) (Table 3.17). Of the classified first degrees, 12 per cent were graded first class and similar proportions of men (13 per cent) and women (12 per cent) achieved this level. A higher proportion of women than men achieved upper second class degrees, 47 per cent compared with 41 per cent, while similar proportions of women and men achieved lower second class qualifications, 27 per cent and 30 per cent respectively. A third class (or pass) qualification was achieved by 7 per cent of all first degree students.

National Vocational Qualifications (NVQs) and Scottish Vocational Qualifications (SVQs) provide alternatives to the more traditional academic qualifications, being aimed at a particular occupation or group of occupations (see Appendix,

Table 3.17

Higher education qualifications attained:[1] by sex and class of qualification, 2007/08

United Kingdom

Percentages

	Men	Women	All
First degree			
First class	12.8	11.9	12.3
Upper second	41.0	46.8	44.3
Lower second	29.8	27.3	28.4
Third class/Pass	8.7	6.0	7.2
Unclassified	7.6	8.0	7.8
All (=100%) (thousands)	143.7	191.0	334.9
Higher degree			
Doctorate	13.4	11.0	12.3
Other higher degree	86.6	89.0	87.7
All (=100%) (thousands)	68.3	67.2	135.6
Other postgraduate			
Postgraduate certificate in education	25.8	37.1	33.0
Other postgraduate	74.3	62.9	67.0
All (=100%) (thousands)	23.7	42.7	66.4
Other undergraduate			
Professional graduate certificate in education	3.7	4.8	4.4
Foundation degree	12.1	10.0	10.7
HND/DipHE[2]	19.6	23.7	22.3
Other undergraduate	64.6	61.6	62.6
All (=100%) (thousands)	49.1	90.4	139.6

1 Full-time and part-time, home and overseas students. See Appendix, Part 3: Stages of education.
2 Higher National Diploma or Diploma in Higher Education.

Source: Higher Education Statistics Agency

Part 3: Qualifications). Between 1987, when they were introduced, and 2007/08 a total of 7.6 million NVQs/SVQs have been awarded in the UK. In 2007/08, around 773,000 NVQs and SVQs were awarded in the UK compared with around 153,000 awarded in 1991/92. The majority (64 per cent) of NVQs and SVQs awarded in 2007/08 were at level 2 (equivalent to five GCSEs at grades A* to C) and awards at this level have increased over five and a half times since 1991/92 (Figure 3.18). A further 25 per cent of awards were at level 3 (equivalent to two GCE A levels) and 4 per cent were at levels 4 and 5 (equivalent to some higher education awards and first or higher degrees).

In 2007/08, 23 per cent of all NVQs and SVQs awarded in the UK were in health, public services and care, with 37 per cent of

Figure 3.18

NVQ/SVQs awarded:[1] by level of qualification

United Kingdom

Thousands

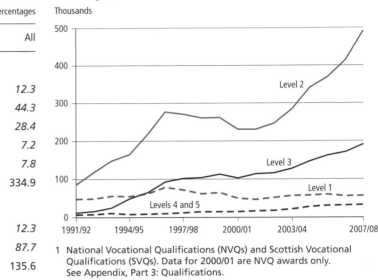

1 National Vocational Qualifications (NVQs) and Scottish Vocational Qualifications (SVQs). Data for 2000/01 are NVQ awards only. See Appendix, Part 3: Qualifications.

Source: Department for Children, Schools and Families

all level 3 NVQs and SVQs awarded in this sector subject area. The next most common subject areas for awards were retail and commercial enterprise (21 per cent of all awards) and business, administration and law (17 per cent).

The Labour Force Survey (LFS) provides data on the highest level of qualifications that people hold. People of working-age (men aged 16 to 64 and women aged 16 to 59) in the UK are more likely to be educated to at least degree level than to be without formal qualifications. Figures for Q2 2009 show that 21 per cent of both men and women held degrees or equivalent and higher compared with 12 per cent of both men and women with no qualifications.

Differences emerge when attainment is analysed by sex and age, essentially reflecting differences between cohorts passing through a changing education and training scene. Among working-age women, those aged 50 and over were more likely than women in other age groups to not have any qualifications (20 per cent in Q2 2009), followed by 16 to 19-year-olds (17 per cent). Among working-age men, 19 per cent aged 16 to 19 and 17 per cent of those aged 50 and over did not have any qualifications, both higher proportions than men in other working-age groups.

The high figures for 16 to 19-year-olds are largely accounted for by the fact that the majority of those who are 16 in Q2 will not have had their Year 11 results and therefore will not yet have the first set of qualifications counted in the LFS. When 16-year-olds are not included in the calculation, the figure for the proportions who held no qualifications fell to 7 per cent for

Figure 3.19

No qualifications held: by sex and age, 2009[1]

United Kingdom
Percentages

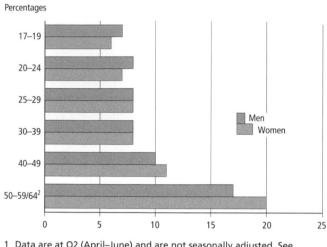

1 Data are at Q2 (April–June) and are not seasonally adjusted. See Appendix, Part 4: Labour Force Survey.
2 Men aged 50 to 64 and women aged 50 to 59.

Source: Labour Force Survey, Office for National Statistics

17 to 19-year-old men and 6 per cent for women of the same age (Figure 3.19).

Educational resources

Public expenditure on education in the UK as a proportion of gross domestic product (GDP), using the Classification of the Functions of Government (see Appendix, Part 3: Classification of the Functions of Government (COFOG)) increased from 5.4 per cent in 2007/08 to 6.1 per cent in 2008/09 (Figue 3.20). This was the highest proportion since records began in 1978/79 when it was 5.1 per cent. As these data are for state-funded institutions only they will differ from the European Union figures (which include private funding) analysed below.

In 2006, total private and public spending on education in the UK as a proportion of GDP was 5.9 per cent. This was relatively high when compared with other EU member states for which data were available. Of the 19 EU member states supplying data, Denmark recorded the highest proportion of GDP spent on education in 2006 (7.3 per cent) followed by Sweden (6.3 per cent) and Belgium and Slovenia (both 6.1 per cent). France (and the UK) followed at 5.9 per cent. The member states with the lowest spend on education were Slovakia (4.3 per cent) and Greece (4.2 per cent in 2005). Among Organisation for Economic Co-operation and Development (OECD) countries, Iceland had the highest spend at 8.0 per cent of GDP closely followed by Israel at 7.8 per cent. Turkey was the lowest at 2.7 per cent with the Russian Federation slightly higher at 3.9 per cent.

Figure 3.20

UK expenditure on education as a proportion of gross domestic product[1]

United Kingdom
Percentages

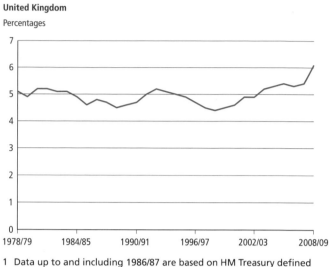

1 Data up to and including 1986/87 are based on HM Treasury defined functions; those from 1987/88 are based on the UN Classification of the Functions of Government (COFOG). Data are public expenditure only. See Appendix, Part 3: Classification of the Functions of Government (COFOG).

Source: HM Treasury; Department for Children, Schools and Families

The number of full-time qualified teachers in public sector mainstream schools in the UK decreased by around 55,000 between 1981/82 and 2007/08 to 437,000. However, although there has been an overall fall in this total there are differences in the patterns for teacher numbers in these schools when analysed by sex. The number of full-time female teachers increased by 5 per cent to 308,000 over the period 1981/82 to 2007/08, while the number of male teachers fell by 35 per cent to 129,000 (Figure 3.21). Throughout this period the majority of full-time teachers in nursery and primary schools have been female with the proportion steadily increasing from 78 per cent in 1980/81 to 85 per cent from 2000/01 to 2007/08. The pattern for secondary schools teachers however is different to that of nursery and primary. In 1980/81, the majority (55 per cent) of full-time teachers in secondary schools in the UK were male. This proportion gradually fell throughout the 1980s and by 1993/94 had fallen to around 50 per cent. It should be noted however that this was driven by a sharper fall (41,000) over this period in the number of male secondary teachers compared with a smaller fall in female secondary teacher numbers (13,000). The proportional decline in male teachers continued after 1993/94 although, unlike previous years, it was driven less by change in male secondary teacher numbers, which fell by 14,000 between 1993/94 and 2007/08, but more by female secondary teacher numbers which increased by 21,000 over the same period. In 2007/08, 42 per cent of secondary school teachers were male.

Figure 3.21

Full-time teachers:[1] by sex and type of school

United Kingdom
Thousands

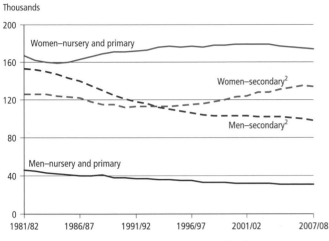

1 Qualified teachers in public sector mainstream schools.
2 From 1993/94 data exclude sixth-form colleges in England and Wales, which were reclassified as further education colleges on 1 April 1993.

Source: Department for Children, Schools and Families; Scottish Government; Northern Ireland Department of Education

There has been a steady increase in the numbers of support staff in maintained schools in the UK, from 88,700 in 1996 to 268,000 in 2009. These include teaching assistants, technicians and other support staff but exclude administrative staff.

Primary schools accounted for the majority of support staff between 1996 and 2009 with between 55 and 59 per cent of all support staff working in these schools. Secondary schools accounted for between 26 per cent and 32 per cent, with nursery and special schools accounting for the remainder (13 to 17 per cent).

The number of initial teacher training places in England peaked in 2008/09 at around 37,000 places, with a decrease to around 36,000 in 2009/10. There are differences in the trends for primary and secondary courses. There were around 15,000 primary teaching places in 2003/04 and this number has increased to around 18,000 in 2009/10. This compares with around 19,000 secondary school places in 2003/04 decreasing to around 17,000 in 2006/07 and 2007/08. There was a slight increase to over 19,000 in 2008/09 however this number then dropped to just over 18,000 in 2009/10. When these data are broken down by subject level it was shown that the most popular subject for secondary teacher training was science, with around 19 per cent of all teacher training places. This was followed by technology with around 15 per cent of places, including design and technology, information and communication technology, and business studies. The least popular subject was citizenship with 1.5 per cent of places. In Scotland the number of initial teacher training places also peaked in 2008/09 at 3,900 before decreasing to 3,600 in 2009/10.

3

Chapter 4

Labour market

- Between Q2 2008 and Q2 2009, the employment rate (working-age people) in the UK fell from 75 per cent to 73 per cent whereas the unemployment rate (people aged 16 and over) increased from 5.4 per cent to 7.8 per cent. (Figure 4.1)

- The proportion of working-age households in the UK in which no-one was in work increased to 16.9 per cent (the equivalent of 3.3 million households) in the 12 months to Q2 2009. (Table 4.3)

- The proportion of jobs in the manufacturing sector in the UK fell from 28.5 per cent in 1978 to 10.0 per cent in 2009. (Table 4.8)

- In Q2 2009, the average working week in the UK was 44 hours for full-time male employees and 40 hours for full-time female employees. (Table 4.10)

- In 2008–09, a total of 3.9 million job separations occurred in the UK. (Table 4.13)

- In 2008, there were a total of 758,900 working days lost in the UK due to industrial disputes involving 511,200 workers in 144 stoppages. (Table 4.21)

DATA

Download data by clicking the online pdf

www.statistics.gov.uk/socialtrends

The number of people in the UK labour force (see Glossary) has grown since 1971, as the population has increased. In Q2 2009, there were 31.4 million people in the UK labour force, approaching two in three (63 per cent) of the 49.4 million people in the total adult population aged 16 and over. Between 1971 and 2009 the employment patterns of men and women have differed, as have their unemployment and economic inactivity patterns. The composition of the labour force has also changed: employment in service industries has increased while employment in manufacturing has fallen. More recently, the recession in the UK economy has impacted on the labour market participation of both men and women.

Labour market profile

The labour market comprises those who are economically active and in the labour force (those who are employed and unemployed) and the economically inactive (those who are not part of the labour force). This latter group consists of those people who are out of work, but who do not satisfy all of the International Labour Organisation criteria for unemployment, because they either are not seeking work or are unavailable to start work. In the UK, people over state pension age (SPA), currently 65 for men and 60 for women, make up the largest proportion of this group. State pension age is changing for both men and women. Between 2010 and 2020 the SPA for women will gradually increase to 65, the same as for men, and between 2024 and 2046 it is planned that SPA for both men and women will gradually increase to 68.

The number of people who are economically active is primarily determined by the size of the population and both have increased since Labour Force Survey (LFS) records began in 1971. For example, the number of economically active people aged 16 and over in the UK increased by 23 per cent from 25.6 million people in Q2 1971 to 31.4 million in Q2 2009, while the total number of people aged 16 and over increased by 22 per cent from 40.6 million people to 49.4 million.

Labour Force Survey (LFS)

The LFS is the largest regular household survey in the UK and much of the labour market data published in this chapter are measured by the LFS. Calendar quarter 2 (Q2) data from the LFS refers to the months April to June in a given year. The earliest year for which LFS data are available is 1971 but only for a limited number of variables. Where time series data are quoted in this chapter, the earliest available comparable year is usually used. For more information on the LFS, including differences between calendar and seasonal quarters, see the Appendix, Part 4: Labour Force Survey.

Among those of working age (see Glossary) the number of economically active people in the UK increased by 5.1 million from 24.8 million to 30.0 million over the period Q2 1971 to Q2 2009, while the population in this age group also increased by a similar amount. As a result the working-age economic activity rate has remained relatively stable, at 78 per cent in Q2 1971 and 79 per cent in Q2 2009 with a high of 81 per cent in 1990 and a low of 77 per cent in 1983 (Figure 4.1).

The proportion of the working-age population in the UK who were in employment (the employment rate) decreased from 76 per cent in the mid-1970s to a low of 68 per cent in Q2 1983. Since then, employment rates have generally risen although there was a fall following the recession in the early 1990s, and another fall in the 12 months to Q2 2009 when the rate was 73 per cent following another recession. This was the lowest Q2 employment rate since 1996 (72 per cent). The fall in the employment rate in the 12 months to Q2 2009 was mirrored by a rise in the unemployment rate from 5 per cent to 8 per cent.

Working-age men and women have different patterns of labour market participation at most ages. In Q2 2009, 15 per cent of men aged 16 to 19 worked full time, the equivalent of 250,000 men of this age (Figure 4.2). Men in this age group were least likely of all working-age men to be in full-time employment, although participation in post-compulsory education is a factor in the proportion of young

Figure 4.1

Economic activity and inactivity rates[1]

United Kingdom
Percentages

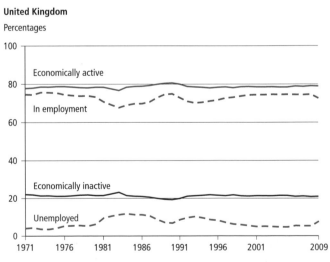

1 Data are at Q2 each year and are seasonally adjusted. Rates are expressed as a proportion of men aged 16 to 64 and women aged 16 to 59 with the exception of unemployment rates which are expressed as a proportion of people aged 16 and over. See Appendix, Part 4: Labour Force Survey.

Source: Labour Force Survey, Office for National Statistics

Figure 4.2

Economic activity and inactivity status: by sex and age, 2009[1]

United Kingdom
Thousands

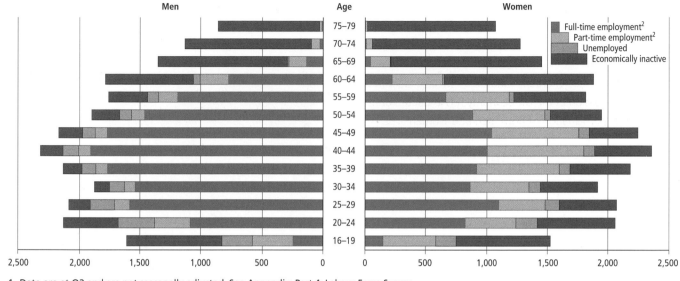

1 Data are at Q2 and are not seasonally adjusted. See Appendix, Part 4: Labour Force Survey.
2 The Labour Force Survey asks people to classify themselves as full time or part time, based on their own perceptions.

Source: Labour Force Survey, Office for National Statistics

people of this age who are economically inactive. Men in their 30s and 40s were most likely to be in full-time employment (each around 82 per cent), and were the least likely of all working-age men to be economically inactive. From the age of around 50, men begin to withdraw from full-time employment and there is an increase in both part-time employment and economic inactivity. However, after state pension age around one in five men (21 per cent) aged 65 to 69 continued to work either full or part time.

For women the picture is different. At 53 per cent, full-time employment was highest for women aged 25 to 29, after which the proportion fell to 45 per cent of 30 to 34-year-olds and 42 per cent of 35 to 39-year-olds (which could reflect family formation – see Chapter 2: Households and families). The proportion of women in full-time employment then rose to 46 per cent for 45 to 49-year-olds. Part-time employment and economic inactivity were generally more common among women of working age than among men, particularly in the younger age groups. Ten years before state pension age, similar proportions of men and women were economically inactive (18 per cent of 55 to 59-year-old men and 22 per cent of 50 to 54-year-old women). However, in the five years immediately before state pension age, a higher proportion of men than women were economically inactive (41 per cent of 60 to 64-year-old men compared with 33 per cent of 55 to 59-year-old women). A contributory factor to this may be that

working-age men are more likely than working-age women to have an occupational or personal pension and can therefore afford to retire earlier.

Using the Labour Force Survey it is possible to analyse the economic activity of households as well as individuals. Between Q2 1999 and Q2 2008, the proportion of working-age households which were workless (see Glossary) decreased from 17.1 per cent to 15.8 per cent. However, reflecting the upturn in the unemployment rate in Figure 4.1, the proportion of households which were workless increased to 16.9 per cent (the equivalent of 3.3 million households) in the 12 months to Q2 2009 and this pattern was consistent across most of the household types shown in Table 4.3 overleaf. Among those households with dependent children, the workless rate was highest for lone parent households at 40.4 per cent (unchanged from 12 months earlier), for couple households it was 5.9 per cent (an increase of 0.9 percentage points) and for other households it was 11.5 per cent (an increase of 2.6 percentage points). Of those households without dependent children, the workless rate for one person households was 30.1 per cent and the workless rate for other households, including couple households, was 13.2 per cent.

Over the same period, the proportion of working-age households that were working (see Glossary) increased from 55.8 per cent in Q2 1999 to 57.2 per cent in Q2 2008,

Table 4.3

Workless working-age households:[1,2] by type of household and presence of dependent children[3]

United Kingdom

Percentages

	1999	2000	2001	2002	2003	2004	2005	2006	2007	2008	2009
One person households	28.8	28.3	28.3	28.3	27.1	27.4	28.4	27.3	27.7	27.8	30.1
Couples with dependent children	5.9	5.6	5.6	5.5	5.1	5.1	5.0	5.1	5.6	5.0	5.9
Lone parents with dependent children	48.1	45.2	44.2	43.5	43.2	41.9	40.8	39.4	40.0	40.4	40.4
Others with dependent children	19.2	15.4	15.9	13.7	10.2	14.2	15.2	12.5	10.2	8.9	11.5
All with dependent children	15.6	14.5	14.5	14.5	14.1	14:0	13.7	13.4	13.8	13.5	14.4
Other household types	13.6	13.4	13.4	13.1	12.7	12.7	12.9	12.4	12.6	12.3	13.2
All household types	17.1	16.6	16.6	16.6	16.0	16.0	16.2	15.6	16.0	15.8	16.9

1 Data are the number of working-age workless households expressed as a percentage of the relevant working-age household type (for example workless lone parent households as a percentage of all lone parent households).
2 Data are at Q2 each year and are not seasonally adjusted. Men aged 16 to 64 and women aged 16 to 59 where economic activity status was known. See Appendix, Part 4: Labour Force Survey.
3 Children aged under 16 and those aged 16 to 18 who have never been married and are in full-time education.

Source: Labour Force Survey, Office for National Statistics

although the peak was in Q2 2007 (58.1 per cent). In the 12 months to Q2 2009, the proportion of working-age households that were working fell to 54.7 per cent (the equivalent of 10.7 million households).

Employment

Figure 4.1 showed some fluctuation in the overall employment rate between 1971 and 2009 associated with conditions in the wider economy. Figure 4.4 illustrates that over the period 1971 to 2009 employment rates for men and women converged, but did not equalise. This convergence largely took place in the 1970s and 1980s. Between Q2 1971 and Q2 1993 the gap in employment rates between men and women fell from 35 percentage points to 10 percentage points, as the rate for men fell to 75 per cent and the rate for women rose to 65 per cent. Since then, the trend towards convergence has slowed. The gap in employment rates between men and women was between 8 and 11 percentage points in the period Q2 1992 to Q2 2008 but was narrowest in Q2 2009 at 7 percentage points.

The impact of previous recessions on men's and women's employment rates can also be seen in Figure 4.4. For example, in the periods of economic growth between the recessions of the 1980s and the early 1990s the male and female employment rates both increased. However, the recession of the early 1990s caused the employment rate to fall more for men than it did for women. The Q2 employment rate for men reached 82 per cent in 1990 and fell by 7 percentage points to a low of 75 per cent in 1993, before it started to pick up again as the economy recovered. In contrast, the female employment

rate fell from 67 per cent in 1990 to 65 per cent in 1993, a fall of 2 percentage points. This pattern seems to be occurring again during the recession that began in 2008. Between Q2 2008 and Q2 2009 employment rates for men fell from 79 per cent to 76 per cent, while for women the rate fell from 70 per cent to 69 per cent.

Employment rates differ not only between men and women but also across the UK. The Annual Population Survey showed that in 2008 working-age employment rates were highest in

Figure 4.4

Employment rates:[1] by sex

United Kingdom

Percentages

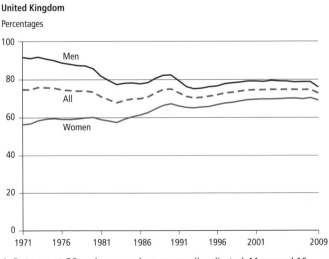

1 Data are at Q2 each year and are seasonally adjusted. Men aged 16 to 64 and women aged 16 to 59. See Appendix, Part 4: Labour Force Survey.

Source: Labour Force Survey, Office for National Statistics

Figure 4.5

Employment rates:[1] by region,[2] 2008[3]

United Kingdom
Percentages

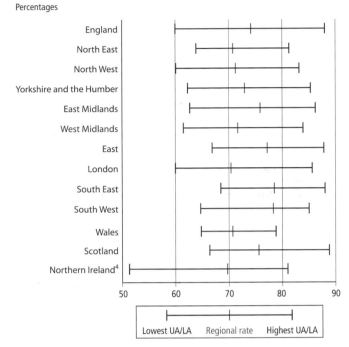

1 Men aged 16 to 64 and women aged 16 to 59.
2 By region and lowest and highest unitary authorities (UA) or local authority (LA) districts. No reliable estimates are available for the Isles of Scilly.
3 Data are at January to December from the Annual Population Survey and will therefore differ from headline quarterly employment figures published from the Labour Force Survey. See Appendix, Part 4: Annual Population Survey.
4 Local area Northern Ireland estimates are provided at district council area level.

Source: Annual Population Survey, Office for National Statistics

Scotland (76 per cent), followed by England (74 per cent), Wales (71 per cent) and Northern Ireland (70 per cent) (Figure 4.5). The English region with the highest working-age employment rate was the South East (79 per cent) and the lowest was London (70 per cent).

Data from the Annual Population Survey show that differences in employment rates of local areas within regions of England, or countries of the UK, were greater than the differences between regions and countries. London had the greatest contrast between employment rates in local authorities in 2008, with a difference of 26 percentage points between Newham (60 per cent) and the City of London (86 per cent). Newham had the lowest rate in Great Britain, with similar rates in Manchester and Liverpool in the North West (both 60 per cent).

There was a difference of 30 percentage points between the lowest and highest employment rates in Northern Ireland, although these data were for district council areas, which

generally have smaller populations than the local unitary authorities within Great Britain shown in Figure 4.5.

Wales had the narrowest spread of working-age employment rates, with 14 percentage points between Blaenau Gwent (65 per cent) and Flintshire (79 per cent). The local authorities with the highest employment rates in Great Britain were Hart in the South East of England, the Shetland Islands, and East Cambridgeshire in the East of England (each with a rate of around 88 per cent).

In 2008, the overall EU-27 working-age employment rate (see Appendix, Part 4: Eurostat rates) was 66 per cent (Table 4.6 overleaf). The UK had the fifth highest employment rate (72 per cent) after Denmark (78 per cent), the Netherlands (77 per cent), Sweden (74 per cent) and Austria (72 per cent). The UK was also one of eight member states with a rate above the 2010 target of 70 per cent which was set at the meeting of the European Union heads of state and ministers at the European Council in Lisbon in 2000. Since that meeting employment rates have increased in most member states, the exception being Portugal (a fall of 0.2 percentage points) and Romania (a fall of 4.0 percentage points). The largest increase was in Bulgaria (13.6 percentage points).

The average employment rate for working-age men in the EU-27 was 73 per cent in 2008. The UK had the fifth highest male rate (77 per cent) across the member states. Employment rates for men ranged from 63 per cent in Hungary to 83 per cent in the Netherlands.

In 2008, the average employment rate for working-age women across the EU-27 was 59 per cent, close to the 2010 target of 60 per cent. This target was set at the Stockholm Council in 2001. By 2008, 10 member states had still not reached the intermediate target set for 2005 of 57 per cent. The UK, along with Austria, had the sixth highest female rate (66 per cent) in 2008. The lowest employment rates for women were in the southern European countries of Malta, Italy and Greece, all of which had female employment rates below 50 per cent. In contrast, the northern European countries of Denmark (74 per cent), Sweden (72 per cent), and the Netherlands (71 per cent) all had employment rates for women above 70 per cent.

There are a range of factors underlying these differences. As well as economic cycle effects, which vary across countries in a given year, employment rates are also affected by population structures and differing cultures, retirement ages and participation in post-compulsory full-time education across the EU.

Table 4.6

Employment rates:[1] by sex, EU comparison, 2008

Percentages

	Men	Women	All		Men	Women	All
Denmark	81.9	74.3	78.1	Spain	73.5	54.9	64.3
Netherlands	83.2	71.1	77.2	Lithuania	67.1	61.8	64.3
Sweden	76.7	71.8	74.3	Bulgaria	68.5	59.5	64.0
Austria	78.5	65.8	72.1	Luxembourg	71.5	55.1	63.4
United Kingdom	77.3	65.8	71.5	Belgium	68.6	56.2	62.4
Finland	73.1	69.0	71.1	Slovakia	70.0	54.6	62.3
Cyprus	79.2	62.9	70.9	Greece	75.0	48.7	61.9
Germany	75.9	65.4	70.7	Poland	66.3	52.4	59.2
Estonia	73.6	66.3	69.8	Romania	65.7	52.5	59.0
Slovenia	72.7	64.2	68.6	Italy	70.3	47.2	58.7
Latvia	72.1	65.4	68.6	Hungary	63.0	50.6	56.7
Portugal	74.0	62.5	68.2	Malta	72.5	37.4	55.2
Ireland	74.9	60.2	67.6				
Czech Republic	75.4	57.6	66.6	EU-27 average	72.8	59.1	65.9
France	69.8	60.7	65.2				

1 See Appendix, Part 4: Eurostat rates, and Accession to the European Union (EU).

Source: Labour Force Survey, Eurostat

Patterns of employment

In Q2 2009, 16 per cent of those in employment in the UK were employed as managers or senior officials – the largest occupational group (see Appendix, Part 4: Standard Occupational Classification 2000 (SOC2000)). This compared with 7 per cent who were employed in each of sales and customer service, and process, plant and machine operation occupations (Table 4.7).

The pattern of occupations followed by men and women is quite different; in Q2 2009 men were most likely to be employed as managers or senior officials (19 per cent) while women were most likely to be employed in administrative and secretarial work (19 per cent). Around 1 in 6 women (16 per cent) worked in personal service (for example hairdressers and child care assistants) and more than 1 in 10 (11 per cent) worked in sales and customer service – occupations which were less common among men. Only the professional occupations, associate professional and technical occupations (such as nurses, financial advisers and IT technicians), and the elementary occupations (such as catering assistants, bar staff and shelf fillers) were almost equally likely to be followed by both men and women: between around 1 in 6 and 1 in 9 were employed in each of these occupations.

The data in Table 4.7 are derived from the LFS, where respondents are asked to classify their occupation and other

measures of employment themselves. However, the measurement of employee jobs, on which Table 4.8 is based, is derived from surveys of employers and the resulting data are based on number of jobs rather than number of people in

Table 4.7

All in employment: by sex and occupation, 2009[1]

United Kingdom

Percentages

	Men	Women	All
Managers and senior officials	19	12	16
Professional	14	13	14
Associate professional and technical	14	16	15
Administrative and secretarial	5	19	11
Skilled trades	18	2	11
Personal service	3	16	9
Sales and customer service	5	11	7
Process, plant and machine operatives	11	2	7
Elementary	12	11	11
All occupations[2] (=100%) (millions)	15.4	13.4	28.8

1 Data are at Q2 and are not seasonally adjusted. People aged 16 and over. See Appendix, Part 4: Labour Force Survey, and Standard Occupational Classification 2000 (SOC2000).
2 Includes people who did not state their occupation.

Source: Labour Force Survey, Office for National Statistics

Table 4.8

Employee jobs: by industry[1]

United Kingdom

Percentages

	1978	1988	1998	2008	2009	Change 1978 to 2008	Change 2008 to 2009
Agriculture and fishing	1.7	1.4	1.3	1.0	1.0	-0.7	-
Energy and water	2.8	1.8	0.8	0.7	0.7	-2.1	-
Manufacturing	28.5	20.7	17.0	10.5	10.0	-18.0	-0.6
Construction	5.7	5.1	4.4	4.8	4.8	-0.8	-
Distribution, hotels and restaurants	19.5	21.3	23.8	23.6	23.5	4.1	-0.1
Transport and communications	6.5	5.9	5.7	5.9	5.8	-0.7	-0.1
Finance and business services	10.5	14.8	18.1	21.4	20.8	10.9	-0.6
Public administration, education and health	21.1	24.5	24.2	26.9	28.1	5.8	1.2
Other services[2]	3.8	4.5	4.7	5.3	5.4	1.5	0.1
All industries (=100%) (millions)	24.3	23.7	24.7	27.2	26.5	2.9	-0.7

1 Data are at June each year and are not seasonally adjusted. See Appendix, Part 4: Standard Industrial Classification 2003 (SIC2003).
2 Community, social and personal services including sanitation, dry cleaning, personal care, and recreational, cultural and sporting activities.

Source: Short-Term Employment Surveys, Office for National Statistics

employment. One person may have more than one job, and jobs may vary in the hours worked.

Table 4.8 shows the changes in employee jobs by industry over the period 1978 to 2009. There were 24.3 million jobs in the UK in 1978, and over the last 30 years the number of jobs increased to 27.2 million in 2008. However, it fell to 26.5 million in 2009.

In 1978, the manufacturing sector accounted for the highest proportion of jobs at 28.5 per cent. This proportion has fallen steadily over the last 30 years to reach 10.0 per cent in 2009, the lowest proportion since records began, and represents an overall fall of around two-thirds since 1978. Conversely, the finance and business services sector has shown an increase of around 10 percentage points over the same period from 10.5 per cent in 1978 to 20.8 per cent in 2009. This sector however, has fallen slightly from 21.4 per cent in 2008.

In 2008, the public administration, education and health sector had the largest proportion of jobs at 26.9 per cent. This compares with 21.1 per cent in 1978, an increase of 5.8 percentage points. Between 2008 and 2009, the number of jobs in this sector increased by 1.2 percentage points to 28.1 per cent, and remained the highest proportion of all industrial sectors. These trends are reflected in the pattern of male and female jobs. In June 1978, the industry with the highest proportion of employee jobs for both men and women was manufacturing, at 34 per cent for men (4.8 million) and 21 per cent for women (2.2 million). These proportions fell to their lowest ever in June 2009 at 15 per cent for men

(2.0 million) and 5 per cent for women (0.7 million). Conversely, the industry with the highest proportion of employee jobs in 2009 was public administration, education and health at 16 per cent for men (2.1 million) and 41 per cent for women (5.4 million). These proportions had increased from 13 per cent for men (1.8 million) in June 1978 and 33 per cent for women (3.4 million).

Another important distinction in the analysis of employment is between private and public sector employment (for example central government, local government and public corporations). The public sector employment series (see Appendix, Part 4: Public sector employment) showed that in Q2 2009, 20.9 per cent of all people aged 16 and over in employment in the UK worked in the public sector, the equivalent of 6.039 million people. This is the highest Q2 total since the series began. The Q2 2009 public sector estimate was 289,000 higher than the same quarter in 2008 and the largest annual change in public sector employment since Q2 1993 when the total number fell by 311,000 (Figure 4.9 overleaf). This recent increase is because, unlike Q2 2008, the Q2 2009 estimate includes employment in Royal Bank of Scotland Group and Lloyds Banking Group following their classifications to the public sector as public corporations effective from October 2008. The largest increase over the 12 months to Q2 2009 was therefore in public corporations (62.9 per cent).

When public sector employment is analysed by industry (see Appendix, Part 4: Standard Industrial Classification (SIC2003)),

Figure 4.9

Annual change in public sector employment[1,2]

United Kingdom

Thousands

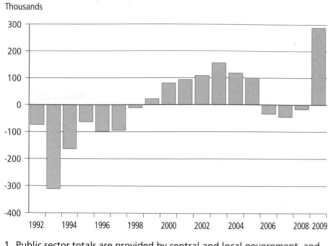

1 Public sector totals are provided by central and local government, and public corporations. Data are seasonally adjusted, annual changes in public sector employment measured at Q2 each year. Headcount of people aged 16 and over. See Appendix, Part 4: Public sector employment, and Labour Force Survey.
2 Estimates for 2008 and 2009 are based partly on projections for some sources.

Source: Office for National Statistics; public sector organisations

Table 4.10

Average usual weekly working hours:[1] by occupation,[2] 2009[3]

United Kingdom

Hours

	Men	Women	All employees
Managers and senior officials	46	43	45
Professional	44	44	44
Associate professional and technical	43	40	42
Administrative and secretarial	40	38	39
Skilled trades	43	40	43
Personal service	41	38	39
Sales and customer service	40	38	39
Process, plant and machine operatives	45	40	44
Elementary	42	38	41
All occupations	44	40	42

1 Average (mean) usual working hours of full-time employees aged 16 and over. Includes regular paid and unpaid overtime. Time rounded to nearest hour respondents worked on their main job. Excludes those who did not state their usual hours and those whose occupation was not known.
2 See Appendix, Part 4: Standard Occupational Classification 2000 (SOC2000).
3 Data are at Q2 and are not seasonally adjusted. See Appendix, Part 4: Labour Force Survey.

Source: Labour Force Survey, Office for National Statistics

the industry with the largest number of people in employment was the National Health Service (1.6 million) followed by education (1.4 million) and public administration (1.2 million).

People may work either full time or part time: in Q2 2009 1.9 million men and 5.7 million women reported to the LFS that they worked part time, though this was defined according to their own perceptions rather than a specified number of hours. However, to analyse someone's working hours simply by whether they work full time or part time can mask a variety of work patterns, and the number of hours a week somebody in employment usually works can be more informative. The 1998 Working Time Regulations implemented the EU Working Time Directive on working time in the UK and these apply to full-time, part-time and temporary workers. Employers should limit working time to 48 hours a week (averaged over a 17-week period) unless they offer individuals the right to opt out of this maximum working week. In Q2 2009, 17 per cent of full-time employees in the UK usually worked more than 48 hours a week (including regular paid and unpaid overtime).

Data from the LFS show that the usual average (mean) working week (including regular paid and unpaid overtime) of full-time employees of all occupations in the UK was 42 hours in Q2 2009 (Table 4.10). Overall the longest average working week among full-time employees was reported by those who were managers and senior officials (45 hours) and the shortest by those who worked in administrative and secretarial

occupations, personal service, and sales and customer service occupations (each 39 hours). For male employees, managers and senior officials had the longest average working week (46 hours) while for female employees, those with the longest average working week were women in professional occupations (44 hours).

The opportunity to work flexible hours can help people to balance home and work responsibilities. Legislation in the UK provides parents and carers (under certain criteria) with the right to request a flexible work pattern. Almost a quarter (23 per cent) of full-time employees and over a quarter (27 per cent) of part-time employees had some form of flexible working arrangement in Q2 2009 (Table 4.11). Female employees were more likely than male employees to have a flexible working arrangement and the most common form for full-time employees of both sexes was flexible working hours. This was also the most common arrangement among men who worked part time and second most common for women, with term-time working the most popular option for part-time female employees.

The Eurobarometer survey provides data on attitudes of working women across the EU-27 to their work-life balance.

Table 4.11

Employees with flexible working patterns:[1] by sex and type of employment,[2] 2009[3]

United Kingdom   Percentages

	Men	Women	All employees
Full-time employees			
Flexible working hours	10.9	15.3	12.6
Annualised working hours	4.9	4.9	4.9
Term-time working	1.2	6.7	3.3
Four and a half day week	1.2	0.5	0.9
Nine day fortnight	0.5	0.4	0.4
Any flexible working pattern[4]	19.0	28.1	22.5
Part-time employees			
Flexible working hours	8.6	10.3	9.9
Term-time working	3.6	11.6	9.9
Annualised working hours	3.3	4.6	4.3
Job sharing	1.0	2.1	1.9
Any flexible working pattern[4]	18.4	29.6	27.1

1 Percentages are based on totals that exclude people who did not state whether or not they had a flexible working arrangement. Respondents could give more than one answer. People aged 16 and over. See Appendix, Part 4: Flexible working arrangements.
2 The Labour Force Survey asks people to classify themselves as either full time or part time, based on their own perceptions.
3 Data are at Q2 and are not seasonally adjusted. See Appendix, Part 4: Labour Force Survey.
4 Includes other categories of flexible working not separately identified.

Source: Labour Force Survey, Office for National Statistics

In 2009, two-thirds (66 per cent) of women in employment in the UK agreed that they managed to balance their personal and working lives, which was slightly lower than the average for the EU-27 (70 per cent). Proportions who said they managed to achieve a balance ranged from 57 per cent of women in Greece and 61 per cent in France and the Czech Republic, to 83 per cent of women in Hungary and Romania, and 84 per cent in the Netherlands. Women were more likely to say that their personal life was hindered by the demands of their working life than their working life being hindered by their personal life in all member states with the exceptions of Slovenia and Denmark.

Costs of sickness absence to employers include statutory sick pay, loss of production, and the expense of covering absence with temporary staff. At the same time there are also indirect costs such as lower morale among those covering for absence and potential for lower customer satisfaction. Sickness absence rates, defined as the proportion of employees with at least one day's absence from work in the reference week because of sickness or injury, for all employees in the UK

decreased between the 12 months ending June 2001 (3.3 per cent) and the 12 months ending June 2006 (2.5 per cent). Since this period, sickness absence rates for all working-age employees have remained stable at around 2.5 per cent, although there was a slight fall to 2.3 per cent in the 12 months to June 2009.

Sickness absence rates for working-age women were 2.6 per cent compared with 1.9 per cent for men in the 12 months to June 2009. Sickness absence also varied between occupations from 1.7 per cent for managers and senior officials to 2.9 per cent for employees in administrative and secretarial occupations. Those who had a gross weekly income of £600 and over were also less likely than those on lower incomes to be absent from work because of sickness (Figure 4.12). The sickness absence rate was 2.0 per cent for those receiving a gross weekly income of £600 and over compared with 2.3 per cent for those receiving less then £300. However, sickness absence rates were higher for those receiving between £300 and £599 per week than those at each end of the income distribution.

Job separations occur either when an employee leaves a paid job of their own accord – a voluntary separation – or when the employer initiates the separation and terminates employment – an involuntary separation (see Appendix, Part 4: Job separations). Between Q2 1997 and Q2 2008 in the UK, the proportion of working-age people in paid employment who

Figure 4.12

Sickness absence rates of employees:[1] by gross weekly income, 2008–09

United Kingdom

Percentages

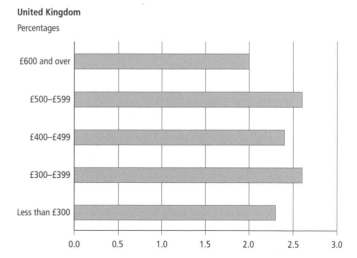

1 Percentages are based on 4-quarter averages (Q3 to Q2) and are not seasonally adjusted. Data are the proportion of male employees aged 16 to 64 and female employees aged 16 to 59 who had at least one day's absence from work because of sickness in the reference week. See Appendix, Part 4: Labour Force Survey.

Source: Labour Force Survey, Office for National Statistics

Table 4.13

Job separations:[1] by reason, 2008–09[2]

United Kingdom

Percentages

	Men	Women	All
Involuntary separations			
Made redundant/voluntary redundancy	29.8	19.0	25.0
Temporary job ended	15.2	13.3	14.3
Dismissed	3.6	2.7	3.2
All involuntary separations (millions)	1.1	0.6	1.7
Voluntary separations			
Resigned	24.3	30.9	27.2
Gave up work for family/personal reasons	2.8	10.4	6.2
Gave up work for health reasons	2.3	3.2	2.7
Early retirement/retired[3]	2.7	1.4	2.1
Left for some other reason	19.3	19.1	19.2
All voluntary separations (millions)	1.1	1.1	2.2
All job separations (=100%) (millions)	2.2	1.7	3.9

1 See Appendix, Part 4: Job separations.
2 Percentages are based on 4-quarter averages (Q3 to Q2) and are not seasonally adjusted. Men aged 16 to 64 and women aged 16 to 59. Excludes those where reason for leaving job was not known. See Appendix, Part 4: Labour Force Survey.
3 Combined response of those who took early retirement, and retired at or after state pension age (currently 65 for men and 60 for women).

Source: Labour Force Survey, Office for National Statistics

left their job voluntarily fell from 3.2 per cent to 2.3 per cent while the proportion who left involuntarily fell from 1.6 per cent to 1.0 per cent. However between Q2 2008 and Q2 2009 there was a further decrease in voluntary separations (to 1.5 per cent) but an increase in involuntary separations (to 1.5 per cent). This decrease in voluntary separations may reflect workers being less likely to instigate a job move in a time of economic recession while the increase in involuntary separations reflects increases in redundancy levels (see Figure 4.14).

In 2008–09 a total of 3.9 million job separations occurred in the UK, of which 2.2 million were voluntary and 1.7 million were involuntary (Table 4.13). The most common reason for leaving a job for people of working age was resignation, accounting for 27 per cent, followed by being made redundant (including voluntary redundancy) at 25 per cent. Leaving for some other reason than those shown in the table was the next most common reason (19 per cent) followed by the ending of a temporary job (14 per cent). Giving up work for family or personal reasons accounted for 6 per cent of job separations and this reason was more common for women (10 per cent) than men (3 per cent). It should be noted that because these data are self-reported there could be reporting errors with the

Figure 4.14

Redundancy rates:[1] by sex

United Kingdom

Rates per 1,000 employees

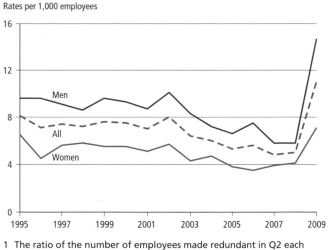

1 The ratio of the number of employees made redundant in Q2 each year to the number of employees in Q1, multiplied by 1,000. Data are seasonally adjusted. People aged 16 and over. See Appendix, Part 4: Labour Force Survey.

Source: Labour Force Survey, Office for National Statistics

reason for the job separation: for example, dismissals may be under-reported.

The shedding of jobs through redundancy fell for both men and women in the UK between Q2 1995 and Q2 2008, although with slight fluctuations (Figure 4.14). However, in Q2 2009, estimates from the LFS show a sharp rise in the overall redundancy rate from 5.0 redundancies per 1,000 employees aged 16 and over in Q2 2008 to 11.0 per 1,000 employees and suggest that a higher proportion of men were made redundant than women during the recession which began in 2008. The redundancy rate for men in Q2 2009 was 14.7 per 1,000 employees, compared with 7.1 per 1,000 employees for women. This compares with redundancy rates of 5.8 per 1,000 employees in Q2 2008 for men and 4.1 per 1,000 employees for women. The increase over the 12 months in redundancy rates for men was therefore 8.9 per 1,000 employees but for women it was 3.0 per 1,000 employees.

Job losses have occurred across the entire economy in Q2 2009, but data by industry show the highest concentrations in construction (27.9 redundancies per 1,000 employees in Q2 2009) and manufacturing (20.1 redundancies per 1,000 employees in Q2 2009). A year earlier in Q2 2008, construction recorded 9.1 redundancies per 1,000 employees and manufacturing recorded 7.1 redundancies per 1,000 employees. These industries were also ones where men were more likely to work than women. The finance and business services industry, which has grown in recent years (see Table 4.8) was also heavily affected with an increase in redundancy rates to 18.1 per 1,000 employees in Q2 2009 compared with 5.1 in Q2 2008.

Unemployment

The unemployment rate fluctuates through the economic cycle. During periods of economic growth the number of jobs generally grows and unemployment falls, although any mismatches between the skill needs of the new jobs and the skills of those available for work may slow this process. Conversely, as the economy slows, and particularly if it goes into recession, so unemployment tends to rise, though a rise in unemployment tends to lag behind an economic slowdown. Since 1971 when Labour Force Survey (LFS) records began, total unemployment for people aged 16 and over, using Q2 data, peaked in 1984 (11.9 per cent) and again in 1993 (10.4 per cent) (Figure 4.15). Although still lower than in 1993, in 2009 there was another increase to 7.8 per cent during the recent recession. Unemployment rates for men aged 16 and over rose to 12.2 per cent in Q2 1983, equivalent to 1.9 million unemployed men. The unemployment peak for women over this period was in Q2 1984 when the rate was 11.8 per cent, equivalent to 1.3 million unemployed women aged 16 and over. The recession in the early 1990s had a much greater effect on unemployment among men than women, and the unemployment rate for men peaked at 12.3 per cent in Q2 1993, the highest rate since the series began. In the same quarter, the female unemployment rate also rose, but to a

lower level of 8.0 per cent. Rates for both men and women increased in the 12 months to Q2 2009 from 5.8 per cent to 8.8 per cent for men (equivalent to 1.5 million men aged 16 and over) and from 4.9 per cent to 6.6 per cent for women (equivalent to 0.9 million women of the same age).

Between Q2 1992 (from when LFS data can be analysed by age) and Q2 2009, unemployment rates for younger people generally increased whereas rates for older workers decreased. The unemployment rate for 16 to 17-year-olds increased by 12.8 percentage points to 31.7 per cent over the period and although there was also an increase for 18 to 24-years-olds, it was smaller – from 15.6 per cent to 17.2 per cent. It is worth noting that the unemployment rate for those aged 16 to 17 will be based on a smaller sample than those aged 18 to 24 not only because of the narrower age band but also because of the high proportion of 16 to 17-year-olds who are in further education and therefore economically inactive rather than unemployed. The rates for men and women aged 25 to 34, 35 to 49, and 50 to 59/64 all fell over the same period. However, in the 12 months to Q2 2009 rates increased for all age bands and the largest increase was for those aged 16 to 17 (by 5.8 percentage points).

The LFS asks unemployed respondents who have worked within the last eight years about their last job (Table 4.16). This information can be used to calculate unemployment rates

Figure 4.15

Unemployment rates:[1] by sex

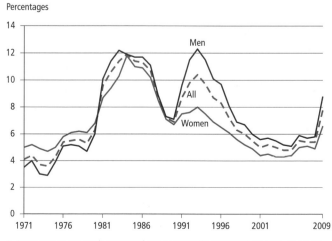

United Kingdom
Percentages

1 Data are at Q2 each year and are seasonally adjusted. People aged 16 and over. See Appendix, Part 4: Labour Force Survey.

Source: Labour Force Survey, Office for National Statistics

Table 4.16

Unemployment rates:[1] by previous occupation, 2009[2]

United Kingdom   Percentages

	Men	Women	All
Managers and senior officials	3.4	2.9	3.2
Professional	2.5	2.0	2.3
Associate professional and technical	4.4	3.0	3.7
Administrative and secretarial	7.2	4.2	4.8
Skilled trades	8.4	3.7	8.0
Personal service	4.6	3.6	3.8
Sales and customer service	11.5	7.9	9.1
Process, plant and machine operatives	9.7	11.5	9.9
Elementary	15.0	9.6	12.7

1 As a proportion of all persons in employment in the relevant occupation plus those unemployed who last worked in that occupation.
2 Data are at Q2 and are not seasonally adjusted. People aged 16 and over. See Appendix, Part 4: Labour Force Survey, and Standard Occupational Classification 2000 (SOC2000).

Source: Labour Force Survey, Office for National Statistics

Table 4.17

Unemployment rates:[1] by region and local area,[2] 2008[3]

United Kingdom

Percentages

	Regional rate	Unitary authority/local authority district			
		Lowest rate within region		Highest rate within region	
England	5.8	Eden/Purbeck	2.6	Tower Hamlets	11.7
North East	7.5	Teesdale	4.4	Middlesbrough	9.8
North West	6.3	Eden	2.6	Manchester	9.9
Yorkshire and the Humber	6.3	Craven	3.0	Kingston upon Hull	9.8
East Midlands	5.8	South Northamptonshire	3.0	Leicester	11.4
West Midlands	6.9	Stratford-on-Avon	3.2	Birmingham	10.9
East	4.9	Uttlesford	3.0	Luton	8.5
London	6.9	Richmond upon Thames	3.6	Tower Hamlets	11.7
South East	4.4	Elmbridge/Surrey Heath/Hart	2.8	Hastings	7.8
South West	4.1	Purbeck	2.6	Torbay	6.0
Wales	6.3	Monmouthshire	4.2	Blaenau Gwent	9.2
Scotland	4.9	Shetland Islands	2.4	North Ayrshire	7.3
Northern Ireland	4.0	..	..	..	..

1 People aged 16 and over.
2 Excludes the City of London and the Isles of Scilly as the sample size is too small to provide an estimate. See Appendix, Part 4: Model-based estimates of unemployment.
3 Data are at January to December from the Annual Population Survey and will therefore differ from headline quarterly unemployment figures published from the Labour Force Survey. See Appendix, Part 4: Annual Population Survey.

Source: Annual Population Survey, Office for National Statistics

according to a person's previous occupation (see Appendix, Part 4: Standard Occupational Classification 2000 (SOC2000)). In Q2 2009 unemployment rates were highest among those who previously worked in the elementary occupations (12.7 per cent) and lowest among those who previously worked in professional occupations (2.3 per cent) with a higher proportion of men being unemployed than women in all occupational groups with the exception of process, plant and machine operatives.

According to the Annual Population Survey, unemployment rates in 2008 among the countries of the UK ranged from 6.3 per cent in Wales to 4.0 per cent in Northern Ireland, with a rate of 5.8 per cent in England and 4.9 per cent in Scotland (Table 4.17). As with employment rates, differences in unemployment rates within the English regions and countries of the UK are greater than differences between them (see also Appendix, Part 4: Model-based estimates of unemployment). The region with the largest difference was the East Midlands, with 8.4 percentage points between the highest and lowest unemployment rates in Leicester (11.4 per cent) and South Northamptonshire (3.0 per cent), whereas the South West had the smallest range of 3.4 percentage points between Torbay (6.0 per cent) and Purbeck (2.6 per cent).

The local authority area with the lowest unemployment rate in Great Britain in 2008 was the Shetland Islands in Scotland (2.4 per cent), followed by Aberdeenshire, also in Scotland (2.5 per cent). The local authority with the highest rate was Tower Hamlets (11.7 per cent). Five other areas in Great Britain had unemployment rates above 10 per cent. These were Leicester in the East Midlands (11.4 per cent), Birmingham (10.9 per cent) and Sandwell (10.7 per cent), both in the West Midlands, Newham (10.3 per cent) in London, and Wolverhampton (10.1 per cent) also in the West Midlands.

Economic inactivity

Economically inactive people are those who are neither in employment nor classed as unemployed (see Glossary), especially those of working age, who could move into the labour force in the future and as such are a potential source of labour market supply.

The overall economic inactivity rate for people in the UK aged 16 and over in Q2 2009 was 37 per cent (equivalent to 18.0 million people) and has remained relatively stable since records began in 1971. It should be noted however, that these figures include those over state pension age, the majority of whom are

Figure 4.18

Economic inactivity rates:[1] by sex

United Kingdom

Percentages

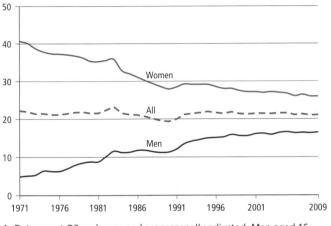

1 Data are at Q2 each year and are seasonally adjusted. Men aged 16 to 64 and women aged 16 to 59. See Appendix, Part 4: Labour Force Survey.

Source: Labour Force Survey, Office for National Statistics

Table 4.19

Economic inactivity rates: by ethnic group[1] and sex, 2009[2]

United Kingdom   Percentages

	Men	Women	All
White British[3]	30	43	37
Other White[3]	24	39	31
Mixed	28	37	33
Indian	23	42	32
Pakistani	28	66	46
Bangladeshi	25	69	46
Other Asian	25	41	34
Black Caribbean	31	34	32
Black African	29	44	37
Other Black	..	53	48
Chinese	38	43	40
Other ethnic group	28	46	37

1 Excludes those who did not state their ethnic group. See Appendix, Part 1: Classification of ethnic groups.
2 Data are at Q2 and are not seasonally adjusted. Men aged 16 to 64 and women aged 16 to 59. See Appendix, Part 4: Labour Force Survey.
3 Data are for Great Britain only.

Source: Labour Force Survey, Office for National Statistics

retired. Those under state pension age are therefore more likely to be a potential source of labour supply, and in Q2 2009 around a quarter (27 per cent) of those economically inactive of this age stated that they did want a job. The economic inactivity rate among working-age people (see Glossary) in the UK showed a small peak in Q2 1983 at 23 per cent, having been stable at a rate of around 21 per cent in the 1970s (Figure 4.18). The rate dropped gradually from the mid-1980s to a low of 19 per cent in 1990 and was 21 per cent in Q2 2009. Economic inactivity rates for men and women converged between Q2 1971 and Q2 2009, with the male rate rising and the female rate falling. This trend began levelling out at the start of this century and the gap between the sexes has remained between 10 and 11 percentage points since 2001, until it fell to 9 percentage points in Q2 2009. The economic inactivity rate for working-age men more than trebled from 5 per cent in Q2 1971 to 17 per cent in Q2 2009 (equivalent to 3.3 million men in Q2 2009). The economic inactivity rate for working-age women fell by 15 percentage points from 41 per cent in Q2 1971 to 26 per cent in Q2 2009 (equivalent to 4.7 million women in Q2 2009) although the rate has remained stable since 1999 at around 26 to 27 per cent.

In Q2 2009, the ethnic group with the highest economic inactivity rate among people of working age in the UK was Other Black at 48 per cent, closely followed by the Pakistani and Bangladeshi ethnic groups, each at 46 per cent (Table 4.19). The high proportions for these two Asian groups were mainly driven by high economic inactivity rates for

women – Pakistanis at 66 per cent and Bangladeshis at 69 per cent, with the men in these groups having rates of 28 per cent and 25 per cent respectively. The ethnic groups with the lowest economic inactivity rates were Other White (this figure is for Great Britain) at 31 per cent overall (24 per cent for men and 39 per cent for women), with Indian and Black Caribbean groups at 32 per cent. The Indian male rate was 23 per cent, the lowest of all groups, and the Black Caribbean male rate was 31 per cent, only exceeded by the rate for Chinese males at 38 per cent.

Between Q2 2001 and Q2 2009, the biggest rise in rates was for the Other Black ethnic group increasing from 33 per cent to 48 per cent, a rise of 15 percentage points. The largest fall, however, was in the Bangladeshi group, falling from 56 per cent in Q2 2001 to 46 per cent in Q2 2009, although this group peaked at 58 per cent in Q2 2005. The fall in the Bangladeshi group was driven by falls for both men (from 34 per cent to 25 per cent) and women (from 80 per cent to 69 per cent).

There are a variety of reasons why a person may be economically inactive. In Q2 2009, the main reason among working-age men was being a student (34 per cent), or long-term sickness or disability (33 per cent). For working-age women, looking after family or home was the most common

Table 4.20

Economic inactivity rates:[1] by region and local area,[2] 2008[3]

United Kingdom

Percentages

| | Regional rate | Unitary authority/local authority district | | | |
		Lowest rate within region		Highest rate within region	
England	21.1	St. Edmundsbury	8.3	Liverpool	35.1
North East	23.3	Berwick-upon-Tweed	11.9	Middlesbrough	29.4
North West	23.7	South Ribble	13.3	Liverpool	35.1
Yorkshire and the Humber	21.9	Selby	13.5	Kingston upon Hull	31.7
East Midlands	19.2	Blaby	12.1	Nottingham	28.8
West Midlands	22.7	Bromsgrove	12.5	Birmingham	30.6
East	18.7	St. Edmundsbury	8.3	Cambridge	29.4
London	24.3	Merton	16.6	Newham	33.3
South East	17.7	Hart	10.5	Hastings	25.6
South West	18.2	Stroud	12.0	West Somerset	33.5
Wales	24.3	Flintshire	18.3	Ceredigion	30.6
Scotland	20.4	Shetland Islands	10.8	Glasgow City	28.9
Northern Ireland	27.4	Antrim[4]	19.0	Cookstown[4]	40.3

1 Men aged 16 to 64 and women aged 16 to 59.
2 Excludes the City of London and the Isles of Scilly as the sample size is too small to provide an estimate.
3 Data are at January to December from the Annual Population Survey and will therefore differ from headline quarterly economic inactivity figures
    published from the Labour Force Survey. See Appendix, Part 4: Annual Population Survey.
4 Local area Northern Ireland estimates are provided at district council area level.

Source: Annual Population Survey, Office for National Statistics

reason, reported by 44 per cent. Reasons for economic inactivity also vary by age. For those aged 16 to 24, being a student was the main reason for both men and women. This pattern changes with age in both sexes – at ages 25 to 34, long-term sickness or disability became the main reason for men (38 per cent), which continued through to state pension age. Looking after family or home was the main reason for economic inactivity among women aged 25 to 34 (71 per cent) and this remained the main reason for those aged 35 to 49 (60 per cent), with long-term sickness or disability becoming the main reason in the pre-state pension age group (50 to 59) at 40 per cent.

According to the Annual Population Survey, Scotland had the lowest national working-age economic inactivity rate of the countries of the UK in 2008, at 20 per cent (Table 4.20). The rate for England was 21 per cent, followed by Wales at 24 per cent and Northern Ireland had the highest economic inactivity rate at 27 per cent. London had the highest regional rate in England, at 24 per cent, while the South East had the lowest (18 per cent).

There were further, and wider, variations in economic inactivity rates at local area level. In Great Britain, the local authority with

the highest economic inactivity rate was Liverpool, at 35 per cent, and the lowest was St. Edmundsbury, at 8 per cent. Comparing the economic inactivity rates within the regions and countries in Great Britain shows that the region with the greatest difference between highest and lowest was the North West, with 22 percentage points between Liverpool at 35 per cent and South Ribble at 13 per cent. Wales had the smallest difference with 12 percentage points between Ceredigion at 31 per cent and Flintshire at 18 per cent.

Among the district councils of Northern Ireland, Antrim had the lowest economic inactivity rate at 19 per cent with Cookstown the highest at 40 per cent, a difference of 21 percentage points.

Employment relations

In the UK in 2008 there were a total of 758,900 working days lost due to industrial disputes involving 511,200 workers in 144 stoppages (Table 4.21). This compares with 1.041 million working days lost in 2007 involving 744,800 workers but a similar number of stoppages (142). Around four-fifths (81 per cent) of working days lost in 2008 were in public administration and defence which also accounted for the

Table 4.21

Labour disputes:[1] by industry group,[2] 2008

United Kingdom

	Working days lost (thousands)	Workers involved (thousands)	Stoppages (numbers)
Agriculture, hunting, forestry and fishing	0.1	0.1	2
Mining, quarrying, electricity, gas and water	0.7	0.8	1
Manufacturing	6.9	4.9	21
Construction	2.7	2.7	4
Transport, storage and communication	24.8	19.0	28
Public administration and defence	614.3	370.3	16
Education	103.4	110.3	40
All other services	6.7	3.1	32
All industries and services	758.9	511.2	144

1 See Appendix, Part 4: Labour disputes.
2 See Appendix, Part 4: Standard Industrial Classification 2003 (SIC2003).

Source: Office for National Statistics

majority of workers involved at 72 per cent. The education sector accounted for the highest proportion of stoppages at 28 per cent (40 stoppages). The same sector also accounted for the second highest share of working days lost at 14 per cent

(103,400 days), and for workers involved at 22 per cent (110,300 workers).

There were 6,900 working days lost in the UK manufacturing industry in 2008 (equivalent to 2 working days lost per 1,000 employees) compared with 15,600 in 2007. This is a record low for working days lost in manufacturing and partly reflects the decline of the industry in the UK (see also Table 4.8). In 2007, the transport, storage and communications sector accounted for 422 working days lost per 1,000 employees. This figure fell sharply to 16 working days lost per 1,000 employees in 2008.

One possible way to address some types of disagreements or issues within the workplace is through employment tribunals, which are judicial bodies that aim to resolve disputes between employers and employees over employment rights. Their aim is to provide fast, accessible and relatively informal justice. In Great Britain a claim may be brought to tribunal by an employee under more than one jurisdiction (or reason) but will only be counted as one claim. In 2007/08 more than 189,000 claims were registered with employment tribunals in Great Britain which covered nearly 297,000 jurisdictions of complaint (Table 4.22).

Of these jurisdictions, equal pay was the most common at 21 per cent of the total, closely followed by the Working Time Directive at 19 per cent. The proportion of claims for unfair dismissal almost halved between 2002/03 and 2007/08 from

Table 4.22

Employment tribunal claims:[1] by jurisdiction of complaint

Great Britain   Percentages

	2000/01	2002/03	2004/05	2006/07	2007/08
Equal pay	7.9	2.9	5.3	18.5	21.1
Working Time Directive	2.9	3.7	2.1	8.9	18.8
Unfair dismissal[2]	23.1	27.0	25.5	18.7	13.8
Sex, disability, race and age[3]	16.0	11.6	12.8	16.1	13.4
Unauthorised deduction of wages[4]	19.1	22.9	24.0	14.6	11.6
Breach of contract	14.4	17.2	14.6	11.4	8.4
Redundancy pay	4.3	5.0	4.4	3.2	2.5
Others	12.3	9.7	11.4	8.6	10.4
All jurisdictions (=100%) (thousands)	218.1	172.3	156.1	238.5	297.0

1 A claim may be brought under more than one jurisdiction or subsequently amended or clarified in the course of proceedings. See Appendix, Part 4: Employment tribunals.
2 Includes the jurisdiction 'unfair dismissal as a result of a transfer of an undertaking'.
3 Data for jurisdictions concerning age are included from 2006/07 onwards following the introduction of *The Employment Equality (Age) Regulations 2006* which came into force in October 2006.
4 Prior to 2002/03 this jurisdiction was known as the *Wages Act*.

Source: Employment Tribunals Service, Ministry of Justice

27 per cent to 14 per cent while claims for equal pay increased more than sevenfold during same period. Claims under the Working Time Directive increased around sixfold since 2001/02. There were around 2,900 claims of age discrimination in 2007/08, an increase of around 2,000 since new legislation came into force in October 2006. In Northern Ireland, 2,163 claims were made under 4,383 jurisdictions in 2007/08. Of these claims, those under the jurisdiction of unauthorised deduction of wages accounted for 21 per cent of the total, although it must be noted that around a third of these cases related to the same complaint made by a number of people against one respondent. This was closely followed by claims for unfair dismissal at 20 per cent.

Once a year in Q4, the Labour Force Survey (LFS) asks questions on trade union membership of all those in employment in the UK, including the self-employed and employees. This section concentrates on employees since they have less direct control over many aspects of their working lives than the self-employed or family workers.

The rate of union membership, or union density, in the UK fell by 0.6 percentage points to 27.4 per cent in Q4 2008 from

28.0 per cent in Q4 2007. Union density among female employees in the UK dropped by 0.4 percentage points in Q4 2008 compared with a 0.8 percentage point drop for males over the same period. In 2002, union density among female employees exceeded the rate for men for the first time. The gap between women and men has since increased each year to reach 4 percentage points in 2008.

In 2007 there was a marked difference in the union density of the Scandinavian countries compared with the rest of the EU. Sweden, Finland and Denmark all had a union density of around 70 per cent. This compared with Spain and Poland at around 14 per cent (data for 2006) and France, with the lowest union density at 8 per cent.

Among the Group of Seven (G7) of the world's largest industrial market economies, Italy ranked as the highest unionised, with 33 per cent of the working population being members of a trade union. Canada was second, at 29 per cent, followed by the UK at 28 per cent, and Germany at 20 per cent. Japan ranked fifth with 18 per cent and the USA was sixth with 12 per cent. France was the lowest, at 8 per cent in 2007.

Glossary

Economically active (or the **labour force**) – those aged 16 and over who are **in employment** or are **unemployed**.

Economic activity rate – the proportion of the population, for example in a given age group, who are **economically active**.

In employment – a measure, obtained from surveys of those aged 16 and over who are **employees**, **self-employed**, people doing unpaid work for a family-run business, and participants in government-supported employment and training programmes.

Employment rate – the proportion of any given population group who are **in employment**. The main presentation of employment rates is the proportion of the population of **working age** who are in employment.

Employees (Labour Force Survey measure) – a measure obtained from surveys of people aged 16 and over who regard themselves as paid employees. People with two or more jobs are counted only once.

Self-employed – a measure obtained from surveys of people aged 16 and over who regard themselves as self-employed: that is, those who in their main employment work on their own account, whether or not they have employees.

Unemployment – a measure, based on International Labour Organisation guidelines and used in the Labour Force Survey, which counts as unemployed those aged 16 and over who

are without a job, are available to start work in the next two weeks, who have been seeking a job in the last four weeks, or are out of work and waiting to start a job already obtained in the next two weeks.

Unemployment rate – the proportion of the **economically active** who are **unemployed**. The main presentation of unemployment rates is the proportion of the economically active population aged 16 and over who are **unemployed**.

Economically inactive – those aged 16 and over who are neither **in employment** nor **unemployment**. For example, those looking after a home, retirees, or those unable to work because of long-term sickness or disability.

Economic inactivity rate – the proportion of a given population group who are **economically inactive**. The main presentation of economic inactivity rates is the proportion of the population of **working age** who are economically inactive.

Working age – Men aged 16 to 64 and women aged 16 to 59.

Working-age household – a household that includes at least one person of **working age**.

Working household – a household where all individuals aged 16 and over are **in employment**.

Workless household – a household that includes at least one person of **working age** where no one aged 16 and over is **in employment**.

Chapter 5

Income and wealth

- Between 2007 and 2008, household disposable income per head in the UK grew by 1.4 per cent in real terms, compared with a fall of 0.1 per cent in gross domestic product per head. (Figure 5.1)

- Household net wealth per head in the UK fell by 15 per cent in real terms between 2007 and 2008, the first fall since 2001. (Figure 5.4)

- Between April 1998 and April 2009, the gender pay gap in the UK decreased from 27.3 per cent to 22.0 per cent for all employees, from 17.4 per cent to 12.2 per cent for full-time employees, and from –4.0 to –2.0 per cent for part-time employees. (Figure 5.11)

- In the UK in 2007/08 people living in workless households, where one or more people were unemployed, were concentrated in the bottom fifth of the income distribution: 70 per cent were in the bottom group and only 2 per cent in the top fifth. (Table 5.17)

- The likelihood of living in a household below 60 per cent of median disposable income in the UK in 2007/08 was higher than average for pensioners, at 23 per cent, although this proportion has fallen substantially from 37 per cent reported in 1990–91. (Figure 5.19)

- The most important element of household wealth in the UK in 2008 was held in the form of residential buildings, amounting to £3,693 billion. However, between 2007 and 2008 this element of wealth fell substantially in real terms, by 12 per cent. (Table 5.21)

DATA

Download data by clicking the online pdf

www.statistics.gov.uk/ socialtrends

Over the last four decades the UK has experienced many changes to its economy and society, and these two aspects are related. Living standards depend on the level of economic activity and on the redistribution of economic resources within society as a whole, and have a major influence on social well-being. Generally, income is analysed at the level of either the family or the household, because these are the units across which income and outgoings are considered to be pooled, so that the income of the family or household can be regarded as representative of the standard of living of each person living in it. However, for some purposes, such as the analysis of income from employment, income is analysed for individuals.

Overview

The level of economic activity in a country is usually measured by its gross domestic product (GDP). This indicator, and its value per head, is also often used to measure societal well-being. However, in recent years there has been an increasing acknowledgment that 'there is more to life than GDP', recognising that GDP is, in some respects, too simplistic a measure to reflect comprehensively the level of well-being within a society.

The total income generated in a country, as measured by GDP, is shared between individuals (in the form of wages and salaries), between companies and other organisations (for example in the form of profits retained for investments), and government (in the form of taxes on production). If GDP is growing in real terms (after adjustments to remove inflation) this means that the economy is expanding. Between 1971 and 2008, GDP per head in the UK more than doubled in real terms (Figure 5.1). However, this trend has not been one of consistent annual growth. Over this period there were times when the economy contracted, for example at the time of the international oil crisis in the mid-1970s, and again during periods of world recession in the early 1980s and early 1990s. The UK economy grew each year since 1992 until 2008 when it contracted again as the latest global economic recession began. Between 2007 and 2008 GDP per head decreased by 0.4 percentage points.

Household disposable income (total income from wages, salaries and state benefits, after the deduction of taxes) per head in the UK increased by more than 140 per cent in real terms between 1971 and 2008. During the 1970s and the 1980s growth fluctuated, and in some years there were small year-on-year falls, but since 1982 there has been growth overall. Between 2003 and 2007, growth in real household disposable income per head has been lower than growth in GDP per head. However, between 2007 and 2008, household

Figure 5.1

Real household disposable income per head[1] and gross domestic product per head[2]

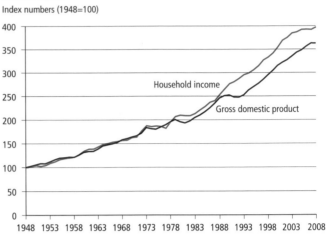

United Kingdom

Index numbers (1948=100)

1 Adjusted to real terms using the expenditure deflator for the household sector. See Appendix, Part 5: Household income data sources.
2 Adjusted to real terms using the GDP deflator.

Source: Office for National Statistics

disposable income per head increased by 5.5 percentage points while GDP per head decreased by 0.4 percentage points.

A comparison of GDP per head in 2008 across the 27 member states of the EU shows that the UK had the seventh highest level of economic activity (Table 5.2). Luxembourg had the highest level of GDP per head, partly because of the importance of its financial sector, but mainly because of the large share of cross-border workers in total employment. These workers contribute to the generation of GDP, but are not included in the resident population used to calculate GDP per head. Ireland had the second highest GDP per head, and showed a substantial improvement of its position in the ranking during the past decade, having been in 10th position in 1997. However, Luxembourg and Ireland also showed the biggest drops in GDP per head relative to the EU-27 average between 2007 and 2008, of 14 and 10 percentage points.

In 2008 all of the EU-15 countries, who were members before 2004, had GDP per head higher than the 12 member states that joined in 2004 and 2007, with the exception of Portugal. However, the data show an overall decrease between 2007 and 2008. GDP per head in many of the EU-15 countries fell relative to the EU-27 average between 2007 and 2008, whereas in some of the more recent members such as Poland and Bulgaria, the gap between them and the EU-27 average narrowed. This is probably a result of the global financial crisis, as the financial sector has a major role in the economies of the richest countries. It also follows a general trend, as the gap

Table 5.2

Gross domestic product[1] per head: EU comparison

Index EU-27=100

	1997	2001	2007	2008
Luxembourg	215	234	267	253
Ireland	115	133	150	140
Netherlands	127	134	131	135
Austria	131	125	124	123
Sweden	123	121	122	121
Denmark	133	128	120	118
United Kingdom	118	120	119	118
Germany	124	117	115	116
Belgium	126	124	118	115
Finland	111	116	116	115
France	115	116	109	107
Spain	93	98	105	104
Italy	119	118	102	101
Greece	85	87	95	95
Cyprus	86	91	91	95
Slovenia	78	80	89	90
Czech Republic	73	70	80	80
Malta	81	78	78	76
Portugal	76	77	76	75
Slovakia	51	52	67	72
Estonia	42	46	68	67
Hungary	52	59	63	63
Lithuania	38	42	60	61
Poland	47	48	54	58
Latvia	35	39	58	56
Romania	..	28	42	46
Bulgaria	26	29	37	40

1 Gross domestic product per inhabitant at current market prices compiled on the basis of the European System of Accounts 1995, expressed in purchasing power standards, an artificial currency unit that eliminates price level differences between countries. See Appendix, Part 5: Purchasing power parities.

Source: Eurostat

between the average for the 12 new member states and the average for the EU-27 has narrowed since 1997. UK GDP per head was 18 percentage points above the EU-27 average in 2008, little change compared with 2007.

Analysing real household disposable income per head shows how people's income has been changing on average. However, income is not evenly distributed across the population and people at different points in the income distribution can experience different levels of income growth. Figure 5.3 shows

Figure 5.3

Distribution of real[1] household disposable income[2]

United Kingdom/Great Britain[3]

£ per week at 2007/08 prices

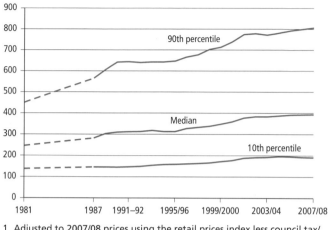

1 Adjusted to 2007/08 prices using the retail prices index less council tax/domestic rates.
2 Equivalised household disposable income before deduction of housing costs, using OECD equivalisation scale. See Appendix, Part 5: Households Below Average Income (HBAI), and Equivalisation scales for variations in source and definition on which the time series is based.
3 Data for 1994/95 to 2001/02 are for Great Britain only.

Source: Households Below Average Income, Department for Work and Pensions

Analysing income distribution

Equivalisation – in analysing the distribution of income, household disposable income is usually adjusted to take account of the size and composition of the household. This recognises that, for example, to achieve the same standard of living a household of five requires a higher income than a single person. This process is known as equivalisation (see Appendix, Part 5: Equivalisation scales).

Quintile and deciles groups – the main method of analysing income distribution used in this chapter is to rank units (households, individuals or adults) by a given income measure, and then to divide the ranked units into groups of equal size. Groups containing 20 per cent of units are referred to as 'quintile groups' or 'fifth'. Thus the 'bottom quintile group' of income is the 20 per cent of units with the lowest incomes. Similarly, groups containing 10 per cent of units are referred to as 'decile groups' or 'tenths'.

Percentiles – an alternative method is to present the income level above or below which a certain proportion of income units fall. Thus the 90th percentile is the income level above which 10 per cent of units fall when ranked by a given income measure. This is also known as the top decile point. The median is the midpoint of the distribution above and below which fifty per cent of units fall.

how incomes have changed at the 90th and 10th percentiles of the distribution, and at the median, since 1981 (see the Analysing income distribution text box for an explanation of these terms). During the 1980s there was little change in income in real terms (that is adjusted to remove the effects of inflation) at the bottom of the distribution, while income at the top of the distribution grew strongly. The early 1990s was a period of economic downturn, and there was little real growth in income anywhere in the distribution. Between 1995/96 and 2007/08, income at all three points of the distribution shown in Figure 5.3 grew by similar amounts in real terms, with median income increasing by a quarter. Thus the income distribution and the extent of inequality have changed considerably over the last three decades. The closer the percentiles are to the median line, the smaller the inequality within the distribution. Inequality grew during the 1980s, was stable during the first half of the 1990s, and then fluctuated slightly between 1994/95 and 2007/08.

The terms wealthy and high income are often used interchangeably, however they relate to quite distinct concepts. Income represents a flow of resources over a specified period of time received either in cash or in kind, for example, earnings or state benefits. Wealth on the other hand describes the ownership of assets valued at a particular point in time. People's ownership of wealth contributes to their economic well-being as it is a source of financial security. Wealth may help maintain a stable standard of living when income is falling in real terms, for example during a period of economic recession. Wealth can also provide a current income flow, for example, interest on savings.

The UK National Accounts (see Appendix, Part 5: Net wealth of the household sector) indicate that the wealth owned by the household sector (net of liabilities) totalled £6,575 billion in 2008, or an average of £107,000 per head. Household net wealth per head in the UK grew more than 60 per cent in real terms between 1987 and 2008 but there has not been steady growth over the period (Figure 5.4). Two of the main components of household net wealth are residential housing (less the value of the loans outstanding on their purchase) and stocks and shares. Therefore trends in wealth reflect both the state of the housing market (see Chapter 10: Housing) and that of the stock market. The impact of economic recession in 2008 on both the housing sector and on financial markets helps to explain why there was a substantial fall between 2007 and 2008 of 15 per cent in real terms in household net wealth per head. This is the first annual fall in household net wealth per head since 2001.

As with income, it is not only the overall level of wealth that is of interest but how it is distributed between individuals. Over

Figure 5.4

Real household net wealth per head[1]

United Kingdom
Index numbers (1987=100)

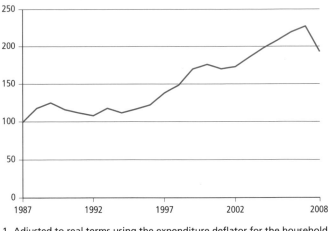

1 Adjusted to real terms using the expenditure deflator for the household sector. See Appendix, Part 5: Household income data sources.

Source: Office for National Statistics

the 20th century the distribution of wealth in the UK became more equal. In 1911, it is estimated that the wealthiest 1 per cent of the population held around 70 per cent of the total UK wealth. After World War Two this proportion had fallen to 42 per cent in 1960. Using a different methodology and data source, during the 1970s and the 1980s the share of the wealthiest 1 per cent of the population is estimated to have fallen from 22 per cent in the late 1970s to reach 17 to 18 per cent during the second half of the 1980s. Since the beginning of the 1990s the distribution appears to have widened again. HM Revenue and Customs estimates indicate that in 2002 the wealthiest 1 per cent of the population owned 23 per cent of total marketable wealth.

The figures on wealth presented above were derived from tax records produced by HM Revenue and Customs. The Wealth and Assets Survey (WAS), on the other hand, provides household data on the distribution of wealth within the British population. It shows that during 2006/08 wealth within the British population was more unevenly distributed than income (Table 5.5). Total wealth has been used to rank households into decile groups, and provide a breakdown of each of the four components of wealth. In 2006/08, the tenth decile group owned 44 per cent (£3,955 billion) of the total household wealth within the British population (£8,958 billion). In the ninth and tenth deciles, net property wealth accounted for 39 and 32 per cent of total wealth respectively, while private pension wealth contributed 40 per cent in the ninth decile and 48 per cent in the tenth decile. The first seven deciles together owned about a quarter (£2,233 billion) of household total

Table 5.5

Breakdown of aggregate wealth: by wealth decile[1] group, 2006/08[2]

Great Britain   £ million

	Property wealth (net)	Financial wealth (net)	Physical wealth	Pension wealth	Total wealth
1st	-7,700	-12,100	15,500	3,900	-500
2nd	1,100	-1,600	37,200	6,600	43,300
3rd	20,600	3,200	65,100	28,500	117,500
4th	108,400	13,500	70,000	61,700	253,600
5th	218,400	24,500	82,500	88,300	413,800
6th	316,900	39,300	94,200	141,700	592,100
7th	403,400	73,900	106,400	229,300	813,100
8th	489,900	116,500	123,000	391,900	1,121,300
9th	642,400	193,400	149,600	663,400	1,648,700
10th	1,283,800	544,700	222,900	1,903,600	3,954,900

1 Total wealth has been used to rank households into decile groups, from the least wealthy households in the 1st decile group to the wealthiest in the 10th decile group.
2 The survey period covers July 2006 to June 2008.

Source: Wealth and Assets Survey, Office for National Statistics

wealth. The value of wealth for the lowest decile group was negative (£500 million below zero), due to negative values for the property and financial wealth among these households. They did, however, have some physical wealth and a small amount of private pension wealth.

Different people have different needs, and their level of income and wealth is far from a complete measure of their well-being. People's satisfaction with their financial situation will depend on their material needs and expectations, and on their perceptions relative to the economic condition of the world around them. The recent economic crisis not only affected household finances in a tangible way, but also influenced the way people evaluate the economic situation of their family and country.

During Spring 2009, when asked to judge the current economic situation in the world and in the UK, people in England generally expressed negative evaluations; 78 per cent of respondents judged the economic situation in both the world and in the UK as either 'bad' or 'very bad', compared with 4 and 6 per cent who, respectively, judged these as either 'good' or 'very good' (Table 5.6). People aged 16 to 21

Table 5.6

Perceptions of the current economic situation:[1] by age, 2009[2]

England   Percentages

	16–21	22–29	30–39	40–49	50–59	60 and over	All individuals
The economic situation in the world							
Good[3]	9	4	3	5	2	1	4
Neither good or bad	26	19	17	13	14	12	16
Bad[4]	62	75	79	83	82	83	78
Don't know	3	2	1	1	2	4	2
The economic situation in the UK							
Good[3]	8	6	5	6	4	3	6
Neither good or bad	27	19	13	13	11	10	15
Bad[4]	62	73	81	81	84	84	78
Don't know	3	1	1	0	2	3	2
The financial situation in your household							
Good[3]	39	31	36	42	41	46	39
Neither good or bad	42	46	45	40	45	43	44
Bad[4]	16	23	19	17	13	9	16
Don't know	3	1	0	1	1	1	1

1 Respondents aged 16 and over were asked 'How would you judge the current situation in each of the following?' regarding the aspects shown.
2 Data are at February to March.
3 Those who responded either 'good' or 'very good'.
4 Those who responded either 'bad' or 'very bad'.

Source: Omnibus Survey, Department for Environment, Food and Rural Affairs

appeared slightly less negative, with 62 per cent considering the world and UK situations as 'bad' or 'very bad'. Respondents in this age group were more positive regarding the financial situation of their own household, with 39 per cent considering it to be either 'good' or 'very good', and 42 per cent considering it to be 'neither good nor bad', while 16 per cent expressed a negative view. People aged over 45 were more optimistic than younger respondents regarding the financial situation of their own household. Respondents also expressed negative views when asked about future changes in the UK economy. Almost half (47 per cent) stated that it would probably 'get worse' during the next 12 months, a third (32 per cent) said that it will 'stay the same' while a sixth (16 per cent) expected improvements.

Composition of income

Alongside strong growth in household disposable income per head, there has been considerable stability in income composition since 1987 (the earliest year for which comparable data are available). In 2008, 51 per cent of total household income in the UK was derived from wages and salaries, compared with 52 per cent in 1987, and social security benefits were the second largest source of income, at 19 per cent of the total, the same proportion as in 1987 (Figure 5.7). Income from investments fell from 15 to 13 per cent over the period and self-employment income, including income from rentals, rose from 11 to 12 per cent of the total.

Figure 5.7

Composition of total household income, 2008

United Kingdom

Percentages

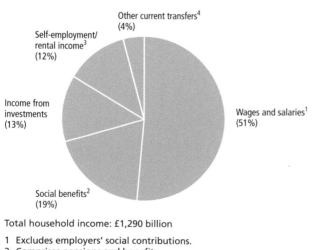

- Other current transfers[4] (4%)
- Self-employment/ rental income[3] (12%)
- Income from investments (13%)
- Social benefits[2] (19%)
- Wages and salaries[1] (51%)

Total household income: £1,290 billion

1 Excludes employers' social contributions.
2 Comprises pensions and benefits.
3 Includes self-employment income for sole-traders.
4 Mostly other government grants, but includes transfers from abroad and non-profit making bodies.

Source: Office for National Statistics

The data in Figures 5.1, 5.4 and 5.7 are derived from the UK National Accounts, whereas Figure 5.3 and the tables and charts in most of the remainder of this chapter are derived from surveys of households or surveys of businesses. There are a number of definitional differences between these two types of data source which are explained in the Appendix, Part 5: Household income data sources.

Data from the Family Resources Survey show that wages and salaries were the main sources of income for the majority of the working-age population in the UK during 2007/08. However, there were differences in the composition of income between households of different types, for example according to their region, their composition, their ethnic group and the age of the household reference person.

In addition, income composition varies according to where a household is situated in the income distribution (Table 5.8). In 2007/08, 53 per cent of the total income of UK households in the lowest fifth of the income distribution was derived from state support, while 38 per cent was from earnings. As income rises, earnings and investment income become more important and state support become less important. Earnings constituted 73 per cent of the total income for households in the central part of the distribution, while state support represented 17 per cent of their income. Households in the top fifth of the distribution derived 85 per cent of their total income from earnings, and 8 per cent from investment income. Only 2 per cent of their total income was derived from state support.

Several factors help to explain why households with different levels of income derive their income from different sources. One of the reasons is simply that certain state benefits are designed to be paid only to households with low incomes. Thus, at the bottom of the distribution there is a higher than average concentration of retired and lone parent households, for whom pensions and state support are more important than for households at the top of the distribution.

The composition of household income also varies according to the household reference person's age (see Appendix, Part 5: Household reference person). Wages and salaries were the main source of income in 2007/08 for households where the reference person was of working age and formed over three-quarters of the total weekly income of households in the UK whose reference person was aged between 25 and 54 (Table 5.9). State retirement pension and other forms of pension were more important for households with a reference person aged over 65. They were the main source of income for households where the reference person was aged 65 to 74, representing 36 per cent and 30 per cent of their total weekly income respectively. Together these two sources of income

Table 5.8

Sources of gross income:[1] by income grouping of household, 2007/08

United Kingdom   £ per year[2]

	Bottom fifth	Next fifth	Middle fifth	Next fifth	Top fifth	All households
Earnings	4,600	10,850	19,350	30,350	68,200	26,650
State support	6,500	6,550	4,450	2,850	1,700	4,400
Investment income	400	450	650	1,000	6,600	1,800
Income from occupational pensions	400	950	1,500	2,050	3,150	1,600
Miscellaneous income	350	500	600	600	850	600
Total income	12,250	19,350	26,600	36,800	80,500	35,100

1 Equivalised household disposable income before deduction of housing costs, using OECD equivalisation scale. See Appendix, Part 5: Households Below Average Income (HBAI), and Equivalisation scales for variations in source and definition on which the time series is based.
2 All amounts have been rounded to the nearest £50.

Source: Households Below Average Income, Department for Work and Pensions

constituted more than 70 per cent of the total income of households with a reference person aged 75 and over. Income derived from self-employment represented, on average, 8 per cent of income for all households, and was more important for those where the reference person was aged 35 to 59 (at least 10 per cent). In 2007/08, wages and salaries formed 64 per cent of the total income for households with a reference person aged 16 to 24, 18 percentage points less than for households aged 25 to 34, and 14 percentage points less than for those aged 35 to 44. Fifteen per cent of the youngest households' total income came from other sources, for

example student loans and odd jobs, and 11 per cent from social security benefits.

Earnings

Figure 5.7 showed that in the UK income from employment in the form of wages and salaries is the most important component of income overall. Earnings for full-time employees in the UK in the top decile group of the income distribution grew by 2.1 per cent between April 2008 and April 2009, the lowest annual rate of increase over the period 1998 to 2009

Table 5.9

Sources of total weekly household income: by age of household reference person,[1] 2007/08

United Kingdom   Percentages

	Wages and salaries	Self-employed income	Investments	Tax credits	State retirement pension[2]	Other pensions	Social security disability benefits	Other social security benefits	Other sources
16–24	64	6	-	4	-	-	1	11	15
25–34	82	7	1	3	-	-	1	5	2
35–44	78	10	1	3	-	-	1	5	2
45–54	76	11	2	1	-	2	2	3	2
55–59	68	10	4	-	1	8	3	3	2
60–64	48	8	5	-	9	19	4	4	3
65–74	13	5	6	-	36	30	4	5	2
75–84	5	1	7	-	43	31	5	7	2
85 and over	2	-	7	-	44	28	7	9	1
All households	65	8	3	2	6	7	2	5	2

1 See Appendix, Part 5: Household reference person.
2 May include income support or pension credit.

Source: Family Resources Survey, Department for Work and Pensions

Figure 5.10

Earnings growth in top and bottom decile groups for full-time employees[1] and the retail prices index[2]

United Kingdom

Percentage change over 12 months[3]

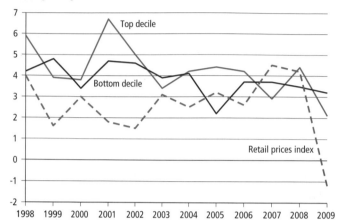

1 Full-time employees on adult rates whose pay for the survey period was unaffected by absence.
2 See Appendix, Part 5: Retail prices index.
3 Data are at April each year.

Source: Annual Survey of Hours and Earnings, Office for National Statistics

(Figure 5.10). Conversely, growth of the bottom decile group remained higher than 3.0 per cent and has been fairly steady since 2006. In the year to April 2009, gross weekly earnings of full-time employees at the bottom of the distribution grew

Annual Survey of Hours and Earnings

The source of much of the data in this section is the Annual Survey of Hours and Earnings (ASHE), which replaced the New Earnings Survey (NES) in 2004 (see Appendix, Part 5: Earnings surveys for a summary of the differences between the two). In Figures 5.10 and 5.11, a series has been used that applies ASHE methodology to NES data for 1997 to 2004. ASHE includes supplementary information that was not available in the NES (for example, on employees in businesses outside the PAYE system), and data for 2004 are presented both with and without this supplementary information. Data for 2005 onwards include the supplementary information and so care should be taken in comparing these with estimates for 2003 and earlier. From 2006 onwards, the Office for National Statistics (ONS) has also introduced a small number of methodological changes. These include changes to the sample design as well as the introduction of an automatic occupation coding tool. Again, care should be taken when comparing these estimates with those for 2005 and earlier, as the changes introduce a small discontinuity.

faster than those in the top decile group (3.2 per cent compared with 2.1 per cent).

Between 1998, when the National Minimum Wage (NMW) was introduced, and 2009, the earnings for the top decile group increased on average by 4.2 per cent per year against an average annual increase of 3.8 per cent for those in the bottom decile. The relationship between earnings growth and price inflation, measured by the retail prices index (RPI, see Appendix, Part 5: Retail prices index) is also important. If earnings rise slower than prices, this means that employees' pay is increasing more slowly than the prices they have to pay for goods and services. In most years since 1997, gross weekly earnings of full-time employees at both the top and bottom end of the distribution grew at a greater annual rate than the RPI; in April 2009 the RPI showed negative year-on-year growth (-1.2 per cent).

Government legislation may also have an effect on wages. The *Equal Pay Act 1970* and subsequent revisions, together with the *Sex Discrimination Act 1975*, established the principle of equal pay for work which can be established to be of equal value to that done by a member of the opposite sex, employed by the same employer, under common terms and conditions of employments. The impact of this legislation, together with other factors such as the opening of more highly paid work to women, has been to narrow the difference between the earnings of male and female workers, although it has not yet been eliminated.

The gender pay gap, defined as the difference between men's and women's median earnings as a percentage of men's median earnings, fell from 17.4 per cent in the UK in April 1998 to 12.2 per cent in April 2009 for full-time employees (Figure 5.11). For part-time employees, the gap fell from –4.0 to –2.0 and for all employees the gender pay gap decreased from 27.3 to 22.0 per cent over the same period. Between 2007 and 2009, using revised Annual Survey of Hours and Earnings (ASHE) Methodology (see Appendix, Part 5: Earnings surveys), the gender pay gap decreased by 0.3 percentage points for full-time employees, although there were reported small percentage increases for part-time and all employees (0.2 and 0.1 percentage points respectively).

The gender pay gap varies for workers of different ages. Data from ASHE show that in April 2007, median hourly earnings (excluding overtime) for men and women working full-time were similar when entering the job market at 18 to 21 years old, but a gender pay gap appeared after approximately 10 years, for those aged from 30 to 39. The gender pay gap increased for the 40 to 49 age group reaching 18.4 per cent of median men's earnings, and remained relatively high for those aged 50 to 59 (16.9 per cent).

Figure 5.11

Pay gap between men's and women's median hourly earnings[1]

United Kingdom

Percentages

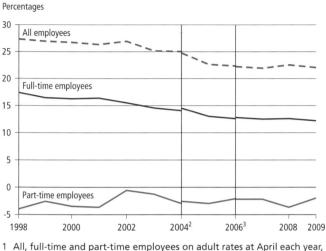

1 All, full-time and part-time employees on adult rates at April each year, whose pay for the survey period was unaffected by absence. Excludes overtime.
2 Higher percentage includes supplementary information. See Appendix, Part 5: Earnings surveys.
3 Discontinuity in 2006 as a result of further methodological changes.

Source: Annual Survey of Hours and Earnings, Office for National Statistics

Taxes

Taxes are the main means by which governments raise revenue. Over the centuries tax liabilities were typically based on a variety of measures of the value of property.

Today the major taxes paid by individuals are income tax, social contributions and taxes on expenditure. Under the UK income tax system, every individual is entitled to a personal allowance and those with an annual income below this do not pay any income tax. For 2009/10 the personal allowance was set at £6,475 per year for those aged under 65, with different allowances (i.e. £9,490) for those aged 65 and over. The income tax regime on earnings for 2009/10 includes two different rates of tax. Taxable income up to £37,400 (after the deduction of allowances and any other tax relief to which the individual may be entitled) is charged at 20 per cent. Taxable income higher than £37,400 is charged at 40 per cent. HM Revenue and Customs estimated that in 2009/10 there will have been around 29.3 million taxpayers in the UK, 1.7 million fewer than in 2008/09 (Table 5.12).

Social contributions, in the form of national insurance contributions, are another form of direct taxation, and for employees, payments are made both by the individual and their employer. In 2009/10, employees with earnings of less than £110 per week in the UK paid no contributions, and neither did their employers. Employees paid Class 1

Table 5.12

Income tax payable: by annual income,[1] 2009/10[2]

United Kingdom

	Number of taxpayers (thousands)	Total tax liability after tax reductions[3] (£ million)	Average rate of tax (percentages)	Average amount of tax (£)
£6,475–£7,499	990	92	1.3	93
£7,500–£9,999	2,650	1,030	4.4	387
£10,000–£14,999	6,290	6,090	7.8	967
£15,000–£19,999	5,060	9,900	11.3	1,960
£20,000–£29,999	6,680	22,200	13.6	3,320
£30,000–£49,999	5,270	30,700	15.5	5,820
£50,000–£99,999	1,800	26,500	22.4	14,700
£100,000–£149,999	304	10,500	28.6	34,500
£150,000–£199,999	117	6,190	30.8	52,800
£200,000–£499,999	134	12,700	33.0	94,900
£500,000–£999,999	26	6,060	34.5	234,000
£1,000,000 and over	11	8,680	36.0	781,000
All incomes	29,300	141,000	17.3	4,790

1 Total income of the individual for income tax purposes including earned and investment income. Figures relate to taxpayers only.
2 Based on 2006–07 Survey of Personal Income and projected in line with the April 2009 Budget.
3 In this context tax reductions refer to allowances given at a fixed rate, for example the married couple's allowance.

Source: HM Revenue and Customs

contributions equal to 11 per cent of their earnings between £110 and £844 per week, and an additional 1 per cent on earnings above £844 per week.

Different taxes affect households with different levels of income in different ways. Income tax and national insurance contributions are progressive, in that the amount of tax and contributions payable increases as income increases both in absolute terms and as a proportion of income. During 2007/08, households in the bottom quintile group of the income distribution paid 10.8 per cent of their gross incomes in direct taxes, around £1,200 on average per year, while the quintile group with the highest incomes paid 24.9 per cent of their gross income in direct taxes, equivalent to an average of £18,500 per year (Table 5.13 overleaf). Therefore, these taxes reduce inequality of income between households.

In addition to direct taxes, households pay indirect taxes through their expenditure. Indirect taxes include value added tax (VAT), customs duties and excise duties, and are included in the price of goods and services; these taxes are specific to

Table 5.13

Taxes as a percentage of gross income: by income grouping[1] of household, 2007/08

United Kingdom

Percentages

	Bottom fifth	Next fifth	Middle fifth	Next fifth	Top fifth	All households
Direct taxes						
Income tax[2]	3.2	6.9	10.7	13.5	18.4	13.7
Employees' national insurance contributions	1.5	3.1	4.6	5.5	4.7	4.5
Council tax and Northern Ireland rates[3]	6.1	4.0	3.4	2.8	1.8	2.8
All direct taxes	10.8	14.1	18.6	21.8	24.9	21.0
Indirect taxes						
Value added tax	10.8	7.2	6.5	5.8	4.5	5.8
Duty on alcohol	1.5	1.0	0.9	0.8	0.6	0.8
Duty on tobacco	2.6	1.8	1.2	0.7	0.3	0.8
Duty on hydrocarbon oils and vehicle excise duty	3.2	2.3	2.2	1.9	1.2	1.8
Other indirect taxes	9.9	6.3	5.3	4.4	3.5	4.7
All indirect taxes	27.9	18.6	15.9	13.7	10.0	13.9
All taxes	38.7	32.7	34.6	35.4	34.9	35.0

1 Equivalised household disposable income before deduction of housing costs has been used to rank the households into quintile groups. See Appendix, Part 5: Equivalisation scales.
2 After deducting tax credits and tax relief at source on life assurance premiums.
3 After deducting discounts, council tax benefits and rates rebates.

Source: Office for National Statistics

particular commodities. Indirect taxes are regressive, since their payment forms a higher proportion of income for households with lower incomes. Households in the bottom quintile group of the income distribution paid 27.9 per cent of their gross income in indirect taxes, compared with 10.0 per cent of gross income paid by households in the top quintile group. If expressed as a percentage of total expenditure rather than of income, households in the top quintile group of the distribution still paid a lower proportion in indirect taxes than those at the bottom (16 per cent compared with 20 per cent). However, in cash terms the top quintile group paid more than double the amount of indirect taxes when compared with low income households, as a result of the higher levels of expenditure of those households with higher incomes.

Income distribution

Various components of income differ in importance for different types of households and levels of earnings vary between individuals. The result is an uneven distribution of total income between households. However, this inequality is reduced to some extent by the deduction of taxes and social contributions, and their subsequent redistribution to the households in the form of benefits from the Government. For this reason, the analysis of the income distribution is usually based on household disposable income.

Figure 5.14 is based on the Households Below Average Income (HBAI) analysis, summarising the income distribution in 2007/08 and showing considerable inequality. Each bar represents the number of people in the UK (both adults and children) who were living in households with equivalised weekly disposable income in a particular £10 band (see Analysing income distribution text box for definition of equivalisation). There is a greater concentration of people at the lower levels of weekly income, with nearly two-thirds of individuals living in households with incomes below the mean. The tail at the upper end of the distribution is even longer than shown: there were an estimated 3.3 million individuals living in households with disposable income above £1,000 per week. The highest bar in Figure 5.14 represents 1.4 million people with an income between £300 and £310 per week. The substantial number of individuals living in households with relatively high incomes skews the distribution and produces a large difference between the overall mean income of £487 per week and the median of £393 per week.

Figure 5.14

Distribution of weekly household disposable income,[1] 2007/08

United Kingdom
Millions of individuals

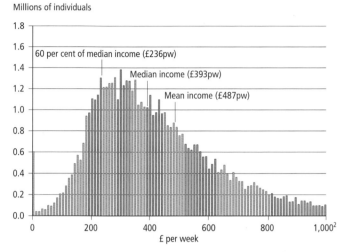

1 Equivalised household disposable income before deduction of housing costs (in £10 bands), using OECD equivalisation scale. The £10 bands are grouped into decile groups in alternating colours. See Appendix, Part 5: Households Below Average Income (HBAI), and Equivalisation scales.
2 There were also an additional 3.3 million individuals with income above £1,000 per week.

Source: Households Below Average Income, Department for Work and Pensions

The extent of inequality within the income distribution is commonly measured by the Gini coefficient. This indicator is expressed as a percentage, taking values between 0 and 100, with higher values denoting higher levels of inequality. A value of 0 indicates complete equality in the distribution of income (all people in the population receiving exactly the same income), while a value of 100 indicates complete inequality (one person in the population receives all the income, others receiving none). For further details see Appendix, Part 5: Gini coefficient.

Data from Eurostat show that during 2007 the level of inequality, as measured by the Gini coefficient, varied substantially among the European Union (EU-27) member states, with an average value of 31 (Figure 5.15). The lowest levels of inequality were recorded in Slovakia, Slovenia and Sweden, all with a Gini coefficient lower than 25. The countries where the inequality of income was highest were Romania (38), Portugal (37), Latvia (35) and Bulgaria (35). The Gini coefficient for the UK was 33, a slight increase from 2006 when it was 32.

The Organisation for Economic Co-operation and Development (OECD) estimates that over the two decades from the mid-1980s to the mid-2000s, income inequality as measured by the Gini coefficient increased in more than two-thirds of those 24 OECD countries for which information is available. The average growth was about 0.02 percentage points, most of it experienced in the first decade. The increases were greatest in

Figure 5.15

Income inequality:[1] EU comparison, 2007

Percentages

1 As measured by the Gini coefficient, which can take values between 0 and 100, with 0 representing complete equality and 100 representing complete inequality. See Appendix, Part 5: Gini coefficient.

Source: EU Survey of Income and Living Standards, Eurostat

Finland, Norway, Sweden, Germany, Italy, New Zealand and the United States, while decreases in inequality were registered in France, Greece, Ireland, Spain and Turkey.

In the UK, income inequality increased substantially during the last four decades, with the Gini coefficient for disposable income growing from 27 per cent in 1977 to 34 per cent in 2007/08 (Figure 5.16 overleaf). However, this trend has not been continuous. During periods of economic growth, such as the late 1980s and the late 1990s, the level of inequality rose rapidly, corresponding with the increase in income from employment. Conversely, during periods of recession (the early 1980s and the early 1990s) the Gini coefficient either grew more slowly or fell. This is due to households at the top of the income distribution tending to benefit more from growth in employment income, while households at the bottom of the distribution rely more on state benefits and pensions, which tend to remain more stable whatever the

Figure 5.16

Inequality[1] of disposable income for all households

United Kingdom
Percentages

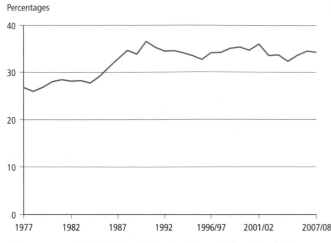

1 As measured by the Gini coefficient, which can take values between 0 and 100, with 0 representing complete equality and 100 representing complete inequality. See Appendix, Part 5: Gini coefficient.

Source: Office for National Statistics

prevailing economic conditions. In the UK, since 2001/02, the Gini coefficient decreased by 1.8 percentage points, from 36.0 per cent to 34.2 per cent. The level of inequality in the UK during 2007/08 was much lower among retired households (Gini coefficient for disposable income equal to 27) than among non-retired households (Gini coefficient for disposable income equal to 34).

Research conducted by the Institute for Fiscal Studies (IFS) into how inequality evolved during previous UK recessions concluded that there is no unique pattern of trends in inequality during a downturn. The research noted that a reduction in inequality might be expected as a result of the economic recession of 2008, involving large-scale job losses and reduced bonuses in the high-earning financial sector. However, low-earning workers seem to be the most affected by growing unemployment, which would tend to reduce incomes towards the bottom of the distribution and thus increase inequality.

A wide variety of factors influence the position of households within the income distribution in the UK and the economic activity of the household members is one of the most important. During 2007/08, single people and people living in couple households where both were in full-time employment had a higher likelihood (38 per cent) of being in the top quintile group of the income distribution compared with other households, and only 3 per cent of them were in the bottom quintile group (Table 5.17). People living in households where

Table 5.17

Distribution of household disposable income:[1] by economic activity status of household, 2007/08

United Kingdom   Percentages

	Bottom fifth	Next fifth	Middle fifth	Next fifth	Top fifth	All (=100%) (millions)
One or more full-time self employed	21	15	17	19	28	5.8
Single/couple all in full-time work	3	8	20	31	38	15.1
Couple, one full-time, one part-time work	4	16	28	29	23	8.4
Couple, one full-time work, one not working	17	29	21	17	16	7.1
No full-time, one or more in part-time work	28	27	20	14	11	5.7
Workless, one or more aged 60 and over	29	29	21	13	7	10.2
Workless, one or more unemployed	70	17	8	3	2	1.6
Workless, other inactive	51	27	12	6	4	6.0

1 Equivalised household disposable income before deduction of housing costs has been used to rank the individuals into quintile groups. See Appendix, Part 5: Households Below Average Income (HBAI), and Equivalisation scales.

Source: Households Below Average Income, Department for Work and Pensions

one or more person was self-employed were also more likely than other individuals to be in the top quintile group of the distribution. People living in households with only one member working full time and the other one either being employed part time or not working, were more concentrated in the middle part of the distribution. At the bottom of the distribution there was a higher concentration of people living in households with members working only part time or that were workless and composed of retired, inactive or unemployed people. People living in workless households, where one or more people were unemployed, were most likely to be found in the bottom quintile group (70 per cent).

Ethnicity also affects an individual's position in the income distribution. Averaged over the three years 2005/06 to 2007/08, households whose reference person (see Appendix, Part 5: Household reference person) belonged to the White ethnic group were fairly evenly spread within the distribution of disposable income. On the other hand, people in households from many other ethnic groups were much more concentrated

5

in the bottom part of the distribution. This was particularly the case for households with a reference person from the Pakistani/Bangladeshi groups, of whom 55 per cent were in the bottom quintile of the income distribution, and for those from the African/Other Black group, of whom 30 per cent were in the bottom quintile group.

Low income

The incidence of low income, the factors contributing to low income and ways to reduce their effects have been an enduring focus of attention of governments since the first poor laws were introduced in the 16th century up to the present day. Having a low income has often been associated with being disadvantaged and thus excluded from many of the opportunities available to the average citizen.

To measure poverty, the approach generally used in more developed countries is to fix a low income threshold in terms of a fraction of the median income of the population. The proportion of people living in households with incomes below various fractions of current median income are then referred to as those with relative low income. The low income threshold generally adopted in the UK, and used in the remainder of this section, is 60 per cent of current equivalised median household disposable income before the deduction of housing costs

(see Appendix, Part 5: Equivalisation scales). In 2007/08 this represented a household income of £236 per week. The proportion of people living in low income households in the UK during 2007/08 was 18 per cent, similar to the proportion recorded in 1987.

The proportion of people living in low income households in the UK has fluctuated during the past 20 years. During the late 1980s and the early 1990s the proportion of people living in low income households rose, peaking at 22 per cent of the population in 1990–91 and 1991–92 (Figure 5.18). The trend was then generally downwards during the 1990s and early 2000s, to reach 17 per cent in 2004/05, though the proportion of low income household rose again, up to 18 per cent, during the three years to 2007/08. This pattern is also reflected in the proportion of people with income less than 50 per cent of the median.

Different groups within the population have different probabilities of living in a low income household, and there were variations in these probabilities during the past 20 years. People of working age were less likely to live in a low income household than either pensioners or children throughout the period, and this probability varied little between 1990–91 and 2007/08 (Figure 5.19). The likelihood of living in a low income household fell substantially for pensioners, from 37 per cent in 1990–91 to 23 per cent in 2007/08, but most of this change occurred between 1990–91 and 1993/94.

Figure 5.18

Proportion of people whose income is below various percentages of median household disposable income[1]

United Kingdom/Great Britain[2]

Percentages

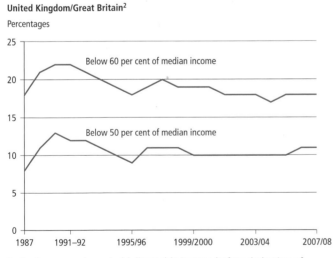

1 Contemporary household disposable income before deduction of housing costs, using OECD equivalisation scale. See Appendix, Part 5: Households Below Average Income (HBAI), and Equivalisation scales, for variations in source and definition on which the time series is based.
2 Data for 1994/95 to 2001/02 are for Great Britain only.

Source: Households Below Average Income, Department for Work and Pensions

Figure 5.19

Individuals living in households below 60 per cent of median household disposable income[1]

United Kingdom/Great Britain[2]

Percentages

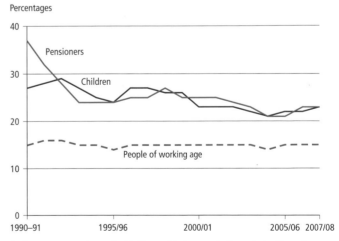

1 Contemporary household disposable income before deduction of housing costs, using OECD equivalisation scale. See Appendix, Part 5: Households Below Average Income (HBAI), and Equivalisation scales for variations in source and definition on which the time series is based.
2 Data for 1994/95 to 2001/02 are for Great Britain only.

Source: Households Below Average Income, Department for Work and Pensions

The proportion of children living in low income households also fell over this period, from 27 per cent in 1990–91 to 21 per cent in 2004/05. However, this proportion has since risen slightly to reach 23 per cent in 2007/08. The Government has a target of halving the number of children in poverty in the UK between 1998/99 and 2010/11. Research by the IFS indicates that having fallen by an average of 60,000 children per year between 1998/99 and 2007/08, the number of children living in low income households would have to fall by an average of 400,000 a year between 2007/08 and 2010/11 in order for the target to be reached.

The likelihood of a child living in a low income household is also related to some of the household's characteristics. During 2007/08, children living either in lone parent families, in workless families, in families with three or more children, or in families with a head of household belonging to an ethnic minority group, had a greater than average risk of living in a low income household.

Although low income is clearly a central factor to poverty and social exclusion, it is now widely accepted that there is a broad range of other elements which are important to people's well-being. For example, the extent to which individuals or households have access to goods or activities considered to be necessary for an acceptable standard of living within a society provides a wider measure of people's living standards. The inability to afford some or all of the items identified is referred to as material deprivation.

Several studies show a close relationship between low income and material deprivation, with the experience of deprivation declining as income increases. In 2007 in Great Britain, 10 per cent of families in the highest 20 per cent of the income distribution stated they were unable to afford at least one out of seven selected deprivation items (Table 5.20). On the other hand, 67 per cent of the families in the bottom quintile group could not afford at least one of the items. In particular, more than half of the families in this group were unable to afford a one week holiday away from home (without staying with relatives).

Other factors, such as household composition and ethnicity, are related to material deprivation. In 2007, 38 per cent of lone parent households were able to afford all of the items listed, compared with 74 per cent of couple parents. Similarly, 38 per cent of households belonging to a Black ethnic group were able to afford all the items, compared with 52 per cent and 66 per cent of Asian and White households respectively.

Wealth

Wealth can be held in different forms. Financial wealth is composed of assets such as saving accounts, which may provide sources of current income, and those such as pension rights which may provide entitlement to a future income flow. Ownership of non-financial wealth, such as property, does not necessarily provide an income flow, but may provide financial security.

Aggregate data on the wealth of the household sector in the UK, compiled by the National Accounts (see Appendix, Part 5: Net wealth of the household sector), indicate that the total UK wealth, net of liabilities, was worth £6,575 billion in 2008, 56.2 per cent of it in the form of residential buildings (Table 5.21). The value of this form of wealth (after deducting the value of loans outstanding on the purchase of housing) grew strongly at an average of 5.2 per cent per year between 1991 and 2006, reflecting the boom in the housing market over the period. However, between 2006 and 2007, the value of residential buildings less loans secured on dwellings only grew by 1.3 per cent in real terms. In 2008 this sector was severely affected by the economic recession, resulting in a fall of 12.0 per cent in real terms compared with 2007.

The second most important element of household wealth is financial assets held in pension funds and life assurance, which

Table 5.20

Deprivation items a family cannot afford: by income grouping,[1] 2007

Great Britain   Percentages[2]

	Bottom fifth	Next fifth	Middle fifth	Next fifth	Top fifth
Two pairs of shoes for each adult	13	9	4	1	1
Car or van	27	13	5	1	0
Celebration with presents at special occasions	12	6	4	1	0
Toys/sports gear for each child	8	5	2	0	0
One week holiday (not staying with relatives)	56	46	26	15	7
Night out once a month	32	26	20	11	5
Friends/relatives for a meal once a month	18	11	6	3	1
None of these	33	44	64	79	90

1 Equivalised household disposable income before deduction of housing costs has been used to rank the households into quintile groups. See Appendix, Part 5: Equivalisation scales.
2 Percentages do not sum to 100 per cent as respondents could give more than one answer.

Source: Families and Children Study, Department for Work and Pensions

Table 5.21

Composition of the net wealth[1] of the household sector

United Kingdom   £ billion at 2008 prices[2]

	1991	2001	2005	2006	2007	2008
Non-financial assets						
Residential buildings	1,733	2,481	3,630	3,916	4,197	3,693
Other	509	576	774	823	869	768
Financial assets						
Life assurance and pension funds	911	1,795	2,061	2,195	2,232	1,844
Securities and shares	392	736	698	695	648	463
Currency and deposits	584	801	1,019	1,076	1,137	1,175
Other assets	122	149	153	181	171	180
Total assets	4,251	6,538	8,334	8,886	9,253	8,123
Financial liabilities						
Loans secured on dwellings	501	713	1,049	1,139	1,215	1,223
Other loans	113	164	219	228	227	218
Other liabilities	69	72	99	132	124	125
Total liabilities	683	950	1,367	1,499	1,566	1,566
Total net wealth	3,569	5,588	6,967	7,387	7,687	6,575

1 At end of each year. See Appendix, Part 5: Net wealth of the household sector.
2 Adjusted to 2008 prices using the expenditure deflator for the household sector. See Appendix, Part 5: Household income data sources.

Source: Office for National Statistics

amounted to £1,844 billion in 2008. This element of household wealth fell by 11 per cent in real terms between 2001 and 2002, reflecting the fall in stock market values over the period, but recovered back to the 2001 level by 2004 and grew until 2007. Between 2007 and 2008 it fell substantially in real terms, by 15 per cent.

The saving ratio is defined as the proportion of total resources that households do not spend on goods and services but put aside every year as savings. The household saving ratio in 2008 was 1.7 per cent of total resources, the lowest recorded since 1970 (Figure 5.22). This figure is also substantially lower than the average of 7.6 per cent recorded between 1970 and 2008. During the past 40 years the saving ratio has been affected by contractions in the economy. During the 1970s and early 1980s there was an upward trend in saving, peaking in 1980 at 12.3 per cent of household resources. During the mid and late 1980s the saving ratio began to decline, falling to 3.9 per cent in 1988. It then rose again until 1993, when it started to decline, falling to 3.9 per cent in 2005, and continuing this downward trend up to the end of 2008. Data for the first two quarters of 2009 indicated that the household saving ratio was rising again, reaching 4.8 per cent on average for the two quarters.

Therefore it seems that households have reacted to the economic recession of 2008 and 2009 by increasing the proportion of income they saved, a similar pattern to previous recessions.

Figure 5.22

Household saving ratio[1]

United Kingdom
Percentages

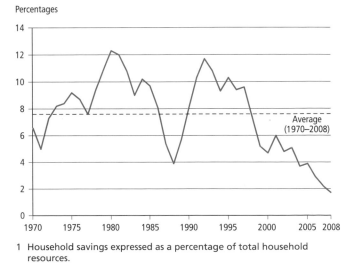

1 Household savings expressed as a percentage of total household resources.

Source: Office for National Statistics

People's perceptions and expectations towards their financial well-being affect their likelihood of saving. Between 2006 and 2008 in Great Britain, respondents to the Wealth and Assets Survey who had not been saving during the past 12 months, were more likely to save in the next 12 months if they expected improvements in their financial situation. Of those who expected their financial situation to improve, 37 per cent said they thought they would save in the next 12 months. Among those who expected their financial situation to remain the same, the proportion of respondents intending to save was 15 per cent, while those who expected their financial situation to get worse were much less likely to report this intention (9 per cent).

Chapter 6

Expenditure

- Between 1970 and 2008, the proportion of total household expenditure spent on services increased from around a third (35 per cent) to just over half (52 per cent) of total UK domestic household expenditure. (Table 6.2)

- Average weekly expenditure by households in Northern Ireland in 2008 was 8 per cent higher than the UK average of £471.00, while weekly expenditure in England was 1 per cent higher. In Wales and Scotland, household weekly expenditure was lower than the UK average, by 12 and 7 per cent respectively. (Table 6.4)

- In 2007/08, the average household expenditure by children aged 7 to 15 in the UK was £12.50 per week and the average expenditure per child was £7.60. (Page 81)

- Between 1987 and 2008, total household debt as a percentage of household disposable income rose from 103 pr cent to 169 per cent, slightly lower than the peak of 174 per cent in 2007. (Figure 6.11)

- The number of people declared bankrupt in England and Wales aged between 35 and 44 increased from 6,358 in 2000 to 20,366 in 2008. (Figure 6.15)

- Between 1971 and 2008 the price of a packet of 20 filter tipped cigarettes in the UK increased by approximately 20 times and the price of a pint of beer by 18 times. (Table 6.21)

DATA

Download data by clicking the online pdf

www.statistics.gov.uk/ socialtrends

Trends in household expenditure provide an insight into changes in society, reflecting changes in consumer preferences, the growth in choices available to consumers, and the impact of their increased purchasing power. The amount households spend on goods and services of various kinds also provides an insight into their living standards and material well-being. The region in which people live, their age, sex, ethnicity and income are some of the factors that affect levels and patterns of household spending.

Household and personal expenditure

Changes in the pattern of expenditure can be the result of changes in prices, or in the volume of goods or services purchased, or a combination of the two. Volume indices are useful for analysing time trends in consumption as they remove the effect of price changes, which can differ depending on the category of expenditure. They are calculated by adjusting the total value of expenditure within each category to account for the corresponding price changes over time. The volume of total

Figure 6.1

Volume of domestic household expenditure[1] on goods and services

United Kingdom

Index numbers (1970=100)

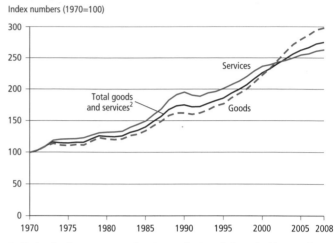

1 Chained volume measure. See Appendix, Part 6: Household expenditure.
2 Excludes expenditure by UK households abroad.

Source: Office for National Statistics

Table 6.2

Household expenditure: by purpose[1]

United Kingdom

Percentages

	1970	1981	1991	2001	2008
Food and non-alcoholic drinks	21	17	12	9	9
Alcoholic drinks and tobacco	8	6	4	4	3
Clothing and footwear	10	7	6	6	5
Housing[2], water and fuel	15	17	18	18	21
Household goods and services	7	7	6	6	5
Health	1	1	1	2	2
Transport	11	15	14	15	15
Communication[2]	1	2	2	2	2
Recreation and culture	9	9	10	11	11
Education	1	1	1	1	1
Restaurants and hotels[2]	10	10	12	11	11
Miscellaneous goods and services[3]	7	8	13	14	13
Total domestic household expenditure	100	100	100	99	98
of which goods	66	60	52	48	46
of which services	35	40	48	51	52
UK tourist expenditure abroad	1	2	3	4	4
less Foreign tourist expenditure	2	2	2	2	2
All household expenditure[4] (=100%) (£ billions)	31	148	365	648	891

1 Current prices. According to the Classification of Individual Consumption by Purpose (COICOP). See Appendix, Part 6: Household expenditure.
2 Housing excludes mortgage interest payments and council tax (domestic rates in Northern Ireland). Communication includes mobile phone equipment and services. Restaurants and hotels includes purchases of alcoholic drinks in pubs, restaurants and hotels.
3 Includes personal care, social protection, insurance and financial services.
4 Includes expenditure by UK households in the UK and abroad.

Source: Office for National Statistics

domestic spending on goods and services in the UK increased steadily between 1970 and 2008, with the exceptions of 1974, 1975, 1977, 1980, 1981 and 1991 (Figure 6.1). These years correspond closely to periods of economic recession in the UK. This period of general growth in expenditure corresponded to a period of growth in real household incomes (see Chapter 5: Income and wealth, Figure 5.1).

Between 1970 and 1991, the volume of consumption of services increased by 91 per cent while the consumption of goods increased more slowly, by 60 per cent. However, after 1991 the consumption of goods increased more quickly than that of services, by 84 per cent and 39 per cent respectively between 1992 and 2008.

There have been substantial changes over the last 40 years in the way in which households in the UK allocate expenditure

between different goods and services. Between 1970 and 2008, the proportion of total household expenditure spent on services increased from around a third (35 per cent) to just over half (52 per cent) of total domestic household expenditure (Table 6.2). From 1998, the proportion of total household expenditure spent on services exceeded that for goods and this trend continued through to 2008. There was also a substantial shift in the pattern of expenditure between 1970 and 2008 according to its purpose. In 1970, food and non-alcoholic drinks was the largest category of household expenditure, accounting for 21 per cent of the total, but by 2008 this had fallen to 9 per cent. This does not necessarily mean that the amount of food and non-alcoholic drinks purchased fell: it implies that expenditure on other goods and services has risen more rapidly.

In 2008 housing, water and fuel was the largest category of expenditure, accounting for 21 per cent of total domestic

Table 6.3

Volume of household expenditure: by purpose[1]

United Kingdom						Index numbers (1970=100)
						£ billions (current prices)
	1970	1981	1991	2001	2008	2000
Food and non-alcoholic drinks	100	105	117	137	149	79
Alcoholic drinks and tobacco	100	98	91	87	89	30
Clothing and footwear	100	122	190	350	520	46
Housing[2], water and fuel	100	118	141	154	163	185
Household goods and services	100	122	167	274	300	46
Health	100	126	185	191	233	14
Transport	100	142	200	273	325	135
Communication[2]	100	191	308	795	1,132	19
Recreation and culture	100	169	298	581	930	102
Education	100	162	202	258	231	13
Restaurants and hotels[2]	100	132	175	202	211	94
Miscellaneous goods and services[3]	100	126	251	351	408	116
Total domestic household expenditure	100	125	172	232	275	878
of which goods	100	120	160	233	298	413
of which services	100	132	191	239	263	465
UK tourist expenditure abroad	100	208	321	754	893	33
less Foreign tourist expenditure	100	153	189	225	269	20
All household expenditure[4]	100	125	174	240	284	891

1 Chained volume measure. According to the Classification of Individual Consumption by Purpose (COICOP). See Appendix, Part 6: Household expenditure.
2 Housing excludes mortgage interest payments and council tax (domestic rates in Northern Ireland). Communication includes mobile phone equipment and services. Restaurants and hotels includes purchases of alcoholic drinks in pubs, restaurants and hotels.
3 Includes personal care, social protection, insurance and financial services.
4 Includes expenditure by UK households in the UK and abroad.

Source: Office for National Statistics

household expenditure, compared with 15 per cent in 1970. Other categories showing an increase over the period were transport (from 11 per cent to 15 per cent), miscellaneous goods and services, which include personal care, social protection, insurance and financial services (from 7 per cent to 13 per cent), and recreation and culture (from 9 per cent to 11 per cent). The categories that showed large decreases in the proportion of total spending between 1970 and 2008, other than food and non-alcoholic drinks, were clothing and footwear (from 10 per cent to 5 per cent), and alcoholic drinks and tobacco (from 8 per cent to 3 per cent).

Table 6.3 illustrates the volume growth of each category of household expenditure. Over the period 1970 to 2008, the category with the strongest growth was communication, with more than an elevenfold increase in the volume of expenditure. The communication category includes mobile phone equipment and services, and Internet subscription charges. Recreation and culture showed the next largest growth in volume expenditure over the period with a ninefold increase. Within the recreation and culture category, goods that showed the greatest increases in the volume of spending were information processing equipment

(which includes personal computers and printers), audio visual equipment (which includes CD and DVD players) and photographic and optical equipment (which include cameras and camcorders). Alcoholic drinks and tobacco was the only category where volume of expenditure fell over the period. This category only includes alcoholic drinks purchased for consumption at home, while spending in pubs and bars is included in the restaurants and hotels category.

The volume of spending by UK tourists abroad in 2008 was around nine times that in 1970, while expenditure by foreign tourists in the UK increased much less, by over two-and-a-half times. However, the level of spending in 2008 for both of these categories was relatively small compared with spending on housing, water and fuel or on transport. In 2008, the largest category of expenditure (at 2008 prices) was spending on housing, water and fuel, at £184.5 billion, while expenditure on transport was the second largest category of household expenditure, at £135.3 billion.

Levels of household expenditure varied across the different countries of the UK in 2008. Households in Northern Ireland

Table 6.4

Household expenditure:[1] by country, 2008

United Kingdom

£ per week

	England	Wales	Scotland	Northern Ireland	United Kingdom
Food and non-alcoholic drink	50.60	54.40	47.90	57.30	50.70
Alcohol and tobacco	10.60	11.90	11.10	13.60	10.80
Clothing and footwear	21.60	17.70	19.70	35.80	21.60
Housing (net),[2] fuel and power	54.00	50.10	47.40	47.40	53.00
Household goods and services	30.40	25.90	29.70	30.60	30.10
Health	5.30	2.50	5.40	5.50	5.10
Transport	63.60	59.70	62.10	68.20	63.40
Communication[3]	12.20	9.70	10.70	14.40	12.00
Recreation and culture	59.80	62.00	61.20	59.90	60.10
Education	6.30	5.20	5.90	5.10	6.20
Restaurants and hotels[4]	38.70	28.50	32.50	44.40	37.70
Miscellaneous goods and services	36.20	28.90	32.10	43.50	35.60
Other expenditure items	87.60	57.20	74.30	80.80	84.70
All household expenditure	476.90	413.70	440.00	506.50	471.00

1 See Appendix, Part 6: Living Costs and Food Survey. Expenditure rounded to the nearest 10 pence.
2 Excludes mortgage interest payments, water charges and council tax (domestic rates in Northern Ireland). These are included in 'Other expenditure items'.
3 Includes mobile phone equipment and services.
4 Includes purchases of alcoholic drinks in pubs, restaurants and hotels.

Source: Living Costs and Food Survey, Office for National Statistics

spent on average £506.50 per week, 8 per cent more than the UK average of £471.00, while weekly expenditure in England (£476.90) was 1 per cent higher than the UK average (Table 6.4). Conversely, household weekly expenditure in Wales at £413.70 and in Scotland at £440.00 were both lower than the UK average, by 12 per cent and 7 per cent respectively.

Household expenditure patterns also varied between the different countries of the UK. These differences may arise because of differences in price levels between countries, or differences in the volume of consumption of the various categories, or a combination of the two factors. The categories of expenditure which varied most between different countries included clothing and footwear, transport, and restaurants and hotels. Households in Northern Ireland tended to spend more on these items compared with households in England, Scotland and Wales. There was a large variation in the other expenditure items category, two-thirds of which is made up of other housing-related costs, particularly mortgage interest payments and council tax. Households in England had the highest weekly expenditure on this category (£87.60) which was 53 per cent more than household expenditure in Wales (£57.20).

The patterns of household expenditure vary across ethnic groups in the UK. Over the four year period 2004/05 to 2007/08, total expenditure per head was highest among households where the household reference person (HRP) defined themselves as White (£503.20), and lower among households where the HRP was Asian, Black or Mixed (see the text box in Chapter 2: Households and families for an explanation of household reference person) (Table 6.5). Average spending per head was lowest in households where the HRP was Black or Black British, at £356.10 per week, this was around three-quarters (76 per cent) of the average for all households of £466.70 per week.

The pattern of expenditure also varied between ethnic groups. For example, households where the HRP was Asian or Asian British spent £29.60 on clothing and footwear, while households where the HRP was White spent £23.00 per week and households where the HRP was Black or Black British spent £18.30 per week. To some extent these differences result from differences in household income – see Chapter 5: Income and wealth. For example, households where the HRP was from an ethnic minority group spent lower proportions of their total

6

Table 6.5

Household expenditure[1] per head: by ethnic group,[2] 2004/05–2007/08[3]

United Kingdom   £ per week

	White	Mixed	Asian/Asian British	Black/Black British	Other	All households
Food and non-alcoholic drink	47.90	43.30	46.30	34.80	43.70	46.50
Alcohol and tobacco	12.00	7.30	4.20	5.00	7.20	11.10
Clothing and footwear	23.00	23.00	29.60	18.30	24.60	22.20
Housing (net),[4] fuel and power	63.70	54.70	56.10	60.00	80.40	44.90
Household goods and services	28.20	19.70	32.70	19.60	18.30	30.90
Health	5.70	3.00	3.70	2.80	3.10	5.40
Transport	62.40	50.90	57.70	41.40	60.50	60.30
Communication[5]	13.30	13.80	14.50	15.10	13.50	11.50
Recreation and culture	54.70	37.90	33.10	27.80	47.10	57.30
Education	11.90	6.50	15.70	8.30	21.40	6.50
Restaurants and hotels[6]	38.30	32.90	25.80	17.90	36.70	35.50
Miscellaneous goods and services	33.30	32.50	36.50	24.10	28.90	34.90
Other expenditure items	106.10	119.30	103.50	77.80	83.90	96.50
All household expenditure	503.20	449.10	464.20	356.10	471.90	466.70

1 See Appendix, Part 6: Living Costs and Food Survey. Expenditure rounded to the nearest 10 pence.
2 See Appendix, Part 1: Classification of ethnic groups.
3 Combined data from 2004/05 to 2007/08.
4 Excludes mortgage interest payments, water charges and council tax (domestic rates in Northern Ireland). These are included in 'Other expenditure items'.
5 Includes mobile phone equipment and services.
6 Includes purchases of alcoholic drinks in pubs, restaurants and hotels.

Source: Living Costs and Food Survey, Office for National Statistics

expenditure on categories that could be regarded more as 'luxury' or discretionary items such as recreation and culture, and restaurants and hotels, compared to households where the HRP was White. Conversely, ethnic minority households allocated higher proportions of their total expenditure to communication and housing, fuel and power. However, variations in some categories of expenditure may be explained by other factors related to ethnicity. For example, expenditure on alcoholic drinks and tobacco in households where the HRP was Asian or Asian British, Black or Black British or Other compared with households where the HRP was White was much lower than could be explained just by differences in total expenditure.

The spending power of a household depends on their total income. In order to analyse expenditure patterns according to income, the households in Table 6.6 have been ranked in

ascending order according to their income. They have then been divided into five equal sized groups, known as quintile groups, with households with the lowest income in the bottom quintile group. Equivalised income, that is income after the size and composition of households has been taken into account, has been used to rank households to recognise their differing demands on resources (see Chapter 5: Income and wealth, Analysing income distribution text box for definitions of equivalisation and quintile groups).

In 2008, weekly household expenditure in the UK ranged from £176.90 in the lowest income quintile group to £877.40 in the highest (Table 6.6). Households in the lowest income quintile group spent a much larger proportion of their expenditure on housing, fuel and power than those in the highest income quintile groups (21 per cent and 7 per cent respectively). This was also the same for expenditure on food and non-alcoholic drink (17 per cent and 8 per cent respectively). The categories with the greatest absolute difference in expenditure between the two quintile groups were other expenditure items, transport and recreation and culture. Households in the highest income quintile group spent on average £167.00 (91 per cent), £122.00 (89 per cent) and £93.30 (83 per cent) more than households in the lowest income quintile group.

Table 6.6

Household expenditure:[1] by selected income quintile group,[2] 2008

United Kingdom   £ per week

	Bottom quintile	Top quintile	All households
Food and non-alcoholic drink	29.70	72.60	50.70
Alcohol and tobacco	6.40	14.40	10.80
Clothing and footwear	7.50	42.40	21.60
Housing (net),[3] fuel and power	37.40	63.40	53.00
Household goods and services	12.20	57.20	30.10
Health	2.20	9.00	5.10
Transport	14.60	136.60	63.40
Communication[4]	6.50	17.70	12.00
Recreation and culture	19.60	112.90	60.10
Education	0.90	20.80	6.20
Restaurants and hotels[5]	10.50	78.30	37.70
Miscellaneous goods and services	12.90	68.40	35.60
Other expenditure items	16.60	183.60	84.70
All household expenditure	176.90	877.40	471.00

1 See Appendix, Part 6: Living Costs and Food Survey. Expenditure rounded to the nearest 10 pence.
2 Households are ranked according to their income and then divided into five groups of equal size. The bottom fifth, or bottom quintile group, is then the 20 per cent of households with the lowest incomes. See Chapter 5: Income and wealth, Analysing income distribution text box.
3 Excludes mortgage interest payments, water charges and council tax (domestic rates in Northern Ireland). These are included in 'Other expenditure items'.
4 Includes mobile phone equipment and services.
5 Includes purchases of alcoholic drinks in pubs, restaurants and hotels.

Source: Living Costs and Food Survey, Office for National Statistics

Average weekly expenditure also varies by the age of the HRP. Households in the UK, where the HRP was aged between 30 and 49 years, had the highest average expenditure in 2008, at £581.90 per week; while those with an HRP aged over 75 had the lowest average household expenditure, at £216.80 per week (Table 6.7). To some extent these differences will be the result of differing household sizes as well as differences in household income. The proportion of spending on food and non-alcoholic drink increased with the age of the HRP, from 9 per cent among households with an HRP aged under 30 to 16 per cent among households with an HRP aged 75 and over. Conversely, spending on household goods and services fell from 8 per cent of total weekly expenditure among households with an HRP aged 75 and over to 5 per cent among households with an HRP aged under 30 years.

Expenditure on recreation and culture, as a proportion of total weekly expenditure, increased from 9 per cent among households with an HRP aged under 30 to 18 per cent among those with an HRP aged 65 to 74, after which the proportion fell again to 14 per cent among those with an HRP aged 75 and over. Households where the HRP was aged 65 to 74 spent relatively smaller proportions of their total expenditure on essential items such as clothing and footwear, and housing, fuel and power (4 per cent and 12 per cent respectively). In

Table 6.7

Household expenditure:[1] by age of household reference person,[2] 2008

United Kingdom

£ per week

	Under 30	30–49	50–64	65–74	75 and over	All households
Food and non-alcoholic drink	38.70	57.00	55.50	48.20	34.90	50.70
Alcohol and tobacco	10.50	12.30	12.80	9.30	4.40	10.80
Clothing and footwear	23.20	27.50	23.70	12.70	7.70	21.60
Housing (net),[3] fuel and power	76.20	59.50	49.10	42.00	36.10	53.00
Household goods and services	23.90	35.70	32.90	26.20	17.60	30.10
Health	2.80	4.20	7.70	4.60	4.90	5.10
Transport	55.80	77.90	80.30	41.20	16.00	63.40
Communication[4]	13.20	14.20	13.20	8.20	5.90	12.00
Recreation and culture	41.50	67.20	70.90	63.70	29.60	60.10
Education	3.00	8.90	8.80	1.30	0.40	6.20
Restaurants and hotels[5]	38.20	46.40	44.10	25.10	12.60	37.70
Miscellaneous goods and services	31.30	45.40	36.60	24.00	20.10	35.60
Other expenditure items	83.00	125.70	73.60	47.20	26.80	84.70
All household expenditure	441.20	581.90	509.20	353.60	216.80	471.00

1 See Appendix, Part 6: Living Costs and Food Survey. Expenditure rounded to the nearest 10 pence.
2 See Chapter 2: Households and familes text box for an explanation of household reference person.
3 Excludes mortgage interest payments, water charges and council tax (domestic rates in Northern Ireland). These are included in 'Other expenditure items'.
4 Includes mobile phone equipment and services.
5 Includes purchases of alcoholic drinks in pubs, restaurants and hotels.

Source: Living Costs and Food Survey, Office for National Statistics

contrast, households where the HRP was aged under 30 spent 22 per cent of their total expenditure on these two categories.

Spending by children contributes to total household expenditure. Although the majority of expenditure on items for children is made by their parents, many children receive pocket money and are able to make their own decisions as to how to spend it. Pocket money is not the only potential source of children's income, particularly for older children. They may also earn money through paid work or may receive cash gifts from parents and relatives.

The Living Costs and Food Survey collects information about the expenditure patterns of children in the UK. Children aged 7 to 15 are asked to keep diaries in which they record their expenditure over a two week period. In 2007/08, the average household expenditure by children aged 7 to 15 was £12.50 per week and the average expenditure per child was £7.60. The largest category of children's expenditure was recreation and culture, accounting for 36 per cent (£4.40) of their average weekly spending (Figure 6.8). Spending on snacks and takeaway meals was the next largest expenditure category, accounting for 24 per cent (£3.00) of their weekly spending followed by clothing and footwear at 18 per cent (£2.20).

Figure 6.8

Children's[1] expenditure on selected items, 2007/08

United Kingdom

Percentages

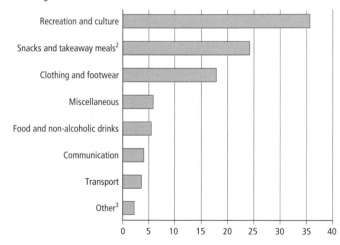

1 Children aged 7 to 15.
2 'Snacks and takeaway meals' reflect the Classification of Individual Consumption by Purpose (COICOP) category 'Restaurants and hotels'. See Appendix, Part 6: Household expenditure. For children, expenditure on hotels is negligible.
3 Includes expenditure on clubs and gifts.

Source: Living Costs and Food Survey, Office for National Statistics

Transport and fare costs accounted for only 4 per cent of children's expenditure, as children's fares tend to be paid for by parents and guardians, and public transport fares for young people are subsidised.

Income and expenditure patterns are reflected in both the ownership of goods, or in some cases, in the inability of families to afford some goods and services. Table 6.3 showed that the volume of expenditure on goods has increased rapidly in recent years, and this has meant that the ownership of new durable goods has extended rapidly to a greater proportion of households. Ownership of new durable goods tends to rise rapidly over the first few years they are available, and then levels off. For example, the proportion of UK households with a DVD player rose from 31 per cent in 2002/03 to 86 per cent in 2007, and in 2008 reached 88 per cent (Figure 6.9). Similarly, the spread of Internet connections and mobile phones slowed in recent years after a sharp rise in the late 1990s and early 2000s. The percentage of households that had an Internet connection increased from 9 per cent in 1998/99 to 49 per cent in 2003/04. However, between 2003/04 and 2008, the proportion grew by only 17 percentage points. Similarly, ownership of a mobile phone increased from 27 per cent in 1998/99 to 76 per cent in 2003/04 but by only 3 percentage points between 2003/04 and 2008.

Growth in the ownership of CD players, which have been available for longer than DVD players, has been slower over the last 14 years. In 1994/95, 46 per cent of households had a CD player compared with 86 per cent in 2008. Ownership of other durable goods such washing machines and microwaves which have been available for even longer and which were already

relatively widely owned in 1994/95 also increased more slowly over the last 14 years. Between 1994/95 and 2008, the proportion of households with a washing machine increased from 89 per cent to 96 per cent while ownership of a microwave increased from 67 per cent to 92 per cent.

Consumer credit

Individuals may spend more than their income by running down savings, selling assets, or borrowing money. Individuals can borrow money from five main sources – banks, building societies, other specialist lenders, retailers, and other organisations such as the Government and pension funds. Total net lending to individuals is the difference between gross lending and gross repayments of debt in a given period. Lending to individuals consists of lending secured on dwellings (mortgages) and consumer credit, as well as all lending to housing associations.

The increase in total lending between 1993 and 2006 (at 2008 prices) was driven primarily by loans for house purchases, which are secured against those dwellings. Lending secured against dwellings fell in the recession of the early 1990s and reached a low point in the fourth quarter (Q4) of 1992 (£4.9 billion) (Figure 6.10). This type of lending started to increase gradually after 1996, and then more rapidly from 2000 onwards with the acceleration in house prices. In Q4 2003, net lending secured on dwellings peaked at £33.3 billion, followed by a decline and subsequently another peak at a

Figure 6.9

Household ownership of selected durable goods

United Kingdom

Percentages

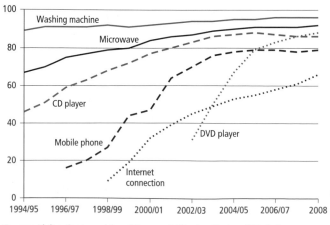

Source: Living Costs and Food Survey, Office for National Statistics

Figure 6.10

Net[1] lending to individuals[2]

United Kingdom

£ billion per quarter at 2008 prices[3]

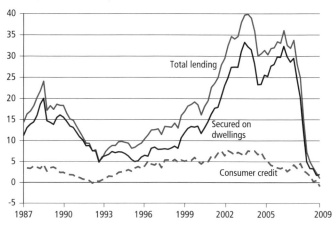

1 New loans less repayments on existing loans.
2 Data are seasonally adjusted. Lending secured on dwellings and consumer credit. Also includes lending to housing associations.
3 Adjusted to 2008 prices using the retail prices index. See Appendix, Part 5: Retail prices index.

Source: Bank of England

similar level in Q4 2006. It then declined again, with the pace of decline increasing sharply at the beginning of the economic downturn which began in 2008 and by Q3 2009 stood at £1.9 billion. There is more information on housing finance in Chapter 10: Housing.

Consumer credit consists of credit card lending, overdrafts and non-secured loans, and advances to individuals, less repayments of such lending. This type of lending has not shown the same level of volatility as net lending secured on dwellings. Nevertheless it too fell during the recession of the early 1990s, from £4.2 billion in Q3 1988 (at 2008 prices) to -£0.2 billion in Q2 1992. (A negative figure means that repayments of debt exceeded the value of new loans.) Consumer credit lending then increased gradually from 1993 and then stabilised from Q1 2002 (£7.5 billion) until Q1 2005. During 2005, consumer credit fell rapidly and in Q3 2009, it reached -£1.0 billion, lower than the previous trough in Q2 1992.

High levels of borrowing over a long period can lead to an increase in household debt relative to its disposable income. UK household debt has risen to historically high levels in recent years as consumers have borrowed to raise spending levels relative to income. In 1987, total household debt (both secured and unsecured) as a percentage of household disposable income, known as the debt ratio, was just over 100 per cent (Figure 6.11). In other words, household debt and household income were almost equal. Between 1987 and 1990 the debt ratio rose from 103 per cent to 115 per cent. This was the result of a 55 per cent increase in household debt over that period while household income only increased by 39 per cent. The

Figure 6.11

Household debt[1] as a proportion of household income

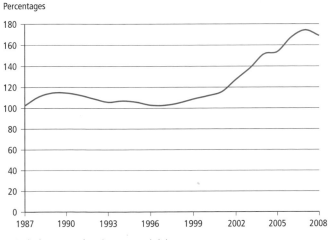

United Kingdom
Percentages

1 Includes secured and unsecured debt.

Source: Office for National Statistics

debt ratio decreased after 1990 and reached a low point of 103 per cent in 1997, but then increased steadily between 1999 and 2007. Over this period household debt increased by 125 per cent while household income increased by only 40 per cent. The debt ratio fell by 5 percentage points between 2007 and 2008 to reach 169 per cent, though this was still over one-and-a-half times the ratio in 1987.

The increase in household debt has led banks to write-off increasing amounts of bad debt. Figures from the Bank of England show that in 2008 banks wrote off £6.9 billion of loans to individuals, compared with £3.0 billion in 2002 and £1.5 billion in 1993 (all at 2008 prices). This increase in individual write-offs was largely driven by other consumer credit (personal loans and overdrafts) which rose from £0.9 billion in 1993 to £3.2 billion in 2008.

According to the Families and Children Study, 46 per cent of all families with children in Great Britain had borrowed money (excluding mortgages) from different sources in 2007 (Table 6.12 overleaf). The most common source of family borrowing was a bank overdraft (29 per cent) or a fixed-term loan from a bank or building society (9 per cent). Families also used less formal types of credit, for example borrowing from friends or relatives (9 per cent). Borrowing in 2007 was more common among lone parents (52 per cent) than couple families with children (44 per cent). Lone parents were also more likely than couple families to have borrowed money from friends or relatives (16 per cent compared with 7 per cent). Another factor associated with borrowing among families was the age of the youngest family member, with the likelihood of having any borrowing being highest for families whose youngest child was aged under 5.

The pattern of borrowing reported by families in 2007 differs in some respects from 2002. In 2002, 52 per cent of all families had borrowed money compared with 46 per cent in 2007. Although around the same proportion had borrowed money through a bank overdraft in 2002 (28 per cent), a higher proportion had a fixed-term loan from a bank or building society (15 per cent) or a loan from a finance company (10 per cent).

Homeowners are likely to have better access to credit than those who are not as they are able to use the value of their property as security for their borrowing. Housing equity withdrawal is defined as new borrowing secured on homes that is not used for house purchase or home improvements. This form of borrowing can represent a substantial supplement to a household's income and can be used to increase consumption expenditure, pay off other debts, or invest in financial assets.

Table 6.12

Borrowing: by family type and age of youngest child, 2007

Great Britain

Percentages

	Any borrowing	Bank overdraft	Bank/building society loan	Finance company loan	Friend or relative loan	Social fund loan	Behind in any payments
Family type							
Couple	44	30	10	5	7	1	1
Lone parent	52	26	7	6	16	12	3
Age of youngest child							
0–4	50	32	9	6	11	5	2
5–10	48	30	10	6	11	4	2
11–15	41	27	11	5	6	2	1
16–18	33	23	5	4	5	0	1
All families	46	29	9	5	9	4	1

Source: Families and Children Study, Department for Work and Pensions

During most of the 1970s, housing equity withdrawal in the UK was around 1 per cent of post-tax income, but then grew to reach a peak of approximately 8 per cent in the late 1980s (Figure 6.13). As a result of the fall in house prices in 1989, housing equity withdrawal then fell in the 1990s and remained below 2 per cent of post-tax income until 1999. Between 2001 and 2006 housing equity withdrawal rose rapidly again, peaking first at 8.5 per cent of post-tax income in Q3 2003 and

Figure 6.13

Housing equity withdrawal[1] as a proportion of post-tax income[2]

United Kingdom

Percentages

1 New borrowing secured on dwellings that is not invested in house purchases or home improvements.
2 Post-tax income is household's total income less direct and indirect taxes.

Source: Bank of England

then again at 6.2 per cent in Q1 2007, caused by a combination of relatively low interest rates and increasing house prices (see also Chapter 10: Housing). Housing equity withdrawal began to fall again in 2007, became negative in the second quarter of 2008, and has remained negative for the first, second and third quarters of 2009, meaning that repayments of these loans exceeded the value of new loans.

High levels of borrowing have been accompanied by an increase in the number of individual insolvencies as debtors found themselves unable to keep up with repayments. Some of the statutory insolvency instruments available to individuals experiencing financial difficulty include bankruptcy, debt relief orders and individual voluntary arrangements (IVAs) in England and Wales; bankruptcy and IVAs in Northern Ireland; and sequestrations and protected trust deeds in Scotland. An individual can be declared bankrupt when the courts conclude that there is no likelihood of the debt being repaid. However, in some circumstances the courts encourage a voluntary arrangement to be set up between the debtor and their creditors. Debt relief orders were introduced in April 2009 and are designed for those individuals with low liabilities, no assets and minimal surplus income. They are made by the Official Receiver through an administrative procedure which does not require the debtor to attend court.

The number of bankruptcies and IVAs in England and Wales remained generally stable from 1970 until 1990 when they started to rise (Figure 6.14). Bankruptcies were the first to increase, starting in 1991 followed closely by an increase in

Figure 6.14

Individual insolvencies

England & Wales
Thousands

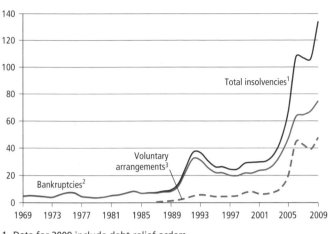

1 Data for 2009 include debt relief orders.
2 Individuals declared bankrupt by a court.
3 Individuals who make a voluntary agreement with their creditors.
   Includes Deeds of Arrangement, which enable debtors to come to an
   agreement with their creditors.

Source: Insolvency Service

IVAs from 1992. Total insolvencies stabilised in the 1990s but then rose rapidly to reach a peak of 107,290 in 2006. However, total insolvencies fell in 2007 and 2008 before increasing sharply to 134,142 individual insolvencies in 2009. This was an increase of 26 per cent on 2008, and was nearly 10 times the number of insolvencies recorded in the recession of 1990 when, as Figure 6.11 showed, the household debt ratio was much lower than in 2008.

Insolvency levels in Northern Ireland have followed a similar trend to England and Wales. Total insolvencies increased from 573 in 1999 to 1,338 in 2007. In 2008, there were 1,638 insolvencies, comprising 1,079 bankruptcies and 559 IVAs. Because of Scotland's different judicial system, the schemes in place are not the same as those in England, Wales and Northern Ireland. However, individual sequestrations (which are comparable to bankruptcies in England, Wales and Northern Ireland) in Scotland more than doubled between 2007/08 and 2008/09, from 6,158 to 14,648.

According to the Insolvency Service, people aged 35 to 44 were the age group in England and Wales most likely to be declared bankrupt in 2008 (Figure 6.15). The number of people declared bankrupt aged 35 to 44 increased from 6,358 in 2000 to 20,366 in 2008. The number of women in bankruptcy increased around fourfold between 2000 and 2008. Women also made up the majority of young people falling into bankruptcy, with 1,562 women under the age of 25 declaring themselves bankrupt in 2008 compared with 1,253 men of the

Figure 6.15

Bankruptcies:[1] by age

England & Wales
Thousands

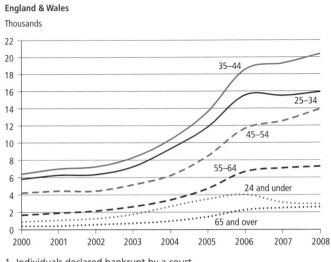

1 Individuals declared bankrupt by a court.

Source: Insolvency Service

same age. The largest proportional increase in bankruptcies was among those aged 65 and over, rising from 403 in 2000 to 2,595 in 2008.

As Figure 6.14 showed, the number of new IVAs was relatively stable between 2000 and 2003 but between 2003 and 2004 they rose rapidly from 7,574 to 10,731, and continued to rise to reach 42,240 in 2007. The number of new cases then declined slightly to 39,116 in 2008. The number of new IVA cases also varied across the different regions in England. In 2008 the number of IVAs was highest in the South East with 6,046 cases, followed by the North West with 5,188 cases. The number of new IVA cases was lowest for the East Midlands and the North East with 3,597 and 2,070 new cases respectively.

Transactions

The ways in which transactions are carried out in the UK have changed dramatically over the last decade with an increase in the use of debit cards and automated payments and a decline in the use of cheques and cash. According to the Payments Council and the UK Cards Association, in 2008 consumers made transactions on the high street and online totalling £524.6 billion. Just over a third (36 per cent, or £190.4 billion) of the value of these transactions was made by debit card and a further 20 per cent (£103.3 billion) was by credit, and charge cards (Table 6.16 overleaf). However, the second most common payment method was cash, accounting for 29 per cent (£153.3 billion) of transactions. Payment by cheque was the least common method, accounting for 12 per cent (£63.1 billion) of transactions. From 2006 onwards, the

Table 6.16

Total consumer spending: by method of payment[1]

United Kingdom   Percentages

	2005	2006	2007	2008
Debit cards	29.5	33.6	34.6	36.3
Credit, and charge cards	19.4	19.8	20.1	19.7
Cash	33.1	31.2	30.4	29.2
Cheques	15.9	12.9	14.1	12.0
Other[2]	2.1	2.6	0.8	2.8
Total spending (=100%) (£ billions)	494.5	503.0	510.6	524.6

1 Total UK consumer spending includes all transactions on the high
   street above £1, and to online retailers by value.
2 Includes telephone or Internet banking initiated payments, vouchers,
   and other payment methods.

Source: The Payments Council

Figure 6.17

Non-cash transactions:[1] by method of payment

United Kingdom

Billions

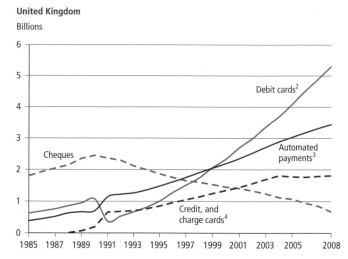

1 Figures are for payments made by households. Cheque encashments
   and cash withdrawals from cash machines and branch counters using
   credit, charge and debit cards are not included. Based on data supplied
   by UK card issuers.
2 Visa, Debit and Switch cards in all years; includes Electron cards from
   1996 and Solo cards from 1997.
3 Direct Debits, standing orders, direct credits, and inter-branch
   automated items.
4 Visa, MasterCard, travel/entertainment cards and store cards.

Source: The Payments Council; The UK Cards Association

majority of transactions (measured by value) were by plastic card (which includes debit cards, credit and charge cards). Debit cards accounted for a greater proportion of total plastic card spending than credit and charge cards throughout the period 2005 to 2008. Debit card usage increased from 60 per cent of total plastic card spending to 65 per cent, while spending by credit, and charge cards decreased from 40 per cent in 2005 to 35 per cent in 2008.

The use of other payment methods, such as telephone and Internet banking, accounted for a very small proportion of transactions, fluctuating between 1 and 3 per cent of transactions between 2005 and 2008.

Consumer spending by cash continued its downward trend from £163.6 billion in 2005 to £153.3 billion in 2008, though it still accounted for the second highest proportion of the value of transactions. In terms of the volume of transactions, figures from the UK Payments Administration show that the number of cash machine withdrawals are expected to continue to rise and peak in 2011 at 2.9 billion withdrawals, before falling back due to lower use of cash for everyday transactions. In 2008 there were 34.3 million regular users of cash machines, each of whom on average withdrew approximately £380 every month in six withdrawals.

Cheques made up the largest volume of non-cash transactions (1.8 billion) in 1985, followed by debit cards (0.62 billion) and automated payments (0.4 billion) (Figure 6.17). An increase in the use of electronic payment methods for regular payments such as mortgages, and of plastic cards for face-to-face, online and telephone retail payments has led to a decline in the use of cheques. Since their use peaked in 1990 at 2.4 billion payments, the volume of consumer payments made by cheque

has fallen by 73 per cent to 0.7 billion in 2008, less than half the volume of transactions in 1985. The volume of transactions using credit and charge cards rose steadily between 1989 and 2004, but has stabilised since 2005 at around 1.8 billion, coinciding with a reduction in net consumer credit available to consumers (see Figure 6.10). In 2008 the number of credit, and charge cards transactions was 1.8 billion.

The volume of automated payments and debit card transactions in 2008 were both approximately nine times greater than they were in 1985. Debit card payments accounted for the largest volume of non-cash payments in 2008 with 5.3 billion transactions, followed by automated payments transactions (3.4 billion) and credit, and charge card transactions (1.8 billion).

As more people have gained access to the Internet (see Figure 6.9), it has been increasingly used by individuals for various financial transactions such as paying bills, transferring funds between accounts and purchasing goods and services. People may also buy goods and services directly from manufacturers or wholesalers or from overseas providers rather than using traditional retail channels.

Figures from the ONS Internet Access survey showed that when interviewed between January and March 2009, 64 per cent of all recent Internet users in the UK had purchased goods or

Table 6.18

Internet purchases by adults,[1] 2009

United Kingdom	Percentages
Films, music	50
Clothes or sports goods	49
Household goods[2]	47
Holiday accommodation	42
Books, magazines or newspapers	41
Travel arrangements[3]	40
Tickets for events	37
Electronic equipment	28
Video games, software and upgrades	26
Food or groceries	22
Other computer software and upgrades	20
Shares, financial services or insurance	17
Telecommunication services[4]	14
Computer hardware	14
Medicine	5
Other goods and services	5

1 Adults in the UK who had purchased or ordered online in the last
  12 months prior to interview in January to March 2009.
2 Includes household furniture and toys.
3 Includes transport tickets and car hire.
4 Includes TV and broadband subscriptions.

Source: Office for National Statistics

services over the Internet at least once. Of these, 83 per cent (26 million) had purchased items within the three months prior to interview. Men were more likely to have purchased goods and services over Internet in 2009 than women (69 per cent and 60 per cent respectively).

Table 6.18 shows Internet purchases made by adults in the UK in the 12 months prior to interview. Half of adults (50 per cent) making online purchases bought films and music, followed by purchases of clothing and sport goods (49 per cent of adults) and household goods (47 per cent). Less than a fifth of people making online purchases bought shares, financial services or insurance (17 per cent) or telecommunication services (which include TV and broadband subscriptions) (14 per cent).

Prices

The way people choose to spend their money is affected by the prices of goods and services. There are two main measures of UK consumer price inflation – the consumer prices index (CPI) and the retail prices index (RPI). The CPI was launched in 1996 (although estimates are available from 1988), and since December 2003 has been used as the main domestic measure

of UK inflation for macroeconomic purposes. The RPI was introduced in 1947 and is the longest standing measure of inflation in the UK. Both the CPI and RPI measure the average change, from month to month, in the prices of goods and services purchased in the UK by consumers.

However, although the RPI and CPI are broadly similar, there are some important differences between the two indices. For example, the CPI excludes a number of items included in the RPI mainly related to housing costs – council tax, mortgage interest payments and house depreciation. The CPI represents a broader population than the RPI. The RPI excludes households whose total household income lies within the top 4 per cent of all households and excludes around 20 per cent of pensioner households – those that derive at least three-quarters of their income from state pension or benefits. Since 1996 the CPI inflation rate has usually been lower than the RPI rate, with the major exception being during late 2008 and 2009.

To ensure that the CPI and RPI are kept up-to-date, the 'shopping basket' of items whose prices are measured to produce the CPI and RPI are reviewed every year. Each year some items are taken out of the basket and some are introduced to reflect changes in the availability of goods and services and to make sure the CPI and RPI are up-to-date and representative of current consumer spending patterns.

Levels of inflation in the UK have varied considerably over the past four decades (Figure 6.19). Annual inflation, as measured by the RPI, exceeded 20 per cent during some periods in the

Figure 6.19

Retail prices index[1] and consumer prices index[2]

United Kingdom

Percentage change over 12 months

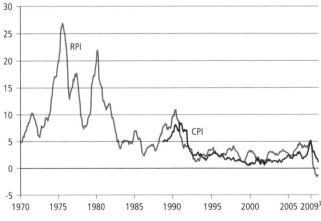

1 See Appendix, Part 5: Retail prices index.
2 See Appendix, Part 6: Consumer prices index. Data for years prior to
   1996 are estimates.
3 Data for 2009 are up to and including September.

Source: Office for National Statistics

1970s and 1980s, went above 10 per cent again in 1990, but has remained below 5 per cent since August 1991. Since 1997 the Bank of England has been responsible for setting interest rates to meet the Government's inflation target, which was initially 2.5 per cent as measured by the RPI (excluding mortgage interest payments). Since December 2003 the target rate of inflation has been 2.0 per cent as measured by the CPI. Inflation, as measured by the CPI, remained at or below 2.0 per cent between 1997 and mid-2005. Between mid-2005 and March 2008, inflation tended to be slightly higher than the target rate and, with the exception of March 2007 when it was 3.1 per cent, it remained within 1 percentage point of it. However, from April 2008 the CPI began to rise, and peaked at 5.2 per cent in September 2008, 3.2 percentage points above the Government's target rate. From September 2008 CPI inflation generally fell each month, reaching 1.1 per cent per annum in September 2009.

Figure 6.20 shows the percentage change for the main components of the UK CPI between 2007 and 2008. The

Figure 6.20

Percentage change[1] in consumer prices index: by purpose of expenditure, 2008

United Kingdom
Percentage change over 12 months

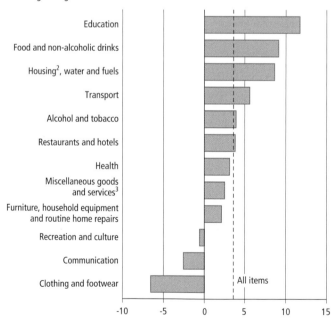

1 Percentage change between 2007 and 2008. See Appendix, Part 6: Consumer prices index.
2 Housing excludes mortgage interest payments and council tax (domestic rates in Northern Ireland). Communication includes mobile phone equipment and services. Restaurants and hotels includes purchases of alcoholic drinks in pubs, restaurants and hotels.
3 Includes personal care, personal effects (for example jewellery and watches), social protection, insurance and financial services.

Source: Office for National Statistics

components showing some of the largest rate of increase in prices were food and non-alcoholic drinks and housing, water and fuel (9.1 percent and 8.6 per cent respectively). In contrast, the prices of items in some categories, such as clothing and footwear and communication, fell between 2007 and 2008, by 6.6 and 2.6 per cent respectively.

The extent to which price change contributes towards the overall level of price inflation depends not just on the size of the price change but also on the importance of the items, or groups of items, within total household expenditure. For example, price increases in housing, water, and fuels; food and non-alcoholic drinks; and transport all contributed to growth in the overall index. This is because these component groups had increases in price of over 3 per cent and each accounted for a relatively high proportion (10 per cent) of average household expenditure. In contrast, although education recorded the largest price rise of any component, 11.7 per cent between 2007 and 2008, it had relatively little effect on the overall CPI because household expenditure on education accounted for only 2 per cent of total expenditure.

The items in the 'basket of goods and services' used to determine both the CPI and RPI are subject to change over time, to take account of changing consumer preferences and changes in the availability of goods and services. For example, lard, bottled pale lager and vinyl records were in the basket in 1970 but have since been removed. In contrast, items like milk, sugar and coffee have been included in the basket since 1970. This makes it possible to show how the prices of these individual items have changed over time. For example, between 1971 and 2008, the price of a packet of 20 filter tipped cigarettes in the UK increased by approximately 20 times and the price of a pint of beer by 18 times (Table 6.21). Part of this increase was due to increased duties levied on cigarettes and alcohol. The price of white fish fillets also increased 18 times over this period. The price of unleaded petrol more than doubled since 1991, which was largely due to a combination of a rise in the world market price and rises in taxes and duties, including fuel duty and value added tax (VAT) (see also Chapter 12: Transport, Figure 12.12). The price of mushrooms and bananas increased between 1971 and 1991, but then fell between 1991 and 2008.

The CPI index is harmonised across the European Union (EU) and can therefore be used to compare levels of inflation among EU member states. In 2008 the Netherlands had the lowest level of annual inflation, at 2.2 per cent (Table 6.22). Portugal and Germany had the second and third lowest rates of inflation at 2.7 and 2.8 per cent respectively. In 2008, the UK had the same rate of inflation as Denmark, and was

Table 6.21

Cost of selected items

United Kingdom   Pence[1]

	1971	1981	1991	2001	2008
White fish fillets, per kg	58	244	630	866	1048
500g back bacon[2]	37	142	235	343	410
Eggs (large), per dozen	26	78	118	172	285
250g cheddar cheese	13	58	86	128	174
1 pint pasteurised milk[3]	6	19	32	37	42
800g white sliced bread	10	37	53	51	119
New potatoes,[4] loose per kg	13	31	34	87	110
Mushrooms, loose per kg	60	211	290	262	263
Tomatoes, loose per kg	35	98	148	125	171
Apples (dessert), per kg	22	55	120	116	147
Bananas, per kg	18	63	119	106	90
Packet of 20 cigarettes (filter tip)[5]	27	97	186	412	531
Pint of beer[6]	15	65	137	203	274
Whisky (per nip)	..	..	95	148	196
Litre of unleaded petrol	..	..	45	76	107

1 The average price in pence sterling in the corresponding calendar year.
2 In 1971 and 1981 the price is for unsmoked. In 1991 the price is an average of vacuum and not vacuum-packed.
3 Delivered milk included from 1996.
4 In season new potatoes prior to 1993.
5 Change from standard to king size in 1991.
6 Bottled until 1981 and draught lager after.

Source: Office for National Statistics

slightly lower than the average inflation rate across the EU-27, 3.6 per cent compared with 3.7 per cent. France had an inflation rate of 3.2 per cent which was 0.5 percentage points below the EU-27 average. Rates in excess of 10 per cent were recorded in four countries, all of which were some of the most recent to join the EU: Estonia, Lithuania, Bulgaria and Latvia. Of these, Latvia had the highest average inflation rate at 15.3 per cent, four times higher than the EU-27 average.

The international spending power of sterling depends both on exchange rates, and on the ratios of prices between the UK

Table 6.22

Percentage change[1] in consumer prices:[2] EU comparison, 2008

Percentage change over 12 months

Latvia	15.3	Finland	3.9
Bulgaria	12.0	Slovakia	3.9
Lithuania	11.1	Denmark	3.6
Estonia	10.6	United Kingdom	3.6
Romania	7.9	Italy	3.5
Czech Republic	6.3	Sweden	3.3
Hungary	6.0	Austria	3.2
Slovenia	5.5	France	3.2
Malta	4.7	Ireland	3.1
Belgium	4.5	Germany	2.8
Cyprus	4.4	Portugal	2.7
Greece	4.2	Netherlands	2.2
Poland	4.2		
Luxembourg	4.1	EU-27 average	3.7
Spain	4.1		

1 Percentage change between 2007 and 2008.
2 See Appendix, Part 6: Consumer prices index.

Source: Office for National Statistics; Eurostat

and other countries, which are measured by purchasing power parities (See Appendix, Part 5: Purchasing power parities). These can be used to calculate comparative price levels that provide a measure of the differences in price levels between countries, and can show which countries in the EU-27 would be cheaper or more expensive to UK residents. In December 2008, 11 countries of the EU-27 would have appeared more expensive to UK residents: Denmark, Ireland, Finland, Luxembourg, Sweden, France, Italy, the Netherlands, Austria, Germany and Belgium. Prices in Denmark were 42 per cent higher than in the UK. Prices in Spain, Greece and Cyprus were slightly cheaper than in the UK, while prices in the Eastern European countries were substantially cheaper. Prices in Bulgaria and Romania were 51 per cent and 62 per cent of the level in the UK. Prices in the UK were approximately 1 per cent below the EU-27 average.

6

6

Chapter 7

Health

- Life expectancy at birth in the UK has risen by more than 30 years for both males and females since 1901. Males born in 2008 could expect to live 77.8 years compared with 81.9 years for females. (Figure 7.1)

- Infant and neonatal mortality rates in the UK were at their lowest recorded levels in 2008, having fallen by around 90 per cent since 1930 to reach 4.7 deaths per 1,000 live births and 3.2 deaths per 1,000 live births respectively. (Figure 7.5)

- In England and Wales, mentions of MRSA on death certificates increased from 51 in 1993 to a peak of 1,652 in 2006, and have since fallen by 26 per cent to 1,230 in 2008. (Figure 7.7)

- Between 1995 and 2008, age-standardised mortality rates in the UK fell by around a quarter for both prostate cancer (23 per cent) and breast cancer (27 per cent), to reach 24 deaths per 100,000 males and 27 deaths per 100,000 females respectively in 2008. (Table 7.10)

- In Great Britain in 2008, around 1 in 5 males (21 per cent) aged 16 and over drank more than double the recommended daily allowance at least once in the week prior to interview, compared with around 1 in 7 females (14 per cent). (Table 7.13)

- In England, the proportion of the adult population classified as obese increased from 16 per cent in 1994 to 25 per cent in 2008. (Table 7.17)

Over the last 40 years patterns of health and ill health have changed steadily in the UK due to improvements in nutrition, the advancement of medical science and technology and the development of health services. Individual behaviours such as diet, vaccination, smoking and drinking can also impact on morbidity and mortality, and by being aware of these and adopting a healthy lifestyle people may be able to improve their own health status.

Key health indicators

Life expectancy is an important indicator of the state of the nation's health. Since the start of the 20th century there have been large improvements in life expectancy at birth for both males and females. In 1901, males born in the UK could expect to live to 45.0 years, and females 48.7 years (Figure 7.1). However, by 2008, life expectancy at birth had risen to 77.8 years for males and 81.9 years for females. Female life expectancy has been consistently higher than for males since 1901, with the greatest difference being between 1969 and 1970 when females could expect to live to around 75 years, more than six years longer than males born in the same year. Since then the gap has narrowed and this trend is expected to continue until 2015, when the difference is projected to level off at 3.6 years. Life expectancy at birth is projected to continue to rise for both sexes, to reach 81.5 years for males and 85.1 years for females by 2021.

Figure 7.1

Expectation of life[1] at birth: by sex

United Kingdom

Years

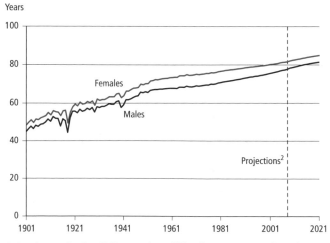

1 See Appendix, Part 7: Expectation of life. The average number of years a new-born baby would survive if he or she experienced age-specific mortality rates for that time period throughout his or her life.
2 2008-based projections for 2009 to 2021.

Source: Office for National Statistics

Among the constituent countries of the UK, gender disparities in life expectancy were greatest in Scotland and Northern Ireland between 2006 and 2008, where females could expect to live five years longer than males born in the same year. In Scotland, females could expect to live for 80 years while for males this figure was 75 years. Equivalent figures in Northern Ireland were 81 years and 76 years respectively.

In 2007, life expectancy at birth for males in the UK of 77.4 years was higher than the European Union (EU-27) average of 75.8 years. Sweden had the highest life expectancy at birth for males in the EU, at 79.0 years. Female life expectancy at birth in the UK, at 81.6 years, was slightly lower than the EU average of 82.0 years, while France had the highest female life expectancy at birth, at 84.4 years.

Over the last 40 years the main causes of mortality have decreased as medical technology and treatments have improved, along with improvements in key lifestyle risk factors such as smoking. However, circulatory disease, including cardiovascular disease (a term covering diseases of the heart or blood vessels such as coronary heart disease, angina and stroke), has remained the leading cause of mortality among males. It was also the leading cause of mortality for females throughout this period until 2006, after which cancers became more prevalent (Figure 7.2).

In 1971, the age-standardised death rates (See Appendix, Part 7: Standardised rates) for circulatory diseases were 6,936 deaths per million males and 4,285 deaths per million females. By 2008, these rates had fallen by two-thirds to 2,298 deaths per million males and 1,494 deaths per million females. In 2006, cancer became the most common cause of death among females, when there were 1,569 cancer deaths per million females compared with 1,559 deaths per million females from circulatory disease. Since 2006, the gap between circulatory diseases and cancer mortality rates for females has widened. By 2008 the death rates for circulatory diseases were 1,494 deaths per million females while the female cancer mortality rate rose slightly to 1,589 deaths per million females.

Male death rates from respiratory diseases have also shown a large decline over the last 40 years, from 2,015 deaths per million males in 1971 to 901 deaths per million males in 2008, a fall of 55 per cent. In 1971, the death rate for respiratory disease for females was less than half the rate for males, at 909 per million females. By 2008 this had fallen 26 per cent to 674 deaths per million females. Death rates for cancers in 2008 were also at their lowest levels among males since 1971, falling 22 per cent from 2,811 per million males in 1971 to 2,180 per million males in 2008.

Figure 7.2

Mortality:[1] by sex and leading cause groups

United Kingdom[2]

Rates per million population

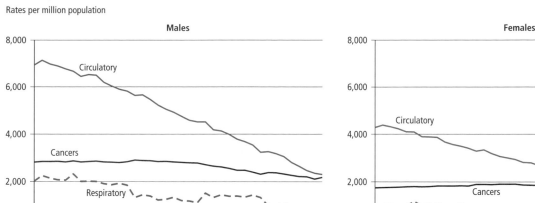

1　Data are for all ages and have been age-standardised using the European standard population. See Appendix, Part 7: Standardised rates, International Classification of Diseases, and European standard population.
2　Data for 2000 are for England and Wales only.

Source: Office for National Statistics

Immunisation and vaccination are important strategies to protect people against certain diseases. Between 1971 and 2008/09 there have been large increases in the proportions of children who have completed primary courses of immunisation by their second birthday (Figure 7.3). The proportion of two-year-olds immunised against diphtheria, tetanus and polio has increased by 33 percentage points over the last 37 years to reach 98 per cent in the UK in 2008/09. Immunisation of two-year-olds against whooping cough has shown a 34 percentage point increase over the same period. However, immunisation against whooping cough fell to 45 per cent in 1981 primarily due to anxiety regarding the side-effects of the vaccine in the mid-1970s. Since this issue has been resolved, there has been a 53 percentage point increase to 98 per cent in 2008/09. Between 1971 and 1991/92, the measles, mumps and rubella (MMR) immunisation rate among two-year-olds nearly doubled from 46 per cent to 90 per cent. Concerns over the safety of the MMR vaccine led to a fall in the proportion of children immunised to 84 per cent in 2001/02, although it has since increased a little to reach 87 per cent in 2008/09.

There are slight differences between the immunisation rates of the constituent countries of the UK in 2008/09. Scotland and Northern Ireland had the highest diphtheria, tetanus, polio and whooping cough immunisation rates in the UK, with 98 per cent of children immunised, compared with 97 per cent in Wales and 94 per cent in England. Similarly, Scotland had the highest MMR immunisation rate (92 per cent) followed by

Figure 7.3

Completed primary immunisation courses[1] at two years of age

United Kingdom[2]

Percentages

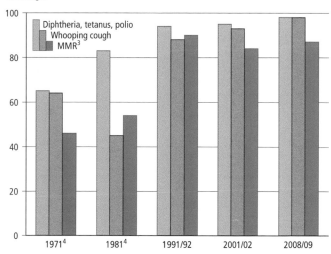

1　Primary immunisation courses are the first immunisations given to babies at two, three and four months.
2　England and Wales data are based on actual numbers of immunisations; Northern Ireland data based on populations by calendar year; Scotland data based on all children reaching a specified age who were alive and registered on the Scottish Immunisation Recall System at the end of the reporting period.
3　Prior to 1988 the vaccination immunised against measles only.
4　Data are for Great Britain.

Source: The NHS Information Centre for health and social care; Welsh Assembly Government; NHS in Scotland; Communicable Disease Surveillance Centre, Northern Ireland

Figure 7.4

Take-up of influenza vaccine: people aged 65 and over

England[1]
Percentages

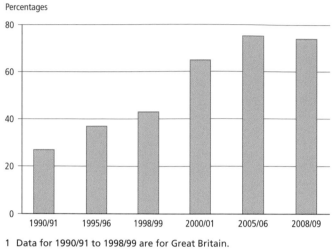

1 Data for 1990/91 to 1998/99 are for Great Britain.

Source: Health Protection Agency

Figure 7.5

Infant[1] and neonatal[2] mortality

United Kingdom
Rates per 1,000 live births

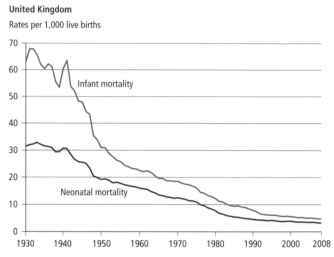

1 Deaths in the first year of life per 1,000 live births.
2 Deaths in babies under 28 days per 1,000 live births. Includes perinatal mortality: deaths under 7 days.

Source: Office for National Statistics; General Register Office for Scotland; Northern Ireland Statistics and Research Agency

Northern Ireland (91 per cent), Wales (88 per cent) and England (85 per cent).

Immunisation against influenza is intended primarily for people in high risk groups, such as the elderly aged 65 and over or those with chronic heart disease, lung disease, renal disease or diabetes. In 2000/01 the Government began a free immunisation campaign for all those aged 65 and over, with a World Health Organisation target that 75 per cent of this age group will be immunised by 2010. In Great Britain in 1990/91, 27 per cent of those aged 65 and over had been immunised against flu and by the start of the NHS influenza immunisation campaign in 2000/01 the proportion in England had risen to 65 per cent (Figure 7.4). The proportion immunised peaked in 2005/06 at 75 per cent, but by 2008/09 had fallen slightly to 74 per cent.

Among the constituent countries of the UK, immunisation was highest in England and Northern Ireland in 2008/09, at 74 per cent, followed by Scotland with 71 per cent. Wales had the lowest rate, at 64 per cent.

Infant and neonatal mortality (defined as deaths in the first year of life and deaths of babies under 28 days respectively) in the UK has decreased since 1930 and this is one of the factors contributing to an overall increase in life expectancy (Figure 7.5). Infant mortality rates fell from 63.1 to 4.7 per 1,000 live births between 1930 and 2008. Neonatal mortality rates have also shown substantial decreases over the last eight decades, falling by around 90 per cent from 31.5 to 3.2 per 1,000 live births between 1930 and 2008. Both infant and neonatal mortality rates were at their lowest recorded levels in 2008.

In England and Wales, infant mortality is higher among boys than girls. In 2008 there were 1,920 deaths among boys under the age of one, compared with 1,449 among girls. Over two-thirds of these deaths for both boys and girls (68 per cent each) were classed as neonatal deaths.

During the period 1978 to 2008, the main underlying causes of death among older people aged 65 and over in the UK were cancers, diseases of the circulatory system and diseases of the respiratory system (Table 7.6).

With the exception of those aged 65 to 74, diseases of the circulatory system remained the most common causes of death among older people over this period, although they have also recorded the largest declines in death rates over the same period of 52 per cent among men and 48 per cent among women. The decline was highest among people aged 65 to 74. Between 1978 and 2008 there was a 70 per cent fall in the death rate from circulatory disease among men aged 65 to 74, from 24,141 to 7,234 deaths per million men, and a 71 per cent fall among women, from 12,534 to 3,683 deaths per million women. There was a downward trend in mortality rates from circulatory disease in the older age groups for both men and women, though not as great. Among those aged 75 to 84, the rates fell by 58 per cent between 1978 and 2008 to reach 22,404 deaths per million men and by 59 per cent to 15,755 deaths per million women. Among those aged 85 and over the rates fell by 46 per cent to 60,576 deaths per million men and by 42 per cent to 56,477 deaths per million women.

Table 7.6

Selected causes of death in people aged 65 and over

United Kingdom   Rates per million population

	65–74		75–84		85 and over	
	Men	Women	Men	Women	Men	Women
Cancer						
1978	13,284	6,809	22,238	10,658	25,980	15,457
1988	12,868	7,606	23,670	12,193	31,533	17,563
1998	11,375	7,377	21,234	11,994	31,139	16,349
2008	9,381	6,370	19,450	12,212	31,858	18,453
Diseases of the circulatory system						
1978	24,141	12,534	53,518	38,139	112,018	96,596
1988	20,149	10,497	47,265	32,731	89,182	86,502
1998	14,409	7,607	36,688	25,303	77,778	68,221
2008	7,234	3,683	22,404	15,755	60,576	56,477
Diseases of the respiratory system						
1978	5,788	2,224	20,450	9,696	57,604	38,453
1988	3,856	1,828	13,312	5,557	39,941	25,075
1998	3,971	2,698	14,624	8,909	47,384	33,502
2008	2,586	1,800	9,344	6,777	31,664	25,056

Source: Office for National Statistics; General Register Office for Scotland; Northern Ireland Statistics and Research Agency

Between 1978 and 2008, death rates for men for all age groups aged 65 and over from diseases of the respiratory system also declined substantially. These declines range from 55 per cent for men aged 65 to 74 years to 45 per cent for those aged 85 and over. Among women aged 65 and over the decrease was smaller, 33 per cent, although the death rates were considerably lower than for men throughout the period.

The death rates from cancers among people aged 65 and over have not followed the same trend as those for diseases of the circulatory and respiratory systems. There were decreases in the death rates between 1978 and 2008 for cancers among men of 29 per cent in the 65 to 74 age group and of 13 per cent for the 75 to 84 age group. However, among men aged 85 and over there was a 23 per cent increase in the death rate from cancers, from 25,980 per million men in 1978 to 31,858 per million in 2008. Among women there were increases in the death rate from cancers among the 75 to 84 age group, of 15 per cent, and among those aged 85 and over of 19 per cent.

There has been a rise in healthcare associated infections since 1993. One of the more common infections is *Staphylococcus aureus* (*S. aureus*), a common germ, and meticillin-resistant

Staphylococcus aureus (MRSA) a variety of *S. aureus* resistant to the antibody meticillin which is used to treat the infection.

In England and Wales between 1993 and 2006, the number of death certificates that mentioned *S. aureus* or MRSA as a contributory factor in death increased each year (Figure 7.7 overleaf). In 1993 there were 481 deaths where *S. aureus* or MRSA was mentioned on the death certificate, of which 11 per cent mentioned MRSA only. The figures peaked in 2006 when there were 3,802 mentions of *S. aureus* or MRSA on death certificates, of which MRSA accounted for 43 per cent. Since then the number of mentions on death certificates has fallen. In 2008 there were 2,730 mentions of *S. aureus* or MRSA on death certificates, the lowest level since 2003, and a 25 per cent fall since 2007.

The number of death certificates where *S. aureus* or MRSA was identified as the underlying cause of death also increased between 1993 and 2008. In 1993 there were 170 deaths where *S. aureus* or MRSA was identified as the underlying cause, of which MRSA accounted for 9 per cent. In 2006, the figure peaked at 1,226 deaths, but has since fallen by 57 per cent to 533 deaths in 2008. In comparison, in Northern Ireland the number of death certificates where *S. aureus* or

Figure 7.7

Deaths involving MRSA[1]

England & Wales
Number

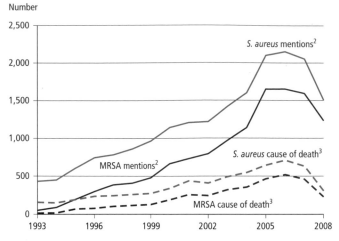

1 Deaths where *Staphylococcus aureus* or meticillin-resistant *Staphylococcus aureus* (MRSA) was mentioned on the death certificate as a contributory factor. See Appendix, Part 7: MRSA.
2 Death certificates where *Staphylococcus aureus* or MRSA was mentioned.
3 Death certificates where *Staphylococcus aureus* or MRSA was given as the underlying cause of death.

Source: Office for National Statistics

MRSA was identified as the underlying cause of death rose from 1 case in 1998 to 38 cases in 2008.

The age-specific mortality rates for *S. aureus* and MRSA increase with age and are highest among those aged 85 and over. Between 2004 and 2008 in England and Wales the 'All *S. aureus*' (including MRSA) mortality rate was 776.0 per million males and 397.7 per million females for this age group. In comparison, the mortality rate was 2.7 per million males and 2.1 per million females aged under 45 years. In Northern Ireland in 2008, the mortality rate among those aged 75 and over (500.1 per million population) was more than 10 times higher than for those aged 45 to 74 (47.0 per million population). In England and Wales between 2004 and 2008, 89 per cent of all *S. aureus* deaths took place in NHS hospitals (8,378 deaths), though this represented less than 0.6 per cent of all deaths in an NHS hospital over this period.

Since 1974 there have been improvements in the treatment of, and immunisation against, infectious diseases. This is reflected in the decline in notification rates of certain diseases such as measles, scarlet fever and tuberculosis (Table 7.8). In 1974 there were almost 110,000 notified cases of measles in England and Wales, a rate of 223.0 per 100,000 population. Thirty years later in 2004 the number had fallen to 2,356 cases, a rate of 4.4 per 100,000 population, at least in part as a result of improved immunisation rates (see Figure 7.3). Although the number of notifications rose slightly in 2008 to 5,088 cases, this was still a decline of 95 per cent compared with 1974.

There have also been large declines in notified cases of whooping cough, scarlet fever and dysentery in England and Wales over the last thirty years. Between 1974 and 2008, the number of cases of whooping cough fell by around

Table 7.8

Notifications of selected infectious diseases and conditions

England & Wales

Thousands

	1974	1984	1994	2004	2008
Food poisoning	6.2	20.7	81.8	70.3	69.0
Mumps[1]	..	..	2.5	16.4	7.8
Tuberculosis	10.7	6.1	5.6	6.7	7.3
Measles	109.6	62.1	16.4	2.4	5.1
Infective jaundice/Viral hepatitis[2]	7.6	5.8	3.7	3.9	4.8
Scarlet fever	10.4	6.3	6.2	2.2	2.9
Whooping cough	16.2	5.5	4.0	0.5	1.5
Acute meningitis	2.2	1.2	1.8	1.3	1.2
Dysentery (amoebic and bacillary)	8.2	6.8	7.0	1.2	1.2
Rubella[1]	..	..	6.3	1.3	1.1
Typhoid and paratyphoid fevers	0.2	0.2	0.4	0.3	0.4
Malaria	0.6	1.4	1.1	0.6	0.4

1 Rubella and mumps became notifiable on 1 October 1988.
2 Infective jaundice was redesignated Viral hepatitis on 1 October 1988.

Source: Office for National Statistics; Health Protection Agency; Department of Health, Social Services and Public Safety, Northern Ireland

Figure 7.9

Incidence of selected major cancers:[1] by sex

England

Thousands

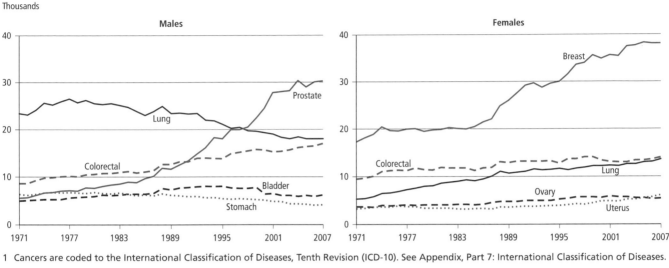

1 Cancers are coded to the International Classification of Diseases, Tenth Revision (ICD-10). See Appendix, Part 7: International Classification of Diseases.

Source: Office for National Statistics

91 per cent, from 16,230 to 1,512. Cases of scarlet fever fell from 10,409 to 2,920; and cases of dysentery fell from 8,211 to 1,166. Over the same period there has been a substantial increase in notifications of food poisoning. In 1994, there were 81,833 cases of food poisoning, 13 times higher than in 1974 (6,239 cases). Although the number of notifications has fallen since 1994, the number of cases in 2008, at 68,962, was still eleven times higher than in 1974, and the rate per 100,000 population had risen from 11.5 in 1974 to 126.7 in 2008.

In Northern Ireland and Scotland, there have also been considerable changes in notifications of certain infectious diseases. Between 1990 and 2008, cases of measles and rubella fell by 93 per cent and 95 per cent respectively in Northern Ireland and by 97 per cent and 96 per cent respectively in Scotland. As in England and Wales, there were large increases in cases of food poisoning in Northern Ireland and Scotland. Between 1990 and 2008 in Northern Ireland there was a 55 per cent increase in cases, from 819 in 1990 to 1,267 in 2008, and a 73 per cent increase between 1985 and 2007 in Scotland, from 4,156 to 7,186 cases. This represented a rate of 71.4 per 100,000 population in Northern Ireland in 2008, almost half the rate in Scotland of 139.7 per 100,000.

Cancer

At some time in their lives, around one in three people will develop cancer. Cigarette smoking is strongly linked to cases of lung cancer, and remains the single biggest risk factor for the disease. In England, the incidence of lung cancer has fallen

sharply in males since the 1970s, from a peak of 26,500 cases in 1977 to around 18,000 in 2007 (Figure 7.9), mainly as a result of the decline in cigarette smoking, see the Smoking, drinking and drugs section later in this chapter. Historically, lung cancer incidence and the number of smokers have been lower among females than males. In 2007, incidence of lung cancer reached around 13,600 cases among females and although this is an increase from 5,300 cases in 1971, it is just over a half of the peak male figure of 26,500 in 1977.

Between 1971 and 1997 the incidence of lung cancer was higher among males in England than any other major cancer, but since 1998 prostate cancer has become the most prevalent male cancer, reaching over 30,000 cases in 2007. Between 1971 and 2007, the most prevalent cancer among females in England was breast cancer, and its incidence more than doubled over the period, from 17,200 to 38,000 cases. In 2007, breast cancer accounted for just under a third of all newly diagnosed cases of cancer in females.

Incidence of prostate cancer among males in England increased more than fivefold between 1971 and 2007, from 5,500 to 30,200 cases, and in 2007 it accounted for a quarter of all newly diagnosed cases of cancer in males. Increased detection due to the use of Prostate Specific Antigen (PSA) testing could account for some of the increase. Among the major cancers, incidence of colorectal cancer among males in England has almost doubled from 8,600 cases in 1971 to 16,900 in 2007. Among females, ovarian cancer has the lowest incidence of the major cancers with 5,400 cases in 2007, around 4 per cent of all cancer cases among females.

Table 7.10

Mortality rates of major cancers:[1] by sex

United Kingdom   Rates per 100,000 population

	1995	2000	2005	2006	2007	2008
Males						
Prostate	31	28	26	25	25	24
Lung	76	63	53	52	52	52
Colorectal	29	26	23	23	22	23
Females						
Breast	37	32	28	28	27	27
Lung	31	30	30	31	31	33
Colorectal	19	16	14	14	14	14

1 Data are for all ages and have been age-standardised using the European standard population. See Appendix, Part 7: Standardised rates, International Classification of Diseases, and European standard population.

Source: Office for National Statistics; Cancer Research UK

Despite increases in the incidence rates of most major cancers, age-standardised mortality rates (see Appendix, Part 7: Standardised rates) for cancer have continued to fall in the UK

(Table 7.10). In the UK, despite incidence rates increasing, mortality rates for colorectal cancer have decreased by around a fifth among males. From 29 per 100,000 in 1995 to 23 per 100,000 in 2008, and just over a quarter among females, 19 per 100,000 females to 14 per 100,000 respectively. The mortality rates for prostate cancer among males and for breast cancer among females have also fallen substantially, by around a quarter (23 per cent and 27 per cent respectively).

Between 1995 and 2008 mortality rates for lung cancer among males fell 32 per cent, from 76 per 100,000 males in 1995 to 52 per 100,000 in 2008. Among females the rate has increased slightly from 31 per 100,000 females to 33 per 100,000 over the same period.

In England in 2007, 8 out of the 17 most common cancers for males aged 15 to 99 had five-year age-standardised survival rates (see Appendix, Part 7: Age-standardised survival rates) of more than 50 per cent, compared with 8 out of the 18 common cancers among females. Among males in England in 2007, the highest five-year age-standardised survival rate was for testicular cancer at 96 per cent, and among females, melanoma (skin cancer) at 90 per cent (Figure 7.11).

Figure 7.11

Five-year relative survival for common cancers:[1] by sex

England

Percentages

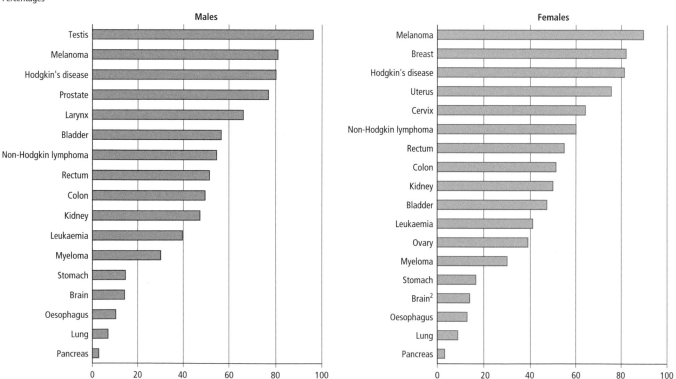

1 Patients aged 15 to 99 years diagnosed between 2001 and 2006, and followed up to 2007. See Appendix, Part 7: Age-standardised survival rates.
2 Not age-standardised.

Source: Office for National Statistics

Among both sexes in England in 2007, the lowest five-year survival rates were for pancreatic cancer, at around 3 per cent. Of the major cancers (see Figure 7.9), lung cancer has the lowest five-year survival rate among both sexes, 7 per cent of males and 9 per cent of females, compared with the survival rate for prostate cancer in males of 77 per cent, and that for breast cancer among females of 82 per cent. Similarly in Northern Ireland in 2006, five-year survival from the major cancers was lowest for lung cancer, 18 per cent, and among males highest for prostate cancer, 80 per cent, and for breast cancer among females, 85 per cent.

Improvements in screening services help identify incidences of cancer during its early stages and may mean it can be treated more effectively. Between 1998 and 2008 the take-up of breast cancer screening among women in the UK has remained at around 75 per cent of the target population (see Appendix, Part 7: Breast and Cervical cancer screening target population). In England, mortality rates from breast cancer have fallen 22 per cent from 69 per 100,000 of the target population in 1998 to 54 per 100,000 in 2007. During the same period cervical cancer screening in the UK has fallen slightly to around 78 per cent of the target population, ranging from 75 per cent in Northern Ireland to 79 per cent in England and Scotland in

2008/09. In England, between 1998 and 2007 the female mortality rate from cervical cancer has remained at around 3 deaths per 100,000.

Smoking, drinking and drugs

People who smoke are more at risk than non-smokers of contracting respiratory cancer (of the lung, larynx and pharynx), other respiratory diseases and emphysema. Over the last decade the proportion of adult regular smokers, defined as those who smoke at least one cigarette a week, has fallen in Great Britain. In 1998, almost one in three men (30 per cent) smoked on a regular basis as did around one in four women (26 per cent) (Table 7.12). By 2008 these proportions had fallen to 22 per cent and 21 per cent respectively.

Among regular smokers between 1974 and 2008, there was a substantial fall for both sexes in the proportion classed as heavy smokers (those smoking 20 or more cigarettes a day). In 1974 more than a quarter of men (26 per cent) and 13 per cent of women in Great Britain who smoked regularly were classed as heavy smokers. By 1998, these proportions had fallen to 11 per cent and 7 per cent respectively, and by 2008, these proportions had fallen further to 7 per cent and 5 per cent respectively.

Table 7.12

Adults'[1] cigarette smoking habits: by sex[2,3]

Great Britain   Percentages

	1998	2000	2001	2002	2003	2004	2005[4]	2006	2007	2008
Men										
Current cigarette smokers	30	29	28	27	28	26	25	23	22	22
Of which:										
Light to moderate smokers (less than 20 per day)	19	18	19	17	18	18	17	15	16	15
Heavy smokers (20 or more per day)	11	10	10	10	10	9	8	8	7	7
Ex-regular cigarette smokers	29	27	27	28	27	28	27	27	28	30
Never or only occasionally smoked cigarettes	42	44	45	46	45	46	47	50	50	49
Women										
Current cigarette smokers	26	25	26	25	24	23	23	21	20	21
Of which:										
Light to moderate smokers (less than 20 per day)	19	19	19	18	18	17	17	16	15	15
Heavy smokers (20 or more per day)	7	6	7	7	7	6	6	5	5	5
Ex-regular cigarette smokers	20	20	21	21	21	20	21	21	21	22
Never or only occasionally smoked cigarettes	53	54	53	54	55	57	57	58	59	58

1 Aged 16 and over.
2 From 1998 onwards data are weighted to compensate for nonresponse and to match known population distributions.
3 In 2008 the General Household Survey was renamed the General Lifestyle Survey. See Appendix, Part 2: General Household Survey.
4 Includes data from last quarter of 2004/05 due to survey change from financial year to calendar year.

Source: General Lifestyle Survey (Longitudinal), Office for National Statistics

The proportion of people who have never smoked, occasionally smoked, or have quit smoking has increased among both men and women over the last four decades. In 1974, around half (48 per cent) of men had never or occasionally smoked or had stopped smoking, by 1998 this had risen to 71 per cent and by 2008 this proportion had risen to more than three-quarters (79 per cent). In comparison, the proportion of females who were not regular smokers rose from three-fifths (60 per cent) in 1974 to 73 per cent in 1998, and then four-fifths (80 per cent) in 2008. In Great Britain in 2008/09, 71 per cent of regular smokers gave better health in general as the main reason for wanting to stop smoking, while 6 per cent wanted to stop as a result of the smoking ban in public places.

In 2008, among the constituent countries of Great Britain, the highest proportion of smokers was in Scotland, 23 per cent of men and 24 per cent of women. Wales had the lowest proportion of men smoking at 20 per cent, and England had the lowest proportion of women smoking at 20 per cent.

International organisations such as the World Health Organisation agree that alcohol can cause a wide range of diseases such as liver cancer and cirrhosis of the liver. Current guidelines from the Chief Medical Officer for England suggest that consuming three to four units of alcohol per day for men and two to three units for women should not lead to significant health risks (see Appendix, Part 7: Alcohol consumption for further information regarding units). Individuals identified at highest risk of alcohol-related harm are those who regularly drink at least twice the recommended daily limit.

In 2008, 16 per cent of men aged 16 and over in Great Britain drank up to double the recommended daily alcohol guideline at least once in the week prior to interview, as did a very similar proportion of women (15 per cent) (Table 7.13). However, a higher proportion of men than women drank more than double the recommended daily units at least once in the previous week, around one in five men (21 per cent) compared with around one in seven women (14 per cent). Two-thirds (63 per cent) of men and around three-quarters (71 per cent) of women drank within the recommended guidelines in the previous week.

The younger adult population are more likely to binge-drink, defined as consuming more than double the recommended daily limit. In 2008 in Great Britain, 30 per cent of men aged 16 to 24 drank more than eight units at least once in the previous week, four times higher than those aged 65 and over. Similarly for women, around a quarter (24 per cent) aged 16 to 24 drank more than double the recommended daily allowance at least once in the previous week, 12 times higher than those aged 65 and over. However, men and women aged 16 to 24 were also

Table 7.13

Adults' maximum alcohol consumption:[1,2] by sex and age, 2008[3]

Great Britain — Percentages

	16–24	25–44	45–64	65 and over	All aged 16 and over
Men					
4 units or less					
Drank nothing in the previous week	37	28	26	34	30
Up to 4 units	21	30	33	44	33
More than 4 units					
More than 4 units and up to 8 units	12	15	20	14	16
More than 8 units	30	27	21	7	21
Women					
3 units or less					
Drank nothing in the previous week	48	41	40	57	45
Up to 3 units	16	22	28	33	26
More than 3 units					
More than 3 units and up to 6 units	12	16	19	8	15
More than 6 units	24	20	13	2	14

1 Maximum drunk on any one day in the week prior to interview. In 2008 a wine glass size question was added and used to calculate the number of units of wine consumed.
2 Department of Health guidelines recommend men should not regularly drink more than 3 to 4 units of alcohol per day, and women should not drink more than 2 to 3 units of alcohol per day.
3 In 2008 the General Household Survey was renamed the General Lifestyle Survey. See Appendix, Part 2: General Household Survey.

Source: General Lifestyle Survey 2008 (Longitudinal), Office for National Statistics

more likely than those aged 25 to 64 to have drunk no alcohol at all in the week prior to interview.

Among the constituent countries of Great Britain in 2008, men aged 16 and over in Scotland were most likely not to have drunk any alcohol; more than a third (35 per cent), and around half (52 per cent) of women in Wales did not drink in the week prior to interview. Among men in Great Britain, those in England were most likely to binge-drink (22 per cent), whereas those in Wales were least likely (16 per cent). Among women in Great Britain, those in Wales were more likely to have drunk less than three units in the previous week (26 per cent), while those in England were more likely to binge-drink, 15 per cent, compared with 13 per cent in Scotland.

Figure 7.14

Alcohol-related deaths:[1] by age

United Kingdom
Thousands

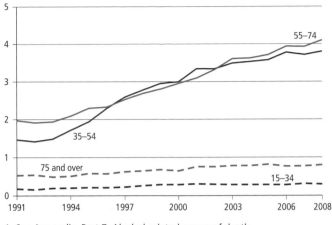

1 See Appendix, Part 7: Alcohol-related causes of death.
Source: Office for National Statistics

In 2008, there were 9,031 alcohol-related deaths in the UK, more than double the number in 1991, at 4,144. Alcohol-related deaths have increased in all age groups since 1991 (Figure 7.14). Those aged 15 to 34 years in the UK were less likely to die of an alcohol-related death than any other age group. In 2008, 328 alcohol-related deaths were recorded in this age group, just under half the number among those aged 75 and over (787).

Between 1991 and 2008 the greatest increases in alcohol-related deaths in the UK were among the 'middle-aged' population. Deaths among those aged 35 to 54 more than doubled from 1,466 in 1991 to 3,814 in 2008, while deaths among those aged 55 to 74 rose from 1,969 to 4,101 over the same period, an increase of 108 per cent and the highest number of deaths of all the age groups shown.

Alcohol-related death rates were highest among the 55 to 74 age group among both men and women, 45.8 per 100,000 men and 21.5 per 100,000 women respectively in 2008. This was just over 15 times higher than the rate among men aged 15 to 34, at 2.9 per 100,000, and more than 16 times higher than among women, at 1.3 per 100,000.

Alcohol-related deaths are consistently higher among men than women. In 2008, men accounted for 66.4 per cent of all alcohol-related deaths, an increase of over 5 percentage points from 1991. The number of alcohol-related deaths among men more than doubled in the UK between 1991 and 2008, a 137 per cent increase from 2,532 deaths to a peak of 5,999. In comparison, deaths among women increased by 88 per cent over the same period, from 1,612 to also peak in 2008 at 3,032.

Figure 7.15

Deaths related to drug misuse:[1] by sex

England & Wales
Thousands

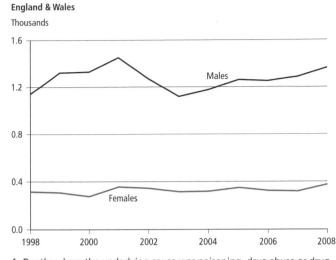

1 Deaths where the underlying cause was poisoning, drug abuse or drug dependence, and where any of the substances controlled under the *Misuse of Drugs Act 1971* were involved. See Appendix, Part 7: Death related to drug misuse.
Source: Office for National Statistics

Deaths related to drug misuse also increased over the last decade in England and Wales, though less rapidly than for alcohol-related deaths (Figure 7.15). Among males, figures peaked in 2001 at 1,450 deaths, before falling to 1,118 in 2003. Over the last five years, figures have steadily risen to reach 1,364 in 2008. Among females, figures have remained fairly stable over the same period, between 300 and 400 deaths, peaking in 2008 at 374 deaths. Between 1998 and 2008 the total number of deaths relating to drug misuse increased by 19 per cent, from 1,457 to 1,738. The percentage increase was the same for both males and females.

Deaths relating to drug misuse were consistently higher among males than females. On average, males accounted for four-fifths (80 per cent) of all drug-related deaths in England and Wales over the last decade. Similarly, in Northern Ireland deaths related to drug misuse between 1997 and 2007 were higher for males than females; a total of 201 deaths compared with 115 female deaths during the period. Among both males and females, those aged between 30 and 39 accounted for the largest proportion of deaths from drug misuse in 2008. There were 490 deaths of males in this age group, representing 36 per cent of all male deaths relating to drug misuse, and deaths among females in the same age group totalled 112, representing 30 per cent of all female deaths relating to drug misuse. In Northern Ireland, those aged 35 to 44 accounted for 19 of the 48 deaths relating to drug misuse in 2007.

In 2008, the main cause of death from drug poisoning in the UK was accidental poisoning, accounting for 36 per cent of all

7

deaths relating to drug misuse. In England and Wales heroin and morphine were the most common substances mentioned on a death certificate. In 2008 there were 897 mentions of heroin and morphine, just over five times higher than 1993 when there were 155 mentions.

Health-related behaviour

Health status is an important indicator of the overall well-being of the population. In the UK in 2007, 70 per cent of males and 66 per cent of females assessed themselves as having 'good health'. A further 21 per cent of males and 22 per cent of females considered themselves to be in 'fairly good health'. The younger population are more than twice as likely to report good health as the elderly population. Among males, on average, 86 per cent of those aged between 16 and 24 reported good health compared with 34 per cent of those aged 75 and over, while the proportions of females in these age groups reporting good health were 78 per cent and 32 per cent respectively.

The population aged 65 and over are generally the most likely age group to suffer from a limiting chronic illness in Great Britain (Table 7.16). Arthritis and rheumatism are the most

commonly reported chronic sickness in 2008 among both men and women aged 45 and over, while among those aged between 16 and 44 years asthma was the most prevalent. Among men, those aged 75 and over were almost 11 times more likely to suffer from arthritis and rheumatism than those aged 16 to 44 years, 118 per 1,000 men and 11 per 1,000 respectively in 2008. Among women, the prevalence rates for arthritis and rheumatism for those aged 75 and over were almost 16 times higher than for those aged 16 to 44, at 236 per 1,000 women and 15 per 1,000 respectively.

For those aged 45 and over in Great Britain in 2008, musculoskeletal conditions were more common among both men and women than heart and circulatory, and respiratory conditions. Respiratory conditions were the leading cause of chronic sickness among those aged between 16 and 44, with asthma affecting 29 per 1,000 men and 47 per 1,000 women.

Obesity is associated with a number of serious chronic conditions such as Type 2 diabetes, hypertension and hyperlipidaemia (high levels of fat in the blood that can lead to narrowing and blockage of blood vessels), which are all major risk factors for cardiovascular disease. Obesity can reduce

Table 7.16

Self-reported longstanding illness: by sex and age,[1,2] 2008

Great Britain

Rates per 1,000 population

	Men				Women			
	16–44	45–64	65–74	75 and over	16–44	45–64	65–74	75 and over
Musculoskeletal								
Arthritis and rheumatism	11	64	114	118	15	97	193	236
Back problems	21	47	33	31	18	41	31	36
Other bone and joint problems	13	37	46	87	12	41	67	117
Heart and circulatory								
Heart attack	*	22	54	58	*	8	26	45
Stroke	1	6	24	33	*	6	16	27
Other heart complaints	4	50	110	117	5	23	59	111
Other blood vessel/embolic disorders	*	9	20	29	1	5	7	18
Respiratory								
Asthma	29	30	30	41	47	45	52	44
Bronchitis and emphysema	0	4	26	33	*	6	16	16
Hay fever	5	3	*	0	3	*	*	0
Other respiratory complaints	3	17	24	34	3	6	13	27

1 Population aged 16 and over reporting a longstanding illness or disability that limited their activities.
2 In 2008 the General Household Survey was renamed the General Lifestyle Survey. See Appendix, Part 2: General Household Survey.

Source: General Lifestyle Survey 2008 (Longitudinal), Office for National Statistics

Table 7.17

Adults'[1] body mass index (BMI): by weight classification[2]

England

Percentages

	1994	1996	1998	2000	2002	2004	2006	2007	2008
Underweight (BMI less than 18.5)	1.7	1.7	1.7	1.5	1.7	1.6	1.6	1.6	1.8
Normal (18.5 to less than 25)	45.2	42.2	40.6	38.6	37.7	36.7	36.8	37.7	36.8
Overweight (25 to less than 30)	37.4	38.7	38.3	38.8	38.1	38.8	37.6	36.7	36.9
Obese[3] (30 and over)	15.7	17.5	19.4	21.2	22.5	22.9	23.9	24.0	24.5
Morbidly obese (40 and over)	1.0	0.9	1.3	1.5	1.8	1.7	2.1	1.8	2.0

1 People aged 16 and over.
2 See Appendix, Part 7: Body mass index.
3 Includes morbidly obese.

Source: Health Survey for England, The NHS Information Centre for health and social care

overall quality of life, create a strain on health services and in some cases lead to premature death.

In England in 2008, more than one in three adults (36.9 per cent) aged 16 or over had a body mass index (BMI) considered overweight; a slight decrease from the proportion in 1994 (37.4 per cent) (Table 7.17). However, the proportion of the population classed as obese according to their BMI rose by almost 10 percentage points over the same period, from 15.7 per cent in 1994 to 24.5 per cent in 2008. In comparison, in Scotland more than one in four adults (26.8 per cent) in 2008 were classed as obese, compared with more than one in five adults in Wales (21.0 per cent).

In England, the proportion of adults considered morbidly obese has doubled over the last 15 years, from 1 per cent of the adult population aged 16 and over in 1994 to 2 per cent in 2008. The proportion of the adult population considered underweight has remained relatively unchanged over the same period, at less than 2 per cent.

Among adults in England in 2008, more than three-quarters (77.1 per cent) of those aged between 65 and 74 were obese or overweight, compared with around a third (33.5 per cent) of those aged between 16 and 24. In both Wales and Scotland in 2008, being overweight or obese was most common among adults aged 55 to 64, (68.0 per cent and 78.9 per cent respectively). Those aged 16 to 24 were least likely to be classified as overweight or obese, 30.0 per cent and 38.0 per cent respectively.

In England, the proportion of children aged under 16 classed as overweight or obese has risen from 25 per cent in 1995 to 30 per cent in 2008. In both Wales and Scotland in 2008, the proportions of overweight or obese children aged between 2 and 15 were very similar to those in England, at 33 per cent

and 32 per cent respectively. Overweight and obesity were slightly more prevalent among boys than girls, 34 per cent and 31 per cent respectively in Wales, and 36 per cent and 27 per cent respectively in Scotland.

Diet has an important influence on obesity and thus on health. A poor diet can result in a higher risk of disease. A diet low in fruit and vegetables can result in chronic conditions such as cardiovascular disease, stroke and diabetes, while a diet high in saturated fat can result in raised blood cholesterol and coronary heart disease. Since 2005 the Government's food and health action plan has set out a strategy recommending at least five portions of fruit and vegetables per day, and reducing the average fat intake to 35 per cent of food energy.

Since 1954 there has been an upward trend in the consumption of fruit and vegetables (Figure 7.18 overleaf). Great Britain was affected by war-time rationing which officially ended when rationing of meat and bacon ended in 1954. In Great Britain in 1954, on average, 594 grams of fruit were consumed per person per week. By 2008 consumption of fruit in the UK had doubled to 1,199 grams per person per week.

Of the selected foods, between 1954 and 1997 vegetables and potatoes were the main constituent in the diet of UK households. In 1954, 1,761 grams of potatoes and 894 grams of vegetables were consumed per person per week. By 2008 less than half the amount of potatoes (776 grams) was consumed, although vegetable consumption had risen to 1,118 grams. The consumption of sugars and preserves has fallen substantially to 127 grams per person per week in 2008, more than four times lower than its peak of 625 grams in 1958.

Among the constituent countries of the UK between 2006 and 2008, households in England consumed the greatest quantity

Figure 7.18

Food consumption: by selected foods

United Kingdom[1]

Grams per person per week

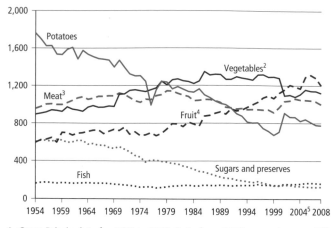

1 Great Britain data for 1954 to 1973. Data from 1974 onwards covers UK.
2 Includes consumption of fresh and processed vegetables, but excludes potatoes.
3 Includes consumption of carcass meat, non-carcass meat and other meat products.
4 Includes consumption of fresh and processed fruit.
5 Between 2001–02 and 2005–06 data are for financial year.

Source: Department for Environment, Food and Rural Affairs

of 'healthy' foods per person per week, such as fruit (1,277 grams) and fish (169 grams), while consuming the least amount of soft drinks (1,670 ml), and confectionary (125 grams). Households in Wales consumed the most vegetables (1,197 grams), but also consumed the most cheese (119 grams) and alcoholic drinks (814 ml). Households in Northern Ireland consumed less fruit (1,095 grams), vegetables (885 grams), and fish (116 grams) per person per week than the rest of the UK. The diets of Scottish households contained more saturated fat than in the rest of the UK, accounting for 14.9 per cent of the daily energy intake, although along with England, consumed the lowest amount of cholesterol, 269 milligrams per person per day.

Mental health

Common mental disorders (CMDs) are the most widespread of the mental health conditions, with stress-related disorders estimated to result in over 40 million working days lost each year in the UK. CMDs can result in physical impairment and problems with social functioning, and are a significant source of distress to individuals and those around them. They include different types of depression and anxiety and cause emotional distress and interfere with daily function (see Appendix, Part 7: Common mental disorders).

In England in 2007, around one in six adults (16 per cent) had suffered from a CMD in the week prior to interview

Figure 7.19

Prevalence of common mental disorders:[1] by sex, 2007

England

Percentages

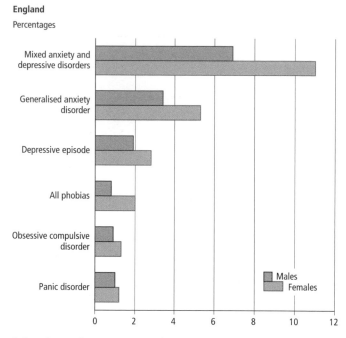

1 Prevalence of a common mental disorder in the week prior to interview. See Appendix, Part 7: Common mental disorders.

Source: Adult Psychiatric Morbidity Survey, The NHS Information Centre for health and social care

(Figure 7.19). The most common mental disorder among both men and women was mixed anxiety and depressive disorders, with 7 per cent of men and 11 per cent of women affected. Prevalence of all types of CMD was higher among women than men, with around one in five women (19.7 per cent) affected compared with around one in eight men (12.5 per cent).

In England, the prevalence of CMD in 2007 was highest overall among adults aged 45 to 54, with around one in five (19.9 per cent) suffering with a disorder in the week prior to interview. This was twice as high as the rate for those aged 75 and over, among whom one in ten (9.9 per cent) were sufferers. Among men, CMDs were more prevalent in those aged 35 to 44, with around one in seven (15 per cent) living with a CMD, while among women prevalence was highest among those aged 45 to 54, with one in four (25.2 per cent) living with a CMD.

In 2007, antidepressant prescriptions dispensed in the community (see Appendix, Part 7: Prescription Cost Analysis System) peaked at 33.8 million items in England, nearly four times higher than in 1991 when there were 9 million items dispensed. However, around three-quarters (76 per cent) of adults with a CMD were not on medication despite having a level of neurotic symptoms sufficient to warrant treatment. In

Figure 7.20

Suicide rates:[1] by sex and age

United Kingdom
Rates per 100,000 population

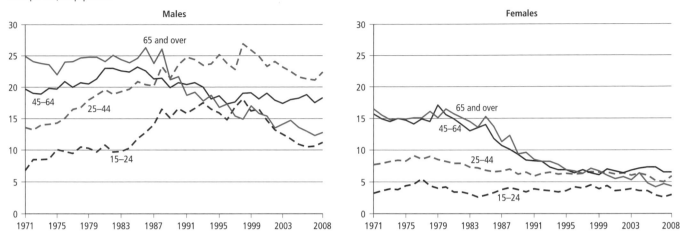

1 Deaths given an underlying cause of intentional self-harm or injury/poisoning of undetermined intent. See Appendix, Part 7: International Classification of Diseases. Rates have been age-standardised using the European standard population. See Appendix, Part 7: Standardised rates, and European standard population.

Source: Office for National Statistics; General Register Office for Scotland; Northern Ireland Statistics and Research Agency

2007 the Government began a programme of increasing access to psychological therapies and it is hoped that increases in the availability of brief, evidence-based talking therapies will help alleviate the distress associated with CMDs. Just one in ten people (10 per cent) with any type of CMD in England sought counselling in 2007, of which 5 per cent received both medication and counselling.

Mental health problems can ultimately lead people to commit suicide. Trends in suicide rates have varied among age groups and between the sexes in the UK since 1971 (Figure 7.20). The largest fall in suicide rates between 1971 and 2008 was among the elderly population. For males aged 65 and over the rate fell by 50 per cent from 24.9 per 100,000 males in 1971 to 12.6 per 100,000 in 2008. For females aged 65 and over, the rate fell more rapidly from 16.5 per 100,000 females in 1971 to 4.3 per 100,000 in 2008, a fall of 74 per cent.

Among females, suicide rates have fallen for most age groups since 1971. Between 1971 and 1996, suicide rates were generally higher among those aged 65 and over, but since then the suicide rate has been higher among those aged 45 to 64. Since 1979 the suicide rate has fallen considerably among both age groups; the rate among the latter age group was 6.6 per 100,000 females in 2008 compared to 4.3 per 100,000 for those aged 65 and over, nearly four times lower than its peak in 1980 of 16.5 per 100,000. The lowest suicide rate was among the youngest age group, those aged 15 to 24, where the rate has

remained relatively stable between 3 and 4 suicides per 100,000 females between 1971 and 2008.

Suicide rates for males were higher in all age groups compared with females between 1971 and 2008. Suicide rates among males aged 15 to 24 and those aged 25 to 44 both increased by around 64 per cent and were around four times higher than for females in these age groups. In 2008, the suicide rate for males aged 15 to 24 was 11.1 per 100,000 males, compared with 3.0 per 100,000 females, while the rate for those aged 25 to 44 was 22.3 per 100,000 males and 5.9 per 100,000 females.

Sexual health

The Government's National Strategy for Sexual Health and HIV aims to reduce the spread of sexually transmitted infections (STIs) through more rapid detection and treatment. Sexual health promotion carried out by the Health Protection Agency seeks to reduce levels of high risk sexual behaviour and new cases of HIV and STIs.

Trends in contraceptive use in Great Britain show that three-quarters (75 per cent) of women aged between 16 and 49 used at least one method of contraception in 2008/09 (Table 7.21 overleaf). Between 2000/01 and 2007/08, the most common form of contraceptive was the pill, whose use rose slightly from 25 per cent to 28 per cent of women over the period. However, the use of the male condom increased by 4 percentage points between 2000/01 and 2008/09 so that

Table 7.21

Current use of contraception:[1,2] by type

Great Britain

Percentages[3]

	2000/01	2001/02	2002/03	2003/04	2004/05	2005/06	2006/07	2007/08	2008/09
Non-surgical									
Pill	25	28	25	25	25	24	27	28	25
Male condom	21	21	20	23	22	21	22	24	25
Withdrawl	3	4	3	3	4	4	3	4	4
Intrauterine device (IUD)	5	3	5	4	4	5	4	4	6
Injection	3	3	3	3	4	3	3	3	3
Cap/diaphragm	1	1	1	1	1	1	1	0	0
Other	3	4	3	3	4	4	7	7	8
Surgical									
Sterilised	11	10	11	11	10	10	9	7	6
Partner sterilised	11	12	12	12	12	11	11	10	11
Total using at least one method	**73**	**75**	**74**	**75**	**75**	**74**	**76**	**74**	**75**
Total not using a method	**27**	**25**	**26**	**25**	**25**	**26**	**24**	**26**	**25**

1 Women aged 16 to 49 currently using contraceptives in a sexual relationship.
2 Data for 2000/01 to 2006/07 are weighted for unequal chance of selection. From 2007/08 data are also weighted to population totals.
3 Percentages do not sum to 100 per cent as respondents could give more than one answer.

Source: Contraception and Sexual Health, Office for National Statistics

in 2008/09, the pill and the male condom were equally the most common methods of contraception among women aged 16 to 49, both being used by 25 per cent of women.

The use of surgical procedures as a contraceptive peaked between 2002/03 and 2003/04, when around 23 per cent of women or their partners were sterilised. Since then, surgical sterilisation has fallen to 17 per cent in 2008/09. Between 2000/01 and 2008/09 the most common reason for women not using any form of contraception (13 per cent) was because they were not in a heterosexual relationship, while 2 per cent not using a form of contraception said they were trying to get pregnant. Women aged between 16 and 19 were least likely to use a contraceptive, 43 per cent did not use at least one method in 2008/09. Among men aged 16 to 69 in Great Britain, 17 per cent said that they used a condom sometimes, while 43 per cent always used one.

For women in Great Britain, condom use is more prevalent among those aged 16 to 24, 70 per cent had used condoms in 2008/09. Men aged 16 to 24 were more likely than any other age group to have used condoms, with 88 per cent having done so in 2008/09.

Unprotected sex raises the risk of contracting STIs, such as HIV, chlamydia and gonorrhoea. As with other infectious diseases, strategies for the prevention and control of STIs are based on reducing the duration of infection through early testing and

treatment, and reducing transmission of infection through regular condom use.

The number of new STI episodes seen at genitourinary (GUM) clinics has risen over the last decade (Figure 7.22). Between

Figure 7.22

New diagnoses of selected sexually transmitted infections[1]

United Kingdom

Number

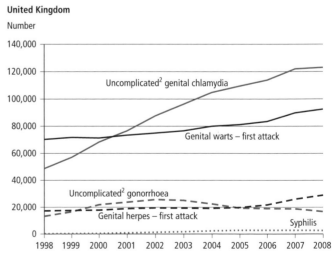

1 Cases of sexually transmitted infections seen at genito-urinary medical clinics.
2 An infection is considered 'uncomplicated' when the infection has not ascended to the upper genital tract.

Source: Health Protection Agency

2001 and 2008 genital chlamydia was the most prevalent STI seen at GUM clinics in the UK with over 123,000 new cases seen in 2008. Although prevalence of syphilis was the lowest of all STIs shown throughout the previous decade, new episodes were more than 18 times higher in 2008 than in 1998, having increased from 139 to 2,524 cases.

Between 1998 and 2000, genital warts were the most common reason for new STI episodes seen at GUM clinics with, on average, around 71,000 cases per year. Although the number of new cases has risen steadily over the last decade, it has risen at a slower rate compared with chlamydia (32 per cent compared with 152 per cent).

In the UK in 2008, males accounted for 89 per cent of new episodes of syphilis, just over two-thirds (67 per cent) of gonorrhoea, and more than half (53 per cent) of genital wart cases. New episodes of herpes were more common among females, accounting for more than 61 per cent of new episodes.

Despite recent increases in STIs, there have been significant decreases in infections since 1949 in the UK. Cases of syphilis fell, from 16,000 in 1949 to around 200 cases in 1999. Although by 2008 they had risen to around 2,500 cases, this was still more than six times lower than the 1949 level. Cases of gonorrhoea more than doubled from 29,000 in 1949 to 61,000 in 1979, falling to less than 17,000 in 2008, almost half the number of cases in 1949.

Unprotected sexual intercourse is the predominant transmission mode of both HIV and other STIs. In 2008 the rate of new HIV diagnoses in the UK was 109.2 per million population, almost double the rate in 1985 of 66.5 per million. There has been a fall over the last five years, from a peak of 148.0 new diagnoses per million in 2004. Within the UK in 2008, diagnoses were highest in England, at 120.1 per million population, almost three times higher than in Wales, at 44.4 per million. For comparison, rates in Scotland were 58.0 per million population and Northern Ireland 51.8 per million.

7

7

Chapter 8

Social protection

- Social security benefit expenditure in the UK in 2008/09 was £152 billion, an increase of 5 per cent (in real terms) since 2007/08, and over the longer term an increase of 122 per cent since 1978/79. (Figure 8.1)

- UK expenditure on social protection in 2006, excluding tax credits, was equivalent to 26.4 per cent of gross domestic product, the ninth highest of all EU member states. (Figure 8.5)

- In 2007/08, 31 per cent of all pensioners in the UK had no pension provision other than state retirement pension and minimum income guarantee or pension credit. (Table 8.14)

- In 2008, nearly six in ten (59 per cent) adults aged 18 and over in Great Britain agreed that the Government should be mainly responsible for ensuring that people have enough to live on in retirement. (Table 8.17)

- Lone parents were more likely than couples in Great Britain in 2007 to make use of most types of informal child care, except for grandparents, who were used by a third (33 per cent) of both couples and lone parents. (Table 8.20)

- At March 2008 there were just over 36,000 children on the 'at risk' register in the UK, an increase of 4 per cent since March 2007 and an increase of 10 per cent since 2003. (Table 8.21)

DATA

Download data by clicking the online pdf

www.statistics.gov.uk/ socialtrends

Social protection encompasses the assistance provided to those in need or at risk of hardship, through the provision of financial assistance and services. It is provided by central government, local authorities, private bodies such as voluntary organisations (the 'third sector') and individuals. It provides a safety net to protect the vulnerable in society who are unable to make provision for themselves for a minimum decent standard of living, such as those with caring requirements, low income and age-related problems. Social protection policies aim to reduce poverty and wealth gaps through the national minimum wage, means-tested benefits, payments such as working tax credits to low earners and assistance with child care. Assistance is provided through direct cash payments such as social security benefits or pensions, payments in kind such as free prescriptions, and the provision of services such as local authority home care help. Unpaid care, often provided by family and neighbours, also plays an important part.

Expenditure

The Department for Work and Pensions (DWP) in Great Britain and the Department for Social Development in Northern Ireland are responsible for the administration and payment of all social security benefits, except for child benefit and tax credits which are the responsibility of HM Revenue and Customs (HMRC). Social security benefits include payments relating to unemployment, disability allowances, state retirement pension and pension credit. Allowing for inflation, social security benefit expenditure in the UK increased by 122 per cent from £69 billion in 1978/79 to £152 billion in 2008/09 (Figure 8.1). Spending on specific benefits is influenced by a range of factors. Expenditure on various elements of unemployment is affected by the economic cycle while expenditure on the elderly, primarily pensions, is affected by demographic changes. Government priorities also have an impact as its policies attempt to address other issues affecting society. Apart from year-on-year falls in social security benefit expenditure between 1987/88 and 1989/90 and a small year-on-year fall between 1996/97 and 1997/98, expenditure has risen steadily each year. Between 1990/91 and 1993/94 there was a rapid increase in spending on social security benefits, from £95 billion to £123 billion, reflecting increases in the number of people who were unemployed or economically inactive during the economic recession in the early 1990s (see Glossary in Chapter 4: Labour market, page 58). Expenditure continued to rise at a steady pace by around £2 billion per year, except between 2000/01 and 2001/02 when it rose by £5.5 billion. This was because it was the first full year of working family tax credits, which were introduced in October 1999.

Figure 8.1

Social security benefit expenditure[1] in real terms[2]

United Kingdom

£ billion at 2008/09 prices

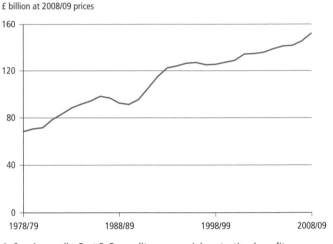

1 See Appendix, Part 8: Expenditure on social protection benefits.
2 Adjusted to 2008/09 prices using the GDP market prices deflator (Q2 2009).

Source: Department for Work and Pensions; HM Revenue and Customs; Veterans Agency; Department for Social Development, Northern Ireland

Of the £152 billion UK benefit expenditure in 2008/09, £136 billion was managed by the DWP in Great Britain. Most of this, £81.7 billion (60 per cent of the Great Britain total), was paid to people of state pension age (age 65 and over for men and 60 and over for women) though this total excludes £1 billion of war pensions payments made by the Veterans Agency to ex-services personnel and their dependents throughout the UK. Expenditure directed at people of working age accounted for £34 billion (25 per cent). A further £2.6 billion (2 per cent) was for the benefit of children, although was payable to adults with responsibility for children. These payments include elements of income support, disability allowances, housing benefit and council tax benefit paid because of the presence of children in the family, but exclude child benefit payments which are the responsibility of HMRC. Expenditure on those with disabilities is not related to age and is therefore spread across people of state pension age, of working age and children, and totalled £17.5 billion (13 per cent).

Child benefit payments, administered by HMRC, totalled £11.3 billion in the UK in 2008/09. HMRC has also provided financial assistance since 1999/2000 in the form of tax credits. Child tax credit is available to families with children on low or moderate incomes, whereas working tax credit is available to adults who are in work but on low or moderate incomes and can be claimed in addition to child tax credit. In the 10 years since their introduction, expenditure on tax credits has risen from £1.1 billion in 1999/2000 to £24 billion in 2008/09 when they were being paid to around 5.7 million families in the UK.

8

In Northern Ireland, the Department for Social Development administers benefits and in 2008/09 spent nearly £4.5 billion on welfare benefits and payments. Of this total, £482 million (11 per cent) was spent on housing benefits and assistance with domestic rates. Around half (49 per cent) of the remaining £3.9 billion was directed at those over state pension age, 26 per cent to those of working age and 25 per cent was directed at those with disabilities and carers.

The British Social Attitudes Survey includes questions on attitudes towards various aspects of welfare expenditure. In 2008, adults aged 18 and over in Great Britain were asked to give their opinion on whether the Government should spend more or less on benefits for people in a range of circumstances. The general pattern of people's views in 2008 was very similar to those reported in 1998, but there were some shifts in attitudes to government spending on particular types of benefit. In 1998, over a third (36 per cent) of adults felt that government spending on benefits paid to the unemployed should be less or much less, while in 2008 this had risen to over half (56 per cent) of adults (Table 8.2). Conversely, in 1998, 22 per cent felt that spending on benefits paid to the unemployed should be much more or more, while in 2008 the proportion of people with that opinion had dropped by 7 percentage points to 15 per cent. Nearly three-quarters (74 per cent) of adults felt that spending on benefits for the disabled who could not work should be much more or more in 1998 but in 2008 this had fallen 11 percentage points to 63 per cent. In 1998, around a quarter (24 per cent) thought that spending on benefits for the disabled who cannot work should remain at the same level, this had increased to a third

(33 per cent) in 2008. There were also slight increases between 1998 and 2008 in the proportion of adults who felt that government spending on benefits for single parents and carers of the sick and disabled should be much more or more.

As well as provision of benefits that provide people with additional income, government also provides services to those in need. In 2007/08, local authorities in England and Wales spent £22 billion on personal social services, more than double the £10.5 billion spent in 1997/98, although these figures have not been adjusted to remove the effect of inflation over this period. Personal social services includes provision of home help and home care, services for looked after children and children on child protection registers, and foster care provided by local authorities. Nearly £9.3 billion was spent on older people aged 65 and over (Figure 8.3 overleaf). This was the largest category of expenditure in 2007/08, at 42 per cent, although this proportion had fallen from 49 per cent in 1997/98. Spending on older people also recorded the largest rise in expenditure over the period, increasing by £4.1 billion. Spending on children and families increased from £2.4 billion in 1997/98, accounting for 22 per cent of total expenditure, to £5.8 billion or 26 per cent of total expenditure in 2007/08. Spending on adults aged under 65 with learning difficulties, physical disabilities, or mental health needs totalled £6.5 billion (29 per cent of expenditure), up from £2.7 billion (26 per cent of expenditure) in 1997/98. The main reason underlying this increase was higher expenditure on adults with learning difficulties.

Eurostat collects social protection expenditure information across the 27 member states of the European Union (EU-27) as

Table 8.2

Attitudes to government spending on social security benefits[1]

Great Britain   Percentages

	Much more		More		Same as now		Less		Much less	
	1998	2008	1998	2008	1998	2008	1998	2008	1998	2008
Benefits for unemployed	4	2	19	12	41	30	31	46	5	10
Benefits for disabled who cannot work	13	9	61	53	24	33	2	4	-	-
Benefits for parents who work on very low incomes	8	9	63	61	27	27	3	4	-	-
Benefits for single parents	5	5	30	33	43	44	18	15	4	2
Benefits for retired	17	15	56	58	25	24	2	2	-	-
Benefits for carers for those who are sick or disabled	18	22	65	63	16	14	1	1	-	-

1 Respondents aged 18 and over were asked 'Some people think that there should be more government spending on social security, while other people disagree. For each of the groups I read out please say whether you would like to see more or less government spending on them than now. Bear in mind that if you want more spending, this would probably mean that you would have to pay more taxes. If you want less spending, this would probably mean paying less taxes.' Excludes those who responded 'don't know' or did not answer.

Source: British Social Attitudes Survey, National Centre for Social Research

Figure 8.3

Local authority personal social services expenditure:[1] by recipient group

England & Wales

£ billion

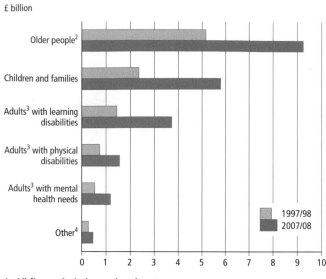

1 All figures include overhead costs.
2 Aged 65 and over, includes people of this age group with learning disabilities, physical disabilities and mental health needs.
3 Adults aged under 65.
4 Includes other expenditure on adults aged under 65 and expenditure on service strategy.

Source: The NHS Information Centre for health and social care; Welsh Assembly Government

part of the European System of Integrated Social Protection Statistics (ESSPROS). ESSPROS defines social protection as encompassing all interventions from public or private bodies intended to relieve households and individuals of the burden of a defined set of risks or needs.

In 2007/08, total UK expenditure on social protection as defined by ESSPROS was estimated at £347 billion. This was equivalent to around £5,783 per person. However, social protection is not spread evenly over the whole population. The largest expenditure was on benefits for old age and 'survivors', defined as the surviving partners and dependent children of a deceased person, accounting for 45 per cent (£156 billion) of the UK total (Figure 8.4). Expenditure on sickness, health care and disability accounted for 40 per cent (£140 billion), while expenditure on services and benefits specifically for families and children accounted for 6 per cent (£21 billion). In real terms (after allowing for inflation) there was a 19 per cent rise in total social protection expenditure between 1990/91 and 2007/08. Expenditure on sickness, health care and disability increased by 33 per cent over the period and spending on benefits for old age and survivors increased by 26 per cent, which may reflect the fact that the UK has an ageing population. Over the same period, expenditure on housing increased by 15 per cent to £20 billion while expenditure on families and children

Figure 8.4

Expenditure on social protection benefits[1] in real terms:[2] by function

United Kingdom

£ billion at 2007/08 prices

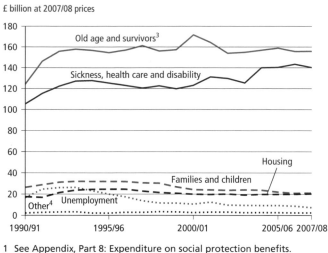

1 See Appendix, Part 8: Expenditure on social protection benefits.
2 Adjusted to 2007/08 prices using the GDP market prices deflator.
3 Survivors are those whose entitlement derives from their relationship to a deceased person (for example, widows, widowers and orphans).
4 Includes expenditure on legal aid and local authority social services.

Source: Office for National Statistics

decreased by 20 per cent to £21 billion. Expenditure on unemployment rose sharply in 1991/92 then, with the exception of a £1.9 billion rise in 2001/02, fell steadily to reach £7 billion in 2007/08. These figures do not include expenditure on tax credits, which increased from £1 billion in 1999/2000 to £20 billion in 2007/08. While these credits can be claimed by people in all categories shown in Figure 8.4, those in the families and children category would be the largest beneficiaries.

In 2006, UK spending on social protection, excluding tax credits, was equivalent to 26.4 per cent of gross domestic product (GDP), slightly below the EU-27 average of 26.9 per cent (Figure 8.5). However, when expressed in terms of expenditure per head and in purchasing power standard (PPS), UK expenditure was 7,410 PPS (see Appendix, Part 5: Purchasing power parities), higher than the EU-27 average of 6,349 PPS per head. As a percentage of GDP, expenditure on social protection was highest in France, at 31.1 per cent, followed by Sweden (30.7 per cent) and Belgium (30.1 per cent). Of all the EU-27 countries, Latvia recorded the lowest expenditure on social protection as a percentage of GDP, at 12.2 per cent, followed by Estonia and Lithuania (12.4 per cent and 13.2 per cent respectively). Of the EU-15 countries Ireland spent the least at 18.2 per cent, less than a number of the recent accession countries such as Slovenia (22.8 per cent), Hungary (22.3 per cent), Poland (19.2 per cent), the Czech Republic (18.7 per cent) and Cyprus (18.4 per cent).

8

Figure 8.5

Expenditure[1] on social protection as a percentage of gross domestic product: EU comparison, 2006

Percentages

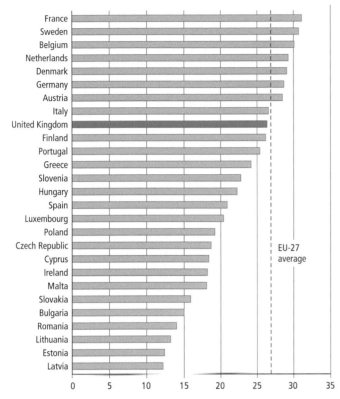

1   Social protection expenditure and receipts are calculated in line with the methodology of the 'European System of Social Protection Statistics' (ESSPROS) manual. Expenditure includes social benefits, administrative costs and other expenditure linked to social protection schemes.

Source: Eurostat

Carers and caring

Since the early 1990s government policy has been to provide help and assistance, through local authorities and councils, to people who need care to continue to live in their own homes as independently as possible. This can include financial help or the provision of services to those who qualify. Such services may involve routine household tasks within or outside the home, personal care of the client, or respite care to support the client's regular carers.

As well as council-run care homes, councils and local authorities provide home care services to those with physical disabilities (including frailty associated with ageing), dementia, mental health problems and learning difficulties to allow them to continue living in their own homes. In 2008, an average of 35 hours per week of home care was provided by councils in England to households in receipt of care, an increase of 69 per cent from 2000 (Figure 8.6). The increase in provision occurred in both sectors between 2000 and 2008. Independent (non-local authority) and council provision each

Figure 8.6

Average number of contact hours of home care per household per week: by sector[1,2]

England

Hours

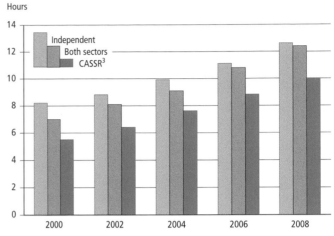

1   Excludes all households where home care was not provided.
2   Excludes households receiving home care purchased with a direct payment.
3   Councils with adult social services responsibilities.

Source: The NHS Information Centre for health and social care

increased by around four and a half hours. Where both sectors were involved, provision increased by nearly five and a half hours. Although independent care remains the largest source of provision its share dropped from 40 per cent in 2000 to 36 per cent in 2008, council provision increased from 27 per cent to 29 per cent and care provision from both sectors increased from 34 per cent to 35 per cent.

Informal carers are adults or children who provide any regular service or help to someone who is sick, disabled or elderly, but not in a paid capacity. The most common type of informal carer in the UK in 2007/08 was providing care to someone living outside their own household (61 per cent). Family members were the main recipients of informal care from both household and non-household members. There was little difference between men and women in the pattern of relationships between the carer and the person being cared for. The largest group cared for by both men and women were parents who were non-household members (34 per cent and 39 per cent respectively) (Figure 8.7 overleaf). Within the household, partners, spouses or cohabitees were the most common recipients of care from both men (23 per cent) and women (16 per cent). Around 7 per cent of male carers and 10 per cent of female carers provided care to non-family members, whether within their own household or not.

Many carers balance their caring responsibilities with paid work. Those in full-time employment made up the largest group (31 per cent) of carers in the UK in 2007/08, regardless

8

Figure 8.7

Informal carers: by sex and relationship to person being cared for, 2007/08

United Kingdom

Percentages

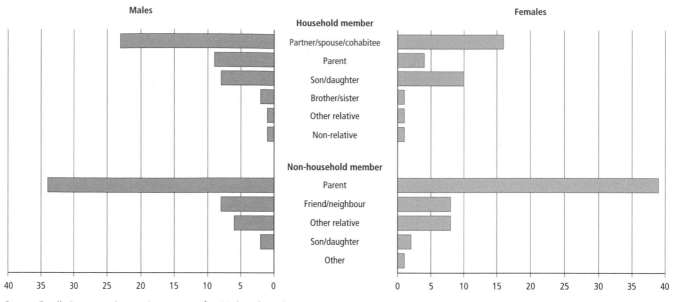

Source: Family Resources Survey, Department for Work and Pensions

of whether they were providing care within or outside their household. The next largest group was those in retirement (23 per cent), followed by those who were economically inactive (17 per cent) or part-time employees (15 per cent). The proportion of male carers in full-time employment was much higher than the proportion of female carers (42 per cent compared with 24 per cent) but the reverse was true for those

Figure 8.8

Carer's allowance: cases in payment[1,2]

United Kingdom

Thousands

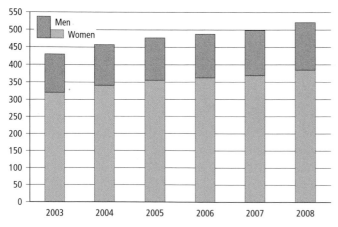

1 At August each year. Includes all in receipt of carer's allowance.
2 Excludes cases where payment has been suspended.

Source: Department for Work and Pensions; Department for Social Development, Northern Ireland

in part-time employment (5 per cent of men and 20 per cent of women). However, there was little difference for those in retirement (24 per cent and 22 per cent respectively).

People providing informal care, depending on their own circumstances and those of the person(s) they care for, may be eligible for benefits in recognition of the assistance they provide. Only those aged 16 and over and spending at least 35 hours per week or more caring for someone who is in receipt of either the highest or middle rate of disability living allowance care component, or some form of attendance allowance, are eligible. In the UK in 2008 there were 521,000 people in receipt of carer's allowance (Figure 8.8), an increase of around 22,000 from 2007, and around 91,000 since 2003. While the numbers have increased each year, men and women, as proportions of the total receiving carer's allowance have remained stable at around 26 per cent and 74 per cent respectively.

Sick and disabled people

Sick and disabled people, depending upon the nature and severity of their condition, are entitled to a number of financial benefits. Incapacity benefit (IB) and severe disablement allowance (SDA) are benefits principally for people of working age, who are unable to work because of illness and/or disability, although a small number of beneficiaries are of over state pension age. These benefits can be claimed in addition to other benefits. In 2008/09 there were just under 2.7 million working age recipients of IB and other benefits in the UK

Table 8.9

Recipients of selected benefits for sick and disabled people[1]

United Kingdom															Thousands

	2005/06	2006/07	2007/08	2008/09
Working-age recipients of incapacity and other benefits[2,3,4]	2,787	2,742	2,696	2,679
Incapacity benefit only	794	753	718	597
Incapacity benefit and disability living allowance	550	553	558	552
Incapacity benefit and income support/pension credit	626	615	601	527
Incapacity benefit, income support/pension credit and disability living allowance	484	499	517	536
Severe disability allowance (including other benefits)	255	241	229	218
Employment and support allowance only[3,4]	.	.	.	151
Employment and support allowance and disability living allowance[3,4]	.	.	.	22
Income support/pension credit only	825	829	809	815
Attendance allowance/disability living allowance[5,6]	4,479	4,601	4,723	4,860
Attendance allowance	1,524	1,567	1,603	1,638
Disability living allowance	2,955	3,033	3,120	3,222

1 See Appendix, Part 8: Expenditure on social protection benefits. At February each year.
2 Includes other benefit combinations not listed here.
3 From 27 October 2008 employment and support allowance (ESA) replaced incapacity benefit and income support paid on the grounds of incapacity for new claims.
4 Employment and support allowance (ESA) data for 2008/09 are provisional.
5 Individuals receiving both attendance allowance and disability living allowance are counted twice.
6 Includes those in receipt of an allowance but excludes those where payment is currently suspended (for example, because of a stay in hospital).

Source: Work and Pensions Longitudinal Study, Department for Work and Pensions; Department for Social Development, Northern Ireland

(Table 8.9). This was around 18,000 less than in 2007/08, continuing the downward trend from 2005/06 when the number of recipients stood at 2.8 million. This resulted mainly from a fall in recipients of IB only and of those receiving IB plus income support/pension credit. However, in October 2008 employment and support allowance (ESA) replaced IB and income support paid on the grounds of incapacity for new claims. The introduction of this new benefit means that the net reduction in recipients is less than the fall in the number of those claiming IB and its various combinations.

Disability living allowance (DLA) is a benefit for people who are disabled, have personal care needs, mobility needs, or both, and who are aged under 65. Attendance allowance (AA) is paid to people who are ill or disabled after their 65th birthday and who need someone to help with their personal care. In 2008/09 there were 4.9 million people in receipt of DLA and/or AA in the UK, compared with 4.5 million in 2005/06. Of those in receipt of these benefits, around two-thirds were claiming DLA and while the number of those in receipt of DLA or AA has increased, the ratio between them has remained steady.

The main support given to sick and disabled people is care provided through the National Health Service (NHS). In 2008 there were more than 10,100 general practitioner (GP) surgeries in the UK employing more than 41,300 GPs. In 2000 there were more surgeries (10,800) but fewer GPs (34,300), reflecting a trend towards larger surgeries where GPs are able to share practice staff and resources. There has also been an increase in the number of dentists providing NHS services since 2000, rising from just under 21,900 to just under 26,200 in 2008.

In England in 2009 there were more than 3,600 adult critical care beds available, representing 2.3 per cent of all available beds (Figure 8.10 overleaf). These beds are used by patients receiving either intensive care or high dependency care. The number of critical care beds has risen each year since 2000, when they represented 1.3 per cent of available beds. In 2009 there were 1,275 more open and staffed critical care beds than in 2000, a 54 per cent increase over the decade. Over the same period the average number of all available beds fell by 27,000, from 186,300 to 159,400, a fall of 14 per cent. The number of beds used for intensive care patients has increased each year, from 1,555 in 2000 to 2,030 in 2009. However, over the same period the number of beds used for high dependency patients has risen by a much greater amount, doubling from 807 in 2000 to 1,607 in 2009.

8

Figure 8.10

Number of open and staffed adult critical care beds[1,2,3]

England

Thousands

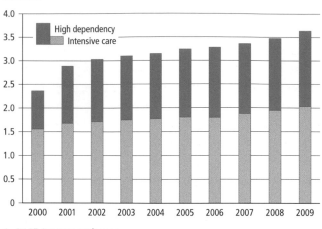

1 At 15 January each year.
2 Open and staffed beds are those where a hospital ward is open for use.
3 See Appendix, Part 8: In-patient activity.

Source: Department of Health

Any person admitted to a hospital ward for assessment or treatment, as opposed to attending a hospital clinic or accident and emergency department, is classified as an in-patient. The number of 'finished consultant episodes' (where the patient completed a period of care under one consultant, including an in-patient stay) classified as 'acute' has risen steadily in the UK, more than doubling between 1991/92 and 2007/08 to reach 15.0 million (Table 8.11). Over the same period the number of 'acute in-patient episodes' per bed per year more than doubled from 51.4 to 124.2. This increase has been accompanied by a reduction in the average length of stay from 6.0 days to 3.9 days over the same period and reflects the policy that patients spend less time recuperating from operations in hospital. Between 1991/92 and 2007/08, the number of finished consultant episodes for the mentally ill has fallen from 281,000 to 196,000. The number of in-patient episodes per bed per year for the mentally ill generally increased over the same period from 4.5 to 6.0 and the average duration of stay more than halved from 114.8 days in 1991/92 to 52.4 in 2007/08. The number of finished consultant episodes for people with learning disabilities fell by nearly two-thirds from 62,000 to 22,000 between 1991/92 and 2007/08. The number of in-patient episodes per bed more than doubled from 2.4 to 5.6 and the average duration of stay fell from 544 days to 52.5 although the number in 1991/92 was particularly high and the figure in recent years has been much lower.

Primary care services are provided by general practitioners (GPs) and practice staff at GP surgeries. These services range from initial diagnosis, vaccinations and general health advice,

Table 8.11

NHS in-patient activity for sick and disabled people[1]

United Kingdom

	1981	1991/92	2001/02	2003/04	2005/06	2007/08
Acute[2]						
Finished consultant episodes (thousands)	5,693	6,974	12,177	12,885	13,959	15,008
In-patient episodes per available bed (numbers)	31.1	51.4	94.6	99.0	108.7	124.2
Mean duration of stay (days)	8.4	6.0	5.1	4.9	4.3	3.9
Mentally ill						
Finished consultant episodes (thousands)	244	281	259	238	211	196
In-patient episodes per available bed (numbers)	2.2	4.5	6.6	6.2	5.9	6.0
Mean duration of stay[3] (days)	..	114.8	48.9	49.3	55.6	52.4
People with learning disabilities						
Finished consultant episodes (thousands)	34	62	41	34	27	22
In-patient episodes per available bed (numbers)	0.6	2.4	5.7	5.4	5.5	5.6
Mean duration of stay[3] (days)	..	544.0	109.7	42.7	70.0	52.5

1 See Appendix, Part 8: In-patient activity.
2 General patients on wards, excluding elderly, maternity and neonatal cots in maternity units.
3 Scotland data unavailable from 2001/02 onwards.

Source: The NHS Information Centre for health and social care; Welsh Assembly Government; NHS in Scotland; Department of Health, Social Services and Public Safety, Northern Ireland

Table 8.12

NHS GP consultations:[1] by site of consultation, 2008[2]

Great Britain   Percentages[3]

	16–44	45–64	65–74	75 and over	Total[4]
Surgery	90	90	87	79	89
Telephone	12	13	12	11	11
Home	1	1	4	13	3

1 NHS GP consultations in the 14 days prior to interview.
2 In 2008 the General Household Survey was renamed the General Lifestyle Survey. See Appendix, Part 2: General Household Survey.
3 Percentages do not sum to 100 per cent as respondents could give more than one answer.
4 Includes children.

Source: General Lifestyle Survey (Longitudinal), Office for National Statistics

through to the provision of secondary care services. How people consult their GP has changed over time: 78 per cent of consultations took place at a GP surgery in 1975, 19 per cent in the home and 3 per cent were conducted over the telephone. In 2008 almost nine in ten (89 per cent) consultations took place at GP surgeries, with smaller proportions taking place over the telephone (11 per cent) or in the home (3 per cent) (Table 8.12). The site of consultation also varies by age. In 2008

only 1 per cent of people aged between 16 and 44 received a home visit, compared with 4 per cent of those aged 65 to 74 and 13 per cent of those aged 75 and over.

The British Social Attitudes Survey includes questions on attitudes towards various aspects of NHS care and services as well as private medical and dental care services. In 2008 there was a marked difference between satisfaction levels with general practitioners (GPs), hospital services and NHS dental services. Of all NHS and private medical services, GP services recorded the highest satisfaction levels; 77 per cent of adults aged 18 and over in Great Britain reported that they were either very satisfied or quite satisfied (Table 8.13). This was followed by NHS ambulance services (71 per cent) and NHS services for children and young people (60 per cent). The lowest satisfaction levels were recorded for NHS dentists, with under half (45 per cent) of respondents being either very or quite satisfied with how this service is run. The proportion of respondents that felt very or quite satisfied with private dentists was slightly higher, at 48 per cent. However, dissatisfaction levels were very different, with 37 per cent of respondents either quite or very dissatisfied with NHS dental services compared with 13 per cent for private dental services.

People's opinions of NHS hospital services, other than accident and emergency and services for children, were sought for in-patient and out-patient services separately, and both

Table 8.13

Satisfaction with the way in which NHS and private medical services are run, 2008[1]

Great Britain   Percentages

	Very satisfied	Quite satisfied	Neither satisfied nor dissatisfied	Quite dissatisfied	Very dissatisfied
Local doctors or GPs	31	46	10	10	3
NHS dentists	13	32	18	18	20
Being in hospital as an in-patient	18	38	24	13	7
Attending hospital as an out-patient	16	48	20	12	4
Accident and emergency departments	18	39	20	16	7
NHS Direct, the telephone or internet advice	15	33	38	8	6
NHS services for children and young people	17	43	32	6	2
NHS ambulance service	29	42	23	5	2
Private medical treatment	22	28	45	3	2
Private dentists	19	29	38	8	5

1 Respondents aged 18 and over were asked 'From your own experience, or from what you have heard, please say how satisfied or dissatisfied you are with the way in which each of these parts of the National Health Service (NHS) runs nowadays.' Excludes those who responded 'don't know' or did not answer.

Source: British Social Attitudes Survey, National Centre for Social Research

Table 8.14

Pension receipt: by type of pensioner unit,[1] 2007/08

United Kingdom

Percentages

	Pensioner couples	Single male pensioners	Single female pensioners	All pensioners
State retirement pension[2]/minimum income guarantee/pension credit only	19	31	42	31
Plus				
Occupational, but not personal pension[3]	56	54	27	43
Personal, but not occupational pension[3]	11	9	4	8
Both occupational and personal pension[3]	9	2	1	5
Other, no occupational or personal pension[4]	1	2	22	11
Other combinations, no retirement pension/minimum income guarantee/pension credit	2	1	1	1
None	2	1	2	2
All people	100	100	100	100

1 See Appendix, Part 8: Benefit units.
2 Includes receipt of other contributory benefits. See Appendix, Part 8: Pension schemes.
3 Occupational and personal pensions include survivor's benefits.
4 Includes widow, trade union, annuity and trust pensions.

Source: Pensioners' Income Series, Department for Work and Pensions

recorded higher satisfaction levels than private medical treatment. Just under two-thirds (64 per cent) of respondents reported that they were very or quite satisfied with NHS hospital out-patient services and 56 per cent reported that they were very or quite satisfied with NHS hospital in-patient services, compared with 50 per cent for private medical treatment. However, dissatisfaction levels are much lower for private treatment, with 5 per cent reporting that they were quite or very dissatisfied with private medical treatment compared with 20 per cent reporting that they were quite or very dissatisfied with NHS hospital in-patient services and 16 per cent with NHS hospital out-patient services. The high proportions who were neither satisfied nor dissatisfied with private medical treatment may reflect the relatively higher proportion of respondents with little or no direct or indirect experience of private treatment.

Older people

In the UK much of central government expenditure on social protection for older people is through payment of the state retirement pension. Nearly everyone of state pension age (currently age 65 for men and 60 for women) receives this pension, whatever the level of their other income. Some also receive income-related state benefits, such as council tax benefit or pension credit.

People can also make their own provision for retirement to supplement the state pension through occupational, personal or stakeholder pensions (see Chapter 5: Income and wealth, Table 5.9). In 2007/08, 31 per cent of all pensioners in the UK had no pension provision other than state retirement pension and minimum income guarantee or pension credit (Table 8.14). Single women were more likely to have a state pension only (42 per cent) compared with single men or pensioner couples (31 per cent and 19 per cent respectively). Over half (54 per cent) of single male pensioners in the UK had an occupational pension in addition to the state pension, compared with 27 per cent of single female pensioners and 56 per cent of pensioner couples. Just over a fifth (22 per cent) of single women received a state pension plus another pension, other than an occupational or personal pension, such as a widow's pension, annuity pension, trust or trade union pension. The proportions of pensioners who received a personal pension as well as the state pension were much lower than those who received an occupational pension; 9 per cent of single male pensioners, 4 per cent of single female pensioners and 11 per cent of pensioner couples. The lower proportions for women may be in part because women traditionally had lower employment rates than men (see Chapter 4: Labour market, Figure 4.4). Women were also less likely to have been self-employed, an employment status where a personal pension is the main source of private pension provision.

Table 8.15

Receipt of selected social security benefits among pensioners: by type of benefit unit,[1] 2007/08

United Kingdom

Percentages

	Single male pensioners	Single female pensioners	Pensioner couples
Income-related			
Council tax benefit	34	38	18
Pension credit	22	29	13
Housing benefit	23	23	7
Any income-related benefit[2]	39	43	20
Non-income-related[3]			
Incapacity or disablement benefits[4]	32	28	33
Any non-income-related benefit[2]	100	100	100
Any benefit[2]	100	100	100

1 Pensioner benefit units. See Appendix, Part 8: Benefit units.
2 Includes benefits not listed here. Components do not sum to the total as each benefit unit may receive more than one benefit.
3 Includes state retirement pension.
4 Includes incapacity benefit, disability living allowance (care and mobility components), severe disablement allowance, industrial injuries disability benefit, armed forces compensation scheme and attendance allowance.

Source: Family Resources Survey, Department for Work and Pensions

Income-related benefits are more common among single pensioners than pensioner couples. In 2007/08, 39 per cent of single male pensioners and 43 per cent of single female pensioners in the UK received income-related benefits, compared with 20 per cent of pensioner couples (Table 8.15). Among single pensioners, a greater proportion of women than men received income support, minimum income guarantee or pension credit (29 per cent compared with 22 per cent) because they were less likely to receive the full rate of state retirement pension. For pensioner couples the proportion was again lower, at 13 per cent. Single women were also more likely to claim council tax benefit (38 per cent) than either single men (34 per cent) or couples (18 per cent). However, the proportions claiming housing benefit were the same for both single men and single women (23 per cent), while for couples the figure was much lower at 7 per cent. Receipt of non-income-related benefits showed less variation between both men and women and single people and married couples. Around a third of pensioners received disability-related benefits, whether single (32 per cent of males and 28 per cent of females) or in a couple (33 per cent).

Figure 8.16

State retirement pension[1]

United Kingdom

£ per week[2]

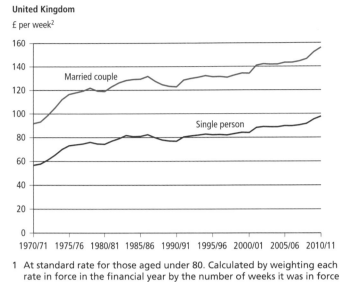

1 At standard rate for those aged under 80. Calculated by weighting each rate in force in the financial year by the number of weeks it was in force for.
2 Adjusted to 2009/10 prices using the GDP deflator (Q2 2009).

Source: HM Treasury

Pension credit is a means-tested benefit comprising guarantee credit and savings credit. Guarantee credit is for people aged 60 and over living in the UK. It ensured a minimum income of £130 per week for single pensioners and £198.45 for pensioner couples in 2009/10. The savings credit element is for those with some savings, whether single or living with a partner, where either partner is aged 65 and over. The maximum savings credit payable in 2009/10 was £20.40 per week for single people or £27.03 for people with a partner. Savings credit is generally available to single people with an income of up to £181 per week and couples with an income of up to £266 per week, although these thresholds may be higher depending on a range of factors such as disability, caring duties or certain housing costs such as mortgage interest payments.

The basic state pension in the UK at April 2009 was £95.25 per week for a single person and £152.30 for couples (Figure 8.16), provided that a claimant's own national insurance (NI) contributions were sufficient. Adjusted to 2009/10 prices using the gross domestic product (GDP) deflator, the single person's state pension increased by £38.52 (68 per cent) between 1970/71 and 2009/10 and the married couple's state pension increased by £60.40 (66 per cent). Although the single person's pension has increased more than the married couple's pension the difference between them has hardly changed because they have been uprated by the same proportion each year.

The increase in the state retirement pension since 1970/71 has not been a constant one and there have been occasions when,

8

in real terms (after adjustment to remove inflation), it has fallen, most noticeably between 1986/87 and 1990/91 when it fell by £5.61 for single people and by £8.93 for married couples. There have also been other years when there was negative growth in state retirement pension but these year-on-year falls have usually been followed by increases in the subsequent year. The decade which showed the greatest rise in state pensions was the 1970s, when the single person's pension increased by £17.91 and the married couple pension by £27.57. The 2000s showed the next largest increase, £11.14 for single people and £17.85 for married couples and the 1980s recorded the smallest increases, £2.36 for single people and £3.80 for married couples. Since 2006/07 there has been growth each year in state retirement pension for single people and married couples.

Views about who should be responsible for the financial security of those in retirement vary with age and, to a lesser extent, sex. Nearly six in ten (59 per cent) adults aged 18 and over in Great Britain agreed that the Government should be mainly responsible for ensuring that people have enough money to live on in retirement, followed by individuals and their families (30 per cent) and employers (11 per cent) (Table 8.17). Generally people in the older age categories were

Table 8.17

Attitudes towards financial security in retirement:[1] by age and sex, 2008

Great Britain

Percentages

	Mainly the Government	Mainly a person's employer	Mainly a person themselves and their family
Men			
18–24	46	21	33
25–40	55	11	34
41–64	53	11	37
65 and over	62	8	30
Women			
18–24	63	17	20
25–40	57	12	32
41–59	66	9	25
60 and over	66	6	28
All people	59	11	30

1 Respondents aged 18 and over were asked 'Who do you think should mainly be responsible for ensuring that people have enough money to live on in retirement?' Excludes those who responded 'don't know' or did not answer.

Source: British Social Attitudes Survey, National Centre for Social Research

more likely than those in the younger age categories to believe that the Government should be responsible for ensuring that people have enough money to live on in retirement, especially among men; 62 per cent of men aged 65 and over held this view compared with 46 per cent of those aged between 18 and 24. For women the differences between age groups was much smaller with those aged between 25 and 40 least likely to expect the Government to be the main provider of retirement income (57 per cent), compared with 66 per cent of women aged 60 and over. Conversely, both men and women aged 18 to 24 were most likely to believe that responsibility lay with the employer (21 per cent and 17 per cent respectively). These proportions decreased with age for both men and women, with 8 per cent of men aged 65 and over and 6 per cent of women aged 60 and over agreeing that a person's employer should be mainly responsible. Apart from women aged 25 to 40, men irrespective of age were more likely than women to agree that individuals and their families should be mostly responsible for the financial security of the retired.

Families and children

The Government provides a number of social security benefits targeted at families with children in the UK. They include income-related benefits paid to low income families, such as housing benefit, council tax benefit and income support and non-income-related benefits, such as child benefit and incapacity or disablement benefits. In 2007/08, 91 per cent of lone parents with dependent children in the UK and 56 per cent of couples with dependent children received income-related benefits (Table 8.18). The most common type of income-related benefit was child tax credit which was payable to 73 per cent of lone parents with dependent children and 53 per cent of couples with dependent children. Among lone parents with dependent children, 34 per cent received working tax credit and 39 per cent income support. In comparison, 14 per cent of couples with dependent children received working tax credit and 3 per cent received income support. This may reflect the employment status of lone parent mothers, who head the majority of lone parent families and are less likely to be employed than mothers with a partner (see also Chapter 2: Households and families).

The General Lifestyle Survey includes questions on the reasons for use of health services (other than a doctor) by children. In 2008, 15 per cent of all children aged under five in Great Britain were seen by an NHS health care professional in the 14 days prior to interview, the same figure as in 2005. Six per cent of all children aged under five were seen at a child health clinic and a

Table 8.18

Receipt of selected social security benefits among families: by type of benefit unit,[1] 2007/08

United Kingdom   Percentages

	Lone parent with dependent children[2]	Couple with dependent children[2]
Income-related		
Council tax benefit	45	8
Housing benefit	43	7
Working tax credit/income support/pension credit	73	17
Jobseeker's allowance	1	2
Any income-related benefit	91	56
Non-income-related		
Child benefit	96	96
Incapacity or disablement benefits[3]	10	8
Any non-income-related benefit	96	96
Any benefit or tax credit[4]	98	97

1 Families where household reference person is under state pension age. See Appendix, Part 8: Benefit units.
2 Children aged under 16, or aged 16 to 19 and not married or in a civil partnership and living with their parents and in full-time non-advanced education or in unwaged government training.
3 Incapacity benefit, disability living allowance (care and mobility components), severe disablement allowance, industrial injuries disability benefit, armed forces compensation scheme, attendance allowance and disabled persons tax credit.
4 Includes all benefits not listed here. Components do not sum to the total as each benefit unit may receive more than one benefit.

Source: Family Resources Survey, Department for Work and Pensions

further 5 per cent saw a health visitor at a GP surgery (Table 8.19). Older children were less likely to make use of these services, with only 3 per cent visiting a GP surgery to see either a practice nurse (2 per cent) or a health visitor (1 per cent). Again, this is unchanged since 2005.

According to the Department for Work and Pensions 2007 Families and Children Study (FACS 2007), 61 per cent of working lone parent mothers and 55 per cent of couples in Great Britain, where the mother worked, made use of some form of child care (Table 8.20 overleaf). The proportion of couples and lone parents using formal child care was similar (28 per cent of couples compared with 29 per cent of lone parents). However, lone parents were more likely to use informal child care than couples, 48 per cent compared with 39 per cent. Child care can be provided informally by family members, partners, ex-partners or friends. Lone parents were more likely than couples to make use of most types of

Table 8.19

Children using health services:[1,2] by age, 2008[3]

Great Britain   Percentages[4]

	0–4	5–15
Child health clinic	6	0
Health visitor at the GP surgery	5	1
Practice nurse at the GP surgery	4	2
None of the above	86	97

1 Services used in the 14 days prior to interview.
2 Excludes visits to the doctor.
3 In 2008 the General Household Survey was renamed the General Lifestyle Survey. See Appendix, Part 2: General Household Survey.
4 Percentages may not add to 100 per cent as respondents could give more than one answer.

Source: General Lifestyle Survey (Longitudinal), Office for National Statistics

informal child care except for grandparents who were used by a third (33 per cent) of both couples and lone parents. Lone parents were more likely to rely on ex-partners for child care than couples (18 per cent of lone parents compared to 1 per cent of couples). As children get older, the use of formal child care decreases. In 2007, 62 per cent of children aged under five, whose mothers worked, were looked after under formal child care arrangements. The proportion of children of primary school age (aged 5 to 10) was almost half this figure (32 per cent), and decreased further to around 6 per cent when they reached secondary education age (aged 11 to 16). Use of informal child care decreased more slowly with age than use of formal child care, with around half (51 per cent) of children under 10, and around a quarter (26 per cent) of children aged 11 to 16 receiving this form of child care.

The use of child care by households with non-working mothers was much lower than in those with working mothers. In 2007, the use of both formal and informal child care by households with non-working mothers was around half that where the mother was in work, 14 per cent of couples and 15 per cent of lone parents used formal child care and 18 per cent of couples and 25 per cent of lone parents used informal child care.

The FACS 2007 showed that lone parents with dependent children in Great Britain were more likely than couples with dependent children to have loans other than a mortgage, 52 per cent compared with 44 per cent. Lone parents were also more reliant on loans from friends or relatives, 16 per cent compared with 7 per cent of couples, and less likely to have bank overdrafts or loans. Lone parents were also more likely to

8

Table 8.20

Child care arrangements for children with working mothers: by family characteristics, 2007

Great Britain

Percentages[1]

	Child care not required	Formal child care[3]	Informal child care[2]				
			Ex partner/ non-resident parent	Grand-parent	Older sibling/ other relative	Other informal[4]	Total informal
Family type							
Lone parent	39	29	18	33	5	17	48
Couple	45	28	1	33	3	12	39
Family type working status							
Lone parent: 1 to 15 hours	45	12	27	25	5	24	52
Lone parent: 16 hours and above	38	30	17	34	5	18	47
Couple – both: 16 hours and above	42	31	1	35	3	12	41
Couple – one only: 16 hours and above	54	20	1	27	2	11	34
Age of child							
0 to 4	20	62	3	43	9	7	50
5 to 10	33	32	6	42	12	12	52
11 to 16	72	6	4	18	8	5	26

1 Percentages do not sum to 100 per cent as respondents could give more than one answer.
2 Respondents could give more than one source of informal child care.
3 Includes nurseries/crèches, nursery schools, playgroups, registered childminders, after school clubs/breakfast clubs, and holiday play schemes.
4 A friend, neighbour or babysitter, who came to the home.

Source: Families and Children Study, Department for Work and Pensions

apply for a Social Fund loan, 12 per cent of lone parents compared with 1 per cent of couples (see Appendix, Part 8: Social fund). Unsurprisingly, single parents working up to 15 hours per week were more likely than those working 16 hours or more to borrow money using these methods. Just over a

fifth (21 per cent), of lone parents working up to 15 hours borrowed from friends or neighbours compared with 12 per cent of those working 16 hours or more. The difference was greater for those with Social Fund loans, where a quarter (25 per cent) of lone parents working up to 15 hours received

Table 8.21

Children and young persons on the at risk register[1]

United Kingdom

Thousands

	2003	2004	2005	2006	2007	2008
Neglect	13.1	13.4	13.9	14.5	15.5	16.3
Emotional abuse	6.0	6.1	6.3	7.0	8.3	9.3
Physical abuse	5.8	5.5	5.2	4.9	4.8	4.7
Sexual abuse	3.3	3.1	3.0	2.9	2.6	2.6
Multiple/not specified	4.5	4.0	3.5	3.2	3.4	3.1
Total number of children	32.7	32.1	31.9	32.5	34.6	36.0

1 At 31 March each year. Children and young persons aged under 18.

Source: Department for Children, Schools and Families; Local Government Data Unit – Wales; Scottish Government; Department of Health, Social Services and Public Safety, Northern Ireland

such a loan compared with 2 per cent of those working 16 hours or more.

When a child is assessed as being subject to a continuing risk of significant harm they may be placed on a local authority's 'at risk' register. These registers are maintained and managed by social services departments. As at March 2008 there were just over 36,000 children on at risk registers throughout the UK (Table 8.21), an increase of 10 per cent (almost 3,300 children) since 2003. However, this increase was not reflected in all the categories of reasons for being on the register. The number of children on the register because of neglect and emotional abuse increased by similar amounts (3,258 and 3,271 respectively) but those in all other categories fell. The number of children on the register because of physical abuse fell by more than 1,000 and sexual abuse by nearly 800. The number of children classified to multiple reasons or unspecified reasons fell by almost 1,400 but this may be due in part to more children being classified to specific categories. Neglect was the most common reason given for a child being placed on the register in 2008 (45 per cent) followed by emotional abuse (26 per cent).

8

Chapter 9

Crime and justice

- The British Crime Survey (BCS) showed that there were 10.7 millions crimes committed against adults living in private households in England and Waes in 2008/09, 8.7 million fewer crimes than in 1995. (Table 9.2)

- According to the BCS in England and Wales in 2008/09, victims of domestic violence were most likely to report being a repeat victim, with 38 per cent of domestic violence victims experiencing this crime more than once in the 12 months prior to interview. (Figure 9.4)

- The number of crimes reported to the police in England and Wales in which a firearm excluding air weapons had been used was 8,208 in 2008/09, a fall of 17 per cent compared with the previous year. (Figure 9.6)

- In 2008, there was a total of £609.9 million worth of plastic card fraud losses on UK issued cards, the highest recorded since 1998, when £135.0 million worth of fraud losses occurred. Losses of £379.7 million (62 per cent) occurred in the UK, compared with £230.1 million (38 per cent) of fraud which occurred abroad. (Figure 9.8)

- Police officers from ethnic minority groups accounted for 4.4 per cent of total police officer strength in England and Wales at 31 March 2009. (Table 9.19)

- In 2008/09, a total of 31,259 complaint cases were made by members of the public against those serving with the police in England and Wales, an increase of 8 per cent on the previous year and the most complaints recorded in a single year since 1990. (Figure 9.21)

DATA

Download data by clicking the online pdf

www.statistics.gov.uk/socialtrends

Many people will be affected by crime during the course of their lives, either directly through loss or suffering, or indirectly through, for example, experiencing heightened levels of fear. This can restrict people's behaviour, or mean that they feel they have to take additional security measures in the course of their daily life. Crime and its associated problems are a continuing concern for society and the Government. There are two main sources of statistics on crime levels: household population surveys of people's experiences of crime, and police records of crime (see Measures of crime text box).

Crime levels

This chapter discusses the incidence and the prevalence of crime (see also Appendix, Part 9: Prevalence rates and incidence rates). The prevalence of crime, or the percentage of people who were victims, is covered in the Offences and

Measures of crime

There are two main measures of the extent of crime in the UK: surveys of the public, and crime recorded by the police. The British Crime Survey (BCS) interviews adults aged 16 and over who are living in private households in England and Wales. The Scottish Crime and Justice Survey (SCJS) and the Northern Ireland Crime Survey (NICS) interview adults aged 16 and over in Scotland and Northern Ireland respectively. In some ways the BCS, the SCJS and the NICS give a better measure of many types of crime than police-recorded crime statistics. These surveys show the large number of offences that are not reported to the police and also give a more reliable picture of trends, as they are not affected by changes in levels of reporting to the police or by variations in police recording practice (see Appendix, Part 9: Types of offence in England and Wales, in Scotland, and in Northern Ireland).

Recorded crime data cover offences reported to, and recorded by, the police. The National Crime Recording Standard (NCRS), introduced in England and Wales in 2002 and the Scottish Crime Recording Standard (SCRS), introduced in 2004, were implemented with the aim of taking a more victim-centred approach and providing consistency between police forces (see Appendix, Part 9: National Crime Recording Standard).

Police-recorded crime and survey-measured crime have different coverage. Unlike crime data recorded by the police, surveys are generally restricted to crimes against adults living in private households and their property and do not include some types of crime (for example, fraud, murder and victimless crimes such as drug use, where there is not a direct victim).

See also Appendix, Part 9: Availability and comparability of data from constituent countries

victims section later in the chapter. The incidence of crime, or the number of crimes experienced, is analysed in this section.

In 2008/09, there were 5.2 million crimes recorded by the police across the UK (Table 9.1), this was a fall of 5 per cent from 5.4 million offences in 2007/08. In England and Wales, recorded crime also fell by 5 per cent between 2007/08 and 2008/09, to reach 4.7 million notifiable offences. Nearly three-quarters (71 per cent) of recorded crimes in England and Wales were property crimes; these include theft and handling stolen goods, burglary, offences involving a vehicle, criminal damage and fraud and forgery. Almost a fifth (19 per cent) of all recorded crime involved violence against the person.

The definition of crime in Northern Ireland is broadly comparable with that in England and Wales. The police in Northern Ireland recorded 110,000 crimes in 2008/09. Theft and handling stolen goods accounted for 24 per cent of all recorded crimes, a lower proportion than in England and Wales or Scotland. In Northern Ireland criminal damage and violence against the person formed higher proportions of recorded crime, at 26 per cent and 27 per cent respectively.

Table 9.1

Crimes recorded by the police: by type of offence,[1] 2008/09

United Kingdom			Percentages
	England & Wales	Scotland	Northern Ireland
Theft and handling stolen goods	36	34	24
Theft from vehicles	8	4	3
Theft of vehicles	3	3	3
Criminal damage	20	29	26
Violence against the person[2]	19	3	27
Burglary	12	7	11
Drugs offences	5	11	3
Fraud and forgery	3	2	3
Robbery	2	1	1
Sexual offences	1	1	2
Other offences[3]	2	12	3
All notifiable offences (=100%) (thousands)	4,702	377	110

1 See Appendix, Part 9: Types of offences in England and Wales, in Scotland and in Northern Ireland, and Availability and comparability of data from constituent countries.
2 Data for Scotland are serious assaults only. Those for England and Wales and Northern Ireland are all assaults including those that cause no physical injury.
3 Northern Ireland includes 'offences against the state'. Scotland excludes 'offending while on bail'.

Source: Home Office; Scottish Government; Police Service of Northern Ireland

In Scotland the term 'crime' is reserved for the more serious offences, broadly equivalent to 'indictable' and 'triable-either-way' offences in England and Wales, while less serious crimes are called 'offences' (see Appendix, Part 9: Types of offences in England and Wales, in Scotland and Northern Ireland). The most common recorded crime in Scotland in 2008/09 was theft and handling stolen goods (34 per cent), followed by criminal damage (29 per cent) and drugs offences (11 per cent).

The British Crime Survey (BCS) estimates of crime are considerably higher than the number of crimes recorded by the police. Many crimes reported to the BCS are not reported to the police, for a variety of reasons. For example, people may consider that the crime was too trivial, or that it was not worthwhile reporting because there was no loss involved. Whether or not a crime had been reported to the police varies by type of offence. Of the comparable crimes covered in both the BCS and police records, (see Appendix, Part 9: Comparable crimes) in 2008/09 theft of a vehicle was the most likely crime captured in the BCS to be reported to the police: 89 per cent of all thefts of vehicles in England and Wales had been reported. Burglaries in which something was stolen had the second highest reporting rate (83 per cent). This is at least in part because both these types of crime need to be reported to the police if the victim wishes to make an insurance claim.

Of the 10.7 million crimes reported to the British Crime Survey (BCS) in England and Wales in 2008/09, almost two-thirds (6.8 million offences) were household crimes (Table 9.2). The

remainder, 3.9 million offences, were personal crimes. The total number of crimes estimated by the BCS rose steadily throughout the 1980s and early 1990s and peaked in 1995, at 19.4 million. Estimated crime levels then declined steadily until 2004/05 and have remained broadly stable since.

The Scottish Crime and Justice Survey (SCJS) estimated that around 1.04 million crimes were committed against adults in private households in Scotland in the 12 months prior to interview in 2008/09, 70 per cent of which were property crimes. The remaining crimes were violent crimes of assault and robbery.

Estimates from the Northern Ireland Crime Survey (NICS) estimated that 176,000 crimes were committed against adults living in private households in the 12 months prior to interview in 2008/09. This was a fall of almost 12 per cent compared with the total of 199,000 in 2007/08, and was two-fifths (40 per cent) lower than the peak recorded in 2003/04 (295,000 crimes).

Offences and victims

According to the 2008/09 British Crime Survey (BCS), around 23 per cent of all adults aged 16 and over in England and Wales had experienced one or more BCS crimes in the 12 months prior to interview. The most common crime experienced was vandalism, with 2.8 million incidents in the 12 months prior to interview (Table 9.3 overleaf). There were 1.5 million incidents of vehicle-related theft (including theft of, or from, motor vehicles, but not bicycles), a fall of two-thirds (66 per cent) since 1995. In 2008/09, vehicle-related thefts accounted for 14 per cent of BCS crime, compared with 23 per cent in 1995.

In Northern Ireland in 2008/09, around 13 per cent of households were victims of at least one Northern Ireland Crime Survey (NICS) crime during the 12 months prior to interview, which is the lowest level of victimisation since the survey began in 1994/95. In Scotland in 2008/09, 20 per cent of adults were the victim of at least one Scottish Crime and Justice Survey (SCJS) crime during the 12 months prior to interview.

Being a victim of crime can be traumatic and the impact can vary depending on the type of offence and the circumstances under which it occurs. For example, the impact can be worse when a person is repeatedly victimised. In the BCS, repeat victimisation is defined as being a victim of the same offence, or group of offences, more than once within a 12 month period. According to the BCS in England and Wales in 2008/09, 9 per cent of victims who experienced theft from the person in

Table 9.2

British Crime Survey offences[1]

England & Wales			Millions
	All household crime	All personal crime	All BCS crime
1983	7.7	4.2	11.9
1987	9.0	4.4	13.4
1991	10.4	4.7	15.1
1995	12.4	6.9	19.4
1999	9.4	5.6	15.0
2003/04	7.2	4.5	11.7
2007/08	6.5	3.8	10.2
2008/09	6.8	3.9	10.7

1 Until 2000 respondents were asked to recall their experience of crime in the previous calendar year. From 2001/02 onwards the British Crime Survey (BCS) became a continuous survey and the recall period was changed to the 12 months prior to interview.

Source: British Crime Survey, Home Office

9

Table 9.3

Incidents of crime: by type of offence[1]

England & Wales

Millions

	1981	1991	1995	2001/02	2006/07	2007/08	2008/09
Household crime							
Vandalism	2.7	2.8	3.4	2.6	3.0	2.7	2.8
All vehicle-related theft[2]	1.8	3.8	4.4	2.5	1.7	1.5	1.5
Burglary	0.7	1.4	1.8	1.0	0.7	0.7	0.7
Bicycle theft	0.2	0.6	0.7	0.4	0.5	0.4	0.5
Other household theft[3]	1.5	1.9	2.3	1.4	1.2	1.1	1.2
All household crime	6.9	10.4	12.4	7.9	7.1	6.5	6.8
Personal crime							
Theft from the person	0.4	0.4	0.7	0.6	0.6	0.6	0.7
Other thefts of personal property	1.6	1.7	2.1	1.4	1.1	1.0	1.1
All BCS violence	2.1	2.6	4.2	2.7	2.5	2.2	2.1
Assault with minor injury	0.6	0.8	1.4	0.7	0.6	0.5	0.5
Assault with no injury	0.8	1.0	1.6	1.0	1.0	0.9	0.8
Wounding	0.5	0.6	0.9	0.6	0.6	0.5	0.5
Robbery	0.2	0.2	0.3	0.4	0.3	0.3	0.3
All personal crime	4.1	4.7	6.9	4.7	4.2	3.8	3.9
All crimes reported to BCS	11.0	15.1	19.4	12.6	11.3	10.2	10.7

1 Until 2000 respondents were asked to recall their experience of crime in the previous calendar year. From 2001/02 onwards the British Crime Survey (BCS) became a continuous survey and the recall period was changed to the 12 months prior to interview.
2 Includes theft of, or from, a vehicle, as well as attempts.
3 Includes thefts and attempted thefts from domestic garages, outhouses and sheds, not directly linked to the dwelling, as well as thefts from both inside and outside a dwelling.

Source: British Crime Survey, Home Office

the 12 months prior to interview had been victims of this offence more than once during the period (Figure 9.4). Victims of domestic violence were most likely to report being a repeat victim, with 38 per cent of domestic violence victims experiencing this crime more than once in the 12 months prior to interview, and around a fifth (21 per cent) were victimised at least three times. The second most common offence reported by the same victim on more than one occasion within the last 12 months was vandalism (28 per cent).

In England and Wales there were 2.1 million violent offences reported in the BCS in 2008/09, a fall of 614,000 incidents since 2001/02. Assault without injury accounted for the largest proportion of violent offences (40 per cent) followed by assault with minor injury (25 per cent), wounding (22 per cent) and robbery (13 per cent). These proportions were very similar to those in 2007/08. The number of violent crimes increased during the 1980s to reach a peak of more than 4 million incidents by 1995. Incidents of BCS violent crime have fallen markedly since the mid-1990s to a level similar to 1981 (2.1 million crimes).

The risk of becoming a victim of violent crime varies according to personal characteristics. Except in cases of domestic violence, men are most likely to be victims of violent crime. In England and Wales in 2008/09, the overall risk of an adult becoming a victim of violent crime at least once in the 12 months prior to interview was 3.2 per cent (Figure 9.5). This proportion rose to 13.2 per cent for men aged 16 to 24, compared with 5.5 per cent of women of the same age. The risk to a single person of becoming a victim of violence (7.6 per cent) was more than five times higher than the risk to a married person (1.4 per cent) and around twice as high as the risk to a cohabiting person (3.8 per cent) or a divorced person (3.2 per cent). The level of risk is also related to lifestyle. For example, those who visited a nightclub on average at least once a week were considerably more at risk (12.4 per cent) than those who had not visited a nightclub in the last month (2.5 per cent).

Firearms are defined as having been used in an incident if they are fired, used as a blunt instrument against a person, or used as a threat. The number of reported crimes in England and Wales involving the use of a firearm was 14,250 in 2008/09,

Figure 9.4

Repeat victimisation:[1] by type of offence, 2008/09

England & Wales

Percentages

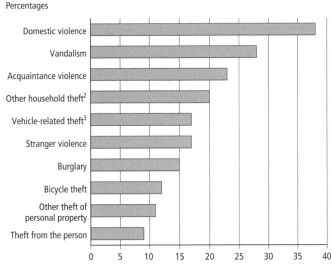

1 Victims of the same offence, or group of offences, more than once in the last 12 months.
2 Includes thefts and attempted thefts from domestic garages, outhouses and sheds, not directly linked to the dwelling, as well as thefts from both inside and outside a dwelling.
3 Includes theft of, or from, a vehicle, as well as attempts.

Source: British Crime Survey, Home Office

a decrease of 18 per cent from the previous year, 2007/08, when 17,343 offences were recorded, and a fall of 41 per cent since the peak of 24,094 offences recorded in 2003/04 (Figure 9.6). In 2008/09, 8,208 offences were committed in which firearms were reported to have been used (excluding air weapons) of which 2,671 were fired with 39 offences resulting

Figure 9.5

Adults most at risk of violence,[1] 2008/09

England & Wales

Percentages

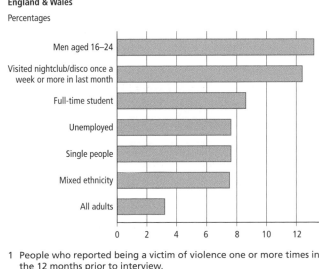

1 People who reported being a victim of violence one or more times in the 12 months prior to interview.

Source: British Crime Survey, Home Office

Figure 9.6

Crimes[1] reported to the police in which a firearm had been used

England & Wales

Thousands

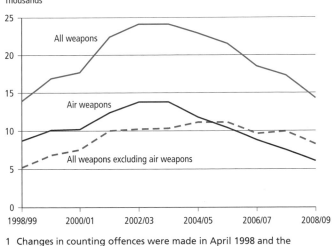

1 Changes in counting offences were made in April 1998 and the National Crime Recording Standard was implemented in April 2002. See Appendix, Part 9: National Crime Recording Standard.

Source: Home Office

in a fatal injury. During the same period, of the total number of firearm offences (excluding air weapons) committed, 5,337 offences were reported in which the weapon was not fired but was used as a blunt instrument or to threaten a person. The number of firearm offences (excluding air weapons) involving any kind of injury almost halved between 2007/08 and 2008/09, falling from 3,241 to 1,764.

An air weapon differs from the conventional firearm by the fact that it, and the pellets discharged, do not contain any explosive substance and most are of such limited powers that they are not required to be licensed, except those classified as dangerous weapons by the Firearms Rules 1969. In 2008/09, the number of reported crimes in England and Wales involving the use of an air weapon was 6,042, of which 5,340 reported incidents involved the air weapon being fired and 702 incidents were reported in which the air weapon was not fired but was used as a blunt instrument or to threaten a person.

Around half of firearm offences in 2008/09 (excluding those involving air weapons) involved a handgun (52 per cent). Imitation firearms were used in 18 per cent of incidents, shotguns in 8 per cent, and rifles in 1 per cent. Other firearms including CS gas, stun guns, and paintball guns accounted for 9 per cent of all firearm offences. The firearm was unidentified in 12 per cent of offences.

Table 9.3 showed that there were 1.5 million vehicle-related thefts against the household population in England and Wales in 2008/09. Of these, 70 per cent of offences were thefts from

9

Figure 9.7

Vehicle-related theft[1]

England & Wales

Incidents

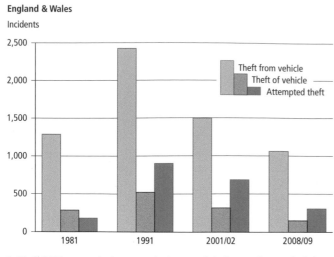

1 Until 2000 respondents were asked to recall their experience of crime in the previous calendar year. From 2001/02 onwards the British Crime Survey became a continuous survey and the recall period was changed to the 12 months prior to interview.

Source: British Crime Survey, Home Office

Figure 9.8

Plastic card fraud losses[1] on UK-issued cards

£ million

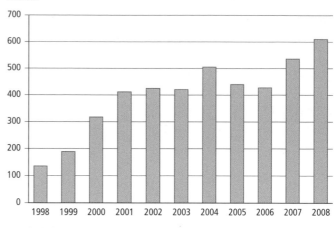

1 Value of transactions resulting from fraudulent use of UK credit and debit cards, both in the UK and overseas.

Source: The UK Cards Association

vehicles and 10 per cent were thefts of vehicles, while 20 per cent were attempted thefts either from or of the vehicle (Figure 9.7). In a pattern similar to violent crime, the number of offences in each of the vehicle-related theft categories had fallen by around two-thirds since they peaked in 1995 (see Table 9.3).

The fall in vehicle-related crime may be at least in part the result of better vehicle security. The proportion of vehicles in England and Wales fitted with security devices has risen over time and in 2008/09 the majority of vehicles had some form of security device installed: 91 per cent of main cars (that is, the car most used by the household) had central locking, and 80 per cent had immobilisers.

The risk of being a victim of vehicle-related theft varies according to the employment status of the household reference person (see Reference persons text box on page 15). For example, in England and Wales in 2008/09, 10.1 per cent of households headed by a student had experienced vehicle-related theft, compared with 2.5 per cent of households headed by a retired person. The household's accommodation was also a risk factor: households living in flats or maisonettes were more likely to be victims of vehicle-related theft (8.3 per cent) than those living in detached houses (4.7 per cent). The risk to households with three or more cars (11.1 per cent) was more than double the risk to households with only one car (5.1 per cent).

In 2008, the value of transactions resulting from fraudulent use of UK credit and debit cards, both in the UK and overseas,

totalled £609.9 million, an increase of 14 per cent on the previous year and over 350 per cent since 1998 (Figure 9.8). However, this amounted to 0.1 per cent of the total value of transactions made in 2008 using plastic cards issued in the UK. Losses of £379.7 million (62 per cent) occurred in the UK, compared with £230.1 million (38 per cent) of fraud which occurred abroad. More than half (54 per cent) of all losses on UK issued cards were through card-not-present transactions, and more than a quarter (28 per cent) resulted from the use of counterfeit cards. The remaining losses were a result of lost or stolen cards (9 per cent), card identity theft (8 per cent) and mail non-receipt, in which cards are stolen while in transit from the issuer to the cardholder (2 per cent).

Card-not-present fraud, where genuine card details are used to make a purchase online, over the phone or by post, increased by 350 per cent between 2000 (72.9 million frauds) and 2008 (328.4 million frauds). However, over the same period, the value of online shopping alone increased more than tenfold, from £3.5 billion in 2000 to £41.2 billion in 2008.

Counterfeit card fraud involves the unauthorised use of card details taken from the magnetic strip of a genuine card. Although the value of this type of card fraud taking place in UK increased by 9 per cent between 2007 and 2008, it fell by 68 per cent between 2004 and 2008 because of the introduction of chip and PIN, which requires people to enter a unique code, rather than signing their name, when purchasing goods. Counterfeit card fraud accounted for 58 per cent of losses in value that occurred abroad involving UK issued cards, as fraudsters use the cards in countries that do not yet have chip and PIN.

Perceptions of crime

Table 9.2 showed that there were an estimated 10.7 million crimes committed in England and Wales in 2008/09, a fall of 45 per cent since the peak of 19.4 million crimes recorded in 1995. However, when asked if they believed crime levels had changed nationally and locally over the last two years, the 2008/09 British Crime Survey (BCS) reported that 75 per cent of respondents thought that crime levels across the whole country had increased over the last two years, but around half this proportion (36 per cent) thought that there was more crime in their local area.

This pattern of belief that crime had increased to a much greater extent nationally than in their local area was reflected in perceptions of the levels of individual types of crime. Almost four-fifths (78 per cent) of people living in private households in England and Wales in 2008/09 believed that knife crime had increased a lot nationally over the last two years, while 16 per cent thought it had increased a little (Table 9.9). At a local level, 8 per cent of people believed that knife crime had increased a lot and 21 per cent thought that it had increased a little. In contrast, BCS data show that knives were used in less than 8 per cent of all violent crimes in each year since 1995 (7 per cent in 2008/09).

Bank and credit card fraud were perceived to have gone up at a local level more than any other crime, with 22 per cent of people questioned stating that they thought bank and credit card fraud had gone up a lot in their area and 31 per cent thinking that it had gone up a little.

Table 9.9

Perceptions of changing crime levels: by type of crime,[1] 2008/09

England & Wales   Percentages

	National level		Local level	
	Increased a lot	Increased a little	Increased a lot	Increased a little
Knife crime	78	16	8	21
Bank/credit card fraud	70	21	22	31
Gun crime	62	25	4	12
People getting beaten up	55	29	9	25
Muggings/street robberies	45	34	7	23
Vandalism	40	33	9	28
Homes being broken into	31	34	9	25
Cars being broken into	34	30	9	23
Cars being stolen	31	31	6	20

1 British Crime Survey respondents were asked if they thought specific crimes had increased locally or nationally. Data are the proportion of people who answered 'increased a lot' or 'increased a little'.

Source: British Crime Survey, Home Office

The *Crime and Disorder Act (1998)* defined anti-social behaviour as 'acting in a manner that caused or was likely to cause harassment, alarm or distress, to one or more persons not of the same household (as the defendant)'. In 2008/09, 17 per cent of people questioned in England and Wales believed that there were high levels of anti-social behaviour in their area (Table 9.10). The most common anti-social behaviours

Table 9.10

Anti-social behaviour indicators[1,2,3]

England & Wales   Percentages

	1992	1996	2000	2002/03	2004/05	2006/07	2008/09
Teenagers hanging around on the streets	20	24	32	33	31	33	30
Rubbish or litter lying around	30	26	30	33	30	31	30
People using or dealing drugs	14	21	33	32	26	28	28
Vandalism, graffiti and other deliberate damage to property	26	24	32	35	28	28	27
People being drunk or rowdy in public places	.	.	.	23	22	26	26
Noisy neighbours or loud parties	8	8	9	10	9	11	10
Abandoned or burnt-out cars[4]	.	.	14	25	12	9	6
High level of perceived anti-social behaviour[5]	.	.	.	21	17	18	17

1 Until 2000 respondents were asked to recall their experience of crime in the previous calendar year. From 2001/02 the British Crime Survey became a continuous survey and the recall period was changed to the 12 months prior to interview.
2 People saying anti-social behaviour is a 'very/fairly big problem' in their area.
3 Percentages do not sum to 100 per cent as respondents could give more than one answer.
4 Question only asked of a quarter of the sample in 2002/03.
5 This measure is derived from responses to seven individual anti-social behaviour strands. See Appendix, Part 9: Anti-social behaviour indicators.

Source: British Crime Survey, Home Office

identified were teenagers hanging around on the streets and rubbish or litter lying around, both reported by 30 per cent of survey respondents, followed by people using or dealing drugs (28 per cent); vandalism, graffiti and other deliberate damage to property (27 per cent); and people being drunk or rowdy in public (26 per cent). Between 2002/03 and 2008/09, the proportion of people who perceived abandoned or burned out cars to be a problem fell from 25 per cent to 6 per cent.

Perceived levels of anti-social behaviour varied according to household and area characteristics, age and sex. For example, 19 per cent of households in urban areas felt there to be a high level of anti-social behaviour in their area compared with 8 per cent of households in rural areas. People in social rented accommodation perceived higher levels of anti-social behaviour (29 per cent) than private renters (18 per cent) or owner-occupiers (13 per cent). Older people aged 65 and over (13 per cent) were less likely to feel that there was a high level of anti-social behaviour in their area compared to young people aged 16 to 24 (24 per cent). Young women were the most likely to feel that there was a high level of anti-social behaviour in their area: 29 per cent of women aged 16 to 24 compared with 20 per cent of men in the same age group. The gap between the sexes narrowed in the older age groups and at the oldest ages there was no difference: 9 per cent of both men and women aged 65 to 74 and 4 per cent of both men and women aged 75 and over felt there was a high level of anti-social behaviour problems in their area.

Offenders

Recorded crime figures based on administrative data collected by the police show that in 2008, 1.69 million offenders were found guilty of, or cautioned for, indictable and summary (including motoring) offences in England and Wales. (See Appendix, Part 9: Types of offence in England and Wales). Most of the offenders were male (76 per cent), of whom around 11 per cent were aged under 18.

In 2008, 32,700 people aged 10 to 14 were found guilty of, or cautioned for, an indictable offence in England and Wales. Males in this age group were more likely than females to be offenders, 22,200 compared with 10,500 (Figure 9.11). Of all offenders who were found guilty of, or cautioned for, an indictable offence in 2008, 35 per cent were aged 20 to 29, the highest proportion for any age group. The proportion of the population who were offenders declined with age as males and females entered their 30s. Less than 15 per cent of males and females over the age of 40 were found guilty of, or cautioned for, an indictable offence in 2008. For those aged 60 and over the proportion of the population who were offenders was negligible.

Figure 9.11

Offenders:[1,2,3] by age

England & Wales

Thousands

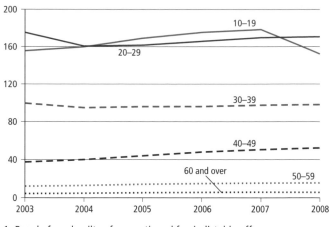

1 People found guilty of, or cautioned for, indictable offences.
2 For motoring offences only persons found guilty are included; these offences may attract written warnings, which are not included in this chart.
3 Data for April, July and August 2008 excludes convictions data for Cardiff magistrates' court.

Source: Office for Criminal Justice Reform, Ministry of Justice

In Northern Ireland, 7,600 offenders were found guilty of, or cautioned for, indictable offences in 2006. Of these, 88 per cent were male. Young men aged 19 and 20 were most likely to be offenders, with 4 per cent of this age group being found guilty of, or cautioned for, an indictable offence. The proportion of women who were offenders was less than 1 per cent for all age groups.

The type of indictable offences for which people were found guilty of, or cautioned for, were similar for men and women in England and Wales in 2008. For both men and women, the most common indictable offence was theft and handling stolen goods accounting for 31 per cent of all male offences (125,200) and 52 per cent of all female offences (48,900) (Figure 9.12). The second most common offences for men were drug offences (88,800) at 22 per cent followed by violence against the person (65,100) at 16 per cent of all male offences. Theft and handling stolen goods, violence against the person and drug offences accounted for the majority of all offences by females (78 per cent). 'Other offences', which include fraud and forgery and indictable motoring offences, accounted for 16 per cent of offences for both men and women.

In Northern Ireland, the most common offences to be found guilty of, or cautioned for, in 2006 were violent offences (violence against a person, sexual offences, and robbery) and acquisitive offences (theft, burglary and fraud and forgery)

Figure 9.12

Offenders found guilty of, or cautioned for, indictable offences:[1] by sex and type of offence, 2008

England & Wales

Thousands

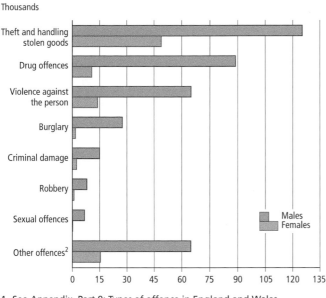

1 See Appendix, Part 9: Types of offence in England and Wales.
2 Includes fraud and forgery and indictable motoring offences.

Source: Office for Criminal Justice Reform, Ministry of Justice

both at 34 per cent, followed by criminal damage and drug related offences, at 17 per cent and 10 per cent respectively.

Not all offences have to be dealt with by the court, the police can deal with some people using a range of alternatives such as a simple caution, conditional caution, penalty notice for disorder or fixed penalty notice for motoring offences. Once the police obtain enough evidence for conviction, the offenders are charged and taken to court where, if found guilty, the court imposes a sentence. Sentences in England, Wales and Northern Ireland can include immediate custody, a community sentence, a fine or, if the court considers that no punishment is necessary, a discharge. In 2008, of the 495,200 offenders found guilty of, or cautioned for, indictable offences in England and Wales, 63 per cent (310,000 offenders) were sentenced (Table 9.13). The type of sentence given depends on the offence committed and other factors that may be applied on a case-by-case basis (see Appendix, Part 9: Sentences and orders). In 2008, the most common type of sentence was a community sentence (32 per cent), with more than two-fifths (44 per cent) of offenders sentenced for criminal damage receiving this sentence. Suspended sentence order was the least common sentence given at 9 per cent, with violence against a person and motoring offenders being the most likely offenders (18 per cent) to receive this sentence.

Table 9.13

Offenders sentenced for indictable offences: by type of offence[1] and type of sentence,[2] 2008

England & Wales   Percentages

	Discharge	Fine	Community sentence	Suspended sentence order	Immediate custody	Other	All sentenced (=100%) (thousands)
Theft and handling stolen goods	20	13	37	6	19	6	109.5
Drug offences	16	33	23	6	18	4	52.4
Violence against the person	5	4	36	18	33	4	39.8
Burglary	3	2	40	10	42	4	23.6
Fraud and forgery	14	12	28	15	30	3	16.9
Criminal damage	21	11	44	5	12	8	9.4
Motoring	3	20	27	18	30	2	4.6
Robbery	0	0	34	5	60	2	8.5
Sexual offences	3	2	27	8	58	2	5.1
Other offences	9	28	23	10	24	7	40.3
All indictable offences	13	16	32	9	25	5	310.0

1 See Appendix, Part 9: Types of offence in England and Wales.
2 Data are based on the principle offence basis, where an offender has been sentenced for more than one offence the principle offence is the one for which the heaviest sentence was imposed. See Appendix, Part 9: Sentences and orders.

Source: Ministry of Justice

Prisons and sentencing

Prison is the usual eventual destination for offenders given custodial sentences, and also for those who break the terms of their non-custodial sentence. Sentenced prisoners are classified into different risk-level groups for security purposes. Women prisoners are held in separate prisons or in separate accommodation in mixed prisons. Young offenders receiving custodial sentences have traditionally been separated from adult offenders, enabling them to receive additional educational and rehabilitative treatment.

The size of the prison population in England and Wales (those held in prison but excluding those in police cells, see Appendix, Part 9: Prison population for more details) has risen by 79 per cent over the years from 17,435 in 1900 when the records began to reach 82,572 in 2008. During this period the population of females in prisons almost doubled from 2,976 in 1900 to 4,414 in 2008, but decreased as a proportion of the male population from 17 per cent in 1900 to 5 per cent in 2008 (Figure 9.14). The prison population was relatively stable during the 1970s and early 1990s, but in the mid-1990s it began to increase. The largest increase during the 1990s occurred between 1996 and 1997 at 11 per cent. Apart from decreases of less than 1 per cent in 1993 and again in 1999, the prison population has increased annually since 1991.

Of the 70,800 British nationals in prison in England and Wales in 2008, the majority were White (79 per cent of male inmates and 83 per cent of female inmates) (Table 9.15). The second largest ethnic group within the prison population in 2008 was

Figure 9.14

Average prison population:[1,2] by sex

England & Wales

Thousands

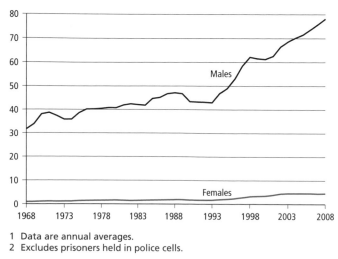

1 Data are annual averages.
2 Excludes prisoners held in police cells.

Source: Ministry of Justice

Table 9.15

Prison population of British nationals: by ethnic group[1]

England & Wales   Percentages

	2004	2005	2006	2007	2008
Males					
White	75	82	81	80	79
Mixed	2	3	3	3	3
Asian or Asian British	4	5	5	5	5
Black or Black British	9	10	11	11	11
Chinese and other ethnic group	-	-	-	-	-
Total male population (=100%) (thousands)	60.8	62.1	62.7	64.5	67.3
Females					
White	78	82	83	84	83
Mixed	4	5	4	4	4
Asian or Asian British	1	2	2	2	2
Black or Black British	9	10	10	9	9
Chinese and other ethnic group	-	-	-	-	-
Total female population (=100%) (thousands)	3.6	3.5	3.4	3.2	3.5

1 See Appendix, Part 1: Classification of ethnic groups.
Source: Ministry of Justice

Black or Black British, at 11 per cent of male inmates and 9 per cent of female inmates. The proportions of male and female inmates who were from the Mixed ethnic group were similar (3 per cent and 4 per cent respectively) but there were more Asian or Asian British males in prison (5 per cent of all inmates) than Asian or Asian British females (2 per cent).

On 30 June 2009 the prison population was 83,454, with a further 258 people held in secure training centres and 175 in local authority children's homes, an increase in total prison population of less than 1 per cent compared with June 2008. The increased prison population may partly result from a rise in the use of longer prison sentences. Average custodial sentence lengths given by the Crown court have increased from 21.8 months in 1998 to 24.5 months in 2008. Over the same period, the average length of custodial sentences given by the magistrates' courts has been stable at around three months.

In 2007, there were 2.7 million motoring offences in England and Wales dealt with by official police action or penalty notice charge, of which 2.6 million were fixed penalty notices issued by the police (including traffic wardens) which were paid and thus resulted in no further action. Speed and traffic light cameras in England and Wales provided evidence for almost

Table 9.16

Fixed penalties[1] for motoring offences detected by cameras: by type of offence

England & Wales   Thousands

	Speeding offences	Traffic light offences	All offences
2001	878	46	923
2002	1,135	71	1,206
2003	1,670	115	1,785
2004	1,787	113	1,900
2005	1,764	123	1,887
2006	1,634	119	1,752
2007	1,260	109	1,369

1 Includes paid, fixed penalties only. Offences where the fixed penalty was not paid are not counted, as further action was taken.

Source: Home Office

1.4 million of these fixed penalties, an increase of nearly half (48 per cent) compared with 2001 (Table 9.16). The majority (92 per cent) of those offences for which evidence had been provided by a camera were speeding offences, with the remainder being traffic light offences. Overall, cameras were used to provide evidence for 86 per cent of speeding offences in 2007 that resulted in fixed penalty notices being issued. Cameras were also used in 53 per cent of offences of neglect of traffic signs and directions and pedestrian rights, which includes traffic light offences.

Fixed penalty notices are motoring offences that are issued on the spot, and can be endorsable (accompanied by points added on the driving licence) or non-endorsable (no points added). There was a fall in the number of fixed penalty notices issued in England and Wales for the use of a hand-held mobile phone while driving, from 167,000 offences in 2006 to 122,000 offences in 2007. This is partly because, at the end of February 2007, the offence was changed from a non-endorsable offence to an endorsable offence, increasing the penalty and adding points to the offender's licence.

In 2007, 90 per cent of fixed penalty notices issued by the police were paid. Fixed penalty notices issued for endorsable offences were more likely to be paid without further enforcement action than were those for non-endorsable offences: 98 per cent of fixed penalty notices issued for endorsable offences were paid compared with 74 per cent of non-endorsable offences where the driver was present and 73 per cent of non-endorsable offences where the driver was not present.

Anti-social behaviour orders (ASBOs) were introduced in England and Wales under the *Crime and Disorder Act (1998)*

Figure 9.17

Number of anti-social behaviour orders (ASBOs) issued:[1] by age

England & Wales

Numbers

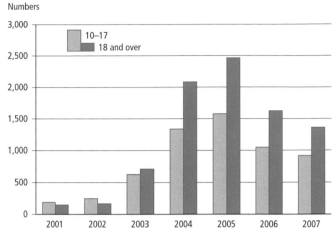

1 Issued at all HM Courts and reported to the Home Office by the Courts Service.

Source: Home Office

and have been available since April 1999. ASBOs are civil orders that impose restrictions on the behaviour of individuals who have behaved in an anti-social way in order to protect communities from often longstanding and intimidating activity. They can be made against anyone aged 10 and over.

The number of ASBOs issued in England and Wales increased from 350 in 2001 to a peak of 4,122 in 2005, since when they have fallen back to 2,299 in 2007. The increase between 2003 and 2005 followed the introduction of the *Anti-Social Behaviour Act* in 2003. This Act strengthened the ASBO by increasing the number of categories for which ASBOs can be awarded, enhancing their legal status and banning spray paint sales to people under the age of 16, and also gave local councils the power to order the removal of graffiti from private property. It also covers truancy, people making false reports of emergency, misuse of fireworks, private drunkenness and gang activity.

Of the 2,299 ASBOs issued in 2007, 17 ASBOs were to persons of unknown age. Of the 2,282 ASBOs issued to persons of known age 1,362 were issued to individuals aged 18 and over, and 920 were issued to 10 to 17-year-olds (Figure 9.17). A larger proportion of males than females were issued ASBOs in 2007. Of the total number of ASBOs issued in this year, half (50 per cent) were issued to men aged 18 and over and more than a third (36 per cent) were issued to males aged 10 to 17, while 9 per cent were issued to women aged 18 and over and 4 per cent were issued to females aged 10 to 17. The remaining 1 per cent were issued to males whose age was unknown.

Table 9.18

People sentenced to life imprisonment:[1] by sex

England & Wales   Numbers

	Males	Females	All people
1998	380	14	394
2000	446	21	467
2002	536	19	555
2004	548	22	570
2006	531	16	547
2008	495	28	523

1 See Appendix, Part 9: Sentences and orders.

Source: Ministry of Justice

Between June 2000 and December 2007 a total of 14,972 ASBOs were issued in England and Wales. Of these, more than half (53 per cent) were proved in court to have been breached at least once and 39 per cent were proved to have been breached more than once.

Life imprisonment, or its equivalent, must be imposed on all persons aged 10 and over convicted of murder. This sentence may also be imposed for a number of the most serious crimes, including manslaughter, robbery, rape, assault with intent to do grievous bodily harm, aggravated burglary, and certain firearms offences. In 2008, 523 people were sentenced to life imprisonment in England and Wales, a fall of 4 per cent compared with 2006 (Table 9.18). The great majority of people sentenced to life imprisonment were men (95 per cent) and just over one in ten (11 per cent) were aged 18 to 20 and one in twenty (almost 5 per cent) were males aged 10 to 17.

In Scotland, 32 people were sentenced to life imprisonment in 2008, excluding those given indeterminate sentences. This was a decrease of 21 persons on the previous year. More than three-quarters (78 per cent) were men aged 21 and over, and 19 per cent were men aged 18 to 20. No life sentences have been issued to anyone aged under 18 in Scotland since 2004.

Resources

There were 43 police forces in England and Wales employing 143,770 full-time equivalent police officers at 31 March 2009, the highest number of police officers ever recorded. Of these, 6,290 police officers were from an ethnic minority group, equivalent to 4.4 per cent of the total police strength and double the proportion recorded in 2000 (2.2 per cent) (Table 9.19). The proportion of police officers belonging to an ethnic minority was lower at senior ranks. In 2009, 2.8 per cent

Table 9.19

Ethnic[1] minority police officers as a proportion of all police officers: by rank[2]

England & Wales   Percentages

	2008	2009
Association of Chief Police Officers	3.3	4.0
Chief Superintendents	2.3	2.8
Superintendents	2.9	3.2
Chief Inspectors	3.0	2.7
Inspectors	2.6	3.1
Sergeants	3.0	3.2
Constables	4.4	4.8
All ethnic minority police officers	4.1	4.4

1 See Appendix, Part 1: Classification of ethnic groups.
2 As at 31 March in each year.

Source: Home Office

of officers at chief superintendent level were from an ethnic minority compared with 4.8 per cent of officers who were constables. One per cent of officers did not state their ethnicity in 2009. Of the officers who stated they were from an ethnic minority group, 39.3 per cent were Asian or Asian British, 27.0 per cent were from the Mixed ethnic group, 22.7 per cent were Black or Black British and 11.0 per cent were from the Chinese or Other ethnic group.

The proportion of ethnic minority officers varies by police force in England and Wales. The largest proportion of ethnic minority officers were based in the Metropolitan Police force (8.8 per cent) which accounted for 45 per cent of all ethnic minority police officers in England and Wales, followed by West Midlands (7.7 per cent), accounting for 11 per cent, Leicestershire (6.6 per cent) accounting for 2 per cent and Bedfordshire (6.1 per cent) accounting for 1 per cent. Police officers from ethnic minority groups accounted for less than 1 per cent of the total police strength in four police force areas in 2009: North Wales (0.8 per cent), Devon and Cornwall (0.8 per cent), Dyfed Powys (0.7 per cent) and Humberside (0.9 per cent).

A quarter (25.1 per cent) of all police officers in England and Wales were women at 31 March 2009. This proportion was lower in the more senior ranks with 13.0 per cent of officers at rank of chief inspector or above being female compared with 27.9 per cent who were constables.

According to the 2008/09 British Crime Survey just over two-thirds (67 per cent) of people in England and Wales had overall confidence in the police in their local area, a

Table 9.20

Ratings and perceptions of local police

England & Wales

Percentages

	2005/06	2006/07	2007/08	2008/09
Ratings of local police[1]				
How good a job do you think the police are doing	50	51	53	53
Perceptions of police in local area[2]				
Would treat you with respect if you had contact with them	82	83	83	84
Treat everyone fairly regardless of who they are	63	62	64	65
Understand the issues that affect this community	60	60	62	65
Are dealing with the things that matter to people in the community	49	49	51	54
Can be relied on to be there when you need them	47	47	48	48
Can be relied on to deal with minor crimes	42	41	43	46
Overall confidence in the local police[2,3]	63	64	65	67

1 Proportion of respondents who rated police as excellent/good.
2 Proportion of respondents who strongly agreed/tended to agree with the statement.
3 Based on the question 'Taking everything into account I have confidence in the police in this area'.

Source: British Crime Survey, Home Office

2 percentage point increase since 2007/08 (Table 9.20). More than half (53 per cent) of people thought that their local police force was doing a good or excellent job, the same proportion as the previous year, and a 3 percentage point increase since 2005/06. In general, these indicators showed that the majority of people in England and Wales agreed that their local police treat people with respect (84 per cent), that they treat everyone fairly (65 per cent), and that they understand the issues affecting the community (65 per cent). People were less likely to agree that their local police force could be relied upon to be there when needed (48 per cent) or to deal with minor crimes (46 per cent).

The proportion of people who agreed that their local police force was doing a good or excellent job in 2008/09 varied according to certain demographic characteristics. For example, women were more inclined than men to rate the police as doing a good or excellent job (56 per cent compared with 51 per cent) and people from non-White groups were more likely than White people to rate the police as doing a good or excellent job (57 per cent compared with 53 per cent). However, 67 per cent of men thought that the police would treat people fairly, compared with 63 per cent of women. Similarly, 84 per cent of White people thought that the police would treat people with respect, compared with 81 per cent of people from non-White groups.

In 2008/09, a total of 31,259 complaint cases were made by members of the public against those serving with the police in

England and Wales, an increase of 8 per cent on the previous year and the most complaints recorded in a single year since 1990 (Figure 9.21). Complaints were made by 31,673 individuals in England and Wales in 2008/09, a rate of approximately one complainant per complaint. Almost two-thirds (63 per cent) of complainants were White,

Figure 9.21

Number of complaint cases recorded[1,2] by police forces

England & Wales

Thousands

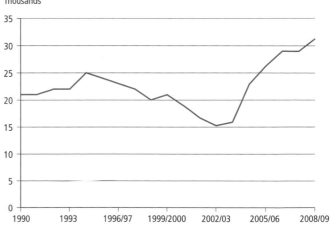

1 Complaints made by members of the public against those serving with the police. Includes completed complaint cases and pending cases at end of reporting year.
2 Data from 2004/05 are post-*Police Reform Act 2002*.

Source: Independent Police Complaints Commission

7 per cent were Black, 6 per cent were Asian, 3 per cent were in the Other ethnic group and the ethnicity of around a fifth (22 per cent) of complainants was unknown.

A complaint may comprise one or more allegations, for example, a person may complain that a police officer was rude to them (one complaint) or that he was rude to them and that he pushed them (two allegations but treated as one complaint). There were 53,534 allegations in England and Wales in 2008/09, a rise of 11 per cent on 2007/08. The most common types were 'incivility, impoliteness and intolerance' (21 per cent), which includes abusive, offensive or rude language or behaviour, and 'other assault' (13 per cent), which includes allegations that unreasonable force was used. Allegations of 'other neglect or failure in duty' (24 per cent) includes allegations such as a failure to record or investigate matters and keep interested parties informed. Allegations of discriminatory behaviour formed 3 per cent of the total, the majority of which (76 per cent) concerned allegations of racial discrimination.

The British Crime Survey asked people in England and Wales how confident they were that the Criminal Justice System (CJS) was fair and effective. Overall, 59 per cent of people questioned in 2008/09 thought that the CJS was fair although fewer people (38 per cent) thought that it was effective. However, levels of confidence in the CJS, particularly in its effectiveness, vary considerably by the respondent's occupation (Table 9.22). For example, 72 per cent of full-time students felt that the CJS was fair and 60 per cent thought that it was effective. In comparison, 56 per cent of those in intermediate or routine and manual occupations felt that the CJS was fair and 35 per cent of those in managerial and professional or intermediate occupations thought that it was effective.

Table 9.22

Confidence in the criminal justice system (CJS): by respondent's occupation, 2008/09

England & Wales   Percentages

	Confidence that the CJS is fair	Confidence that the CJS is effective
Managerial and professional occupations	59	35
Intermediate occupations	56	35
Routine and manual occupations	56	38
Never worked and long-term unemployed	68	52
Full-time students	72	60
Not classified	49	32

Source: British Crime Survey, Home Office

White people were less likely to have confidence in the CJS than people from other ethnic groups. In 2008/09, 57 per cent of White people thought that the CJS was fair and 36 per cent thought that it was effective. In comparison, 72 per cent of Asian or Asian British people thought that the CJS was fair and 61 per cent thought that it was effective. For Black and Black British people, the equivalent figures were 60 per cent and 51 per cent.

People who had any type of contact with the police in the 12 months prior to interview were slightly less likely to believe that the CJS was fair (57 per cent) or effective (37 per cent) that those who had not had contact with the police (61 per cent and 40 per cent).

Housing

- Between 1971 and 2007, there was a 38 per cent increase in the number of dwellings in Great Britain, from 18.8 million to 25.9 million, exceeding the increase in the number of households. (Figure 10.1)

- Between 1997/98 and 2008/09, the proportion of households accepted as homeless in England because family and friends were unable or unwilling to accommodate them increased from 26 per cent to 37 per cent, reaching a peak of 38 per cent in 2005/06. (Figure 10.8)

- In 2007/08, 68 per cent of owner-occupiers in England were very satisfied with their current accommodation, compared with 49 per cent of social renters and 47 per cent of private renters. (Table 10.13)

- The proportion of first-time buyers in the UK aged under 25 fell from 30 per cent in 1990 to 18 per cent in 2008, reaching a low of 16 per cent in 2003. (Figure 10.16)

- The average house price in the UK was 12.5 per cent lower in the first quarter (Q1) of 2009 than in Q1 2008. This is the largest annual decline since the series began in 1969. (Figure 10.18)

- Between 1988 and 2008, deposits for first-time buyers in the UK tended to rise each year, increasing from 12 per cent to 22 per cent of purchase price, and with a peak of 23 per cent in 2003. (Figure 10.20)

DATA

Download data by clicking the online pdf

www.statistics.gov.uk/
socialtrends

A range of social, economic and demographic factors affect where a person lives, the tenure, type and condition of their home, their living conditions, and their satisfaction with the area where they live. Over the last 40 years there have been some notable changes in people's living situations, from who they live with, to the type of homes in which they live. There have also been changes in the level of housebuilding and in the condition of the existing housing stock. Conditions in both the housing market and the wider economy in the last few years have made it more difficult for people to arrange finance to purchase a home for the first time, or to move.

Housing stock and housebuilding

The number of dwellings in Great Britain increased dramatically over the last century, from 7.7 million in 1901 to 25.9 million in 2007 (Figure 10.1). Although the stock of dwellings increased in every decade from 1900, the increase was slower between 1911 and 1921 and in the 1920s. This was partly because the First World War led to a slow-down in new building and because some existing buildings were in need of repair.

The housing stock has almost doubled since 1951, reflecting the greater demand for homes caused by the growing population (see Chapter 1: Population, Table 1.1) and, more particularly, a trend towards smaller households that has emerged since the 1970s (see Chapter 2: Households and families). During the period 1971 to 2007 the number of dwellings increased by 38 per cent, from 18.8 million to

25.9 million, which exceeded the 31 per cent increase in the number of households in Great Britain, from 18.6 million to 24.4 million (see also Chapter 2: Households and families). Over the same period the population increased much less: by 9 per cent from 54.3 million to 59.2 million. More recently, between 2006 and 2007, there was a 1 per cent increase in both the number of dwellings (from 25.7 million to 25.9 million) and number of households (from 24.2 million to 24.4 million) and a 0.5 per cent increase in the population (58.9 million to 59.2 million).

The increase in the stock of dwellings slowed down during the 1990s, which is reflected in the number of housebuilding completions in England. Between 1991/92 and 1996/97 the number of new homes built, which includes houses, bungalows and flats (see Appendix, Part 10: Housebuilding completions), fell by 6 per cent from 155,100 new homes to 146,300 new homes, and fell to a low of 129,900 new homes built in 2001/02 (Table 10.2). The number of dwellings completed each year rose throughout the first half of the 2000s, to a peak of just over 168,100 in 2007/08, equivalent to an increase of 29 per cent over the period from 2001/02. However, from 2007/08 the number of new homes being built started to decline. Between 2007/08 and 2008/09 the number

Figure 10.1

Dwelling stock[1,2]

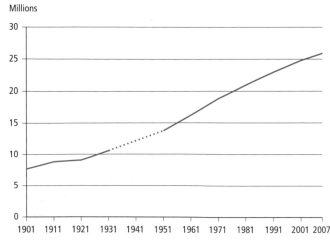

Great Britain

Millions

1 See Appendix, Part 10: Dwelling stock.
2 No census was undertaken in 1941, so data for this year is plotted as the mid-point between 1931 and 1951.

Source: Communities and Local Government

Table 10.2

Housebuilding completions:[1] by number of bedrooms

England					Percentages
	1991/92	1996/97	2001/02	2007/08	2008/09
Houses					
1 bedroom	4	1	-	-	-
2 bedrooms	22	21	11	8	10
3 bedrooms	28	36	28	25	23
4 or more bedrooms	20	26	37	19	17
All houses	74	84	77	52	50
Flats					
1 bedroom	15	7	6	11	13
2 bedrooms	10	8	15	36	36
3 bedrooms	1	1	1	1	1
4 or more bedrooms	-	-	-	-	-
All flats	26	16	23	48	50
All houses and flats (=100%) (thousands)	155	146	130	168	134

1 See Appendix, Part 10: Housebuilding completions.

Source: Communities and Local Government

of completions decreased by 20 per cent to just over 133,800, the lowest number recorded since 2001/02. In Scotland and Wales, housebuilding completions also fell by similar proportions in 2008/09, 17 per cent and 18 per cent respectively. There were 21,400 completions in Scotland and 7,100 in Wales.

In 1991/92 almost three-quarters (74 per cent) of housebuilding completions in England were houses and around a quarter (26 per cent) were flats. However, new dwellings constructed over the past 10 years have reflected changes to the type and size of households. A shift to the construction of smaller homes meant that by 2008/09 half (50 per cent) of homes completed were flats. The largest increase over the period 1991/92 to 2008/09 was in the construction of two bedroom flats, which increased from 10 per cent to 36 per cent of total completions.

The density of new homes has also increased. In 2007, new dwellings in England were built at an average of 44 per hectare, compared with 41 in 2006 and 26 in 1991. The East of England and the East Midlands had the lowest density of newly built homes, at 35 and 37 dwellings per hectare respectively. Although London had the highest density of new homes of any English region, at 76 dwellings per hectare, this was a decrease of 28 per cent on 2005, when the density of new homes was 106 per hectare.

There has been concern in recent years about the level of building in flood risk areas. The Environment Agency estimates that around 2 million properties in England and Wales are at risk from flooding and that changes in our climate, such as more severe storms and wetter winters, will increase that risk. New developments built in flood risk areas, particularly on floodplains, can increase the risk of flooding by reducing the capacity for floodwaters to drain away. In 2007/08 the Environment Agency objected to 6,200 planning applications on the grounds of flood risk, compared with 4,750 objections in the previous year.

In England in 2007, 9 per cent of all new dwellings were built in areas of high flood risk. The proportion varied by English region, from 2 per cent of properties built in the North East to 17 per cent in both Yorkshire and the Humber and London.

Affordable housing (see Appendix, Part 10: Affordable homes schemes) includes social rented and intermediate affordable housing, which is provided to eligible households whose needs are not met by the commercial market. Between 1995/96 and 2004/05 there was a steady decline in the number of additional homes supplied to the market for social renting, from 57,000 to 22,000 (Figure 10.3).

Figure 10.3

Additional affordable homes provided to the market: by type of scheme[1]

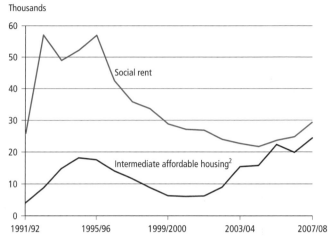

England

Thousands

1 See Appendix, Part 10: Affordable homes schemes.
2 Intermediate affordable housing is the sum of intermediate rent and low cost home ownership. Intermediate rent allows those unable to buy a home to rent from a registered social landlord (RSL) at a discounted price. Low cost home ownership schemes such as shared ownership allow people to purchase part of a home and pay rent on the remainder.

Source: Communities and Local Government

However, between 2004/05 and 2007/08 there were increases in the number of additional homes supplied for this purpose. The largest increase (19 per cent) in this period was between 2006/07 and 2007/08, from around 25,000 to around 29,000.

As well as homes for social rent, a number of affordable homes are made available through other schemes, such as intermediate affordable housing. Intermediate affordable housing is housing where prices or rents are above social rent but below open market rents or prices. This includes intermediate rent and low cost home ownership, such as shared equity schemes (see Appendix, Part 10: Affordable homes schemes). During the 1990s, the number of additional homes supplied as intermediate affordable housing was well below the number of homes supplied for social rent but, since 2005/06 they have been much closer in number. The number of additional homes supplied as intermediate affordable housing was highest in 2007/08, at over 24,000 homes, more than a sixfold increase from 1991/92 and a 23 per cent increase on 2006/07. This increase follows an increase in government funding for such schemes and a broadening of the products available for low cost home ownership (such as the Home Buy range and the First Time Buyer's initiative). In 2007/08 there were more than 17,000 new builds for low cost home ownership, the highest level since the series began.

10

Tenure and accommodation

Between quarter 2 (Q2) 1997 and Q2 2005, the number of owner-occupied households in the UK rose by 1.6 million, from 16.2 million to 17.7 million (Figure 10.4). By Q2 2009, this figure had fallen slightly to 17.5 million households. In contrast, the number of households renting from the social sector fell consistently between Q2 1997 (5.3 million) and Q2 2005 (4.5 million) but had risen to 4.6 million in Q2 2007 and Q2 2008 before returning to 4.5 million in Q2 2009. There was a gradual increase in the number of privately rented households between Q2 1997 and Q2 2005, from 2.4 million to 2.8 million. In Q2 2009, there were 3.8 million privately rented households, an increase of 9 per cent on the previous year.

Over the last decade there has been an increase in the proportion of younger households in the UK (that is where the household reference person is aged under 30) living in privately rented properties, from around 30 per cent in Q2 1997 to 49 per cent in Q2 2009 (Figure 10.5). Conversely, over the same period, the proportion of these younger households buying their homes with a mortgage decreased from 43 per cent to 29 per cent. Various lifestyle changes may have contributed to this pattern, for example, people are now generally marrying later in life than they did 10 years ago (see also Chapter 2: Households and families, Partnerships). In addition, more young people are going to university and some leave home to live in shared accommodation before setting up their own homes.

Figure 10.4

Households: by tenure[1,2]

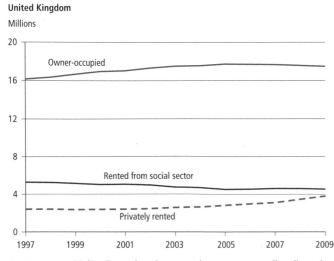

United Kingdom
Millions

1 Data are at Q2 (April–June) each year and are not seasonally adjusted. See Appendix, Part 4: Labour Force Survey.
2 See Appendix, Part 10: Private and social sectors, and Tenure.

Source: Labour Force Survey, Office for National Statistics

Figure 10.5

Households aged under 30:[1,2] by tenure[3]

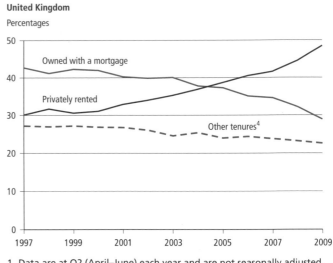

United Kingdom
Percentages

1 Data are at Q2 (April–June) each year and are not seasonally adjusted. See Appendix, Part 4: Labour Force Survey.
2 Data are based on household reference persons aged under 30. See Appendix, Part 10: Household reference person.
3 See Appendix, Part 10: Tenure.
4 Includes those who owned outright, rented from the local authority or registered social landlord (RSL), squatters and those where tenure was not known.

Source: Labour Force Survey, Office for National Statistics

In recent years increasing house prices have made it more difficult to purchase a home, meaning that people who may otherwise have bought a property are increasingly staying in, or moving back to, their parental homes, or are living in rented accommodation. There was a gradual decline over the period in the proportion of younger households in other tenures, including renting from registered social landlords and from local authorities.

Tenure varies not only according to the age of the household but also by their economic activity status. In Q2 2009 in the UK almost three-fifths (57 per cent) of those who owned their homes outright were retired and around two-fifths (36 per cent) were in employment (Table 10.6). This compares with 6 per cent who were economically inactive for a reason other than retirement (including long-term sick, those looking after the family or home and students) and 2 per cent who were unemployed. The majority of households buying their homes with a mortgage were working, 84 per cent in full-time employment and 8 per cent in part-time employment.

In Q2 2009, 68 per cent of private renters were in employment, compared with 33 per cent of social renters. Conversely, social renters were more likely than private renters to be economically inactive. A similar proportion of social and private renters were unemployed in the quarter.

Table 10.6

Economic activity status of household reference person:[1] by tenure,[2] 2009[3]

United Kingdom

Percentages

| | In employment | | Total in employment | Unemployed | Economically inactive | |
	Full-time	Part-time			Retired	Other[5]
All owner-occupied	57	9	66	1	28	4
Owned outright	26	10	36	2	57	6
Owned with a mortgage	84	8	92	1	3	3
Rented from social sector	22	10	33	7	30	29
Privately rented	57	11	68	6	9	17
All tenures[4]	51	9	60	3	26	11

1 See Appendix, Part 10: Household reference person.
2 See Appendix, Part 10: Tenure.
3 Data are at Q2 (April–June) and are not seasonally adjusted. See Appendix, Part 4: Labour Force Survey.
4 Includes squatters and those where tenure was not known.
5 Includes students, those looking after the family or home, those who are either temporarily or long-term sick or disabled, and discouraged workers.

Source: Labour Force Survey, Office for National Statistics

Over the last decade, of those who owned their own homes outright, there were slight increases in the proportions who were in employment (from 31 per cent in Q2 1998 to 36 per cent in Q2 2009) and among those buying with a mortgage (from 88 per cent in Q2 1998 to 92 per cent in Q2 2009).

As well as age and economic activity status, tenure varies markedly according to the size and composition of the household. In Q2 2009 in the UK, lone parent households with dependent children were more likely than any other type of household to rent property rather than own it. Two-thirds (66 per cent) of lone parent households with dependent children rented their home, mostly from registered social landlords or local authorities (43 per cent), while around a third (34 per cent) lived in owner-occupied accommodation. In contrast, three-quarters (75 per cent) of couple households with dependent children were owner-occupiers and 25 per cent rented (12 per cent from the social sector).

According to the bedroom standard, a household is classified as being overcrowded if the number of bedrooms available is less than the number deemed necessary according to the size and composition of the household (see Appendix, Part 10: Bedroom standard). During the period 2005/06 to 2007/08, on this definition around 3 per cent of homes in England were overcrowded, and 25 per cent had a number of bedrooms that was equal to the standard, in other words they had exactly the number of bedrooms that were needed by the household (Table 10.7). Thirty five per cent had one bedroom more than was needed, and 37 per cent of homes over this period were

classified as being under-occupied, that is they had two or more bedrooms more than was deemed necessary.

The likelihood of being overcrowded varied by tenure. Those living in rented accommodation were more likely to have fewer bedrooms than were needed: 6 per cent of social renters and 5 per cent of private renters lived in overcrowded accommodation over the period 2005/06 to 2007/08. This compares with 2 per cent among those buying their homes with a mortgage and 1 per cent of those who owned their homes outright.

Table 10.7

Overcrowding and under-occupation:[1] by tenure,[2] 2005/06–2007/08[3]

England

Percentages

	Overcrowded	Equal to standard	1 bedroom above standard	Under-occupied
All owner-occupied	1	15	37	47
Owned outright	1	9	33	58
Owned with a mortgage	2	19	41	38
Rented from social sector	6	53	29	12
Privately rented	5	44	35	17
All tenures	3	25	35	37

1 See Appendix, Part 10: Bedroom standard.
2 See Appendix, Part 10: Tenure.
3 Data are three-year rolling averages.

Source: Survey of English Housing, Communities and Local Government

10

The number of households accepted as homeless and in priority need increased sharply from 1997/98 to reach a peak of around 135,000 in 2003/04. Since then, the number has halved to just over 53,000 in 2008/09. Living in overcrowded accommodation, or at least not having any spare bedrooms, means that households have less space available for household members and less space for others to come and stay. The inability, or unwillingness, of friends or relatives to accommodate people in need of a place to stay has been the most common reason for households in England to be accepted as homeless and in priority need since 1997/98 (Figure 10.8) (see Appendix, Part 10: Homeless in priority need). In 1997/98, 26 per cent of these households were homeless for this reason although similar proportions were homeless because of relationship breakdowns (25 per cent) or because their private rented accommodation (including that tied to a job) had come to an end (23 per cent). Between 1997/98 and 2008/09, the proportion of households accepted as homeless because of family and friends being unable to accommodate them increased from 26 per cent to 37 per cent of total acceptances, reaching a peak of 38 per cent in 2005/06. Over the same period the proportion becoming homeless due to relationship breakdowns fell by 7 percentage points, from 25 per cent to 18 per cent.

Figure 10.8

Households accepted as homeless: by main reason for loss of last settled home[1]

England

Percentages

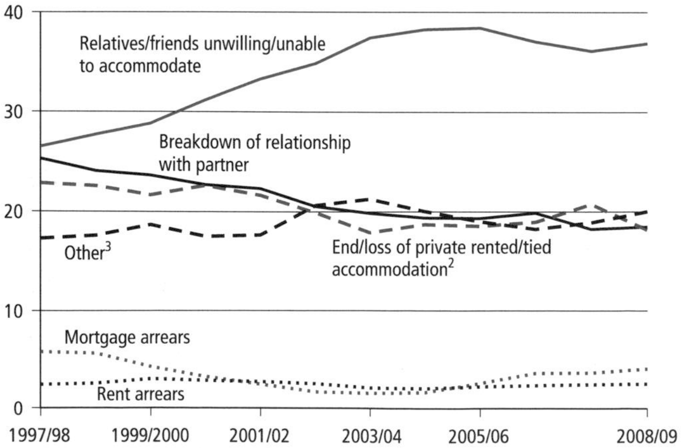

1 Households found to be eligible for assistance, unintentionally homeless and falling within a priority need group, and consequently owed a main homelessness duty by a local housing authority.
2 Mainly the ending of an assured tenancy.
3 Includes households leaving an institution (such as hospital, prison or a residential home), and those returning from abroad, sleeping rough or in hostels, or made homeless by an emergency such as fire or flooding.

Source: Communities and Local Government

Between 2007/08 and 2008/09, there was a slight decrease in the proportion of households accepted as homeless because their rented or tied accommodation came to an end, from 21 per cent to 18 per cent. There were increases for all the other reasons over the same period, including a small rise in 2008/09 in the proportion of households accepted as homeless because of rent and mortgage arrears, which may reflect the difficulties associated with households' finances in the recession.

Housing condition and satisfaction with the area

In recent years there has been an increasing focus on environmental issues, which has resulted in attempts by both government and environmental groups to encourage people to reduce their use of energy and therefore their impact on global warming. The energy used in constructing, occupying and operating buildings is estimated to represent around 50 per cent of greenhouse gas emissions in the UK, so there has been a particular focus on reducing the emissions of buildings and services. Legislation was passed in 2006 to update the Building Regulations 2000, to ensure all new buildings (residential and commercial) available to purchase or rent in England and Wales meet higher standards of energy efficiency. This provided methods to calculate performance of buildings and the setting of energy performance standards for new buildings. In addition, the requirement to have an Energy Performance Certificate (EPC) which states the energy efficiency of a home, has come into force on a phased basis from 1 August 2007, and is now a mandatory part of the Home Information Pack for all homes sold.

The energy efficiency rating of a home is based on the Standard Assessment Procedure (SAP) which is an index of energy costs based on annual space and water heating costs. The index rates properties on a scale from 1 (highly energy inefficient) to 100 (highly energy efficient) with 100 representing zero energy cost (see Appendix, Part 10: Standard Assessment Procedure (SAP)). The energy efficiency of all homes in England has steadily improved from an average SAP rating of 42 in 1996 to 50 in 2007.

For EPCs the energy performance rating is presented in a banding system, with band A containing the most energy efficient properties down to band G with the least energy efficient. Very few homes in England (0.2 per cent) were in the highest bands for energy efficiency (A and B) in 2007 – 35,000 properties. Four per cent of properties (880,000) were in the least energy efficient band (band G). The majority of homes were in band E, 8.9 million, or band D, 7.3 million, (40 per cent and 33 per cent respectively). In Scotland in 2007, the majority of homes were in band D (48 per cent) and band E (27 per cent) with only 1 per cent in band G.

The energy efficiency of the home varies by tenure, with social rented homes more likely than privately rented homes to be energy efficient (Figure 10.9). In 2007, more than a quarter (26 per cent) of homes rented from registered social landlords (RSLs) in England achieved a band C rating, followed by local authority homes (15 per cent). Conversely, only 4 per cent of owner-occupied accommodation achieved this band rating. Owner-occupied and private rented accommodation was most likely to be in band E (44 per cent and 36 per cent respectively) compared with 30 per cent of local authority homes and 23 per cent of RSL homes.

As well as being more likely than other housing tenures to be energy inefficient, private housing, which includes private rented and owner-occupied dwellings, is also more likely to fail the criteria of a 'decent' home. A home must meet all four of the criteria in order to be defined as 'decent' (see Appendix, Part 10: Decent home standard). In 2007, 36 per cent of private

housing and 29 per cent of social housing in England failed to meet the statutory minimum standard for housing. Private housing was more likely to fail the decent home standard for each of the criteria, with the exception of modern facilities; 5 per cent of social homes failed this criterion compared with 3 per cent of private homes. The largest difference between social and private housing was in failure to meet the Housing Health and Safety Rating System (HHSRS) which almost a quarter (24 per cent) of private homes failed compared with 13 per cent of social homes.

Privately rented homes were the most likely of all tenure types to fail at least one of the four decent homes criteria, with 45 per cent rated as non-decent compared with between 26 per cent and 34 per cent in the other tenures (Figure 10.10). Almost a third (31 per cent) of privately rented homes failed the HHSRS compared with just over a fifth (22 per cent) of owner-occupied homes. Failure to meet the HHSRS was also the most common reason for failing the decent home standard among local authority homes, with 15 per cent not meeting the criteria. However, among homes rented from registered social landlords (RSLs), the most common reason for failing the decent home standard was lack of thermal comfort (13 per cent) closely followed by failure under the HHSRS (12 per cent).

Figure 10.9

Energy efficient homes: by rating[1] and tenure,[2] 2007

England

Percentages

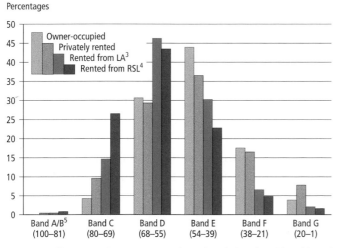

1　Energy efficiency ratings are grouped into bands (EER bands) and based on Standard Assessment Procedure (SAP) ratings which are shown in brackets. See Appendix, Part 10: Standard Assessment Procedure (SAP), and Energy Efficiency Rating (EER) Bands.
2　See Appendix, Part 10: Tenure.
3　Local authority.
4　Registered social landlord.
5　EER bands A and B are grouped because of insufficient numbers of properties in band A.

Source: English House Condition Survey, Communities and Local Government

Figure 10.10

Homes failing decent homes criteria:[1] by tenure[2] and reason, 2007

England

Percentages

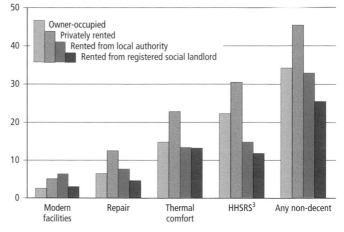

1　For definitions of the different criteria used in the decent home standard, see Appendix, Part 10: Decent home standard.
2　See Appendix, Part 10: Tenure.
3　The Housing Health and Safety Rating System (HHSRS) replaced the fitness standard as the statutory element of the decent home standard in April 2006. See Appendix, Part 10: Housing Health and Safety Rating System (HHSRS).

Source: English House Condition Survey, Communities and Local Government

As well as the condition of a home, the quality of the environment in which it is situated is also important. There are several aspects of a residential area that can be considered problematic and can contribute to it being considered a poor environment in which to live. For example, poor quality environments include those with poor upkeep, graffiti, rubbish or dog mess, those containing boarded-up buildings, intrusive industry, and traffic problems. Sixteen such environmental problems, as assessed by professional surveyors, can be grouped into three main types of problem to measure poor quality environments. These are upkeep, traffic and utilisation (see Appendix, Part 10: Poor quality environments).

In 2007, there were an estimated 3.2 million households in England living in poor quality environments. The overall proportion of households in poor quality environments remained fairly stable between 2003 and 2007 at around 15 to 16 per cent (Table 10.11). Over the same period, the most common environmental problems identified by surveyors were those relating to upkeep: in 2007, they identified 10 per cent of all households as having upkeep as a problem, the equivalent of 2.2 million households. Substantial traffic problems meant that 7 per cent of households (1.5 million) were considered to be in poor quality environments. A smaller proportion of households, around 2 per cent, were in areas with problems of utilisation, for example abandoned and boarded-up residential property. The environment in which a household is situated could be in more than one category of problem.

Table 10.11

Households living in poor quality environments:[1] by type of problem

England | | | | Percentages

	Upkeep	Traffic	Utilisation[2]	Any poor quality environment
2003	10.1	7.7	2.2	15.9
2004	10.1	7.0	1.9	15.4
2005	10.8	7.4	1.9	16.1
2006	10.4	7.6	1.7	15.9
2007	10.1	6.8	1.7	15.0

1 Based on surveyor's assessments of problems in the immediate area of the home. Percentages do not sum to totals as households could be assessed as living in more than one type of poor environment. See Appendix, Part 10: Poor quality environments.
2 Abandonment or non residential use of property, for example vacant sites and boarded up buildings.

Source: English House Condition Survey, Communities and Local Government

Householders' own views of the problems in the immediate environment of their homes differed to those of the surveyors. Traffic has been the most common concern reported by householders since 2003/04, and more than half (52 per cent) of householders stated this was a problem in their area in 2007/08 (Table 10.12). This was the same proportion as in 2006/07 but an increase of 11 percentage points since

Table 10.12

Households[1] experiencing problems[2] in local area: by type of problem

England | | | | | | | | | | Percentages

	1994/95	1997/98	1999/2000	2001/02	2002/03	2003/04	2004/05	2005/06	2006/07	2007/08[3]
Traffic	..	..	41	40	54	53	52	53	52	52
Crime	74	68	56	58	55	53	48	49	45	..
Litter and rubbish	46	41	42	45	45	45	43	43	43	43
Vandalism and hooliganism	59	55	40	45	43	43	40	41	40	39
Noise	25	24	23	22	27	27	27	28	27	27
Graffiti	32	29	22	26	25	24	23	23	23	22
Dogs	42	34	29	28	25	24	23	23	22	23
Neighbours	14	13	13	12	14	14	15	15	16	..
Racial harassment	5	4	4	4	4	4	5	6	6	7
Other harassment	..	..	..	..	6	5	5	6	6	..

1 Excludes households where the respondent was not the household reference person nor spouse or partner.
2 Householders were shown a list of problems and asked whether they thought each was a 'serious problem in this area', 'a problem in this area but not serious', or whether it was 'not a problem in this area'. All households reporting problems are included, whether serious or not.
3 The range of questions was reduced in 2007/08 so data are not available for crime, neighbours and other harassment.

Source: Survey of English Housing, Communities and Local Government

Table 10.13

Satisfaction with current accommodation: by tenure,[1] 2007/08

England   Percentages

	Owner-occupied	Rented from social sector	Privately rented	All households
Very satisfied	68	49	47	62
Fairly satisfied	28	33	38	30
Neither satisfied nor dissatisfied	2	5	6	3
Slightly dissatisfied	2	7	6	3
Very dissatisfied	-	6	4	2

1 See Appendix, Part 10: Tenure.

Source: Survey of English Housing, Communities and Local Government

1999/2000. In 2006/07, crime, the most common concern until 2002/03, was viewed as a problem by 45 per cent of householders, a proportion that has steadily declined from 74 per cent in 1994/95. The perceived problem with the largest decrease between 1994/95 and 2007/08 was vandalism and hooliganism, which decreased by 20 percentage points from 59 per cent to 39 per cent. Upkeep, the most common group of problems identified by surveyors, were also a concern of householders in 2007/08 – over two-fifths (43 per cent) stated that litter and rubbish was a problem in their area and around a fifth (22 per cent) viewed graffiti as a problem.

With such variation in the condition of people's homes as well as the quality of the environment in which they live, it is interesting to note that in England in 2007/08 more than four-fifths (82 per cent) of households were satisfied with both their home and the area in which they lived, a slight increase from 80 per cent reported a decade earlier. The majority of householders (92 per cent) were very or fairly satisfied with their current accommodation in 2007/08 (Table 10.13). Around three-fifths (62 per cent) of householders were very satisfied with their accommodation.

Overall satisfaction with current accommodation varied by tenure, with more than two-thirds (68 per cent) of owner-occupiers in England saying they were very satisfied with their homes in 2007/08, compared with around half of social and private renters (49 per cent and 47 per cent respectively). Only 2 per cent of owner-occupiers expressed slight dissatisfaction with their homes while 10 per cent of private renters and 13 per cent of social renters were either slightly or very dissatisfied with their accommodation.

Housing mobility

In 2007/08, 2.4 million households in England had lived at their current address for less than one year. Around 390,000 of these were new households formed during 2007/08 and the rest were continuing households. The most commonly cited reason for moving, averaged across all tenure groups, was to move to larger accommodation (17 per cent) followed by the wish to live independently (11 per cent) (Table 10.14 overleaf). A further 10 per cent of households moved home because they either changed job or wanted to live nearer to their jobs, and the same proportion because they wanted to live in a better area.

Reasons for moving varied according to the tenure of the household. In 2007/08, around a fifth (21 per cent) of owner-occupiers, according to their post-move tenure, moved because they wanted a larger house or flat, compared with 15 per cent of social renters and 14 per cent of private renters. Among owner-occupiers, 7 per cent moved because they wanted smaller accommodation. The majority of these are likely to be older households who own their properties outright and want to release equity or downsize to something more suitable for their needs. Only 4 per cent of private and social renters respectively moved for this reason. The second most common reason for moving among owner-occupiers was because they wanted to buy (15 per cent) followed by wanting to move to a better area (13 per cent). Among social renters, almost a fifth (19 per cent) moved because they wanted to live independently, while a similar proportion of private renters (17 per cent) moved because they had a new job or they wanted to live nearer to their existing job.

In 2007/08, 56 per cent of private renters (1.3 million) and 24 per cent of social renters (900,000) said they expected to buy their own home eventually. This compares with 60 per cent of private renters and 31 per cent of social renters in 2002/03. Of those who expected to buy in the future, private renters were more optimistic than social renters about when they would expect to become homeowners. Around a third (32 per cent) thought they would buy their own home in two to five years time and over a quarter (28 per cent) thought it would be less than two years before they bought a home (Figure 10.15 overleaf). Among social renters, 12 per cent thought they would buy a home within two years, more than a quarter (26 per cent) thought it would be between two and five years, and more than three-fifths (62 per cent) thought it would be five years or more before they bought a home.

There are a number of schemes for Low Cost Home Ownership (LCHO) that can act as a stepping stone between renting and purchasing a property, available to both private and social

10

Table 10.14

Main reason for moving: by post-move tenure,[1] 2007/08

England | | | | Percentages

	Current tenure			
	Owner-occupied	Rented from social sector	Privately rented	All tenures
Different size accommodation				
Wanted larger house or flat	21	15	14	17
Wanted smaller house or flat	7	4	4	5
Personal reasons				
Divorce or separation	5	5	7	6
Marriage or cohabitation	6	2	6	5
Other personal reasons	8	13	8	9
To move to a better area	13	7	8	10
Change of job/nearer to job	5	2	17	10
Accommodation no longer available	0	8	7	4
Wanted to buy	15	-	-	7
Couldn't afford mortgage or rent	-	2	2	1
To live independently	11	19	8	11
So children can get into a better school	1	-	1	1
Other reasons	7	22	18	14
All households (=100%) (thousands)	984	371	1,003	2,358

1 Household reference persons resident for less than one year. Includes both new and continuing households. See Appendix, Part 10: Tenure, and Household reference person.

Source: Survey of English Housing, Communities and Local Government

Figure 10.15

Buying aspirations of renters:[1] by when they expect to purchase a home, 2007/08

England

Percentages

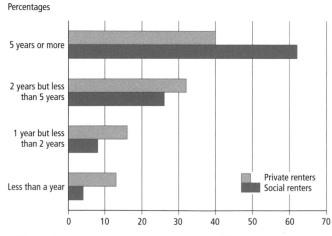

1 Those who expect to purchase a home eventually.

Source: Survey of English Housing, Communities and Local Government

renters (see also Figure 10.3 and Appendix, Part 10: Affordable homes schemes). One of the primary LCHO schemes is shared ownership, in which people share ownership of a property with a local authority, registered social landlord or other provider, and pay rent on the remaining part. Shared ownership may be targeted to key workers (such as teachers, nurses, police officers and prison officers) and others who are unable to afford the full costs of purchasing property, as it enables them to get on the property ladder and begin to build up equity. However, shared ownership does not always enable householders to move eventually to owner-occupation. A recent study by the Joseph Rowntree Foundation into housing mobility in this intermediate tenure group found that some shared owners who wanted to purchase their own home were unable to do so and some went on to live in rented accommodation. Lack of mobility has particularly been a concern during the recession. Falling house prices have meant that some shared owners were unable to bridge the equity gap between their current holdings and open market values and could not afford to move to full ownership.

During the 1990s it became increasingly difficult for young people to become homeowners. The proportion of first-time buyers (which includes some buyers who have previously owner a property, but are not in owner occupation at the time of purchase) in the UK aged under 25 fell from 30 per cent in 1990 to 16 per cent in 1999 (Figure 10.16). Over the same period the proportion of older first-time buyers, people aged 35 to 44, increased from 15 per cent to 20 per cent. The proportion of first-time buyers aged under 25 remained fairly stable between 2000 and 2003, fluctuating between 16 and 17 per cent, before increasing to 19 per cent in 2005. Most recently, between 2007 and 2008, there was a fall of almost 1 percentage point in the proportion of first-time buyers aged under 25. Over the same period the proportion of first-time buyers aged 25 to 34 decreased (from 56 per cent to 53 per cent) and the proportion of those aged 35 to 44 increased from 18 per cent to 19 per cent. The average age of first-time buyers in 2008 was 32, compared with 33 in 1990.

The proportion of existing owner-occupiers in the UK aged under 35 has declined since 1990. In 2008, 2 per cent of existing owner-occupiers were aged under 25 and 27 per cent were aged 25 to 34, compared with 8 per cent and 43 per cent respectively in the UK in 1990. Between 2007 and 2008 there was a decrease in the proportion of existing owner-occupiers aged 25 to 34 (from 31 per cent to 27 per cent) and an increase in the proportion of those aged 45 to 54 (from 21 per cent to 24 per cent). The average age of existing

owner-occupiers was 41 in 2008, compared with 40 in 2006 and 2007, and was the oldest age recorded since the series began in 1990, when the average age was 36.

These changes in the age breakdown of existing owner-occupiers and first-time buyers reflect both changes in society as well as an increasing difficulty for younger people to both get on the property ladder and the additional time it takes to do this. It may also reflect the difficulty faced by people who bought their homes within the last few years, at the peak of house prices, to move in the housing market conditions of 2008.

Housing market and finance

The state of the housing market can affect an individual's housing mobility, and is closely linked to conditions in the wider economy. Over the past 40 years, the economy and the housing market have mirrored one another, with booms and slumps in one tending to influence the other. During the 1980s the number of property transactions in England and Wales increased, mainly as a result of existing owner-occupiers moving home and an increase in the availability of affordable private stock because of the 'right-to-buy' initiative. Changes to the mortgage lending market in the 1980s may also have been a contributing factor to the 1980s property boom, when new households opted for ownership rather than renting. Following sharp increases in the interest rate in the two years from 1988 from 7.4 per cent in

Figure 10.16

Distribution of borrowers' ages:[1] by type of buyer

United Kingdom
Percentages

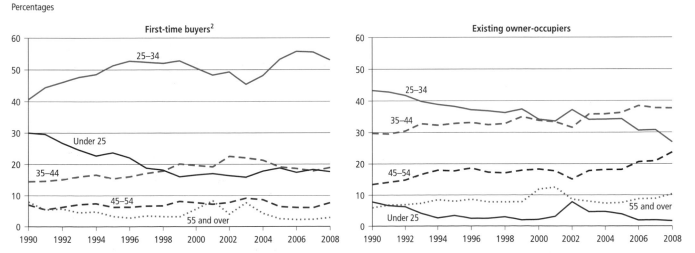

1 Based on the age of main borrower.
2 Includes some buyers who have previously owned a property, but are not in owner occupation at the time of purchase.

Source: Regulated Mortgage Survey, Council of Mortgage Lenders/BankSearch

mid-1988 to around 15 per cent two years later, the annual number of property transactions halved from a peak of 2.2 million in 1988 to 1.1 million by 1992, after which it fluctuated for several years in a generally upward direction. There was a similar boom in the housing market in the early to mid-2000s when the number of property transactions, including commercial premises, reached 1.8 million in 2007, the highest number recorded since 1988.

In April 2008 the way that property transactions were counted was changed, with data based on the new system backdated to April 2005 to allow a consistent time series (see Appendix, Part 10: Property transactions). Under the new system, transactions are based on actual completions instead of the number of stamp duty land tax certificates issued, and properties valued at less than £40,000 are excluded. By removing transactions at the very bottom of the market, the resulting data became closer to the sales of dwellings because many properties under £40,000 are likely to be of land only, or of land and buildings other than dwellings, rather than land and dwellings.

There were 1.7 million residential property transactions in the UK in 2006, and although the total number of transactions remained high in 2007, at 1.6 million, the count in December 2007 was over 30 per cent lower than in January 2007 (Figure 10.17). A sharp decline in the number of property transactions continued throughout most of 2008 and the overall number of transactions for that year was around 900,000.

The number of transactions in early 2009 dropped to 54,000 in January and 53,000 in February but then there were monthly increases to a total of 76,000 in July 2009, which is 10 per cent higher than in July 2008.

Directly linked to the number of property transactions are changes in the average dwelling price. The decline in the number of transactions throughout 2008, as noted above, was accompanied by a 1 per cent decrease in the average dwelling price in the UK (based on mix-adjusted methodology) between 2007 (£213,807) and 2008 (£211,388) (see Appendix, Part 10: Average dwelling prices). However, while first-time buyers benefited from a 5 per cent decrease in the average dwelling price over this period, to an average price of £155,165, the purchase price for homes among existing owner-occupiers increased by 3 per cent to reach £244,750.

Large decreases in house prices were not seen until 2009. Between the first quarter (Q1) of 2008 and Q1 2009, the annual house price in the UK had dropped by 12.5 per cent, the largest annual decline since the series began in 1969 (Figure 10.18). This was the third consecutive quarter to show an annual house price decrease, there was a 3.7 per cent decrease between Q3 2007 and Q3 2008 and an 8.7 per cent decrease between Q4 2007 and Q4 2008.

The annual decrease in house prices in Q3 2008 was the first time house prices had experienced negative growth since Q4 1995, when there was a 0.3 per cent decrease. The only

Figure 10.17

Property transactions[1]

United Kingdom

Thousands

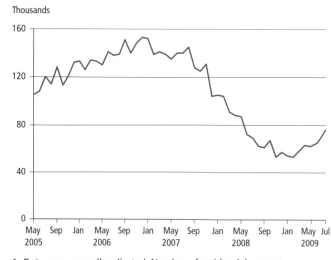

1 Data are seasonally adjusted. Number of residential property transactions with a value of £40,000 or more. Transactions are allocated to the month in which the transaction was completed.

Source: HM Revenue and Customs

Figure 10.18

Annual house price change[1,2]

United Kingdom

Percentages

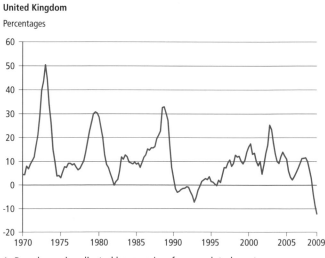

1 Based on mix-adjusted house prices for completed mortgages. See Appendix, Part 10: Average dwelling prices.
2 Data are annual house price changes for each quarter, up to Q1 (Jan–Mar) 2009. Data are not seasonally adjusted.

Source: Communities and Local Government

period of sustained price falls was the recession of the early 1990s during which house prices declined in each period from Q2 1990 to Q3 1993 compared with the same quarter a year earlier.

Falling house prices raise the possibility of homeowners falling into negative equity, which occurs when the value of an asset used to secure a loan is less than the outstanding balance on the loan. This is particularly of concern for those who purchased their homes in the run up to the peak in house prices in 2007. In April 2009 the Council of Mortgage Lenders (CML) estimated that, among the homeowners who took out mortgages in the UK between Q2 2005 and Q4 2008, there were 900,000 (around 13 per cent) in some degree of negative equity. However, the average amount of negative equity was quite small with shortfalls being less than 10 per cent of the value of the property for two-thirds of borrowers in negative equity. For the remaining homeowners in negative equity, the majority had a shortfall of between 10 and 20 per cent of their property's value, with very few cases having a shortfall exceeding this.

There were large geographical differences in the experience of negative equity in the UK at the end of 2008 (Figure 10.19). Households in Wales were more likely to have homes in negative equity (6.1 per cent) at the end of 2008 than the other countries of the UK, where 5.2 per cent of owner-occupied homes in England, 4.8 per cent in Northern Ireland, and 1.0 per cent in Scotland experienced negative equity. In England, the Northern region had the highest concentration of negative equity, with 9.2 per cent of owner-occupiers estimated to be in negative equity, followed by Yorkshire and Humberside at 6.7 per cent. The lowest concentration of negative equity was in East Anglia, at 0.9 per cent, with the next lowest being in the South West, at 4.3 per cent. For all regions in the UK, the greatest numbers of negative equity cases are for mortgages taken out when house prices peaked in 2007.

Although the average house price has declined over the last year and the UK base interest rate has dropped to its lowest level in over three centuries, these changes have not necessarily been reflected in home affordability. The decline in housing prices has been accompanied by a decrease in funds available for mortgages and stricter lending criteria. In the last 20 years mortgage repayments for first-time buyers (including some buyers who have previously owned a property, but are not in owner occupation at the time of purchase) and existing owner-occupiers in the UK have been similar as a proportion of income, with first-time buyers spending a slightly higher proportion of their income on mortgage payments

Figure 10.19

Proportion of owner-occupiers in negative equity:[1] by region, 2008[2]

United Kingdom
Percentages

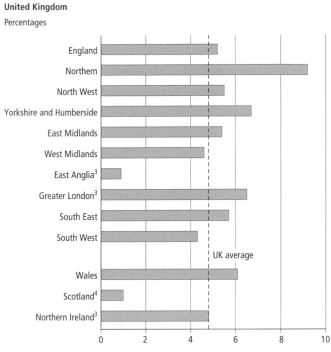

1 Relative negative equity, which is negative equity cases in each region as a proportion of the total owner-occupied housing stock in that region.
2 Those in negative equity at the end of 2008. Based on mortgages taken out in the period 2005 to 2008.
3 Based on mortgages taken out in the period 2006 to 2008 only.
4 Based on mortgages taken out in the period 2007 to 2008 only.

Source: Regulated Mortgage Survey, Council of Mortgage Lenders/ BankSearch

(Figure 10.20 overleaf). However, since 2000 the gap between existing owners and first-time buyers has widened. In 2000 there was around half a percentage point difference between these two groups, with first-time buyers spending 19.4 per cent of their income on mortgage repayments compared with 18.9 per cent for existing owners. In 2008 the difference was 3.4 percentage points (22.7 per cent for first-time buyers and 19.4 per cent for existing owner-occupiers).

As well as the amount of income spent on monthly mortgage repayments, there are also large differences between first-time buyers and existing owner-occupiers in the proportion of the purchase price used as a deposit for house purchase. This is mostly explained by the fact that existing owners will have built up equity in their previous home to use as a deposit for their purchase. Between 1988 and 2008 deposits for existing owner-occupiers in the UK fluctuated between 31 per cent and 37 per cent of the house purchase price, although the figure of 37 per cent in 2008 was the highest proportion recorded over the period, perhaps reflecting the changes in mortgage availability experienced during the economic downturn in this

10

Figure 10.20

Mortgages repayments and deposits:[1] by type of buyer

United Kingdom
Percentages[2]

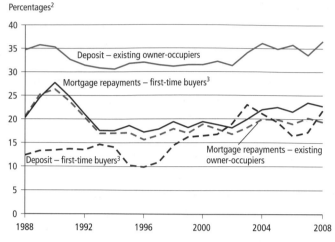

1 Mortgage repayments as a percentage of income, and deposit as a percentage of purchase price. See Appendix, Part 10: Mortgage repayments and deposits.
2 Based on mortgages for house purchases.
3 Includes some buyers who have previously owned a property, but are not in owner occupation at the time of purchase.

Source: Regulated Mortgage Survey, Council of Mortgage Lenders/ BankSearch

Figure 10.21

Households experiencing mortgage difficulties:[1] by type of household,[2] 2006/07–2007/08[3]

England
Percentages

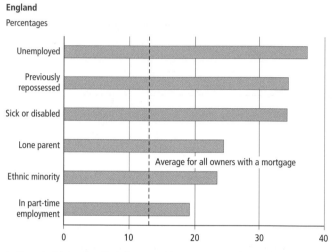

1 Households buying their homes with a mortgage who are in arrears or experiencing difficulties.
2 Data are for household reference persons, and respondents could be included in more than one household type. See Appendix, Part 10: Household reference person.
3 Data are two-year rolling averages.

Source: Survey of English Housing, Communities and Local Government

year and the requirement by lenders for larger deposits. Deposits for first-time buyers increased from 12 per cent in 1988 to 22 per cent in 2008, although they were at their highest in 2003 at 23 per cent. Between 2007 and 2008 there was a 5 percentage point increase in the proportion of the house price used as a deposit for the purchase, again reflecting the lack of mortgages and the requirement of lenders for larger deposits.

In England in the period 2006/07 to 2007/08, more than 1 in 10 (13 per cent) of all households buying their homes with a mortgage were experiencing mortgage arrears or difficulties (Figure 10.21). There were variations in households' experiences of mortgage difficulties, with those who were vulnerable for a variety of reasons being much more likely to experience difficulties than the average. Households with an unemployed household reference person (HRP) were almost three times more likely than average to have mortgage arrears or difficulties (37 per cent). This was almost double the proportion of those in part-time employment (19 per cent).

Around a third (34 per cent) of households with a sick or disabled HRP and just under a quarter (24 per cent) of lone parents were either in arrears or experiencing difficulties with their mortgage repayments in the period 2006/07 to 2007/08. These household types are often on low incomes and are

therefore more vulnerable to increases in mortgage payments due to changing interest rates.

Having had previous experience of financial problems also increased the likelihood of a household experiencing mortgage difficulties or being in arrears. More than a third (34 per cent) of those who had previously had their property repossessed were experiencing mortgage difficulties or arrears in the period 2006/07 to 2007/08.

Mortgage repayments become increasingly difficult when base interest rates and mortgage interest rates increase. This is particularly true for those whose financial circumstances change, for example as a result of job loss, or who had borrowed a high proportion of the value of their properties and had high mortgage repayments. When people fall behind with their mortgage repayments and are unable to reach an alternative arrangement with their mortgage lender, a county court possession summons may be issued, with the view to obtaining a court order.

Not all orders result in repossession. Courts often make suspended orders, which provide for arrears to be paid off within a reasonable period. However, when repayments cannot be made, the mortgage lender may ultimately repossess the property, either on a voluntary basis or through recourse to the courts. At its peak in 1991, around 75,500 properties were repossessed in the UK, some 0.8 per cent of all mortgages,

10

Figure 10.22

Properties taken into repossession[1]

United Kingdom

Thousands

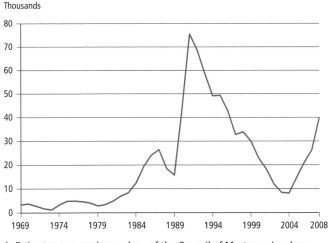

1 Estimates cover only members of the Council of Mortgage Lenders; these account for around 97 per cent of first charge mortgages. See Appendix, Part 10: Mortgage arrears and repossessions.

Source: Council of Mortgage Lenders

following sharp increases in the interest rate in the two years from 1988 (from 7 per cent in mid-1988 to around 15 per cent two years later) (Figure 10.22). However, due to improving macroeconomic and housing market conditions, and lower interest rates, repossessions then fell through to 2004, when 8,200 homes (less than 0.1 per cent of all mortgages) were repossessed. Between 2004 and 2008 the number of repossessions has increased almost fivefold, to reach 40,000.

This includes an increase of 13,800 repossessions between 2007 and 2008, reflecting an impact of the recession that began in 2008.

In Q1 2009 there were 12,700 repossessions, a 49 per cent increase on Q1 2008, 1,400 of which were buy-to-let mortgages; these are mortgages taken out by landlords who plan to purchase a property, or portfolio of properties, for subsequent letting. However, although the number of repossessions have increased, the number of mortgages in arrears have risen more markedly. In Q1 2009 the Council of Mortgage Lenders (CML) reported that there were a total of 203,900 mortgage loans in arrears of more than 2.5 per cent of the mortgage balance, a 62 per cent increase from Q1 2008, when 127,000 loan arrears were reported. To reduce the pressure on homeowners who have experienced difficulty meeting their mortgage payments, the Government set up initiatives in 2009 such as the Mortgage Rescue Scheme and Homeowners Mortgage Support schemes. Lenders also operate a wide range of forbearance policies of their own, working with borrowers, for example by allowing borrowers longer to get their finances on track or by lowering interest rates to reduce their mortgage repayments.

In June 2009 the CML forecast that there will be 65,000 repossessions in 2009, still below the 1991 peak of 75,500, provided that the government initiatives set up in 2009 (which allow people who fall into arrears because of sickness, redundancy or loss of income to defer a proportion of their interest payments on their loans for two years) are effective.

10

Chapter 11

Environment

- In 1970, coal was the most commonly used fuel for electricity generation (67 per cent) in the UK. In 2008, its place had been taken by natural gas (40 per cent). (Figure 11.1)

- Domestic energy consumption for lighting and electrical appliances in the UK between 1970 and 2007 increased by 155 per cent, while energy used for cooking in the home decreased by 41 per cent over the same period. (Table 11.4)

- Thirty eight per cent of household waste in England was recycled in 2008/09, compared with 36 per cent in Wales, 35 per cent in Scotland and 34 per cent in Northern Ireland. (Table 11.7)

- In 2008, there were 442 recorded serious pollution incidents to water, 199 incidents to land and 126 incidents to the air in England and Wales. Overall, the number of recorded incidents was the lowest on record. (Figure 11.11)

- In 2009, over three-quarters (78 per cent) of people aged 15 and over in the EU-27 reported that they separate most of their waste as a way of fighting climate change, with 87 per cent of people in the UK doing so. (Table 11.16)

- In 2008, 743,500 hectares of agricultural land in the UK was organically managed, compared with 30,700 hectares in 1993. (Figure 11.18)

DATA

Download data by clicking the online pdf

www.statistics.gov.uk/ socialtrends

The environment is a term used to encompass all living and non-living things occurring naturally on Earth. Environmental problems such as pollution, temperature change and loss of biodiversity do not respect national boundaries and are global concerns. Governments in the UK and the rest of the European Union have developed environment-related policies and regulations and have adopted strategies for sustainable development to try and protect the environment. Reducing the negative impacts of human activity is a major concern, such as the treatment of waste or the use of energy resources. The use of land, farming practices, and the protection of the countryside and wildlife are also important issues that have to be addressed in order to pass on a healthy and environmentally sound world for future generations.

Use of resources

Energy generation from renewable resources such as wind and hydro is seen as environmentally friendly and the Government is committed to increasing the contribution of renewable resources to future electricity generation. However, it is the conventional fuels and methods which continue to be the main generators of electricity. Before 1987, data on the fuels used for electricity generation in the UK were provided only by the major power producers, transport undertakings and industrial hydro and nuclear stations. Nevertheless the data do give an indication of the trends in the mix of fuels used for electricity generation over the last 40 years. Between 1970 and 2008, the total fuel used for electricity generation rose by around 28 per cent from 64 million tonnes of oil equivalent to 82 million tonnes. In 1970 coal was the most commonly used fuel for electricity generation, as it had been for many decades, providing over two-thirds (67 per cent) of the fuel input (Figure 11.1). Coal continued to be the most widely used fuel for electricity generation throughout the 1970s, 1980s and most of the 1990s, but by 1999 its share had fallen to 32 per cent from around 65 per cent 10 years earlier. However, in recent years the contribution of coal has risen again as it has been used to substitute for the output of nuclear and gas-fired stations when they are unavailable, and as a more economic substitute for highly priced gas. In 2008, coal provided 37 per cent of all fuels used for generation. Oil use accounted for 29 per cent of fuel input in 1972, but its use declined after the oil supply crisis in 1973 apart from a temporary increase during the 1984 miners' dispute, when the contribution of coal fell to 45 per cent while the contribution of oil peaked at 33 per cent.

Nuclear energy grew steadily from around 11 per cent of fuel input in 1970 and peaked in 1998 at 29 per cent. In the following years, closure of some old nuclear stations and increased periods when stations were temporarily shutdown

Figure 11.1

Fuels used for electricity generation[1]

United Kingdom
Percentages

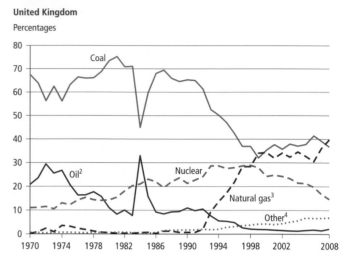

1 Data for all generating companies are only available from 1987 onwards, and the figures for 1987 to 1989 include a high degree of estimation. Before 1987 the data are for major power producers, transport undertakings and industrial hydro and nuclear stations only.
2 Includes oil used in gas turbine and diesel plant or for lighting up coal fired boilers, Orimulsion, and from 1987, refinery gas.
3 Includes colliery methane from 1987 onwards.
4 Includes coke oven gas, blast furnace gas, waste products from chemical processes, refuse derived fuels and renewable sources.

Source: Department of Energy and Climate Change

for maintenance and repair have reduced the level. In 2008, nuclear power accounted for 15 per cent of all fuels used for electricity generation.

Between 1975 and 1990, a European Community (EC) Directive limited the use of natural gas in public supply power stations during this period. After 1991 the amount of gas used in electricity generation grew rapidly, from 2 per cent of all generation in 1992, before exceeding both coal and nuclear in 1999, at 34 per cent. In 2006, due to high gas prices, its share of generation fell to its lowest level since 1998 (31 per cent). However, in 2008 its share had increased to a new peak of around 40 per cent.

Renewable energy is energy that is naturally replenished. It is sourced from natural resources such as sunlight, wind, rain, tides, and geothermal heat. In June 2009, the UK signed up to the European Union (EU) Renewable Energy Directive. This includes a target by which the UK has to provide 15 per cent of energy from renewable sources by 2020 for electricity, heat and transport. This target is equivalent to a sevenfold increase in UK renewable energy consumption from 2008 levels. In 2008, renewable energy accounted for 5.5 per cent of all electricity generated in the UK, the equivalent of 4.3 million tonnes of oil equivalent (Table 11.2). This represented an increase of around 5 per cent since 2007 and 564 per cent since 1991. Biofuels accounted for the largest

Table 11.2

Electricity generation: by renewable sources

United Kingdom			Thousand tonnes of oil equivalent	
	1991	2001	2007	2008
Wind and wave[1]	0.7	83.0	453.5	610.3
Hydro	397.6	348.7	437.5	444.4
Biofuels				
Landfill gas	68.2	822.2	1,533.9	1,560.3
Co-firing with fossil fuels	..	..	641.4	528.9
Municipal solid waste combustion[2]	70.5	387.1	486.8	506.8
Sewage sludge digestion	107.6	119.0	162.5	185.1
Other biomass[3]	0.6	282.2	356.6	439.6
Solar photo-voltaics	..	0.2	1.2	1.5
Total	645.2	2,042.4	4,073.4	4,281.6

1 Includes shoreline wave but this is less than 0.05 thousand tonnes of oil equivalent.
2 Biodegradable part only.
3 Includes electricity from farm waste digestion, poultry litter combustion, meat and bone combustion, straw and short rotation coppice.

Source: Department of Energy and Climate Change

proportion of electricity generated from renewable sources (3.2 million tonnes of oil equivalent), followed by wind power (0.6 million tonnes of oil equivalent), and hydroelectricity (0.4 million tonnes of oil equivalent). Over recent years wind power has been the fastest growing major renewable source, with its use in electricity generation increasing over seven times between 2001 and 2008.

Across the European Union (EU-27) countries, 16 per cent of gross electricity consumption was generated from renewable sources in 2007, a rise of 3 percentage points since 1997 (Table 11.3). The proportion of renewable sources used to generate electricity varies across the EU-27. Around 60 per cent of gross electricity consumed in Austria was generated from renewable sources, due to its extensive use of hydropower, though this represents a fall from 68 per cent in 1997. Just over half (52 per cent) of Sweden's electricity consumption and over a third (36 per cent) of Latvia's electricity consumption was generated from renewable sources, again due to their high use of hydropower. However, the proportion of renewable sources used for generating electricity was under 10 per cent in half of the countries in the EU-27, with Cyprus and Malta producing no electricity from renewable sources and Estonia just 2 per cent.

Domestic energy consumption in the UK was 24 per cent higher in 2008 than in 1970, although it fell by 3 per cent

Table 11.3

Proportion of gross electricity consumption generated by renewable sources: EU comparison

				Percentages
	1997	2001	2006	2007
Austria	68	67	57	60
Sweden	49	54	48	52
Latvia	47	46	38	36
Portugal	38	34	29	30
Denmark	9	17	26	29
Romania	31	28	31	27
Finland	25	26	24	26
Slovenia	27	31	24	22
Spain	20	21	18	20
Slovakia	15	18	17	17
Germany	4	7	12	15
Italy	16	17	15	14
France	15	17	13	13
Ireland	4	4	9	9
Netherlands	4	4	8	8
Bulgaria	7	5	11	8
Greece	9	5	12	7
United Kingdom	2	3	5	5
Czech Republic	4	4	5	5
Hungary	1	1	4	5
Lithuania	3	3	4	5
Belgium	1	2	4	4
Luxembourg	2	2	3	4
Poland	2	2	3	4
Estonia	0	0	1	2
Cyprus	0	0	0	0
Malta	0	0	0	0
EU-27 average	13	14	15	16

Source: Eurostat

between 2000 and 2008. In 1970, most domestic energy came from coal (39 per cent) and natural gas (24 per cent), but by 2008 just over two-thirds (68 per cent) of domestic energy consumption came from natural gas, with coal supplying just 1 per cent. Most domestic energy use is for space heating, accounting for around 56 per cent (24.9 million tonnes of oil equivalent) in 2007 (Table 11.4 overleaf). The amount of energy consumed by domestic space heating increased by around 12 per cent between 1970 and 2007, but this increase was lower than for some other energy demands due to

11

Table 11.4

Domestic energy consumption: by final use

United Kingdom					Million tonnes of oil equivalent	
	1970	1980	1990	2000	2006	2007
Space heating[1]	22.1	23.8	23.7	28.7	26.5	24.9
Water heating	9.9	10.0	10.1	10.7	11.3	11.3
Lighting and appliances	2.7	4.1	5.5	6.1	6.7	6.8
Cooking	2.2	2.0	1.5	1.3	1.3	1.3
Total	36.9	39.8	40.8	46.9	45.8	44.2

1 The heating of a space, usually enclosed, such as a house or room.

Source: Department of Energy and Climate Change; Building Research Establishment

improvements in levels of home insulation, double glazing and more efficient heating in the home (see also Chapter 10: Housing). For example, over the same period domestic energy consumption for water heating rose by 14 per cent to reach 11.3 million tonnes of oil equivalent in 2007. However, the largest percentage rise in domestic consumption between 1970 and 2007 was for lighting and electrical appliances which increased by 155 per cent, reflecting the increasing number of electrical appliances in households. However, this category accounted for only 15 per cent of total consumption (6.8 million tonnes of oil equivalent) in 2007, compared with water heating which accounted for 26 per cent. Energy used for cooking in the home accounted for around 3 per cent of household consumption in 2007 (1.3 million tonnes of oil equivalent). However, energy used for this purpose decreased by 41 per cent since 1970 mainly because of changes in technology and lifestyle such as use of microwave ovens and a greater availability of convenience food.

Water is a precious resource and essential for human life. Although two-thirds of the world's surface is covered with water, freshwater lakes, rivers and underground aquifers hold only 2.5 per cent of the world's water with the remainder being saltwater oceans and seas. According to the Water Services Regulation Authority (OFWAT) average household consumption per head of water across England and Wales in 2007/08 was 148 litres per day. Public demand for water continues to increase because of the increasing number of households, increasing use of domestic appliances, in particular dishwashers and washing machines, and warmer weather leading to more garden watering.

Water is a renewable resource, but there are limits to fresh water availability. Water abstraction is the process of taking water from any source, either temporarily or permanently.

Table 11.5

Water abstraction: by purpose[1]

England & Wales			Thousand megalitres[2] per day		
	1995	2000	2005	2006	2007
Public water supply	17.3	17.0	17.4	17.0	16.4
Electricity supply industry	8.2	13.9	10.0	10.4	10.2
Fish farming, cress growing and amenity ponds	4.3	4.7	3.7	3.6	3.6
Industry	2.3	4.4	4.2	3.7	2.5
Other[3]	1.0	1.1	0.4	0.4	0.3
Total	33.2	41.2	35.6	35.1	33.0

1 Estimated abstractions from all sources except tidal. See Appendix, Part 11: Water abstractions.
2 A megalitre is equal to one million litres.
3 Includes spray irrigation, agriculture, private water supply and mineral washing.

Source: Environment Agency

It can be carried out by a variety of means including a pump, pipes, an engineering structure in a watercourse, a borehole or a well. Most water is used for industry or to produce water for household consumption. Over-abstraction can lead to rivers drying up or the level of groundwater aquifers reducing beyond useful provision. In 2007, a daily average of around 33,000 megalitres of water was abstracted from non-tidal surface water and groundwater in England and Wales (Table 11.5). Of this, half (50 per cent) was for the public water supply, at around 16,400 megalitres, while 31 per cent was for the electricity supply industry, equivalent to around 10,200 megalitres. Since 1995, the largest proportional increase was in water use by the electrical supply industry which rose by 24 per cent from 8,200 megalitres to 10,200 megalitres. Since 1995, the amount of water abstracted for the public water supply has changed little.

Waste management

Each year the UK generates around 100 million tonnes of waste from households, commerce and industry. Most of this ends up in landfill, where biodegradable waste generates methane, a powerful greenhouse gas (see Figure 11.14). In addition, energy is used to make new products to replace items that could have been recycled, which also contributes to climate change.

In 2008/09, around 24 million tonnes of household waste was produced in England, the equivalent of around 473 kilograms per person per year (Figure 11.6). This was 47 kilograms per person less than the peak of 520 kilograms in 2002/03. In

Figure 11.6

Household waste and recycling[1]

England

Kilograms per person per year

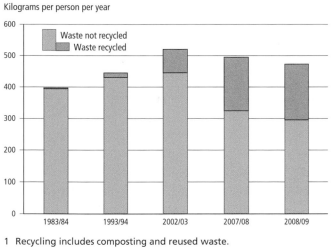

1 Recycling includes composting and reused waste.

Source: Department for Environment, Food and Rural Affairs

2008/09, 38 per cent (178 kilograms) of total household waste per person was recycled, composted or reused, while the remainder (295 kilograms per person) went to landfill or was incinerated. In comparison, in 1983/84 an average of 397 kilograms per person of household waste was produced, of

which less than 1 per cent (3 kilograms per person) was recycled, composted or reused.

The recycling rate for household waste (total household recycling as a proportion of total household waste) in England was 38 per cent in 2008/09 (Table 11.7). In Wales 36 per cent of household waste was recycled, in Scotland 35 per cent was recycled, while in Northern Ireland 34 per cent of household waste was recycled. There were wide variations in household recycling rates achieved by regions and waste disposal authorities or councils across the UK in 2008/09. Among the English regions, the highest recycling rates were in the East and the East Midlands (both 44 per cent), while London had the lowest recycling rate (29 per cent). Across the waste disposal authorities and unitary councils in England, recycling rates varied from 18 per cent in the council of the Isles of Scilly, to 53 per cent in Rutland County Council. The waste authority with the highest recycling rate in Wales was Conwy, where 44 per cent of all household waste was recycled, while the lowest was in Blaenau Gwent (23 per cent). In Scotland the highest rate was in South Ayrshire (48 per cent) and the lowest in Glasgow City Council (16 per cent). In Northern Ireland the highest recycling rate was in Antrim Borough Council (48 per cent) and the lowest in Strabane District Council (26 per cent).

Table 11.7

Household waste recycling rates:[1] by region and waste disposal authority, 2008/09

United Kingdom

Percentages

	Regional rate	Waste disposal authority			
		Lowest rate within region		Highest rate within region	
England	38	Council of the Isles of Scilly	18	Rutland County Council	53
North East	31	Middlesbrough Borough Council	23	Redcar and Cleveland Borough Council	40
North West	37	Wigan MBC[2]	28	Cheshire County Council	48
Yorkshire and the Humber	34	Calderdale MBC[2]	26	North Lincolnshire Council	49
East Midlands	44	Leicester City Council	31	Rutland County Council	53
West Midlands	37	Coventry City Council	27	Shropshire County Council	48
East	44	Thurrock Council	30	Cambridgeshire County Council	52
London	29	London Borough of Tower Hamlets	19	London Borough of Bexley	51
South East	38	Portsmouth City Council	25	Buckinghamshire County Council	44
South West	42	Council of the Isles of Scilly	18	Devon County Council	52
Wales	36	Blaenau Gwent	23	Conwy	44
Scotland	35	Glasgow City Council	16	South Ayrshire	48
Northern Ireland	34	Strabane District Council	26	Antrim Borough Council	48

1 Includes composting and reused waste.
2 MBC is Metropolitan Borough Council.

Source: Department for Environment, Food and Rural Affairs; Welsh Assembly Government; Scottish Environment Protection Agency; Department of Environment, Northern Ireland

In 2008/09, 9.3 million tonnes of household waste was collected for recycling in England, an increase of around 5 per cent (0.4 million tonnes of waste) since 2007/08 and 471 per cent since 1996/97 equivalent to 7.6 million tonnes of waste (Table 11.8). Compost constituted the largest proportion in 2008/09, accounting for 38 per of the total amount, equivalent to over 3.5 million tonnes. The collection of co-mingled materials, which is the collection of a number of recyclable materials in the same box or bin (for example paper, cans and plastics) accounted for the next highest proportion at 20 per cent (around 1.8 million tonnes). The amounts of compost and co-mingled materials collected from households have both increased more rapidly than other materials, by 3.2 million tonnes and 1.7 million tonnes respectively between 1996/97 and 2008/09.

According to a report published in 2009 by the Waste and Resources Action Programme (WRAP), UK households waste around 8.3 million tonnes of food and drink every year, representing 22 per cent of food and drink purchases. Most of this waste (around 5.8 million tonnes) is collected by local

authorities, with the majority going to landfill. The remainder is composted at home, fed to animals or tipped down the sink. WRAP estimate that around two-thirds of this waste (5.3 million tonnes) could have been avoided through better management by households. Of this 'avoidable' waste, 2.9 million tonnes was thrown away before it was used because it had gone off or was past its 'use by' or 'best before' date. A further 2.2 million tonnes was left over after use, either after cooking or after a meal.

Pollution

The air today is considerably cleaner than at any time since the industrial revolution, but can still cause health problems. Air pollution is currently estimated to reduce the life expectancy of every person in the UK by an average of seven to eight months while also contributing to associated health costs. It also has a detrimental effect on the UK's ecosystems and vegetation. The *Environment Act 1995*, which covers England, Scotland and Wales, and the *Environment (Northern Ireland) Order 2002*, requires all local authorities in the UK to review and assess air quality in their area. In 2007, the *Air Quality Strategy for England, Scotland, Wales and Northern Ireland* was presented to Parliament. This strategy provided a long-term vision for improving air quality in the UK and offered options for further measures to reduce the risk to health and the environment from air pollution.

Air pollution comes from a variety of sources. Road transport is the main source of nitrogen dioxide and carbon monoxide. Power stations and other industrial sources are also a significant source of nitrogen dioxide. Industry is the main source of sulphur dioxide, but the burning of wood and coal for home heating can also be a source. Emissions of the major air pollutants in the UK have been generally falling since the 1970s, and the rate of decline has accelerated since 1989 (Figure 11.9). The release of carbon monoxide into the atmosphere is a health issue as it prevents the normal transport of oxygen through the blood, leading to a reduction in the supply of oxygen to the heart. Between 1970 and 2008, emissions of carbon monoxide have decreased by 71 per cent from 9.8 million tonnes per year to 2.8 million tonnes. The reduction since the early 1990s is mainly due to the introduction of catalytic converters in petrol-driven cars and improved vehicle engine efficiency.

Similarly the release of sulphur dioxide and nitrogen dioxide can impact on health, as they are acidic gases that irritate the airways of the lungs and so can increase symptoms for those suffering from lung disease and asthma. Emissions of sulphur dioxide in the UK decreased between 1970 and 2008 by

Table 11.8

Materials collected from households for recycling[1]

England | | | Thousand tonnes

	1996/97[2]	2001/02	2007/08	2008/09
Compost[3]	278	954	3,189	3,512
Co-mingled[4]	77	221	1,563	1,823
Paper and card	555	981	1,599	1,471
Glass	306	426	902	844
Scrap metal and white goods	199	369	598	555
Textiles	30	46	113	112
Cans[5]	18	26	83	91
Plastics	5	8	66	79
Other[6]	152	155	728	771
Total	1,620	3,186	8,841	9,258

1 Includes data from different types of recycling schemes collecting waste from household sources, including private/voluntary schemes such as kerbside and 'bring' systems where recyclables are delivered to a central collection point. Reuse and waste that is rejected by a reprocessor are included in these figures.
2 Excludes material from private/voluntary schemes. The total for these schemes is 57,000 tonnes, but cannot be split down into different materials.
3 Includes organic materials (kitchen and garden waste) collected for centralised composting. Excludes home composting.
4 Co-mingled materials are separated after collection.
5 Includes ferrous and aluminium cans.
6 Includes oils, batteries, aluminium foil, books and shoes.

Source: Department for Environment, Food and Rural Affairs

Figure 11.9

Emissions of selected air pollutants[1]

United Kingdom
Million tonnes

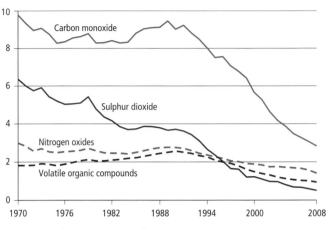

1 See Appendix, Part 11: Air pollutants.

Source: Department for Environment, Food and Rural Affairs; AEA Energy and Environment

92 per cent from 6.4 million tonnes to 0.5 million tonnes, while over the same period nitrogen oxide emissions decreased by just over half (53 per cent) from 3.0 million tonnes to 1.4 million tonnes. These decreases are largely a result of cleaner power stations, less use of coal and, again, the use of catalytic converters in cars.

The measurement of levels of ozone and particulate matter (PM) in the air is important as these two pollutants have significant impacts on public health through long-term exposure. They can cause biological mutations, poor lung development, breathing difficulties and premature death. Particulate matter in the atmosphere can originate from natural sources such as sand or sea spray, or be man made such as construction dust or soot and were, for example, the cause of smog in the UK during the 1950s. Attention nowadays is concentrated on particulate matter that is less than 10 microns in diameter or about one-seventh of the thickness of a human hair. These are known as PM_{10} and are more likely to have a toxic effect as they can be breathed more deeply into the lungs. Annual average particulate levels monitored at urban background sites (see Appendix, Part 11: Types of monitoring sites) in the UK have generally decreased since 1993 (the earliest available data) when they were 36 micrograms per cubic metre (Figure 11.10). In 2009, the level was 19 micrograms per cubic metre, the same level as 2008. Annual average particulate levels monitored at roadside sites stood at 22 micrograms per cubic metre in 2009, compared with 26 micrograms per cubic metre in 2008 and 37 micrograms per cubic metre in 1997 (the earliest available data).

Figure 11.10

Air quality: by levels of ozone[1] and particulate matter[2,3]

United Kingdom
Micrograms per cubic metre

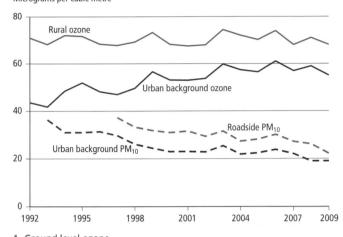

1 Ground level ozone.
2 Particulate matter that is less than 10 microns in diameter (PM_{10}). See Appendix, Part 11: Air pollutants.
3 Rural sites include monitoring sites in remote and rural areas. Urban sites include suburban, central urban and industrial urban areas. Roadside sites include kerbside monitoring sites and roadside sites next to major roads. See Appendix, Part 11: Types of monitoring sites.

Source: Department for Environment, Food and Rural Affairs; AEA Energy and Environment

Ground level ozone is not the same as the ozone layer in the atmosphere, which is affected by ozone depleting substances such as chlorofluorocarbons (CFCs) that are released into the atmosphere. Ozone is a secondary pollutant produced by reactions between nitrogen dioxide, hydrocarbons and sunlight. Levels are usually highest in rural areas, particularly in hot, still, sunny weather conditions, giving rise to 'summer smog'. Rural ozone levels averaged 68 micrograms per cubic metre in 2009 compared with 71 micrograms per cubic metre in 2008 and 59 micrograms per cubic metre in 1987. However, there is not a clear long term trend. Urban background ozone levels were 55 micrograms per cubic metre in 2009 compared with 59 micrograms per cubic metre in 2008. These levels have increased since 1992 (the first year data were available), possibly due to the reduction in emissions of nitrogen oxides, which act to destroy ozone close to its source. Both particulate and ozone concentrations are strongly influenced by weather, which contributes to the fluctuations over time.

Pollution incidents of air, water and land are monitored by the Environment Agency. There are four categories of pollution incidents, of which two are deemed serious. Category 1 incidents, classified as 'most severe', are defined as those that have a persistent and/or extensive effect on the quality of the air, land or water. They may cause major damage to the ecosystem; cause major damage to agriculture and/or

11

Figure 11.11

Serious pollution incidents[1]

England & Wales

Numbers

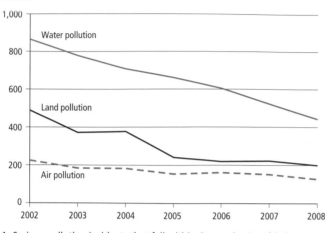

1 Serious pollution incidents that fall within Categories 1 and 2. See Appendix, Part 11: Pollution incidents.

Source: Environment Agency

Figure 11.12

Difference in average surface temperature: deviation from 1961–90 average[1]

Global and Central England[2]

Degrees Celsius

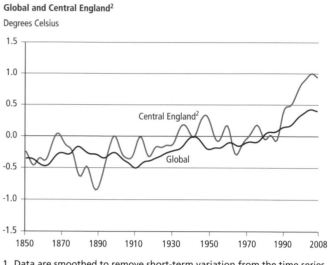

1 Data are smoothed to remove short-term variation from the time series to get a clearer view of the underlying changes. See, Appendix, Part 11: Average temperatures.
2 Central England temperature is representative of a roughly triangular area of the UK enclosed by Bristol, Lancashire and London.

Source: Hadley Centre for Climate Prediction and Research

commerce; or have a serious impact on the human population. Category 2 incidents, classified as 'severe', have similar, but less serious effects (see Appendix, Part 11: Pollution incidents).

In 2008, the Environment Agency recorded 723 Category 1 or Category 2 incidents overall in England and Wales, the lowest on record. This was a fall of 51 per cent since 2002 and 13 per cent since 2007. Of these serious incidents, 442 were water pollution, 199 land pollution and 126 air pollution (some of these incidents can result in pollution to more than one medium) (Figure 11.11). All sectors have seen a decrease since 2002 and reached their lowest level of incidents in 2008. In 2008, specific waste materials such as asbestos, household rubbish and vehicle parts were the most common pollutant, and were found at 21 per cent of serious incidents, followed by inert material and waste, which was found at 13 per cent of incidents.

Global warming and climate change

Climate change is defined as any long-term change in the pattern of weather, temperature, wind and rainfall over periods of time that range from decades to millions of years. It can be expressed as a change in weather conditions over time or as the probability that extreme conditions will occur in the future. Before the industrial revolution, the climate was influenced by natural occurrences such as volcanic eruptions and tropical storms. Global temperature has risen by about 0.76 degrees Celsius (°C) between the last half of the 19th century and the period 2000 to 2008 when compared to the 1961–90 average temperature (see Appendix, Part 11: Average temperatures)

(Figure 11.12). The increase over the past 20 years (1989 to 2008) has been much greater than the whole period (1850 to 2008) at 0.3°C. In 2007 the Intergovernmental Panel on Climate Change (IPCC) asserted in the 2007 Fourth Assessment Report (AR4) that human activity was the main cause of the warming, particularly in the last 50 years.

According to the Met Office, the first decade of the 21st century has been warmer worldwide than any other decade since global surface temperature measurements began in 1850. The warmest year to date globally was 1998, caused in part by the global effects of the strongest El Nino ocean warming event in the last century. The next warmest years globally were 2005, 2003 and 2002. Figure 11.12 shows that in 'Central England' (a triangular area enclosed by Bristol, Lancashire and London) average surface temperature has risen by about 1°C since 1980 when compared to the 1961–90 average, after remaining relatively stable for most of the 20th century. This is a more rapid rise than the global average land-surface temperature. The warmest year on record in 'Central England' was 2006, with an average temperature of 10.8°C, followed by 1990, 1999 and 1949. The highest temperature ever recorded in the UK was 38.5°C, measured on 10 August 2003 at Brogdale (near Faversham in the south east of England). Conversely, the lowest temperature recorded in the UK was -27.2°C at Braemar in the Grampians in Scotland, on 10 January 1982 and Altnaharra, in the Highlands in Scotland on 30 December 1995.

Average annual rainfall across the UK varies enormously from around 5,000 millimetres in parts of the western highlands of Scotland to around 500 millimetres in parts of East Anglia and on the borders of the Thames estuary. Overall, the wettest areas are the western uplands which are most exposed to the Atlantic depressions, and these account for most of the UK's rainfall.

Since the early 20th century there has been a tendency for winter (December to February) rainfall to be higher than summer (June to August) rainfall in England and Wales, although wide seasonal variations occur (Figure 11.13). The 10-year rolling average shows a trend of increasing winter rainfall and decreasing summer rainfall since the late 19th century.

During November 2009, which was the wettest November since records began in 1914, many parts of North-West Britain were affected by sustained heavy rainfall leading to widespread flooding. The largest rainfall accumulations were associated with a near-stationary low-pressure system which allowed an exceptionally warm and moist subtropical airflow to track across Northern Ireland, Cumbria and South-West Scotland. Extreme rainfall totals were recorded in the mountainous terrain of the Lake District. At Seathwaite in Cumbria, 372.4 millimetres of rain fell between 8.00 am on Wednesday 18 November 2009 and 4.00 am on Friday 20 November 2009, and the provisional total at Seathwaite over the 24 hours ending at 12.45 am on 20 November 2009 was

314.4 millimetres, the highest ever recorded in a UK rain gauge.

The emission of the key greenhouse gases – carbon dioxide (CO_2), methane (CH_4) and nitrous oxide (N_2O) – is generally considered to be an influence on the global climate. The accumulation of these gases in the Earth's atmosphere causes heat from the sun to be trapped near the Earth's surface, generally known as the 'greenhouse effect'.

According to the Office for National Statistics' Environmental Accounts (see Appendix, Part 11: Environmental Accounts), the total emissions of greenhouse gases in the UK fell from 809 million tonnes of CO_2 equivalent in 1990 to 707 million tonnes in 2007. Most of the reduction occurred between 1990 and 1999, when they fell by 10.1 per cent. However, between 1999 and 2007 the total decreased by just 2.9 per cent. Greenhouse gas emissions from households accounted for around a fifth (21.4 per cent) of all emissions in the UK in 2007 (151 million tonnes of CO_2 equivalent). The largest source of emissions among the non-household sectors was the electricity, gas and water supply industry, which contributed over a quarter (27.7 per cent) of all emissions (196 million tonnes of CO_2 equivalent) (Figure 11.14). Emissions from this sector decreased by 1.9 per cent between 2006 and 2007, a contributing factor could be the continuing switch away from

Figure 11.13

Winter and summer rainfall[1,2]

England & Wales

Millimetres

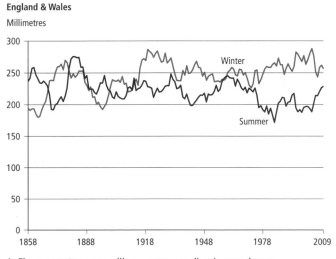

1 Figures are ten-year rolling averages ending in year shown.
2 Winter is December to February, summer is June to August.

Source: Climate Research Unit, University of East Anglia; Hadley Centre for Climate Prediction and Research; Centre for Ecology & Hydrology (Wallingford)

Figure 11.14

Source of greenhouse gas emissions:[1] by selected UK sector[2]

United Kingdom

Million tonnes of carbon dioxide equivalent

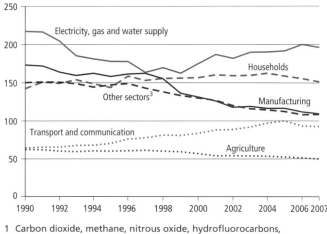

1 Carbon dioxide, methane, nitrous oxide, hydrofluorocarbons, perfluorocarbon and sulphur hexafluoride expressed as million tonnes of carbon dioxide equivalent.
2 Data from Office for National Statistics' Environmental Accounts. See Appendix, Part 11: Environmental Accounts.
3 Includes mining and quarrying, construction, wholesale and retail trade, other business services, public administration, education, health and social work and other services.

Source: Office for National Statistics; AEA Energy and Environment

coal to other forms of electricity generation such as the combustion of natural gas. However, emissions from this sector have generally been rising in the last 10 years. The other main non-household contributors were the manufacturing industry, which emitted 15.5 per cent (110 million tonnes of CO_2 equivalent) of UK emissions, and the transport and communications industry, which emitted 13.0 per cent (92 million tonnes of CO_2 equivalent). Since 1990, emissions from the manufacturing industry have fallen 36.8 per cent from 173 million tonnes to 110 million tonnes in 2007 probably due to cleaner production practices. However, greenhouse gas emissions from the transport and communication industry have risen by 43.6 per cent between 1990 and 2007, from around 64 million tonnes of CO_2 equivalent. This rise mainly reflects increases in emissions from the UK-owned road and air transport industries. Greenhouse gas emissions from road transport from all UK industries have risen from 13.8 per cent to 17.7 per cent of total UK emissions, while greenhouse gas emissions from the UK-owned air industry more than doubled from 2.5 per cent in 1990 to 6.2 per cent of total UK emissions in 2007. Between 1990 and 2007, the proportion of greenhouse gas emissions from agriculture changed very little, accounting for between 7 and 8 per cent of all emissions each year.

The Kyoto Protocol is an international legally-binding agreement adopted at Kyoto in 1997 under the UN Framework Convention on Climate Change to reduce the emissions of greenhouse gases. Under the 1997 Kyoto Protocol, the UK has a legally binding target to reduce its emissions of a 'basket' of six greenhouse gases by 12.5 per cent over the period 2008 to 2012. This reduction is against 1990 emission levels for carbon dioxide, methane and nitrous oxide, and 1995 levels for hydrofluorocarbons (HFCs), perfluorocarbons (PFCs) and sulphur hexafluoride (SF_6) – see Appendix, Part 11: Global warming and climate change. Within the basket, each gas is weighted by its global warming potential, a measure of how much a given mass of greenhouse gas is estimated to contribute to global warming. Additionally, in October 2008 the Government announced that the UK was committed to cutting the basket of greenhouse gas emissions by 80 per cent compared with 1990 levels by 2050. The Government also intended to move towards a goal of reducing CO_2 emissions to 20 per cent below 1990 levels by 2010. In 2008, emissions of the basket of six greenhouse gases were at their lowest compared with the 1990 base year level, at 628 million tonnes of CO_2 equivalent, a fall of around 19 per cent (Figure 11.15). CO_2 is the main greenhouse gas and accounted for 85 per cent of total UK emissions in 2008. Net emissions for 2008 are estimated at 533 million tonnes of CO_2 equivalent, 2 per cent lower than in 2007. This decrease is partly explained by the

Figure 11.15

Emissions of greenhouse gases[1]

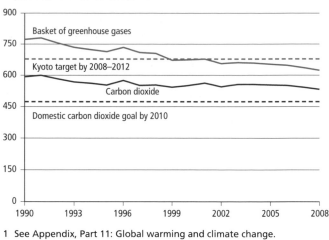

United Kingdom
Million tonnes of carbon dioxide equivalent

1 See Appendix, Part 11: Global warming and climate change.

Source: Department of Energy and Climate Change; AEA Energy and Environment

switch from coal to natural gas in electricity generation, and by a lower use of fossil fuel by both households and industry. However, in 2008 CO_2 emissions were an estimated 58 million tonnes above the 2010 domestic target of 474.3 million tonnes.

People aged 15 and over in the European Union (EU-27) were asked in 2009 what environmental actions aimed at fighting climate change they had carried out. Just over three-quarters (78 per cent) reported separating most of their waste for recycling and this was, on average, the most common action taken (Table 11.16). Waste separation was most common in France where over nine in ten people (91 per cent) reported doing so, followed by Germany (88 per cent), Belgium, Ireland, Luxembourg and the UK (all at 87 per cent). In 18 countries in the EU-27, 70 per cent or more of people reported that they separated most of their waste for recycling while less than 50 per cent of people in only one country (Romania) reported doing so. The next most common environmental action aimed at fighting climate change was reducing consumption of energy at home, which 63 per cent of the citizens surveyed reported doing. This was most common in Denmark (84 per cent) followed by Germany and the Netherlands (both 76 per cent). Just over six in ten (62 per cent) people in the UK reported reducing consumption of energy at home, while it was least common in Latvia where nearly four in ten (38 per cent) did so.

Over half (55 per cent) of people in the EU member states reported that they had reduced their water consumption at home. This was most common in Cyprus (78 per cent),

Table 11.16

Selected environmental actions aimed at fighting climate change:[1] EU comparison, 2009

Percentages

	Separating most waste for recycling	Reducing consumption of energy at home	Reducing consumption of water at home	Reducing consumption of disposable items
Austria	83	66	46	56
Belgium	87	66	60	56
Bulgaria	50	55	43	23
Cyprus	55	71	78	13
Czech Republic	82	73	65	44
Denmark	67	84	71	43
Estonia	78	55	61	52
Finland	82	74	60	45
France	91	66	70	54
Germany	88	76	69	55
Greece	64	66	68	19
Hungary	52	69	67	34
Ireland	87	61	43	45
Italy	70	53	47	38
Latvia	53	38	49	46
Lithuania	61	46	54	35
Luxembourg	87	75	71	61
Malta	77	74	73	50
Netherlands	80	76	42	42
Poland	59	53	49	44
Portugal	71	55	56	21
Romania	38	52	49	37
Slovakia	72	68	60	30
Slovenia	81	68	69	48
Spain	78	51	50	16
Sweden	82	74	43	54
United Kingdom	87	62	37	32
EU-27 average	78	63	55	41

1 Respondents aged 15 and over were shown a list from which they chose the actions they had personally taken, aimed at helping to fight climate change.

Source: Eurobarometer

Malta (73 per cent) and Luxembourg and Denmark (both 71 per cent) while just under four in ten (37 per cent) reported doing this in the UK where this was least common. Reducing consumption of disposable items was an action carried out to help fight climate change by around four in ten people

(41 per cent) in the EU-27. This was most common in Luxembourg (61 per cent) and Belgium and Austria (both 56 per cent), compared with 32 per cent of people in the UK. This action was less common in Cyprus (13 per cent) and Spain (16 per cent).

Countryside, farming and wildlife

Much of the natural landscape of the UK is the product of many centuries of human intervention, mainly farming and agriculture. In June 2008, 77 per cent of the total land area of the UK, some 17.5 million hectares, was land on agricultural holdings. Permanent grassland and sole right rough grazing accounted for 60 per cent of agricultural land and a further 35 per cent was 'croppable land', that is land currently under crops, bare fallow, uncropped land or temporary grass. Just over half of 'croppable land' in June 2008 was occupied by cereal crops, some 3.3 million hectares (Table 11.17 overleaf). The most widely grown cereal crop, which covered over 60 per cent of the area (2.0 million hectares), was wheat, which is used in bread, cakes and many other food products. The next most widely grown cereal crop was barley, grown on 1.0 million hectares. Around a third of this crop is used to make malt, a key ingredient of beer and whisky. Oats to be used for human consumption such as breakfast cereals were grown on 0.1 million hectares. Oilseed rape, which is crushed to extract oil for the food and animal feed industries, was grown on 0.6 million hectares. Potatoes and horticulture such as vegetables, fruits, plants and flowers were grown on the remaining 0.3 million hectares.

The number of cattle and calves in the UK in 2008 was estimated at around 10.1 million, of which 1.9 million were breeding dairy herd and 1.7 million breeding beef herd. The remainder of the cattle are made up of cattle too young to breed, those that are old enough but not yet had offspring and male cattle (either bulls for breeding or cattle to be eaten). Of the 33.1 million sheep, half (16.6 million) were lambs under one-year-old and female breeding stock accounted for 0.4 million of the estimated 4.7 million pigs. Poultry numbers were estimated at around 166 million, the majority being chickens for consumption (110 million) and egg layers (26 million). The remaining poultry are made up of pullets, those in the breeding flock and other types of poultry such as ducks and geese.

Organic farming is a form of agriculture that largely excludes the use of synthetic fertilizers and pesticides, plant growth regulators and livestock feed additives. To maintain soil productivity, to supply plant nutrients and to control weeds, insects and pests, organic farmers use methods such as crop

11

Table 11.17

Crop areas and livestock numbers, 2008[1]

United Kingdom	Thousand hectares
Crop areas	
Cereals	3,274
Wheat	2,080
Barley	1,032
Oats	135
Rye, mixed corn, and triticale	27
Other arable crops (excluding potatoes)	1,152
Oilseed rape	598
Sugar beet not for stockfeeding[2]	120
Peas for harvesting dry and field beans[2]	148
Linseed[2]	16
Other crops	269
Potatoes	144
Horticulture	170
Vegetables grown in the open	122
Orchard fruit[3]	24
Soft fruit[4]	10
Plants and flowers[5]	13
Glasshouse crops	2
Total crop area	4,740
Livestock numbers (thousand head)	
Cattle and calves	10,107
Sheep and lambs	33,131
Pigs	4,714
Poultry	166,200

1 As at June.
2 Data are not available for Wales.
3 Includes non-commercial orchards.
4 Includes wine grapes.
5 Hardy nursery stock, bulbs and flowers.

Source: Department for Environment, Food and Rural Affairs

rotation, crop residues, animal manures and mechanical cultivation. In 2008, 743,500 hectares was organically managed in the UK; being either fully organic or in conversion, representing around 4 per cent of total agricultural holdings (Figure 11.18). The majority (84 per cent) of this land was permanent and temporary pasture, the remainder included cereals and other crops, vegetables including potatoes, and woodland. The late 1990s and early 2000s saw increases in the area of organically managed land to reach around 741,200 hectares in 2002, as some farmers sought alternatives to conventional farming in response to falling farm incomes and increases in the payment rates from organic farming support

Figure 11.18

Organically managed land[1]

United Kingdom

Thousand hectares

1 Due to the nature of the inspections, the data is collected at varying times through the year. Therefore, the data presented here does not give an exact snapshot of organic farming at any specific time of year.
2 Converting land to organic production can take two to three years.

Source: Department for Environment, Food and Rural Affairs

schemes. There was a small decline in the area of organically managed land between 2003 and 2007. However, in 2008 it increased by 9 per cent, with the area of in-conversion land falling by 6 per cent to 149,100 hectares and the area of fully organic land rising by 13 per cent to 594,400 hectares. Around 9 per cent of agricultural land in Wales was either in conversion or fully organic, equivalent to 125,000 hectares. In both Scotland and England, 4 per cent of agricultural land was either in conversion or fully organic, equivalent to 375,000 hectares and 231,000 hectares respectively, and 1 per cent (12,500 hectares) in Northern Ireland.

The UK has a responsibility to ensure the conservation and enhancement of habitats and species in both a national and international context. Special Areas of Conservation (SACs) and Sites of Community Importance (SCIs) are areas which have been given special protection under the European Union's Habitats Directive (see Appendix, Part 11: Special areas of conservation) in order that they can provide increased protection to a variety of wild animals, plants and habitats. As of 31 August 2008 there were 614 designated SACs and SCIs in the UK, excluding seven candidate SACs and five possible or draft SACs (Table 11.19), covering more than 2.6 million hectares. Just over three-quarters (76 per cent) of the number of SACs and SCIs were wholly in England and Scotland. The sites vary in size and habitat. For example, the largest SAC, at 151,000 hectares, is the Moray Firth, whose primary reason for being an SAC is that it supports the only known resident population of bottlenose

11

Table 11.19

Special areas of conservation or sites of community importance, 2008[1]

United Kingdom   Numbers

	Special area of conservation		Sites of community importance	
	Number	Area (hectares)	Number	Area (hectares)
England	228	809,144	2	36,712
England/Scotland	3	112,478	0	0
England/Wales	5	5,552	2	89,520
Wales	85	590,871	0	0
Scotland	235	921,207	1	16
Northern Ireland	52	65,913	1	408
Total	608	2,505,165	6	126,656

1 As at 31 August. See Appendix, Part 11: Special areas of conservation.

Source: Joint Nature Conservation Committee

dolphin in the North Sea. The smallest SAC is Hestercombe House in Somerset at 0.1 hectares, whose primary reason for being an SAC is that it is a large maternity site for the lesser horseshoe bat.

Bat species include some of the UK's most widespread wild mammals, found throughout urban areas, farmland, woodland and river/lake systems. Bats serve as a good indicator for the wider health of the UK's wildlife. Pressures faced by bats include landscape change, agricultural intensification, urban development and habitat fragmentation which are also relevant to many other wildlife species. The National Bat Monitoring Programme run by the Bat Conservation Trust (BCT) produces statistically robust population trends for 11 of the 17 resident species. Based on data up to 2008, three of the species (lesser horseshoe, Natterer's bat and common pipistrelle) have shown increases in the UK since 1999, although these increases are likely to be slight compared with long-term declines. Possible factors for the increases include targeted conservation work, legal protection of roosts and improvements in water quality. Three further species/species groups (greater horseshoe, whiskered/Brandt's bat and noctule) have also shown increases since 1999, but further years' monitoring is needed before these trends can be interpreted with confidence. The population of the remaining species are currently thought to be stable, though BCT's concerns about the vulnerability of the populations of noctule and the brown long-eared bat has led to these species being added to the list of priority Biodiversity Action Plan species. This list contains species and habitats that

have been listed as priorities for conservation action under the UK Biodiversity Action Plan (UK BAP).

Wild bird populations are also good indicators of the general state of the countryside and its associated wildlife. They occupy a wide range of different habitats and as they tend to be near to, or at the top of the food chain, they can reflect changes in insects, plants and other aspects of the environment. Overall the population index of wild birds in the UK, which measures the populations of 114 species, has remained relatively stable between 1970 and 2008 (see Appendix, Part 11: Wild bird species) (Figure 11.20). However, trends for different species vary. Although the population of farmland birds (19 species) increased by 2 per cent between 2007 and 2008 – the first annual increase since 2000 – this population has seen the largest decline and was 47 per cent lower in 2008 than in 1970. This was principally driven by declines in farmland 'specialists' such as the tree sparrow, corn bunting, grey partridge and starling whose populations have each declined by over 70 per cent since 1970. However, there have been exceptions for some specialists, for example, the goldfinch and stock dove increased by over 50 per cent over the same period.

The woodland bird population index fell by 14 per cent between 1970 and 2008, though it increased by 7 per cent between 2007 and 2008. Both woodland specialists and generalists increased in numbers between 2007 and 2008 (8 per cent and 3 per cent respectively). However, some woodland specialists such as the lesser redpoll, spotted

Figure 11.20

Population of wild birds:[1] by species group

United Kingdom

Index numbers (1970=100)

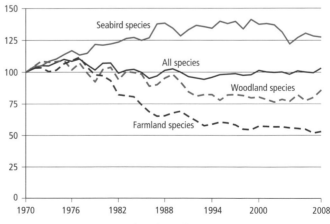

1 It was not possible to complete the Breeding Birds Survey in 2001 because of restrictions imposed during the outbreak of foot-and-mouth disease. Estimates for that year are based on the average for 2000 and 2002 for individual species. See Appendix, Part 11: Wild bird species.

Source: British Trust for Ornithology; Royal Society for the Protection of Birds; Department for Environment, Food and Rural Affairs

11

flycatcher, willow tit, marsh tit, wood warbler and tree pipit saw reductions of more than 70 per cent since 1970, while some specialists such as the great spotted woodpecker and the green woodpecker more than doubled their population over the same period. Between 1970 and 2008, the seabird population index has increased by around 27 per cent. During this period numbers of the great skua, northern gannet and common guillemot have doubled or more than doubled. However, some seabird species such as the herring gull have shown a continual decline and have decreased by around 60 per cent since 1970.

Fish are a vital element of the ocean's ecosystem. The level of spawning stock biomass (the total weight of all sexually mature fish in a population) is used to determine whether the population of each stock is at a sustainable level. Historically, trends in spawning stock biomass vary from species to species and fluctuate over relatively short periods depending on the success of breeding from year to year. Some stocks are at historically low levels as a result of both over-exploitation through fishing activity and natural factors. Pollution of the sea has little impact because concentrations of contaminants in sea water are generally low.

To prevent over-exploitation of fish stocks there has to be a balance between fishing activity and the natural ability of fish stocks to regenerate. For example, cod, a popular food in the UK, is caught throughout the North Sea and because of over fishing has been reduced to very low levels. In 1964 the stocks of cod in the North Sea were estimated at around 167,000 tonnes and by 2006 stocks had fallen to an all time low of 34,000 tonnes, a decrease of around 79 per cent (Figure 11.21). Numbers had recovered slightly by 2008 with stocks

Figure 11.21

North Sea fish stocks[1]

Thousand tonnes

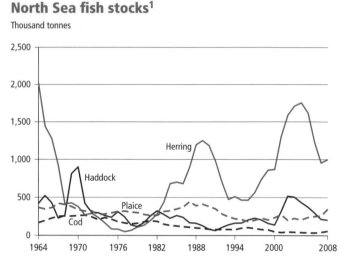

1 Spawning stock biomass (the total weight of all sexually mature fish in a population).

Source: Centre for Environment, Fisheries and Agriculture Science; International Council for the Exploration of the Sea

standing at around 57,000 tonnes. The North Sea herring was seriously over fished in the 1970s and between 1964 and 1977 herring stocks declined by around 98 per cent, from just over 2 million tonnes to 47,000 tonnes. This led to the closure of the fishery between 1978 and 1982 and although there was some recovery in the late 1980s, numbers declined again during the 1990s following a second period of excessive fishing and low numbers of young fish entering the stock. Stocks in 2008 stood at 999,000 tonnes. Overall in 2008, just 36 per cent of the 25 assessed fish stocks around the UK were categorised as being both at full reproductive capacity and being harvested sustainably.

Chapter 12

Transport

- The total distance travelled by people in Great Britain increased by 275 per cent between 1952 and 2007, to 817 billion passenger kilometres per year. (Page 170)

- Between 1989–91 and 2008, the proportion of children in Great Britain of primary school age travelling to school by car rose steadily, from 27 per cent to 43 per cent. (Table 12.3)

- The proportion of households in Great Britain without access to a car decreased from 86 per cent in 1951 to 22 per cent in 2008. Over the same period, the proportion of households with access to two cars increased from 1 per cent to 27 per cent. (Figure 12.6)

- Vehicle maintenance costs rose by 236 per cent between 1987 and 2009 in the UK, compared with a rise in the 'All items' retail prices index of 110 per cent. (Figure 12.11)

- There were 176,814 reported personal injury accidents on roads in the UK in 2008. Of these, 66 per cent occurred on roads (excluding motorways) with a 30 mph speed limit, a fall of 4 per cent from 2007. (Table 12.17)

- Of the 68.2 million trips made abroad by UK residents in 2008, 82 per cent were made by air travel, compared with 69 per cent of all visits made in 1998. (Table 12.19)

The 20th century saw dramatic changes in how people in the UK travel and in the distances they travel. At the turn of the century, the rail network was largely in place. Horse-drawn transport still ruled the roads as cars were a rarity. However, in the 1920s, when the car started to become a reality for the few, the way in which people travelled across the country changed. Motorised buses and mass-produced cars replaced horse-drawn transport. By the late 1950s, the freedom of the 'open road' instigated by the popularity of owning a car started to dominate the way people travelled. New roads were built to accommodate the growth in travel by motorised vehicles, while the rail network started to see a decline in journeys and passenger numbers. Commercial air flights also became a reality for many people during the second half of the last century, further boosted by the emergence of 'budget' airlines. Although travel by car is still the dominant mode of travel in the 21st century, bus and rail travel has begun to increase and travelling by air shows signs of slowing down, partly perhaps as people reflect on the way we travel and its effect on the environment around us.

Travel patterns

Since the early 1950s the total distance travelled by people in Great Britain has increased fourfold, from 218 billion passenger kilometres in 1952 to 817 billion passenger kilometres in 2007. In 1952, bus and coach travel accounted for the largest share of overall distance travelled, at 42 per cent, equivalent to 92 billion passenger kilometres, while travel by car and van accounted for 27 per cent (58 billion passenger kilometres) (Figure 12.1). In 2007, bus and coach travel had declined to 6 per cent (50 billion passenger kilometres), while travel by car and van accounted for the largest share of distance travelled, at 84 per cent (689 billion passenger kilometres).

In the 1950s and 1960s the annual distance travelled by car and van saw a rapid increase from 58 billion passenger kilometres in 1952 to 286 billion passenger kilometres in 1969, while bus and coach travel fell from 92 billion to 63 billion passenger kilometres over the same period. The 1970s, 1980s, and 1990s saw similar patterns of growth and decline for these two modes of transport, with car and van travel rising from 297 billion passenger kilometres in 1970 to 642 billion passenger kilometres in 1999, while bus and coach travel declined from 60 billion to 46 billion passenger kilometres over the same period. Between 2000 and 2007, the annual average distance travelled by car and van was 671 billion passenger kilometres while for bus and coach it was 48 billion passenger kilometres.

Although rail travel increased from 38 billion to 59 billion passenger kilometres between 1952 and 2007, it has fallen from 17 per cent to 7 per cent as a proportion of the total

Figure 12.1

Passenger transport:[1] by mode

Great Britain
Percentages

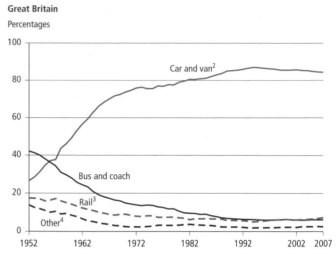

1 Road transport data from 1993 onwards are not directly comparable with earlier years. See Appendix, Part 12: Road traffic.
2 Includes taxis.
3 Data relate to financial years (for example 1970/71).
4 Data include bicycle, motorcycle and air. Data for air are domestic flights only and include Northern Ireland, the Channel Islands and the Isle of Man.

Source: Department for Transport

distance travelled. Travel by rail reached its lowest point in 1982 when 31 billion passenger kilometres were travelled, but six years later this had risen to 41 billion passenger kilometres. Rail travel declined again during the early to mid-1990s but there has been a steady increase in passenger kilometres travelled throughout the late 1990s and into the new century. From 2000, the distance travelled by rail continued to rise steadily by an average of 3 per cent a year (see also the section on Public transport later in this chapter).

In 1952, a total of 23 billion passenger kilometres were travelled by bicycle, accounting for 11 per cent of the total distance travelled during that year. By 2007, this had fallen to 4 billion passenger kilometres, accounting for 0.5 per cent of all travel. The distance travelled by motorcycle also declined over the same period, from 7 billion passenger kilometres in 1952 to 6 billion in 2007.

The distance travelled by domestic air flights in 2007 was 50 times greater than that travelled in 1952, accounting for 10 billion passenger kilometres. Although air travel showed the fastest growth of all types of transport over the period, it still represented only 1 per cent of the total domestic distance travelled in Great Britain in 2007 (see also the section on International travel at the end of this chapter).

An average of 992 trips per person were made in Great Britain in 2008, with the majority (410 trips) being made by car or van

Table 12.2

Trips per person per year:[1] by mode

Great Britain

Number of trips

	1995 –1997	1998 –2000	2002	2003	2004	2005	2006	2007	2008
Car/van driver	425	434	435	425	422	435	430	408	410
Car/van passenger	239	238	239	232	229	236	228	218	227
Walk[2]	292	271	244	246	246	245	249	216	221
Bus[3]	68	65	65	67	65	64	65	66	65
Rail[4]	19	21	22	22	24	23	24	25	27
Bicycle	18	17	16	15	16	14	16	14	16
Other[5]	25	26	26	27	25	27	24	24	26
All modes	1,086	1,071	1,047	1,034	1,026	1,044	1,037	972	992

1 See Appendix, Part 12: National Travel Survey.
2 Due to methodological changes short walks were under-recorded in 2002 and to a lesser extent in 2003. Due to design changes made to the travel diary in 2007 there has been a fall in short trips made in 2007 and 2008. Under-recording of short walks affects the average time and length of trips, especially for walking and school trips.
3 Includes buses in London, local and non-local buses.
4 Includes London Underground.
5 Includes motorcycles, taxis and other private and public transport.

Source: National Travel Survey, Department for Transport

drivers (Table 12.2). The number of trips made per person per year increased by 2 per cent between 2007 and 2008, but the overall trend since 1995–97 has been downwards. There was a decrease of 4 per cent between 2006 and 2008, and of 9 per cent from the 1995–97 average of 1,086 trips made per person per year.

People made a total of 221 trips on foot in 2008, on average, accounting for 22 per cent of the total number of trips made that year. This is an increase of 2 per cent from 2007, but a decrease of 11 per cent from 2006, and a 24 per cent decrease from the 1995–97 average. Although there were only 16 trips made per person per year by bicycle in 2008 (representing 2 per cent of the total number of trips made), this mode of transport has shown the largest proportional growth in trips per person between 2007 and 2008, at 17 per cent. Rail trips are the only mode to have increased across the whole period, increasing by 44 per cent in 2008 from the 1995–97 average of 19 trips per person per year.

Trips by car accounted for just under two-thirds of all trips made in 2008. The most common reason for making a trip by car was for leisure purposes, with 186 trips made per person on average, 94 trips made as a car driver and the remainder as a car passenger. For car drivers, commuting was the second most common reason for making a trip by car, with 90 trips being made per person, while for car passengers it was for shopping (42 trips per person).

The most common reason for making a trip on foot was for shopping or just walking (45 trips and 43 trips per person respectively). There were 13 trips per person made by rail for commuting and 6 trips per person made by rail for leisure purposes. The most common reason for using a local bus was shopping (19 trips per person), while the joint second most common reasons for using a local bus were leisure and commuting (13 trips per person for each purpose).

Over the last two decades, the way in which children in Great Britain travel to school has changed. In general fewer are walking and more are travelling by car (Table 12.3 overleaf). Between 2002 and 2008, the proportion of children of primary school age (aged 5 to 10) walking to school has remained fairly stable, ranging from 51 per cent of trips to school for this age group in 2002 to 48 per cent in 2008, but it has fallen by 14 percentage points since 1989–91. Conversely, the proportion of trips to school by car for this age group increased by 16 percentage points between 1989–91 and 2008, from 27 per cent to 43 per cent.

The proportion of trips to school made on foot by secondary school aged children (aged 11 to 16) also fell between 1989–91 and 2002, but by less than for primary school children, from 48 per cent to 38 per cent. By 2008, this proportion had increased slightly to 40 per cent.

The proportion of trips to school made by other modes of transport, which are mainly trips by private or local bus,

12

Table 12.3

Trips[1] to and from school: by age of child and selected mode[2]

Great Britain Percentages

	Age 5–10			Age 11–16		
	Walk	Car/van	Other[3]	Walk	Car/van	Other[3]
1989–1991	62	27	10	48	14	38
1990–1992	61	28	11	48	14	38
1991–1993	60	29	10	46	15	39
1992–1994	61	30	10	44	16	39
1993–1995	60	31	9	42	18	39
1994–1996	59	32	9	42	20	37
1995–1997	53	38	9	42	20	38
1996–1998	53	37	10	42	21	37
1997–1999	53	39	9	42	21	37
1998–2000	56	37	8	43	20	38
1999–2001	53	40	7	42	19	39
2002	51	41	8	38	24	39
2003	51	41	9	40	23	37
2004	49	43	9	43	22	34
2005	49	43	8	44	22	34
2006	52	41	8	41	20	38
2007	51	41	9	43	22	35
2008	48	43	9	40	21	39

1 Trips of under 80 kilometres (50 miles) only.
2 From 1995–97 data are weighted to account for nonresponse bias. Data prior to 2002 are three-year rolling averages. See Appendix, Part 12: National Travel Survey.
3 Mostly private and local bus.

Source: National Travel Survey, Department for Transport

remained relatively stable for children in both age groups. In 2008 these other modes accounted for a much higher proportion of trips to school among children aged 11 to 16 (39 per cent) than among children aged 5 to 10 (9 per cent).

The average length of a trip to school has increased. In the period 1995–97 the average trip to school for children aged 5 to 10 was 1.3 miles, but this rose to 1.6 miles in 2008. Over the same period, for children aged 11 to 16 the average distance to school increased from 2.9 to 3.4 miles.

The National Travel Survey (see Appendix, Part 12: National Travel Survey), published by the Department for Transport, asked parents in Great Britain about their children's independence in terms of travelling to school unaccompanied by an adult. The majority of children aged 7 to 10 were usually accompanied to school by an adult in 2008 (86 per cent), an increase from 78 per cent in 2002. The main reasons for accompanying their children were traffic

danger (58 per cent) and fear of assault or molestation (29 per cent).

Almost a third (31 per cent) of children aged 11 to 13 were usually accompanied to school by an adult in 2008, the main reasons were traffic danger (34 per cent), convenience (30 per cent) and the school being too far away (29 per cent).

Motor vehicles

At the end of 2008 there were 34.2 million motor vehicles licensed in Great Britain, compared with a total of 2.3 million in 1930 and 15.0 million in 1970. Growth in the number of motor vehicles owned, contributing to the greater distances travelled by individuals, along with greater numbers of road haulage and public transport vehicles, have led to an increase in the average daily flow of vehicles on the roads.

Between 1965 and 2008 the average daily traffic flow on all roads in Great Britain rose by 150 per cent to 3,500 vehicles per day (Table 12.4). Motorways had the highest flow of vehicles, at 76,900 vehicles per day in 2008; this was just over four times the flow in 1965 (18,300 vehicles). There were also large increases in traffic flow on major roads in rural areas over the same period (197 per cent), while the increase on urban major roads was 99 per cent.

In 1914, the total road length in Great Britain was 285,000 kilometres, 38 per cent less than the total road length in 2008 (394,500 kilometres). Total road length increased by nearly

Table 12.4

Average daily flow[1] of motor vehicles: by class of road[2]

Great Britain Thousands

	1965	1975	1985	1995	2005	2008
Motorways	18.3	30.2	37.0	61.9	75.5	76.9
All 'A' roads	5.5	7.0	8.9	11.8	13.1	13.0
Urban major roads	9.9	11.5	12.9	19.9	20.1	19.7
Rural major roads	3.7	5.1	7.2	9.3	10.9	11.0
All major roads[3]	5.1	7.6	10.3	15.1	17.5	17.6
All minor roads	0.7	0.9	1.1	1.3	1.5	1.5
All roads	1.4	1.9	2.4	3.0	3.5	3.5

1 Flow at an average point on each class of road.
2 Motorways include trunk motorways and principal motorways. Urban major roads include roads in built up areas prior to 1995. Rural major roads include roads in non-built up areas prior to 1995. See Appendix, Part 12: Road traffic.
3 Includes all trunk and principal motorways and 'A' roads.

Source: National Road Traffic Survey, Department for Transport

6,000 kilometres over the 10 years since 1998, an increase of 1.5 per cent, of which over 5,000 kilometres has been on the minor road network, mainly due to the construction of new housing areas (see also Chapter 10: Housing).

Motorways and 'A' roads accounted for 0.9 per cent and 12 per cent respectively of road length in Great Britain in 2008. They carried a much higher proportion of traffic: motorways accounted for 20 per cent of all traffic, while 'A' roads accounted for 44 per cent. Minor roads, accounting for 87 per cent of the total road length, carried 37 per cent of all traffic.

At the end of 2008 there was a total of 28.4 million cars licensed in Great Britain. Although this is an increase of 163,000 cars since the end of 2007 it is the lowest year-on-year growth since 1999, at 0.6 per cent (Table 12.5). The highest year-on-year increase over the last decade was recorded between 2003 and 2004, at 3 per cent, equivalent to 788,000 cars.

There were a total of 14.4 million cars licensed with an engine capacity of 1,551 to 2,000 cubic centimetres (cc) at the end of 2008, accounting for just over half (51 per cent) of the total number of cars licensed in that year. The second largest share of cars licensed were those with an engine capacity of 1,001 to 1,550cc, at 31 per cent (8.9 million cars). The number licensed with an engine capacity of less than 1,000cc was 1.3 million, which accounted for 4 per cent of the total number of cars licensed.

The proportion of cars licensed with an engine capacity of more than 2,501cc, and those licensed with an engine capacity of 2,001 to 2,500cc, each represented 7 per cent of the total

number of cars licensed in 2008 (1.9 million and 2.0 million respectively). The trend since 1999 has been towards larger engine sizes; the number of cars licensed with an engine capacity of 2,501 to 3,000cc has increased by 83 per cent, while those with an engine capacity of less than 1,000cc has declined by 19 per cent over the same period.

The average age of cars licensed at the end of 2008 was 7.0 years; this is an increase on the 2007 average of 6.8 years and the 2003 average of 6.6 years. The average age of licensed motorcycles has followed a similar trend, increasing from a 2003 average of 9.4 years to 10.4 years in 2008.

The proportion of households in Great Britain without access to a car has decreased nearly fourfold since the early 1950s, with 86 per cent of households not having access to a car in 1951 compared with 22 per cent in 2008 (Figure 12.6 overleaf). The proportion of households with access to one car increased over the same period, from 13 per cent to 44 per cent, and has remained relatively stable since the early 1970s, at around 44 to 45 per cent. However, there has been steady growth over the period in the proportion of households with access to two cars, which increased from 1 per cent in 1951 to 27 per cent in 2008. The proportion of households with access to three or more cars has also steadily increased, from 1 per cent in 1970 to 7 per cent in 2008.

In Great Britain people living in urban areas have better access to more frequent public transport than people living in rural areas, making it easier for them to manage without a car (see Appendix, Part 12: Area type classification). In 2008, 43 per cent of households in London boroughs did not own or

Table 12.5

Cars licensed: by engine capacity[1]

Great Britain   Millions

	1 to 1,000cc	1,001 to 1,550cc	1,551 to 2,000cc	2,001 to 2,500cc	2,501 to 3,000cc	3,001cc and over	All cars
1999	1.5	8.4	11.8	1.1	0.6	0.5	24.0
2000	1.5	8.4	12.1	1.2	0.7	0.5	24.4
2001	1.5	8.6	12.5	1.3	0.7	0.6	25.1
2002	1.4	8.6	12.9	1.5	0.7	0.6	25.8
2003	1.4	8.7	13.2	1.6	0.8	0.6	26.2
2004	1.3	8.8	13.7	1.7	0.9	0.7	27.0
2005	1.3	8.8	14.0	1.8	1.0	0.7	27.5
2006	1.3	8.8	14.1	1.9	1.1	0.7	27.8
2007	1.2	8.8	14.3	2.0	1.1	0.8	28.2
2008	1.3	8.9	14.4	2.0	1.2	0.8	28.4

1 Engine capacity is measured in cubic centimetres (cc) and is a measure of the combustion space in the cylinders of an internal combustion engine.

Source: Department for Transport

12

Figure 12.6

Households with regular use of a car[1,2]

Great Britain

Percentages

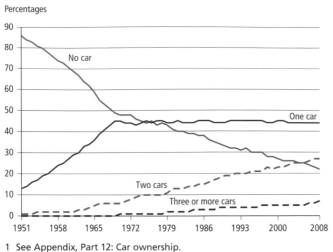

1 See Appendix, Part 12: Car ownership.
2 In 2008 the General Household Survey was renamed the General Lifestyle Survey. See Appendix, Part 2: General Household Survey.

Source: National Travel Survey, Department for Transport; General Lifestyle Survey (Longitudinal), Office for National Statistics

have access to a car, compared with 32 per cent of households in other built-up metropolitan areas, and 10 per cent in rural areas. Nearly half (47 per cent) of households in rural areas had access to two or more cars compared with 17 per cent in London boroughs, and around a quarter (26 per cent) in other metropolitan areas.

Public transport

In recent years there have been a number of measures aimed at reducing people's reliance on cars. The 1998 Government White Paper *A New Deal for Transport* gave public transport a higher profile, with the aim of encouraging people to use modes of travel other than the car. The paper stated that, as a result of privatisation and deregulation which had dominated transport policy for 20 years, there had been a decline in bus and rail services and over-reliance on the car. The intention of the paper was to introduce powers to promote service stability, more flexible ticketing, and better passenger information. It also aimed to provide better access to public transport designed for everyone to use easily. The paper introduced local transport plans in which local authorities set out their strategies for transport together with long-term targets (for example improving road safety and public transport).

In 2008/09, there were a total of 7.8 billion journeys made by passengers on public transport in Great Britain; this was 55 per cent less than the number of passenger journeys made in 1955, when 17.3 billion journeys had been made (Table 12.7). Local buses accounted for the largest share of passenger journeys in 1955, around 15.6 billion journeys, equivalent to 90 per cent of passenger journeys made in that year. Although the number of passenger journeys made by local bus has declined, this mode of transport still represents the largest share of passenger journeys made in 2008/09 (30 per cent), carrying around twice as many passengers compared with all forms of rail travel.

Passenger journeys made on domestic flights increased through the decades to 2005/06. However, since 2005/06 passenger journeys have declined, with 1 million fewer journeys made in 2007/08 compared with 2005/06, and a further decline of 1 million journeys made in 2008/09 to 21 million passenger journeys. Although the use of the bus as a

Table 12.7

Passenger journeys: by mode of public transport

Great Britain

Millions

	1955	1965	1975	1985/86	1995/96	2005/06	2007/08	2008/09
Local buses[1,2]	15,592	11,239	7,533	5,819	4,494	4,795	5,165	5,236
National rail	994	865	730	686	761	1,082	1,232	1,274
London Underground	676	657	601	732	784	970	1,096	1,089
Other rail and metros[3]	..	24	15	72	83	173	198	200
Air passengers[4]	1	5	6	9	14	23	22	21
All passenger journeys	17,263	12,790	8,885	7,318	6,136	7,043	7,713	7,820

1 Includes traditional trams and trolleys.
2 Data from 2007/08 onwards are not comparable with earlier years because of changes to methodology.
3 Comprises the Glasgow Subway, Tyne and Wear Metro, Docklands Light Railway, Manchester Metrolink, Supertram, West Midlands Metro, Croydon Tramlink, and Nottingham Tram.
4 UK airlines only, domestic passengers on scheduled and non-scheduled flights. Data are for calendar years.

Source: Department for Transport

mode of transport in Great Britain has declined since the 1950s, it remains the most common form of public transport in terms of the number of journeys taken.

A total of 9.7 billion passenger journeys were made on local buses in Great Britain in 1968, representing 2.8 billion vehicle kilometres. Over the next three decades the trend in local bus use was generally downwards, and then started to increase from 1999/2000. By 2008/09 passenger journeys had declined by nearly half (46 per cent) since 1968. Over the same period, the overall distance travelled by bus declined by only 1 per cent (Figure 12.8).

Passenger bus journeys reached their lowest level in 1998/99, at 4.3 billion, a fall of 55 per cent compared with 1968, while the overall distance travelled by bus reached its lowest level in 1985/86, at 2.0 billion kilometres, a fall of just over a quarter (26 per cent) compared with 1968. In the last 10 years the decline in bus use has reversed, with bus passenger journeys increasing by 20 per cent.

People in households in Great Britain are asked to rate the frequency and reliability of their local buses through the National Travel Survey, conducted by the Department for Transport. Findings show that since 2002 the proportion of households rating their local bus service as frequent or reliable has remained reasonably constant, at around four-fifths. However, the proportion rating it as very frequent has increased from 22 per cent in 2002 to 30 per cent in 2008, and the proportion rating it as very reliable increased from 24 per cent to 28 per cent over the same period.

Figure 12.8

Local bus travel[1]

Great Britain

Index numbers (1968=100)

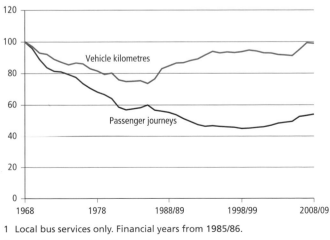

1 Local bus services only. Financial years from 1985/86.

Source: Department for Transport

Figure 12.9

Passenger rail[1] journeys

Great Britain

Millions

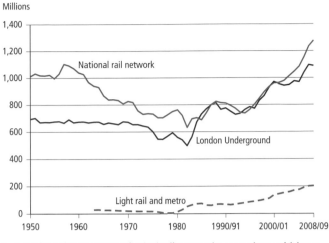

1 Excludes railways operated principally as tourist attractions, which are Great Orme and Blackpool tramways.

Source: Office of Rail Regulation; London Underground; light railway operators; Department for Transport

In Great Britain, an average of 1.7 billion passenger journeys were made on the national rail network per year during the 1950s (including the London Underground). However, passenger journeys declined through the 1960s, 1970s and early 1980s to reach a low of 1.2 billion passenger journeys in 1982 (Figure 12.9). Apart from a period in the early 1990s when journey numbers fell, the number of journeys generally increased between 1982 and 2008/09.

In 2008/09, more than 2.5 billion passenger journeys were made (including underground and metro systems), of which 1.3 billion were made on the national rail network, the sixth consecutive year that passenger journeys on the national network exceeded 1 billion. Prior to this, the last time passenger journeys exceeded 1 billion was in 1961, just before the Beeching closures when more than 4,000 miles of railway branch lines and 3,000 stations were closed in the decade after 1963.

In 2008/09, passengers using the London Underground network exceeded 1 billion for the third consecutive year. Overall, the national rail network and London Underground accounted for almost all rail journeys in 2008/09, at 50 per cent and 42 per cent respectively.

Light railways and trams accounted for 8 per cent of rail journeys in 2008/09, compared with 2 per cent in 1963 when data were first collected for these modes of transport. Passenger journeys on light railways and trams more than doubled from 83 million to 200 million between the mid-1990s and 2008/09. This increase was partly due to the fact that

Table 12.10

Passenger satisfaction with the railways, 2009[1]

Great Britain

Percentages

	Satisfactory or good	Neither satisfactory nor unsatisfactory	Unsatisfactory or poor	Change since spring 2006[2]
Station facilities				
How request to station staff was handled	82	7	10	0
Provision of information about train times/platforms	78	12	10	1
Connections with other forms of public transport	73	15	12	1
Personal security whilst using the facilities	63	29	8	6
Facilities and services	50	20	30	0
Facilities for car parking	44	18	38	-3
Train facilities				
Length of time the journey was scheduled to take[3]	83	9	7	1
Punctuality/reliability[4]	80	7	13	1
Frequency of the trains on that route	75	9	15	-1
Upkeep and repair of the train	72	16	12	2
Comfort of the seating area	69	18	13	1
Sufficient room for all passengers to sit/stand	66	14	20	4
Availability of staff	41	29	30	2
Value for money for the price of ticket	40	21	39	-1
Toilet facilities	36	24	40	-3
Overall satisfaction	81	11	8	1

1 Data are at spring.
2 Improvement/decline in the proportion of passengers who rated railway services as satisfactory or good since spring 2006.
3 Relates to the speed of the journey.
4 The train arriving/departing on time.

Source: National Passenger Survey, Passenger Focus

several new light railways and tram lines were built or extended between 1997 and 2008/09, such as the Croydon Tramlink in south London and Metrolink in Manchester.

The National Passenger Survey, conducted by Passenger Focus (an independent national rail consumer watchdog) in spring 2009, asked adult rail customers aged 16 and over in Great Britain about their satisfaction with various aspects of travelling on railways. More than four-fifths (81 per cent) of passengers were satisfied with their rail journey and associated facilities overall (Table 12.10). This was around the same proportion as in spring 2006 (80 per cent). When asked about station facilities, 82 per cent of customers were satisfied about how station staff handled requests, while 78 per cent were satisfied with the provision of information about train times and platforms. The indicator recording the highest proportional increase in satisfaction since spring 2006 was personal security while using the facilities, an increase of 6 percentage points, to 63 per cent.

When asked about train facilities, 83 per cent of customers were satisfied with the speed of the journey and 80 per cent were satisfied with punctuality and reliability. The indicator with the largest percentage point increase in satisfied customers since spring 2006 was sufficient room for all passengers to sit or stand, an increase of 4 percentage points to 66 per cent. The indicators that had the highest proportion of dissatisfied customers were toilet facilities on the train (40 per cent), value for money for the price of the ticket (39 per cent) and the availability of staff on the train (30 per cent).

Prices and expenditure

Motoring costs in the UK, as measured by the 'All motoring expenditure' component of the retail prices index (RPI), rose by 77 per cent between January 1987 and January 2009, less than the rise in the 'All items' RPI measure of general inflation of 110 per cent.

Figure 12.11

Passenger transport prices[1]

United Kingdom
Index numbers (1987=100)

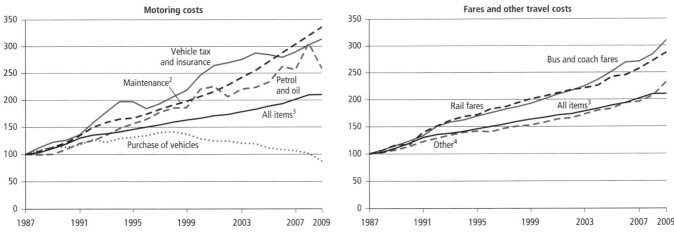

1 At January each year based on the retail prices index (RPI). See Appendix, Part 5: Retail prices index.
2 Includes spare parts and accessories, roadside recovery services, MOT test fee, car service, labour charges and car wash.
3 The RPI measure of general inflation.
4 Includes taxi and minicab fares, self-drive and van hire charges, ferry and sea fares, air fares, road tolls, purchase of bicycles/boats and car park charges.

Source: Office for National Statistics

Since 1987, different components of motoring costs have seen varying price increases and decreases compared with the 'All items' RPI measure (Figure 12.11). For example, maintenance costs rose by 236 per cent between January 1987 and January 2009 whereas the cost of purchasing vehicles fell by 14 per cent over the same period. However, the cost of purchasing a vehicle rose at a rate similar to the 'All items' measure of the RPI between 1987 and 1998, and since then has fallen by 39 per cent.

The price of petrol and oil more than doubled between 1987 and 2000, and then rose to a peak in January 2008 of 205 per cent above its 1987 level. However, petrol and oil prices fell in January 2009 compared with the 12 months previously.

Between January 2008 and January 2009 motoring costs contributed to an overall fall in the annual RPI rate. Contributing factors were petrol and oil prices falling by 15 per cent, a fall in the cost of the purchase of motor vehicles and the price of maintenance of motor vehicles rising by less than in January 2008.

Overall the 'All fares and other travel' component of the RPI rose by 163 per cent between January 1987 and January 2009. There was a large upward effect from bus and coach fares, which rose by 209 per cent over the period. Other travel costs, such as taxi fares and the purchase of bicycles, also increased over the period, by 132 per cent.

There is considerable volatility in the prices of petrol and diesel, reflecting the market for crude oil which in turn is influenced by world events. November 2007 was the first time both premium unleaded petrol and diesel prices rose to over £1.00 per litre in the UK (Figure 12.12).

Between January 1999 and November 2009, the average pump prices of both premium unleaded and diesel (including tax and

Figure 12.12

Premium unleaded petrol[1] and diesel pump prices

United Kingdom
Pence per litre

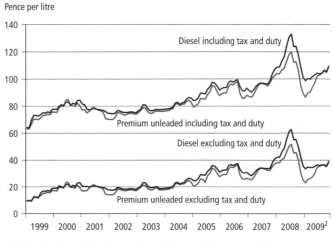

1 Unleaded petrol that is rated at 95 Research Octane Number. Does not include super unleaded petrol.
2 Data for 2009 are to November only.

Source: Department of Energy and Climate Change

12

duty) reached their highest levels in July 2008, at 119.6 pence per litre and 133.0 pence per litre respectively. The prices then began to fall – premium unleaded petrol fell to under £1.00 (94.7 pence per litre) in November 2008, while diesel fell to under £1.00 in January 2009 (98.7 pence per litre). These reductions were relatively short-lived with premium unleaded returning to over £1.00 per litre in June 2009 while diesel returned to over £1.00 per litre in February 2009. In November 2009, the average pump price of premium unleaded petrol in the UK was 108.3 pence per litre, a rise of 72 per cent since January 1999. The average price of diesel rose by 67 per cent over the same period to 109.5 pence per litre.

Tax and duty form a major component of petrol prices. In January 1999 the tax component in the price of both unleaded petrol and diesel was 85 per cent, the highest proportion reached for both products over the period shown. In November 2009 the tax and duty component for unleaded petrol and diesel accounted for nearly two-thirds (65 per cent and 64 per cent respectively) of the cost of the products.

In 2008, transport and travel costs accounted for 16 per cent of all household expenditure in the UK. This proportion has remained relatively stable since 1998/99. After taking into account the effects of inflation, there was little change overall in expenditure on transport and travel costs between 1998/99 and 2008, showing a decline in real terms of 4 per cent over this period, compared with 2 per cent growth in real terms in total household expenditure (Table 12.13).

Between 1998/99 and 2008 the largest percentage increase in motoring expenditure was on petrol, diesel and other oils, at 24 per cent (a rise of £4.00 per week), followed by motor vehicle insurance and taxation which increased by 18 per cent (a rise of £1.60). Between 2007 and 2008 expenditure on petrol, diesel and other oils increased by 11 per cent (a rise of £2.00) while motor vehicle insurance and taxation increased by 2 per cent (a rise of £0.20). However, average expenditure on the purchase of cars, vans and motorcycles fell by 32 per cent between 1998/99 and 2008, and in 2008 was only just above average expenditure on petrol, diesel and other oils (£21.10

Table 12.13

Household expenditure on transport in real terms[1]

United Kingdom £ per week

	1998/99	2000/01	2002/03[2]	2004/05	2006[3]	2007	2008
Motoring costs							
Cars, vans and motorcycle purchase	31.10	28.80	32.20	28.60	24.80	23.70	21.10
Repairs, servicing, spares and accessories	8.20	7.80	8.80	8.90	8.50	8.40	8.60
Motor vehicle insurance and taxation[4]	9.10	10.30	13.30	12.60	11.30	10.60	10.70
Petrol, diesel and other oils	17.00	19.90	18.00	18.50	19.40	19.00	21.00
Other motoring costs	2.40	2.30	2.30	2.70	2.50	2.50	2.10
All motoring expenditure	67.90	69.10	74.70	71.30	66.50	64.20	63.70
Fares and other travel costs							
Rail and tube fares	2.40	2.50	2.20	2.30	2.30	2.60	2.40
Bus and coach fares	1.60	1.70	1.70	1.70	1.40	1.30	1.40
Taxi, air and other travel costs[5]	5.50	6.50	6.40	5.30	7.00	6.60	6.70
All fares and other travel costs[6]	9.60	10.60	10.30	9.30	10.70	10.50	10.50
Motoring and all fares	77.50	79.70	85.00	80.60	77.20	74.70	74.10
Total expenditure[7]	462.00	483.60	491.50	496.00	486.70	477.40	471.00

1 At 2008 prices deflated by the 'all items' retail prices index. Expenditure rounded to the nearest 10 pence. See Appendix, Part 5: Retail price index and Part 6: Living Costs and Food Survey.
2 Data for 2002/03 onwards include children's expenditure, and are weighted based on the population figures from the 2001 Census.
3 From 2006 onwards, figures are based on weighted data, with nonresponse weights and population figures based on the 2001 Census.
4 Excludes boat insurance.
5 Includes combined fares.
6 Includes expenditure on bicycles and boats – purchases and repairs.
7 Total expenditure is classified according to the Classification of Individual Consumption by Purpose (COICOP). See Appendix, Part 6: Household expenditure.

Source: Living Costs and Food Survey, Office for National Statistics

compared with £21.00). Household expenditure on this component decreased by 11 per cent between 2007 and 2008 (a decrease of £2.60).

Household expenditure on bus and coach fares decreased by 17 per cent between 1998/99 and 2008, though they increased by 6 per cent between 2007 and 2008. Although expenditure on rail and tube fares was unchanged between 1998/99 and 2008, expenditure on these fares fell by 6 per cent between 2007 and 2008. There was a 20 per cent increase in expenditure on taxis, air and other travel costs between 1998/99 and 2008, but only a 1 per cent increase since 2007.

Of the £63.70 spent on motoring per week in 2008, half (50 per cent) was spent on the operation of personal transport (£31.80 per week). The majority of this was spent on petrol, diesel and other oils (£21.00 per week), with repairs, servicing, spares and accessories together with other motoring costs making up the remainder. In comparison, 41 per cent of motoring expenditure in 1998/99 was spent on the operation of personal transport (£27.70 per week) including £17.00 being spent on petrol, diesel and other oils per week.

Transport safety

The Government has targets for substantial improvements in road safety. By 2010 in Great Britain, the aim is to reduce the number of people killed or seriously injured in road accidents per 100 million vehicle kilometres by 40 per cent compared with the average in 1994–98. Similar targets exist for Northern Ireland (see Appendix, Part 12: Road safety).

In April 2009, the Government published proposals for a new, post 2010 road safety strategy *A Safer Way: consultation on making Britain's roads the safest in the world*. By 2020, the aim is to reduce the number of annual road deaths and serious injuries on Britain's roads by at least 33 per cent compared with the average in 2004–08, and to reduce the number of annual road deaths and serious injuries to children and young people (aged 0 to 17) by at least 50 per cent against the 2004–08 average.

In Great Britain, 2,538 people died in 2008 as a result of road accidents which were reported to the police, 14 per cent fewer than in 2007, with deaths among car users decreasing by 12 per cent over the same period. There was a 7 per cent decrease in those slightly injured and a 6 per cent decrease in the number of people seriously injured as a result of reported road accidents over the same period. There was a 16 per cent decrease in the number of motorcycle user fatalities in accidents and an 11 per cent decrease in the number of

Table 12.14

Passenger death rates:[1] by mode of transport[2]

Great Britain				Rate per billion passenger kilometres	
	1981	1991	1996	2001	2008
Motorcycle	115.8	94.6	108.4	112.1	88.8
Walking	76.9	69.8	55.9	47.5	30.9
Bicycle	56.9	46.5	49.8	32.6	24.2
Car	6.1	3.7	3.0	2.8	1.9
Van	3.7	2.1	1.0	0.9	0.5
Bus or coach	0.3	0.6	0.2	0.2	0.1
Rail[3]	1.0	0.8	0.4	0.3	0.3
Water	0.4	-	0.8	0.4	0.9
Air	0.2	-	-	-	-

1 See Appendix, Part 12: Passenger death rates.
2 Motorcycle, bicycle, car and van includes driver and passenger fatalities. Water includes fatalities on UK registered merchant vessels. Air includes fatalities involving UK registered airline aircraft in UK and foreign airspace.
3 Financial years up to 1996 (1995/96). Includes train accidents and accidents occurring through movement of railway vehicles.

Source: Department for Transport

pedestrian deaths between 2007 and 2008. Reported child casualties fell by 8 per cent in 2008 with the number of children killed or seriously injured falling by 9 per cent. The number of pedal cyclists killed fell by 15 per cent while the number of seriously injured rose by 1 per cent to 2,450.

The safety levels of most forms of transport in Great Britain are much improved compared with the early 1980s, and improvements in most areas have continued since the mid-1990s. Motorcycling, walking and cycling continued to have the highest fatality rates per kilometre travelled, compared with other forms of transport (Table 12.14).

In 2008 the highest death rate was again among motorcycle users, at 88.8 deaths per billion passenger kilometres travelled. This was 47 times greater than the death rate for car users, but a reduction of 27.0 deaths per billion passenger kilometres travelled since 1981.

Although walking had the second highest death rate in 2008 (30.9 deaths per billion passenger kilometres) it recorded the largest decrease since 1981, 46.0 deaths per billion passenger kilometres.

Fifty one per cent of all deaths to reported road users in Great Britain in 1930 were of pedestrians (Table 12.15 overleaf). This was over four times higher than pedal cyclists and other road users (both 12 per cent), and double the proportion of motorcycle users (25 per cent). The proportion of reported

Table 12.15

Reported road users killed: by type of user

Great Britain   Percentages

	Pedestrians	Motorcycle users[1]	Pedal cyclists[1]	Others[2]	All
1930	51	25	12	12	100
1940	55	15	16	15	100
1950	45	23	16	17	100
1960	39	25	10	26	100
1970	39	10	5	46	100
1980	33	20	5	44	100
1990	32	13	5	50	100
2000	25	18	4	53	100
2007	22	20	5	53	100
2008	23	19	5	54	100

1 Data for 1940 to 1970 exclude sidecar passengers and second riders of tandems.
2 Includes car drivers and passengers and cases where type of road user was not reported.

Source: Department for Transport

deaths for pedestrians peaked at 55 per cent in 1940, followed by a steady decline to reach a low of 22 per cent in 2007.

There was a 1 percentage point increase between 2007 and 2008 in reported deaths of pedestrians as a proportion of the total deaths, though the number of pedestrian fatalities fell by 11 per cent over the same period. Reported deaths for other road users, which include car users, as a proportion of total deaths increased to 54 per cent in 2008. The number of motorcycle users killed as a proportion of total fatalities fluctuated between 25 per cent and 19 per cent over the period 1930 to 2008, while pedal cyclists have declined from 12 per cent of the total in 1930 to 5 per cent in 2008.

In Northern Ireland, 33 per cent of those killed in road traffic accidents in 1990 were pedestrians and 6 per cent were motorcycle users. By 2008, the proportion of pedestrians killed fell to 18 per cent, while motorcycle users increased to 15 per cent. The proportion of those killed in road traffic accidents who were car users increased from 49 per cent of the total in 1990 to 58 per cent in 2008, while pedal cyclists killed decreased from 6 per cent to 2 per cent of total deaths over the same period.

In 2008 in Great Britain there were 149,188 car user casualties reported, 1,257 of which were fatalities, compared with 28,482 pedestrian casualties of which 572 were fatalities. In the same period there were a total of 493 motorcycle users and 115 pedal cyclists killed. In Northern Ireland there were

Table 12.16

Attitudes towards drink driving,[1] 2008

Great Britain   Percentages

	Agree[2]	Neither agree nor disagree	Disagree[3]
If someone has drunk any alcohol they should not drive	86	5	9
Anyone caught drink driving should be banned for at least five years	81	8	11
Most people don't know how much alcohol they can drink before being over the legal drink-drive limit	78	5	17

1 Adults aged 18 and over were asked whether they agreed or disagreed with the statements shown.
2 Those who said they either agreed or agreed strongly.
3 Those who said they either disagreed or disagreed strongly.

Source: British Social Attitudes Survey, National Centre for Social Research

4,894 casualties from car use in 2008/09, of which 44 incidences resulted in fatalities. In comparison there were 856 pedestrian casualties, 21 of which were fatalities, and 443 motorcyclist casualties of which 16 were fatalities.

According to the British Social Attitudes Survey, 86 per cent of adults in Great Britain in 2008 agreed or agreed strongly that if someone has drunk any alcohol they should not drive, while 81 per cent agreed or agreed strongly that anyone caught drink driving should be banned for at least five years (Table 12.16). However, 78 per cent of adults agreed or agreed strongly that most people don't know how much alcohol they can drink before being over the legal drink-drive limit.

The Northern Ireland Road Safety Monitor, conducted by the Northern Ireland Omnibus survey, reported that 66 per cent of respondents in 2009 felt that motorists should not be allowed to drive after drinking any alcohol. Also, 88 per cent of respondents agreed that the police should be able to stop people at random and breathalyse them to test for driving under the influence of alcohol.

The Road Safety Act 1967 established a legal alcohol limit for drivers, set at 80 milligrams of alcohol in 100 millilitres of blood and made it an offence to drive when over this limit. The Act also gave the police the power to carry out breathalyser testing to determine whether an individual's alcohol level is above the limit of 35 micrograms of alcohol in 100 millilitres of breath.

Of the 294,000 injury accidents recorded during 2008 in Great Britain, the police requested breathalyser tests at 163,000 of

Table 12.17

Accidents:[1] by class of road and speed limit

United Kingdom Thousands

	1994–98 average[2]	2000	2001	2002	2003	2004	2005	2006	2007	2008
Motorways	8.1	9.6	9.3	9.1	8.9	9.2	8.7	8.5	8.1	7.4
Other roads[3]										
20 mph[4]	0.2	0.4	0.5	0.7	0.7	0.9	1.0	1.0	1.2	1.3
30 mph	158.1	155.6	151.6	145.4	140.1	133.0	128.0	121.3	117.3	112.3
40 mph	18.8	20.1	19.4	19.2	17.9	17.7	16.0	15.6	15.4	14.5
50 mph	3.2	4.1	4.6	4.6	4.8	4.8	4.9	5.2	5.1	4.9
60 mph	46.1	43.8	42.5	41.1	39.7	39.3	37.7	35.8	34.1	30.3
70 mph	8.4	8.4	8.5	8.5	8.1	8.1	7.5	7.3	6.9	6.1

1 Includes all severities of accidents (fatal, fatal and serious, and slight).
2 Figures have been rounded to the nearest whole number.
3 Includes 'A', 'B' and 'C' roads, and unclassified roads. Excludes cases where road class was not reported.
4 The option to record accidents at 20 mph in Northern Ireland was only introduced in April 2007.

Source: Department for Transport; Police Service for Northern Ireland

these incidents (55 per cent). Just over 5,500 of these incidents (3.4 per cent) resulted in failed breathalyser tests (recording above the legal limit). There had been 413,000 injury accidents in 1998 and breathalyser tests were requested in 210,000 of them, of which 7,500 were failed tests (3.6 per cent). In 1979, 41,000 tests were requested, resulting in 14,000 failures (34 per cent).

The number of deaths from road accidents involving illegal alcohol levels in the UK declined steadily from less than 1,000 in 1987 to approximately 600 a year in the early to mid-1990s. Following a further decline to around 500 deaths in 1998 and 1999, the number of deaths was relatively stable again, at around 600 a year between 2000 and 2006, before falling to around 400 deaths in 2008. Serious injuries from road accidents involving illegal alcohol levels decreased by more than half during the 1980s and 1990s to around 2,600 in 1999, and in 2008 fell to around 1,800.

Speeding is a traffic offence with potentially serious consequences, and driving at excessive speed continues to be a problem that results in accidents, fatalities and serious injuries. Government research has shown that at 40 miles per hour (mph), 85 per cent of accidents resulted in fatalities, compared with 20 per cent at 30 mph and 5 per cent at 20 mph. It has also been estimated that for each 1 mph reduction in average speed, accident frequency is reduced by 5 per cent.

There were 176,814 reported personal injury accidents on roads in the UK in 2008. Two-thirds (66 per cent) of accidents

on roads (excluding motorways) occurred on roads with a 30 mph speed limit (Table 12.17). This represented 112,255 accidents, a fall of 4 per cent from 2007 and a fall of more than a quarter (29 per cent) from the 1994–98 average. Accidents that occurred on roads with a speed limit of 50 mph rose from 3,192 in 1994–98 to a peak of 5,244 in 2006, but since declined by 3 per cent between 2006 and 2007 and again in 2008 by 4 per cent.

Reported personal injury accidents that occurred on roads with a 20 mph speed limit have increased each year since 2000, with the largest year-on-year change reported between 2000 and 2001 (30 per cent). However, this remains the category with the smallest number of accidents.

Accidents which occurred on roads with a 60 mph and 70 mph speed limit declined by 11 and 12 per cent respectively between 2007 and 2008, the largest year-on-year reductions across all speed limits.

In Great Britain in 2008 there were 230,905 reported road casualties of all severities, 7 per cent fewer than in 2007. There was a 14 per cent reduction overall in those killed. Among the different categories of road users there was a 12 per cent reduction in deaths of car occupants, 11 per cent reduction in deaths of pedestrians, 16 per cent reduction for motorcyclists and a 15 per cent reduction for pedal cyclists.

Across the Group of Seven (G7), the world's largest industrial market economies, the UK had the lowest road death rate for all persons, at 4.3 per 100,000 population in 2008, a reduction

Table 12.18

Road deaths: G7 comparison

		Rate per 100,000 population	
	1998	2003	2008
USA	15.4	14.8	12.3
Italy	11.9	11.7	7.9
Canada	9.7	8.7	7.3
France	15.2	10.2	6.9
Germany	9.5	8.0	5.5
Japan	5.5	7.0	4.7
United Kingdom	6.1	6.1	4.3

Source: International Road Traffic and Accident Database (Organisation for Economic Co-operation and Development); International Transport Forum; Eurostat and CARE (EU road accidents database)

of 1.8 deaths per 100,000 population since 1998 (Table 12.18). Japan had a rate of 4.7 road deaths per 100,000 population, a reduction of 0.8 deaths per 100,000 population since 1998, when it had the lowest road death rate of the countries in the G7. The USA had the highest recorded road death rate for all persons, at 12.3 per 100,000 population in 2008. This was a reduction of 3.1 deaths per 100,000 population since 1998 and 2.5 deaths from 2003. However, the largest decline in road death rates between 1998 and 2008 across the G7 was in France, where the rate fell by 8.3 deaths per 100,000 population.

Across the 27 European Union member states (EU-27), the average road death rate was 8.6 per 100,000 population in 2007. Compared with other EU countries, the UK had the third lowest death rate, at 5.0 per 100,000 population, while Lithuania had the highest rate, at 21.8 per 100,000 population.

The UK also has a relatively good record in terms of road fatalities involving children. In 2007 the UK road accident death rate for children aged under 15 was 0.9 per 100,000 population. Latvia had the highest rate in the EU-27, 3.5 per 100,000 population.

International travel

UK residents made 68.2 million trips abroad in 2008, an increase of 45 per cent compared with 1998 (Table 12.19). In 1998, 69 per cent of all visits abroad by UK residents were made by air, and by 2008 this had increased to 82 per cent. The proportion of trips made by sea declined between 1998 and 2008, from 18 per cent to 11 per cent of the total.

Trips made by the Channel Tunnel also declined as a proportion of the total, from 13 per cent to 7 per cent. Holidays accounted for two-thirds of trips made abroad by UK residents in 2008, the same proportion as ten years previously. See also the Holidays section in Chapter 13: Lifestyles and social participation.

In 2008, overseas residents made 31.7 million visits to the UK, around a third (36 per cent) more than in 1998 (23.3 million visits). Of the total number of trips made to the UK by overseas residents in 2008, 24.0 million were made by air, of which 34 per cent were to visit friends or relatives in the UK and 31 per cent were for holidays. In 1998, 15.7 million visits made to the UK by overseas residents were by air, of which just over a third (35 per cent) were for a holiday.

Between 1980 and 2008 there has been a substantial rise in the number of air passengers at UK airports. Over this period there was a 204 per cent increase in the number of domestic passengers at UK airports, from 7.5 million to 22.8 million, and

Table 12.19

International travel by UK residents: by mode of travel and purpose of visit

United Kingdom   Percentages

	1998				2008			
	Air	Sea	Channel Tunnel	All modes	Air	Sea	Channel Tunnel	All modes
Holiday	70	65	52	66	66	73	65	66
Visiting friends and relatives	12	6	7	10	19	13	10	18
Business	17	9	16	15	13	7	18	13
Other	2	20	24	8	2	7	7	3
All purposes (=100%) (millions)	32.4	8.4	6.1	46.9	56.0	7.4	4.8	68.2

Source: International Passenger Survey, Office for National Statistics

12

Figure 12.20

Air passengers at UK civil airports

United Kingdom

Millions

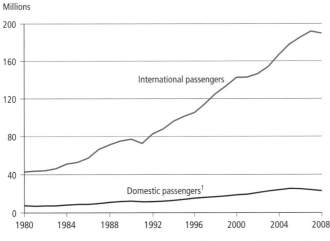

1 Numbers have been halved as domestic traffic is counted both at the airport of departure and at the airport of arrival.

Source: Civil Aviation Authority

Figure 12.21

Air passengers travelling overseas from UK civil airports:[1] by type of airline

Millions

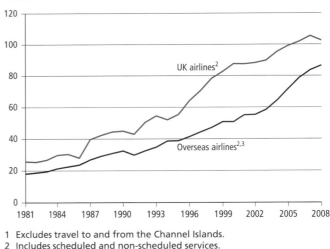

1 Excludes travel to and from the Channel Islands.
2 Includes scheduled and non-scheduled services.
3 Includes airlines of UK Overseas Territories.

Source: Civil Aviation Authority

the number of international passengers increased by 342 per cent, from 42.9 million to 189.8 million (Figure 12.20). However, 2008 saw a decrease in the number of both international and domestic passengers, with international passengers declining by 1 per cent and domestic passengers declining by 5 per cent compared with 2007.

This is not the first time UK airports have seen a decline in passengers. In 1981 there was a decline in domestic passengers of around 7 per cent compared with the previous year, and in 1991 there was an annual fall of 6 per cent for both international and domestic passengers. These reductions can be attributed to the recessions that took place during the early 1980s and 1990s. Similarly, the most recent decline may be attributed to the economic downturn that began in the UK in 2008.

The Department for Transport forecasts that demand for air travel is set to continue. Mid-range estimates made in January 2009 suggest that between 2010 and 2030 passenger numbers at UK airports will grow from 270 million to 464 million. International passengers are forecast to increase by more than two-thirds from 215 million to 363 million passengers, while domestic passengers are set to double from 50 million to 101 million passengers annually.

In 2008, 189 million passengers were carried between the UK and abroad, an increase of 332 per cent on 1981, and around the same level as recorded in 2007. UK airlines accounted for 103 million passengers carried in 2008, 54 per cent of the total number of passengers (Figure 12.21). However, there was a

decrease of 3 per cent in passenger numbers carried by UK airlines overseas between 2007 and 2008, while passengers carried by overseas airlines increased by 3 per cent over the same period.

In 2008, there were around 1.5 million flights between the UK and abroad, a 0.5 per cent decrease from the previous year but an increase of 204 per cent compared with 1981, when there were around 496,000 flights. UK airlines made around 795,000 flights abroad in 2008, accounting for 53 per cent of the total, and 76 per cent of these were scheduled services.

Overseas airlines made a total of just over 711,000 flights between the UK and abroad in 2008, 97 per cent of which were scheduled services. Overall, between 1981 and 2008 the number of scheduled services from the UK to overseas destinations increased by 327 per cent, while the number of passengers using non-scheduled services increased by 12 per cent over the same period.

In 2008, 22.8 million international sea passenger journeys to and from the UK were made, 4 per cent lower than the number made in 2007 and 33 per cent lower than 1995 (Table 12.22 overleaf). With the exceptions of Portsmouth, Poole, Grimsby and Immingham, Felixstowe, and Harwich, all UK ports experienced a decline in passenger journeys between 2007 and 2008, the largest being a year-on-year decrease of 50 per cent at Ipswich, where passenger journeys fell from 4,000 to 2,000. The largest year-on-year increase of 29 per cent was at

Table 12.22

International sea passenger journeys: by short sea ferry route[1]

United Kingdom   Millions

	1995	1998	2001	2004	2007	2008
Thames & Kent	21.5	20.4	16.0	14.4	14.5	14.0
South Coast	5.8	5.2	4.9	4.6	3.5	3.4
West Coast	3.6	4.6	3.9	3.7	3.3	3.1
East Coast	3.4	3.0	3.1	3.1	2.4	2.3
All routes	34.3	33.2	27.8	25.8	23.7	22.8

1 International routes to Belgium, Denmark, Faroe Isles, Finland, France, Germany, Ireland, Netherlands, Norway, Spain, and Sweden. See Appendix, Part 12: International sea passengers.

Source: Department for Transport

Grimsby and Immingham, where passenger journeys rose from 63,000 to 81,000.

Dover, the UK's largest ferry port, handled 13.8 million passenger journeys in 2008, 3.3 per cent fewer than in 2007.

There were around 2.0 million passengers both at Portsmouth (a reduction of 0.1 per cent compared with 2007) and at Holyhead (a reduction of 6.6 per cent). There were also 17.7 million passenger journeys through the Channel Tunnel, marginally up on 2007.

A number of events are thought to have contributed to the decline in sea passenger numbers since the mid-1990s. Between 1994 and 1995, the first full year the Channel Tunnel was operational, sea passenger traffic through Dover and other ports from Medway to Plymouth declined by 8 per cent. The temporary increase in sea passenger numbers in 1997 may have been a consequence of the Channel Tunnel fire in November 1996. In 2000 and 2001, sea passenger numbers are likely to have fallen due to the abolition of duty free sales, blockaded channel ports, restrictions on travel because of the fuel crisis, and the foot and mouth outbreak. In 2002, sea passenger journeys increased relative to the depressed levels in 2000 and 2001 and then declined again subsequently.

Chapter 13

Lifestyles and social participation

- Music album sales in the UK were dominated in 1975 by vinyl albums (92 million trade deliveries), in 1989 by cassettes (83 million deliveries) and in 1992 by CDs (71 million deliveries). In 2008, digital album downloads represented 7 per cent (10.3 million albums) of the total. (Figure 13.5)

- In the 12 months to June 2009, less than half (42 per cent) of people aged 15 and over in Great Britain read a national daily newspaper, compared with 72 per cent in the 12 months to June 1978. (Table 13.6)

- In 2008, there were 164 million admissions to the cinema in the UK, compared with 1.6 billion at the peak of cinema attendance in 1946. (Figure 13.8)

- Between 2007 and 2008, there was a 0.2 per cent increase in holiday visits taken abroad by UK residents, reaching a record 45.5 million holiday trips. (Figure 13.10)

- The proportion of pupils that participated in at least three hours of high quality PE and out-of-hours school sport increased from 47 per cent in Year 1 to 65 per cent in Year 6, but decreased in each subsequent school year in England in 2008/09. (Figure 13.13)

- In the second quarter of 2009, 57 per cent of adults aged 16 and over in England carried out informal volunteering at least once in the 12 months prior to interview, and 43 per cent did some sort of formal volunteering. (Table 13.15)

A person's lifestyle is defined by the way they live and the individual choices they make. These are influenced by personal characteristics and circumstances, social interactions and relationships and interests. Traditional activities such as watching television, spending time with family and friends, reading, going on holiday, playing sports and interacting within communities are still as popular as they were 40 years ago. However, over the last four decades new technology has advanced at a rapid pace and affected people in many different ways, providing greater access to information and an increased choice of leisure and entertainment.

Leisure and entertainment activities

Watching television has been a common leisure activity for many decades. People began to buy or rent television sets in significant numbers in the 1950s. Since the early 1990s, according to the General Lifestyle Survey, more than 90 per cent of households in Great Britain had a television set. In 2007/08, 85 per cent of adults aged 16 and over in England watched television in their free time (Table 13.1). It was also among the most common activities for all age groups and was the most popular activity for those aged 35 and over.

Spending time with family and friends and listening to music were jointly the most common leisure activities for more than eight in ten (both 83 per cent) young people aged 16 to 24 closely followed by watching television (82 per cent). The next

most common activities for this age group were shopping, going to the cinema, going to pubs, bars and clubs, and sports and exercise. The pattern of free time activities for those aged 25 to 34 was very similar, such as spending time with family and friends (84 per cent) and watching television (83 per cent). However, this age group was more likely than those aged 16 to 24 to eat out at restaurants (66 per cent compared with 55 per cent) and go for days out (63 per cent compared with 50 per cent). The proportions of people reading and gardening increased with age and were most likely to be carried out by people aged 45 and over.

Conversely, the proportions of people taking part in sport or exercise, going to pubs, bars and clubs, and going to the cinema decreased with age, with 34 per cent, 25 per cent and 18 per cent respectively of those aged 65 and over taking part.

The most common leisure activities performed in their free time for both men and women were watching television (both 85 per cent) and spending time with friends and family (77 per cent of men compared with 84 per cent of women). The next most common activities for men were listening to music (71 per cent) and eating out at restaurants (60 per cent), while for women the next most common activities were shopping (76 per cent), reading and listening to music (both 73 per cent).

The economic downturn that began in 2008 meant that people were considering cutting down their spending on some

Table 13.1

Selected activities performed in free time:[1] by age, 2007/08

England   Percentages

	16–24	25–34	35–44	45–64	65 and over	All aged 16 and over
Watching television	82	83	84	85	89	85
Spending time with friends/family	83	84	82	79	76	80
Listening to music	83	74	72	70	65	72
Shopping	69	67	65	64	67	66
Reading	47	60	63	71	74	65
Eating out at restaurants	55	66	66	66	58	63
Days out	50	63	66	65	58	61
Sport/exercise	59	58	57	51	34	51
Gardening	12	32	48	61	61	47
Going to pubs/bars/clubs	60	56	47	42	25	45
Going to the cinema	64	53	48	37	18	42

1 Respondents were shown a list of activities and asked to pick the things they did in their free time. The most popular activities performed by all adults aged 16 and over are shown in the table.

Source: Taking Part: The National Survey of Culture, Leisure and Sport, Department for Culture, Media and Sport

leisure activities. However, according to Ofcom (the independent regulator for the UK communications industries), people were less likely to consider cutting back their spending on communication services than on other activities. In the second quarter of 2009, adults aged 16 and over in the UK who had a landline telephone, a mobile phone, a pay television service and a broadband Internet service, were asked which items they would cut back on if they were forced to cut spending. Nearly half (47 per cent) said that they would cut back on nights and meals out, while four in ten (41 per cent) reported that they would cut back on holidays or weekends away and new furniture or home improvements. However, less than two in ten of these people stated that they would cut back on their communication services. Reducing spending on their mobile phone was reported by 19 per cent, while 16 per cent said that they would spend less on their television subscriptions. One in ten (10 per cent) would spend less on their broadband subscription or home telephone calls.

In 2008, the process known as the 'digital switchover' began, where the UK's analogue television broadcast signal started being switched off and replaced with a digital signal television region by television region. This process will continue until 2012. Any household that has not converted to digital when the switchover takes place will no longer be able to receive television programmes. The switchover is an obvious reason for households in the UK to convert to digital. Nearly nine in ten homes (89 per cent) in the UK had a digital television service at the end of the first quarter (Q1) of 2009 (Figure 13.2), a rise of

73 percentage points since 2000. Much of the recent growth in take-up of digital television services has been driven by the take-up of a digital terrestrial television service. In Q1 2000, 3 per cent of households had this service connected to their main television set. By Q1 2009, this had increased more than twelvefold to 38 per cent of households.

More than a third of homes (37 per cent) received a digital satellite service on their main television set, while around 13 per cent of homes received a digital cable service.

According to the Taking Part Survey, national or local news was the most common type of programme viewed on television in England in 2007/08. News programmes were watched by more than seven in ten (72 per cent) adults aged 16 and over (Table 13.3). Films and comedy programmes were the next most commonly viewed programmes (66 per cent and 59 per cent respectively). Apart from watching the news, which was viewed by a similar proportion of both men and women (73 per cent and 71 per cent respectively), the viewing habits of men and women varied. Around seven in ten men watched live sport coverage and films (72 per cent and 68 per cent respectively) followed by comedy programmes (64 per cent), wildlife programmes (52 per cent) and other sport programmes (46 per cent). Men were also more likely than women to watch

Figure 13.2

Household take-up of digital television: by type of service[1]

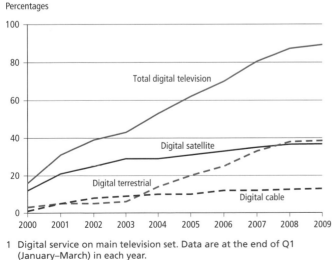

United Kingdom
Percentages

1 Digital service on main television set. Data are at the end of Q1 (January–March) in each year.

Source: Ofcom

Table 13.3

Selected types of television programmes viewed:[1] by sex, 2007/08

England — Percentages

	Men	Women	All aged 16 and over
News[2]	73	71	72
Films	68	64	66
Comedy	64	54	59
Live sport coverage	72	37	54
Wildlife	52	50	51
Soaps	29	58	44
History	44	34	39
Food and cookery	30	46	39
Contemporary or period drama	25	45	35
Quiz shows	31	37	35
Current affairs or politics	36	29	33
Other sport	46	17	31

1 Respondents were asked 'Thinking about when you watch television, what type of programmes do you watch nowadays?'
2 National or local news.

Source: Taking Part: The National Survey of Culture, Leisure and Sport, Department for Culture, Media and Sport

history programmes and current affairs or politics programmes. Nearly two-thirds of women watched films (64 per cent), followed by soaps (58 per cent), comedy (54 per cent) and wildlife (50 per cent). Women were also more likely to watch food and cookery programmes and contemporary or period dramas.

It is also possible to watch television programmes online using catch-up TV services. All major public services and some multi-channel broadcasters now offer a selection of their programmes online, ranging from seven-day catch-up programming to archive material. According to Ofcom, nearly a quarter (23 per cent) of people in the UK with the Internet at home claimed that someone in their household had watched catch-up television in the first quarter of 2009.

In 2009, 37.4 million adults aged 16 and over (76 per cent of the UK adult population) had accessed the Internet in the three months prior to interview, an increase of around 10 per cent (around 3.5 million adults) since 2008. Nearly two-thirds (64 per cent) of all adults had bought or ordered goods online at least once. Of those who had used the Internet in the three months prior to interview and had bought or ordered online in the 12 months prior to interview, the most popular purchases were films or music (50 per cent), clothes or sports goods (49 per cent) and household goods (47 per cent), for example furniture and toys.

Across the 27 European Union member states (EU-27), 37 per cent of adults aged 16 to 74 had bought or ordered goods and services for private use over the Internet in the 12 months prior to interview in 2009, but countries varied widely in its use (Figure 13.4). Use of the Internet to buy or order goods and services was highest in the UK where two-thirds (66 per cent) of adults had done so, followed by Denmark (64 per cent), Sweden and the Netherlands (both 63 per cent). However, in the majority of countries in the EU-27, less than 30 per cent of adults who had used the Internet in the 12 months prior to interview for private use had bought or ordered goods online.

Only 2 per cent of adults in Romania, 5 per cent in Bulgaria and 8 per cent in Lithuania had done so. There could be many reasons for this difference, such as the number of adults with Internet connections, familiarity with Internet shopping or people's confidence in transacting online.

According to a 2009 Eurobarometer report, around three-quarters of adults in the Netherlands (78 per cent) and the UK (76 per cent) felt that Internet connections were completely safe or rather safe, compared with 41 per cent in Romania and just 17 per cent of adults in Bulgaria.

Figure 13.4

Buying or ordering goods or services over the Internet:[1] EU comparison, 2009

Percentages

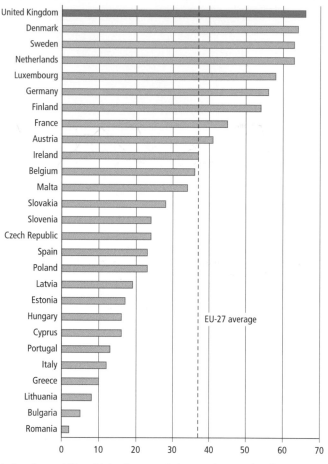

1 People aged 16 to 74, buying or ordering goods or services for private use over the Internet in the 12 months prior to interview.

Source: Eurostat

According to Ofcom, nearly four in ten (39 per cent) adults in the UK who used the Internet had downloaded or listened to music online in April to May 2009. While an increasing amount of music or speech is downloaded from the Internet, some traditional ways of listening to this medium remain popular. In 2008, according to BPI, compact discs (CDs) made up 92 per cent (131.2 million) of total albums delivered to retailers, distributors, wholesalers and mail order companies in the UK. Digital album downloads represented 7 per cent (10.3 million) of the total and vinyl albums around 0.3 per cent (0.4 million) (Figure 13.5). This was very different to the early 1970s when the CD, although invented, had yet to be introduced to the market place. In 1973 the vinyl album or 'Long Player' dominated album sales, with around 81 million trade deliveries compared with around 10 million audio cassettes (see Appendix, Part 13: Sales of phonographic albums, cassettes, CDs and singles).

Figure 13.5

Sales[1] of CDs, vinyl albums, cassettes, singles, and album downloads

United Kingdom
Millions

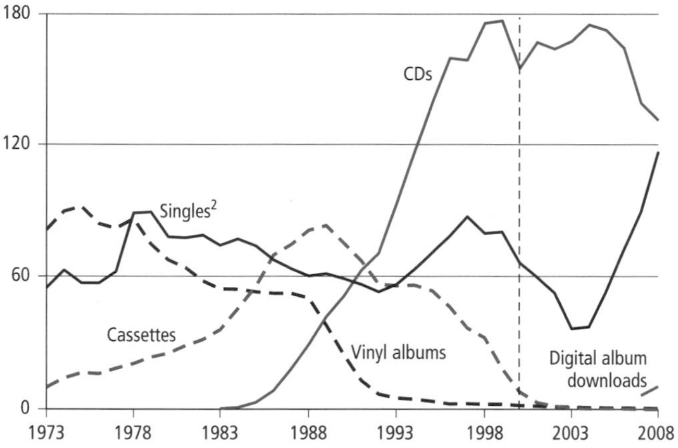

1 Trade deliveries. See Appendix, Part 13: Sales of phonographic albums, cassettes, CDs and singles. From 2000 onwards, volume data are reported as 'packages' rather than units. In previous years, double disc sets counted as two units, triple disc sets as three units etc. Consequently, historical sales volumes are not comparable.
2 All formats combined (7", 12", cassette, CD and downloads).

Source: BPI Surveys and Official Charts Company

Vinyl albums peaked in the mid-1970s with around 92 million deliveries in 1975, while audio cassette sales continued to rise through the 1970s, peaking in 1989 with 83 million deliveries.

CDs were introduced into the retail market in the early 1980s, and by 1992 dominated album sales with around 71 million trade deliveries, compared with around 56 million audio cassettes and 7 million vinyl albums. Sales of singles on 7" or 12" vinyl records or on cassette or CD peaked in 1979 (89 million deliveries) and have fluctuated since then. However, unlike the album market which is dominated by CD sales, sales of singles are now almost entirely comprised of sales of digital downloads. The launch of the first mainstream online store in the UK in 2004 meant that sales of singles rose from around 36 million in 2003 to around 117 million in 2008.

The top five selling albums in the UK between 1956 and 2009 were *Greatest Hits* – Queen (first released in 1981, 5.7 million), *Sgt. Pepper's Lonely Hearts Club Band* – The Beatles (1967, 4.9 million), *Gold* – Greatest Hits – Abba (1992, 4.6 million), *What's The Story Morning Glory* – Oasis (1996, 4.4 million) and *Brothers in Arms* – Dire Straits (1985, 4.1 million). The top five selling singles were *Candle in the Wind '97* – Sir Elton John (1997, 4.9 million), *Do they know it's Christmas* – Band Aid (1984, 3.6 million), *Bohemian Rhapsody* – Queen (1975, 2.1 million), *Mull of Kintyre* – Wings (1977, 2.1 million) and

Table 13.6

Readership of national daily newspapers[1]

Great Britain   Percentages

	1971	1978	1981	1991	2001	2009
The Sun	17	29	26	22	20	16
Daily Mail	12	13	12	10	12	10
Daily Mirror	34	28	25	22	12	7
The Daily Telegraph	9	8	8	6	5	4
The Times	3	2	2	2	3	4
Daily Express	24	16	14	8	4	3
Daily Star	.	.	9	6	3	3
The Guardian	3	2	3	3	2	2
The Independent	.	.	.	2	1	1
Financial Times	2	2	2	2	1	1
Any national daily newspaper[2]	..	72	72	62	53	42

1 In the 12 months to June each year. Proportion of adults aged 15 and over who have read or looked at the individual newspaper for at least two minutes on the day before interview.
2 Includes the above newspapers and *The Daily Record* in 1981, and *The Sporting Life* and the *Racing Post* in 2001 and 2009.

Source: National Readership Survey

Rivers of Babylon/Brown Girl in the Ring – Boney M (1978, 2.0 million).

The National Readership Survey estimates that the proportion of people reading a national daily newspaper has been declining over the past three decades. In the 12 months to June 2009, on an average day less than half (42 per cent) of all people aged 15 and over in Great Britain read a national daily newspaper (Table 13.6), compared with 72 per cent of people in the 12 months to June 1978. In 1971, the most commonly read newspapers were the *Daily Mirror*, which was read by just over a third (34 per cent) of adults, followed by the *Daily Express*, read by just under a quarter (24 per cent). Both these papers had been in publication since the early 1900s and were well established. The third most read newspaper in 1971 was *The Sun* read by 17 per cent of adults on an average day. *The Sun*, as a tabloid newspaper, was a relative newcomer at this time having been relaunched from a broadsheet newspaper in 1969. In 2009, *The Sun* was the most commonly read newspaper with a readership of 16 per cent of adults. However, this was around half of the proportion of its readers compared with its peak of around 29 per cent in the late 1970s. The *Daily Mail* was the second most commonly read newspaper in 2009 with around 10 per cent of adults reading it, a proportion that has changed very little since 1971. The proportion of those reading the *Daily Express* however has decreased quite rapidly by around 21 percentage points since 1971.

Possible reasons for the recent decline in national daily newspaper readership could include the advent of free newspapers such as *Metro*, which is distributed in major cities and was estimated to be read by 7 per cent of the adult population in Great Britain in the 12 months to June 2009. Also there is greater availability of national and local news on the television (see Table 13.3), the radio and online. In 2009 over half (52 per cent) of adults aged 16 and over in the UK who used the Internet in the three months prior to interview had read or downloaded online news, newspapers or magazines.

According to the Taking Part Survey, in 2007/08, 64 per cent of adults aged 16 and over in England read for pleasure. The National Year of Reading was celebrated in 2008, aimed at encouraging reading both for pleasure and as a means of improving learning, achievement and individual prospects. It highlighted reading as an essential skill for children.

According to a 2007 survey by the National Literacy Trust, nearly six in ten (58 per cent) children aged 9 to 14 in England reported that they enjoyed reading either very much or quite a lot. Just over half (51 per cent) of boys stated they enjoyed reading either very much or quite a lot compared with just under two-thirds (64 per cent) of girls. However, 10 per cent of boys and 6 per cent of girls did not enjoy reading at all and the remainder did not enjoy reading very much (39 per cent of boys and 30 per cent of girls). More girls than boys reported that they read outside of school every day or almost every day (42 per cent and 34 per cent respectively).

Magazines were the preferred reading material outside of school for both boys and girls, with over six in ten (63 per cent) boys and eight in ten (80 per cent) girls reading this sort of material (Figure 13.7). The next most common types of reading material for both boys and girls were Internet based. Websites were read by marginally more boys than girls (58 per cent and 56 per cent respectively) while emails were read by more girls (59 per cent of girls compared with 45 per cent of boys). Boys were more likely to read newspapers and comics or graphic novels compared with girls, while girls preferred blogs and networking websites and fiction books. When asked how reading made them feel, the majority of both boys and girls said that it made them calm (57 per cent and 64 per cent respectively) and happy (27 per cent and 34 per cent respectively). However, 29 per cent of boys and 25 per cent of girls also stated that reading made them bored.

One of the successes attributed to the National Year of Reading was that public libraries in England received 2.3 million new

Figure 13.7

Type of reading material read[1] by children[2] outside of school, 2007

England
Percentages

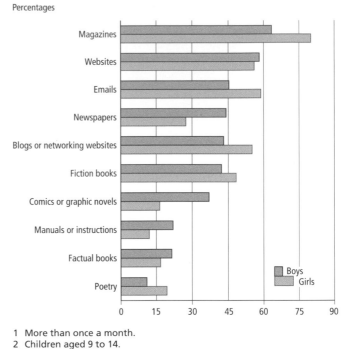

1 More than once a month.
2 Children aged 9 to 14.
Source: National Literacy Trust

members between April and the end of December 2008. According to the Public Lending Right, the most borrowed fiction title for adults in 2007/08 was *The House at Riverton* by Kate Morton. The most borrowed adult non-fiction book was *Semi-detached* by Griff Rhys Jones, while the most borrowed classic title was *Catcher in the Rye* by JD Salinger. For children the most borrowed fiction title was *Harry Potter and the Deathly Hallows* by JK Rowling, the most borrowed non-fiction title was *Jacky Daydream* by Jacqueline Wilson (illustrated by Nick Sharratt) and the most borrowed children's classic was *Charlie and the Great Glass Elevator* by Roald Dahl (illustrated by Quentin Blake).

Harry Potter was also a big success at the cinema. According to the UK Film Council, the top five grossing films at the UK cinema box office between 1975 and 2008 (after adjustment to remove inflation) were *Titanic* (1998), *Harry Potter and the Philosopher's Stone* (2001), *Lord of the Rings: The Fellowship of the Ring* (2001), *Mamma Mia!* (2008) and *Jaws* (1975).

In 2008 there were 164 million admissions to the cinema in the UK, a rise of 1 per cent since 2007 (Figure 13.8). These numbers however are a fraction of what they were decades earlier, before widespread availability of television sets. There were over 1,000 million admissions each year between 1940

Figure 13.8

Cinema admissions

United Kingdom
Millions

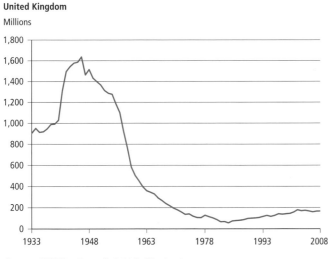

Source: UK Film Council; British Film Institute

and 1956, peaking just after World War Two in 1946 when there were 1,600 million admissions. Between 1957 and the mid-1980s admissions fell rapidly to reach a low point of around 54 million admissions in 1984. Since then, the number of admissions has gradually risen and from the early 2000s has remained relatively stable.

According to the UK Film Council, six out of ten (60 per cent) people aged seven and over in the UK went to the cinema at least once in 2008, while nearly one in five (18 per cent) went at least once a month. There was no marked differences in the proportion of men and women going to the cinema at least once a year, or in those who went to the cinema at least once a month. Just under half (48 per cent) of the cinema going audience in 2008 was aged 7 to 24, just over a third (34 per cent) was aged 25 to 44, and 18 per cent was aged 45 and over.

In 2009 the National Lottery celebrated its 15th birthday, the first draw having taken place on 19 November 1994. As of December 2009, the National Lottery had raised £23 billion for good causes, £36 billion in prizes had been paid out, and 2,200 millionaires or multi-millionaires had been created. According to the National Lottery Commission, around 70 per cent of adults in the UK play the Lottery on a regular basis. National Lottery games consist of draw-based games, such as Lotto, scratchcards which pay out an instant prize, and online Interactive Instant Win Games. The most popular game in 2008/09 was the bi-weekly Lotto draw, which accounted for 52 per cent of all National Lottery sales (Figure 13.9). National Lottery scratchcards formed the next highest proportion of sales (24 per cent) followed by

Figure 13.9

National Lottery game sales: by type of game, 2008/09

United Kingdom
Percentages

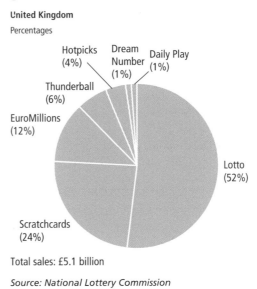

Total sales: £5.1 billion

Source: National Lottery Commission

EuroMillions (12 per cent) and Thunderball (6 per cent), which are both draw based games.

According to the Omnibus Survey commissioned by the Gambling Commission, around 11 per cent of adults aged 18 and over in Great Britain participated in gambling through a computer, mobile phone or interactive/digital television over the four quarters to September 2009. This was an increase of around 3 percentage points since 2006. The most common remote gambling activities were buying tickets for the National Lottery draw (8 per cent), betting, for example on horse racing, greyhound racing or football, and online Interactive Instant Win Games (both 3 per cent).

Holidays

According to the 2008 UK Tourism Survey, 75.4 million holiday trips were taken in the UK, including at least a one night stay, by adults aged 16 and over who were resident in the UK. Holiday trips include those which are for pleasure and leisure, and visiting friends or relatives. Just under a third (32 per cent) of holiday trips were to a large city or town and just over a quarter (26 per cent) to the seaside.

Many holiday trips, as well as days out, involve a visit to the UK's many tourist attractions such as museums and art galleries, historic properties, gardens and farms. Of the attractions that declared visitor numbers in England in 2008, the most visited attractions with free admission were the British Museum and the Tate Modern gallery, both in London, with around 5.9 million and 4.9 million visitors respectively. The most visited attractions that charged admission were Westminster Abbey and Kew Gardens, also both in London, with around 1.5 million and 1.3 million visitors respectively. The most visited attractions with free admission in Scotland in 2008 were the Kelvingrove Art Gallery and Museum in Glasgow and the National Gallery of Scotland complex in Edinburgh, with around 1.4 million and 0.8 million visitors respectively. Edinburgh Castle and Edinburgh Zoo were the most popular attractions charging admission, with around 1.1 million and 0.7 million visitors respectively. In Wales the most popular free attractions were the Wales Millennium Centre and St Fagans: National History Museum in Cardiff (1.1 million and 0.6 million visitors respectively). LC (a leisure complex in Swansea) and Pembrey Country Park were the most visited charged attractions, with around 0.4 million visitors each. In Northern Ireland, the most popular free attractions (excluding country parks and gardens) were the Oxford Island National Nature Reserve and the Island Arts Centre with around 0.3 million visitors each in 2008. The Giants Causeway Visitor Centre and W5, an interactive science discovery centre, were the most popular attractions (excluding country parks and gardens) that either had an admission or parking charge, with 0.8 million and 0.3 million visitors respectively.

UK residents made a record 45.5 million holiday trips abroad in 2008 (Figure 13.10). However, this was the smallest year-on-year increase (0.2 per cent) since 1996 when the number of holiday trips fell by nearly 4 per cent compared with 1995. The number of holiday trips abroad has increased by 41 per cent since 1998, when 32.3 million holiday trips were made, and by

120 per cent since 1988 when 20.7 million holiday trips were made. In 1971, UK residents made just 6.7 million holiday trips abroad, which was around 15 per cent of the total number of holiday trips made in 2008. Package holidays (see Appendix, Part 13: Package holiday) are still often chosen by UK residents when they holiday abroad, though their popularity is declining. The 17.9 million package holidays in 2008 made up 39 per cent of all holiday trips abroad that year, compared with a peak of 20.6 million in 2002, when more than half (52 per cent) of all overseas holidays were of this type.

Holiday trips to North America were least likely to be package holidays in 2008, with around three in ten (31 per cent) being package holidays compared with nearly four in ten (38 per cent) to Europe and over five in ten (55 per cent) to all other countries. The majority (57 per cent) of all holiday visits included a stay of four to 13 nights. Around two in ten (22 per cent) were longer than this (stays of 14 to 27 nights) and 16 per cent were shorter than four nights.

Spain was the most popular destination for holidays in 2008, accounting for over a quarter (27 per cent) of holidays abroad by UK residents (Table 13.11). France was the second most popular destination (17 per cent of all holidays) followed by the United States of America, Italy and Portugal (each accounting for 5 per cent of all holidays). Spain and France have repeatedly

Figure 13.10

UK residents' holiday visits abroad[1]

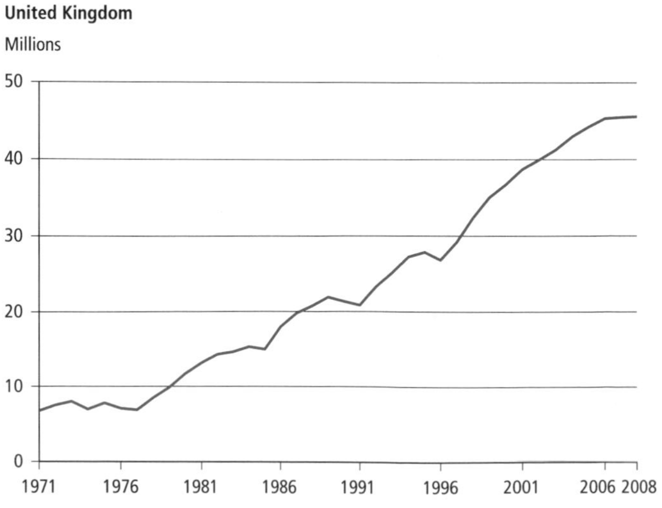

United Kingdom

Millions

1 A visit made by a UK resident for holiday purposes. Excludes business trips, visits to friends or relatives and other miscellaneous visits.

Source: International Passenger Survey, Office for National Statistics

Table 13.11

UK residents' holiday visits abroad: by destination[1]

United Kingdom   Percentages

	1981	1991	2001	2007	2008
Spain	22	21	28	26	27
France	27	26	18	17	17
Italy	6	4	4	6	5
United States	5	7	6	5	5
Portugal	3	5	4	4	5
Greece	7	8	8	5	4
Turkey	-	1	2	3	4
Ireland	4	3	4	3	3
Cyprus	1	2	4	2	2
Netherlands	2	4	3	2	2
Other countries	23	20	20	26	26
All destinations (=100%) (millions)	13.1	20.8	38.7	45.4	45.5

1 As a proportion of all holidays taken abroad by residents of the UK. Excludes business trips, visits to friends or relatives and other miscellaneous visits.

Source: International Passenger Survey, Office for National Statistics

been the most popular holiday destinations for UK residents since the early 1980s. Over the period, holidays to Spain have increased as a proportion of the total while those to France have decreased. In 1981, 27 per cent of holiday trips were to France and 22 per cent to Spain, while in 2008, 27 per cent of holiday trips were to Spain and 17 per cent to France.

Between 2004 and 2008 the number of trips to some new holiday destinations have shown large proportional growth. Holiday trips to Slovakia have shown the largest proportional growth with an increase of 438 per cent, followed by Poland (355 per cent) and Latvia (222 per cent). The largest percentage decreases, between 2004 and 2008, were to Sri Lanka where holiday trips fell by nearly half (45 per cent), followed by the Czech Republic (38 per cent), South Africa (25 per cent) and Denmark (24 per cent).

Despite some broadening of the holiday season, the times of year when holidays are taken remain largely unchanged. In 2008, 36 per cent of holidays abroad were taken in July to September, coinciding with the main school holidays, compared with 19 per cent in January to March, 27 per cent in April to June, and 18 per cent in October to December.

Sporting activities

Increasing the number of adults aged 16 and over who participate in sport by 2012/13 is an important government target. Participation in a moderate intensity sport for at least 30 minutes at least three times a week is one indicator of sporting activity. According to the Active People Survey commissioned by Sport England, 6.9 million (16.6 per cent) adults aged 16 and over in England were taking part in sport to this extent in 2008/09.

Adults aged 16 and over in England were asked in the 2007/08 Taking Part Survey what sports they had participated in during the 12 months prior to interview. The most common sport in which both men and women participated was indoor swimming or diving (28 per cent of men and 35 per cent of women) (Table 13.12). The next most common sport for men was snooker, pool or billiards in which nearly a quarter (23 per cent) participated, followed by cycling and health, fitness, gym or conditioning activities (both 21 per cent). Outdoor football was also popular among two in ten (20 per cent) men. More than two in ten (22 per cent) women participated in health, fitness, gym or conditioning activities and 16 per cent participated in keepfit, aerobics and dance exercise. Similar proportions of men and women took part in tenpin bowling (15 per cent and 13 per cent respectively).

Sport and physical education (PE) play an important part in the life of children of school age, helping to reduce obesity and improve fitness levels, team spirit, concentration and self-esteem.

Table 13.12

Top ten active sports:[1] by sex, 2007/08

England   Percentages

Men		Women	
Indoor swimming or diving	28	Indoor swimming or diving	35
Snooker, pool, billiards[2]	23	Health, fitness, gym or conditioning activities	22
Cycling[3]	21	Keepfit, aerobics and dance exercise[6]	16
Health, fitness, gym or conditioning activities	21	Outdoor swimming or diving	14
Outdoor football[4]	20	Tenpin bowling	13
Golf, pitch and putt, putting	18	Cycling[3]	13
Outdoor swimming or diving	16	Jogging[5]	8
Tenpin bowling	15	Snooker, pool, billiards[2]	7
Darts	12	Badminton	7
Jogging[5]	12	Yoga	6

1 Adults aged 16 and over.
2 Excludes bar billiards.
3 Includes for health, recreation, training or competition.
4 Includes 5-a-side and 6-a-side.
5 Includes cross-country and road running.
6 Includes exercise bike.

Source: Taking Part: The National Survey of Culture, Leisure and Sport, Department for Culture, Media and Sport

School Sport Partnerships (SSPs) are 'families' of schools working together to develop physical education and sport opportunities for all young people. They are made up of secondary, primary (infant and junior schools) and special schools and usually have a Specialist Sports College acting as the hub of the family. In the 2008/09 academic year there were 21,526 schools and 356 further education colleges in England arranged into 450 different partnerships.

Previous editions of Social Trends have shown the proportion of pupils in England that undertook at least two hours of high quality PE and out-of-hours school sport each week. By 2007/08, the proportion of pupils achieving this had reached 90 per cent across Years 1 to 11. In 2008/09 the Department for Children, Schools and Families reported on the proportion of pupils who had participated in at least three hours of high quality PE and sport in a typical week. Overall, half (50 per cent) of pupils aged 5 to 19 participated in at least three hours of PE and sport. This included nearly six in ten (57 per cent) pupils in primary and special schools and just over four in ten (42 per cent) secondary school pupils. The proportion of pupils that participated in at least three hours of high quality PE and out-of-hours school sport increased every school year up to Year 6, from 47 per cent in Year 1 to 65 per cent in Year 6 (Figure 13.13). In Year 7 this had decreased to 53 per cent and continued to fall by each subsequent school year, to reach 19 per cent in Year 13.

Across all types of schools and school years, pupils in England spent on average 1 hour 55 minutes each week on curriculum PE in 2008/09. A similar amount of time was recorded for pupils in Years 1 to 9, who spent on average 2 hours 5 minutes each week on curriculum PE. However, the average amount of time recorded for pupils in Years 10 and 11 decreased to around 1 hour and 40 minutes, and fell further to around half an hour for pupils in Years 12 and 13. More than nine in ten schools offered football, dance, gymnastics and athletics during the academic year 2008/09 and more than eight in ten schools offered cricket, rounders, swimming and netball.

According to a report by the NHS Information Centre for health and social care, around two-thirds (68 per cent) of adults aged 16 to 64 in England stated that they would like to do more physical activity than they did at the time of interview in 2007. Women were slightly more likely than men to want to do more physical activity (66 per cent of men and 69 per cent of women). The most common practical barriers that prevented both men and women doing more physical activities were work commitments (45 per cent of men and 34 per cent of women) and not

Figure 13.13

Pupils who participate in physical education and out-of-hours sport[1] at school:[2] by year group,[3] 2008/09

England
Percentages

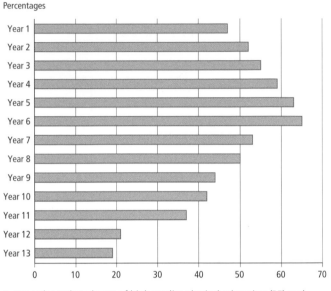

1 For at least three hours of high quality physical education (PE) and out-of-hours school sport in a typical week during term time.
2 Schools that are part of a School Sport Partnership (SSP), which are groups of schools working together to develop PE and sport opportunities.
3 See Appendix, Part 3: Stages of education.

Source: Department for Children, Schools and Families

having enough leisure time (38 per cent of men and 37 per cent of women) (Figure 13.14). Caring for children or older people was the barrier that showed the greatest difference between men and women, with a quarter (25 per cent) of women stating this reason compared with 13 per cent of men. Fewer than two in ten men (17 per cent) and just over one in ten women (12 per cent) stated that they didn't need to do any more physical activities than they did already. People were also asked about psychological barriers to doing more physical activities. 'Not being motivated' was the most common psychological reason for both men and women (21 per cent of men compared with 25 per cent of women), while just over two in ten (21 per cent) women felt they were 'not the sporty type' compared with 14 per cent of men.

There are very few sports clubs or organisations that do not rely on volunteers to help them in their activities, such as refereeing, club administration or cutting the grass on a pitch. According to the Active People Survey, just over two million adults contributed at least one hour a week to sport volunteering in 2007/08 in England. This is equivalent to just under 5 per cent of the adult population.

Figure 13.14

Practical barriers to doing more physical activity, exercise or sport:[1] by sex, 2007

England
Percentages

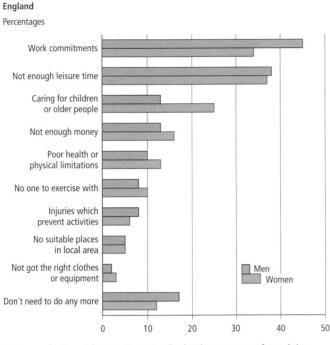

1 Respondents aged 16 to 64 were asked 'What stops you from doing more physical activity, exercise or sport than you do now?'

Source: The NHS Information Centre for health and social care

Social and political participation

Volunteering is a way in which individuals can contribute to their community. Two types of volunteering are sometimes distinguished to help understand patterns of activity; informal volunteering, which is giving unpaid help as an individual to other individuals who are not relatives, and formal volunteering, which involves giving unpaid help through groups, clubs and organisations to benefit other people or the environment. In April to June 2009, informal volunteering was carried out by 57 per cent of adults aged 16 and over in England at least once in the 12 months prior to interview, and a third (33 per cent) did so at least once in the month prior to interview (Table 13.15). Over four in ten (43 per cent) people did some kind of formal volunteering at least once in the 12 months prior to interview, and just under three in ten (28 per cent) in the month prior to interview. There was some variation in levels of volunteering by age. The proportion of people undertaking formal volunteering at least once in the 12 months prior to interview was lower for those aged 75 and over (30 per cent) than for any other age group. Those undertaking informal volunteering at least once in the 12 months prior to interview varied between 45 per cent of those aged 75 and over and 62 per cent of those aged 26 to 34. Just over a fifth (22 per cent) of those aged 26 to 34

Table 13.15

Participation in voluntary activities: by age, 2009[1]

England

Percentages

	At least once a month		At least once in last year	
	Informal volunteering	Formal volunteering	Informal volunteering	Formal volunteering
16–25	40	25	61	44
26–34	34	22	62	41
35–49	30	31	60	48
50–64	28	30	53	43
65–74	37	34	54	45
75 and over	30	23	45	30
All aged 16 and over	33	28	57	43

1 Data are at April to June.

Source: Citizenship Survey, Communities and Local Government

formally volunteered at least once a month, compared with just over a third (34 per cent) of those aged 65 to 74. Four in ten (40 per cent) of those aged 16 to 25 informally volunteered at least once a month, compared with under three in ten (28 per cent) of those aged 50 to 64.

According to the 2007/08 Taking Part Survey carried out by the Department for Culture, Media and Sport, the most common types of voluntary work undertaken by adults aged 16 and over in the 12 months prior to interview in England were raising or handling money or taking part in sponsored events – these activities were undertaken by just over a third (34 per cent) of volunteers (Table 13.16 overleaf). Just under a third (32 per cent) organised or helped to run an event, and almost a quarter (23 per cent) were members of a committee. Men were more likely to coach or tutor with just over two in ten (22 per cent) doing this, compared with just over one in ten (11 per cent) women. Men were also more likely to be a member of a committee, lead a group or provide transport. However, most types of voluntary work were performed by similar proportions of men and women.

According to the 2007/08 Scottish Household Survey, in Scotland as in England, most activities were done by similar proportions of men and women. However, men were more likely to volunteer to educate, train or coach (18 per cent of men compared with 10 per cent of women), while women were more likely to raise money (38 per cent of women compared with 27 per cent of men).

Volunteering is also one way to meet other people from different backgrounds. In April to June 2009, eight in ten

Table 13.16

Selected types of voluntary work undertaken: by sex, 2007/08[1]

England

Percentages

	Men	Women	All aged 16 and over
Raising or handling money or taking part in sponsored events	33	36	34
Organising or helping to run an activity or event	31	32	32
Member of a committee	26	21	23
Coaching or tuition	22	11	15
Leading a group	15	10	13
Giving advice, information or counselling	13	11	12
Secretarial, administrative or clerical work	11	12	12
Befriending or mentoring people	10	13	12
Visiting people	10	12	11
Providing transport or driving	12	8	10

1 As a proportion of all who had done voluntary work in the 12 months prior to interview.

Source: Taking Part: The National Survey of Culture, Leisure and Sport, Department for Culture, Media and Sport

(80 per cent) adults in England aged 16 and over mixed socially at least once a month with people from different ethnic or religious backgrounds. This was either at work, at a place of education, through a leisure activity, at a place of worship, at the shops or through volunteering. (see Appendix, Part 13: Mixing socially). More than two in ten (22 per cent) did this through formal volunteering and just under two in ten (19 per cent) through informal volunteering (Figure 13.17). The most likely place to mix socially with people from different ethnic or religious backgrounds was at the shops (62 per cent), followed by work, school or college (53 per cent), or a pub, club, café or restaurant (47 per cent). People from ethnic minority groups were more likely than white people to mix socially with people from different ethnic or religious backgrounds (95 per cent compared with 79 per cent). Young people were more likely than older people to mix socially with people from different backgrounds. Over nine in ten (94 per cent) of those aged 16 to 24 mixed socially at least once a month compared with just over half (51 per cent) of those aged 75 and over. Younger people tended to mix at work school or college while older people tended to mix at the shops.

While volunteering generally involves giving time to help the community, many people also care for others through giving gifts of money to charity, from large charitable organisations to the smallest community groups. In 2008/09 the total estimated amount donated to charity by individuals in the UK was around £9.9 billion, an 11 per cent reduction in real terms (i.e. after adjustment to remove inflation) from 2007/08. In a typical month in 2008/09, over half (54 per cent) of adults gave to

charity. This is equivalent to 26.9 million adults, with women more likely to donate than men (58 per cent of women compared with 49 per cent of men). The average (mean) donation per donor was £31. However, this reflects the impact of the number of very large donations on the average donation

Figure 13.17

Proportion of people mixing with others from different ethnic or religious backgrounds:[1] by location, 2009[2]

England

Percentages

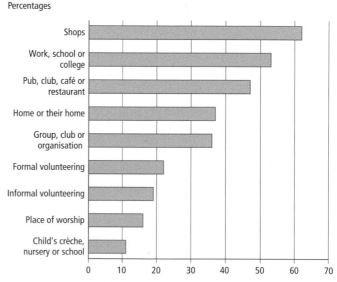

1 See Appendix, Part 13: Mixing socially.
2 At least once a month. Data are at April to June.

Source: Citizenship Survey, Communities and Local Government

Figure 13.18

Proportion of total amount given to charity: by cause, 2008/09

United Kingdom
Percentages

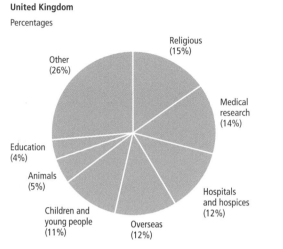

Total amount donated to charity: £9.9 billion

Source: Charities Aid Foundation; National Council for Voluntary Organisations

value, so median donation (£10 per donor) is a better indicator of the average. The highest number of donations was made to medical research charities, supported by two in ten (20 per cent) donors in 2008/09. This was followed by hospitals and hospices (15 per cent) and charities supporting young people (14 per cent). There is however a wide range in the size of donations, and the number of people supporting a charity is not necessarily a good indicator of the level of financial support received. Charities that represent religious causes received the highest level of financial donations (around 15 per cent), followed by medical research (14 per cent) (Figure 13.18). Just under two-thirds (64 per cent) of the total amount donated to charities in 2008/09 went to religious causes, medical research, hospitals and hospices, overseas, and children and young people. Just under half (48 per cent) of these donations were in the form of cash, while almost a third (31 per cent) used Direct Debit and just under a quarter (24 per cent) of supporters purchased goods from a charity.

Many people consider voting as their civic duty, and a way of participating in their community. Since 1979 elections have been held for the European Parliament, and the latest one was held on 4 June 2009. Just over a third (35 per cent) of the UK population voted, which was a decrease of around 4 percentage points compared with the previous election in 2004, when the UK turnout peaked at around 39 per cent (Figure 13.19). The political parties that won the most seats out of the 72 allotted to the UK in 2009 were the Conservative Party (25 seats), UK Independence Party (13 seats), Labour Party (13 seats) and the Liberal Democrats (11 seats). Turnout

Figure 13.19

European Parliament[1] election turnout

Percentages

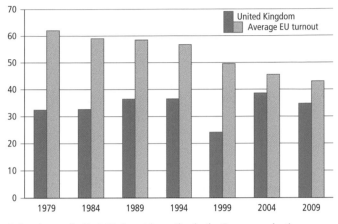

1 See Appendix, Part 13: Countries voting in the European elections.
Source: European Parliament

for these European Parliament elections has been steadily declining across the EU from around 62 per cent in 1979 to 43 per cent in 2009. The highest turnout rates in 2009 were in Luxembourg (91 per cent) and Belgium (90 per cent) where voting is mandatory. The lowest turnouts were in Slovakia (20 per cent) and Lithuania (21 per cent).

In a Eurobarometer survey conducted in January and February 2009, citizens of the 27 European Union member states were asked what campaign themes would be a priority for them in the 2009 European election. Nearly three in five (57 per cent) stated unemployment, followed by economic growth (52 per cent), inflation and purchasing power (40 per cent) and the future of pensions (32 per cent).

Religion

Religion can provide a spiritual element and a moral framework to a person's life, and may also provide contact with other individuals and participation in the local community. Having faith in a higher being is probably as old as humanity itself but it is not always evident what that higher being is, or whether we believe at all. According to a survey by YouGov in 2007, when asked which statement came closest to their belief, just over a quarter (26 per cent) of adults aged 18 and over in Great Britain believed in 'something' but they were not sure what that 'something' was. This was also one of the two most common statements with which men agreed (22 per cent) and the most common statement with which women agreed (29 per cent) (Figure 13.20 overleaf).

More than two in ten (22 per cent) of all adults reported that they agreed with the statement 'I believe in a personal god

Figure 13.20

Belief in God,[1] 2007[2]

Great Britain

Percentages

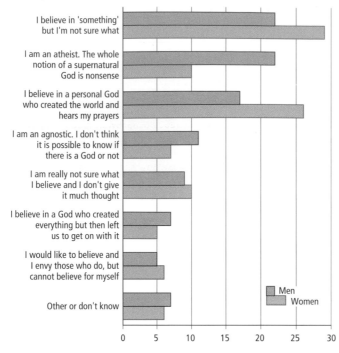

■	Men
□	Women

1 Respondents aged 18 and over were shown the above statements and asked 'Which of these comes closest to your belief?'
2 Data are at February.

Source: YouGov

Table 13.21

Attendance at church services or meetings,[1] 2008

Great Britain   Percentages

	Men	Women	All
Once a week or more	11	12	11
At least once in two weeks	2	2	2
At least once a month	5	8	7
At least twice a year	8	12	10
At least once a year	6	8	7
Less often than once a year	5	5	5
Never or practically never	63	52	57
Varies too much to say	1	1	1

1 Respondents aged 18 and over were asked 'Apart from such special occasions as weddings, funerals and baptisms, how often nowadays do you attend services or meetings connected with your religion?'

Source: British Social Attitudes Survey, National Centre for Social Research

who created the world and hears my prayers', which was the second most common statement that women agreed with (26 per cent). Sixteen per cent of all adults agreed with the statement 'I am an atheist. The whole notion of a supernatural god is nonsense'. This was also the other most common statement that men agreed with (22 per cent).

According to the 2008 British Social Attitudes Survey, religion played a somewhat, very or extremely important part in the lives of 47 per cent of people aged 18 and over in Great Britain. Around three in ten (31 per cent) stated that it was somewhat important, one in ten (10 per cent) very important and 5 per cent extremely important. However, over half

(53 per cent) of all adults reported that religion was not at all important in their daily life. A higher proportion of men (61 per cent) than women (45 per cent) felt this way.

The British Social Attitudes Survey also asked people how often they attended services or meetings connected with their religion (apart from special occasions such as weddings, funerals and baptisms). In Great Britain in 2008, 57 per cent of adults aged 18 and over stated that they never or practically never attended (Table 13.21). Men were more likely than women to not attend, 63 per cent of men compared with 52 per cent of women. Around 14 per cent of adults regularly attended church services or meetings (defined as attending once a week or more, or at least once in two weeks). In 2008, there was little difference in the proportions of men and women attending regularly (12 per cent and 15 per cent respectively). Regular church attendance also varied between young and older people. Nearly two in ten (19 per cent) of those aged 65 and over regularly attended a religious service and were more likely than all younger age groups to do so.

References, further reading and websites

Chapter 1: Population

References and further reading

Annual Report of the Registrar General for Northern Ireland, Northern Ireland Statistics and Research Agency, available at: www.nisra.gov.uk/demography/default.asp22.htm

Annual Report of the Registrar General for Scotland, General Register Office for Scotland, available at: www.gro-scotland.gov.uk/statistics/annrep/index.html

Birth Statistics, England and Wales (Series FM1), Office for National Statistics, Internet only publication, available at: www.statistics.gov.uk/statbase/Product.asp?vlnk=5768

British Citizenship Statistics, United Kingdom, 2008, Home Office, available at: www.homeoffice.gov.uk/rds/pdfs08/hosb0508.pdf

Census 2001: First results on population for England and Wales, Office for National Statistics, TSO, available at: www.statistics.gov.uk/census2001/downloads/pop2001ew.pdf

Control of Immigration: Statistics, United Kingdom, 2007, Home Office, TSO, available at: www.homeoffice.gov.uk/rds/pdfs08/hosb1008.pdf

Europe in Figures – Population, Eurostat, available at: epp.eurostat.ec.europa.eu/cache/ITY_OFFPUB/KS-CD-06-001-01/EN/KS-CD-06-001-01-EN.PDF

Health Statistics Quarterly, Office for National Statistics, Palgrave Macmillan, available at: www.statistics.gov.uk/statbase/Product.asp?vlnk=6725

International Migration Statistics (Series MN), Office for National Statistics, Internet only publication, available at: www.statistics.gov.uk/statbase/Product.asp?vlnk=507

Key Population and Vital Statistics (Series VS/PP1), Office for National Statistics/TSO, available at: www.statistics.gov.uk/statbase/Product.asp?vlnk=539

Mid-2008 Population Estimates Scotland, General Register Office for Scotland, Internet only publication, available at: www.gro-scotland.gov.uk/statistics/publications-and-data/population-estimates/mid-year/mid-2007-pop-est/index.html

Mid-year Population Estimates, Northern Ireland, Northern Ireland Statistics and Research Agency, available at: www.nisra.gov.uk/demography/default.asp17.htm

Mid-year Population Estimates, United Kingdom, Office for National Statistics, available at: www.statistics.gov.uk/statbase/Product.asp?vlnk=15106

Mortality Statistics for England and Wales (Series DH2), Office for National Statistics, Internet only publications, available at: www.statistics.gov.uk/statbase/Product.asp?vlnk=618

National Population Projections, UK (Series PP2), Office for National Statistics, available at: www.statistics.gov.uk/StatBase/Product.asp?vlnk=8519

Population in Europe 2008: first results, Eurostat, available at: epp.eurostat.ec.europa.eu/cache/ITY_OFFPUB/KS-SF-08-081/EN/KS-SF-08-081-EN.PDF

Population Projections, Northern Ireland, Northern Ireland Statistics and Research Agency, available at: www.nisra.gov.uk/demography/default.asp20.htm

Population Projections, Scotland, General Register Office for Scotland, available at: www.gro-scotland.gov.uk/statistics/publications-and-data/popproj/projected-population-of-scotland-(2006-based)/index.html

Population Projections for Wales (sub-national), Welsh Assembly Government / Welsh Office Statistical Directorate, available at: www.wales.gov.uk/docrepos/40382/40382313/statistics/population/pop-2007/sb49-2007?lang=en

Population Trends, Office for National Statistics, Palgrave Macmillan, available at: www.statistics.gov.uk/STATBASE/Product.asp?vlnk=6303

Kramer S, *The Fragile Male,* British Medical Journal, available at: www.bmj.com/cgi/content/full/321/7276/1609 (requires site registration)

Wales's Population, 2009 (A Demographic overview), Welsh Assembly Government, available at: www.wales.gov.uk/docs/statistics/2009/090326walespop09en.pdf

Bradford B, *Who are the 'Mixed' ethnic group?* Office for National Statistics, Internet only, available at: www.statistics.gov.uk/CCI/article.asp?ID=1580&Pos=1&ColRank=1&Rank=224

World Population Prospects: The 2008 Revision, United Nations, available at: www.un.org/esa/population/publications/wpp2008/

Other useful websites

National Statistics
www.statistics.gov.uk

Scottish Government
www.scotland.gov.uk

General Register Office for Scotland
www.gro-scotland.gov.uk

Welsh Assembly Government (Statistics)
www.wales.gov.uk/statistics

Northern Ireland Statistics Research Agency
www.nisra.gov.uk

Eurostat
epp.eurostat.ec.europa.eu

Home Office Immigration and Asylum Statistics
www.homeoffice.gov.uk/rds/immigration-asylum-stats.html

United Nations Population Division
www.un.org/esa/population/unpop.htm

Chapter 2: Households and families

References and further reading

Abortion Statistics, England and Wales: 2008, Department of Health available at: www.dh.gov.uk/en/Publicationsandstatistics/Publications/PublicationsStatistics/DH_099285

Abortion Statistics, 2008, Information Services Division Scotland, available at: www.isdscotland.org/isd/1918.html

Adoption Statistics (Series FM2), Office for National Statistics, available at: www.statistics.gov.uk/statbase/Product.asp?vlnk=581

Annual Report of the Registrar General for Northern Ireland, Northern Ireland Statistics and Research Agency, available at: www.nisra.gov.uk/demography/default.asp22.htm

Annual Report of the Registrar General for Scotland, General Register Office for Scotland, available at: www.gro-scotland.gov.uk/statistics/index.html

Birth Statistics, England and Wales (Series FM1), Office for National Statistics, available at: www.statistics.gov.uk/statbase/Product.asp?vlnk=5768

Continuous Household Survey, Northern Ireland Statistics and Research Agency, available at: www.csu.nisra.gov.uk/survey.asp134.htm

Alcohol–related deaths 1992–2008, Office for National Statistics, available at: www.statistics.gov.uk/CCI/nugget.asp?ID=1091&Pos=1&ColRank=28&Rank=1000

Annual Report of the Registrar General for Northern Ireland, Northern Ireland Statistics and Research Agency, available at: www.nisra.gov.uk/demography/default.asp50.htm

Annual Report of the Registrar General for Scotland, General Register Office for Scotland, available at: www.gro-scotland.gov.uk/statistics/publications-and-data/annual-report-publications/rgs-annual-review-2007/index.html

At Least Five a Week – Evidence on the Impact of Physical Activity and its Relationship to Health, A Report from the Chief Medical Officer, Department of Health, available at: http://www.dh.gov.uk/en/Publicationsandstatistics/Publications/PublicationsPolicyAndGuidance/DH_4080994

Choosing Health – Making Healthy Choices Easier, Cm6374, Department of Health, TSO, available at: http://www.dh.gov.uk/en/Publicationsandstatistics/Publications/PublicationsPolicyAndGuidance/DH_4094550

Contraception and Sexual Health, 2008/09, Office for National Statistics, Palgrave Macmillan, available at: www.statistics.gov.uk/StatBase/Product.asp?vlnk=6988&Pos=6&Col

Deaths involving MRSA: England and Wales, 2008, Health Statistics Quarterly, 2009, Vol. 43, page 39, available at: www.statistics.gov.uk/statbase/Product.asp?vlnk=6725

Family Food – Report on the Expenditure and Food Survey, Department for Environment, Food and Rural Affairs, available at: www.defra.gov.uk/evidence/Statistics/foodfarm/food/familyfood/index.htm

General Lifestyle Survey (Longitudinal) 2008, Internet only publication, Office for National Statistics, available at: www.statistics.gov.uk/ghs

Deaths related to drug poisoning in England and Wales, 2008, Health Statistics Quarterly, 2009, Vol. 43, page 49, available at: www.statistics.gov.uk/statbase/Product.asp?vlnk=6725

Health in Scotland. The Annual Report of the Chief Medical Officer on the State of Scotland's Health, Scottish Executive, available at: www.scotland.gov.uk/Publications/2007/11/15135302/0

Health Statistics Quarterly, Office for National Statistics, available at: www.statistics.gov.uk/statbase/Product.asp?vlnk=6725

Health Statistics Wales, Welsh Assembly Government, available at: www.wales.gov.uk/topics/statistics/theme/health/?lang=en

Health Survey for England, Information Centre for health and social care, available at: www.ic.nhs.uk/statistics-and-data-collections/health-and-lifestyles-related-surveys/health-survey-for-England

Mortality Statistics for England and Wales (Series DH1, 2, 3, 4), Internet only publications, Office for National Statistics, available at:
www.statistics.gov.uk/statbase/Product.asp?vlnk=620
www.statistics.gov.uk/statbase/Product.asp?vlnk=618
www.statistics.gov.uk/statbase/Product.asp?vlnk=6305
www.statistics.gov.uk/statbase/Product.asp?vlnk=621

On the State of the Public Health – The Annual Report of the Chief Medical Officer of the Department of Health, Department of Health, available at: www.dh.gov.uk/en/Publicationsandstatistics/Publications/AnnualReports/DH_076817

Opinions (Omnibus) Survey, Office for National Statistics, available at: www.ons.gov.uk/about/who-we-are/our-services/omnibus-survey/

Quinn M, Wood H, Cooper N and Rowan S (2005) *Cancer Atlas of the United Kingdom and Ireland 1991–2000*, Office for National Statistics, Palgrave Macmillan, available at: www.statistics.gov.uk/statbase/Product.asp?vlnk=14059

Registrations of cancer diagnosed in 2006, England, Office for National Statistics, available at: www.statistics.gov.uk/downloads/theme_health/MB1-37/MB1_37_2006.pdf

Report of the Chief Medical Officer, Department of Health, Social Services and Public Safety, Northern Ireland, available at: www.dhsspsni.gov.uk/index/phealth/cmoannualreport.htm

Results of the ICD-10 bridge coding study, England and Wales, 1999, Health Statistics Quarterly, no 14, pp 75–83, Office for National Statistics, available at: www.statistics.gov.uk/downloads/theme_health/HSQ14_v4.pdf

Sexually transmitted Infections and Young People in the UK: 2008 report, Health Protection Agency Centre for Infections, available at: http://www.hpa.org.uk/web/HPAweb&HPAwebStandard/HPAweb_C/1216022460726

Tackling Health Inequalities: Status Report on the Programme for Action, Department of Health, available at: www.dh.gov.uk/en/Publicationsandstatistics/Publications/PublicationsPolicyAndGuidance/DH_062903

United Kingdom Health Statistics 2009, Office for National Statistics, Online publication only, available at: www.statistics.gov.uk/statbase/Product.asp?vlnk=6637

Welsh Health: Annual Report of the Chief Medical Officer, Welsh Assembly Government, available at: www.wales.gov.uk/topics/health/ocmo/publications/annual/report08/?lang=en

World Health Statistics, World Health Organisation, available at: www.who.int/whosis/en/

Other useful websites

Department for Environment, Food and Rural Affairs
www.defra.gov.uk

Department of Health
www.dh.gov.uk

Department of Health, Social Services and Public Safety, Northern Ireland
www.dhsspsni.gov.uk/stats&research/index.asp

General Register Office for Scotland
www.gro-scotland.gov.uk

Health Protection Agency
www.hpa.org.uk

The NHS Information Centre for health and social care
www.ic.nhs.uk

Information Services Division Scotland
www.isdscotland.org

Northern Ireland Cancer Registry
www.qub.ac.uk/nicr

Northern Ireland Statistics and Research Agency
www.nisra.gov.uk

Scottish Government
www.scotland.gov.uk

Welsh Assembly Government
www.wales.gov.uk

Chapter 8: Social protection

References and further reading

Annual Statistical Publication Notices, Scottish Government, available at: www.scotland.gov.uk/Topics/Statistics/

Benefit expenditure and caseload information, Department for Work and Pensions, available at: www.dwp.gov.uk/asd/asd4/expenditure.asp

British Social Attitudes – The 26th Report, National Centre for Social Research, Sage publications, available at: www.natcen.ac.uk/study/british-social-attitudes-26th-report

Children looked after statistics in Scotland, Scottish Government, available at: www.scotland.gov.uk/Topics/Statistics/Browse/Children/PubChildrenLookedAfter

Community Care Statistics 2008: Home Help/Care Services for Adults, England – National Health Service, available at:
www.ic.nhs.uk/pubs/commcarestats08home

Philo D, Maplethorpe N, Conolly A and Toomse M (2009) *Families with children in Britain: Findings from the 2007 Families and Children Study (FACS)*, Department for Work and Pensions, Corporate Document Services, available at:
www.dwp.gov.uk/asd/asd5/facs/

Family Resources Survey, Department for Work and Pensions, available at:
www.dwp.gov.uk/asd/frs

General Household Survey 2008, Internet only publication, Office for National Statistics, available at:
www.statistics.gov.uk/ghs

Health Statistics Wales, Children and young people, Welsh Assembly Government, available at:
www.wales.gov.uk/topics/childrenyoungpeople/?lang=en

Hospital Statistics for Northern Ireland, Department of Health, Social Services and Public Safety, Northern Ireland, available at:
www.dhsspsni.gov.uk/index/stats_research/stats-activity_stats-2.htm

Mooney E, Fitzpatrick M and Hewitt R (2007) *Children Order Statistical Bulletin*, Department of Health, Social Services and Public Safety, Northern Ireland, available at:
www.dhsspsni.gov.uk/stats-cib-children_order_bulletin

Referrals, assessments and children and young people on child protection registers, England (First Release), Department for Children, Schools and Families, available at:
www.dcsf.gov.uk/rsgateway/DB/SFR/s000873/index.shtml

Social loan fund, Jobcentreplus, available at:
www.jobcentreplus.gov.uk/JCP/Customers/WorkingAgeBenefits/Dev_008613.xml.html

Social Services Statistics Wales, Local Government Data Unit, available at:
www.dataunitwales.gov.uk

Benefit Caseload Statistics, Work and Pensions Longitudinal Study, Tabulation Tool, Department for Work and Pensions, available at:
http://83.244.183.180/100pc/tabtool.html

Other useful websites

National Statistics
www.statistics.gov.uk

Charities Aid Foundation
www.cafonline.org

Department for children, schools and families
www.dcsf.gov.uk

Department of Health, Social Services and Public Safety, Northern Ireland
www.dhsspsni.gov.uk

Department for Social Development, Northern Ireland
www.dsdni.gov.uk

Department for Work and Pensions
www.dwp.gov.uk

Department of Health
www.dh.gov.uk

Eurostat
epp.eurostat.ec.europa.eu

Local Government Data Unit
www.dataunitwales.gov.uk
www.unedddatacymru.gov.uk

National Society for the Prevention of Cruelty to Children
www.nspcc.org.uk

The NHS Information Centre for health and social care
www.ic.nhs.uk

Northern Ireland Statistics and Research Agency
www.nisra.gov.uk/

Northern Ireland Assembly
www.niassembly.gov.uk

The Organisation for Economic Co-operation and Development
www.oecd.org

Scottish Government
www.scotland.gov.uk

Welsh Assembly Government
www.wales.gov.uk

Chapter 9: Crime and justice

References and further reading

A Guide to Anti-social Behaviour Orders and Acceptable Behaviour Contracts (2007), Home Office, available at:
www.crimereduction.homeoffice.gov.uk/asbos/asbos9.pdf

Circumstances of Crime, Neighbourhood Watch Membership and Perceptions of Policing: Supplementary Volume 3 to Crime in England and Wales 2006/07, Home Office, available at:
www.homeoffice.gov.uk/rds/pdfs08/hosb0608.pdf

Crime in England and Wales 2008/09, Volume 1 – Findings from the British Crime Survey and police recorded crime, Home Office, available at:
www.homeoffice.gov.uk/rds/pdfs09/hosb1109vol1.pdf

Criminal Justice System Strategic Plan 2008-2011, Office for Criminal Justice Reform, available at:
www.cjsonline.gov.uk/downloads/application/pdf/1_Strategic_Plan_ALL.pdf

Criminal Statistics England and Wales 2008, Ministry of Justice, available at:
www.justice.gov.uk/publications/criminalannual.htm

Experiences of Crime: Findings from the 2008/09 Northern Ireland Crime Survey, Research and Statistical bulletin 7/2009, Northern Ireland Office, available at:
www.nio.gov.uk/statistics-research/publications.htm

Fraud The Facts 2009, Analysis of Policing and Community Safety, available at:
www.cardwatch.org.uk/images/uploads/publications/Fraud%20the%20Facts%202009.pdf

Home Office Research Findings, Home Office, available at:
www.homeoffice.gov.uk/rds/pubsintro1.html

Home Office Statistical Bulletins, Home Office, available at:
www.homeoffice.gov.uk/rds/hosbpubs1.html

Homicides, Firearm offences and Intimate Violence 2008/09: Supplementary Volume 2 to Crime in England and Wales 2008/09, Home Office, available at:
www.homeoffice.gov.uk/rds/pdfs10/hosb0110.pdf

Northern Ireland Crime Survey Bulletins, Northern Ireland Office, available at:
www.nio.gov.uk/statistics-research/publications.htm

Northern Ireland Judicial Statistics, Northern Ireland Court Service, available at:
www.courtsni.gov.uk/en-GB/Publications/Targets_and_Performance/

Offender Management Caseload Statistics 2008, Ministry of Justice, available at:
www.justice.gov.uk/publications/prisonandprobation.htm

Offending, Crime and Justice Survey, 2006, Home Office, available at:
www.homeoffice.gov.uk/rds/pdfs08/hosb0908.pdf

Police Service of Northern Ireland Annual Statistics, 2007/08, Police Service of Northern Ireland, available at:
www.psni.police.uk/index/updates/updates_statistics/update_crime_statistics.htm

Police Powers and Procedures England and Wales 2007/08, Home Office, available at:
www.homeoffice.gov.uk/rds/pdfs09/hosb0709.pdf

Police Service Strength England and Wales 30th September 2009, Home Office, available at:
www.homeoffice.gov.uk/rds/pdfs10/hosb0310.pdf

Population in Custody: Monthly tables June 2009, England and Wales, Ministry of Justice, available at: www.justice.gov.uk/publications/docs/population-in-custody-06-2009.pdf

Hough M, Hunter G, Jacobson J and Cossalter S, *Research Report 04, The impact of the Licensing Act 2003 on Levels of Crime and Disorder: An Evaluation,* Institute of Public Policy Research, Kings College London, available at: www.homeoffice.gov.uk/rds/pdfs08/horr04c.pdf

Recorded Crime & Clearances 1st April 2008 – 31st March 2009, PSNI Annual Statistical Report; Report No.1, Police Service of Northern Ireland, available at: www.psni.police.uk/1._08_09_recorded_crime.pdf

Recorded Crime in Scotland 2007/08, Scottish Government, available at: www.scotland.gov.uk/Publications/2008/09/29155946/0

Scotland Crime and Justice Statistics, Scottish Government, available at: www.scotland.gov.uk/Topics/Statistics/Browse/Crime-Justice

Sentencing Statistics, 2007 England and Wales (annual), Ministry of Justice, available at: www.justice.gov.uk/about/docs/sentencing-statistics-2007.pdf

Story of The Prison Population 1995 – 2009, Ministry of Justice, available at: www.justice.gov.uk/publications/docs/story-prison-population.pdf

Other useful websites

Court Service
www.hmcourts-service.gov.uk

Criminal Justice System
www.cjsonline.gov.uk

Crown Prosecution Service
www.cps.gov.uk

Department of Constitutional Affairs
www.dca.gov.uk

Home Office
www.homeoffice.gov.uk

Ministry of Justice
www.justice.gov.uk

Northern Ireland Court Service
www.courtsni.gov.uk

Northern Ireland Office
www.nio.gov.uk

Northern Ireland Prison Service
www.niprisonservice.gov.uk

Prison Service for England and Wales
www.hmprisonservice.gov.uk

Police Service of Northern Ireland
www.psni.police.uk

Scottish Government
www.scotland.gov.uk

Scottish Prison Service
www.sps.gov.uk

Welsh Assembly Government
www.wales.gov.uk/

Chapter 10: Housing

References and further reading

Achieving mobility in the intermediate housing market: moving up and moving on? Joseph Rowntree Foundation, The Chartered Institute of Housing, 2008, available at: www.jrf.org.uk/sites/files/jrf/2296-housing-shared-ownership.pdf

e-digest Statistics about: Land Use and Land Cover – Urbanisation in England, Department for Environment, Food and Rural Affairs, available at: www.defra.gov.uk/evidence/statistics/environment/land/ldurban.htm

English House Condition Survey 2007, Communities and Local Government, TSO, available at: www.communities.gov.uk/publications/corporate/statistics/ehcs2007headlinereport

Homeowner housing equity through the downturn, Council of Mortgage Lenders, available at: www.cml.org.uk/cml/publications/research

Housing in England: Survey of English Housing, Communities and Local Government, TSO, available at: www.communities.gov.uk/publications/corporate/statistics/sehprelimresults0708

Housing Statistics 2008, Communities and Local Government, TSO, available at: www.communities.gov.uk/publications/corporate/statistics/housingstatistics2008

Scottish House Condition Survey, Scottish Government, available at: www.scotland.gov.uk/Topics/Statistics/SHCS

Statistical Bulletins on Housing, Scottish Government, available at: www.scotland.gov.uk/Topics/Housing

Survey of English Housing, Department for Communities and Local Government, available at: www.communities.gov.uk/housing/housingresearch/housingsurveys/surveyofenglishhousing/

Other useful websites

National Statistics
www.statistics.gov.uk

Communities and Local Government
www.communities.gov.uk

Council of Mortgage Lenders
www.cml.org.uk

Department for Social Development, Northern Ireland
www.dsdni.gov.uk

HM Revenue and Customs
www.hmrc.gov.uk

Joseph Rowntree Foundation
www.jrf.org.uk/

Land Registry
www.landregistry.gov.uk

Neighbourhood Renewal Unit
www.neighbourhood.gov.uk

Northern Ireland Statistics and Research Agency
www.nisra.gov.uk

Scottish Government
www.scotland.gov.uk

Welsh Assembly Government
www.wales.gov.uk

Chapter 11: Environment

References and further reading

Agriculture in the United Kingdom, Department for Environment, Food and Rural Affairs, available at: http://www.defra.gov.uk/evidence/statistics/foodfarm/general/ak/index/htm

Air Quality Strategy for England, Scotland, Wales and Northern Ireland, Department for Environment, Food and Rural Affairs, TSO, available at: www.defra.gov.uk/environment/quality/air/airquality/strategy/index.htm

Digest of United Kingdom energy statistics (DUKES), Department of Energy and Climate Change, available at: www.decc.gov.uk/en/content/cms/statistics/publications/dukes/dukes.aspx

e-Digest of Environmental Statistics, Department for Environment, Food and Rural Affairs, available at:
www.defra.gov.uk/evidence/statistics/environment/index.htm

Energy consumption in the UK, Department of Energy and Climate Change, available at:
www.decc.gov.uk/en/content/cms/statistics/publications/ecuk/ecuk.aspx

Energy Trends, Department of Energy and Climate Change, available at:
www.decc.gov.uk/en/content/cms/statistics/publications/trends/trends.aspx

Europeans' attitudes towards climate, Eurobarometer, available at:
www.ec.europa.eu/public_opinion/archives/ebs/ebs_322_en.pdf

Household Food and Drink in the UK, Waste & Resources Action Programme, available at:
www.wrap.org.uk/retail/case_studies_research/report_household.html

Hydrological Summaries for the United Kingdom, Centre for Ecology and Hydrology Wallingford and British Geological Survey, available at:
www.ceh.ac.uk/data/nrfa/water_watch.html

Municipal Waste Management, Welsh Assembly Government, available at:
www.new.wales.gov.uk/topics/environmentcountryside/epq/waste_recycling/municipalwastemanagement/;jsessionid=9WkSJvKD2YyvlldLQdXLQTJB2jgzxMwTtV8Cr3Tw8Pf284S60rh3!-1130397166?lang=en

National Bat Monitoring Programme Annual Report 2008, Bat Conservation Trust, available at:
www.bats.org.uk/pages/nbmp_reports.html

Waste and Recycling Statistics, Department for Environment, Food and Rural Affairs, available at:
www.defra.gov.uk/evidence/statistics/environment/waste/index.htm

Organic Statistics UK, Department for Environment, Food and Rural Affairs, available at:
statistics.defra.gov.uk/esg/statnot/orguk.pdf

Pollution incidents, Environment Agency, available at:
www.environment-agency.gov.uk/research/library/data/34363.aspx

Population of wild birds: 1970-2008, Department for Environment, Food and Rural Affairs, available at:
www.defra.gov.uk/evidence/statistics/environment/wildlife/kf/wdkf03.htm

Special Areas of Conservation (SAC), Joint Nature Conservation Committee, available at:
www.jncc.gov.uk/page-23

Sustainable Development Indicators in your Pocket 2009, Department for Environment, Food and Rural Affairs, available at:
www.defra.gov.uk/sustainable/government/progress/data-resources/sdiyp.htm

The Environment in your Pocket 2009, Department for Environment, Food and Rural Affairs, available at:
www.defra.gov.uk/evidence/statistics/environment/eiyp/index.htm

Websites

Bat Conservation Trust
www.bats.org.uk

Centre for Ecology and Hydrology
www.ceh-nerc.ac.uk

Centre for Environment, Fisheries & Aquaculture Science
www.cefas.co.uk/

Department of Energy and Climate Change
www.decc.gov.uk

Department for Environment, Food and Rural Affairs
www.defra.gov.uk

Department of the Environment Northern Ireland
www.doeni.gov.uk

Environment Agency
www.environment-agency.gov.uk

Eurobarometer
www.ec.europa.eu/public_opinion/index_en.htm

Eurostat
epp.eurostat.ec.europa.eu

Joint Nature Conservation Committee
www.jncc.gov.uk

Northern Ireland Statistics and Research Agency
www.nisra.gov.uk

Scottish Environment Protection Agency
www.sepa.org.uk

Scottish Government
www.scotland.gov.uk

Waste & Resources Action Programme
www.wrap.org.uk/

Welsh Assembly Government
www.wales.gov.uk

Chapter 12: Transport

References and further reading

British Social Attitudes – The 26th Report, National Centre for Social Research, Sage publications, available at:
www.natcen.ac.uk/study/british-social-attitudes-26th-report

European Union Energy and Transport in Figures, 2007, European Commission, available at:
ec.europa.eu/dgs/energy_transport/figures/pocketbook/2007_en.htm

Focus on Personal Travel: 2005 edition, Department for Transport, TSO, available at:
www.dft.gov.uk/pgr/statistics/datatablespublications/personal/focuspt/2005/focusonpersonaltravel2005edi5238

General Household Survey (Longitudinal) 2008, Internet only publication, Office for National Statistics, available at:
www.statistics.gov.uk/ghs

Injury Road Traffic Collisions and Casualties 2008/09, Police Service of Northern Ireland, available at:
www.psni.police.uk/6._08_09_rtcs.pdf

National Passenger Survey Spring 2009, Passenger Focus, available at:
www.passengerfocus.org.uk/your-experiences/content.asp?dsid=496

National Rail Trends 2008–09 Yearbook, Office of Rail Regulation, available at:
www.rail-reg.gov.uk/upload/pdf/yearbook0809-v22.pdf

National Travel Survey Bulletins, Department for Transport, available at:
www.dft.gov.uk/pgr/statistics/recentpubs/recentpublications

A New Deal for Transport: Better for Everyone (2005), Department for Transport, TSO, available at:
www.dft.gov.uk/about/strategy/whitepapers/previous/anewdealfortransportbetterfo5695

Northern Ireland Transport Statistics Annual 2008-2009, Department for Regional Development Northern Ireland, available at:
www.drdni.gov.uk/transport_statistics_annual_2008-09.pdf

Office of Rail Regulation Annual report 2008-09, Office of Rail Regulation, available at:
www.rail-reg.gov.uk/server/show/nav.1240

Road Accidents Scotland 2007, Scottish Government, available at:
www.scotland.gov.uk/Topics/Statistics/Browse/Transport-Travel/PubRoadAcc

Road Casualties Great Britain 2008 – Annual Report, Department for Transport, TSO, available at:
www.dft.gov.uk/pgr/statistics/datatablespublications/accidents/casualtiesgbar/

Road Casualties: Wales 2006, Welsh Assembly Government, available at: www.wales.gov.uk/cisd/publications/statspubs/roadcasualties/ency. pdf?lang=en

Scottish Government Transport publications and bulleting pages, Scottish Government, available at: www.scotland.gov.uk/Topics/Statistics/Browse/Transport-Travel/ Publications

Scottish Household Survey 2007/2008, Scottish Government, available at: www.scotland.gov.uk/Topics/Statistics/16002

Scottish Transport and Travel Statistics, Scottish Government, available at: www.scotland.gov.uk/Topics/Statistics/Browse/Transport-Travel

Securing the Future – UK Government sustainable development strategy (2005), Department for Environment, Food and Rural Affairs, TSO, available at: www.defra.gov.uk/sustainable/government/progress/index.htm

Traffic Speeds and Congestion 2008, Department for Transport, available at: www.dft.gov.uk/pgr/statistics/datatablespublications/roadstraffic/ speedscongestion/roadstatstsc/roadstats08tsc

Transport Statistics Bulletins and Reports, Department for Transport, available at: www.dft.gov.uk/pgr/statistics/recentpubs/recentpublications

Transport Statistics for Great Britain 2008, Department for Transport, TSO, available at: www.dft.gov.uk/pgr/statistics/datatablespublications/ tsgb/2008edition/

Transport Trends 2007, Department for Transport, TSO, available at: www.dft.gov.uk/pgr/statistics/datatablespublications/trends/ current/transporttrends2007

Travel Trends, Office for National Statistics, Palgrave Macmillan, available at: www.statistics.gov.uk/statbase/Product.asp?vlnk=1391

Vehicle Licensing Statistics 2008, Department for Transport, available at: www.dft.gov.uk/pgr/statistics/datatablespublications/vehicles/ licensing/vehiclelicensingstatistics2008

Welsh Transport Statistics, Welsh Assembly Government, available at: www.wales.gov.uk/topics/statistics/theme/transport/?lang=en

Other useful websites

National Statistics
www.statistics.gov.uk

Civil Aviation Authority, Economic Regulation Group
www.caa.co.uk/homepage.aspx

Department of Energy and Climate Change
www.decc.gov.uk

Department of the Environment Northern Ireland
www.doeni.gov.uk

Department for Regional Development Northern Ireland
www.drdni.gov.uk

Department for Transport
www.dft.gov.uk

European Commission Directorate-General Energy and Transport
www.ec.europa.eu/dgs/energy_transport/index_en.html

National Centre for Social Research
www.natcen.ac.uk

Office of Rail Regulation
www.rail-reg.gov.uk

Passenger Focus
www.passengerfocus.org.uk

Police Service of Northern Ireland
www.psni.police.uk

Scottish Government
www.scotland.gov.uk

Welsh Assembly Government
www.wales.gov.uk

Chapter 13: Lifestyles and social participation

References and further reading

Active People Survey, 2008/09, SportEngland, available at: www.sportengland.org/research/active_people_survey.aspx

British Social Attitudes – The 26th Report, National Centre for Social Research, Sage publications, available at: www.natcen.ac.uk/study/british-social-attitudes-26th-report

Citizenship Survey: April – June 2009, England and Wales, Communities and Local Government, available at: www.communities.gov.uk/publications/corporate/statistics/ citizenshipsurveyq1200910

Confidence in Information Society, Eurobarometer, available at: www.ec.europa.eu/public_opinion/flash/fl_250_sum_en.pdf

Health Survey for England 2007: Healthy lifestyles: knowledge, attitudes and behaviour, The Health and Social Care Information Centre, available at: www.ic.nhs.uk/pubs/hse07healthylifestyles

Internet Access, Households and Individuals 2009, Statistical Bulletin, Office for National Statistics, available at: www.statistics.gov.uk/pdfdir/iahi0809.pdf

Quick S, Dalziel D, Thornton A and Simon A, *PE and Sport Survey 2008/09*, Department for Children, Schools and Families, available at: www.dcsf.gov.uk/research/data/uploadfiles/DCSF-RR168.pdf

Scottish Household Survey Annual Report 2007/2008, People and Culture in Scotland and People and Sport in Scotland, Scottish Government, available at: www.scotland.gov.uk/Topics/Statistics/16002/Publications

Survey data on remote gambling participation, Year to September 2009, Gambling Commission, available at: www.gamblingcommission.gov.uk/research__consultations/ research/survey_data_on_remote_gam/survey_data_on_remote_ gambling.aspx

Taking Part: The National Survey of Culture, Leisure and Sport, Department for Culture, Media and Sport, available at: www.culture.gov.uk/reference_library/research_and_statistics/ 4828.aspx

The Communications Market 2009, Ofcom, available at: www.ofcom.org.uk/research/cm/cmr09/

Travel Trends: Data and commentary from the International Passenger Survey, Office for National Statistics, available at: www.statistics.gov.uk/downloads/theme_transport/Travel_ Trends_2008.pdf

UK Film Council Statistical Yearbook 2009, available at: www.ukfilmcouncil.org.uk/yearbook

UK Giving 2009, Charities Aid Foundation and National Council of Voluntary Organisations, available at: www.cafonline.org/pdf/UK_Giving_2009.pdf

UK Tourist 2008, VisitBritain, available at: www.enjoyengland.com/Images/The%20UK%20Tourist%202008_ tcm21-170509.pdf

Visitor Attractions Survey 2008 Northern Ireland, Northern Ireland Tourist Board, available at: www.nitb.com/DocumentPage.aspx?path=2e3c2831-b6cb-4bcd- a276-e0283e5bd203,e9a63dbc-7319-4780-8d0e- ca576a0a741d,67089e4c-9428-4179-9d4b-93731ed7f797,d74f29fc- 273c-4016-9d3a-524a7af4ba2a

Visitor Attractions Trends in England 2008, VisitEngland, available at: www.enjoyengland.com/Images/Annual%20Visits%20to%20 Visitor%20Attractions%20Survey%202008%20-%20Final%20 Report_tcm21-172083.doc

Visits to tourist attractions 2008, Welsh Assembly Government, available at:
www.wales.gov.uk/topics/tourism/research/tourisminwales/attractionssurvey/?lang=en

Clark C, Osborne S and Akerman R, *Young people's self-perception as readers: An investigation including family, peer and school influences*, available at:
www.literacytrust.org.uk/research/Self-perception_as_readers_report_2008.pdf

Other useful websites

Charities Aid Foundation
www.cafonline.org

Communities and Local Government
www.communities.gov.uk

Department for Children, Schools and Families
www.dcsf.gov.uk

Department for Culture, Media and Sport
www.culture.gov.uk

Eurobarometer
www.ec.europa.eu/public_opinion/

Gambling Commission
www.gamblingcommission.gov.uk

National Centre for Social Research
www.natcen.ac.uk

National Literacy Trust
www.literacytrust.org.uk

National Lottery Commission
www.natlotcomm.gov.uk

National Readership Survey
www.nrs.co.uk

Northern Ireland Tourist Board
www.nitb.com

Ofcom
www.ofcom.org.uk/research

Public Lending Right
www.plr.uk.com

Sport England
www.sportengland.org

The Health and Social Care Information Centre
www.ic.nhs.uk

UK Film Council
www.ukfilmcouncil.org.uk

VisitBritain
www.visitbritain.co.uk

Geographical areas

The European Union

Two countries which joined the EU on 1 January 2007

Ten countries which joined the EU on 1 May 2004

EU-15 members

Non-EU members

Azores (Portugal)

Madeira Islands (Portugal)

Canary Islands (Spain)

Government Office Regions[1]

SCOTLAND

ENGLAND

— GOR boundary

NORTHERN IRELAND

NORTH EAST

YORKSHIRE AND THE HUMBER

NORTH WEST

EAST MIDLANDS

WEST MIDLANDS

EAST OF ENGLAND

WALES

LONDON

SOUTH WEST

SOUTH EAST

1 Counties or unitary authorities shown in England were effective until 31 March 2009.

Police Force areas[1]

GREAT BRITAIN

— Police Force area boundary

Northern

Grampian

Tayside

Fife

Central

Strathclyde

Lothian and Borders

Dumfries and Galloway

Northumbria

NORTHERN IRELAND

Cumbria

Durham

Cleveland

North Yorkshire

Lancashire

W. Yorks

Humberside

Merseyside

GMP

S. Yorks

Lincolnshire

Cheshire

Derbs

North Wales

Notts

Staffs

Leics

Norfolk

Dyfed-Powys

W. Mids

Warks

Northants

Cambs

Mercia

Beds

Suffolk

Gwent

Gloucs

Herts

Essex

South Wales

Thames Valley

City

Avon and Somerset

Wiltshire

Met

Surrey

Kent

Devon and Cornwall

Dorset

Hampshire

Sussex

1 Counties or unitary authorities shown in England were effective until 31 March 2009. GMP is Greater Manchester Police and Met is Metropolitan Police.

Waste Disposal Authorities

1 Aberdeen City
2 Dundee City
3 Clackmannanshire
4 West Dunbartonshire
5 East Dunbartonshire
6 Inverclyde
7 Renfrewshire
8 Glasgow City
9 North Lanarkshire
10 East Renfrewshire
11 City of Edinburgh
12 Midlothian
13 Ballymoney
14 Magherafelt
15 Ballymena
16 Newtownabbey
17 Carrickfergus
18 Belfast
19 North Down
20 Castlereagh
21 Craigavon
22 Banbridge
23 Newcastle upon Tyne
24 North Tyneside
25 South Tyneside
26 Gateshead
27 Sunderland
28 Hartlepool
29 Darlington
30 Stockton-on-Tees
31 Middlesbrough
32 Redcar and Cleveland

33 Bradford
34 Blackburn with Darwen
35 Calderdale
36 City of Kingston upon Hull
37 Wigan
38 Kirklees
39 Wakefield
40 Barnsley
41 Doncaster
42 North Lincolnshire
43 North East Lincolnshire
44 Halton
45 Warrington
46 Sheffield
47 Rotherham
48 Stoke-on-Trent
49 Derby
50 Nottingham
51 Telford and Wrekin
52 Wolverhampton
53 Walsall
54 Sandwell
55 Dudley
56 Birmingham
57 Solihull
58 Coventry
59 Leicester
60 Rutland
61 Peterborough
62 Milton Keynes
63 Luton
64 Neath Port Talbot
65 Rhondda Cynon Taff
66 Merthyr Tydfil
67 Caerphilly
68 Blaenau Gwent
69 Torfaen
70 Newport
71 The Vale of Glamorgan
72 South Gloucestershire
73 City of Bristol
74 North Somerset
75 Bath and North East Somerset

76 Swindon
77 West Berkshire
78 Reading
79 Wokingham
80 Windsor and Maidenhead
81 Slough
82 Bracknell Forest
83 Thurrock
84 Southend-on-Sea
85 Medway
86 Brighton and Hove
87 Portsmouth
88 Southampton
89 Bournemouth
90 Poole
91 Torbay
92 Plymouth

93 Westminster
94 City of London
95 Tower Hamlets
96 Western Riverside
97 Southwark
98 Lewisham
99 Greenwich
100 Kingston upon Thames
101 Merton
102 Sutton

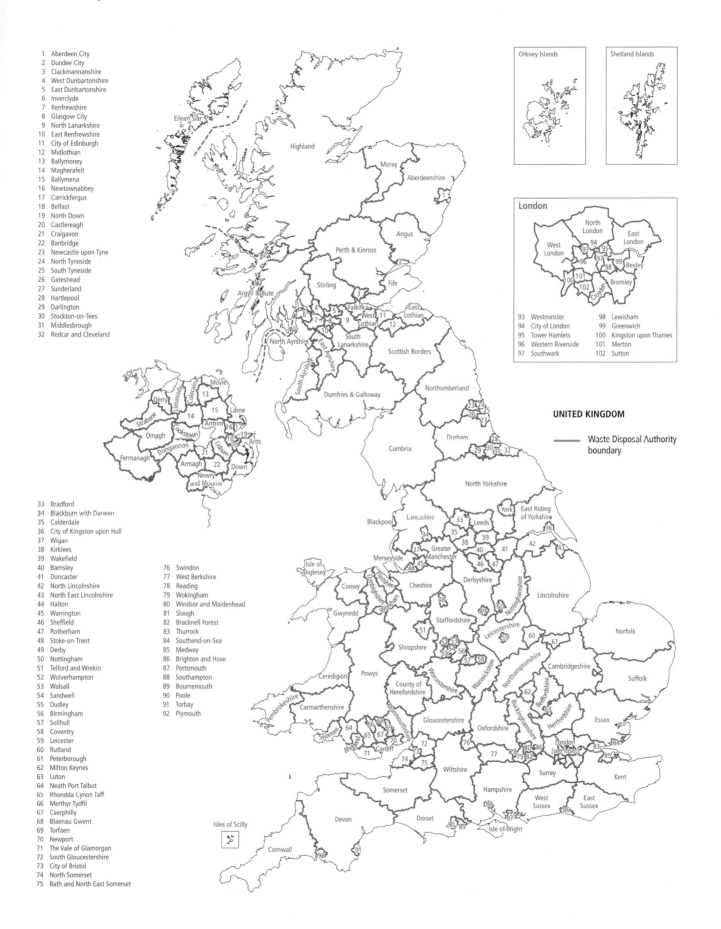

UNITED KINGDOM

—— Waste Disposal Authority
    boundary

Local or Unitary Authorities[1,2]

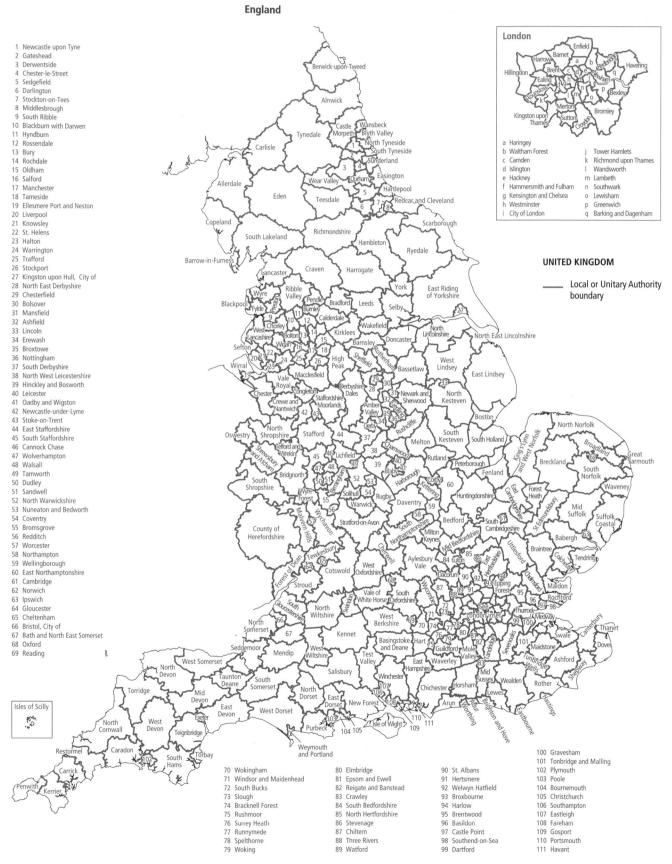

England

1 Newcastle upon Tyne
2 Gateshead
3 Derwentside
4 Chester-le-Street
5 Sedgefield
6 Darlington
7 Stockton-on-Tees
8 Middlesbrough
9 South Ribble
10 Blackburn with Darwen
11 Hyndburn
12 Rossendale
13 Bury
14 Rochdale
15 Oldham
16 Salford
17 Manchester
18 Tameside
19 Ellesmere Port and Neston
20 Liverpool
21 Knowsley
22 St. Helens
23 Halton
24 Warrington
25 Trafford
26 Stockport
27 Kingston upon Hull, City of
28 North East Derbyshire
29 Chesterfield
30 Bolsover
31 Mansfield
32 Ashfield
33 Lincoln
34 Erewash
35 Broxtowe
36 Nottingham
37 South Derbyshire
38 North West Leicestershire
39 Hinckley and Bosworth
40 Leicester
41 Oadby and Wigston
42 Newcastle-under-Lyme
43 Stoke-on-Trent
44 East Staffordshire
45 South Staffordshire
46 Cannock Chase
47 Wolverhampton
48 Walsall
49 Tamworth
50 Dudley
51 Sandwell
52 North Warwickshire
53 Nuneaton and Bedworth
54 Coventry
55 Bromsgrove
56 Redditch
57 Worcester
58 Northampton
59 Wellingborough
60 East Northamptonshire
61 Cambridge
62 Norwich
63 Ipswich
64 Gloucester
65 Cheltenham
66 Bristol, City of
67 Bath and North East Somerset
68 Oxford
69 Reading

70 Wokingham
71 Windsor and Maidenhead
72 South Bucks
73 Slough
74 Bracknell Forest
75 Rushmoor
76 Surrey Heath
77 Runnymede
78 Spelthorne
79 Woking

80 Elmbridge
81 Epsom and Ewell
82 Reigate and Banstead
83 Crawley
84 South Bedfordshire
85 North Hertfordshire
86 Stevenage
87 Chiltern
88 Three Rivers
89 Watford

90 St. Albans
91 Hertsmere
92 Welwyn Hatfield
93 Broxbourne
94 Harlow
95 Brentwood
96 Basildon
97 Castle Point
98 Southend-on-Sea
99 Dartford

100 Gravesham
101 Tonbridge and Malling
102 Plymouth
103 Poole
104 Bournemouth
105 Christchurch
106 Southampton
107 Eastleigh
108 Fareham
109 Gosport
110 Portsmouth
111 Havant

London

a Haringey
b Waltham Forest
c Camden
d Islington
e Hackney
f Hammersmith and Fulham
g Kensington and Chelsea
h Westminster
i City of London
j Tower Hamlets
k Richmond upon Thames
l Wandsworth
m Lambeth
n Southwark
o Lewisham
p Greenwich
q Barking and Dagenham

UNITED KINGDOM

——— Local or Unitary Authority boundary

1 Local or unitary authorities in England, unitary authorities in Wales, council areas in Scotland and district council areas in Northern Ireland.
2 Local or unitary authorities shown in England were effective until 31 March 2009.

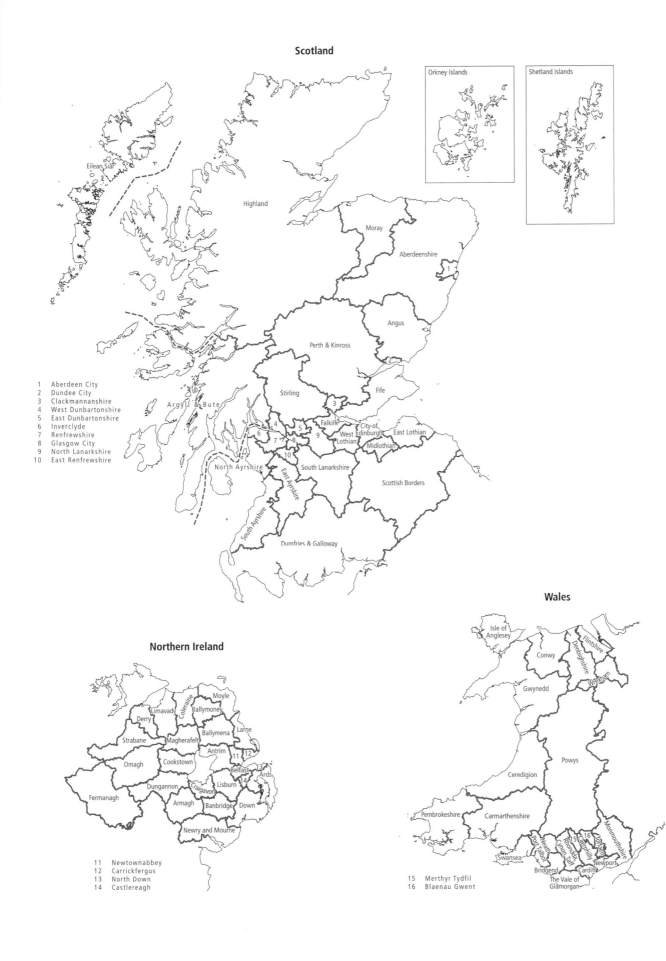

Scotland

Orkney Islands

Shetland Islands

Eilean Siar

Highland

Moray

Aberdeenshire

Angus

Perth & Kinross

Fife

Stirling

Argyll & Bute

Falkirk

City of Edinburgh

East Lothian

West Lothian

Midlothian

1 Aberdeen City
2 Dundee City
3 Clackmannanshire
4 West Dunbartonshire
5 East Dunbartonshire
6 Inverclyde
7 Renfrewshire
8 Glasgow City
9 North Lanarkshire
10 East Renfrewshire

North Ayrshire

East Ayrshire

South Lanarkshire

Scottish Borders

South Ayrshire

Dumfries & Galloway

Northern Ireland

Moyle

Limavady

Coleraine

Ballymoney

Derry

Ballymena

Larne

Strabane

Magherafelt

Antrim

11 12

Omagh

Cookstown

Belfast

13

Dungannon

Craigavon

Lisburn

14

Ards

Fermanagh

Armagh

Banbridge

Down

Newry and Mourne

11 Newtownabbey
12 Carrickfergus
13 North Down
14 Castlereagh

Wales

Isle of Anglesey

Flintshire

Conwy

Denbighshire

Wrexham

Gwynedd

Powys

Ceredigion

Pembrokeshire

Carmarthenshire

Neath Port Talbot

Rhondda Cynon Taff

15

Caerphilly

16

Monmouthshire

Swansea

Bridgend

Cardiff

Newport

The Vale of Glàmorgan

15 Merthyr Tydfil
16 Blaenau Gwent

Major surveys

	Frequency	Sampling frame	Type of respondent	Coverage	Effective sample size[1] (most recent survey included in *Social Trends*)	Response rate (percentages)
Annual Population Survey	Continuous	Postcode Address File	All adults in household	UK	360,000 individuals	54.7[2]
Annual Survey of Hours and Earnings	Annual	HM Revenue & Customs PAYE records	Employee	UK	142,000 employees	82
British Crime Survey	Annual	Postcode Address File	Adult in household	E&W	46,983 addresses	76
British Social Attitudes Survey	Annual	Postcode Address File	One adult aged 18 and over per household	GB	4,486 adults aged 18 and over	54[3]
Census of Population	Decennial	Detailed local	Adult in household	UK	Full count	98
Citizenship Survey	Continuous	Postcode Address File	One adult aged 16 and over per household	E&W	4,189 core; 3,148 boost	59[4]
Continuous Household Survey	Continuous	Valuation and Lands Agency Property	All adults in household	NI	3,980 addresses	65
English House Condition Survey	Continuous[5]	Postcode Address File	Any one householder	E	30,289 addresses	54[5]
Families and Children Study	Annual	Child benefit records[6]	Recipients of child benefit (usually mothers)	GB	8,821 households[6]	89% for panel cases, 76% for booster cases[6]
Family Resources Survey	Continuous	Postcode Address File	All members in household	UK	43,173 households	58
General Household Survey, 2007	Continuous	Postcode Address File	All adults in household	GB	12,023 households	73[7]
General Lifestyle Survey, 2008	Continuous	Postcode Address File	All adults in household	GB	11,700 households	73[7]
Health Survey for England, 2008	Continuous	Postcode Address File	All adults aged 16 and over in household and up to a maximum of 2 children	E	14,250 households[8]	64[8]
International Passenger Survey	Continuous	International passengers	Individual traveller	UK[9]	259,000 individuals	80
Labour Force Survey	Continuous	Postcode Address File	All adults in household	UK	52,000 households	53[10]
Living Costs and Food Survey	Continuous	Postcode Address File in GB, Valuation and Lands Agency list in NI	All adults in households aged 16 and over[11]	UK	10,397 addresses[11]	51[11]
Longitudinal Study of Young People in England	Annual	School records	Young person and his/her parents/guardians	E	11,393 households	92[12]
National Employers Skills Survey	Annual	Experian	Employer	E	79,018 employers	35
National Passenger Survey	Twice yearly	Passengers at 700 stations	Railway passengers	GB	50,000 individuals	35
National Travel Survey	Continuous	Postcode Address File	All household members	GB	13,687 households per year	61[13]
Northern Ireland Crime Survey	Continuous	Land and Property Services Agency (LPSA) list of domestic addresses	One person aged 16 and over from each household	NI	6,420 addresses	67

	Frequency	Sampling frame	Type of respondent	Coverage	Effective sample size[1] (most recent survey included in *Social Trends*)	Response rate (percentages)
Omnibus Survey	Continuous	Postcode Address File	Adults aged 16 and over living in private households	GB	6,000 adults aged 16 and over[14]	61
Opinions Survey	Continuous	Postcode Address File	Adults aged 16 or over living in private households	GB	Approximately 12,000	66
Scottish Crime and Justice Survey	Continuous	Postcode Address File	One adult in household	S	16,003	70.9
Scottish Household Survey	Continuous	Postcode Address File	Highest earning householder or spouse/partner, one random adult (aged 16+) and one random child (under 16)	S	27,238 householder interviews and 24,615 'random adult' interviews	66
Survey of English Housing	Continuous	Postcode Address File	Household	E	25,269 households	62
Survey of Personal Incomes	Annual	HM Revenue & Customs PAYE, Claims and Self-assessment records	Individuals/taxpayers	UK	520,000 individuals	[15]
Taking Part Survey	Continuous	Postcode Address File	One adult aged 16 and over in private households and, where appropriate, one child aged between 11 and 15. For 2008/09 onwards, the survey also includes a questionnaire for children aged 5 to 10	E	24,174 adults aged 16 and over	55
Wealth and Asset Survey	Every 2 years	HM Revenue & Customs, Postcode Address File	Private households and individuals within the household	GB	30,595 households	55
Welsh Health Survey	Continuous	Postcode Address File	All adults in household aged 16+ and up to a maximum of 2 children	W	13,590	74
Work and Pensions Longitudinal Study	Quarterly	Benefit claimants	Benefit claimants/ beneficiaries	GB	All benefit claimants	[15]
Youth Cohort Study	Annual	School records	Young person	E	7,525 young people	69[16]

1 Effective sample sizes include nonrespondents but exclude ineligible households.
2 The Annual Population Survey includes the English Local Labour Force Survey, Welsh Local Labour Force Survey, Scottish Labour Force Survey, Annual Population Survey 'Boost' and waves 1 and 5 of the Quarterly Labour Force Survey.
3 Response rate refers to 2008 survey.
4 Response rate for the core sample only.
5 Although the EHCS runs on a continuous basis, its reporting is based on a rolling two year sample (in this case 2006/07 and 2007/08). The EHCS response combines successful outcomes from two linked surveys where information is separately gathered about the household and the dwelling for each address.
6 The overall response rate given describes, of those who were contacted, the proportion who agreed to take part.
7 Response rate for fully and partially responding households.
8 There were an additional 3,693 households in the boost sample with a response rate of 73 per cent.
9 Includes UK and overseas residents.
10 Response rate to first wave interviews of the quarterly LFS over the period April to June 2009.
11 There is an optional diary for children aged 7 to 15 in Great Britain. Basic sample is for Great Britain only. Response rate refers to Great Britain.
12 Response rate quoted refers to wave 4, which was conducted in 2007.
13 Sixty one per cent of eligible households were recorded as being 'fully productive'. However, a further 7 per cent co-operated partially with the survey, and the data from these households can be used on a limited basis.
14 Achieved sample size per Omnibus cycle. The Omnibus interviews at one household per sampled address and one adult per household. Data are weighted to account for the fact that respondents living in smaller households would have a greater chance of selection.
15 Response rate not applicable as data are drawn from administrative records.
16 Response rate at first sweep.

Symbols and conventions

Reference years	Where, because of space constraints, a choice of years has to be made, the most recent year or a run of recent years is shown together with the past population census years (2001, 1991, 1981, etc) and sometimes the mid-points between census years (1996, 1986, etc). Other years may be added if they represent a peak or trough in the series.
Financial year	For example, 1 April 2006 to 31 March 2007 would be shown as 2006/07.
Academic year	For example, September 2006 to July 2007 would be shown as 2006/07.
Combined years	For example, 2004–07 shows data for more than one year that have been combined.
Geography	Where possible Social Trends uses data for the UK as a whole. When UK data are not available, or data from the constituent countries of the UK are not comparable, data for Great Britain or the constituent countries are used. Constituent countries can advise where data are available that are equivalent but not directly comparable with those of other constituent countries.
Units on tables	Where one unit predominates it is shown at the top of the table. All other units are shown against the relevant row or column. Where a table contains both numbers and percentages, the percentages are shown in italics.
Rounding of figures	In tables where figures have been rounded to the nearest final digit, there may be an apparent discrepancy between the sum of the constituent items and the total as shown.
Provisional and estimated data	Some data for the latest year (and occasionally for earlier years) are provisional or estimated. To keep footnotes to a minimum, these have not been indicated; source departments will be able to advise if revised data are available.
Billion	This term is used to represent one thousand million.
Seasonal adjustment	Unless otherwise stated, unadjusted data have been used.
Dependent children	Those aged under 16, or single people aged 16 to 18 who have not married and are in full-time education unless otherwise indicated.
State pension age (SPA)	The age at which pensions are normally payable by the state pension scheme, currently 65 for men and 60 for women.
EU	Unless otherwise stated, data relate to the enlarged European Union of 27 countries (EU-27) as constituted since 1 January 2007. EU-25 refers to the 25 members of the EU before enlargement in May 2004 from the 15 original members (EU-15).
Ireland	Refers to the Republic of Ireland and does not include Northern Ireland.
Sources	Sources are usually listed as the name by which the source is currently known. In some instances, requests have been made to show the source name at the time the data were compiled. Specific instances have been recorded in relevant appendix entries.
Symbols	The following symbols have been used throughout *Social Trends*:

- .. not available
- . not applicable
- * data have been suppressed to protect confidentiality
- \- negligible (less than one-half the final digit shown)
- 0 nil

Appendix

Part 1: Population

Population estimates and projections

The estimated and projected populations are of the resident population of an area, that is all those usually resident there, whatever their nationality. Members of HM Forces stationed outside the UK are excluded; members of foreign forces stationed in the UK are included. Students are taken to be resident at their term-time addresses. Figures for the UK do not include the population of the Channel Islands or the Isle of Man.

The population estimates for mid-2001 to mid-2008 are based on results from the 2001 Census and have been updated to reflect subsequent births, deaths, net migration and other changes. The estimates used in this publication were released on 27 August 2009 and are available at: www.statistics.gov.uk/statbase/Product.asp?vlnk=15106

The most recent set of national population projections published for the UK are based on the populations of England, Wales, Scotland and Northern Ireland at mid-2008. These were released on 21 October 2009 and further details are available at: www.statistics.gov.uk/CCI/nscl.asp?id=7595

Classification of ethnic groups

The recommended classification of ethnic groups for National Statistics data sources was changed in 2001 to bring it broadly in line with the 2001 Census.

There are two levels to this classification. Level 1 is a classification into five main ethnic groups. Level 2 provides a finer, more detailed classification of Level 1. The preference is for the Level 2 categories to be adopted wherever possible. The two levels and the categories are in the box below.

Direct comparisons should not be made between the figures produced using this new classification and those based on the previous classification.

Further details can be found on the National Statistics website: www.statistics.gov.uk/about/classifications/downloads/ns_ethnicity_statement.doc

National Statistics Socio-economic Classification (NS-SEC)

From 2001 the National Statistics Socio-economic Classification (NS-SEC) was adopted for all official surveys, in place of social class based on occupation and socio-economic group. NS-SEC is itself based on the Standard Occupational Classification 2000 (SOC2000, see Appendix, Part 4) and details of employment status (whether as employer, self employed or employee).

The NS-SEC is an occupationally based classification designed to provide coverage of the whole adult population. The version of the classification, which will be used for most analyses, has eight classes, the first of which can be subdivided. These are:

National Statistics Socio-economic Classification (NS-SEC)

1 Higher managerial and professional occupations, subdivided into:
  1.1 Large employers and higher managerial occupations
  1.2 Higher professional occupations
2 Lower managerial and professional occupations
3 Intermediate occupations
4 Small employers and own account workers
5 Lower supervisory and technical operations
6 Semi-routine occupations
7 Routine occupations
8 Never worked and long-term unemployed

The classes can be further grouped into:

i Managerial and professional occupations	1, 2
ii Intermediate occupations	3, 4
iii Routine and manual occupations	5, 6, 7
iv Never worked and long term unemployed	8

Users have the option to include these classes in the overall analysis or keep them separate. The long-term unemployed are defined as those unemployed and seeking work for 12 months or more. Members of HM Forces, who were shown separately in tables of social class, are included within the NS-SEC. Residual groups that remain unclassified include students and those with inadequately described occupations.

Further details can be found on the National Statistics website: www.statistics.gov.uk/methods_quality/ns_sec/default.asp

International migration estimates

An international migrant is defined as someone who changes his or her country of usual residence for a period of at least a year, so that the country of destination becomes the country of usual residence. The richest source of information on international migrants comes from the International Passenger Survey (IPS), which is a sample survey of passengers arriving

Classification of ethnic groups

Level 1	Level 2
White	White
	British
	Irish
	Other White background
	All White groups
Mixed	White and Black Caribbean
	White and Black African
	White and Asian
	Other Mixed background
	All Mixed groups
Asian or Asian British	Indian
	Pakistani
	Bangladeshi
	Other Asian background
	All Asian groups
Black or Black British	Caribbean
	African
	Other Black background
	All Black groups
Chinese or other ethnic Group	Chinese
	Other ethnic group
	All Chinese or Other groups
All ethnic groups	All ethnic groups
Not stated	Not stated

at, and departing from, the main UK air and sea ports and the Channel Tunnel. This survey provides migration estimates based on respondents' intended length of stay in the UK or abroad.

Adjustments are made to account for people who do not realise their intended length of stay. An estimate is made for the number of people who initially come to or leave the UK for a short period but subsequently stay for a year or longer ('visitor switchers'). The number of people who intend to be migrants, but who in reality stay in the UK or abroad for less than a year ('migrant switchers') are also estimated.

Data from other sources are used to supplement the IPS migration estimates. Home Office asylum seeker data are used to estimate the number of asylum seekers and their dependants who enter or leave the country without being counted in the IPS. Estimates of migration between the UK and Ireland are made using information from the Irish Central Statistics Office.

Internal migration estimates

The estimates of internal migration presented in this volume are based on data provided by the National Health Service Central Register (NHSCR), which records movements of patients between former health authority (HA) areas in England and Wales and area health boards (AHBs) in Scotland and Northern Ireland. Using this data source, the definition of an internal migrant is someone who moves from one former HA or AHB to another and registers with a different NHS doctor. Historically, internal migration estimates were only available at the former HA level; these were equivalent to shire counties, metropolitan districts and groupings of London boroughs. HA-level migration estimates are available from 1975 on a quarterly rolling year basis.

Internal migration estimates by age and sex became available for all local authority areas in 1999. By obtaining a download from each patient register and by combining all the patient register extracts together, the Office for National Statistics creates a total register for the whole of England and Wales. Comparing records in one year with those of the previous year enables identification of people who have changed their postcode. Estimates at local authority level are made by constraining the migration estimates from the patient registers with the NHSCR estimates at the former HA level.

It has been established that internal migration data under-report the migration of men aged between 16 and 36. Currently, however, there are no suitable sources of data available to enable adjustments or revisions to be made to the estimates. Further research is planned on this topic and new data sources may become available in the future.

North–South divide

A 2004 study by the University of Sheffield looked at different statistical, social, cultural and economic factors to define what constitutes the north and south of the UK. Their conclusions placed the dividing line along a diagonal from just above Gloucester in the south to just below Grimsby in the North. This dividing line is approximated using Government Office Region

boundaries to calculate internal migration from north to south.

Refugees

The criteria for recognition as a refugee, and hence the granting of asylum, are set out in the 1951 United Nations Convention relating to the Status of Refugees, extended in its application by the 1967 Protocol relating to the Status of Refugees. The Convention defines a refugee as a person who 'owing to a well-founded fear of being persecuted for reasons of race, religion, nationality, membership of a particular social group or political opinion, is outside the country of his [or her] nationality and unable or, owing to such fear, is unwilling to avail himself [or herself] of the protection of that country; or who, not having a nationality and being outside the country of his [or her] former habitual residence … is unable or, owing to such fear, is unwilling to return to it'.

Part 2: Households and families

Households

Although definitions differ slightly across surveys and the census, they are broadly similar.

A household is a person living alone or a group of people who have the address as their only or main residence and who either share one meal a day or share the living accommodation.

Students: those living in halls of residence are recorded under their parents' household and included in the parents' family type in the Labour Force Survey (LFS), although some surveys/projections include such students in the institutional population.

In the General Household Survey (GHS) (Longitudinal) (see below), young people aged 16 and over who live away from home for purposes of either work or study and come home only for holidays are not included at the parental address.

Families

Children: Never-married people of any age who live with one or both parent(s). They include stepchildren and adopted children (but not foster children) and also grandchildren, where the parent(s) are absent.

Dependent children: In the 1971 and 1981 Censuses, dependent children were defined as never-married children in families who were either under 15 years of age, or aged 15 to 24 and in full-time education. In the 1991 Census, the Labour Force Survey (LFS) and the General Household Survey (GHS) (Longitudinal), dependent children are childless never-married children in families who are aged under 16, or aged 16 to 18 and in full-time education and living in the household and, in the 1991 Census, economically inactive (see Glossary in Chapter 4: Labour Market). In the 2001 Census a dependent child is a person aged under 16 in a household (whether or not in a family) or aged 16 to 18, in full-time education and living in a family with their parent(s).

A family: A married or cohabiting couple, either with or without their never-married child or children (of any age), including couples with no children or a lone parent together with his or her

never-married child or children, provided they have no children of their own. A family could also consist of a grandparent(s) with their grandchild or grandchildren if the parents of the grandchild or grandchildren are not usually resident in the household. In the LFS, a family unit can also comprise a single person. LFS family units include non-dependent children (who can in fact be adult) those aged 16 and over and not in full-time education, provided they are never married and have no children of their own in the household.

One family and no others: A household comprises one family and no others if there is only one family in the household and there are no non-family people.

Multi-family household: A household containing two or more people who cannot be allocated to a single family as defined in 'a family' above. This includes households with two or more unrelated adults and can also include a grandparent(s) with their child or children and grandchild or grandchildren in one household.

A lone parent family: In the census is a father or mother together with his or her never-married child or children. A lone parent family in the LFS consists of a lone parent, living with his or her never-married child or children, provided these children have no children of their own living with them. A lone parent family in the GHS consists of a lone parent, living with his or her never-married dependent child or children, provided these children have no children of their own. Married lone mothers whose husbands are not defined as resident in the household are not classified as lone parents. Evidence suggests the majority are separated from their husband either because he usually works away from home or for some other reason that does not imply the breakdown of the marriage.

Multi-sourced tables

Tables 2.1, 2.2 and 2.3 have multiple sources. To create long time series it is necessary to combine these sources even though they are not always directly comparable. Most of the multi-sourced tables include a combination of the General Household Survey (GHS) (Longitudinal), the Labour Force Survey (LFS) and the Census. For further information about the GHS see below and for the LFS see Appendix, Part 4: Labour Force Survey.

General Household Survey

The General Household Survey (GHS) (Longitudinal) is an interdepartmental multi-purpose continuous survey carried out by the Office for National Statistics (ONS) collecting information from people living in private households in Great Britain. The survey has run continuously since 1971, except for breaks in 1997/78 (when the survey was reviewed) and 1999/2000 when the survey was redeveloped.

In 2005 the GHS adopted a new sample design in line with European requirements, changing from a cross-sectional to a longitudinal design. The purpose of this change was to help monitor European social policy by comparing poverty indicators and changes over time across the European Community. The GHS design changed to a four-yearly rotation where respondents are followed up and re-interviewed up to four times.

Around 75 per cent of the people surveyed in 2006 had also completed an interview in 2005.

Between April 1994 and April 2005, the GHS was conducted on a financial year basis, with fieldwork spread evenly across the year April–March. However, in 2005 the survey period reverted to the calendar year. The 2006 and 2007 surveys ran from January to December.

Further details of the methodological changes made during 2005 can be found in the appendices to the GHS at: www.statistics.gov.uk/ghs

The GHS collects information on a range of topics. These are:

- smoking
- drinking
- households, families and people
- housing and consumer durables
- marriage and cohabitation
- occupational and personal pension schemes

The GHS provides authoritative estimates in the topics of smoking and drinking. A detailed summary and a longer report on these topics can be found at: www.statistics.gov.uk/ghs

In 2008 the GHS was renamed the General Lifestyle Survey (GLF) and is now part of the Integrated Household Survey (IHS). The GLF is a multi-purpose survey conducted by the ONS. For more information see: www.statistics.gov.uk/STATBASE/Product. asp?vlnk=5756&More=Y

Civil partnership

The *Civil Partnership Act 2004* came into force on 5 December 2005 and enables same sex couples aged 16 and over to obtain legal recognition of their relationship. Couples who form a civil partnership have a new legal status, that of 'civil partner'.

Civil partners have equal treatment to married couples in a range of legal matters, including:

- tax, including inheritance tax
- employment benefits
- most state and occupational pension benefits
- income-related benefits, tax credits and child support
- duty to provide reasonable maintenance for your civil partner and any children of the family
- ability to apply for parental responsibility for your civil partner's child
- inheritance of a tenancy agreement
- recognition under intestacy rules
- access to fatal accidents compensation
- protection from domestic violence
- recognition for immigration and nationality purposes

Mean age

The mean age (also known as the average age) is obtained by adding together the ages of all the people concerned and dividing by the number of people. The mean ages of women at the birth of their first child (Figure 2.17) are standardised. A standardised measure uses rates per 1,000 female population by true birth order and single year of age of mother. This serves to eliminate the effect of year to year changes in the age-structure of the female population.

Conceptions

Conception statistics used in Figure 2.20 include pregnancies that result in either a maternity at which one or more live births or stillbirths occur, or a legal abortion under the *Abortion Act 1967*. Conception statistics do not include miscarriages or illegal abortions. Dates of conception are estimated using recorded gestation for abortions and stillbirths, and assuming 38 weeks gestation for live births.

Adoptions

Data on adoptions are derived from the Adopted Children Register, and are based on adoption orders made in England and Wales. The data here relates to those cases notified by the courts to the Registrar General and entered onto the Adopted Children Register in a given year. Figures for 1998 to 2007 may not match those previously published. This is due to amendments in the Adopted Children Register and the addition of late registrations. Imputations are not usually made for missing information in adoptions data. In 1998, however, the parents' marital status was imputed, as it was found that due to a data entry error, a third of all adoption records had no parents' marital status at birth recorded. The imputation method used compared the natural mothers' surname with the natural fathers' surname. If the surnames matched exactly, the system assumed legitimacy; if they were different, it assumed the child had been born outside marriage. This imputation method was checked against data where the parents' marital status was known and was found to be accurate for 98 per cent of all records.

Part 3: Education and training

Stages of education

Education takes place in several stages: early years, primary, secondary, further and higher education, and is compulsory for all children in the UK between the ages of 5 (4 in Northern Ireland) and 16. The non-compulsory fourth stage, further education, covers non-advanced education, which can be taken at both further (including tertiary) education colleges, higher education institutions and increasingly in secondary schools. The fifth stage, higher education, is study beyond GCE A levels and their equivalent, which, for most full-time students, takes place in universities and other higher education institutions.

Early years education
In recent years there has been a major expansion of early years education. Many children under five attend state nursery schools or nursery classes within primary schools. Others may attend playgroups in the voluntary sector or in privately run nurseries. In England and Wales many primary schools also operate an early admissions policy where they admit children

Organisation of compulsory school years

	Pupil ages	Year group
England and Wales		
Key Stage 1	5–7	1–2
Key Stage 2	7–11	3–6
Key Stage 3	11–14	7–9
Key Stage 4	14–16	10–11
Northern Ireland		
Key Stage 1	4–8	1–4
Key Stage 2	8–11	5–7
Key Stage 3	11–14	8–10
Key Stage 4	14–16	11–12
Scotland		
(Curriculum	4/5–6/7	P1–P3
following	6/7–6/8	P3–P4
national	7/8–9/10	P4–P6
guidelines from	9/10–/1011	P6–P7
ages 5 to 14)	10/11–12/13	P7–S2
NQ[1]	13/14–14/15	S3–S4

1 Standard Grades are part of the National Qualifications (NQ) framework in Scotland. They are broadly equivalent to GCSEs.

under five into what are called 'reception classes'. The *Education Act 2002* extended the National Curriculum (see below) for England to include the foundation stage. The foundation stage was introduced in September 2000 and covered children's education from the age of three to the end of the reception year, when most are just five and some almost six years old. The Early Years Foundation Stage (EYFS) came into force in September 2008 and is a play-based early learning framework for care, learning and development for children aged under five replacing the foundation stage profile. It aims to develop young children's learning in six broad areas: personal, social and emotional development; communication, language and literacy; problem solving, reasoning and numeracy; knowledge and understanding of the world; physical development; and creative development. All three and four-year-olds in England are entitled to a free part-time early education place for 12.5 hours per week for 38 weeks of the year. From September 2010, this will be extended to 15 hours a week. In Wales all children are entitled to a free part-time (10 hours per week) education place from the term following their third birthday. From September 2008 the Foundation Phase became statutory for three to four-year-olds and by 2011/12 will be extended to three to seven-year-olds. In Scotland, the 'Curriculum Framework for Three to Five Year Olds' has now been replaced by a 'Curriculum for Excellence' as the main guidance for providers about the delivery of pre-school education. As a result there is now a single curriculum for ages 3 to 18. The delivery of early years education in Northern Ireland also aims to develop young children's learning and a new early years strategy is being drafted by the Department for Education for implementation from 2010.

Figure 3.1 covers children in early years education in maintained nursery and primary schools, independent and special schools. Other provision also takes place in non-school education settings in the private and voluntary sector, such as nurseries (which usually provide care, education and play for children up to the age of five), playgroups and pre-schools (which provide childcare, play and early years education, usually for children aged between two and five), children's centres (for children under five), and through accredited childminders. In Scotland data are based on children who are registered for ante-pre-school and pre-school education in local authority centres at the time of the annual Pre-school Education and Daycare Census, as a proportion of all those who are eligible for early years education. Census dates differed over the years for pre-school education in Scotland as follows: from 1970/71 to 1973/74 and 2000/01 to present day this was January registrations, for 1998/99 this was February registrations and for all other years it was September registrations. For more information on data for Scotland see: www.scotland.gov.uk/Topics/Statistics/Browse/Children/PubPreSchoolEdChildcare

Primary education
The primary stage covers three age ranges: nursery (under 5), infant (5 to 7 or 8) and junior (8 or 9 to 11 or 12). In Scotland and Northern Ireland, there is generally no distinction between infant and junior schools. Most public sector primary schools take both boys and girls in mixed classes. It is usual to transfer straight to secondary school at age 11 (in England, Wales and Northern Ireland) but in England some children make the transition through middle schools catering for various age ranges between 8 and 14. Depending on their individual age ranges, middle schools are classified as either primary or secondary. In Scotland, pupils start school based on their age as at the end of February rather than at the start of the academic year, and so generally start secondary school at age 11 or 12.

Secondary education
Public provision of secondary education in an area may consist of a combination of different types of school, the pattern reflecting historical circumstances and the policy adopted by the local authority. Comprehensive schools largely admit pupils without reference to ability or aptitude and cater for all the children in a neighbourhood. In some areas they co-exist with grammar, secondary modern or technical schools. In Northern Ireland, post-primary education is provided by grammar schools and non-selective secondary schools. In England, the Specialist Schools Programme helps schools, in partnership with private sector sponsors and supported by additional government funding, to establish distinctive identities through their chosen specialisms. Specialist schools have a focus on their chosen subject area but must also meet the National Curriculum requirements and deliver a broad and balanced education to all

pupils. Any maintained secondary school in England can apply to be designated as a specialist school in one of ten specialist areas: arts, business and enterprise, engineering, humanities, languages, mathematics and computing, music, science, sports, and technology. Schools can also combine any two specialisms. Academies, also operating only in England, are all-ability state funded schools that provide free education but have sponsors from a wide range of backgrounds, including universities and colleges, educational trusts, charities, the business sector and faith communities. Sponsors establish a charitable trust, which appoints the majority of governors to the academy governing body. The Department for Children, Schools and Families (DCSF) Secretary of State announced in July 2007 that future academies (that is not including those with a signed agreement already, although they could if they wished) would be required to follow the National Curriculum programmes of study in English, mathematics, science and information and communication technology (ICT). All academies – like the large majority of secondary schools – have specialist school status, and have a specialism in one or more subjects.

Special schools
Special schools (day or boarding) provide education for children who require specialist support to complete their education, for example, because they have physical or other difficulties. Many pupils with special educational needs are educated in mainstream schools. All children attending special schools are offered a curriculum designed to overcome their learning difficulties and to enable them to become self-reliant. Since December 2005 special schools in England have also been able to apply for the special educational needs (SEN) specialism, under the Specialist Schools Programme (see Secondary education above). They can apply for a curriculum specialism, but not for both the SEN and a curriculum specialism.

Pupil referral units
Pupil referral units (PRUs) are legally a type of school established and maintained by a local authority to provide education for children of compulsory school age who may otherwise not receive suitable education. The aim of such units is to provide suitable alternative education on a temporary basis for pupils who may not be able to attend a mainstream school, for example teenage mothers, pupils excluded from school, school-phobics and pupils in the assessment phase of a statement of special educational needs (SEN). The focus of the units should be to get pupils back into a mainstream school.

Further education
The term further education may be used in a general sense to cover all non-advanced courses taken after the period of compulsory education, but more commonly it excludes those staying on at secondary school and those in higher education, that is doing courses in universities and colleges leading to qualifications above GCE A level, Higher Grade (in Scotland), General National Vocational Qualifications/National Vocational Qualifications (GNVQ/NVQ) level 3, and their equivalents. Since 1 April 1993, sixth

form colleges in England and Wales have been included in the further education sector.

Further education figures for 2007/08 shown in Table 3.7 are whole year counts. However, over the period covered in the table, there is a mixture of whole year and annual snapshot counts, as well as a combination of enrolment and headcounts. There are also other factors, such as mode of study, the inclusion/exclusion of students funded by specific bodies or at certain types of institutions, which have not been constant over time.

Higher education
Higher education (HE) is defined as courses that are of a standard that is higher than GCE A level, the Higher Grade of the Scottish Certificate of Education/National Qualification, GNVQ/NVQ level 3 or the Edexcel (formerly BTEC) or Scottish Qualifications Authority (SQA) National Certificate/Diploma. There are three main levels of HE courses:

• undergraduate courses, which include first degrees, first degrees with qualified teacher status, enhanced first degrees, first degrees obtained concurrently with a diploma, and intercalated first degrees (where first degree students, usually in medicine, dentistry or veterinary medicine, interrupt their studies to complete a one-year course of advanced studies in a related topic)

• other undergraduate courses, which include all other HE courses, for example Higher National Diplomas and Diplomas in HE

• postgraduate courses leading to higher degrees, diplomas and certificates, including postgraduate certificates of education (PGCE) and professional qualifications that usually require a first degree as entry qualification

As a result of the *1992 Further and Higher Education Act,* former polytechnics and some other HE institutions were designated as universities in 1992/93. Students normally attend HE courses at HE institutions, but some attend at further education colleges. In Scotland, around one-fifth of HE students study at a college. Some also attend institutions that do not receive public grants (such as the University of Buckingham) and these numbers are excluded from the tables.

Up to 2000/01 figures for HE students in Table 3.7 are annual snapshots taken around November or December each year, depending on the type of institution, except for further education colleges in Scotland from 1998/99, for which counts are based on the whole year. From 2001/02 figures for HE institutions are based on the Higher Education Statistics Agency (HESA) 'standard registration' count, and are not directly comparable with previous years. The Open University is included in these estimates.

Main categories of educational establishments

Educational establishments in the UK are administered and financed in several ways. Most schools are controlled by local authorities (LAs), which are part of the structure of local government, but some are 'assisted', receiving grants direct from central government sources and being controlled by governing bodies that have a substantial degree of autonomy. Completely outside the public sector are non-maintained schools run by individuals, companies or charitable institutions.

Up to March 2001, further education (FE) courses in FE sector colleges in England and Wales were largely funded through grants from the respective Further Education Funding Councils (FEFCs). In April 2001, however, the Learning and Skills Council (LSC) took over the responsibility for funding the FE sector in England, and the National Council for Education and Training for Wales (part of Education and Learning Wales – ELWa) did so for Wales. The LSC in England is also responsible for funding provision for FE and some non-prescribed higher education in FE sector colleges; in addition, it funds some FE provided by LA maintained and other institutions referred to as 'external institutions'. From April 2006 FE funding in Wales, became the responsibility of the Welsh Assembly Government. The Scottish Further and Higher Education Funding Council (SFC) funds FE colleges in Scotland, while the Department for Employment and Learning funds FE colleges in Northern Ireland.

Higher education (HE) courses in HE establishments are largely publicly funded through block grants from the HE funding councils in England and Scotland, the Higher Education Funding Council in Wales, and the Department for Employment and Learning in Northern Ireland. In addition, some designated HE, mainly Higher National Diplomas (HND)/ Higher National Certificates (HNC) is funded by these sources. The FE sources mentioned above fund the remainder.

Special educational needs (SEN) data

Information for England presented in Figure 3.5 is mainly drawn from two sources: the Schools' Census (SC) and the SEN2 Survey. Figures sourced from SC and the SEN2 Survey are not directly comparable.

The SC has collected information on pupils with special educational needs (SEN) on the census date in January from schools since 1985. It is completed by schools and records those pupils with and without statements who are educated at the school, regardless of which local authority (LA) is responsible. Figures for pupils with SEN without statements were collected from maintained primary and secondary schools for the first time in 1995.

The SEN2 Survey has collected information on children with statements on the census date in January and new statements made in the previous calendar year from LAs since 1984. SEN2 is completed by LAs and records those children for whom the LA is responsible (regardless of whether they are educated in the LA's own maintained schools, in schools in other LAs, in the non-maintained or independent sectors or educated other than at school).

In January 2002, the SC introduced a major change in that primary, secondary and special schools reported data at an individual pupil level for the first time. While the overall collection of pupil level data for these schools was successful, it is possible that some discontinuity in the time series data has resulted from this underlying

change in data collection. For instance, the national trend in SEN pupils with statements between 2001 and 2002 in SC is different from that shown in the SEN2 survey. While there are valid reasons as to why the figures will be different between these surveys, it is unusual for the trends to differ to this degree.

Joint Academic Coding System

The Joint Academic Coding System (JACS) was introduced into the Higher Education Statistics Agency (HESA) data collection in 2002/03 and forms the basis of the data presented in Table 3.8. This subject-based classification is used to classify subjects studied at UK higher education institutions and looks similar to that previously used by HESA (HESACODE), although it has been devised in a different way and therefore subject data between the two classifications are not comparable. The JACS system defines the principal subjects studied at UK higher education institutions and aggregates them into 19 headline subject areas, as shown in Table 3.8. The subject areas do not overlap and cover the entire range of principal subjects.

For more information on JACS, see the HESA website: www.hesa.ac.uk/index. php?option=com_content&task=view&id=1 58&Itemid=233

Qualifications

England, Wales and Northern Ireland
In England, Wales and Northern Ireland, the main examination for school pupils at the minimum school leaving age is the General Certificate of Secondary Education (GCSE), which can be taken in a wide range of subjects. This replaced the GCE O Level and Certificate of Secondary Education (CSE) examinations in 1987 (1988 in Northern Ireland). In England, Wales and Northern Ireland, the GCSE is awarded in eight grades, A* to G, the highest four (A* to C) being regarded as equivalent to O level grades A to C or CSE grade 1.

GCE A level is usually taken after a further two years of study beyond compulsory education in a sixth form or equivalent, passes being graded from A (the highest) to E (the lowest).

In September 2000 following the Qualifying for Success consultations in 1997, a number of reforms were introduced to the qualifications structure for young people aged 16 to 19. Under these reforms, students were encouraged to follow a wide range of subjects in their first year of post-16 study, with students expected to study four Advanced Subsidiaries (AS) before progressing three of them on to full A levels in their second year. New specifications introduced in 2001 are in place and A levels now comprise units, normally six for a full A level and three for the AS level, which is one-half a full A level. The full A level is normally taken either over two years (modular) or as a set of exams at the end of the two years (linear). In addition, students are encouraged to study a combination of both general and vocational advanced level examinations.

The AS qualification equates to the first year of study of a traditional A level, while the programmes of study in the second year of the full A level are called 'A2' and represent the

harder elements of the traditional A level. The AS is a qualification in its own right, whereas A2 modules do not make up a qualification in their own right, but when taken together with the AS units they comprise a full A level.

Scotland
In Scotland, National Qualifications (NQs) are offered to students. These include Standard Grades, National Courses and National Units. The Standard Grade is awarded in seven grades, through three levels of study: Credit (1 or 2), General (3 or 4) and Foundation (5 or 6). Students who do not achieve grade 1 to 6, but do complete the course, are awarded a grade 7. Standard Grade courses are made up of different parts called 'elements', with an exam at the end. National Courses are available at Intermediate, Higher and Advanced Higher levels, and consist of National Units that are assessed by the school/college, plus an external assessment. Grades are awarded on the basis of how well a student does in the external assessment, having passed all the National Units. Pass grades are awarded at A, B and C. Grade D is awarded to a student who just fails to get a grade C. Standard Grades 1 to 3 and Intermediate 2 grades A to C are equivalent to GCSE grades A* to C. Standard Grades 4 to 6, Intermediate 1 grades B to C or Access 3 (pass) are equivalent to grades D to G at GCSE level. Intermediate courses can be taken as an alternative to Standard Grade or as a stepping stone to Highers. Access units are assessed by the school/college, with no exam. Groups of units in a particular subject area can be built up at Access 2 and 3 to lead to 'cluster awards'. In Scotland, pupils generally sit Highers one year earlier than pupils in the rest of the UK sit A levels.

Vocational qualifications
After leaving school, people can study towards higher academic qualifications such as degrees. However, a large number of people choose to study towards qualifications aimed at a particular occupation or group of occupations – these qualifications are called vocational qualifications.

Vocational qualifications were initially split into three groups: National Vocational Qualifications (NVQs), General National Vocational Qualifications (GNVQs) and Vocationally Related Qualifications (VRQs), however GNVQs were phased out between 2005 and 2007.

- NVQs are based on an explicit statement of competence derived from an analysis of employment requirements. They are awarded at five levels. Scottish Vocational Qualifications (SVQs) are the Scottish equivalent

- GNVQs were a vocational alternative to GCSEs and GCE A levels. General Scottish Vocational Qualifications (GSVQs) were the Scottish equivalent. They were awarded at three levels: Foundation, Intermediate and Advanced, although Advanced GNVQs were subsequently redesigned and relaunched as Vocational A levels or, more formally, Advanced Vocational Certificates of Education (VCEs)

- there are a large number of other vocational qualifications, which are not NVQs, SVQs, (or former GNVQs or GSVQs). For example, a Business and Technology Education Council (BTEC) Higher National Diploma (HND) or a City & Guilds craft award

Other qualifications (including academic qualifications) are often expressed as being equivalent to a particular NVQ level so that comparisons can be easily made:

- an NVQ level 1 is equivalent to one or more GCSEs at grade G (but is lower than five GCSE grades A* to C), a BTEC general certificate, a Youth Training certificate, and to other Royal Society of Arts (RSA) and City & Guilds craft qualifications

- an NVQ level 2 is equivalent to five GCSEs at grades A* to C, a former Intermediate GNVQ, an RSA diploma, a City & Guilds craft or a BTEC first or general diploma

- an NVQ level 3 is equivalent to two A levels, a former Advanced GNVQ, an International Baccalaureate, an RSA advanced diploma, a City & Guilds advanced craft, an Ordinary National Diploma (OND) or Ordinary National Certificate (ONC) or a BTEC National Diploma

- an NVQ level 4 is equivalent to a first degree, an HND or HNC, a BTEC Higher Diploma, an RSA Higher Diploma, a nursing qualification or other higher education qualification below a higher degree

- an NVQ level 5 is equivalent to a higher degree

Table 3.12 includes Learning and Skills Council (LSC) funded training in England at different levels. The following table provides explanatory notes for each level.

Table 3.16 shows attainment of level 2 qualifications. Achievements in the following qualifications are counted at level 2+:

1 Advanced Extension Award equals 5 per cent

1 free standing mathematics qualification at level 3 equals 10 per cent

1 Key Skills pass at level 3 equals 20 per cent

1 short GCSE at grade A* to C equals 10 per cent

1 full GCSE at grade A* to C equals 20 per cent

1 Double Award GCSE (including vocational GCSEs) at grade A* to C equals 40 per cent

1 part 1 intermediate GNVQ equals 40 per cent

1 full intermediate GNVQ equals 80 per cent

1 AS level (including VCE) at grade A to E equals 50 per cent

1 A/A2 level (including VCE) at grade A to E equals 100 per cent

1 Advanced GNVQ pass equals 100 per cent

1 Advanced Pilot 6 unit GNVQ equals 100 per cent

1 NVQ pass at level 2 or higher equals 100 per cent

1 'full' VRQ2 pass at level 2 or higher equals 100 per cent

1 International Baccalaureate pass equals 100 per cent

1 Apprenticeship pass equals 100 per cent

Below level 2	This is activity funded by the LSC which is below level 2. This excludes any Skills for Life qualifications.
Skills for Life	This is measured by the number of adults aged 16 and over who improve their skills by at least one level through one of the following nationally approved qualifications:

- Certificates in adult literacy, numeracy or English for speakers of other languages (ESOL) Skills for Life at entry level 3, level 1 or level 2

- Key skills in communication or application of number at level 1 or level 2 (partial achievement of a key skills qualification counts where this is an achievement of a test)

- GCSEs in English or mathematics (grades A* to C = level 2, grades D to G = level 1)

Full level 2	The width of the level 2 aims is summed up to establish whether a learner is taking a full level 2 programme. This would include qualifications shown below in the table. Learners only count if the total width of their aims is 100 per cent or more – part level 2 learners are excluded, for example those taking 4 GCSEs.

Aim type	Percentage of full level 2
NVQ level 2	100 per cent
GNVQ Intermediate (part GNVQs constitute 40 per cent)	80 per cent
GCSE Double awards (including vocational GCSEs)	40 per cent
GCSE (including vocational GCSEs)	20 per cent
GCSE short courses	10 per cent
Other Vocationally Related Qualifications which are 80 per cent or more of a full level 2 (325 guided learning hours or more)	100 per cent
An apprenticeship at level 2 is counted as a full level 2.	

Full level 3	The width of the level 3 aims is summed up to establish whether a learner is taking a full level 3 programme. This would include qualifications shown below in the table. Learners only count if the total width of their aims is 100 per cent or more – part level 3 learners are excluded, for example those taking 2 AS level qualifications.

Aim type	Percentage of full level 3
AS Levels (including VCEs)	25 per cent
A/A2 levels (including VCEs)	50 per cent
Advanced GNVQ	100 per cent
Advanced pilot 6 unit GNVQ	100 per cent
NVQ level 3 or above	100 per cent
Other Vocationally Related Qualifications which are 80 per cent or more of a full level 2 (595 guided learning hours or more)	100 per cent
Advanced apprenticeships and Higher Level Apprenticeships are counted as full level 3	

Level 2	LSC-funded level 2 qualifications. This includes all learner that are doing full level 2 programmes as well as those that are doing part level 2 qualifications for example 1 GCSE.
Level 3	LSC-funded level 3 qualifications. This includes all learner that are doing full level 2 programmes as well as those that are doing part level 2 qualifications for example 1 AS level.
Level 4 and above	LSC-funded level 4 and above qualifications.

National Employers Skills Survey

The National Employers Skills Survey (NESS) is an annual series of employer surveys to investigate skills deficiencies and the role of workforce development among employers in England. The aim of the NESS study is to provide the Learning and Skills Council (LSC) and its partners with information on the current and future skill needs of employers in England, and how these needs vary by size of industry, occupation, region and local LSC areas.

In Figure 3.13 employers who had experienced skills gaps were asked to define what skills they felt needed improving for an occupation where staff were considered not fully proficient (if an establishment had two or more occupations with skills gaps then the occupation to be reported on was chosen at random from these).

Scottish Employers Skills Survey

The Scottish Employers Skills Survey (SESS) is a biennial series of employer surveys which aim to gather evidence on skills related issues. The aim of SESS is to help understand more fully from the employers' perspective how the labour and learning markets work.

The National Curriculum

England and Wales

Under the *Education Reform Act 1988*, a National Curriculum has been progressively introduced into primary and secondary schools in England and Wales (and a new primary curriculum is planned for introduction in September 2011). This consists of English (or the option of Welsh as a first language in Wales), mathematics and science. The second level of curriculum additionally comprises the so-called 'foundation' subjects, such as history, geography, art, music, information technology, design and technology, and physical education (and Welsh as a second language in Wales). The *Education Act 2002* extended the National Curriculum for England to include the foundation stage (see Stages of education above). It has six areas of learning:

- personal
- social and emotional development
- communication, language and literacy
- mathematical development
- knowledge and understanding of the world
- physical development and
- creative development

Measurable targets have been defined for the four Key Stages, corresponding to ages 7, 11, 14 and 16 (see above). Pupils are assessed formally at the ages of 7, 11 and 14 by a mixture of teacher assessments and by national tests (statutory testing at Key Stages 1 to 3 has been abolished in Wales with the last tests taking place in 2005 at Key Stage 3) in the core subjects of English, mathematics and science (and in Welsh speaking schools in Wales, Welsh as a first language), though the method varies between subjects and countries. Sixteen-year-olds are assessed by the GCSE examination. Statutory authorities have been set up for England and for Wales to advise the Government on the National Curriculum and promote curriculum development generally.

Expected attainment levels in England

England	Attainment expected
Key Stage 1	Level 2 or above
Key Stage 2	Level 4 or above
Key Stage 3	Level 5 or above
Key Stage 4	GCSE

Northern Ireland

Northern Ireland has its own common curriculum that is similar, but not identical, to the National Curriculum in England and Wales. Assessment arrangements in Northern Ireland

became statutory from September 1996 and Key Stage 1 pupils are assessed at age eight.

Scotland

In Scotland there is no statutory national curriculum. Responsibility for the management and delivery of the curriculum belongs to education authorities and head teachers. Pupils aged 5 to 14 study a broad curriculum based on national guidelines, which set out the aims of study, the ground to be covered and the way the pupils' learning should be assessed and reported. Progress is measured by attainment of six levels based on the expectation of the performance of the majority of pupils on completion of certain stages between the ages of 5 and 14: Primary 3 (age 7/8), Primary 4 (age 8 /9), Primary 7 (age 11/12) and Secondary 2 (age 13/14). It is recognised that pupils learn at different rates and some will reach the various levels before others.

The 5 to 14 curriculum areas in Scotland are:

- language
- mathematics
- environmental studies
- expressive arts
- religious and moral education with personal and social development and
- health education

In Secondary 3 and 4, it is recommended that the core curriculum of all pupils should include study within the following eight modes:

- language and communication
- mathematical studies and applications
- scientific studies and applications
- social and environmental studies
- technological activities and applications
- creative and aesthetic activities
- physical education and
- religious and moral education

For Secondary 5 and 6, these eight modes are important in structuring the curriculum, although each pupil is not expected to study under each mode but rather the curriculum will be negotiated. The Scottish curriculum 3 to 18 is being reviewed under *A Curriculum for Excellence*.

Classification of the Functions of Government (COFOG)

In 2007 Her Majesty's Treasury (HMT) changed the presentation of public expenditure statistical analysis (PESA) categories to bring analysis in closer alignment to the United Nations (UN) Classification of the Functions of Government (COFOG). COFOG describes the functions of government in ten categories (general public services; defence; public order and safety; economic affairs; environment protection; housing and community amenities; health; recreation, culture and religion; education; and social protection) and within these categories there is a further breakdown of the functions into sub-sets. Departmental expenditure is allocated to these sub-sets, which create the overall function categories.

For further details on the classification see: www.hm-treasury.gov.uk/pes_function.htm

Part 4: Labour market

Labour market statistics

For more information on labour market statistics, sources and analysis, including information about all aspects of the Office for National Statistics' labour market outputs, see the online *Guide to Labour Market Statistics* www.statistics.gov.uk/downloads/ theme_labour/guide_to_LMS_FR1.pdf

Labour Force Survey

The Labour Force Survey (LFS) is the largest regular household survey in the UK and much of the labour market data published are measured by the LFS. The concepts and definitions used in the LFS are those agreed by the International Labour Organisation (ILO). The definitions are used by European Union (EU) member states and members of the Organisation for Economic Co-operation and Development.

The LFS results refer to people resident in private households and some non-private accommodation in the UK. For most people residence at an address is unambiguous. People with more than one address are counted as resident at the sample address if they regard that as their main residence. The following are also counted as being resident at an address:

- people who normally live there, but are on holiday, away on business, or in hospital, unless they have been living away from the address for six months or more;
- children aged 16 and under, even if they are at boarding or other schools; and
- students aged 16 and over are counted as resident at their normal term-time address even if it is vacation time and they may be away from it.

People resident in two categories of non-private accommodation are also included in the LFS sample, namely those in NHS accommodation (which used to be called nurses' homes), and students in halls of residence. Students are included through the parental home.

On 22 August 2007 the Office for National Statistics (ONS) published the 2006-based mid-year population estimates for the UK and on 13 September 2007 ONS published the 2006 quarter 2 (Q2) experimental quarterly population estimates for England and Wales. These revised population estimates have been incorporated into LFS sourced tables and figures in the chapter. For more information see: www.statistics.gov.uk/pdfdir/lmsuk0808.pdf

An EU requirement exists whereby all member states must conduct a labour force survey based on calendar quarters. The UK LFS complied with this from May 2006. The survey previously used seasonal quarters where, for example, the March–May months covered the spring quarter, June–August was summer and so forth. This has now changed to calendar quarters where microdata are available for January–March (Q1), April–June (Q2), July–September (Q3) and October–December (Q4).

ONS has produced a set of historical estimates covering the monthly periods between 1971 and 1991, which are fully consistent with post-1992 annual LFS data. The data cover headline measures of employment, unemployment, economic activity, economic inactivity and hours worked. These estimates were published on an experimental basis in 2003 and following further user consultation and quality assurance, these estimates were made National Statistics. As such, they represent ONS's best estimate of the headline labour market series over this period. The labour market chapter uses data from these estimates only where headline data are reported since the historical estimates are not yet available for subgroups of the population, other than by sex and for key age groups.

Annual Population Survey

The Annual Population Survey (APS) was introduced in 2004. The APS included all the data of the annual local area Labour Force Survey (LFS) in the UK, as well as a further sample boost aimed at achieving a minimum number of economically active respondents in the sample in each local authority district in England. This sample boost was withdrawn after 2005. The first APS covered the calendar year 2004, rather than the annual local area LFS period of March to February.

Also, the annual local area LFS data are published only once a year, whereas the APS data are published quarterly, with each publication including a year's data. Like the local area LFS data set, the APS data are published by local authority area. However, the APS data contain an enhanced range of variables providing a greater level of detail than the LFS about the resident household population of an area, in particular on ethnic group, health and sex.

For more information on local area labour market statistics, see: 'Local area labour markets: statistical indicators July 2008': **www.statistics.gov.uk/StatBase/Product. asp?vlnk=14160**

Eurostat rates

There are differences between Eurostat and the Office for National Statistics in the age bases used in calculating published employment rates:

Employed persons are persons:

- aged 15 year and over (16 and over in Spain, UK and Sweden (1995–2001); 15 to 74 year-olds in Denmark, Estonia, Hungary, Latvia, Finland and Sweden (from 2001 onwards),

- who during the reference week performed work, even for just one hour a week, for pay, profit or family gain,

- who were not at work but had a job or business from which they were temporarily absent because of, e.g., illness, holidays, industrial dispute or education and training.

The employment rates published by Eurostat refer to people in the age group 15 to 64 with

the exception of Spain and the UK which are for people aged 16 to 64.

For more information see: **epp.eurostat.ec. europa.eu/portal/page/portal/employment_ unemployment_lfs/methodology/definitions**

Accession to the European Union (EU)

Until 1973 the European Economic Community (EEC) consisted of 6 member states: Belgium, France, West Germany, Italy, Luxembourg and the Netherlands. In 1973, three more states joined – Denmark, Ireland and the United Kingdom. Greece joined the EEC in 1981, followed by Portugal and Spain in 1986.

In 1995 the EEC became the European Union, and membership grew again with Austria, Finland and Sweden joining to make the EU-15. In May 2004, a further ten states joined the EU (EU-25): Cyprus, the Czech Republic, Estonia, Hungary, Latvia, Lithuania, Malta, Poland, the Slovak Republic, and Slovenia. Cyprus and Malta already had close links with the UK, having only gained independence from the UK in 1960 and 1964 and so for the purpose of some analyses the remaining eight countries: the Czech Republic, Estonia, Hungary, Latvia, Lithuania, Poland, the Slovak Republic, and Slovenia are sometimes grouped together as the A8. Finally, in January 2007, Bulgaria and Romania joined the EU (EU-27).

Standard Occupational Classification 2000 (SOC2000)

The Standard Occupational Classification (SOC) was first published in 1990 (SOC90) to replace both the Classification of Occupations 1980, and the Classification of Occupations and Dictionary of Occupational Titles. SOC90 was revised and updated in 2000 to produce SOC2000. There is no exact correspondence between SOC90 and SOC2000 at any level.

The two main concepts that SOC2000 is used to investigate are:

- kind of work performed and

- the competent performance of the tasks and duties

The structure of SOC2000 is four-tier covering:

- major groups/numbers
- sub-major groups/numbers
- minor groups/numbers and
- unit groups/numbers (occupations)

For example, the group/number breakdown for the occupation of a chemist is as follows:

major group	2	Professional occupations
sub-major group	21	Science and technology professionals
minor group	211	Science professionals
unit group	2111	Chemists

SOC2000 comprises 9 major groups, 25 sub-major groups, 81 minor groups and 353

unit groups (occupations). The major groups are:

- managers and senior officials
- professional occupations
- associate professional and technical occupations
- administrative and secretarial occupations
- skilled trades occupations
- personal service occupations
- sales and customer service occupations
- process, plant and machine operatives
- elementary occupations

For more information on SOC2000 see: **www.statistics.gov.uk/methods_quality/ ns_sec/soc2000.asp**

Standard Industrial Classification 2003 (SIC2003)

A Standard Industrial Classification (SIC) was first introduced into the UK in 1948 for use in classifying business establishments and other statistical units by the type of economic activity in which they are engaged. The classification provides a framework for the collection, tabulation, presentation and analysis of data and its use promotes uniformity. In addition, it can be used for administrative purposes and by non-government bodies as a convenient way of classifying industrial activities into a common structure.

Since 1948 the classification has been revised in 1958, 1968, 1980, 1992 and 2003. Table 4.8 uses SIC2003. Revision is necessary because over time new products and the new industries to produce them emerge, and shifts of emphasis occur in existing industries. It is not always possible for the system to accommodate such developments and so the classification is updated.

For further information about SIC see: **www.statistics.gov.uk/methods_quality/sic/ downloads/UK_SIC_Vol1(2003).pdf**

Public sector employment

Public sector employment comprises employment in central government, local government and public corporations as defined for the UK National Accounts. Data are collected from public sector organisations through the Quarterly Public Sector Employment Survey by the Office for National Statistics and other sources. Employment estimates for the private sector are derived as the difference between Labour Force Survey employment estimates for the whole economy (not seasonally adjusted) and the public sector employment estimates.

The public sector employment estimates given in Figure 4.9 include a number of workers with a second job in the public sector whose main job is in the private sector or in a separate public sector organisation. The private sector estimate will thus tend to be correspondingly understated by a small percentage.

Flexible working arrangements

The Labour Force Survey asks questions of all respondents in employment (excluding those on college based schemes) whether they have a flexible working arrangement. The categories are defined as below:

Flexible working hours
Employees can vary their daily start and finish times each day. Over an accounting period (usually four weeks or a calendar month) debit and credit hours can be carried over into another accounting period. Variable start and finish times on their own are not enough for a flexitime system. There must also be a formal accounting period.

Annualised hours contract
The number of hours an employee has to work are calculated over a full year. Instead of, e.g. 40 hours per week, employees are contracted to e.g. 1900 hours per year (after allowing for leave and other entitlements). Longer hours are worked over certain parts of the year and shorter hours at other periods. Variations in hours are related to seasonal factors or fluctuation in demand for the companies' goods or services.

Term-time working
Employees work during the school or college term. Unpaid leave is taken during the school holidays, although their pay may be spread equally over the year.

Job sharing
This is a type of part time working. A full-time job is divided between, usually, two people. The job sharers work at different times, although there may be a changeover period.

Nine day fortnight
This involves individual employees having one day off every other week. The actual day off may vary so long as the employee keeps to an alternating pattern of one five day week followed by one four day week. A nine day fortnight working arrangement involves two five day working weeks being compressed into fewer full days. Such arrangements refer to full-time working only.

Four and a half day week
Typically this involves the normal working week finishing early on Fridays. The short day need not necessarily be Friday, but this is the most obvious and common day. A four and a half day week working arrangement involves the five day working week being compressed into fewer full days. Such arrangements refer to full-time working only.

Zero hours contract
Where an employee is not contracted to work a set number of hours, and is only paid for the number of hours that they actually work.

Job separations

The job separation rate is the number of working-age people who separated from a paid job in the three months before interview divided by the number of people who said they were in employment for more than three months, plus those who had separated from a paid job.

The Labour Force Survey (LFS) asks respondents whether they have left a paid job in the past three months and then finds out the reasons for leaving that job. These reasons are usually grouped into two employee-centric categories: voluntary separations; and involuntary

separations to reflect the dynamics of labour supply and demand.

Involuntary separations
Dismissed
Made redundant/voluntary redundancy
Temporary job finished

Voluntary separations
Resigned
Gave up work for health reasons
Gave up work for family or personal reasons
Took early retirement
Retirement at or after state pension age
Other reason

Voluntary redundancy and the termination of a temporary job are seen as involuntary separations as they are symptoms of a contraction in labour demand. Early retirement is a slightly ambiguous category to place in the voluntary group, as in some cases it may also be used by employers as a tool to shed jobs in times of labour demand contraction. However, it is assumed that in the majority of cases it is the normal retirement age of the organisation which is early and therefore not related to labour demand (for example public sector areas such as the police, civil service, fire brigade, armed forces).

Model-based estimates of unemployment

On 28 July 2006 the Office for National Statistics launched model-based estimates of unemployment for unitary and local authorities as National Statistics. These estimates are the best available for total unemployment in these areas. For local areas, even the annual local area Labour Force Survey or Annual Population Survey have small samples. This means that estimates for these areas are likely to be less reliable than those for larger areas, since the sampling variability is high. In particular, this affects estimates of events that are uncommon, like unemployment. A statistical model was developed to provide reliable unemployment estimates for all local authorities.

For more information, see: 'Local area labour markets: statistical indicators July 2009':
www.statistics.gov.uk/downloads/theme_labour/LALM_statistical_indicators_Jul09.pdf

Labour disputes

Statistics of stoppages of work caused by labour disputes in the UK relate to disputes connected with terms and conditions of employment. Small stoppages involving fewer than ten workers or lasting less than one day are excluded from the statistics unless the aggregate number of working days lost in the dispute is 100 or more. Disputes not resulting in a stoppage of work are not included in the statistics.

Workers involved and working days lost relate to persons both directly and indirectly involved (unable to work although not parties to the dispute) at the establishments where the disputes occurred. People laid off and working days lost at establishments not in dispute, for example because of resulting shortages of supplies, are excluded.

There are difficulties in ensuring complete recording of stoppages, in particular for short

disputes lasting only a day or so, or involving only a few workers. Any under-recording would affect the total number of stoppages much more than the number of working days lost.

For more information, see 'Labour disputes in 2008' see:
www.statistics.gov.uk/elmr/06_09/downloads/ELMR_Jun09_Hale.pdf

Employment tribunals

The Employment tribunals are independent judiciary bodies who determine disputes between employers and employees over employment rights in Great Britain. An Employment tribunal is like a court but it is not as formal. However, like a court it must act independently and cannot give legal advice. Almost all hearings are open to the public.

The figures quoted in Table 4.22 are for jurisdictions. The Tribunals service report also shows the number of claims which is lower than the number of jurisdictions as one claim may be brought under more than one jurisdiction. Jurisdictions include unfair dismissal, redundancy payments and discrimination.

For more information about jurisdictions see:
www.employmenttribunals.gov.uk/FormsGuidance/jurisdictionList.htm

Part 5: Income and wealth

Household income data sources

The data for the household sector as derived from the National Accounts have been compiled according to the definitions and conventions set out in the European System of Accounts 1995 (ESA95). Estimates for the household sector cannot be separated from the sector for non-profit institutions serving households and so the data in *Social Trends* cover both sectors. The most obvious example of a non-profit institution is a charity. This sector also includes many other organisations of which universities, trade unions, and clubs and societies are the most important. Non-profit making bodies receive income mainly in the form of property income (that is, investment income) and of other current receipts. The household sector differs from the personal sector, as defined in the National Accounts prior to the introduction of ESA95, in that it excludes unincorporated private businesses apart from sole traders. The household sector also includes people living in institutions such as nursing homes, as well as people living in private households. More information is given in *United Kingdom National Accounts Concepts, Sources and Methods* published by The Stationery Office and is available on the Office for National Statistics (ONS) website: www.statistics.gov.uk/downloads/theme_economy/Concepts_Sources_&_Methods.pdf

In ESA95, household income includes the value of national insurance contributions and pension contributions made by employers on behalf of their employees. It also shows property income (that is, income from investments) net of payments of interest on loans. In both these respects, national accounts' conventions diverge from those normally used when collecting data on household income from household surveys.

Employees are usually unaware of the value of the national insurance contributions and pension contributions made on their behalf by their employer, and so such data are rarely collected. Payments of interest are usually regarded as items of expenditure rather than reductions of income. In Figure 5.7, household income excludes employers' national insurance and pension contributions and includes property income gross of payment of interest on loans, to correspond more closely with the definition generally used in household surveys.

Survey sources differ from the National Accounts in a number of other important respects. They cover the population living in households and some cover certain parts of the population living in institutions such as nursing homes, but all exclude non-profit making institutions. Survey sources are also subject to under-reporting and non-response bias. In the case of household income surveys, investment income is commonly underestimated, as is income from self-employment. All these factors mean that the survey data on income used in most of this chapter are not entirely consistent with the National Accounts household sector data.

Purchasing power parities

The international spending power of sterling depends both on market exchange rates and on the ratios of prices between the UK and other countries. Purchasing power parities (PPPs) are indicators of price level differences across countries. PPPs tell us how many currency units a given quantity of goods and services costs in different countries. PPPs can thus be used as currency conversion rates to convert expenditures expressed in national currencies into an artificial common currency (the Purchasing Power Standard, PPS), eliminating the effect of price level differences across countries.

The main use of PPPs is to convert national accounts aggregates, like the gross domestic product (GDP) of different countries, into comparable volume aggregates. Applying nominal exchange rates in this process would overestimate the GDP of countries with high price levels relative to countries with low price levels. The use of PPPs ensures that the GDP of all countries is valued at a uniform price level and thus reflects only differences in the actual volume of the economy.

PPPs are also applied in analyses of relative price levels across countries. For this purpose, the PPPs are divided by the current nominal exchange rate to obtain a price level index (PLI) which expresses the price level of a given country relative to another, or relative to a group of countries like the EU-27; more information is available at: **epp.eurostat.ec.europa.eu/ portal/page/portal/purchasing_power_ parities/introduction**

Households Below Average Income (HBAI)

Information on the distribution of income based on the Family Resources Survey is provided in the Department for Work and Pensions (DWP) publication *Households Below Average Income:1994/95 –2007/08,* available both in hard copy and on the DWP website:

research.dwp.gov.uk/asd/hbai/hbai2008/ contents.asp This publication provides estimates of patterns of personal disposable income in the UK, and of changes in income over time. It attempts to measure people's potential living standards as determined by disposable income. Although as the title would suggest, HBAI concentrates on the lower part of the income distribution, it also provides estimates covering the whole of the income distribution.

In 2002/03, the Family Resources Survey was extended to cover Northern Ireland. Data presented from 2002/03 cover the UK rather than Great Britain. NI data have been imputed back to 1998/99, and for aggregate time series, estimates are shown for Great Britain up to 1997/98 and for the UK since 1998/99. Estimates for the UK are very similar to those for Great Britain.

Disposable household income includes all flows of income into the household, principally earnings, benefits, occupational and private pensions, and investments. It is net of tax, employees' national insurance contributions, council tax, contributions to occupational pension schemes (including additional voluntary contributions), maintenance and child support payments, and parental contributions to students living away from home.

Two different measures of disposable income are used in HBAI: before and after housing costs are deducted. This is principally to take into account variations in housing costs that do not correspond to comparable variations in the quality of housing. Housing costs consist of rent, water rates, community charges, mortgage interest payments, structural insurance, ground rent and service charges.

HBAI estimates for 1979 to 1993/94 inclusive have been derived from the Family Expenditure Survey. This survey was conducted on a calendar year basis from 1979 to 1993, and on a financial year basis from 1993/94 onwards. Because of the relatively small sample size of this survey, from 1988 onwards data from two survey years have been pooled to produce HBAI estimates. From 1994/95 onwards, the data source is the Family Resources Survey which is conducted on a financial year basis.

Equivalisation scales

In the analysis of income distribution it is customary to adjust household income using an equivalence scale to take into account variations in the size and composition of households. This reflects the common sense notion that a household of five adults will need a higher income than will a single person living alone to enjoy a comparable standard of living. An overall equivalence value is calculated for each household by summing the appropriate scale values for each household member. Equivalised household income is then calculated by dividing household income by the household's equivalence value. The scales conventionally take a couple as the reference point with an equivalence value of one; equivalisation therefore tends to increase relatively the incomes of single person households (since their incomes are divided by a value of less than one) and to reduce incomes of households with three or more persons.

OECD equivalence scales:

Household member	Before housing costs	After housing costs
First adult	0.67	0.58
Spouse	0.33	0.42
Other second adult	0.33	0.42
Third adult	0.33	0.42
Subsequent adults	0.33	0.42
Children aged under 14 years	0.20	0.20
Children aged 14 years and over	0.33	0.42

McClements equivalence scales:

Household member	Before housing costs	After housing costs
First adult (head)	0.61	0.55
Spouse of head	0.39	0.45
Other second adult	0.46	0.45
Third adult	0.42	0.45
Subsequent adults	0.36	0.40
Each dependant aged:		
0–1	0.09	0.07
2–4	0.18	0.18
5–7	0.21	0.21
8–10	0.23	0.23
11–12	0.25	0.26
13–15	0.27	0.28
16 years and over	0.36	0.38

From 2007, the Department for Work and Pensions (DWP) changed from using the McClements equivalence scales to the Organisation for Economic Co-operation and Development (OECD) equivalence scales in their analysis of the income distribution. For further information see *Households Below Average Income 1994/95–2007/08* available on the DWP website: **research.dwp.gov.uk/asd/hbai/hbai2008/pdf_files/full_hbai09.pdf**

The McClements equivalence scales are still used by DWP to produce the persistent poverty estimates from the British Household Panel Survey (BHPS). The BHPS raw data are supplied by the Institute for Social and Economic Research (ISER). Both the OECD and McClements scales exist in two versions, one for adjusting incomes before housing costs and one for adjusting income after housing costs.

The change from the McClements to the OECD equivalence scale has meant that it is no longer possible to present as long a time series in *Social Trends* as has been presented in previous editions. A full time series is available from 1987 onwards, and estimates are also available for 1979 and 1981.

The McClements scale has also been used to adjust income in Figure 5.14.

Net wealth of the household sector

The National Accounts compiles aggregate data on the wealth of the household sector in the UK. Revised balance sheet estimates of the net wealth of the household (and non-profit institutions) sector were published in an article in *Economic Trends* November 1999 **www.statistics.gov.uk/cci/article.asp?ID=41&Pos=1&ColRank=1&Rank=1**

These figures are based on the new international system of national accounting and incorporate data from new sources. Quarterly estimates of net financial wealth (excluding tangible and intangible assets) are published in *Financial Statistics*.

Figures regarding the distribution of wealth among households are derived from the Wealth and Assets Survey (WAS). Results from the 2006/08 WAS are for Great Britain; wave 1 of the survey covers the period July 2006 to June 2008. Over the two year period the WAS achieved a sample size of 30,595 private households. Grossed to the population, this represents 24,580,000 households. The wealth estimates in this report are derived by adding up the value of different types of asset owned by households, and subtracting any liabilities. The report presents two different totals: total wealth with and without pension wealth.

Information is presented both at aggregate level (for Great Britain as a whole) and at household level. Total wealth with pension wealth is the sum of four components:

- net property wealth
- physical wealth
- net financial wealth
- private pension wealth

Total wealth without pension wealth is the sum of three components: net property wealth, physical wealth and net financial wealth.

The components are, in turn, made up of smaller building blocks:

- Net property wealth is the sum of all property values minus value of all mortgages and value of amounts owed as a result of equity release

- Physical wealth is the sum of values of household contents, collectables and valuables, and vehicles (including personalised number plates)

- Gross financial wealth is the sum of values of formal and informal financial assets, plus value of assets held in the names of children, plus value of endowments purchased to repay mortgages.

Household reference person

The definition of household reference person (HRP) adopted in this chapter is the one used by DWP for FRS and HBAI.

The HRP is classified as the highest income householder (HIH); without regard to gender.

In a single adult household:

- The HIH is the sole householder (i.e. the person in whose name the accommodation is owned or rented).

If there are two or more householders:

- The HIH is the householder with the highest personal income from all sources.

If there are two or more householders who have the same income

- The HIH is the eldest householder

Retail prices index

The retail prices index (RPI) is the most long-standing measure of inflation in the UK. It measures the average change from month to month in the prices of goods and services purchased by most households in the UK. The spending pattern on which the index is based is revised each year, mainly using information from the Living Costs and Food Survey (LCF, see above). It covers the goods and services purchased by private households, excluding:

- high income households, defined as those households with a total income within the top 4 per cent of all households, as measured by each quarter's LCF; and

- 'pensioner' households, which derive at least three-quarters of their total income from state pensions and benefits

It is considered that such households are likely to have atypical spending patterns and so including them in the scope of the RPI would distort the overall average. Expenditure patterns of one person and two person 'pensioner' households differ from those of the households that the RPI is based on. Separate indices have been compiled for such pensioner households since 1969, and quarterly averages are published in *Focus on Consumer Price Indices*, available on the National Statistics website. They are chained indices constructed in the same way as the RPI. It should, however, be noted that the pensioner indices exclude housing costs.

A guide to the RPI can be found on the National Statistics website: **www.statistics.gov.uk/rpi**

Earnings surveys

The Annual Survey of Hours and Earnings (ASHE) replaced the New Earnings Survey (NES) from October 2004. ASHE improves on NES by extending the coverage of the survey sample, introducing weighting and publishing estimates of quality for all survey outputs. The new survey methodology produces weighted estimates, using weights calculated by calibrating the survey responses to totals from the Labour Force Survey by occupation, sex, region and age. It also focuses on median levels of pay rather than the mean. The ASHE survey sample design was improved to include employees who have either changed or started new jobs between the survey sample identification and the survey reference date. Full details of the methodology of ASHE can be found on the ONS website at: **www.statistics.gov.uk/articles/nojournal/ASHEMethod_article.pdf**

Back series using ASHE methodology applied to NES data sets are available for 1997 to 2004 at: **www.statistics.gov.uk/statbase/Product.asp?vlnk=13101**

Because it was not possible to impute for the supplementary information collected in ASHE in the NES data sets, data for 2004 are available on two bases: estimates excluding supplementary information, which are comparable with the 1997 to 2003 back series, and estimates including supplementary information, which are comparable with 2005 onwards.

A small number of methodological changes were also introduced in 2007 to improve the quality of ASHE results. These include changes to the sample design as well as the introduction of an automatic occupation coding tool. These changes were also taken back to 2006 so that data for 2006 are available on two bases: estimates for 2006 comparable with 2004 and 2005, and estimates for 2006 comparable with 2007 onwards.

Gini coefficient

The Gini coefficient is the most widely used summary measure of the degree of inequality in an income distribution. The first step is to rank the distribution in ascending order. The coefficient can then best be understood by considering a graph of the cumulative income share against the cumulative share of households – the Lorenz curve. This would take the form of a diagonal line for complete equality where all households had the same income, while complete inequality, where one household received all the income and the remainder received none, would be represented by a curve comprising the horizontal axis and the right-hand vertical axis. The area between the Lorenz curve and the diagonal line of complete equality and inequality gives the value of the Gini coefficient. As inequality increases (and the Lorenz curve bellies out) so does the Gini coefficient until it reaches its maximum value of 100 with complete inequality.

Part 6: Expenditure

Household expenditure

The estimates of household final consumption expenditure that appear in the National

Accounts measure expenditure on goods and services by UK residents. This includes the value of income in kind; imputed rent for owner-occupied dwellings; and the purchase of second-hand goods less the proceeds of sales of used goods. Excluded are interest and other transfer payments; all business expenditure; and the purchase of land and buildings (and associated costs).

Expenditure is classified according to the internationally recognised Classification of Individual Consumption by Purpose (COICOP), which has 12 categories of household expenditure:

- food and non-alcoholic beverages
- alcoholic beverages and tobacco
- clothing and footwear
- housing, water and fuel
- household goods and services
- health
- transport
- communication
- recreation and culture
- education
- restaurants and hotels
- miscellaneous goods and services

In addition, household final consumption expenditure includes expenditure by UK resident households that takes place abroad, and excludes expenditure by non-residents in the UK.

Estimates of household final consumption expenditure are produced using a range of data sources. Both value and volume estimates are available, which provide reliable information about how expenditure has changed over time.

Until September 2003 UK economic growth was calculated using 'fixed base aggregation'. Under this method the detailed estimates for growth for different parts of the economy were summed to a total by weighting each component according to its share of total expenditure in 1995. The year from which this information was drawn was updated at five-yearly intervals. Since September 2003 UK economic growth has been calculated by 'annual chain-linking'. This uses information updated every year to give each component the most relevant weight that can be estimated. This method has been used for estimating change in household expenditure since 1971.

For further details see Consumer Trends at: www.statistics.gov.uk/consumertrends

Living Costs and Food Survey

Estimates of household expenditure are also available directly from the Living Costs and Food Survey (LCF) (formerly known as the Expenditure and Food Survey – EFS and the Family Expenditure Survey – FES) and are published in Family Spending. The LCF covers all private households (that is, it excludes people living in institutions such as prisons, retirement homes or in student accommodation) and provides information about how expenditure patterns differ across different types of households. However, unlike the National Accounts estimates

(see 'Household expenditure' above), only estimates of the value of expenditure are available (that is, current price estimates) and the survey results are not intended to be used to measure change over time.

The EFS was created in April 2001, by merging the Family Expenditure Survey (FES) with the National Food Survey (NFS). The LCF continues to produce the information previously provided by the FES. From January 2006 survey results are published for calendar years (rather than financial years), in anticipation of the integration of the LCF within the Continuous Population Survey (CPS).

The LCF also uses the Classification of Individual Consumption by Purpose (COICOP, see above), although the definition of household expenditure is not exactly the same as that used in the National Accounts. For example, there are some differences in the treatment of housing-related expenditure. Within the National Accounts, an estimate of imputed rent for owner-occupied dwellings is included in the category 'Housing, water and fuel'. Results from the EFS do not include imputed rent for owner occupiers but mortgage interest payments are included in an additional category 'Other expenditure items'.

For further details see Family Spending at: www.statistics.gov.uk/familyspending

Consumer prices index

The consumer prices index (CPI) is the main measure of inflation used within the Government's monetary policy framework. Prior to 10 December 2003, this index was published as the harmonised index of consumer prices.

The methodology of the CPI is similar to that of the RPI but differs in the following ways:

- in the CPI, the geometric mean is used to aggregate the prices at the most basic level, whereas the RPI uses arithmetic means

- a number of RPI series are excluded from the CPI, most particularly, those mainly relating to owner occupiers' housing costs (for example, mortgage interest payments, house depreciation, council tax and buildings insurance)

- the coverage of the CPI indices is based on the Classification of Individual Consumption by Purpose (COICOP, see above), whereas the RPI uses its own bespoke classification

- the CPI includes series for university accommodation fees, foreign students' university tuition fees, unit trust and stockbrokers charges, none of which are included in the RPI

- the index for new car prices in the RPI is imputed from movements in second-hand car prices, whereas the CPI uses a quality adjusted index based on published prices of new cars

- the CPI weights are based on expenditure by all private households, foreign visitors to the UK and residents of institutional households. In the RPI, weights are based on expenditure by private households only, excluding the highest income households, and pensioner households mainly dependent on state benefits

- in the construction of the RPI weights, expenditure on insurance is assigned to the relevant insurance heading. For the CPI weights, the amount paid out in insurance claims is distributed among the COICOP headings according to the nature of the claims expenditure with the residual (that is, the service charge) being allocated to the relevant insurance heading

A guide to the CPI can be found on the National Statistics website: www.statistics.gov.uk/cpi

Internationally, the CPI is known as the harmonised index of consumer prices (HICP). HICPs are calculated in each member state of the European Union (EU-27), according to rules specified in a series of European regulations developed by Eurostat in conjunction with the EU member states. HICPs are used to compare inflation rates across the EU-27. Since January 1999 the European Central Bank (ECB) has used HICPs as the measure of price stability across the euro area.

Further details can be found on the ECB website: www.ecb.int/mopo/html/index.en.html

CPI estimates for years prior to 1996 had to be estimated using available data sources. For 1988 to 1995 the CPI was estimated from archived RPI price quotes and historical weights data, and aggregated up to the published COICOP weights. Therefore, the estimated CPI is based on the RPI household population and not all private households, and it does not account for all items included in the official CPI.

For more information about how these historical estimates were produced see the 'Harmonised Index of Consumer Prices: Historical Estimates' paper in Economic Trends, no. 541.

Part 7: Health

Expectation of life

The expectation of life is the average total number of years that a person of that age could be expected to live, if the rates of mortality at each age were those experienced in that year. The mortality rates that underlie the expectation of life figures are based, up to 2008, on total deaths occurring in each year for England and Wales, and total deaths registered in each year for Scotland and Northern Ireland.

Standardised rates

Directly age-standardised incidence rates enable comparisons to be made between geographical areas over time, and between the sexes, which are independent of changes in the age structure of the population. In each year the crude rates in each five-year age group are multiplied by the European standard population (see table below) for that age group. These are then summed and divided by the total standard population for these age groups to give an overall standardised rate.

International Classification of Diseases

The International Classification of Diseases (ICD) is a coding scheme for diseases and causes of death. The Tenth Revision of the ICD (ICD10) was introduced for coding the underlying cause of death in Scotland from 2000 and in the rest

International Classification of Diseases for cancers, Ninth and Tenth Revisions

ICD 9			ICD10	
Code 151	Stomach		C16	Stomach
Code 153	Colon		C18	Colon
Code 154	Rectum		C19–C20	Rectum
Code 153, 154	Colorectal		C18–C20	Colorectal
Code 162	Lung		C34	Lung
Code 174	Breast		C50	Breast
Code 179	Uterus		C54	Uterus
Code 183	Ovary		C56	Ovary
Code 185	Prostate		C61	Prostate
Code 188	Bladder		C67	Bladder
C00–C97	(excluding C44 All malignant cancers excluding non-melanoma skin cancer)			

of the UK from 2001. The causes of death included in Figure 7.2 correspond to the following ICD10 codes: circulatory diseases I00–I99: cancer C00–D48: and respiratory diseases J00–J99. Rates for 2000 are for England and Wales only.

The data presented in Figure 7.9 cover three different revisions of the ICD. Although they have been selected according to the codes that are comparable, there may still be differences between years that are the result of changes in the rules used to select the underlying cause of death. This can be seen in deaths from respiratory diseases where different interpretation of these rules were used to code the underlying cause of death from 1983 to 1992, and from 2001 onwards in England and Wales, and 2000 onwards in Scotland.

The cancer trends data presented in Figure 7.9 and Table 7.10 correspond to the following two sets of cancer specific ICD9 and ICD10 codes. ICD9 codes correspond to the period up to 1994, ICD10 codes correspond to the period from 1995 when the coding for cancer incidence was changed.

European standard population

The age distribution of the European standard population is presented in the table below. See also Standardised rates.

European standard population

Age	Population
Under 1	1,600
1–4	6,400
5–9	7,000
10–14	7,000
15–19	7,000
20–24	7,000
25–29	7,000
30–34	7,000
35–39	7,000
40–44	7,000
45–49	7,000
50–54	7,000
55–59	6,000
60–64	5,000
65–69	4,000
70–74	3,000
75–79	2,000
80–84	1,000
85 and over	1,000
Total	100,000

MRSA

International Classification of Diseases codes relating specifically to *Staphylococcus* infection are presented below.

International Classification of Diseases for *Staphylococcus*, tenth revision

Code	Text
A05.0	Food borne staphylococcal intoxication
A41.0–A41.2	Septicaemia due to *Staphylococcus aureus*/other specified staphylococcus/ unspecified staphylococcus
A49.0	Staphylococcal infection, unspecified
B95.6–B95.8	Staphylococcus aureus/other staphylococcus/unspecified Staphylococcus as the cause of diseases classified to other chapters
G00.3	Staphylococcal meningitis
J15.2	Pneumonia due to Staphylococcus
L00	Staphylococcal scalded skin syndrome
M00.0	Staphylococcal arthritis and polyarthritis
P23.2	Congenital pneumonia due to staphylococcus
P36.2	Sepsis of newborn due to *staphylococcus aureus*

Age-standardised survival rates

Relative survival varies with age at diagnosis, and the age profile of cancer patients changes with time, so the overall (all ages) survival estimates are age-standardised using standard weights to improve their comparability over time: see Chapter 3 of *Cancer Survival Trends in England and Wales 1971–1995: deprivation and NHS Region. Studies on Medical and Population Subjects No. 61* (Coleman MP and Babb P, Damiecki P, Grosclaude P, Honjo S, Jones J, Knerer G, Pitard A, Quinn MJ, Sloggett A and De Stavola B L (1999), London: The Stationery Office, 1999.

Breast and Cervical cancer screening target population

The screening programme among constituent countries of the UK differs among their target population invited for screening. For breast cancer screening the target population in England, Scotland and Northern Ireland is women aged 50–64 years screened in the previous three years, while in Wales the target population is women aged 53–64 years.

For England and Northern Ireland the target population for cervical cancer screening relates to women aged 25–64, for Wales 20–64 and for Scotland to women aged 20–60 years screened in the previous five years (five and a half years in Scotland).

Alcohol consumption

Estimates of alcohol consumption in surveys are given in standard units derived from assumptions about the alcohol content of different types of drink, combined with information from the respondent about the volume drunk. Following recent changes to the type of alcoholic drinks available, the alcohol content of drinks, and variable quantities, it became necessary to reconsider the assumptions made in obtaining estimates of alcohol consumption.

The changes in conversion factor are discussed in detail in a paper in the National Statistics Methodology series, which also includes a table giving the original and updated factors for converting alcohol volume to units. See Goddard E (2007) *Estimating alcohol consumption from survey data: updated method of converting volumes to units*, National Statistics Methodology Series NSM 37 (Office for National Statistics 2007), also available at: **www.statistics.gov.uk/statbase/product. asp?vlnk_15067**

It was clear from the research undertaken that all surveys, including the General Household Survey (GHS) (Longitudinal), have been undercounting the number of units in some types of drink – predominantly wine, but also to a lesser degree beer, lager and cider. For example, using the latest method one-half pint of strong beer, lager or cider has 2 units, the number of units in a glass of wine depends on the size of glass and is counted as 2 units if the glass size is unspecified and a bottle of alcopops has 1.5 units.

According to the NHS, one UK unit is 10ml or eight grams of pure alcohol (also called ethanol). Units are calculated by multiplying the amount in millilitres (ml) by the strength (ABV) and dividing the result by 1000. There's a unit for every percentage point of ABV in a litre: e.g. a litre of typical whiskey (37.5 ABV) will contain 37.5 units.

Alcohol-related causes of death

The Office for National Statistics (ONS) definition of alcohol-related deaths includes only those causes regarded as being most directly a result of alcohol consumption. It does not include other disease where alcohol has been shown to have some causal relationship, such as cancers of the mouth, oesophagus and liver.

The definition includes all deaths from chronic liver disease and cirrhosis (excluding biliary cirrhosis), even when alcohol is not specifically mentioned on the death certificate. Apart from deaths due to poisoning with alcohol (accidental, intentional or undetermined), this definition excludes any other external causes of death, such as road traffic and other accidents. The definition allows for consistent comparisons over time for those deaths most clearly associated with alcohol consumption.

For the years 1980–2000 the cause of death was defined using the International Classification of Diseases, Ninth Revision (ICD9) (see above). The codes used by ONS to define alcohol-related deaths are listed below:

International Classification of Diseases for alcohol-related illness, Ninth Revision

Code 291	Alcoholic psychoses
Code 303	Alcohol dependence syndrome
Code 305.0	Non-dependent abuse of alcohol
Code 425.5	Alcoholic cardiomyopathy
Code 571.0	Alcoholic fatty liver
Code 571.1	Acute alcoholic hepatitis
Code 571.2	Alcoholic cirrhosis of liver
Code 571.3	Alcoholic liver damage, unspecified
Code 571.4	Chronic hepatitis
Code 571.5	Cirrhosis of liver without mention of alcohol
Code 571.8	Other chronic non-alcoholic liver disease
Code 571.9	Unspecified chronic liver disease without mention of alcohol
Code E860	Accidental poisoning by alcohol

For the years 2001–08 the International Classification of Diseases, Tenth Revision (ICD10) was used. To maintain comparability with earlier years the following codes were used:

International Classification of Diseases for alcohol-related illness, Tenth Revision

F10	Mental and behavioural disorders due to use of alcohol
G31.2	Degeneration of nervous system due to alcohol
G62.1	Alcoholic polyneuropathy
I42.6	Alcoholic cardiomyopathy
K29.2	Alcoholic gastritis
K70	Alcoholic liver disease
K73	Chronic hepatitis, not elsewhere classified
K74	Fibrosis and cirrhosis of liver (Excluding K74.3-K74.5 – Biliary cirrhosis)
K86.0	Alcohol induced chronic pancreatitis

X45	Accidental poisoning by and exposure to alcohol
X65	Intentional self-poisoning by and exposure to alcohol
Y15	Poisoning by and exposure to alcohol, undetermined intent

Death related to drug misuse

These figures represent the number of deaths where the underlying cause of death is regarded as poisoning, drug abuse or drug dependence and where any substances controlled under the *Misuse of Drug Act (1971)* was mentioned on the death certificate. The data on drug misuse deaths do not include deaths from other causes that may have been related to drug taking (for example, road traffic accidents or HIV/AIDS).

ONS monitors deaths from drug-related poisoning using a special database, developed to enable the analysis of deaths by the specific substances involved. Substances involved in deaths from drug-related poisoning include over-the-counter, prescription and illegal drugs. The deaths included are certified by coroners following post-mortem and inquest. Details of this database were published in 'ONS drug-related deaths database: first results for England and Wales, 1993–1997' in *Health Statistics Quarterly No. 5*. The latest report on deaths from drug-related poisoning was published in *Health Statistics Quarterly No. 39*[1] on 28 August 2008.

Body mass index

The body mass index (BMI) shown in Table 7.17 is the most widely used measure of obesity among adults aged 16 and over. The BMI standardises weight for height and is calculated as weight (kg)/height (m)^2. Underweight is defined as a BMI of less than 18.5; desirable 18.5 to less than 25; overweight 25 to less than 30; and obese 30 and over.

There is ongoing debate on the definition of overweight and obesity in children. For children, BMI changes substantially with age, rising steeply in infancy, falling during the pre-school years and then rising again into adulthood. For this reason, child BMI needs to be assessed against standards that make allowance for age. Because of differences in growth rates, it is not possible to apply a universal formula in calculating obesity and overweight in children. The 1990 UK national BMI percentile classification is therefore used, which gives a BMI threshold for each age above which a child is considered overweight or obese. Those children whose BMI lies between the 85th to 95th percentiles are classified as overweight and those above the 95th percentile are classified as obese, compared with the 1990 BMI UK reference data. The percentiles are calculated for each sex and age. According to this method, 15 per cent of children had a BMI within the 85th to 95th percentile in 1990, and 5 per cent of children were above the 95th percentile, and were thus classified as overweight or obese respectively. Increases over 15 per cent and 5 per cent in the proportion of children who exceed the reference 85th and 95th percentiles respectively, over time, would indicate an

upward trend in prevalence of those overweight and obese.

Common mental disorders

Common mental disorders (CMDs), also known as neurotic disorders, are mental conditions that cause marked emotional distress and interfere with daily function. CMDs comprise different types of depression and anxiety. Symptoms of depressive episodes include low mood and a loss of interest and enjoyment in ordinary things and experiences. They impair emotional and physical well-being and behaviour. Anxiety disorders include generalised anxiety disorder (GAD), panic disorder, phobias and obsessive and compulsive disorder (OCD). See the Adult Psychiatric Morbidity Survey 2007, Chapter 2: Common Mental Disorders, the NHS Information Centre for Health and social care.

International Classification of Diseases codes relating to neurosis are presented below.

International Classification of Diseases for neurosis, tenth revision

F32.00	Mild depressive episode without somatic symptoms
F32.01	Mild depressive episode with somatic symptoms
F32.10	Moderate depressive episode without somatic symptoms
F32.11	Moderate depressive episode with somatic symptoms
F32.2	Severe depressive episode
F40.00	Agoraphobia without panic disorder
F40.01	Agoraphobia with panic disorder
F40.1	Social phobias
F40.2	Specific (isolated) phobias
F41.0	Panic disorder
F41.1	Generalised anxiety disorder
F41.2	Mixed anxiety and depressive disorder
F42	Obsessive–compulsive disorder

Prescription Cost Analysis System

Data from the Prescription Cost Analysis System cover all prescriptions dispensed by community pharmacists and dispensing doctors in England. The system covers prescriptions originating from general practices and also those written by nurses, dentists and hospital doctors provided they are dispensed in the community. Also included are prescriptions written in Wales, Scotland, Northern Ireland and the Isle of Man but dispensed in England. Information on items dispensed in hospitals is not available.

Part 8: Social protection

Expenditure on social protection benefits

Cash benefits
Income support: Periodic payments to people with insufficient resources. Conditions for entitlement may be related to personal resources

and to nationality, residence, age, availability for work and family status. The benefit may be paid for a limited or an unlimited period. It may be paid to the individual or to the family, and be provided by central or local government.

Other cash benefits: Support for destitute or vulnerable people to help alleviate poverty or assist in difficult situations. These benefits may be paid by private non-profit organisations.

Benefits in kind
Accommodation: Shelter and board provided to destitute or vulnerable people, where these services cannot be classified under another function. This may be short term in reception centres, shelters and others, or on a more regular basis in special institutions, boarding houses, reception families, and others.

Rehabilitation of alcohol and drug abusers: Treatment of alcohol and drug dependency aimed at reconstructing the social life of the abusers, making them able to live an independent life. The treatment is usually provided in reception centres or special institutions.

Other benefits in kind: Basic services and goods to help vulnerable people, such as counselling, day shelter, help with carrying out daily tasks, food, clothing and fuel. Means-tested legal aid is also included.

Employment and support allowance
Employment and support allowance (ESA) was introduced in October 2008 to replace incapacity benefit (IB) and incapacity-related income support (IS). The figures relating to ESA in Table 8.9 (Recipients of selected benefits for sick and disabled people) have been thoroughly quality assured to National Statistics standards. However it should be noted that this is a new benefit using a new data source which may not have reached steady state in terms of operational processing and retrospection.

In-patient activity

Critical care beds: are classified as high dependency or intensive care beds based on the treatment of the patient. There are no differences between the beds and they can be used in either ward.

High dependency unit
A high dependency unit (HDU) is a unit for patients who require more intensive observation, treatment and nursing care than can be provided on a ward. It would not normally accept patients requiring mechanical ventilation, but could manage those receiving invasive monitoring.

- An HDU may be a centralised unit or it may be part of a ward. In the latter case a group of beds is usually set aside specially for the purpose. A centralised unit is usually available to all specialties.

- An HDU may be distinguished from an intensive care unit by its level of staffing. A doctor is not always present in a HDU and the nurse: patient ratio is less than 1:1.

- A centralised HDU may be located in the same area as an intensive care unit. A cardiac care unit (CCU) is a unit for patients with cardiac problems who require intensive

observation and monitoring and/or intervention.

Intensive care unit
An intensive care unit (ICU) is an area to which patients are admitted for treatment of actual or impending organ failure. Patients may require technological support (including mechanical ventilation) and/or invasive monitoring. An ICU is usually separate from a ward.

- An ICU is usually available to all specialties but may be restricted to a single specialty e.g. neurosurgery.

- An ICU may be distinguished from a high dependency unit by its level of staffing. A doctor is always present and the nurse: patient ratio is 1:1 or greater.

In Table 8.11 in-patient data for England are based on finished consultant episodes (FCEs). Data for Wales, Scotland and Northern Ireland are based on deaths and discharges and transfers between specialities (between hospitals in Northern Ireland).

An FCE is a completed period of care of a patient using a bed, under one consultant, in a particular National Health Service (NHS) Trust or directly managed unit. If a patient is transferred from one consultant to another within the same hospital, this counts as an FCE but not a hospital discharge. If a patient is transferred from one hospital to another provider, this counts as an FCE and a hospital discharge. Data for England, Wales and Northern Ireland exclude NHS beds and activity in joint-user and contractual hospitals. For Scotland, data for joint-user and contractual hospitals are included.

Acute Hospital Care/Activity – includes services such as: consultation with specialist clinicians; emergency treatment; routine, complex and life saving surgery; specialist diagnostic procedures; close observation and short-term care of patients. 'Acute' hospital care excludes obstetric, psychiatric and long stay care services.

Length of stay
A standard measure used in hospitals, indicating the number of days that a patient occupied a bed in the hospital prior to discharge.

Length of stay is calculated as the difference in days between the admission date and the discharge date, where both are given. Length of stay is based on hospital spells and only applies to ordinary admissions.

0 day stay – patients who are admitted and discharged on the same calendar date.

1 day stay – patients who are admitted and discharged on consecutive days, this will include some patients whose stay is less than 24 hours.

2 or more days stay – all other lengths of stay admissions.

Benefit units

A benefit unit is a single adult or couple living as married and any dependent children living with them in the same household, where the head is below state pension age (60 for women and 65 for men) and where one or both are in receipt of a benefit. A pensioner benefit unit is a single person over state pension age or a couple where one or both adults are over state pension age.

Pension schemes

A pension scheme is a plan offering benefits to members upon retirement. Schemes are provided by the state, employers and insurance firms, and are differentiated by a wide range of rules governing membership eligibility, contributions, benefits and taxation.

Occupational pension scheme: An arrangement (other than accident or permanent health insurance) organised by an employer (or on behalf of a group of employers) to provide benefits for employees on their retirement and for their dependants on their death.

Personal pension scheme: A scheme where the contract to provide contributions in return for retirement benefits is between an individual and an insurance firm, rather than between an individual and an employer or the state. Individuals may choose to join such schemes, for example, to provide a primary source of retirement income for the self-employed, or to provide a secondary income to employees who are members of occupational schemes. These schemes may be facilitated (but not provided) by an employer.

Stakeholder pension scheme: Available since 2001, a flexible, portable, defined-contribution personal pension arrangement (provided by insurance companies with capped management charges) that must meet the conditions set out in the *Welfare Reform and Pensions Act 1999* and be registered with the Pensions Regulator. They can be taken out by an individual or facilitated by an employer. Where an employer of five or more staff offers no occupational pension and an employee earns more than the lower earnings limit (the entrance level for paying tax), the provision of access to a stakeholder scheme with contributions deducted from payroll is compulsory.

Social fund

The social fund is available to people on low incomes faced with expenses they find difficult meeting from their normal income. Payments come in the form of payments, grants or loans and can cover maternity costs, funeral costs, fuel costs, items of clothing and footwear, furniture items and items relating to the safety and well-being of individuals and families.

Maternity grant: also known as Sure Start maternity grant is a fixed amount of £500 to help people on low income buy clothes and equipment for a new born baby, it does not have to be repaid.

Funeral payment: is a payment to people on low income to help with the essential costs of a funeral. Proof has to be provided of expense and the payment does not have to be repaid but it can be recovered from the estate of the person who has died.

Budgeting loan: is a loan to people on low income to help pay essential lump sum payments which are difficult to budget for. It is an interest free loan which must be paid back to the social fund.

Crisis loan: is a loan to people on low income who need money quickly because of expenses in an emergency or disaster. It is an interest free loan which must be paid back to the social fund.

Part 9: Crime and justice

Prevalence rates and incidence rates

Prevalence rates show the proportion of the British Crime Survey (BCS) sample who were victims of an offence once or more during the year. Unlike the BCS incidence rates, they only take account of whether a household or person was a victim of a specific crime once or more in the recall period, but not of the number of times victimised. Prevalence rates are taken as equivalent to 'risk'.

Incidence rates describe the number of crimes experienced per household or adult in the BCS or police-recorded crime statistics.

Types of offence in England and Wales

The figures are compiled from police returns to the Home Office and the Ministry of Justice or directly from court computer systems.

Indictable offences in England and Wales cover those offences that can only be tried at the Crown Court and include the more serious offences.

Summary offences are those for which a defendant would normally be tried at a magistrates' court and are generally less serious – the majority of motoring offences fall into this category.

Triable-either-way offences are triable either on indictment or summarily.

Recorded crime statistics broadly cover the more serious offences. Up to March 1998 most indictable and triable-either-way offences were included, as well as some summary offences; from April 1998, all indictable and triable-either-way offences were included, plus a few closely related summary offences.

Recorded offences are the most readily available measures of the incidence of crime, but do not necessarily indicate the true level of crime. Many less serious offences are not reported to the police and cannot, therefore, be recorded. Moreover, the propensity of the public to report offences to the police is influenced by a number of factors and may change over time.

From 2000 some police forces changed their systems to record the allegations of victims unless there is credible evidence that a crime has *not* taken place. In April 2002 the National Crime Recording Standard (NCRS, see below) formalised these changes across England and Wales.

There have been changes to the methodology of the British Crime Survey (BCS). Between 1982 and 2001 the survey was carried out every two years, and reported on victimisation in the previous calendar year. From 2001/02 onwards the surveys cover the financial year of interviews and report on victimisation in the 12 months before interview on an annual basis.

This change makes the BCS estimates more comparable with figures collected by the police. Because of the significant changes taking place in both these measures of crime, direct comparisons with figures for previous years cannot be made.

Types of offence in Scotland

In Scotland the term 'crime' is reserved for the more serious offences (broadly equivalent to 'indictable' and 'triable-either-way' offences in England and Wales) while less serious crimes are called 'offences'. The seriousness of an act is *generally* based on the maximum sentence that can be imposed.

Police-recorded crime data included in this report are based on a count of the numbers of crimes and offences recorded and cleared up by the police. Amendments (such as the deletion of incidents found on investigation not to be criminal) that arise after the end of the financial year are not generally incorporated. Offences recorded by the British Transport Police, the Ministry of Defence and the Civil Nuclear Constabulary (previously known as the UK Atomic Energy Authority) are also not included.

In a single criminal incident, several crimes or offences may occur, for example, a house may be broken into and vandalised and the occupants assaulted. In multiple offence incidents, all the offences are counted separately rather than the incident as a whole being counted as one offence; that is, the counting system is offence-based rather than incident-based. Statistics are therefore not directly comparable with statistics on action taken against offenders, as one offence may lead to several persons being charged and, equally, an offender may be charged with several offences.

Motor vehicle offences do not include *stationary* motor vehicle offences dealt with by the issue of a fixed penalty ticket. However, offences dealt with under the vehicle defect rectification scheme and offences for which the procurator fiscal offers a fixed penalty are included in the figures. In addition to this, *moving* traffic offences that are the subject of a police conditional offer of a fixed penalty are also included, for example, speeding, traffic directions offences.

Fieldwork for the Scottish Crime and Justice Survey (SCJS) began in April 2008 and the first results were published on 27 October 2009. The 2008/09 SCJS was the ninth in a series of crime surveys in Scotland. Crime and victimisation surveys have been carried out in Scotland since the early 1980s. In 1982 and 1988 a crime survey was carried out in central and southern Scotland as part of the British Crime Survey. The British Crime Survey ceased to cover Scotland when the first independent Scottish Crime Survey was launched in 1993 and extended the same design and sample size (5,000) to cover the whole of Scotland. Further sweeps of the Scottish Crime Survey were conducted in 1996, 2000 and 2003. There were two further sweeps of the survey 2004 and 2006, when the survey was titled the Scottish Crime and Victimisation Survey.

Types of offence in Northern Ireland

In recording crime, the Police Service of Northern Ireland (PSNI) broadly follows the Home Office rules for counting crime. As from 1 April 1998 notifiable offences are recorded on the same basis as those in England and Wales. Before the revision of the rules, criminal damage offences in Northern Ireland excluded those where the value of the property damaged was less than £200. The National Crime Recording Standard (NCRS, see below) was introduced within PSNI in April 2002.

See 'Availability and comparability of data from constituent countries' entry below for information on the differences in the legal system in Scotland compared with England and Wales, and Northern Ireland.

National Crime Recording Standard

Changes in the counting rules for recorded crime on 1 April 1998 affected both the methods of counting and the coverage for recorded crime and had the effect of inflating the number of crimes recorded. For some offence groups – more serious violence against the person and burglary – there was little effect on the numbers recorded. However, the changes had more effect on figures for minor violence and criminal damage.

In April 2002 the National Crime Recording Standard (NCRS) was introduced in England and Wales, and in Northern Ireland, with the aim of taking a more victim-centred approach and providing more consistency between forces. Before 2002 police forces in England and Wales did not necessarily record a crime that was reported if there was no evidence to support the claim of the victim but the NCRS changed this such that the allegations of victims are recorded unless there is credible evidence that a crime has *not* taken place Therefore crimes recorded from 1 April 2002 are not comparable with earlier years.

It is not possible to assess the effect of NCRS on recorded firearm crimes. NCRS inflated the overall number of violence against the person and criminal damage offences, but has less effect on the number of robberies. Many firearm offences are among the less serious categories, and these types of offences are among those most affected by NCRS.

The introduction of the NCRS may have had an effect on the recorded crime detection rate, but this is difficult to quantify.

Scottish Crime Recording Standard
In April 2004 the Association of Chief Police Officers in Scotland (ACPOS) implemented the Scottish Crime Recording Standard (SCRS) following recommendations from Her Majesty's Inspectorate of Constabulary (HMIC), which means that no corroborative evidence is required initially to record a crime-related incident as a crime if so perceived by the victim. In consequence of this more victim-oriented approach, the HMIC expected the SCRS to increase the numbers of minor crimes recorded by the police, such as minor crimes of vandalism and minor thefts. However, the HMIC also expected that the SCRS would not have much impact on the figures for the more serious crimes, such as serious assault, sexual assault, robbery or housebreaking.

Unfortunately it was not possible to estimate the exact impact of SCRS on the recorded crime figures. Around the time that the standard was implemented police also introduced centralised call centres, which encouraged the reporting of incidents to the police.

Availability and comparability of data from constituent countries

There are a number of reasons why recorded crime statistics in England and Wales, Northern Ireland and Scotland cannot be directly compared:

Different legal systems: The legal system operating in Scotland differs from that in England and Wales, and Northern Ireland. For example, in Scotland children aged under 16 accused of offending are normally dealt with by the Children's Hearings system rather than the courts.

Differences in classification: There are significant differences in the offences included within the recorded crime categories used in Scotland and the categories of notifiable offences used in England, Wales, and Northern Ireland. Scottish figures are divided into 'offences' (less serious criminal acts) and 'crimes' (the more serious criminal acts). The seriousness of an act is *generally* based on the maximum sentence that can be imposed. Scottish figures of 'crime' have therefore been grouped in an attempt to approximate to the classification of notifiable offences in England, Wales and Northern Ireland.

Counting rules: In all parts of the UK, only the main offence occurring within an incident is counted.

Burglary: This term is not applicable to Scotland where the term used is 'housebreaking' and includes domestic as well as commercial premises.

Theft from vehicles: In Scotland data have only been separately identified from January 1992. The figures include theft by opening lock-fast places from a motor vehicle and other theft from a motor vehicle.

Comparable crimes

Comparable crimes are a set of offences that are covered by both the British Crime Survey (BCS) and police-recorded crime. Various adjustments are made to the recorded crime categories to maximise comparability with the BCS. Comparable crime is used to compare trends in police and BCS figures, and to identify the amount of crime that is not reported to the police and not recorded by them. The comparable subset includes common assaults (and assaults on a constable), and vehicle interference and tampering. Four-fifths (80 per cent) of BCS offences reported through interviews in the 2007/08 interview sample fall into categories that can be compared with crimes recorded under the new police coverage of offences adopted from 1 April 1998. With the introduction of new police counting rules in 1998/99, the 'old' comparable subset that was used up to and including the 1998 BCS, was updated as it excluded common assaults, other household theft and other theft of personal property.

Anti-social behaviour indicators

The BCS measures 'high' levels of perceived anti-social behaviour from responses to seven individual anti-social behaviour strands:

- Noisy neighbours or loud parties
- Teenagers hanging around on the streets
- Rubbish or litter lying around
- Vandalism, graffiti and other deliberate damage to property
- People using or dealing drugs
- People being drunk or rowdy in public places
- Abandoned or burnt-out cars

Perceptions of anti-social behaviour based on answers to these seven questions are measured using the following scale:

- 'very big problem' = 3
- 'fairly big problem' = 2
- 'not a very big problem' = 1
- 'not a problem at all' = 0

The maximum score for the seven questions is 21. Respondents with 'high' levels of perceived anti-social behaviour in their area (within a 15 minute walk) are those who score 11 or more on this scale.

Sentences and orders

The following are the main sentences and orders that can be imposed upon people found guilty. Some types of sentence or order can only be given to offenders in England and Wales in certain age groups. Under the framework for sentencing contained in the *Criminal Justice Acts 1991, 1993* and the *Powers of Criminal Courts (Sentencing) Act 2000* the sentence must reflect the seriousness of the offence. The sentences explained below are available for adults aged 18 and over but a similar range of sentences is available for juveniles aged 10 to 17 and these have been identified where relevant:

Absolute and conditional discharge: A court may make an order discharging a person absolutely or (except in Scotland) conditionally where it is inexpedient to inflict punishment and, before 1 October 1992, where a probation order was not appropriate. An order for conditional discharge runs for a period of not more than three years as the court specifies, the condition being that the offender does not commit another offence within the period so specified. In Scotland a court may also discharge a person with an admonition.

Community sentences: The term 'community sentence' refers to attendance centre orders, reparation orders, action plan orders, drug treatment and testing orders, community orders, community rehabilitation orders, community punishment orders, community punishment and rehabilitation orders, supervision orders, curfew orders and referral orders. Under the *Criminal Justice and Courts Services Act 2000*, certain community orders current at 1 April 2001 were renamed. Probation orders were renamed community rehabilitation orders, community service orders were renamed community punishment orders and combination orders were renamed community punishment and rehabilitation orders. Some of the above historical community sentences are still available for offences committed before April 2005.

Community order: For offences committed on or after 4 April 2005 the new community order,

introduced under the *Criminal Justice Act 2003*, replaced all existing community sentences for adults. Under this order, one or more of 12 possible requirements must be added, such as supervision, unpaid work and drug treatment. The Act also introduced a new suspended sentence order for offences that pass the custody threshold. One or more of the same set of 12 possible requirements must be added to this order. Unless considered dangerous those sentenced to 12 months or more in custody, who will be released on licence at the halfway point of the sentence, will remain on licence, and subject to recall if they breach the conditions of their licence, for the entire remaining period of their sentence, instead of to the three-quarter point.

Detention and imprisonment
Detention and training order: This was introduced for juveniles aged 10 to 18 under the *Powers of Criminal Courts (Sentencing) Act 2000*. It is for juveniles who have committed a serious crime. They can serve the sentence at a young offender institution, at a local authority establishment, or at a local authority secure training centre. The sentence given is from 4 to 24 months, but sentences can run consecutively.

Imprisonment: Is the custodial sentence for adult offenders. Home Office or Scottish Executive consent is needed for release or transfer. In the case of mentally disordered offenders, hospital orders, which may include a restriction order, may be considered appropriate. A new disposal, the 'hospital direction', was introduced in 1997. The court, when imposing a period of imprisonment, can direct that the offender be sent directly to hospital. On recovering from the mental disorder, the offender is returned to prison to serve the balance of their sentence.

The *Criminal Justice Act 1991* abolished remission and substantially changed the parole scheme in England and Wales. Those serving sentences of less than four years, imposed on or after 1 October 1992, are subject to automatic conditional release and are released, subject to certain criteria, halfway through their sentence. Home detention curfews result in selected prisoners being released up to two months early with a tag that monitors their presence during curfew hours. Those serving sentences of four years or longer are considered for discretionary conditional release after having served half their sentence, but are automatically released at the two-thirds point of sentence.

The *Crime (Sentences) Act 1997*, implemented on 1 October 1997, included, for persons aged 18 or over, an automatic life sentence for a second serious violent or sexual offence unless there are exceptional circumstances. All offenders serving a sentence of 12 months or more are supervised in the community until the three-quarters point of sentence. A life sentence prisoner may be released on licence subject to supervision and is always liable to recall.

In Scotland the *Prisoners and Criminal Proceedings (Scotland) Act 1993* changed the system of remission and parole for prisoners sentenced on or after 1 October 1993. Those serving sentences of less than four years are released unconditionally after having served half of their sentence, unless the court specifically imposes a supervised release order that subjects them to social work supervision after release. Those serving sentences of four years or more are eligible for parole at half sentence. If parole is not granted then they will automatically be released on licence at the two-thirds point of sentence subject to days added for breaches of prison rules. All such prisoners are liable to be 'recalled on conviction' or for breach of conditions of licence, if between the date of release and the date on which the full sentence ends he/she commits another offence that is punishable by imprisonment, or breaches his/her licence conditions. The offender may be returned to prison for the remainder of that sentence whether or not a sentence of imprisonment is also imposed for the new offence.

Management of Offenders, etc (Scotland) Act 2005 introduced home detention curfew in Scotland. From 3 July 2006, certain prisoners serving less than four years and assessed as presenting a low risk of re-offending, can be released on licence between two weeks and four months early. They are subject to electronically monitored restrictions on their movements for up to 12 hours per day for the remainder of their sentence.

Custody probation order:
An order unique to Northern Ireland, reflecting the different regime there that applies in respect of remission and the general absence of release on licence. The custodial sentence is followed by a period of supervision for a period of between one and three years.

Suspended Sentence
The new suspended sentence order (SSO), introduced by the Criminal Justice Act 2003 came into force for offences committed from 4 April 2005 and replaced the previous fully suspended sentence. It applies to persons aged 18 and is a sentence of custody of under 12 months, suspended for a period ranging from six months to two years. During the suspension period the court sets community requirements from the same options as are available for the community order – unpaid work, activity requirement, programme requirement, prohibited activity requirement, curfew requirement, exclusion requirement, supervision requirement, attendance centre requirement (if the offender is aged under 25). During the suspension period the court can periodically review the offender's progress in complying with the orders made. Breaches of the requirements of an SSO are dealt with by the court and the assumption is that failure to comply with the set requirements or the commission of another offence will result in the custodial term being activated. Where the offence was committed before 4 April 2005 the court may, in the case of a person over the age of 21, suspend a custodial sentence for up to two years for between one and two years if there are exceptional circumstances for doing so.

Fines
The *Criminal Justice Act 1993* introduced new arrangements on 20 September 1993 whereby courts are required to fit an amount for the fine that reflects the seriousness of the offence and that takes account of an offender's means. This system replaced the more formal unit fines scheme included in the *Criminal Justice Act 1991*. The 1993 Act also introduced the power for courts to arrange deduction of fines from income benefit for those offenders receiving such benefits.

Prison population

The population in custody includes those held in prison or police cells. It includes prisoners on remand (both untried and those who have been convicted but remain unsentenced), prisoners under sentence and non-criminal prisoners (for example those held under the *1971 Immigration Act*). It also includes those held in police cells.

Part 10: Housing

Dwelling stock

The definition of a dwelling follows the census definition applicable at that time. Currently the 2001 Census definition is used, which defines a dwelling as 'structurally separate accommodation'. This was determined primarily by considering the type of accommodation, as well as separate and shared access to multi-occupied properties.

In all stock figures vacant dwellings are included but non-permanent dwellings are generally excluded. For housebuilding statistics, only data on permanent dwellings are collected.

Estimates of the total dwelling stock, stock changes and the tenure distribution in the UK are made by Communities and Local Government for England, the Scottish Government, the Welsh Assembly Government, and the Northern Ireland Department for Social Development. These are primarily based on census output data for the number of dwellings (or households converted to dwellings) from the censuses of population for the UK. Adjustments are carried out if there are specific reasons to do so. Census year figures are based on outputs from the censuses. For years between censuses, the total figures are obtained by projecting the base census year's figure forward annually. The increment is based on the annual total number of completions plus the annual total net gain from other housing statistics, that is, conversions, demolitions and changes of use.

Estimates of dwelling stock by tenure category are based on other sources where it is considered that for some specific tenure information, these are more accurate than census output data. In this situation it is assumed that the other data sources also contain vacant dwellings, but it is not certain and it is not expected that these data are very precise. Thus the allocation of vacant dwellings to tenure categories may not be completely accurate and the margin of error for tenure categories is wider than for estimates of total stock.

For local authority stock, figures supplied by local authorities are more reliable than those in the 2001 Census. Similarly, it was found that the Housing Corporation's own data are more accurate than census output data for the registered social landlord (RSL) stock. Hence only the privately rented or with a job or business tenure data were taken directly from the Census. The owner-occupied data were taken as the residual of the total from the Census. For non-census years, the same approach was adopted except for the privately rented or with a job or business, for which Labour Force Survey results were used (see Appendix, Part 4: Labour Force Survey).

In the Survey of English Housing, data for privately rented unfurnished accommodation include accommodation that is partly furnished.

For further information on the methodology used to calculate stock by tenure and tenure definitions for the UK, see Appendix B Notes and Definitions in the Communities and Local Government annual volume *Housing Statistics* or the housing statistics page of the Communities and Local Government website at: www.communities.gov.uk/housing/ housingresearch/housingstatistics/

Housebuilding completions

Housebuilding statistics cover building of all permanent dwellings, including houses, bungalows and flats. In principle a dwelling is regarded as completed when it becomes ready for occupation, whether it is occupied or not. In practice there are instances where the timing could be delayed and some completions are missed, for example, because no completion certificates were requested by the owner.

Tenure definition for housebuilding is only slightly different from that used for dwelling stock figures (see above). For further information on the methodology used to calculate stock by tenure and tenure definitions, see Appendix B Notes and Definitions in the Communities and Local Government annual volume *Housing Statistics* or the housing statistics page of the Communities and Local Government website: www.communities.gov.uk/housing/ housingresearch/housingstatistics/

Affordable homes schemes

Affordable housing is provided to specified eligible households whose needs are not met by the market. Figure 10.3 provides data on social rent and intermediate affordable housing. Intermediate affordable housing includes intermediate rent and low cost home ownership which together with social rent make up the gross supply of affordable housing.

Social rented housing is rented housing owned and managed by local authorities and Registered Social Landlords, for which guideline target rents are determined through the national rent regime.

Intermediate affordable housing is housing at prices and rents above those of social rent but below market price or rents, and which meet the criteria for affordable housing. These can include homes for intermediate rent and low cost home ownership schemes such as shared equity (for example Home Buy).

Intermediate rented homes are provided at rent levels above those of social rented but below private rented. The Government offers these to some key workers who do not wish to buy.

Low Cost Home Ownership schemes include:

- *Discounted sale* homes have a simple discount for the purchaser on its market price, so the purchaser buys the whole home at a reduced rate.

- *Shared equity* is where more than one party has an interest in the value of the home, for example an equity loan arrangement or a shared ownership lease. There may be a charge on the loan, and restrictions on price, access and resale.

- *Shared ownership* is a form of shared equity under which the purchaser buys an initial share in a home from a housing provider, who retains the remainder and may charge a rent. The purchaser may buy additional shares and this payment should be 'recycled' for more affordable housing. In most cases, a purchaser may buy the final share and own the whole home, though this may be restricted in some rural areas.

Private and social sectors

'Social sector' housing includes all local authority (or public) housing as well as registered social landlord (RSL) and housing association (HA) housing.

Where the term 'private sector' is used in housing policy and housing statistics, it generally means the 'private housing' sector or non-social housing sector, that is owner-occupied dwellings and those rented privately, including those that go with a job or business and not those owned by RSLs or HAs.

For housebuilding starts and completions data, especially the former, there is a small possibility that some dwellings built for RSLs and HAs could have been counted as 'private enterprise' and vice versa. This is because sometimes the builders themselves are not sure of the precise ownership or the ownership may keep evolving and it is not final until it is sold.

Tenure

There are four tenure categories available for dwelling stock and household figures. These are:

- owner-occupied (or private enterprise in the case of housebuilding statistics, that is dwellings financed and built by private developers for owner-occupiers or private landlords, whether persons or companies). This includes accommodation that is owned outright or is being bought with a mortgage.

- rented privately, defined as all non-owner-occupied property other than that rented from local authorities and registered social landlords (RSLs) plus that rented from private or public bodies by virtue of employment. This includes property occupied rent-free by someone other than the owner. New build privately rented dwellings will be included in the housebuilding private enterprise figures.

- rented from RSLs, but for stock figures non-registered housing associations are excluded and subsumed within owner-occupied as are RSL shared ownership and shared equity dwellings; for housebuilding figures the RSL tenure includes social rent, intermediate rent and low cost home ownership RSL new build dwellings.

- rented from local authorities. In Scotland dwellings rented from local authorities include those rented from Communities Scotland, formerly Scottish Homes.

Household reference person

In Figure 10.5 and Table 10.6 the household reference person (HRP) definition used is based on that used for Office for National Statistics social surveys. From April 2001 the Survey of English Housing (SEH) in common with other Government surveys replaced the traditional concept of the "head of the household" by 'household reference person'. This definition is used in Table 10.14 and Figure 10.21. In both cases the HRP is identified during the interview and is defined as the member of the household who:

- owns the household accommodation or;

- is legally responsible for the rent of the accommodation or;

- has the household accommodation as an emolument or perquisite or;

- has the household accommodation by virtue of some relationship to the owner who is not a member of the household.

The household reference person must always be a householder, whereas the head of the household was always the husband for a couple household, who might not be a householder. For joint householders, the HRP will be the householder with the highest income. If two or more householders have exactly the same income the HRP is the eldest.

Bedroom standard

The bedroom standard concept is used to estimate occupation density by allocating a standard number of bedrooms to each household in accordance with its age/sex/marital status composition and the relationship of the members to one another. A separate bedroom is allocated to each married or cohabiting couple, and any other person aged 21 and over, each pair of adolescents aged 10 to 20 of the same sex and each pair of children aged under 10. Any unpaired person aged 10 to 20 is paired, if possible with a child under 10 of the same sex, or, if that is not possible, is given a separate bedroom, as is any unpaired child under 10. This standard is then compared with the actual number of bedrooms (including bed-sitters) available for the sole use of the household, and deficiencies or excesses are tabulated. Bedrooms converted to other uses are not counted as available unless they have been denoted as bedrooms by the informants; bedrooms not actually in use are counted unless uninhabitable. If a household has fewer bedrooms than implied by the standard then it is deemed to be overcrowded. As a bed-sitter will meet the bedroom standard for a one person household or for a married/cohabiting couple, one person and couple households cannot be overcrowded according to the bedroom standard.

Homeless in priority need

Priority need groups include households with dependent children or a pregnant woman and people who are vulnerable in some way for example because of mental illness or physical disability. In 2002 an Order made under the *Housing Act 1996* extended the priority need categories to include: applicants aged 16 or 17; applicants aged 18 to 20 who were previously in care; applicants vulnerable as a result of time spent in care, in custody, or in HM Forces, and applicants vulnerable as a result of having to flee their home because of violence or the threat of violence.

Where a main duty is owed, the local housing authority must ensure that suitable accommodation is available for the applicant and his or her household. The duty continues until a settled housing solution becomes available for them, or some other circumstance brings the duty to an end. Where households are found to be intentionally homeless, or not in priority need, the authority must make an assessment of their housing needs and provide advice and assistance to help them find accommodation for themselves.

Standard Assessment Procedure (SAP)

The SAP is an index based on calculated annual space and water heating costs for a standard heating regime for a home, and is expressed on a scale of 1 (highly energy inefficient) to 100 (highly energy efficient, with 100 representing zero energy cost).

The detailed methodology for calculating the SAP to monitor the energy efficiency was comprehensively updated in 2005 to reflect developments in the energy efficiency technologies and knowledge of dwelling performance. The rating scale was revised to run between 1 and 100 under the 2005 methodology. Under the 2001 methodology the scale ran between 1 and 120. Therefore, a SAP rating under the 2001 methodology is not comparable with the one calculated under the 2005 methodology.

Energy Efficiency Rating (EER) Bands

The energy efficiency rating is presented in an A to G banding system by way of an Energy Performance Certificate, where band A rating represents low energy costs (the most efficient band) and band G rating represents high energy costs (the least efficient band). The break points in SAP (see above) are used for the EER bands, and are:

- Band A (92–100)

- Band B (81–91)

- Band C (69–80)

- Band D (55–68)

- Band E (39–54)

- Band F (21–38)

- Band G (1–20)

Decent home standard

The definition of a decent home is one that meets all of the following criteria:

- meets the statutory minimum for housing. This was the Fitness Standard up to April 2006 when it was replaced by the Housing Health and Safety Rating System (see below)

- is in a reasonable state of repair

- has reasonably modern facilities and services

- provides a reasonable degree of thermal comfort, that is it has efficient heating and effective insulation

Housing Health and Safety Rating System (HHSRS)

The HHSRS is the statutory tool used to assess the risks posed by a home to occupants in residential properties in England and Wales. It replaced the Fitness Standard in April 2006.

The purpose of the HHSRS assessment is not to set a standard but to generate objective information to determine and inform enforcement decisions. There are 29 types of hazard, each separately rated, based on risk to the potential occupant who is most vulnerable to that hazard. The individual hazard scores are grouped into ten bands where the highest bands A–C (representing scores of 1,000 or more) are considered to pose Category 1 hazards. Local authorities have a duty to act where Category 1 hazards are present. Local authorities may take into account the vulnerability of the actual occupant in determining the best course of action.

For the purposes of the decent homes standard (see above), homes posing a Category 1 hazard are 'non-decent' on the criterion that to be 'decent' a home must meet the statutory minimum requirements.

The English House Condition Survey (EHCS) is not able to replicate the HHSRS assessment in full as part of a large scale survey. Its assessment employs a mix of hazards that are directly assessed by surveyors in the field and others that are indirectly assessed from detailed related information collected.

Not all hazards are covered by the EHCS but it is expected that those included account for more than 95 per cent of all Category 1 hazards. The full list of hazards and details of how the EHCS collects and models information on the HHSRS, is available at: www.communities.gov.uk/housing/housingresearch/housingsurveys/englishhousecondition/ehcsreports/

Poor quality environments

The identification of poor quality environments is based on surveyor's assessments of the severity of problems in the immediate environment of the home. The problems assessed fall into three groups:

- Upkeep – the upkeep, management or misuse of the private and public space and buildings, (specifically, the presence of: scruffy or neglected buildings, poor condition housing; graffiti; scruffy gardens or landscaping; litter, rubbish or dumping; vandalism; dog or other excrement; and nuisance from street parking)

- Traffic – road traffic and other forms of transport (specifically the presence of intrusive motorways and main roads; railway or aircraft noise; heavy traffic; and ambient air quality)

- Utilisation – abandonment or non-residential use of property (specifically, vacant sites; vacant or boarded up buildings; intrusive industry; or non-conforming use of a residential area)

Property transactions

In April 2008 changes were made to the way in which property transactions were counted. Under the new system, transactions are based on actual completions instead of the number of stamp duty land tax certificates issued. Figure 10.17 is based on counts of completed residential transactions for all months from May 2005. Properties valued at less than £40,000 are excluded from the data. Removing transactions at the very bottom end of the market means that Figure 10.17 is closer to showing the sales of residential dwellings, as non dwellings such as small pieces of land, will tend to be in the excluded transactions.

Average dwelling prices

Information on dwelling prices at national and regional levels are collected and published by Communities and Local Government on a monthly basis. Until August 2005 data came from a sample survey of mortgage completions, the Survey of Mortgage Lenders (SML). The SML covered around 50 banks and building societies that are members of the Council of Mortgage Lenders (CML). From September 2005 data come from the Regulated Mortgage Survey (RMS), which is conducted by BankSearch and the CML.

There are two main methods of calculating house prices; simple average prices and mix-adjusted prices. Simple average prices are more volatile as they will be influenced by changes in the mix of properties bought in each period. This effect is removed by applying fixed weights to the process at the start of each year to create mix-adjusted house prices, based on the average mix of properties purchased during the previous three years, and these weights are applied to prices during the year.

The RMS collects 100 per cent of completions data from those mortgage lenders who take part (and as a result the sample size increased to around 50,000 from September 2005). Annual figures have been derived as an average of the monthly prices. The annual change in price is shown as the average percentage change over the year and is calculated from the house price index. The mix-adjusted average price excludes sitting tenant (right-to-buy) purchases, cash purchases, remortgages and further loans.

Mortgage repayments and deposits

Data in Figure 10.20 are based on mortgages for house purchase and therefore include first-time and chain free buyers as well as those moving home, but not those re-mortgaging an existing property. Data for 2005 are based on combined data from the Survey of Mortgage Lenders (SML) and the Regulated Mortgage Survey (RMS) but data from September 2005 onwards is collected via the Regulated Mortgage Survey. Mortgage repayments data up to and including 2000 take into account mortgage tax relief.

Income is the income on which the mortgage was based which may differ from actual income.

Repayments data up to and including 1998 were based on average building society mortgage rates. From 1999, the average mortgage rate is a composite figure which has been constructed from a weighted combination of building society and bank mortgage interest figures to give an overall estimate of the mortgage rate.

The ratios of deposit to price have been calculated on a case-by-case basis and then averaged.

Mortgage arrears and repossessions

Figures are estimates of arrears on all first-charge loans held by Council of Mortgage Lenders (CML) members, both regulated and unregulated, and include buy-to-let. First charge loans are the first mortgage on a property. Any additional loans secured against the property on top of this are not first charge loans. The lender with the first charge has the first call on the property if the borrower defaults on the loan. Figures presented here do not include arrears relating to other secured lending, or to firms that are not CML members. These estimates are based on reporting by a sample of CML members, which are then grossed up to represent the lending undertaken by CML members as a whole. In the first half of 2008 these accounted for about 97 per cent of first charge mortgages.

Figures are revised as better information about rates of growth and performance in different parts of the market becomes available, so care should be taken when looking at changes over time as lenders newly reporting figures may distort comparisons. Trends in the number of months' arrears data may also be distorted by changes in mortgage rates. When rates change this may alter the contractual mortgage repayments due and so affect the number of months that a given arrears amount represents. In the case of variable rate products, with lower mortgage rates a given amount of arrears represents a higher number of monthly payments. Properties in possession are not counted as arrears. Buy-to-let mortgages, where a receiver of rent has been appointed, are also not counted as arrears.

Part 11: Environment

Water abstractions

In England and Wales, the Environment Agency (EA) licenses all abstractions apart from those that are exempt. Estimates of actual abstractions are based on returns from license holders. For the agriculture and private water supply categories only a small, and not necessarily representative, sample of license holders makes returns. Thus confidence in the accuracy of these data is low. However, these abstractions are small in volume and have a limited impact on the annual abstraction figures, although the resource and environmental impact of agricultural abstraction can be significant in local areas during the irrigation season. Conversely, in all of the other categories returns cover a high proportion of the total licensed quantity, where the abstractions are high in volume and/or have a high resource or environmental impact.

Air pollutants

Volatile organic compounds (VOCs) are ozone precursors and comprise a wide range of chemical compounds including hydrocarbons, oxygenates and halogen containing species. Methane (CH_4) is an important component of VOCs but its environmental impact derives principally from its contribution to global warming. The major environmental impact of non-methane VOCs lies in their involvement in the formation of ground level ozone. Most VOCs are non-toxic or are present at levels well below guideline values. Others, such as benzene and 1, 3-butadiene, are of concern because of their potential impact on human health.

PM_{10} is airborne particulate matter. Specifically, it is that fraction of 'black smoke' that is thought most likely to be deposited in the lungs. It can be defined as the fraction resulting from a collection from black smoke by a size selective sampler that collects smaller particles preferentially, capturing 50 per cent of 10 micron aerodynamic diameter particles, more than 95 per cent of 5 micron particles, and less than 5 per cent of 20 micron particles.

Types of monitoring sites

Rural sites are in the open country away from roads, industrial areas and where people live.

Urban background sites are in urban locations (for example, parks and urban residential areas) away from emission sources.

Roadside sites are sites with sample inlets between one metre of the edge of a busy road and the back of the pavement (usually five metres from the roadside).

Pollution incidents

The Environment Agency defines four categories of pollution incidents:

Category 1: The most severe incidents, which involve one or more of the following:

- potential or actual persistent effect on water quality or aquatic life
- closure of potable water, industrial or agricultural abstraction necessary
- major damage to aquatic ecosystems
- major damage to agriculture and/or commerce
- serious impact on man, or
- major effect on amenity value

Category 2: Severe incidents, which involve one or more of the following:

- notification to abstractors necessary
- significant damage to aquatic ecosystems
- significant effect on water quality
- damage to agriculture and/or commerce
- impact on man, or
- impact on amenity value to public, owners or users

Category 3: Minor incidents, involving one or more of the following:

- a minimal effect on water quality
- minor damage to aquatic ecosystems
- amenity value only marginally affected, or
- minimal impact on agriculture and/or commerce

Category 4: Incidents where no impact on the environment occurred.

Average temperatures

The World Meteorological Organisation (WMO) requires the calculation of average temperatures for consecutive periods of 30 years, with the latest covering the period 1961–90. Thirty years was chosen as a period long enough to eliminate year-to-year variations.

Environmental Accounts

Environmental Accounts are satellite accounts to the National Accounts. As such they use similar concepts and classifications of industry to those employed in the National Accounts. They reflect the frameworks recommended by the European Union and United Nations for developing such accounts. For more information, please refer to the UK Environmental Accounts website.

ONS Environmental Accounts measure air emissions on a UK residents basis. This means that all emissions generated from transport at home and abroad by UK resident households and businesses are included. Emissions related to non-resident households and businesses travel and transport within the UK are excluded. Producing statistics on this basis allows for a more consistent comparison with key National Accounts indicators such as GDP and Gross Value Added.

Global warming and climate change

Emissions estimates for the UK are updated annually to reflect revisions in methodology and the availability of new information. These adjustments are applied retrospectively to earlier years and hence there are differences from the data published in previous editions of *Social Trends*.

In Figure 11.15, the Kyoto reduction targets cover a basket of six gases: carbon dioxide (CO_2), methane (CH_4), nitrous oxide (N_2O), hydrofluorocarbons (HFCs), perfluorocarbons (PFCs) and sulphur hexafluoride (SF_6). For the latter three gases signatories to the Kyoto Protocol may choose to use 1995, rather than 1990, as the base year from which to calculate targets, since data for 1995 for these gases tend to be more widely available and more reliable than for 1990. The UK announced in its Climate Change Programme that it would use 1995 as the base year for the fluorinated gases – therefore the 'base year' emissions for the UK target differ slightly from UK emissions in 1990.

Emissions of the six greenhouse gases are presented based on their relative contributions to global warming. Limited allowance is given in the Protocol for the absorption of CO_2 by forests, which act as so-called carbon sinks. Carbon dioxide emissions in Figure 11.15 are reported as total emissions minus removals from the atmosphere by carbon sinks.

Special areas of conservation

Special areas of conservation (SACs) are sites that have been adopted by the European Commission and formally designated by the government of each country in whose territory the site lies. Sites of community importance

(SCIs) are sites that have been adopted by the European Commission but not yet formally designated by the government of each country.

SACs are strictly protected sites designated under the EC Habitats Directive. Article 3 of the Habitats Directive requires the establishment of a European network of important high-quality conservation sites that will make a significant contribution to conserving the 189 habitat types and 788 species identified in Annexes I and II of the Directive (as amended). The listed habitat types and species are those considered to be most in need of conservation at a European level (excluding birds). Of the Annex I habitat types, 78 are believed to occur in the UK. Of the Annex II species, 43 are native to, and normally resident in, the UK.

Wild bird species

Species in italics are specialists, while the remainder are generalists. A generalist species is able to thrive in a wide variety of environmental conditions and can make use of a variety of different resources. Specialist species can only thrive in a narrow range of environmental conditions and/or have a limited diet.

- Woodland species (38): Blackbird, *Blackcap*, Blue Tit, Bullfinch, Capercaillie, Chaffinch, *Chiffchaff*, *Coal Tit*, *Crossbill*, Dunnock, *Garden Warbler*, *Goldcrest*, *Great Spotted Woodpecker*, Great Tit, *Green Woodpecker*, *Hawfinch*, *Jay*, *Lesser Spotted Woodpecker*, Lesser Whitethroat, Long-tailed Tit, *Marsh Tit*, *Nightingale*, *Nuthatch*, *Pied flycatcher*, *Redpoll*, *Redstart*, Robin, *Siskin*, Song Thrush, *Sparrowhawk*, *Spotted Flycatcher*, *Tawny Owl*, *Tree Pipit*, *Treecreeper*, *Willow Tit*, *Willow Warbler*, *Wood Warbler*, Wren.

- Farmland species (19): *Corn Bunting*, *Goldfinch*, Greenfinch, *Grey Partridge*, Jackdaw, Kestrel, *Lapwing*, Linnet, Reed Bunting, Rook, *Skylark*, Starling, *Stock Dove*, *Tree Sparrow*, *Turtle Dove*, Whitethroat, Woodpigeon, *Yellowhammer*, Yellow Wagtail.

- Seabird species (19): Arctic Skua, Arctic Tern, Black-headed Gull, Common Guillemot, Common Gull, Common Tern, Cormorant, Fulmar, Gannet, Great Black-backed Gull, Great Skua, Herring Gull, Kittiwake, Black-backed Gull, Little Tern, Puffin, Razorbill, Sandwich Tern, Shag.

12: Transport

Road traffic

Road traffic is estimated from a network of manual traffic counts, which count traffic for a single 12-hour period, and automatic traffic counters, which count traffic 24 hours a day throughout the whole year. There are around 22,000 manual count points that are counted between every one to eight years, with around 9,000 counts carried out each year. There are around 190 automatic traffic counters.

Improvements were made to the methodology used to estimate minor road traffic in 2004. From 2000 to 2003, trends in traffic flow, derived from a relatively small number of automatic traffic counters, were used to update

1999 base-year estimates. For the annual estimates made from and including 2004, the trends were derived from a set of some 4,200 manual traffic counts instead.

For more details, see *How National Traffic Estimates are made* from the Department for Transport, **www.dft.gov.uk/matrix/estimates. aspx**

National Travel Survey

The National Travel Survey (NTS) is designed to provide a databank of personal travel information for Great Britain. It has been conducted as a continuous survey since July 1988, following ad hoc surveys since the mid-1960s. The NTS is designed to identify long-term trends and is not suitable for monitoring short-term trends.

NTS data are collected via two main sources. Firstly, face to face interviews are carried out to collect information on the sampled households, all individual members within the household and all vehicles to which they have access. Secondly, each household member is then asked to record details of their trips over a seven day period in a travel diary at household and individual level, including information on access to vehicles, allowing travel patterns to be linked with individual and household characteristics. The NTS covers travel by people of all ages, including children.

Travel included in the NTS covers all trips by British residents within Great Britain for personal reasons, including travel in the course of work. It does not include their international travel.

Sample size
During 2008 just under 8,100 households participated fully in the survey by providing information via interview and completing a seven day travel diary. An additional 800 households participated in the interviews but not all respondents completed the diary; although these cases cannot be used for trip-level analysis, their data is included in all analysis at household, individual and vehicle level. The drawn sample size from 2002 nearly trebled compared with previous years following recommendations in a National Statistics Review of the NTS. This enabled most results to be presented on a single year basis from 2002. Previously data were shown as a three-year period because of the smaller sample size.

Discontinuity in 2007 and 2008 trip data
Thorough checking of the 2007 data raised concerns about the quality of the diary data, associated with the introduction of a redesigned diary from January 2007. The diary was redesigned for the 2007 survey to make it both more appealing to respondents and easier for them to use. The diary was subject to extensive testing and appeared to be working well in the first quarter of 2007. However, analysis of the data for the whole of 2007 suggested there was an under-recording of short trips which continued in 2008. An experiment to test the impact of several specific changes to the diary was run in September to December. However, this did not prove conclusive and the results could not be used to generate 'correction factors' to apply to the 2007 data. Therefore, there is an apparent discontinuity in the trip data from 2007.

The change in the travel diary in 2007 seemed to have caused a fall in short, incidental trips. The main modes affected were walks under 1 mile and short car trips under 5 miles. The main purpose affected was shopping, although there was also a fall in short trips, particularly for other 'incidental' purposes, such as personal business and visiting friends. There has been a downward trend in these trip purposes and in short trips over the last 10 years so it is likely that part of the fall in 2007 was genuine.

As the under-recording of trips in 2007 mainly affected short trips, it had little impact on the average distance travelled overall, which remained fairly flat in 2007.

Under-recording of short trips continued in 2008, although the difference compared with earlier years was less pronounced than in 2007. In 2008, there was also a fall in longer trips compared with earlier years. It is likely that this fall was associated with the increase in fuel prices and the economic downturn that began in 2008, although it may also be due to sampling variability. This fall in longer trips affected the average distance travelled, which fell in 2008. Further details on the changes to the travel diary and comparisons of NTS data with other sources over the last 10 years are given in the 2008 NTS Technical Report. **www.dft.gov.uk/pgr/statistics/ datatablespublications/personal/ methodology/ntstechreports/ ntstechrep2008**

Methodological changes
There have been various methodological changes to the NTS since the first survey in 1965. These changes are outlined in detail in the 2008 NTS Technical Report **www.dft.gov.uk/pgr/statistics/ datatablespublications/personal/ methodology/ntstechreports/ ntstechrep2008**

Methodological changes mean that there are some inconsistencies and discontinuities in the time series.

Trips
A trip is defined as a one-way course of travel having a single main purpose. It is the basic unit of personal travel defined in the survey. A round trip is split into two trips, with the first ending at a convenient point about halfway round as a notional stopping point for the outward destination and return origin. A stage is that portion of a trip defined by the use of a specific method of transport or of a specific ticket (a new stage being defined if either the mode or the ticket changes).

Households consist of one or more people who have the sampled address as their only or main residence and who either share at least one main meal a day or share the living accommodation.

Cars are regarded as household cars if they are either owned by a member of the household, or available for the private use of household members. Company cars provided by an employer for the use of a particular employee (or director) are included, but cars borrowed temporarily from a company pool are not.

The main driver of a household car is the household member who drives the furthest in that car in the course of a year.

The purpose of a trip is normally taken to be the activity at the destination, unless that destination is 'home', in which case the purpose is defined by the origin of the trip. The classification of trips to 'work' is also dependent on the origin of the trip. The following purposes of trips are distinguished:

Commuting: Trips to a usual place of work from home, or from work to home.

Business: Personal trips in the course of work, including a trip in the course of work back to work. This includes all work trips by people with no usual place of work (for example, site workers) and those who work at or from home.

Education: Trips to school or college, etc, by full-time students, students on day-release and part-time students following vocational courses.

Escort: Used when the traveller has no purpose of his or her own, other than to escort or accompany another person; for example, taking a child to school.

Escort commuting is escorting or accompanying someone from home to work or from work to home.

Shopping: All trips to shops or from shops to home, even if there was no intention to buy.

Personal business: Visits to services, for example, hairdressers, launderettes, dry-cleaners, betting shops, solicitors, banks, estate agents, libraries, churches; or for medical consultations or treatment, or for eating and drinking, unless the main purpose was social or entertainment.

Social or entertainment: Visits to meet friends, relatives, or acquaintances, both at someone's home or at a pub, restaurant, etc; all types of entertainment or sport, clubs, and voluntary work, non-vocational evening classes, political meetings, etc.

Holidays or day trips: Trips (within Great Britain) to or from any holiday (including stays of four nights or more with friends or relatives) or trips for pleasure (not otherwise classified as social or entertainment) within a single day.

Just walk: Walking for pleasure trips along public highways, including taking the dog for a walk and jogging.

Scotland NTS data is based on a small annual sample size (1,000 households) so results are not possible at Local Authority or Regional Transport Partnership level. For results at this level the Scottish Household Survey is an alternative source.

Car ownership

The figures for household ownership include four-wheeled and three-wheeled cars, off-road vehicles, minibuses, motorcaravans, dormobiles, and light vans. Company cars normally available for household use are also included.

Area type classification

In the National Travel Survey (see above), households in Great Britain are classified according to whether they are within an urban area of at least 3,000 population or in a rural area. Urban areas are subdivided for the purpose of this publication as follows:

- London boroughs – the whole of the Greater London Authority

- Metropolitan built-up areas – the built-up areas of the former metropolitan counties of Greater Manchester, Merseyside, West Midlands, West Yorkshire, Tyne and Wear and Strathclyde (excludes South Yorkshire)

- Large urban – self-contained urban areas over 250,000 population

- Medium urban – self-contained urban areas over 25,000 but not over 250,000 population

- Small/medium urban – self-contained urban areas over 10,000 but not over 25,000 population

- Small urban – self-contained urban areas over 3,000 but not over 10,000 population

- Rural – all other areas, including urban areas, under 3,000 population

Prior to 1996, 'small urban' and 'small/medium urban' were combined into one category covering self-contained urban areas over 3,000 but not over 25,000 population.

England and Wales
The classification specifies urban areas based on the extent of urban development indicated on Ordnance Survey maps. An urban area is a tract of continuously built-up urban land extending 20 hectares or more. Urban areas thus defined but less than 200 metres apart are combined into a single urban area.

Scotland
In Scotland postcodes were classified as urban or rural using population density. Urban postcodes were then aggregated together to form localities using a minimum population of 500 together with other rules.

Road safety

The Government targets regarding road safety for Great Britain are that by 2010, compared with the average for a number of indicators in 1994–98, the proportion of people killed or seriously injured in road accidents per 100 million vehicle kilometres will be reduced by 40 per cent; the proportion of children killed or seriously injured, by 50 per cent, and the proportion of people slightly injured, by 10 per cent.

In April 2009, the Government published proposals for a new post 2010 road safety strategy *A Safer Way: consultation on making Britain's roads the safest in the world*. By 2020, the aim is to reduce the number of annual road deaths and serious injuries on Britain's roads by at least 33 per cent compared with the average in 2004–08, and to reduce the number of annual road deaths and serious injuries to children and young people (aged 0 to 17) by at least 50 per cent against the 2004–08 average.

The Northern Ireland Road Safety Strategy 2002–2012 aims to reduce the proportion of people killed or seriously injured on Northern Ireland's roads each year by a third, compared with the average for the period 1996–2000, and to reduce the proportion of children killed or seriously injured on Northern Ireland's roads each year by a half.

The *Road Safety Act 1967* established a legal alcohol limit for drivers, set at 80 milligrams of alcohol in 100 millilitres of blood and made it an offence to drive when over this limit. The Act also gave the police the power to carry out breath testing in order to determine whether an individual's alcohol level is above the limit of 35 micrograms of alcohol in 100 millilitres of breath.

Passenger death rates

Passenger fatality rates given in Table 12.14 can be interpreted as the risk a traveller runs of being killed per billion kilometres travelled. The coverage varies for each mode of travel and care should be exercised in drawing comparisons between the rates for different modes.

The table provides information on passenger fatalities. Where possible, travel by drivers and other crew in the course of their work has been excluded. Exceptions are for private journeys and those in company owned cars and vans where drivers are included.

Figures for all modes of transport exclude confirmed suicides and deaths through natural causes. Figures for air, rail and water exclude trespassers and rail excludes attempted suicides. Accidents occurring in airports, seaports and railway stations that do not directly involve the mode of transport concerned are also excluded, for example, deaths sustained on escalators or falling over packages on platforms.

The figures are compiled by the Department for Transport. Further information is available in the annual publications *Road Casualties Great Britain: Annual Report* and *Transport Statistics Great Britain*. Both are published by The Stationery Office and are available at: **www.dft.gov.uk/transtat**

The following definitions are used:

Air: Accidents involving UK registered airline aircraft in UK and foreign airspace. Fixed wing and rotary wing aircraft are included but air taxis are excluded. Accidents cover UK airline aircraft around the world not just in the UK.

Rail: Train accidents and accidents occurring through movement of railway vehicles in Great Britain. As well as national rail the figures include accidents on underground and tram systems, Eurotunnel and minor railways.

Water: Figures for travel by water include both domestic and international passenger carrying services of UK registered merchant vessels.

Road: Figures refer to Great Britain and include accidents occurring on the public highway (including footways) in which at least one road vehicle or a vehicle in collision with a pedestrian is involved and which becomes known to the police within 30 days of its occurrence. Figures include both public and private transport.

Bus or coach: Figures for work buses are included. From 1 January 1994, the casualty definition was revised to include only those vehicles equipped to carry 17 or more passengers regardless of use. Prior to 1994 these vehicles were coded according to construction, whether or not they were being used for carrying passengers. Vehicles constructed as buses that were privately licensed were included

under 'Bus and coach' but Public Service Vehicles (PSV) licensed minibuses were included under cars.

Car: Includes taxis, invalid tricycles, three-wheeled and four-wheeled cars and minibuses. Prior to 1999 motor caravans were also included.

Van: Vans mainly include vehicles of the van type constructed on a car chassis. From 1 January 1994 these are defined as those vehicles not 3.5 tonnes maximum permissible gross vehicle weight. Prior to 1994 the weight definition was not more than 1.524 tonnes unladen.

Two-wheeled motor vehicle: Mopeds, motor scooters and motorcycles (including motorcycle combinations).

Pedal cycle: Includes tandems, tricycles and toy cycles ridden on the carriageway.

Pedestrian: Includes persons riding toy cycles on the footway, persons pushing bicycles, pushing or pulling other vehicles or operating pedestrian controlled vehicles, those leading or herding animals, occupants of prams or wheelchairs, and people who alight safely from vehicles and are subsequently injured.

International sea passengers

Table 12.22 provides data for port areas, the ports contained within these areas are listed below:

Thames & Kent
London
Ramsgate
Dover
Folkestone

South Coast
Newhaven
Portsmouth
Southampton
Poole
Weymouth
Plymouth

West Coast
Swansea
Milford Haven
Fishguard
Holyhead
Mostyn
Liverpool
Fleetwood
Other ports

East Coast
Lerwick
Forth
Tyne
Hull
Grimsby & Immingham
Ipswich
Felixstowe
Harwich
Other ports

Part 13: Lifestyles and social participation

Sales of phonographic albums, cassettes, CDs and singles

Trade deliveries are defined as sales of CDs and other physical format sound carriers to retailers, distributors, wholesalers and mail order companies.

Long-playing (LP) record albums are 33⅓ rpm vinyl gramophone records (phonograph records), generally either 10 or 12 inches in diameter.

An audio cassette, often referred to as compact cassette, cassette tape, cassette, or simply tape, is a magnetic tape sound recording format.

A compact disc (also known as a CD) is an optical disc used to store sound recordings.

A single is a type of release, typically a short recording of one or more separate tracks. In most cases, the single is a song that is released separately from an album, but may also appear on an album. The most common form of the vinyl single is the 45 or 7 inch gramophone record, these names being derived from its play speed, 45 rpm and the standard diameter of 7 inches. 12 inch singles were introduced for use by DJs in discos in the 1970s. The longer playing time of these singles allowed the inclusion of extended dance mixes of tracks. Most singles are now on CD or are digitally downloaded.

Package holiday

A package holiday must be sold or offered for sale, be sold at an inclusive price, be pre-arranged and include a minimum of two of the following three elements:

- transport

- accommodation

- other tourist services (not ancillary to transport or accommodation) accounting for a significant proportion of the cost of the package, such as a tour guide

Mixing socially

In the Citizenship Survey (Communities and Local Government),respondents were asked how many times they had mixed socially with people from different ethnic and religious groups to themselves in different areas of their lives. Mixing socially is defined as "mixing with people on a personal level by having informal conversations with them at, for example, the shops, your work or a child's school, as well as meeting up with people to socialise". However, it excludes "situations where you've interacted with people solely for work or business, for example just to buy something.

Countries voting in the European elections

1979
Belgium, Denmark, Germany, Ireland, France, Italy, Luxembourg, Netherlands, and the UK.

1984
Belgium, Denmark, Germany, Ireland, France, Italy, Luxembourg, Netherlands, UK and Greece.

1989
Belgium, Denmark, Germany, Ireland, France, Italy, Luxembourg, Netherlands, UK, Greece, Spain and Portugal.

1994
Belgium, Denmark, Germany, Ireland, France, Italy, Luxembourg, Netherlands, UK, Greece, Spain and Portugal.

1999
Belgium, Denmark, Germany, Ireland, France, Italy, Luxembourg, Netherlands, UK, Greece, Spain, Portugal, Sweden and Austria.

2004
Belgium, Denmark, Germany, Ireland, France, Italy, Luxembourg, Netherlands, UK, Greece, Spain, Portugal, Sweden, Austria, Cyprus, Czech Republic, Estonia, Finland, Hungary, Latvia, Lithuania, Malta, Poland, Slovakia and Slovenia.

2009
Belgium, Denmark, Germany, Ireland, France, Italy, Luxembourg, Netherlands, UK, Greece, Spain, Portugal, Sweden, Austria, Cyprus, Czech Republic, Estonia, Finland, Hungary, Latvia, Lithuania, Malta, Poland, Slovakia, Slovenia, Romania and Bulgaria.

Index

Office for
National Statistics

Social Trends

No. 40
2010 edition

Editor: Matthew Hughes

Assistant editor: Jenny Church

Office for National Statistics

ISBN 978-0-230-24067-4
ISSN 0306–7742 (print), ISSN 2040–1620 (online)

A National Statistics publication

National Statistics are produced to high professional standards as set out in the Code of Practice for Official Statistics. They are produced free from political influence.

Not all of the statistics contained in this publication are National Statistics because it is a compilation from various data sources.

About us

The Office for National Statistics

The Office for National Statistics (ONS) is the executive office of the UK Statistics Authority, a non-ministerial department which reports directly to Parliament. ONS is the UK government's single largest statistical producer. It compiles information about the UK's society and economy, and provides the evidence-base for policy and decision-making, the allocation of resources, and public accountability. The Director General of ONS reports directly to the National Statistician who is the Authority's Chief Executive and the Head of the Government Statistical Service.

The Government Statistical Service (GSS)

The Government Statistical Service is a network of professional statisticians and their staff operating both within the Office for National Statistics and across more than 30 other government departments and agencies.

Palgrave Macmillan

This publication first published 2010 by Palgrave Macmillan.

Palgrave Macmillan in the UK is an imprint of Macmillan Publishers Limited, registered in England, company number 785998, of Houndmills, Basingstoke, Hampshire RG21 6XS. Palgrave Macmillan in the US is a division of St Martin's Press LLC, 175 Fifth Avenue, New York, NY 10010.

Palgrave Macmillan is the global academic imprint of the above companies and has companies and representatives throughout the world. Palgrave® and Macmillan® are registered trademarks in the United States, the United Kingdom, Europe and other countries.

A catalogue record for this book is available from the British Library.

10 9 8 7 6 5 4 3 2 1
18 17 16 15 14 13 12 11 10 09

Contacts

This publication

For information about the content of this publication, contact the Editor
Tel: 01633 455931
Email: social.trends@ons.gsi.gov.uk

Other customer enquiries
ONS Customer Contact Centre
Tel: 0845 601 3034
International: +44 (0)845 601 3034
Minicom: 01633 815044
Email: info@statistics.gsi.gov.uk
Fax: 01633 652747
Post: Room 1.101, Government Buildings, Cardiff Road, Newport, South Wales NP10 8XG
www.ons.gov.uk

Media enquiries
Tel: 0845 604 1858
Email: press.office@ons.gsi.gov.uk

Publication orders
To obtain the print version of this publication, contact Palgrave Macmillan
Tel: 01256 302611
www.palgrave.com/ons
Price: £55.00

Copyright and reproduction

Printing

This book is printed on paper suitable for recycling and made from fully managed and sustained forest sources. Logging, pulping and manufacturing processes are expected to conform to the environmental regulations of the country of origin.

Printed and bound in Great Britain by Hobbs the Printer Ltd, Totton, Southampton

Typeset by Academic + Technical Typesetting, Bristol

Contents